REIMAGINING THE *ANALOGIA ENTIS*

INTERVENTIONS

Conor Cunningham

GENERAL EDITOR

Coming from the Centre of Theology and Philosophy at the University of Nottingham, England, Interventions is a genuinely interdisciplinary series of mediations of crucial concepts and key figures in contemporary thought.

RECENTLY PUBLISHED

Philipp W. Rosemann, *Charred Root of Meaning: Continuity, Transgression, and the Other in Christian Tradition* (2018)

Aaron Riches, *Ecce Homo: On the Divinity of Christ* (2016)

Edward T. Oakes, SJ, *A Theology of Grace in Six Controversies* (2016)

Nicholas M. Healy, *Hauerwas: A (Very) Critical Introduction* (2014)

Johannes Hoff, *The Analogical Turn: Rethinking Modernity with Nicholas of Cusa* (2013)

For a complete list of published volumes in this series, see the back of the book.

REIMAGINING THE
ANALOGIA ENTIS

The Future of Erich Przywara's Christian Vision

Philip John Paul Gonzales

WILLIAM B. EERDMANS PUBLISHING COMPANY
GRAND RAPIDS, MICHIGAN

Wm. B. Eerdmans Publishing Co.
4035 Park East Court SE, Grand Rapids, Michigan 49546
www.eerdmans.com

© 2019 Philip John Paul Gonzales
All rights reserved
Published 2019

Printed in the United States of America

25 24 23 22 21 20 19   1 2 3 4 5 6 7

ISBN 978-0-8028-7671-3

Library of Congress Cataloging-in-Publication Data

Names: Gonzales, Philip John Paul, 1981- author.
Title: Reimagining the Analogia entis : the future of Erich Przywara's
    Christian vision / Philip John Paul Gonzales.
Description: Grand Rapids, Michigan : William B. Eerdmans Publishing Company,
    2018. | Series: Interventions | Revision of author's thesis
    (doctoral)—Katholieke Universiteit Leuven, 2015. | Includes
    bibliographical references and index.
Identifiers: LCCN 2018022303 | ISBN 9780802876713 (hardcover : alk. paper)
Subjects: LCSH: Przywara, Erich, 1889–1972. | Przywara, Erich, 1889-1972.
    Analogia entis. | Analogy (Religion)—History of doctrines—20th century.
    | Philosophical theology. | Knowledge, Theory of (Religion) | Philosophy
    and religion. | Catholic Church—Doctrines—History—20th century.
Classification: LCC B3323.P84 G66 2018 | DDC 193—dc23
    LC record available at https://lccn.loc.gov/2018022303

The author and publisher gratefully acknowledge permission to reuse material from the author's article "Why We Need Erich Przywara," *Communio* 44, no. 1 (Spring 2017): 144–72.

To my beloved Sarah

The journey of this book is twined with the journey of our life and family: from the youthful freedom of Leuven, to France and the vicissitudes of life, to Texas and the thankfulness for a University position, to the gracious gift of Rome still being lived. This book is dedicated to you with joy and thanksgiving, unutterable.

Contents

Foreword by Cyril O'Regan	ix
Preface	xix
Introduction	1

Part 1. Formal and Critical Dialogue

1. A Crossroad Moment for Catholic Thought: The Modernist Crisis	39
2. *Philo*sophy and *Theo*logy: Modernity and Countermodernity	56
3. Visions of Being: Foundation and Nonfoundation	103
4. Differing Reimaginings of the *Analogia Entis*: Anthropocentrism and Theocentrism	137

Part 2. Constructive Reimagining

5. Setting the Stage: Post-Conciliar Trajectories	205
6. The Postmodern Scene of Thought: Breaking Heidegger's Spell	219
7. The Resurgence of Analogical Metaphysics: Desmond, Milbank, and Hart	246
8. Enlisting Apocalyptic *Theo*logy: Cyril O'Regan's Pleromatic Vision	288
9. The *Analogia Entis* Reimagined: A Christian Analogical-Apocalyptic Metaphysics	321
Bibliography	355
Index	371

Foreword

If this offering by Philip Gonzales is anything to go on, rumors of the demise of Catholic thought are greatly exaggerated. In this book Gonzales provides us with an incredibly substantial piece of scholarship that is at the same time wonderfully creative. The creativity is not at all flashy and takes time to exhibit itself. Moreover, by the time it appears we are made to feel the seriousness as well as the munificence of the text that forbids us to garland it with superlatives from the available cornucopia of academic praise. While one senses enthusiasm on every page, one also finds assuredness of tone and maturity of thought, and while the book is a book of large ambitions, there is a wonderful matter-of-factness in terms of tone and a resolute reserve in terms of style. The stated aim of the book is to inject further energy into the ongoing retrieval of the thought of the great twentieth-century Catholic theologian Erich Przywara. It does far more than that. The book represents a boost that shifts Przywara studies onto an entirely different level of reception and appreciation. While not pretending comprehensiveness regarding an oeuvre that is almost impossible to scale, Gonzales explores in detail key texts of the Jesuit theologian, including the pivotal *Analogia Entis* (1932); places Przywara's developing but wondrously consistent thought in its original immediate pre– and post–World War I context, which seemed to suggest a caesura between the new moment and that which went before; and casts Edith Stein as an interlocutor and intellectual companion in the creative and formative period of Przywara's thought from the middle of the 1920s to the commencement of World War II.

Context as well as text matter in Gonzales's analysis. But context truly matters only if we can be persuaded by an encounter with a text that is saturated with meaning. And, on Gonzales's reading, the texts of Przywara

FOREWORD

do so persuade. Still, even probing interpretation of Przywara's texts, together with peeling away the various layers of the cultural context, and sustained treatment of the Stein-Przywara relation at best only partially define this truly ample text. Although there is little or nothing in this text that recalls Nietzsche, nonetheless, for Gonzales genuine recovery of the past cannot proceed in the antiquarian mode. The historical excavation of Przywara's texts and context makes sense only to the extent to which it unveils the philosophical and theological predicaments of the present and suggests a way forward for Christian, and more specifically Catholic, discourses, practices, and forms of life. This interpretive commitment is aptly captured in the subtitle, in which the future is highlighted. Over a third of the text consists of an extended reflection on contemporary forms of philosophical and theological thinking that can be thought to catalyze and further develop Przywara's "creaturely metaphysics" and his profound reflections on the relation between philosophy and theology.

The always generous Gonzales would be the first to admit that the translation of Przywara's classic *Analogia Entis* (1932), together with those essays that Balthasar published along with it in 1961, has effectively revolutionized Przywara studies. Still, however appreciative he is of current translation and interpretation, Gonzales has decidedly charted his own course. The focus is determinate; it is clearly on Przywara's articulation of the analogy of being that received its definitive expression in *Analogia Entis*. Gonzales knows well that in Przywara's extraordinarily difficult classic, which seems to move towards the condition of cipher, the construct of analogy of being is decidedly different than that of a Baroque Catholic commentator on Aquinas such as Thomas Cajetan (1469–1534). In contrast to Cajetan, Przywara's account is urgently metaphysical and considerably more expansive in that it involves not only the naming of God but the entire conspectus of the God-world relation. Gonzales acknowledges that Przywara thinks his rendition of the analogy of being to be faithful to the intention of Aquinas, while also suggesting that it is nothing less than the basic form of all Catholic philosophical thought, Augustine as much as Aquinas, and John of the Cross and Ignatius of Loyola as much as both. In summary, the analogy of being in Przywara is a "creaturely metaphysics" that has at its center the dynamic orientation of a finite subjectivity towards the divine infinite that precisely as such grounds desire and exceeds any and all conceptual framing.

As Gonzales brings out powerfully, in Przywara the human is given, but is not given as fixed. The human person is a venture of self-appropriation that is coherent only because of its reference to the divine ground. If in some sense existence precedes essence, and thus becoming matters, human being is not the creator, which in Thomistic language is the unity between essence (*essentia*) and existence (*esse*). Nor is the finite subject the provider of meaning: dynamic becoming is the becoming of meaning and truth. Correlatively, the divine infinite is not simply the highest instance of Being. One of Przywara's mantras is that the divine infinite or infinite divine cannot be expressed adequately. Perhaps an unacknowledged sign that the level of apophasis in Przywara runs somewhat higher than it does in Aquinas is the threading throughout Przywara's works of the Augustinian "If you comprehend it, it is not God" (*Si comprehendis, non est Deus*) and the famous passage in the Fourth Lateran Council (1215) to the effect that the similarity between God and the world is cut across by the ever greater dissimilarity. These two sayings serve as apophatic canons that allow Przywara in turn to take on board Carmelite masters such as Teresa of Avila and Saint John of the Cross, not only as spiritual writers who fructify his meditative and ecstatic poetry, but as theological masters able to link apophasis and a metaphysics of finitude. Gonzales celebrates as well as demonstrates that a creaturely metaphysics is regulated by a reduction to mystery (*reductio ad mysterium*) that is as dynamic as it is participatory.

For Gonzales, however, in his construction of the analogy of being Przywara critically negotiates with the entire metaphysical tradition, both the classical and the modern: Plato and Aristotle, Kant, Hegel, Nietzsche, and Kierkegaard are all threads in the dense weave of reference that is *Analogia Entis*. More, according to Gonzales, throughout his work Przywara is determining his relation to the phenomenological movement that he, like many Catholic thinkers in the same period, above all Husserl's other assistant, Edith Stein, is sifting through. Respectful of Husserl, Przywara, nonetheless, does not think that the mandate of "back to the things themselves" is in itself sufficient to energize a Catholic philosophy that necessarily has to undergo something of a rebirth. In addition, as Gonzales makes clear, on Przywara's account neither the eidetic nor phenomenological reduction is calculated to give life to a Catholic philosophy and theology that has become sclerotic. Accordingly, the constitutive representative of phenomenology for Przywara is Heidegger rather than Husserl. Heidegger's analytic of *Dasein* in *Being and Time* transforms phenomenology into an ontology of being-in-the-world and poses a question for Catholic thought as to whether Heidegger can be taken on board in a revised metaphysical track, which, while it emphasizes the finite subject as the way of approach, also allows God into discourse. One aspect of Przywara's genius, according to Gonzales, is his yes and no, or to use language which I have used elsewhere, his simultaneous welcoming and unwelcoming of a thinker who early and late found God talk abhorrent in philosophical inquiry. Implicitly in *Analogia Entis* and explicitly in essays both before and after his master text, Przywara gives an accounting that, had it been heeded, might have prevented a considerable amount of philosophical and theological mischief in twentieth- and twenty-first-century Christian and more specifically Catholic thought. Heidegger can be a fellow traveler to the extent to which he offers wonderfully descriptive accounts of a finite subject oriented towards and enveloped by mystery. He cannot be such to the extent to which he prescribes that mystery must be identified with nothing.

One of the more fascinating discussions in Gonzales's replete text is his attention to the overlaps and differences between the metaphysical ventures of Przywara and of Stein. Stein serves as both companion and foil to Przywara: companion in that she too is involved in the attempted energizing of Catholicism by phenomenology, while remaining critical of it to the extent to which it would repress its existential exigence and rule out beforehand either the reality of a divine ground, or its appearance in time and history, or both; companion also in a more general sense, in that her articulation of a metaphysics of finitude represents at once an intervention into the spaces of high philosophy and the Catholic church that, wracked by the modernist controversy, was still searching for ways to encounter, adopt, adapt, and critique modernity. Stein serves also as foil. Gonzales pays Stein the respect of asking whether her thought has the kind of future that he believes Przywara's has, and if not, why not. While he thinks that Stein's commitment to philosophy as rigorous science and the tendency to follow Husserl's back to the cogito hinder her thought in some respects, it is not a zero-sum game between these lovers of the Carmelite mystics. Both can be brought forward. Yet there is an excess in Przywara, and a greater fecundity. Gonzales suggests that the philosophical method or "logic" articulated in *Analogia Entis* has a synthetic capacity that is unique in twentieth-century philosophical and theological thought. This is not only for the reason that in his classic text Przywara gives equal emphasis to the subjective (noetic) and objective (ontic) registers in philosophy and shows their complementarity, but also that he is successful in deconstructing the Promethean drive of philosophy that would set conditions for all discourse and either foreclose all talk of God or stipulate conditions that could constrain divine appearing.

Foreword

To this extent it would not be incorrect to say that in a more nearly metaphysical idiom Przywara anticipates the way in which Jean-Luc Marion subverts potential blockages to the theological from within phenomenology itself, even if Marion might more nearly be cast as a follower of Stein when it comes to a commitment to philosophy as a rigorous science. Other virtues of Przywara's mode of approach that allow real commerce between the discourses of philosophy and theology are more hinted at than explored. Given what Gonzales writes in the second part of the text regarding contemporary activations and developments of Przywara's analogical model and creaturely metaphysics, one is tempted to suggest that another salient characteristic of Przywara's intellectual practice is what one could refer to as "philosophical style." Specifically, what I have in mind is that Przywara's positive articulation of creaturely metaphysics is shadowed by negation and genealogical concerns. Kant's thoroughgoing transcendentalism is rejected, as are Husserl's essentialism and egology. Nietzsche's reduction of metaphysics to temporality, authenticity, and search is rejected, as is its disguised variant in Heidegger. The rejections transcend inventory. The point of such negations is to contest not only particular philosophies but also the "effective history" (*Wirkungsgeschichte*) of texts that block or distort the possibility of the dialogue between reason and faith and philosophy and theology that belongs to the very definition of Catholicism. Put otherwise, a peculiarity of Przywara's theological style is that it is genealogical as well as constructive.

For Gonzales, it makes all the difference in the world whether the kind of thinking illustrated in the work of Przywara has pregnancy and thus a future. Although Hans Urs von Balthasar is not made thematic in his text, Balthasar is very much a presence. Gonzales would agree readily that Balthasar's work is a genuine offshoot of that of Przywara, while having inventions and glories that are solely his own. Yet for Gonzales Przywara's future in metaphysics and theology is not exhausted by the work of Balthasar, even if Balthasar sometimes serves the function of relay. Gonzales finds such a future in the contemporary philosophical and theological scene and selects for extended discussion the philosopher William Desmond (Catholic), and three theologians, David Bentley Hart (Orthodox), John Milbank (Anglican), and Cyril O'Regan (Catholic). He is convinced that all four operate broadly within Przywara's analogical manifold, which allows the conversation between philosophy and theology to be mutually enhancing. Gonzales is not advancing a genetic thesis. He is not saying, for example, that the main works of any of these authors are

FOREWORD

dependent on Przywara, although all four authors are familiar with Przywara's work and would be prepared to see it as constructing the horizon of the finite subject whose end exceeds the order of nature and whose meaning is received rather than constructed. Although Gonzales could not be more even-handed in his treatment, a certain priority has to be granted his teacher and mentor, the Irish philosopher William Desmond, who has been called the "last metaphysician." In his trilogy of *Being and the Between*, *Ethics and the Between*, and *God and the Between*, Desmond has articulated the analogical milieu with a finesse and sense of differentiation and complexity that surpasses not only that of any of his contemporaries, but also that of Przywara himself. Throughout the trilogy, however, Desmond refers to Plato's *metaxu* or "between" rather than analogy. The choice of term is not meretricious, but reflects Desmond's worry that the language of analogy might be too restrictive for the kind of global philosophical work that he intends the metaxological to do. The form of analogy Desmond has in mind, however, is the analogy of Aquinas as read through his later commentators. This, as Gonzales never tires of saying, is not the form of analogy championed by Przywara. Thus, Desmond's extraordinarily creative and original account of the domain of the between can, on Gonzales's account, be seen to flow—albeit noncausally—from Przywara's expansive analogical account of reality.

In making the case that Desmond's metaxology is a nonidentical repetition of Przywara's analogical metaphysics, Gonzales puts his finger on reinforcing continuities between the German and Irish thinkers. One feature of continuity has to do with method, and more specifically how Desmond assimilates the phenomenological tradition. Like Przywara, Desmond has concerns regarding classical phenomenology: metaxology is not a space of disembodied essences or objects that might or might not exist. As a term "metaxology" is meant to speak to a space of singularities, embodiment, community, and ecstatic transcendence beyond the world precisely by traversing it. As in Przywara, in Desmond the eidetic reduction is refused; so also is the phenomenological reduction. The questioning and questing finite subjectivity manifests an ineluctable appetite for the real. While this appetite is a systemic feature of classical philosophy, more than occasionally Desmond seems to suggest its Christian appropriation when he recalls Augustine, whom Przywara leaves us in no doubt is his favorite Christian thinker. Similar to Przywara, Desmond also welcomes the transformation wrung by Heidegger on phenomenology, while resisting the imperialist claims of both his analytic of *Dasein* and his ruminations on *Ereignis* in his later works. When one considers the third volume in the "between" series, that is, *God and the Between*, one notices another aspect of repetition. Desmond, the philosopher, like Przywara, wants to craft a metaphysics of finitude that is not nihilistic; or put more positively, a form of metaphysics hospitable to God as providing support and aim to the erotic striving of a sensing, perceiving, and knowing, embodied and communally related, self. And, lastly, Gonzales suggests to the reader that a carryover from Przywara to Desmond may well be what I have called Przywara's philosophical style, that is, a philosophy that, while rich in articulation of the milieu of finitude, also has genealogical edge and takes issue with much of modern philosophy, and not simply the easy targets of scientism and positivism, but the harder targets of Kant, deconstruction, and other postmodern sophistications. Heidegger too, but also Hegel, who with Heidegger is in *Analogia Entis*, arguably are the two main philosophers that a Catholic thinker is obliged to sift and resist. Repetition is not sameness. Even were we to put the singularity of Desmond's work in suspension, there are, of course, major differences. Desmond is forced to respond to the dominance in the contemporary period of analytic philosophy in a way not done by Przywara, who could more or less assume an ancient and modern philosophical canon, with the modern canon being largely German. Then there is the extra-ecclesial nature of Desmond's philosophical work, which contrasts with the more guided aim of Przywara in *Analogia Entis*, where it is taken for granted that philosophy is there for theology. And, finally, there is Desmond's reluctance to operate in a theological mode despite his acknowledgment of revelation as a key category in the analysis of religion and his acceptance of the legitimacy of theology as reflection on the givens of Christian faith.

In his analyses of each of the three theologians whom he singles out, Gonzales combines enthusiasm with accuracy and, while focused more nearly on what they have in common, never fails to bring out differences in context, emphasis, and vocabulary, and, finally and most importantly, differences in substantive theological position. What unites these discourses, across confessions, to Przywara and to each other is a concern with the genuinely dialogical relation of philosophy and theology, which all agree has been compromised in the modern period. Kant's turn to the subject is regarded as problematic; the neutrality of phenomenology is interrogated; and the Christianity-friendly credentials of the discourses of both Hegel and Heidegger are essentially withdrawn. Yet, in none of these cases is it simply the case that philosophy as such is out of order. Constitutive for all three, as well as for Desmond and Przywara, is the classical model of philosophy as eros for a reality that both realizes and exceeds searching. And each has an elective affinity for forms of Platonism consonant with a Christian discourse of a God of superabundant love who receives in the philosophical and theological tradition both sober and exhuberant forms. There are Nyssa, Augustine, and Maximus; there are also Johannes Scotus Eriugena, Meister Eckhart, and Nicholas of Cusa. In the case of all three theologians there is a "creaturely metaphysics" oriented towards a divine ground that is intrinsically communicative. There are thus an ontology and theology of gift, but precisely because of this an anthropology that underscores participation. In addition, for all three the theological tradition, which exposits and interprets revelation, has rightly emphasized the Trinitarian nature of God as self-communicative good, the Trinitarian understanding of history, and the Trinitarian horizon of the Church along with the mystery of Christ, which is both its object and together with the Holy Spirit its subject.

Gonzales appreciates what these forms of theological thought, which straddle both philosophy and theology, reject and embrace as well as the stories they tell about how the contemporary bedeviled situation came to be. Yet, he also embraces differences in emphasis: the extraordinary emphasis on beauty in Hart, which after Przywara is double-axled (on the one hand an excavation of the theological aesthetics of Nyssa waxed in the Trinitarian explorations of Bulgakov and, on the other, a powerful polemic against modern philosophers such as Kant, Hegel, Heidegger, and their postmodern epigones); the emphasis in Milbank on the Church as an alternate community of vision and witness that is Christologically founded, pneumatically energized, and Trinitarianly directed; and the emphasis on apocalyptic in O'Regan, who thinks of Balthasar's quite literally visionary work as always engaging that of Przywara, while expanding and sharpening it, and tirelessly excavating the treasures of the Church and discovering new spiritual and literary voices that will tell the truth of Christ at a slant, this while engaging Balthasar's assimilation and resistance to Hegel and Heidegger. For Gonzales, O'Regan's work seems to come in the form of a double repetition: he nonidentically repeats Balthasar who creatively repeats Przywara. On Gonzales's view the differences between these thinkers underscore the fecundity of Przywara. Together with Desmond, these three theologians show that reception itself constitutes an analogical space in which plurality is not reducible to unity. And then there is the case of Gonzales himself in this analogical space of reception. He is the one remarking all this in *Reimagining the "Analogia Entis."* If he thinks that his set of four should be applauded for their nonidentical repetition of Przywara's analogy of being, how should we view him? If they are to be applauded for "going on," as Wittgenstein would say, what about Gonzales himself? Is he reporting or getting ready to make the next move, or both, in his fabulous first book? He provides more than a hint in the final two chapters that, with due gratitude for what he has received in his four thinkers as well as Przywara, he plans on going on, aiming to forge a new synthesis, with Desmond's stretching of analogical metaphysics serving as the basic platform, Hart's rhapsodies as the memory of the unforgettable gifts and the even more unforgettable triune giver, Milbank's theopolitical urgency as undergirding the theological aim for embodiment and community, and O'Regan's apocalyptic as a necessary inflection with respect to the vision and call that define Christianity as they compete with other visions and calls in the land of unlikeness laden with counterfeits.

CYRIL O'REGAN
Huisking Professor of Theology
University of Notre Dame

Preface

The infancy of this book began as a doctoral dissertation at the Katholieke Universiteit Leuven, Belgium, eight years ago under the supervision of William Desmond (promoter) and Cyril O'Regan (co-promoter). The writing of it, in its various stages of life, has spanned four countries and the birth of three of our four little girls. Moreover, it marks and maps my own intellectual life—through narrow-minded Thomism, the spell of Heidegger, to the insufficiency of the French theological turn in phenomenology, to my turn to the essential importance of apocalyptic and theo-politics for the life of Christian discourse today—in my struggle and desire for the fullness of Catholic vision and life. This vision and fullness was only first abundantly opened to me through my encounter with Erich Przywara and before him, in a slightly less powerful way, with Hans Urs von Balthasar.

In a word, this text, for me, was/is a kind of intellectual homecoming to the treasures of the living mosaic of the Catholic and Christian tradition. It is an attempt to express something of the pleromatic truth and glory of the Catholic metaphysical tradition, analogically conceived. This is done in view of, and with a deep concern for, the future of Catholic and Christian vision and life within the dramatic and unprecedented exigencies of our time. The humble, yet bold, claim is that there is a *future* for Catholic and Christian metaphysical discourse and that Przywara's voice and vision need to be listened to for the viability and future of Christian thought. The gift of Przywara's thought to the Church, and to Christian thought in general, must thus be recognized and moved forward. This is not to claim that the future of the Church depends on Przywara or any one philosopher or theologian, for such a claim would be heterodox, prideful, absurd, and foolish. Rather, it is to claim that the future of the Church, and of Christian metaphysical thought, depends on the living tradition—a tradition rooted in the one sent forth from the Father, Christ, and Christ's self-gift to the Church given through the Spirit of truth and of life—and that some thinkers have drunk more deeply and fully from the wellsprings of these living waters. Thus, such voices must be heard if the tradition is to be creatively moved forward. Przywara's is such a visionary voice.

This book would not have been possible without the support and encouragement it received, in its doctoral stage (and beyond), from William Desmond and Cyril O'Regan, even as it grew longer and more daringly apocalyptic. Both encouraged risk and creativity beyond mere polished scholarship understood as an end in itself. Without this faith and encouragement this text would not be what it is today. Of course, any shortcomings or weaknesses in my arguments are fully my own. Yet even beyond their exquisite support, supervision, and encouragement, William Desmond and Cyril O'Regan are true living masters of the art and craft of thinking—of Christian thinking and vision. So while I was unlocking textually the pleromatic truth in Przywara, I was watching it being performed and conversing with this same living truth in the persons of William Desmond and Cyril O'Regan. And for that I am forever grateful and in their debt. Likewise, a profound thank-you must also be given to John Milbank, for his reading of the doctoral stages of this work and for our conversations together that have always proved inspiring and richly fertile. It was John Milbank who was so influential in helping me have the courage to write boldly as a Christian, beyond the narrow confines of the secularized academy.

Further, thanks must be given to John Betz for our email correspondence and for providing me with an early manuscript of his and David Bentley Hart's superb translation of *Analogia Entis*. John's fine Przywara scholarship has held me to a very high standard, indeed. Great thanks must likewise be given to my friend, the late Fr. Cyril Crawford, OSB, for our conversations on Przywara, Balthasar, Maximus the Confessor, and the glory of the Catholic tradition, fittingly over Westmalle Tripels at Café Amedee, in Leuven. Unique gratitude must be shown and given to my dearest friend, Patrick Ryan Cooper, for it was, in many ways, in our countless conversations that the vision and form of this book unfolded, as a mirroring of the *commercium* of our friendship. Patrick, you have never let me rest secure that I have come to the fullness of the truth of Catholic vision, even when the difficulty and, at times, the weariness of the search might tempt me to think that I have.

A deep debt of gratitude must be shown and offered to Wm. B. Eerdmans Publishing Company. A profoundly deep and singular thank-you

Preface

must to be given to Bill Eerdmans Jr. for his advocacy, sponsorship, and support of this book and the conviction that it belonged at Eerdmans. Thank you, Bill, for believing in this text. I am truly grateful and honored. A special and heartfelt thank-you is given to Conor Cunningham and Interventions for so swiftly believing in the merits of this book and the need for it to be published. More thanks must be given to James Ernest for his wonderful support of this book. James, it has been a true pleasure working with you and your genuine personal professionalism. Further thanks must be given to Bill, James, and Conor for their support in publishing a book of this length, as it is becoming more and more common among publishers of philosophical and theological monographs to ask their authors, under economic pressures, to publish shorter and thus more marketable books. The spirit and courage of Eerdmans and the genuinely catholic and impressive range of their books are the mark of a true Christian publishing house. A profound thank-you must further be given to Jenny Hoffman, my editor, for the overwhelming mastery of her craft, and her patience and understanding in working with such a long and dense text, as well as my publicist, Laura Bardolph Hubers, for her ceaseless work and energy in promoting a text of this length and density on a thinker whose name is so difficult to pronounce. I must also mention and thank my friend Amos Hunt, whose keen editorial eye and skill aided me greatly before I turned this text in to Eerdmans. Working with Eerdmans has been the delightful and rare experience of publishing a book, not with a company, but with a community of persons. I am, indeed, grateful.

Lastly, a profound word of thanks must be given to my family: To my in-laws, Bruce and Shelia Schofield, for their unwavering support of our young family through graduate school and beyond. To my mother and father, Donald and Leslie Gonzales, for their love, and to my father for showing me, at such a young age, that there is something like the life of the mind. To my four glorious and spirited girls—Sophia, Anastasia, and my twins, Melanie and Serafina—for keeping their father grounded as to why I write and read, as to why I love. To my beloved wife, Sarah, to whom this book is dedicated, without whose selfless and unflappable love none of this would have been possible. We did this together, and—without you—I simply could not have even begun...

Rome, April 5, 2018

Introduction

The Question(s)

This book inquires into the essence of Christian thought by reimagining an analogical style of metaphysics: the *analogia entis*. In doing so, it reopens an exchange—*commercium*—between *philo*sophy and *theo*logy that is faithful to the gifting event of relationality between being and grace. To speak from this event is to speak from within the dynamic, analogical "suspended middle" (*schwebende Mitte*) where gift is laid upon gift. It is to speak from within the Christian metaphysical narrative of creation and re-creation; it is to order *philo*sophy to *theo*logy within an analogy of discourses between *philo*sophy (being) and *theo*logy (grace). To speak thus is to speak forth boldly (with *parrhēsia*) the truth of a Christian space of difference, which is other than and rhetorically and metaphysically counter to the autonomous posture of philosophical modernity. Why? Simply put: this style of metaphysical speaking is responsorial and doxological—not monologically self-referential and self-legitimizing, as is modern philosophy's infatuation with self-presence. It is a response to the call of the living Christian God of creation (being) and redemption (grace), metaphysically performed, sung from within the storied *apokalypsis* of the Christian *mysterium*: the true story of being. I hold, then, that the *analogia entis* offers a potent and genuinely Christian antidote to the self-legitimizing foundational narrative of autonomy upon which philosophical modernity is built. This book seeks to show the *analogia entis* as the way forward to a recovery and retrieval of a pleromatic Christian vision of reality; a vision that resides within the glory of the incarnate, storied truth which is Christianity itself. In other words, Christian vision must always be dramatically enfleshed and performed. An analogical performance recovered in this

INTRODUCTION

way would reopen the possibility of a genuinely postmodern Christian style of thought within this dramatic vesperal hour of history in which we now find ourselves. I claim that a style—such a form of enfleshed pleromatic Christian thought—is most fully contained in that seemingly archaic and arcane metaphysical term: *analogia entis*.

The burden of this book thus rests in showing and unlocking the Christian postmodern truth of the *analogia entis*. To unlock this truth, the following questions must be asked: What enables the *analogia entis* to present a nonfoundational counter to philosophical modernity? What is its grammar? What is its inner logic and what is its central vision? How can the guiding vision of the *analogia entis* specifically express a Christian, and Catholic, pleromatic vision of reality in keeping with the Christian evangel? And if the *analogia entis* finds its fullest expression as a Christian metaphysics, how and why is this so? In other words, what gives the *analogia entis* its particular Christian metaphysical style? And how is the *analogia entis* capable of funding a specifically Christian response and vision that is counter to both philosophical modernity and the nihilism of postmodernity? And, lastly, how is the *analogia entis* capable of showing a way forward for post-Conciliar Catholic thought today?

The Protagonist

Such claims may sound grandiose and rhetorically exaggerated, too metaphysically presumptuous and naïve. For is not the *analogia entis* commonly understood, and either dismissed or defended, as a mere semantic apparatus or retrograde Scholastic *terminus technicus* from the commentarial tradition of narrow-minded post-Cajetan Baroque Scholasticism? Indeed, if the *analogia entis* is conceived in either of these ways, then the jury is in before the case can even be prosecuted. However, such misrepresentations are easily averted when one encounters the speculative metaphysical genius of the extraordinary Jesuit philosopher and theologian Erich Przywara (1889–1972). For it was Przywara who, in the words of Karl Rahner, transmuted the *analogia entis* "from a scholastic technicality into the fundamental structure of Catholic theology."[1] Przywara's creative brilliance

---

1. Cited in John Betz, "After Barth: A New Introduction to Erich Przywara's *Analogia Entis*," in *The Analogy of Being: Invention of the Antichrist or the Wisdom of God?*, ed. Thomas Joseph White, OP (Grand Rapids: Eerdmans, 2011), 38.

daringly and controversially transmuted the worn-out "technical term" *analogia entis* into a fundamental Catholic *Denkform*, thereby championing it as essential to an integral Catholic vision of reality.²

Why then did the *analogia entis* become (and remain) a point of metaphysical and theological contention? Because it is centered in the fundamental Catholic doctrine of the relation between God and creature: creation *ex nihilo*. The *analogia entis* thus stands at the beginning of the Christian narrative of creation, Incarnation, and redemption. In so doing, it entails nearly every essential aspect of Catholic narrative and doctrine. I list briefly its Catholic metaphysical range of influence: First, the *analogia entis*, based in the fundamental doctrine of creation *ex nihilo*, affects how one views the relation between philosophy and theology (and hence also natural theology), nature and grace, faith and reason, as well as the question of the extent of the effect of sin on human nature. Second, the *analogia entis* consequently reaches into Mariology (as Barth rightly saw), implicating the question of the creature's openness to grace and ability

---

2. John Betz rightly notes, "It is of course, not unheard of in the history of Christianity for theological doctrines to turn upon a single phrase—such as *homoousios* (concerning the divinity of Christ as the incarnate Son), *filioque* (concerning the eternal procession of the Holy Spirit from the Son), and the Reformation's shibboleth *sola fide* (concerning salvation), to name some of the most obvious examples. In the first decades of the twentieth century, however, at least in Germany no single phrase was the subject of more theological controversy than the seemingly innocuous metaphysical term *analogia entis*." Betz, "After Barth," 35. Of course, Przywara's most renowned conversation partner concerning the great debate was Karl Barth. Barth famously said, "I regard the *analogia entis* as the invention of the Antichrist, and I believe that because of it it is impossible ever to become a Catholic." Karl Barth, *Church Dogmatics* I/1, trans. G. W. Bromiley (London: T&T Clark, 2004), xiii. Yet, despite Barth's invective against the *analogia entis* as a Catholic philosophical/theological *Denkform*, he still showed overwhelming admiration for Przywara's brilliance. Barth says: "He knows everything, everything which we think we know, except that, always right at the proper moment, he does not make use of it. The Catholic Church is becoming for me more and more the amazing phenomenon. In comparison, our Protestant opponents look very much like dwarfs, don't you think? . . . This Jesuit was really something I had never seen before. He also told me that I too am for him the opponent par excellence. He is a little man with a large head, but that doesn't mean he is not the giant Goliath incarnate." Cited in Betz, "After Barth," 39–40. And again in a *Festschrift* for Przywara in 1959 Barth has this to say: "My meetings with him in Münster and Bonn, the impression of his astonishing gift and art for being true to the world and his church, not only to understand everything but to integrate it into his own ceaselessly penetrating and encompassing thinking and still to remain in an exemplary way Catholic—this remains, confirmed by so many exchanges, unforgettable." Thomas F. O'Meara, OP, *Erich Przywara, S.J.: His Theology and His World* (Notre Dame: University of Notre Dame Press, 2002), 106–7.

INTRODUCTION

to receive the divine.³ Third, again following from the former, Christology is implicated in the range of influence of the *analogia entis*, insofar as it is able to explain (in a nonrationalistic sense) how the divine/human unity, in the Person of Christ, weds creaturely *logos* with the divine *Logos*, without confusion and separation. Fourth, the sphere of influence of the *analogia entis* passes over into the Christian theologoumenon of Trinitarian doctrine by protecting the distinction between the immanent and the economic Trinity. Fifth, the *analogia entis* expresses authentic orthodox spirituality insofar as this spirituality is rooted in an experience of God, who is ever and always both in and beyond the experience of the creature. The *analogia entis* is thus communicative of a spirituality or a "metaphysics of the saints" enacted through humble submission and an active-service that is always respectful of the ever-greater mystery of God's unsurpassable glory.⁴ If the extent of this range sounds daunting, it is. And, although I by no means intend to treat all of these spheres of influence of the *analogia entis* in this work thematically, nevertheless many of these themes will be touched upon. Hence, it will certainly become clear throughout how much the *analogia entis*, as construed by Przywara, can be, and indeed must be, interpreted as a fundamental Catholic *Denkform* that opens up a specifically Christian pleromatic metaphysical vision of reality.

Paternity and Hermeneutic

The paternity of my retrieval and reimagining of the *analogia entis* must then be said to be Przywarian. But what does this mean? On the surface level, it means that my hermeneutic tactic of reimagining the *analogia entis* occurs via a retrieval of Przywara's analogical vision. However, on a deeper

---

3. For the Mariological context of Barth's rejection of the *analogia entis* see Karl Barth, *Church Dogmatics* I/2: *The Doctrine of the Word of God*, trans. G. W. Bromiley (London: T&T Clark, 2010), 139–50. For further reflections on the relation between Mariology and the *analogia entis* in their unitive ability to fund an integrated postmodern Christian vision and grammar see my essay, "Thinking toward an Analogical Mariology," in *Commitments to Medieval Mysticism within Contemporary Contexts*, Bibliotheca Ephemeridum Theologicarum Lovaniensium 290, ed. Patrick Cooper and Satoshi Kikuchi (Leuven: Peeters, 2017), 111–29.

4. I am borrowing this beautiful and extraordinary phrase from Balthasar, who, in the spirit of Przywara, astutely saw how the *analogia entis* is expressive of this reality. See Hans Urs von Balthasar, *The Glory of the Lord: A Theological Aesthetics*, vol. 5: *The Realm of Metaphysics in the Modern Age*, trans. Erasmo Leiva-Merikakis (San Francisco: Ignatius Press, 1991), 48–149.

level, every hermeneutic choice of a metaphysical protagonist or source(s) is always already a decision concerning the desired direction and expanse of metaphysical vision sought after. In light of this: Why Przywara, and why is he needed now? Answer: What is needed today is a dramatic nonidentical reactivation of the Christian pleromatic tradition of metaphysical glory. This is to say that Przywara's vision is read as a mode and style of Christian metaphysics that instantiates the very living glory of the Christian tradition itself. Przywara's hermeneutic of the Christian tradition can be said to manifest the way that the Christian tradition conceives its own revealed history, as paradigmatically seen in its interpretation of the relation between the Old Testament and the New: *vetus in novo patet, novum in vetere latet* (the Old is made manifest in the new, the new is concealed in the old). (Think of Clement of Alexandria.) This hermeneutic motif of the old manifested in the new and the new being hidden in the old is transposed, by Przywara, onto the great tradition of Western philosophy which sees, in line with Augustine, that there is a *una verissimae philosophiae disciplina*.[5] Christian wisdom is anticipated in pagan wisdom, which then, in turn, requires a cleansing and perfecting in the fire of a fully Christian vision of reality, given through the speaking God: Creator and Redeemer.[6] Genuine Christian thinking, of the pleromatic stamp, then always enacts both an Alexandrian *spolia Aegyptiorum* and a Christian reimagining of the tradition. This reimagining of the tradition begins with pagan sources but continues through the great Christian thinkers in their respective historical times, thereby continually reading the new in the ancient and the ancient in the new. The gift of the magisterial tradition is thus a translating and regifting of this gift in light of historical circumstances and challenges. (I will say more on tradition in the following.) The purpose of a Christian pleromatic hermeneutic of reimagining is, in its finality, to radically humble all human systems of thought by "breaking open" finite truth and capturing all truth for Christ.[7] This is the seal of glory of the metaphysical tradition of pleromatic Christian thought as seen in Augustine, Gregory of Nyssa, Denys, Maximus the Confessor, Anselm, Bonaventure, and Aquinas, to name a few. And it is to this lineage that Przywara's analogical vision and hermeneutic of the tradition belongs. He, then, must be said to be enacting what I will

---

5. *Contra Acad.* III, xix, 42.
6. I will say more below on how this hermeneutic is greatly complicated in modernity.
7. For the concept of "breaking open," again in the spirit of Przywara, see Hans Urs von Balthasar, "On the Tasks of Catholic Philosophy in Our Time," *Communio* 20 (1993): 147–87.

INTRODUCTION

term a "pleromatic analogical hermeneutic of nonidentical repetition." It is thus not surprising that Hans Urs von Balthasar reads Przywara as a much-needed "corrective" to post–Vatican II Catholic discourse.[8] Nor is it a surprise that Rahner sees that "the whole Przywara, especially the late Przywara, is yet to come. He stands at a place in the road that many in the church have yet to get past."[9]

---

8. Balthasar says, "[Przywara] had long anticipated the opening of the Church to the world [*das All*] that came with the council, but he possessed in addition the corrective that has not been applied in the way that the council's [teachings] have been inflected and broadly put into practice: namely, the elemental, downright Old Testament sense for the divinity of God, who is a consuming fire, a death-bringing sword, and a transporting love. Indeed, he alone possessed the language in which the word "God" could be heard without that touch of squeamishness that has led to the tepid, half-hearted talk of the average theology today. He lives like the mythical salamander in the fire: there, at the point where finite, creaturely being arises out of the infinite, where the indissoluble mystery holds sway that he baptized with the name *analogia entis*." Cited in O'Meara, *Erich Przywara*, 134.

9. Cited in Betz, "After Barth," 43. This view of the importance and relevance of Przywara's late work is also held by Kenneth Oaks and Joseph Cardinal Ratzinger. And although it is true that Przywara's later work fills out in an extremely fruitful theological and poetic vein his early metaphysical works, in my view, *Analogia Entis* strikes a better analogical balance between the metaphysical and theological. Thus, to my mind, *Analogia Entis* (1932) is, and remains, Przywara's magnum opus. Oaks holds that the later work of Przywara, especially *Alter und Neuer Bund, Logos, Abendland, Reich*, and *Commercium*, present more of a theology of the cross and thus fill out in a more fully theological and scriptural mode Przywara's early metaphysical work. Although aspects of Oaks's reading are certainly correct, I think Oaks too much downplays the continual metaphysical aspect of the entirety of Przywara's work. That is, all of Przywara's later theo-logical work is still entirely predicated and dependent on Przywara's metaphysical vision of the *analogia entis*, which *always* exhibited a deep interpenetration of the metaphysical and *theo*logical. See Kenneth Oaks, "The Cross and the *Analogia Entis* in Erich Przywara," in *The Analogy of Being*, 147–71. Furthermore, Ratzinger speaks of "the profound theology of the *sacrum commercium* in the late work of E. Przywara. There he first gave to his *analogia entis* doctrine its full theo-logical form (theology of the cross), which has been unfortunately hardly noticed." Joseph Cardinal Ratzinger, *Daughter Zion: Meditations on the Church's Marian Belief*, trans. John M. McDermott (San Francisco: Ignatius Press, 1983), 29. It should be noted that Ratzinger's reading of Przywara is going to be heavily influenced by his teacher and mentor, Gottlieb Söhngen, who was a lay scholar of medieval Augustinianism (especially Bonaventure). Söhngen tried to bring Przywara's *analogia entis* into close dialogue with Barth's *analogia fidei* via a heavy emphasis on the importance of Christology as contextualizing the discourse of the *analogia entis* and, therefore, downplaying the metaphysical dimension of analogy. And this is, in my reading, why Ratzinger is (it would seem) more drawn to the late Przywara, rather than the earlier more explicitly metaphysical Przywara, and this is certainly a weak point in Ratzinger's reading of Przywara. This is because it is precisely the brilliance of the text, *Analogia Entis*, that it so deeply unites, in an analogical balance, the metaphysical *and* theological, a balance that,

Introduction

In sum: To call the paternity of this book Przywarian is to claim three things. First, it is to claim that what is deeply needed today is a continual *ressourcement* and dramatic reimagining of the pleromatic Christian tradition of metaphysical glory. Second, it is to further claim that Przywara is one of the magisterial giants of genuine *ressourcement* and creative reimagining of the pleromatic Christian tradition of metaphysical glory in the twentieth century.[10] Third, it is to claim, most remarkably, that Przywara's thought uncannily and powerfully speaks to our postmodern Christian moment. In other words, it is my contention that Przywara's expanse of Christian vision is more relevant today than it was in his own time. In this way, analogously to Heidegger's reading of Hölderlin, the significance of Przywara's thinking is still to come, and this is what both Balthasar and Rahner prophetically saw in different but related ways.[11]

Telos

But if the paternity of this book is Przywarian, it is so in a spirit of sonship that recognizes that Przywara gives us much to think, and thus, still much to do. Therefore, beyond mere scholarship, what is proposed here is not a simple retrieval of Przywara's idiosyncratic analogical vision, but a retrieval, reimagining, and synthesis of Christian analogical vision as a whole. Which, in its pleromatic, yet nontotalistic nature, gives rise to a polyphonic chorus. This is why Przywara's vision is read as a dynamically living model that instantiates the spirit of the broader Christian tradition. And because this is so, one is able to go further than Przy-

---

simultaneously, does justice to the interdependence and interrelation of the two discourses by opening up a moving site of an analogy of discourses.

10. I am in perfect agreement with John Betz that Przywara's magnum opus, *Analogia Entis*: *Metaphysics: Original Structure and Universal Rhythm*, is the greatest work of Catholic metaphysics in the twentieth century. This, no doubt, sounds like a bold overestimation given the brilliance of Catholic minds that filled the twentieth century. But it is my hope that such a statement will sound far more plausible at the conclusion of this book. See Betz, "After Barth," 39.

11. For Rahner see Betz, "After Barth," 43; and for Balthasar see O'Meara, *Erich Przywara*, 137–38. Speaking of Hölderlin: Przywara must be mentioned as one of those responsible for the Hölderlin renaissance in Germany in the first half of the twentieth century. Przywara's works on Hölderlin in 1945 and 1948 must be put in line with other notable works on Hölderlin at that time, such as Romano Guardini's 1939 book, as well as Martin Heidegger's Rome lectures on Hölderlin in 1936.

wara in forms of nonidentical repetitions by enhancing it in postmodern keys and variations. This is why in the second part of this book I will treat figures such as William Desmond (Catholic), John Milbank (high Anglican), and David Bentley Hart (Eastern Orthodox) as diverse nonidentical repetitions of Przywara, and, further, why I also treat Przywara in relation to Cyril O'Regan's Balthasar-inspired rendition of visionary apocalyptic theology in its elective affinity with analogical metaphysical vision. Moreover, these thinkers, like Przywara, exhibit strong affinities with the countermodern strategy of the *Nouvelle Théologie* and *ressourcement*. This strategy seeks a pluriform retrieval of the Christian tradition in an attempt to offer a robust elaboration of a specifically Christian vision and grammar situated within the one concrete transnatural order of grace and redemption. A narrative analogical and countermodern line of strategy and vision is thus advanced and seen in all of the thinkers under discussion.

My reason for electing Desmond, Milbank, and Hart is simple and straightforward. They all advance similar strategies to counter philosophical modernity through the deployment of styles of analogical metaphysics that are highly capacious, thereby offering models of robust Christian vision and grammar. This shared grammar and vision is, in turn, able to fund and articulate adequate responses to both modernity and postmodernity. Invoking these thinkers, and their performances of Christian vision, thus enables me to enhance and supplement Przywara's vision in a contemporary light while at the same time elaborating and synthesizing a shared postmodern Christian vision and trajectory. In short, these three thinkers enable me to constructively narrate, enhance, synthesize, and reimagine the contemporary potential of Przywara's analogical vision and the polyphonic nature of analogical vision as a whole. This enhancement and retelling, via Desmond, Milbank, and Hart, further aids my turn towards what I term an "analogical-apocalyptic metaphysics" whereby I seek to reimagine a Przywarian model of analogical metaphysics in conversation with O'Regan's postmodern visionary apocalyptic *theo*logy. This latter apocalyptic reimagining of the *analogia entis* accomplishes two things. First, it fully solidifies the shared Christian visionary trajectory and response of Przywara, Desmond, Milbank, Hart, and O'Regan in its polyphonic harmony. Second, it secures my move towards presenting a postmodern and post-Conciliar pleromatic visionary style that needs to be dramatically performed. This dramatically performed style of Christian vision, I contend, is required and needed for Christian thinking today.

Introduction

In sum, these four thinkers permit me to render Przywara's analogical vision in a new and contemporary light, thereby ultimately rendering the postmodern and post-Conciliar Christian significance of the *analogia entis* by showing the ability of Przywara's thinking to reunite Christian vision and Christian praxis, that is to say, the ability of his thinking to fund an apocalyptic, enfleshed, dramatic performance of Christian vision or a "metaphysics of the saints." In light of this, at the conclusion of this book, I programmatically trace ways in which the *analogia entis* can be rendered and developed in a more concrete, political, and praxis-based register, as a means of critiquing the anti-Christian system of Capitalism. Przywara's vision thus offers a moving and dynamic model that can be supplemented and enhanced, which is to say thought in light of its future. And, in allowing for this supplementation, Przywara's thinking is a microcosm of the great glory of the living tradition of Catholic thought and life. The *telos* of this book, then, is one of constructive retrieval, synthesis, and reimagining of analogical metaphysical vision in its polyphonic and pleromatic range, via a retrieved enhancement of Przywara's vision, in light of our postmodern and post-Conciliar Catholic context. The end result is a proposed analogical-apocalyptic path forward for Catholic thought in our dramatic and intensifying hour of Christian history as the way to reactivate Christian metaphysical glory on this late and far side of history.

Groundwork

Before this reimagined *telos* can occur, or better, in order for this reimagining of the *analogia entis* to get underway, one must first stop to understand the historical circumstances of Przywara's time and especially the dynamic formal workings of his thought on analogy, thereby establishing the metaphysical depths of its expansive Christian vision and counter-modern essence. This is the purpose of Part 1. My chosen hermeneutical strategy to accomplish this is a comparative one.

This brings me to the second major player in Part 1: Edith Stein (1891–1942). Stein is chosen as a dialogue partner with Przywara for four principal reasons. I begin with the least important and then, by degrees, move to the most important reason. First, Stein was a close intellectual compatriot of Przywara. Second, in the wake of the neo-Scholastic revival and the modernist crisis in the Church, she saw, like Przywara, that Catholic thought must enact a creative "transposition"—to borrow from Maréchal—that brings the great tradition into dialogue with modern and contemporary thought. Thus, both Przywara and Stein agree that *philosophical modernity* needs to be dialogically and creatively engaged by Catholic thought. Third, both agree that this creative Catholic engagement with modernity finds its ultimate expression in a rethinking of the *analogia entis* (and in this belief Stein is no doubt under the influence of Przywara). Fourth, Stein's understanding of the *analogia entis* is hindered and limited due to her philosophical indebtedness to modern anthropocentric foundationalism. Her Christian philosophy is haunted by the modern methodological ghosts of reflexive foundationalism. In this, Stein *unintentionally* opens a space of secularity within her Christian philosophy, which is judged to be inadequate to a distinctively Christian vision of a postmodern bent.

Put simply, Stein presents a vision of Christian philosophy, and the *analogia entis*, that is more man-centered and *anthropocentric*, while Przywara offers a vision that is radically *theocentric*, decentered, and based in God's infinite glory, which smashes to pieces all modern anthropocentric pretense. These two stances, in turn, can be read as expressive of the two basic trajectories of Catholic thought in the twentieth century in relation to philosophical modernity. The *subplot* of this book, then, must be said to be a *partial* retelling (beginning with the impasse of the modernist crisis) of the two primary stances and/or strategies of creative Catholic thought towards philosophical modernity, concentrated and condensed in my analogical narrative. I thus read the *analogia entis* as a microcosm of Catholic thought in the twentieth century, in its struggle with philosophical modernity. From the viewpoint of the knowledge of the development of twentieth-century Catholic thought, Przywara and Stein can be seen as representing or showing affinities with the two most important approaches to modernity in post-Conciliar Catholic discourse.

These two stances are famously seen in the deep divide between the modernity of Rahner's transcendentalism and his embracing of the "turn to the subject," and the student of Przywara, Balthasar, and his countermodern genealogy and revelational-based *theo*logy (immensely indebted to Przywara's thinking on the *analogia entis*). Reading Przywara and Stein in light of this divide, in turn, allows me to secure the narrative analogical and countermodern line of strategy (spoken about in the previous section) between Przywara, *Nouvelle Théologie/ressourcement*, and the postmodern reactivation of this line in Desmond, Milbank, Hart, and O'Regan. Hence, in establishing the distinctively Christian metaphysical range and workings of Przywara's analogical thought, via the comparison with Stein, I read both thinkers from the perspective of the intention of constructive retrieval and reimagining. Which means they are read from the point of view of the knowledge of the general trajectory of twentieth-century Catholic thought and our postmodern and post-Conciliar condition. I am thus judging the inadequacies and adequacies of each thinker's thought from the point of view of the furtherance of Catholic thought, in light of a postmodern and post-Conciliar Christian vision or grammar. In sum, my formal and critical dialogue between Przywara and Stein in Part 1 is written in light of Part 2, the *telos* of this book.

Yet, methodologically and historically speaking, if Przywara and Stein are read from this standpoint, then the inverse is also the case. This is to say, there is always a hermeneutic circle in which the past is judged from the point of view of contemporaneity and contemporaneity is judged from the point of view of the living presence of the past. That is to say, the general contours of the trajectory of twentieth-century Catholic thought, and the problems facing Catholic thought today, cannot be properly understood without consideration of the events that set this trajectory in motion, events that wholly contextualized Przywara and Stein's thought-world: the neo-Scholastic revival and the modernist crisis in the Church. Hence, for example, the interpretation of the relation between philosophy and theology, or more broadly speaking, the question of the relation between nature and grace, is wholly central to how one chooses to engage philosophical modernity. Indeed, this was one of the guiding points of contention of the modernist crisis, as it is in post-Conciliar form in the *Communio/Concilium* divide, as much as it is today in postmodern discourse, as especially accentuated in a thinker like Milbank, for example. Przywara and Stein's problems are ours, albeit in a nonidentically repeated context.

Regarding my reading of Stein, it may be asked: Does my reading run the risk of caricature, in the sense of exaggeration and misrepresentation? I have no doubt that some readers will certainly see it as such. But to those who read it as caricature I would like to remind them that caricature has a justified hermeneutic use. That is, it is useful when one seeks to show that certain seductive concepts or notions are extremely slippery and dangerous. Such is especially the case for Christian metaphysical discourse that sees reflexive foundationalism or the "turn to the subject" as the proper Christian strategy towards philosophical modernity. Moreover, caricature only works if there is some real resemblance—albeit by exaggeration—to the original. Yet something strange happens when—if—there is a caricature of methodological modern foundationalism of Cartesian ilk. Namely, caricature itself becomes greatly hindered because of the methodological securing of the founding appearance of being, that is, of the appearance of the I to itself. This is the pure I—*reine Ich*—which then makes nearly impossible any exaggerated doubling (caricature) because of the methodological self-sameness and self-presence governing this I. This is to say, with the foundational subject there is only the original, and if there are copies—exaggerations/caricature—they bear the copyright of this founding original, thereby disallowing full exaggeration, full caricature, or a real doubling. That said, I contend that Stein's reliance on Husserl—and thus Cartesian paternity—limits the Christian range of her vision. I do not claim that her Christian vision is eviscerated, but that it is handicapped, haunted by the modern methodological starting point of the I. In sum, Stein never escapes the formal principle of phenomenology, which consists in an immediate and intuitive noetic encounter with the *essence* of being, which in turn finds its grounding manifestation in the appearing of the being of the I to itself, thereby making extremely difficult her candidacy for postmodern Christian election.

That said, Stein's *Finite and Eternal Being* is an outstanding achievement, one of the first major Catholic philosophical texts to creatively engage medieval thought with the early phenomenological thinkers. This text is a much-needed example of the proper spirit advanced by certain Catholic intellectuals in their attempt to overcome the impasse of the integralist/modernist divide and the narrow-minded Thomism of the day. We therefore owe homage to Stein's creative daring and spirit, even if I have doubts about the full success of Stein's creative dialogue with philosophical modernity. Thus I hope that my treatment of Stein's understanding of the *analogia entis* will also bring attention to a thinker whose work deserves more attention. And although, on an intellectual front, I call into question her general strategy towards modernity, what can never be called into question is her spirit and the deep integration of her thought and life. This is, paradoxically, seen in the fact that her last intellectual work, *The Science of the Cross*, was written just shortly before she was taken to her death in Auschwitz.

Lastly, it needs to be noted that, in the comparative formal and critical dialogue of Part 1, I limit myself to a close textual comparison of each thinker's magnum opus: *Analogia Entis* for Przywara and *Finite and Eternal Being* for Stein.[12] This is done for two primary reasons. The first

---

12. It must be noted that the new English translation of *Analogia Entis* by David Bentley

Introduction

reason is for comparative and textual reasons, while the second concerns directly the intention of this book. First, as each thinker's magnum opus, each text represents the philosophical core of each thinker's mature vision. Moreover, the guiding theme of each text is the *analogia entis*. And, further, both thinkers had some level of influence on each other's texts, as will be seen. Second, pertaining directly to this book, the reason I limit myself to a comparison of these two texts is in order to establish the metaphysical depth of Przywara's vision, thereby making sure that the roots of his vision are seen in their depths, before allowing for the reimagined expanse of his vision to be given full range in Part 2. In a word, Part 1 concerns the depths and intimate workings of analogical vision in its countermodern essence, while Part 2 concerns its range and reimagined postmodern expanse.

Hart and John Betz is the 1962 edition, which was published with Balthasar's press Johannes Verlag, titled *Analogia Entis I. Metaphysik. Ur-Struktur und All-Rhythmus*. What then is the difference with the 1932 edition? The 1962 version includes the 1932 version, unaltered, with the exception of the very last paragraph, which aids in abating the difficult choice of the word *principle* by Przywara, which was included in the title of the 1932 version. As Przywara says speaking about the misunderstandings and reception of his understanding of the *analogia entis*, "The misunderstanding, for which the author is not himself free of blame, has to do with his having chosen the word 'Principle' for the title of the first volume—in order then, however, from the outset, to understand this 'principle' as a dynamic primordial movement. In the new edition, therefore, the first volume from 1932 bears the title 'Original Structure,' while the subsequent collection of investigations concerning the *analogia* [sic] in various domains bears the title 'Universal Rhythm.'" Erich Przywara, *Preface to the 1962 Edition*, in *Analogia Entis*, xviii–xix. Furthermore, Przywara had always intended to write a second volume of the *Analogia Entis*, an effort that was frustrated due to the war years. That being the case, Przywara and Balthasar decided, in the 1962 version, to collect various essays from Przywara concerning analogy that would have, more or less, comprised his scope and intention of the second volume. These essays, in turn, comprise the second part of the 1962 version titled "Universal Rhythm." Part two thus consists of thirteen essays spanning twenty years from 1939 to 1959 showing the dynamic breadth of the *analogia entis* in a wide range of issues. However, Betz and Hart have also generously included two supplementary essays not included in the 1962 version: one on Edith Stein and Simone Weil and the other on Husserl and Heidegger. For a fuller clarification of this issue see John R. Betz, *Translator's Preface* to *Analogia Entis*, xi–xiii. The difficulty of this text is notorious. Balthasar says of the text, "An exposition of this thought-world, which is compressed into 150 pages, would require 1000 normal pages of philosophical epic." Hans Urs von Balthasar, "Die Metaphysik Erich Przywaras," *Schweizerische Rundschau* 33 (1933): 489. Cited in John R. Betz, Introduction to *Analogia Entis*, 3.

INTRODUCTION

Terms Employed

In the following, in order to avoid unnecessary equivocation, I offer fluid descriptions and guiding features of how I am understanding some of the central terms employed in this book. The terms I will treat are: *metaphysics*, *modernity*, *postmodernity*, and *tradition*.

Metaphysics

The prejudice against metaphysics, in both contemporary Continental and Analytical traditions, is well known and does not need to be rehearsed here. However, I will treat this Continental prejudice specifically in Part 2. That said, I do not subscribe to the view that metaphysics is simply over and done with. Indeed, this book precisely argues for the fittingness of a Christian analogical style of metaphysics as the way forward, thereby advocating an "overcoming of the overcoming" of metaphysics. (Desmond and others are also persuasively arguing along similar lines.) Therefore, something must be said concerning the way I am conceiving the condition of Christian metaphysics and the style of metaphysics I am advancing.

I am simply not convinced that any old form of metaphysics will do in light of the contemporary intellectual, cultural, and political landscape. Indeed, in the way that Balthasar rightly sees that the "epic" theology of the medieval *summa* and the "lyric" theology of spiritual treatises must give way to a theo-dramatic and apocalyptic style of theology, so too must Christian substantialist and essentialist univocal forms of metaphysics, which lack epistemic humility, give way to an aesthetic and dramatically relational analogical metaphysics of creation.[13] That is, one must be enough of an honest realist to see that the Christian tradition, and indeed large aspects of Western philosophy, have not always been respectful of being's mystery and the loving mystery of God's transcendent and free *Being*. I thus think it must be acknowledged that there is such a thing as Christian

---

13. Hans Urs von Balthasar, *Theo-Drama: Theological Dramatic Theory*, vol. 1: *Prolegomena*, trans. Graham Harrison (San Francisco: Ignatius Press, 1988), 42. An apocalyptic and theo-dramatic style of theology is, of course, electively aligned with the aesthetic paradigm shift that Balthasar enacted earlier in his theology; a shift that, in my view, got off the ground in Przywara's massively diverse philosophical and theological project and corpus. For an extensive bibliography of Przywara's works see Leo Zimny, *Erich Przywara: Sein Schrifttum (1912–1962)* (Einsiedeln: Johannes, 1963).

rationalism and logocentrism, and that not a few Christian thinkers fall into this category, indeed, that many a Christian thinker has inadvertently sung a dirge for Christian thought, and even a *requiem aeternam Deo*, by defending certain domesticated interpretations of being and idolatrous concepts of God.

This is one side of my worry, but its opposite must also be avoided, which is to ascribe a logocentric interpretation to the magisterial thinkers of the Christian tradition, like Augustine, Gregory of Nyssa, Anselm, Bonaventure, and Aquinas, for example. This is simply inadmissible. The widespread contemporary dismissal of these magisterial thinkers of the Christian tradition of metaphysics is naïve and uncritical and as such needs to be countered. I further do not view metaphysics as inimical to Christian discourse. Nor do I accept the naïve view of the "Hellenization thesis" of Christianity popularized by Adolf von Harnack, a thesis that has now colonized huge swaths of intellectual Continental terrain. Christianity and Christian thought are partly and irrevocably metaphysical. And metaphysical *theōria* is a constitutive aspect of the Christian story.[14] Metaphysics, then, is not a disease, not a form of idolatry that needs to be overcome and exorcised. Or, at least, it does not necessarily have to be so.

To avoid these worries it is necessary to do two things. First, metaphysics must return to the sources of the theological and metaphysical tradition. This is accomplished in the mode of a varied and inventive restoration of metaphysical mindfulness under the rubric of what I have called a "pleromatic analogical hermeneutic of nonidentical repetition." Second, in this restoration of metaphysics, I see it to be necessary to listen with critical and discerning ears to the voices of critique and suspicion enacted by post-Heideggerian thinkers, and indeed, to the voices of suspicion well before. Yet to have critical eyes and ears, which are open to postmodern suspicion, is also at the same time to be critical of many aspects of postmodern suspicion. In so doing one is able to detect and separate the validity and nonvalidity of the contemporary critique of the Christian

---

14. I am here using the relation between metaphysics and narrative in the same way as Hart. This view sees the Christian narrative to be the true story of being and distrusts "too absolute a distinction between narrative and metaphysics in theology; 'narrative,' as I would be content to use the word, would somewhat elide the distinction between metaphysics and story, myth and *kerygma*, gospel and creed; it is a category wide enough to accommodate every foliation of the Christian story, from legendary to the most intensely theoretical." David Bentley Hart, *The Beauty of the Infinite: The Aesthetics of Christian Truth* (Grand Rapids: Eerdmans, 2003), 32.

theological/philosophical tradition. Therefore, taking some aspects and leaving others as is seen fit, in light of the moving and living glory of the Christian tradition mindfully (re)membered.

In other words, if Christian thought is to be in dialogue with postmodernity then it must be so in light of an affiliated faithfulness to its own tradition and thus its respective ecclesial community. Metaphysical mindfulness is, then, always storied, interested, committed, and affiliated. As such, metaphysical mindfulness is importantly an imaginative and performative act of integration that, in thought's committed story, seeks to integrate ecclesial commitments, practices, and forms of life with the deepest aspects of the theoretical speculation of the Christian tradition. This imaginative and *storied* metaphysics escapes the narrow confines of a logical game of proofs. What is proffered then, in the place of an arid and logical conception of metaphysics, is a performative metaphysical aesthetics and dramatics, a persuasive grammar or vision that shows forth the vibrancy of the pluriform Christian tradition. And all of this is done in acts of varied and dynamic (re)membering that are always ways of thinking the ancient and perennial with a view to its ever-new vibrant and dynamic potential. And because dramatic Christian thinking allows itself to be addressed by the plight of our time—without though simply succumbing to one's time—I accept that all foundations have rightfully been pulled from under our feet. Thinking—as postmodern—is a war of metaphysical rhetoric. And thus Christian thinking proffers its own peaceful story to the postmodern fray and marketplace of ideas, in an attempt to rhetorically persuade by the intrinsic beauty of its peaceful form, vision, and dramatic story.

Much has been said in the above concerning the *analogia entis*, but how specifically am I using it? (I realize that the fullness of its meaning, reality, and range cannot be given in a mere definition. It is my hope that something of its reality will be communicated via this text as a whole.) I am using it in the sense of a Christian metaphysics of creation and participatory relation that succeeds in enacting an analogization of being in the difference between God and creatures. This analogization, in turn, allows one to see created being fully in its unnecessary gifted difference from the *prius* of God's transcendent *Being* of loving freedom. This alone allows for the dramatic and aesthetic reality of the *admirabile commercium* whereby the possibility of the exchange of love is given between God and his creation. This exchange bespeaks the reality of God's shimmering presence, within creation, in virtue of his loving distance from creation. I am further reading the term *analogia entis*, like Hart, as "shorthand" for the pleromatic tradition of Christian metaphysics that was successful in uniting the biblical doctrine of creation *ex nihilo* with a sapiential metaphysics of participation.[15]

I offer seven features of the style of analogical metaphysics that will be advanced: (1) Being is inherently analogical and thus dynamically relational; this implies a critique and eschewing of substantialist, foundational, and essentialist interpretations of being and modes of metaphysics. (2) Following from this, metaphysics is intrinsically participatory and sapiential. (3) The following two criteria are rooted in the ineluctable Christian doctrine of creation *ex nihilo*. (4) Being, in both its created and uncreated guises, is inherently mysterious and overdeterminate, escaping conceptual capture. (5) This aspect of being is safeguarded by a turn to an aesthetics and dramatics of being, thereby marking metaphysics as an imaginative and performative mindfulness set within a committed narrative. (6) Overarching and implicating all of the previous features is that metaphysics, analogically rooted within *creatio ex nihilo*, takes place within and safeguards the God/world distinction from all forms of identity. This is done by recognizing that all created being (and thought) is a servant of the ever-greater absolute of God's absolving love, a love that has creatively set free creation as genuinely and analogically other to God himself. (7) Predicated on this view is that God, as inherently free from and nondependent on the world, is agapeic and not erotic, theogonic, or developmental. Yet I likewise embrace a desiring and erotic element in God, but one that is always regulated and subservient to the free whyless love of the agapeic. God need not create but, paradoxically, desires to create out of his mysterious excess and plentitude of love and replete life. Thus this form of metaphysics counters all forms of identity between God and world, avoiding any form of monistic *identitas entis*. This list does not pretend to be exhaustive; nevertheless it does isolate some of the important elements governing the analogical style of metaphysics presented here.

Modernity

I begin with a wide-ranging description, which will narrow to philosophical modernity. The question of modernity is a matter of "crisis."[16] It is a

---

15. Hart, *Beauty of the Infinite*, 241.
16. I am here thinking of crisis in the way O'Regan is using it in the preface of *The Anat-*

radical time of disquiet and "leveling" (Kierkegaard), where new forms of life, practices, and modes of thought are preordained and superimposed in place of more traditional forms of life, practices, and modes of feeling and thought. Moreover, Hegel's metaphor of the Enlightenment as a "perfume," in the *Phenomenology*, is perhaps one of the most fitting images of the ongoing event of modernity, as O'Regan suggests.[17] Yet how understand this perfume? It is not alluringly seductive, as in *les fleurs du mal*. Nor is it overtly odiferous, repugnant, or miasmic, although its late manifestation certainly was for Nietzsche's keen nose which everywhere smelled the "bad air" of humanity's nihilism. Rather, this "perfume" insinuates itself as a subtle change that occurs in an all-pervasive lowering of the atmosphere in which humanity breathes (one might think of something like Charles Taylor's "immanent frame"). It is the ubiquitous smell of prosaic domestication.

Socially and culturally modernity is a domestication or banishment of performative practices and forms of life that find expression in the symbolic, poetic, festive, and liturgical. Politically and economically it is the domesticating rise of liberalism and its economizing of the political, via Capitalism, and the normalization of the bio-political order (Benjamin/Foucault/Agamben) of the "state of exception" (Schmitt/Agamben), which is the totalitarian offspring of the founding violence of liberal democracy, as Agamben has brilliantly shown. In a word, modernity is the rising, via a "leveling," of a *novus ordo seclorum*. That is, it is the emergence of the rights of an autonomous human order contra the perceived *ancien régime* of the revelatory Christian order and its economy of salvation. Modernity, in its Enlightenment variant, is a Joachimite pneumatic apocalyptic coming of age story of the progressive "education of the human race" (Lessing); a narrative of the rights of the autonomous *nouveau Grand-Être* (Comte): humanity.

Thus, if modernity as such is an event of crisis, then, viewed from a Christian perspective, this event of crisis is qualitatively heightened with the very degeneration of Christianity itself into "modern Christianity" or an enlightened liberal and rationalized Christianity. This is to assert that the occurrence of the autonomous event of modernity is genealogically contiguous with a weakening of Christian metaphysical/theological vi-

---

omy of Misremembering. See Cyril O'Regan, *The Anatomy of Misremembering: Von Balthasar's Response to Philosophical Modernity*, vol. 1: *Hegel* (New York: Crossroad, 2014), 2–27.

17. O'Regan, *Misremembering*, 1:2.

sion and forms of life, as Balthasar and Milbank have shown in related, but differing ways (one might think of Löwith here as well in a related but different way). In a word, modernity is wholly dependent on Christianity, and its weakening, insofar as it seeks to be a definitive ousting of Christian reality. Modernity, in its self-legitimizing self-interpretation, seeks to be a post-Christian reality. The transformation of Christianity into "modern Christianity" is thus a crisis to a degree hitherto unknown in the history of Christianity. The question of the crisis of modernity, and its self-legitimizing narrative, is inextricably bound to a naturalization and rationalization of the supernatural within Christian discourse. Therefore, metaphysically conceived, philosophical modernity is the rupturing of the relation between being and grace. It is the seismic rupturing of being from the revelation of the Christian God of creation and redemption. Modernity is an event of dechristianization and the loss of the "sense of the supernatural" (Jean Borella).

I offer eight features of philosophical modernity: (1) Philosophical modernity, in a Heideggerian and Derridean sense, is grounded upon a self-securing foundationalism or metaphysics of self-presence. This is paradigmatically expressed in the disincarnate and unaffiliated nature of the founding instance of the autonomous *Cogito*. (2) Following from this, the narrative of philosophical modernity views reason as disincarnate, universal, and disinterested. Modern philosophical enlightened reason is thus a view from "nowhere." In a Gadamerian sense, modern enlightened reason is "a prejudice against prejudice."[18] (3) Seen from a Christian perspective, the first two autonomous features bespeak a stance that eschews the Christian metaphysical narrative of creation and grace, due to their gifted nature, which demands heteronomy over self-legitimacy. Philosophical modernity is an autonomous rejection of being-as-gift and the gracing of metaphysics via revelation. (4) This results in a domestication of being's abiding mystery and transcendence, which renders both susceptible to epistemic and univocal capture. (5) Following from the latter two senses, philosophical modernity is, in a Balthasarian sense, an "eclipse of glory" that seeks to close the never-to-be-closed distance between God and creation by rejecting the analogizing of being in its difference from God, which alone allows for the dramatic *commercium* of God's glory to be seen and metaphysically sung. (6) The problem of God, in philosophical modernity, thus reveals the essential *conatus* of modernity to be one of titanism. This is

---

18. Hans-Georg Gadamer, *Truth and Method* (New York: Continuum, 2004), 276.

expressly seen in German Idealism and especially Hegel and Schelling, both of whom advocate "counterfeit doubles" (Desmond) of God or a narratival enacting of an *identitas entis* between God and creation. (7) Philosophical modernity, as expressed in its titanic highpoint in German Idealism, enacts a visionary metaleptic rewriting of the Christian story that shows it to be a nonidentical recrudescence of a Valentinian Gnostic grammar which, in its nonidentical form, puts the emphasis on the developmental nature of the divine, as O'Regan has fiercely shown. (8) Philosophical modernity is thus a reversing of the great Christian Alexandrian slogan of *spoliatio Aegyptiorum* into a *spoliatio Christianorum*. It is a counter "master narrative" to the "pleromatic analogical hermeneutic of nonidentical repetition," which means that wherever the Christian thinker looks there is seen a doubling and counterfeiting, at times a doubling that is a distorted and twisted parody (Nietzsche). And at other times is seen what seems to be a genuine pristine monumental doppelgänger (Hegel). And at other times is seen a submerged, muted double, speaking in its silence and letting be (Heidegger). Christian metaphysical and theological themes are thus ubiquitously present within philosophical modernity as transmuted disfigurations of Christian pleromatic metaphysical and theological glory.

In sum, philosophical modernity seeks to be the overcoming of the Christian metaphysical tradition of pleromatic glory, metaphysically rendered and performed in the *analogia entis*. The *analogia entis*, bound to the one transnatural concrete order of sin and redemption, thus reads the history of philosophy from within the theologoumena of original sin and redemption. Meaning: Philosophy is either redeemed or unredeemed, Christian or anti-Christian. Anonymity and the modern enlightened myth of a "pure knowing" are rendered impossible in this metaphysical narrative. Because metaphysically seen from the revelation of Christ, "every kind of knowing is either Christian or anti-Christian."[19] In modernity philosophy, by and large, denies its creaturely essence, seeking to become and know "like God" (Gen. 3:5). The project of philosophical modernity (and modernity as such) is the greatest attempt, to date, to usurp the majesty of the Christian God. In this, philosophical modernity must be read apocalyptically, in keeping with the "law of polarization" and the "law of inten-

---

19. These are the words of the far-too-little-known, prophetically brilliant theo-political theologian, Erik Peterson. Erik Peterson, "Witness to the Truth," in *Theological Tractates*, trans. and ed. Michael J. Hollerich (Stanford, CA: Stanford University Press, 2011), 166. I will briefly return to the importance of Peterson in Part 2 of this book.

sification," which sees the antichristic spirit of the lie as ever-intensifying after the revelation of Christ, as Balthasar dazzlingly lays out in volumes 4 and 5 of *Theo-Drama*. And this is partly and importantly why an aligning of analogical vision with apocalyptic vision is called for now.

Postmodernity

It is by no means possible here to go into the debate concerning the validity and credence of the word *postmodern* in all of its features. However, without giving an exhaustive definition or description, certain features can be discerned. I limit myself to features of postmodernity of interest directly to philosophy and theology and thus this book. That said, I am working under the assumption that there is credence to the view that postmodernity is a reality of current philosophical and theological discourse and that this reality operates under certain guiding features and as such these features cannot be simply outright dismissed and ignored as many a Christian thinker is wont to do.

These features are the following: (1) Postmodernity is the self-proclaimed thinking of difference/différance (Heidegger/Derrida), Otherness (Levinas), nonidentical repetition or expressive variation (Deleuze), and the multiple (Badiou) against the perceived hegemony of the One, the Same, and thus, the totality of the Western metaphysical tradition (as well as the Christian theological tradition, insofar as this tradition is complicit in metaphysical totality). (2) Following from this flows the commonly accepted view of Lyotard, namely, that postmodernity is the end of all "metanarratives" or master discourses.[20] (3) Postmodernity is thus the rejection of the Enlightenment myth of Reason understood as a universal and disinterested view from "nowhere." (4) The modern foundational subject, in postmodernity, is thus decentered, deconstructed, and subverted. (5) Truth therefore lacks all foundation in the myth of Reason and the foundational construct of the modern subject. Hence truth is reinserted into the storied particularity of diverse and competing narratives or traditions. (6) Postmodernity thus presents a rhetorical competition of rivaling narratives or stories on: philosophy, theology, being, truth, beauty,

20. Lyotard says, "I define *postmodern* as incredulity toward metanarratives." Jean-François Lyotard, *The Postmodern Condition: A Report on Knowledge*, trans. Brian Massumi and Geoff Bennington (Manchester, UK: Manchester University Press, 1994), xxiv.

the arts, goodness, history, politics, cultural and religious traditions, and man and God. In a word, in postmodernity, rivaling stories are told about, and touch upon, nearly everything that comprises the embattled and endangered Occidental tradition. (7) Postmodernity exhibits a prophetic and "apocalyptic tone" (Derrida) heralding "ends" and presaging the coming or advent of something new. Postmodernity is a kind of indiscriminate and indeterminate waiting that is, on the whole, antithetical to the discerning and vigilant apocalyptic watching and waiting for the Christian dramatic hour of the Second Coming. This is seen in its amorphous or nebulous religious element expressed in its twilight critique of idols, which waits in expectation for the unforeseen future and an unmasterable alterity. This vague religiosity of postmodern thought thus exhibits a strong iconoclastic element or a Nietzschean philosophizing with a hammer. (8) Postmodern Continental discourse is riddled, in a far less systematic way than philosophical modernity, with Christian motifs this time parodied in a harlequin, aleatory, and "carnivalesque" (Bakhtin) manner—a kind of profaning "feast of fools" presided over by post-Christian itinerant magicians: the great postmodern thinkers of difference.

Suffice to say that Christian thought is able to find an uneasy alliance with certain features in the above, all the while needing to be profoundly careful and discerning that it does not capitulate too much to the critique of postmodernity to the detriment of a distinctively Christian grammar. In sum, it is easy to become a *postmodern* Christian, thus tying Christianity to postmodernity, instead of reading postmodernity as an opportunity to reestablish a distinctively challenging Christian grammar, vision, and rhetoric that sees nonfoundation as bespeaking the whyless giving of the Christian story of creation and redemption: the true story of being. In pursuing the latter path one can then, in turn, move beyond the secular, anthropocentric, and foundational impasse of modernity, as well as the forgetting and post-Christian misremembering of Christianity in modernity. But, for the Christian, the limitations of postmodernity must also be overcome, most notably seen in a nihilistic coloring that lies in wait for a rebirth that can never come. For if the divine were to be birthed, were to come, then it would enter into the economy of presence and thereby become an idol, and thus, that which it came to save us from. In a word, the Christian narrative of salvation is barred from the discourse of nihilistic postmodernity.

Introduction

Tradition

As I am advocating a retrieval of the pleromatic tradition of metaphysical glory, which seeks to nontotalistically express the expanse of Christian mystery, something must be said concerning how I am viewing the narrative and ecclesial situatedness of analogical mindfulness within the revealed Christian tradition.

Analogical vision is never a bird's-eye view, a fulfilled or realized eschatological whole, which is over and done with. Rather, vision is always analogically inscribed within the movement and figurations of history and the Christian struggle for the polyphonic and pleromatic identity of the living tradition. And as tradition is "a dynamic field of memory," then this vision is always seen from within the standpoint of our contemporaneity and the dramatic figurations and exigencies of our time.[21] Thinking within the Christian tradition is always an attempt to remember rightly the vision of this tradition, as this tradition serves and addresses the present moment. This dynamic remembrance of the tradition in the present moment is, at the same time, a movement and hope towards the future. Thus allowing oneself to be addressed by present needs ensures that Christianity does not become a mere relic or mausoleum of the past, where Christian thinking becomes the entombment of the tradition rather than its perpetuation. Yet, the only way to address these needs is to remember rightly from within an ecclesial memory. This ecclesial art of memory—*ars memoriae*—is a nonidentical act of remembrance of a dynamically living presence. Such presence is inherently Eucharistic. This means, analogical mindfulness enacted within the tradition is first and foremost a putting on of the mind of Christ and thus a conforming ecclesial performance.

Hence, to put on the mind of Christ, which is always the mind of the Church, is, as Przywara profoundly saw, a "noetic mysticism of participation" in the procession of the Son, the Eternal Truth.[22] This is to say that in transcending oneself, and one's narrow subjectivity (*transcende te ipsum*), by putting on the mind of Christ, through the Church, one is "being-formed-in-Christ."[23] And thus one analogically participates in the eternal procession of Truth, that is, of the eternal *Logos* receiving himself

---

21. O'Regan, *Misremembering*, 1:9–10.
22. Erich Przywara, *Analogia Entis: Metaphysics: Original Structure and Universal Rhythm*, trans. John R. Betz and David Bentley Hart (Grand Rapids: Eerdmans, 2014), 187.
23. Przywara, *Analogia Entis*, 186.

INTRODUCTION

from the Father. By our humble submission to Christian truth, dynamically and ecclesially remembered, one thus focuses all of one's life, thoughts, and vision on Christ, as Christ is handed down ecclesially within the varied and creative conformity of this tradition. In doing so, we thus receive ourselves from Christ, as handed on through the tradition. Our lives thus become a free and creative mission, a dramatic performance and a being-sent-forth (as Christ was sent forth by the Father), to uniquely and nonidentically hand on the creative and vivifying gift of this tradition. Moreover, this tradition, which is in conformity to Christ, as the one who is sent by the Father, is guided and guarded by the Spirit of Truth: the Spirit of Christ. And it is through this life-giving Spirit of Truth that we, in turn, receive this gift in order to continually hand over and give away the gift of the tradition. The tradition is a passing over—a gift that is continually received and given away. Further, this tradition is handed on, and passed over, ecclesially through practices, prayers, liturgical worship, forms of speech, forms of life, dogmas, and intensely speculative and theoretical modes of thinking. Christian being and thinking is the free and creative submission to Christ, where all truth is captured for Christ's glory, by those sent forth ecclesially to serve uniquely, through their own specific missions and charisms.[24] Thinking eucharistically shares in Christ's living presence, around which the Christian community is gathered and contained. Christian thinking is Christocentric and Trinitarian and thereby eucharistically and ecclesially enacted in an act of humble submission and dramatic service.

Analogical mindfulness is thus performed within the narrative of the one concrete order of grace and redemption, ruled by the analogical axiom that grace does not destroy, but presupposes and perfects nature. Analogical mindfulness, situated within the narrative order of grace and redemption, is a graced and final form or style of metaphysics that is a situated *creaturely* response to the entire expanse of the revealed Trinitarian backdrop of the Christian *mysterium*. Hence, within this one concrete

---

24. Milbank is perfectly correct to see a form of Romanticism in the Christian understanding of service to the Church through one's own particular gifts (*charismata*). The Church by no means squashes one's own uniqueness, exceptionality, and singularity. But rather particularity is set free within a communion of peaceful and analogical unity-in-difference, through which the Church is comprised of many members, but one Body. Here the self serves the common good through an embracing of her or his own particular mission, uniqueness, and gifts, but gifts that are always used and placed before the good of the community. John Milbank, *Being Reconciled: Towards an Ontology of Pardon* (London: Routledge, 2003), 153.

order, under the banner of the above axiom, one is able to draw from the full breadth and treasures of Christian truth and vision (Trinity, creation, Eucharist, Mystical Body, etc.), without thereby violating creaturely being and thought. In other words, by appealing to such theological motifs, as invoked above, I do not see the integrity of the philosophical act to be endangered, but rather fulfilled through a creaturely participation in theological mysteries, in one concrete graced metaphysics, which will be advanced throughout this book. Such thinking, then, must not be ashamed to be bound to the folly and *skandalon* of the *Mysterium Crucis*. Nor should it be ashamed of being an ecclesial thinking bound to the Augustinian view of the *totus Christus* and the Pauline *Corpus Mysticum*. That is, it cannot be ashamed of being such if it is to counter the artificial and apostate divide that philosophical modernity has enforced between *philo*sophy (being) and *theo*logy (grace).

Overview of the Chapters

The text is divided into two parts or movements. Part 1 is titled "Formal and Critical Dialogue" and comprises four chapters, while Part 2 rides under the banner of "Constructive Reimagining" and comprises five chapters.

Chapter 1 of Part 1 sets up the formal and critical dialogue enacted between Przywara and Stein in chapters 2 through 4. In doing so, it seeks to accomplish two principal things. First, before entering into the formal comparison this chapter seeks to show the critical context of the crossroad moment for Catholic thought which was Przywara and Stein's thought-world. To do this I proceed in two steps. First, I depict the radical time of unrest caused by the two historical events of the neo-Scholastic revival and the modernist crisis in the Catholic Church. These events must be understood because the strategies of twentieth-century Catholic thought, towards philosophical modernity, are largely set into motion by these events. Hence in order to commence telling the *partial* narrative of Catholic thought in the twentieth century (the *subplot*), the historical significance of these events must be highlighted. Second, I then seek to show how Przywara and Stein are united in a shared creative project that seeks to move beyond the historical impasse of the modernist crisis. Both thinkers significantly realize that if this impasse is to be overcome then a creative confrontation with philosophical modernity must take place. This is the first step towards a proper Catholic response towards philosophical modernity. The second, main thing this chapter seeks to accomplish is a signaling to the kernels of what will divide Przywara and Stein in regard to their respective interpretations of analogy and their strategies towards philosophical modernity. I do this by looking at some comments of Stein's on Przywara's *Analogia Entis*, in the preface to *Finite and Eternal Being*. This sets up and shows the seeds of division that the deep textual comparison uncovers in the following three chapters of Part 1.

Chapter 2, "*Philo*sophy and *Theo*logy: Modernity and Countermodernity," seeks to deal with, on a formal level, the relational question of philosophy and theology. This chapter is a tone-setter for what is to follow in chapters 3 and 4 of Part 1, insofar as the differing approaches of Przywara and Stein towards philosophical modernity are precisely reflected in their respective understandings of the relational interplay between philosophy and theology. Prior to entering into the specifics of Przywara's and Stein's understanding of the relation between philosophy and theology, or faith and reason, I look at the substantive importance of this question for Christian discourse in order to see its wide-ranging importance and the impossibility of avoiding this seminal question.

After setting up the question of faith/reason, philosophy/theology, I then turn to Przywara's and Stein's proposed solutions or strategies towards this question. And, as already noted, their responses are wholly central to Part 1, thus serving as a hermeneutic key to Przywara's and Stein's respective narrations on being (chapter 3) and thus also their ultimate interpretations of the *analogia entis* (chapter 4). The core of Przywara's and Stein's answers to this question consists in their different definitions of philosophy. For Stein, philosophy is an inherently autonomous and rational discourse that is not intrinsically and formally related to faith, grace, and the theological. Stein sets forth a creative transformation of Christian philosophy on the model of the foundationalism of Husserl and modern philosophy in general. On the other hand, Przywara eschews modern foundationalism on the model of a participatory, relational, and transitive understanding of philosophy, which is intrinsically and formally open to the faith, grace, and the theological. I argue that Stein risks presenting an overly modern, rationalistic, and foundational interpretation of Christian philosophy that endangers theological truth. Conversely, Przywara presents a relational, sapiential, and participatory vision of philosophy, which is open to the *mysterium* of the theological, thereby offering a supreme analogical balance of unity-in-difference through which the two discourses are united. Przywara thus points the way to a postmodern vision of philosophy, rooted in the mystery of the otherness of theological Wisdom. In doing so, Przywara counters modern foundationalism in a countermodern participatory move. In Przywara's and Stein's visions of philosophy, their approaches to philosophical modernity come unmistakably to the fore. Stein's is dependent on, and has an affinity with, the foundationalism of philosophical modernity. In contradistinction, Przywara's view of philosophy funds a full-fledged countermodern move that pulls all foundational footing away. Philosophy, for Przywara, is ever and always a suspended discourse that ends in a *reductio in mysterium* and analogical participation in the mystery of theological truth.

Chapter 3, "Visions of Being: Foundation and Nonfoundation," seeks to show how Przywara's and Stein's respective strategies towards philosophical modernity, exhibited in their approaches to Christian philosophy, further come to utterance and expression in their visions and narrations of being. Stein's narration on being takes its point of departure from the indubitable ground of her version of the *Cogito*, which is given implicitly in the reflexive awareness of the *being* of the I, implicit in the I think. Stein's guiding logic shows itself to be rooted in the modern foundationalism of the I, especially of the Husserlian ilk. Such a logic is shown to be a logic of reflexive immediacy that is grounded in the intuitive certainty of the coincidence of being with the I. Stein's method is thus one of an immanent phenomenological-ontology rooted in subjectivity. It is acknowledged that Stein moves further than Husserl by bringing out the ontological significance of the being of the I implicit in the I think. But Stein's approach is still found lacking despite her admirable attempt to move beyond the subjectivity of egological foundationalism. This is due to the fact that, no matter how hard Stein tries, she never moves beyond the formal principle of phenomenology, which consists in an immediate and intuitive noetic encounter with the *essence* of being, which finds its grounding manifestation in the appearing of the being of the I to itself. Thus even Stein's move towards a phenomenological-ontology of manifestation is still predicated on the immediacy of the being of the I to itself and thus the methodological certainty of modern foundationalism. Stein's grounding reflexive logic of immediate and secure identity, as the starting point of her philosophy, is too heavy and is never able to be fully dispensed with. It infects and haunts the entirety of her discourse on being, thereby revealing her discourse to be an unintended strain of modernity's foundational and anthropocentric project.

Przywara's narration on being is found to be a narration based on the nonground and nonidentity of analogical difference, or the suspended condition of creaturely being. Przywara's metaphysics of being is founded and grounded upon the nonground of the nonidentical makeup of creaturely being. This means that man's being is a being in inherent becoming. This is metaphysically expressed in the nonidentity of essence and existence in man. The analogical dynamism of nonidentity is admirably seen in Przywara's formula *Sosein in-über Dasein*. Here essence is always in existence, but in a manner that is ever beyond in an eschatologically deferred manner. For Przywara, then, at the heart of creaturely being resides the mystery of analogical difference, which reveals man or creaturely being to be inherently unstable, between, suspended, contingent, and relative. Przywara can be seen to be creatively dynamizing the Thomistic real distinction between essence and existence, with Augustinian movement and restlessness. The human being, for Przywara, is the Augustinian *homo abyssus*, a being that is and is not, *est non est*. There is no ground or foundation for creaturely being to stand on, as creaturely being is forever a suspended and between being-in-becoming. Przywara roots his epistemology in the above analogical dynamism of the nonground and nonidentity of essence and existence in man. In doing so, Przywara deconstructs any and all absolute systems of pure identity, where being and consciousness coincide. Epistemology is unmoored from any and all foundation, because epistemology is a method rooted in its object, namely, the mysterious and abyssal nonground of creaturely being's suspended condition of analogical mediation. Przywara presents an antifoundational epistemology that investigates the suspended analogical condition of creaturely thought, where being and consciousness never fully coincide, but are suspended and open beyond themselves towards the mystery of transcendence and difference. Transcendence and difference thus reside at the heart of creaturely being and knowing. Przywara points the way to an aesthetics and dramatics of creaturely being's abiding and abyssal *mysterium*, which is drastically different from the egological bent of Stein's thinking. Przywara's and Stein's strategies towards philosophical modernity, revealed in their respective interpretations of Christian philosophy, are consistent with their respective logics, visions, and narrations on being.

Chapter 4, "Differing Reimaginings of the *Analogia Entis*: Anthropocentrism and Theocentrism," is wholly predicated on the findings of chapters 2 and 3. It is thus in chapter 4 that Przywara's and Stein's respective narrations on philosophy and being find their consummatory logic, worked out in their differing interpretations of the *analogia entis*. The whole of Part 1 has been leading up to this crescendo. Stein's interpretation

Introduction

of the *analogia entis* is shown to be one that is based on a unified phenomenological theory of being (phenomenological-ontology) grounded in the commonality of the *ens commune*. Analogy, for Stein, consists in a "common constitutive element of meaning" that secures a unified/univocal theory of being's meaning, which comprises both finite and Eternal being. Stein secures this unitive and univocal bridge by appealing to Exodus 3:14 where she reads the "I" in the "I Am" of the divine name as bespeaking the same kind of reflexive experience of the I of finite being's intuitive coincidence of the being of the I with itself (which grounded Stein's philosophy). Here the univocality of the *ens commune* is read from a phenomenological point of view that shows the unitive link and bridge between God and man to be reflexive experience, given to us through an egological reading of the divine name of Exodus 3:14. Stein thus makes use of revelation (Exod. 3:14) in order to elaborate a reflexive-based Christian phenomenological-ontology that, she thinks, is able to offer a unified theory of being's (finite/Eternal) common meaning. Stein presents a vision of the *analogia entis* that is based in the immanent, foundational, and egological sphere of phenomenology, which seeks to bridge the unbridgeable gap between finite and eternal being through the unitive thread of reflexive experience. This, I argue, endangers the glory and *maior dissimilitudo* of God, safeguarded in Przywara's theocentric version of analogy. Stein runs the risk of pulling analogy and God into an anthropological orbit, which opens a space of secularity in her discourse, which is in danger of viewing God in the image of man. Stein's approach is not sufficient to the task of overcoming the anthropological base of philosophical modernity, and thus correlatively, of funding a specifically Christian postmodern vision and grammar. Stein's foundational and univocal logic are shown to be consistent throughout.

Negatively speaking, in chapter 4, Przywara is presented as avoiding all of my above worries. Positively speaking, Przywara is presented as elaborating a rigorous creaturely/analogical logic that is correlatively a logic of God's unsurpassable glory, which adequately depicts the God/creature relation. This relation is fully grounded in the nonground of the Christian God's free, whyless, and abyssal love. The *analogia entis*, for Przywara, is thus representative of the *maior dissimilitudo* of the Fourth Lateran Council, which thereby enacts an asymmetrical reversal that destroys and prohibits any form of metaphysical bridge-building, which would make God subservient to the *tertium quid* of the *ens commune*. Rather, God is shown to be fully and completely the giver of all relation. The relation between God and man is shown to be one of alterity and difference ever set within the very difference of God's free love, which grants and creates creaturely being *ex nihilo*. Przywara founds the *analogia entis* on the *prius* of God's free love. God and man are united in the distance of love, a unity-in-difference of a *communitas analogiae*, an *analogia caritatis*. The analogy of being, then, is precisely seen to be just that, namely, an *analogy*, where what is common between God and creature is the *nothing* of the creature, created out of nothing by God, the Creator out of *nothing*.

Yet this creation out of nothing is precisely the distance of God's love, which paradoxically secures the freedom and reality of the creature and thus the creature's free response to the loving and free God of creation and revelation. Lord and servant are united in the analogical freedom of creation, which respects the freedom of creaturely difference, thereby opening the possibility of the traversal of love's never-to-be closed distance. The *analogia entis*, for Przywara, safeguards both God and creation from identity and fusion by opening up a relational site of *commercium* based in alterity and premised on the *prius* of God's free and creative love. Man is thus sent forth on a dramatic mission of free service, on which man seeks to capture all things for the unsurpassable glory of God's loving and sovereign freedom. Here all anthropological foundationalism is broken open into a theocentric vision of God's glory, where the foundational subject is overcome with a vision of the free doxological Christian self. Such a self is a self sent forth on a performance of mission and service. Importantly here I also signal to the concrete *praxis*-based dimensions of Przywara's *analogia entis*, which become thematic in my elaboration of an "analogical-apocalyptic metaphysics."

In light of the aforesaid, I then present Przywara's theocentric and countermodern vision as preferable to Stein's anthropocentric vision. Przywara is elected to provide a model for a postmodern Christian vision and grammar of analogical being, to be constructively and nonidentically retrieved and reimagined in Part 2.

The first chapter of Part 2—chapter 5, "Setting the Stage: Post-Conciliar Trajectories"—is precisely that, namely, a setup of what is to follow in Part 2. Yet it also serves as transitional-binding between the two parts of the text. In this chapter, I briefly look again at the trajectory of twentieth-century Catholic thought, beginning with the modernist crisis and neo-Scholastic revival up to, and including, post–Vatican II Catholic discourse. This is done in order to see the two guiding strategies towards philosophical modernity in post-Conciliar Catholic thought, namely, the modern transcendentalist approach of Rahner, contra the *Nouvelle*

Introduction

Théologie countermodern approach of de Lubac, and especially Balthasar. This, in turn, enables me to reask the question of the respective stances towards philosophical modernity in Przywara and Stein as seen in Part 1, now from the perspective of the contemporary vantage and trajectory of post-Conciliar Catholic thought. I claim that Stein's approach shows more affinity with the modern transcendentalist route of Rahner, while Przywara's exhibits more of an affinity with the countermodern move of de Lubac and Balthasar.

I do this by classifying the post-Conciliar trajectory in terms of the two journals *Concilium* and *Communio*. I recognize that such a divide is overly simplistic, and if I were telling the full story of Catholic thought in the twentieth century, then this story would have to be greatly complicated. But seeing how the story of twentieth-century Catholic thought is a subplot, I find this approach justifiable. My main purpose here is to secure the affinity of Przywara with the *Nouvelle Théologie* approach, which, in turn, secures an affinity with my Przywarian theological forms of nonidentical repetitions in Milbank, O'Regan, and Hart, as all of these thinkers are critical of the transcendentalist route of Rahner and thus more nearly belong to the spirit of *Nouvelle Théologie*, now expressed in a countermodern postmodern vein. Further, importantly, in this chapter, I also point to the weak points in *Nouvelle Théologie* thinkers in their general lack of any political theology and ideology-critique. Yet in acknowledging this deficiency I also recognize that the view of grace in *Nouvelle Théologie* thinkers, in general, is capable of more fully funding a specifically Christian socio-economic and theo-political critique than is the overly secularized vision of grace presented in *Concilium* thinkers in general. This is important because this lack of integration, exhibited in the deficiencies on both sides of this divide, will be addressed by an "analogical-apocalyptic metaphysics."

Chapter 6, "The Postmodern Scene of Thought: Breaking Heidegger's Spell," is in essence a call to break the Heideggerian hegemony and spell over contemporary Continental religious and theological discourse. Heidegger's metanarrative of the mythicizing of being's forgetfulness, in relation to the question of onto-theology, is thus confronted. Here Heidegger's story and influence are presented as invidious and parasitic on Christian themes and symbolism. I present his visionary story in order to set up three constellations of response to him within the contemporary Continental religious and/or theological "turn." These three constellations are judged by their inability or ability to overcome the Heideggerian metanarrative.

INTRODUCTION

The three constellations presented are as follows: (1) The theological "turn" in contemporary French phenomenology is exhibited in thinkers like Marion, Henri, Chrétien, and Lacoste. Marion is chosen for specific treatment as he is the most renowned and extreme of the group. His approach is judged to be inadequate to sufficiently overcome Heideggerian influence. (2) What I term to be the "noncreedal turn" to religion exhibited in thinkers like Mark C. Taylor, Caputo, and Kearney. Kearney is chosen for special treatment for two reasons. First, practically speaking, I treat Caputo in chapter 8, and as Caputo's deconstructive reading of religion is similar to Taylor's, I will not treat Taylor in order to avoid negative repetition. Second, Kearney is chosen because he points to weaknesses in extreme forms of postmodern religious and/or theological discourse that he himself is unable to overcome because of his commitment to the Heideggerian metanarrative. His approach, as with Marion, is seen to be inadequate in regard to its ability to resist the narrative pull of Heidegger. (3) Thinkers who abjure the Heideggerian metanarrative. From a Christian perspective, this challenging of the Heideggerian metanarrative is seen in Desmond, Milbank, and Hart and, from a materialist atheistic perspective, it is seen in figures like Badiou and Žižek. Desmond and Badiou are singled out for treatment, as they both offer a surprising alliance of the Catholic and the atheist in their respective strategies of breaking the Heideggerian spell. Both show that philosophy is by no means dead, and that the question of being can be asked anew outside a Heideggerian framework. The approaches of Desmond and Badiou are seen to be adequate to breaking the spell of Heidegger and are preferred over the first two constellations of thinkers. This chapter thus sets up the return of expansive styles of analogical discourse in Desmond, Milbank, and Hart, where thinking God in terms of Being is preferred over the cramped and parsimonious accounts of God and the divine as expressed in Heidegger-dependent forms of discourse. A space for postmodern analogical Christian discourse has thus been secured after the breaking of the Heideggerian spell and its narrative web.

Chapter 7, "The Resurgence of Analogical Metaphysics: Desmond, Milbank, and Hart," treats the retrieval and reinvigoration of analogical styles of metaphysics as nonidentical repetitions of Przywara. This is exhibited in the theologically inclined mode of philosophizing enacted by Desmond and the philosophically inclined modes of *theo*logy enacted in Milbank and Hart. All three thinkers are shown to share strong elective affinities with Przywarian analogical vision, thereby affirming Przywara's approach. These thinkers, as nonidentical forms of repetition, are thus also able to offer new inflections on Przywara's vision by translating it into forms of postmodern Christian analogical vision which challenge the general direction of post-Heideggerian and postmodern thinking as a whole, along with the foundationalism of philosophical modernity. All three thinkers, like Przywara in his own time, present creative retrievals of the pluriform Christian metaphysical tradition in order to counter modernity and postmodernity within a specific Christian response, vision, and grammar. This chapter is important for at least three reasons. First, insofar as the three thinkers are presented in their affinity with Przywara, it is important to again underscore that this affinity is a nonidentical one. The implication here is that the broader vision of the capability of the *analogia entis* is coming into focus here, and thus its ability to continually fund Christian vision and identity in new contexts. Second, Desmond, Milbank, and Hart offer stark contrasts with the less content- and vision-filled discourses, as seen in the previous chapter with Marion and Kearney. Third, following from the second, the distinction between empty and full modes of discourse (which will become thematic in O'Regan's distinction between "kenomatic" [empty] forms of apocalyptic theology and "pleromatic" [full] forms of apocalyptic *theo*logy) is already coming to expression in the capacious modes of analogical metaphysics in Desmond, Milbank, and Hart. This chapter must thus be read as the torso of Part 2, for the following reasons. First, in this chapter, for the first time, nonidentical forms of Przywarian vision are treated, thus bringing the narrative line of countermodern descent, alluded to in chapter 5, into full relief. Second, this chapter begins to set up and pave the way for my argument for an elective affinity between analogical metaphysics and pleromatic forms of apocalyptic *theo*logy, to be carried out in chapter 9, insofar as both discourses present full and/or spacious forms of *performative Christian vision*. In sum, in this chapter, the *telos* of the text starts to more fully come into view.

Chapter 8, "Enlisting Apocalyptic *Theo*logy: Cyril O'Regan's Pleromatic Vision," after being set up by the expansive forms of nonidentical repetition of Przywarian analogical vision in Desmond, Milbank, and Hart, turns to the equally expansive vision of pleromatic apocalyptic *theo*logy, as elaborated in O'Regan's apocalyptic project. It is my contention that O'Regan's theo-dramatic and pleromatic apocalyptic form of *theo*logy is the most fruitful path forward for Catholic *theo*logy in a postmodern, post-Conciliar, and post-Christian context. This is due to pleromatic apocalyptic *theo*logy's emphasis on the entire visionary content of the Christian story of creation, Incarnation, and redemption. Such a *theo*logy precisely inflects the importance of Christian identity and the necessity to unmask "counterfeit doubles" of the Christian narrative while, at the same time, putting a point of emphasis on practices and forms of Christian life, where Christian vision is enacted, witnessed to, and thus dramatically made flesh.

For the purposes of this chapter I have chosen to focus on two texts of O'Regan, namely, *Theology and the Spaces of Apocalyptic* and *The Anatomy of Misremembering: Von Balthasar's Response to Philosophical Modernity*, volume 1: *Hegel* (henceforth, *Misremembering*). By doing so, I seek to show what O'Regan means by pleromatic apocalyptic *theo*logy, in distinction from kenomatic and metaxic forms of apocalyptic theology. To better understand the contrast between pleromatic (full) apocalyptic discourse and kenomatic apocalyptic discourse (empty), I take a brief detour or trek through the apocalyptic desert of Caputo's thought, as seen in his apocalypse sans apocalypse presented in *The Prayers and Tears of Jacques Derrida*. This trek through the postmodern desert of Caputo's thought better enables me to return to the guiding criterion of a pleromatic mode of apocalyptic discourse, as laid out by O'Regan at the conclusion of *Theology and the Spaces of Apocalyptic*, thereby seeing the stark contrast between these two discourses. All of this, in turn, enables me to capture the guiding theological intention and vision of the postmodern pleromatic apocalyptic *theo*logy presented in *Misremembering*. The purpose here is to show the extreme importance of O'Regan's guiding intent and apocalyptic vision for Catholic theology as a means forward at the onset of the twenty-first century. This chapter thus allows me to make my move towards showing the profound elective affinities between O'Regan's theo-dramatic and pleromatic form of apocalyptic *theo*logy, with analogical styles of metaphysics, as seen throughout in Przywara, Desmond, Milbank, and Hart and thus my own proposed synthesis and reimagining of the *analogia entis*.

Chapter 9, "The *Analogia Entis* Reimagined: A Christian Analogical-Apocalyptic Metaphysics," is the concluding chapter of this book. There are two main parts to this chapter. First, it begins by synthesizing my search for analogical Christian vision. This is accomplished by showing the tremendous overlap and elective affinities between analogical metaphysical discourse and theo-dramatic/pleromatic apocalyptic theological discourse. Once this overlap has been established, I then seek to show forth the possibility of an "analogical-apocalyptic metaphysics" as a postmodern discourse of discourses. The operating rules for such a discourse are then expanded upon, through which I show how the vision of an analogical metaphysics is deepened by the theo-dramatic vision of pleromatic apocalyptic *theo*logy while, at the same time, analogical discourse reinforces and strengthens the theo-dramatic vision of apocalyptic *theo*logy on a creaturely and metaphysical front. Both discourses are presented as bound together by an analogical unity-in-difference by which each reinforces the other in its elective affinities and attempts to fund and tell the fullness of the Christian visionary and apocalyptic story.

I end with a programmatic tracing of the special task of an "analogical-apocalyptic metaphysics" by seeking to show its distinctive inflection for the apocalyptic meaning of the *fiat*, in which vision and flesh are united in the entire response of the Christian doxological self, thus calling for a marring of *vision* and *praxis*. I begin this by signaling to how, in a fuller expansion of an "analogical-apocalyptic metaphysics," it must directly confront the question of political theology, or better, a theo-politics. I briefly show how the prophetic figure of Erik Peterson is central here in linking my Przywara-inspired "analogical-apocalyptic metaphysics" with O'Regan's Balthasar-inspired rendition of apocalyptic *theo*logy. I then turn to showing an aspect of this theo-political dimension of an "analogical-apocalyptic metaphysics" by showing its ability to unite Christian vision with Christian action and/or *praxis*. This is done through an analogical and apocalyptic challenging of Capitalism's anti-Christian empire. The socio-economic and political conditions of Capitalism must thereby be called into question, insofar as these conditions nearly make impossible Christian practices and forms of life, and thus, both the ground from which Christian vision arises and the ground through which Christian vision is incarnated. Capitalism is presented as wholly antithetical to the *commercium* of the Christian story and thus is seen as an anti-*commercium*. An "analogical-apocalyptic metaphysics" is presented as a call for both Christian vision and action/*praxis* in that it is able to critique, on both a theoretical and active front, the entire range of conditions of Capitalistic ideology. Vision is called to be made flesh and acted out. And, in this, an "analogical-apocalyptic metaphysics" seeks to overcome the weaknesses on both sides of the post-Conciliar Catholic divide by elaborating a form of ideology-critique in which vision and action are united within the *identity* of a specifically robust and spacious Christian grammar. Przywara's analogical vision is reimagined and constructively retrieved in an attempt to develop the underlying social and political implications of such a metaphysics and vision, now made possible through its postmodern enhancement that was carried out through my dialogue with Desmond, Milbank, and Hart and the enlisting of O'Regan's apocalyptic *theo*logy.

PART 1

Formal and Critical Dialogue

CHAPTER 1

A Crossroad Moment for Catholic Thought: The Modernist Crisis

> In the course of Christian history, the spirit from Paul's spirit is seen in every achievement of thought that has succeeded in integrating wholly new images of the world into the *philosophia perennis*, not merely externally, but from within, something that however involves translating the *philosophia perennis* itself into ever new languages which are living at that precise moment and can be understood.
>
> Hans Urs von Balthasar, "Catholic Philosophy"

This chapter serves the function of setting up the formal and critical dialogue that takes place between Przywara and Stein in Part 1. In doing so, it seeks to accomplish two primary things. First, prior to entering into the formal comparison between Przywara and Stein, this chapter seeks to capture something of the critical context of the crossroad moment for Catholic thought which was Przywara and Stein's intellectual world. In order to do this, I proceed in two steps. First, I show the radical time of unrest caused by the two historical events of the neo-Scholastic revival and the modernist crisis in the Catholic Church. Something of these events must be understood because the strategies of twentieth-century Catholic thought towards philosophical modernity are largely set into motion by these events. Thus in order to commence telling the *partial* narrative of Catholic thought in the twentieth century (the *subplot*), something of the historical significance of these events must be conveyed. Second, and more importantly, I then seek to show how Przywara and Stein are united in a shared creative project that seeks to move beyond the historical impasse of the modernist crisis with their proper recognition that a creative dialogue must occur with philosophical modernity. The second, primary thing this chapter seeks to accomplish on the heels of Przywara and Stein's needed creative stance towards philosophical modernity is a signaling to the seeds of what will divide them in regard to their respective interpretations of analogy and their strategies towards philosophical modernity. I signal to this by looking at Stein's comments on Przywara's *Analogia Entis* in the preface to *Finite and Eternal Being*. This, by way of setup, shows the seeds of division that the deep textual comparison reveals in the following three chapters of Part 1.

The Neo-Scholastic Revival and the Modernist Crisis

The neo-Scholastic revival, dating from Pope Leo XIII's encyclical *Aeterni Patris* (1879), was to definitively mark, both philosophically and theologically, the intellectual life of the Catholic Church, for better and worse, until the time of Vatican II.[1] Yet what was the meaning of neo-Scholasticism, its aims and purposes, and what significant questions did it raise? The terms "neo-Scholasticism" and "neo-Thomism" came into use in the late 1870s, and very generally speaking, they can be defined as an attempt by Catholic thinkers to again make contact with the great reservoir of the medieval Scholastic tradition. This tradition was carried on up until the Baroque commentators such as Cajetan and John of Saint Thomas, but was then broken by the Enlightenment narrative.[2]

Przywara mentions four types of neo-Scholasticism prevalent from the 1870s until World War I. The first he terms critical neo-Scholasticism. Critical neo-Scholasticism is typified by five central features: (1) its literalist interpretation of Aquinas, (2) disfavor of the Platonic and Augustinian traditions, (3) opposition towards the Kantian critiques (and modern philosophy in general), (4) valorization of the Baroque Dominican commentators, thus viewing their texts as canonical, (5) suspicion of history and historical context in favor of a closed metaphysics, which is Aristotelian. Critical neo-Scholasticism was largely—but by no means entirely—exemplified in the Angelicum in Rome and the theological and philosophical faculties

---

1. The revival of neo-Scholasticism was not merely confined to the intellectual life of the Church, but was also seen in the neo-Gothic revival in architecture, as well as in attempts to reinvigorate the religious orders and Gregorian chant.

2. This is by no means to assert that the fullness of this tradition was kept by the Baroque commentators.

of Fribourg, Switzerland. The second is termed historical neo-Scholasticism, which sought a rediscovery of the varied and wide-ranging medieval Scholastic and mystical schools. The third form of neo-Scholasticism is nominated productive, by which is meant a stress on external reality and an incorporation of the new discoveries of science and psychology into the neo-Scholastic paradigm (think of Cardinal Mercier). The fourth is designated dialogical, and by this is meant a positive creative engagement with contemporary philosophy, e.g., Bergson, Husserl, and Scheler. Przywara's sympathies no doubt are with the last three and especially the fourth.

Yet the way in which the Neo-Scholastic revival was carried out, unfortunately, privileged the first form of Neo-Scholasticism, namely, critical Neo-Scholasticism. This meant that the historical, productive, and dialogical forms of the revival took backstage to the towering figure of Aquinas, albeit now interpreted in a very narrow light. In *Aeterni Patris* Aquinas was proclaimed the teacher of the Catholic Church and his method was propagated as normative for Catholic intellectuals. This papal approval and avowal was only to increase over time due to the modernist crises in the Catholic Church. In 1914 Pope Pius X published *Doctoris Angelici*, followed by the much-disputed twenty-four theses from the Vatican (1914), *Studiorum Ducem* of Pius XI (1923), and *Humani Generis* of Pius XII (1950) (Réginald Marie Garrigou-Lagrange was largely acknowledged as its ghostwriter). All of these papal documents enforced, in one way or another, the philosophy and theology of Aquinas as the official position of the Catholic Church. And hence, Aquinas was seen as the means of defense against the many problems and questions raised by the ever-accelerating modern world. This would remain the norm in the Catholic Church up until Vatican II.

The problem of the revival of Aquinas was that it widely became a reaction and thus caught in a dialectic with the very problems it was attempting to face. This can be seen in many instances of how neo-Thomism was carried out. Beginning with the fact that it was more of a revival of Aristotle, and his mastery of logic and conceptual clarity, than it was of Aquinas. Consequently, the deeply theo-logical nature of Aquinas's work was lost sight of, as well as his revolutionary and creative synthesis of Aristotle, Augustine, and Pseudo-Dionysius. (The importance of the last is shown brilliantly in the work of the Italian Thomist, Cornelio Fabro.) Further, in the neo-Scholastic handbooks, heavy emphasis was placed on apologetical-logical proofs for the existence of God, natural virtues, and a mechanical presentation of grace. In a word, the theo-logical dimensions were relegated, and logical and conceptual clarity were valorized. Further, in this valorization of conceptual clarity the deep and mysterious relational interplay between philosophy and theology, being and grace was lost sight of, ending in an impoverished and empty state for both philosophy and theology. Thus, ironically, in many branches of the neo-Thomistic revival, an unwitting nod of concession was made to the Cartesian "clear and distinct ideas," as well as to a positivistic reduction of the supernatural character of faith to verifiable facts. And all this despite the desire to return to Aristotelian-Thomistic metaphysics. Critical Thomism, "sawdust Thomism," or "manual Thomism" thus won the day, provoking far more questions and objections than it did answers.

To say that this aspect of the neo-Thomistic revival was troubling is an understatement. To the outside world, and to many Catholic philosophers and theologians, such a stance was absolutely untenable. If this was to be and remain the stance of the Catholic Church, what would happen to the great expansive and plenary mosaic that was and is the Catholic intellectual/spiritual tradition? Was the intellectual tradition to be viewed as entirely static and finished in terms of philosophy and theology, and thus merely meant to be rehashed and repeated? How was the Catholic intellectual tradition to meet the crises, problems, questions, and difficulties of the modern world if it clung to such a narrow interpretation of philosophy and theology? Was not the creative risk and daring, which was characteristic of the greatest pleromatic Christian thinkers of the tradition (Augustine and Aquinas, to name the most obvious), being lost sight of in favor of a reactionary and defensive stance that heralded a certain brand and interpretation of Aquinas as authoritative? Many other such questions as these surfaced at this time in the Catholic Church, a time that was marked by radical unrest and uncertainty. What really did it mean, if anything, to be a Christian philosopher or theologian? How was one to *identify* oneself during this battle between integralism and modernism, which has come to be termed the modernist crisis in the Catholic Church?[3] Catholic intellec-

---

3. By the term "integralism" I mean more or less what Przywara nominated "critical" neo-Scholasticism, or a totalizing closed system of Thomism that, historically, aligned itself with a clerical ultramontane politics (and in France with the political movement *Action Française* and its founder Charles Maurras [1868–1952], which again manifests the hidden affinity between critical neo-Scholasticism and positivism). The term "integralism" can, however, be confusing as it can also be used to express its polar opposite, namely, the Blondelian/Lubacian revolution and deconstruction of the Baroque concept of a "pure nature" separated from grace (the classic texts of this deconstruction are Blondel's *L'Action* [1893] and

tuals were thus thrust into a radical state of self-questioning at a historical time of crossroads.

It was not long before the neo-Scholastic revival, called for by Leo XIII, was enlisted into the ranks of papal policy to combat modernism in all its forms. And it is, therefore, no accident that many of the papal documents written against modernism show a tremendous affinity with the critical/integralist neo-Thomism adopted by Vatican policy. Such documents include: the *Syllabus of Errors*, the encyclical *Pascendi Dominici Gregis*, the antimodernist oath, and the encyclical on Saint Charles Borromeo. All of these documents were written between 1907 and 1910, during the height of the modernist crises under the pontificate of Pius X.

What then exactly is modernism? The word *modernism* is an extremely amorphous and nebulous term and has been in use since the sixteenth century to designate the tendency to hold the modern world in higher esteem than the medieval world and antiquity. Notable thinkers in the modernist movement include Antonio Fogazzaro (1842–1911), Ernesto Buonaiuti (1881–1946) among Italians; Thaddäus Engert (1875–1945), Joseph Schnitzer (1859–1939) among Germans; Alfred Loisy (1857–1940), Lucien Laberthonnière (1860–1932), Henri Brémond (1865–1933), Édouard Le Roy (1870–1954) among the French; and lastly, the Irish-born British modernist George Tyrrell (1861–1909).[4] The movement itself possessed no

---

de Lubac's *Surnaturel* [1946]). Both Blondel and de Lubac held that in concrete historical reality such a view of a "pure nature" is unfounded abstraction. This form of "Integralism" thus rightly posited an integral always already-worked-on relation of nature and grace in concrete historical man. John Milbank makes the distinction between "integralism" and "integrism," the former to denote the Blondelian/Lubacian view of nature/grace and the latter to denote the upholders of a "pure nature" and a closed abstract/metaphysical system. Although this terminological distinction is completely valid it is not often used. And although I am sympathetic with Milbank on these matters I am using the term "integralism" to denote the critical form of neo-Scholasticism that was used in papal policy to combat the modernist movement in the Catholic Church. For the above distinction see John Milbank, *Theology and Social Theory: Beyond Secular Reason*, 2nd ed. (Oxford: Blackwell, 2006), 206–7.

4. Maurice Blondel was close friends with Lucien Laberthonnière and was suspected of modernism, both for his intellectual company and for the alleged "immanentism" of *L'Action* (1893). Jean-Luc Marion describes the whole of twentieth-century Catholic thought as ruled by "the method of immanence" dating from Blondel (he even, strangely, includes Przywara's *Analogia Entis* in this). See Jean-Luc Marion, "Christian Philosophy: Hermeneutic or Heuristic," in *The Visible and the Revealed*, trans. Christina M. Gschwandtner (New York: Fordham University Press, 2008), 66–69. For a critique of Blondel's alleged modernist ideas see Réginald Garrigou-Lagrange, OP, "Where Is the New Theology Leading Us?," *Angelicum* 23 (1946): 126–45. Furthermore, this critique of Garrigou-Lagrange is just one manifestation of the

strict creed and was itself a varied phenomenon, although geographically, it was strongest in Italy and especially France. Genealogically, the movement was influenced by the Kantian critique of metaphysics and emphasis on subjectivity, Schleiermacher's privileging of religious feeling, Newman's stress on conscience and doctrinal development, and Bergson's dynamic metaphysics of intuition and creative evolution (*élan vital*). The philosophical aspects that were isolated and condemned by Pius X in *Pascendi* are as follows: (1) an agnosticism of reason that calls into question the possibility of proving the existence of God by philosophical reasoning alone; (2) an immanentism of the mind that seeks to derive the data of faith and revelation from human consciousness.[5]

What questions did the modernist crisis in the Catholic Church raise? Or, better, what questions did it not raise? Historically, the questions of the neo-Scholastic revival came to be, by and large, the same as the questions raised by the modernist crisis. And to say that these questions were significant and all-encompassing is by no means an understatement. These very questions had to do, precisely, with the core of the Catholic Church and the great intellectual heritage of this tradition. In other words, the questions raised by the modernist crisis came to a head in the prevailing questions that encapsulated the debate. Namely, how was the intellectual life of the Catholic Church to meet the demands of the modern world, if it was to do so at all? And how was the Catholic intellectual tradition to engage the Cartesian "turn to the subject," the Kantian critiques, the Enlightenment tradition, the discovery of historicity, and the modern emphasis on experience? The question of the modernist crisis thus became, by and large, the question of Catholic thought's strategy towards philosophical modernity.[6]

---

difficulty with the integralist attack on modernism, namely, that anyone who was creatively thinking or engaging modern and contemporary philosophy could be labeled a modernist. Moreover, the whole of the movement—of what Réginald Garrigou-Lagrange negatively termed *Nouvelle Théologie*—could then be accused of modernism, or neo-modernism. For a fine study that distinguishes between the modernist movement and *Nouvelle Théologie* see Hans Boersma, *Nouvelle Théologie and Sacramental Ontology: A Return to Mystery* (Oxford: Oxford University Press, 2009).

5. Other facets of Modernism that were condemned in *Pascendi* were a historicist reading of the Bible, the denial of the eternal nature of dogma, and the separation of Church and State. John Paul II in *Fides et Ratio* interestingly still employs the term "modernism" to designate historicist theological approaches that use *only* the most recent philosophical discourse(s) *without* critical appropriation, thus entirely ignoring tradition. See John Paul II, *Fides et Ratio*, Vatican translation (Boston: Pauline Books and Media, 1998), 109.

6. For an excellent magisterial and programmatic approach to Catholic philosophy

The Modernist Crisis

These problems and questions become all the more exacerbated and acute because answers given by both sides of battle/debate were seen, by many, to be completely unsatisfactory solutions to the dire problems facing Catholic philosophers and theologians at this time. The integralist side was caught in a mummified reaction, which rejected everything new as pernicious in favor of a closed narrow-minded system and presentation of Aquinas and the tradition of Christian thought. And with this, the catholic expansiveness of a living tradition was lost sight of in favor of a stultified thought that itself was part of the rationalism and positivism it was attempting to reject. Przywara was then absolutely correct in diagnosing integralism as itself a "historical ideology."[7] On the other side of the dialectic, modernism advocated a clean sweep of the great glory of the living tradition of Christian thought in favor of a rejection of metaphysics, a one-sided emphasis on subjectivity, feeling, and emotion that ended in an anthropological/immanent reduction of the transcendent reality of the living God. Przywara, again, is perfectly right to see the final result of modernism being an "agnostic irrationalism," which logically consummates itself in "pantheism" and "atheism."[8]

How then was one to navigate between the Scylla and Charybdis of the pair modernism/integralism? How was one to be true to the living stream of the great tradition of Christian thought without falling prey to the above dialectic? Clearly what was needed was a balance, a middle, an in-between analogical positioning that would be anything but a lazy compromise or mediatory mitigation of the two opposing views (as the French would say, *couper la poire en deux*). Rather the "middle way" is—as Aristotle reminds us—extreme and radical because it resists the polar tensions of both terms to remain authentically open between both. In sum, an analogical position that escapes dialectical closure was needed.

A Shared Project at a Crossroad Moment

Przywara and Stein's time can only rightly be characterized when it is seen as a radical kairotic moment that demanded a creative Catholic strategy

---

in the wake of the modernist crisis, see Hans Urs von Balthasar, "On the Tasks of Catholic Philosophy in Our Time," *Communio* 20 (1993): 147–87.

7. Thomas F. O'Meara, OP, *Erich Przywara, S.J.: His Theology and His World* (Notre Dame: University of Notre Dame Press, 2002), 22.

8. O'Meara, *Erich Przywara*, 22.

towards philosophical modernity in the wake of the neo-Scholastic revival and the modernist crisis. Hence, before accenting the great differences between Przywara and Stein in regard to philosophical modernity, something of their necessary shared project should be highlighted.

It is in Przywara and Stein's attitude and response to the two aforesaid events that their shared project comes into relief. Przywara was a cradle Catholic and priest, and as a priest, he was personally affected by the modernist crisis.[9] Furthermore, he grew up immersed in the thought of Augustine, Aquinas, and Newman, and it was from this direction that he pursued a dialogue with modern and contemporary thought, especially the early phenomenological thinkers: Husserl, Scheler, and Heidegger, and a deep critical engagement with German Idealism, specifically Hegel. Stein, on the other hand, was a convert.[10] Her philosophical formation began in the prevalent neo-Kantianism of the day and then reached its maturity in the early phenomenological movement under the tutelage of Reinach and Husserl. And it was from this direction that Stein, in turn, pursued her dialogue with medieval metaphysics. Moreover, Stein was not as personally touched by the modernist crisis as was Przywara; nonetheless, as a woman intellectual and a Jewish convert she was entering an embroiled Church and one in which her thoughts, actions, and positions were easily suspect and scrutinized. In other words, Stein was still very much dealing with the lingering (or not-so-lingering) effects of the modernist crisis and the narrow-minded revival of Aquinas. (For example, Maritain did not think her approach to Aquinas to be very orthodox.) As such, it is fascinating to see that both Przywara and Stein felt and believed so urgently in the necessity and need to bring the *philosophia perennis* into dialogue with modern and contemporary thought. Yet, the intellectual roots of each sprung from the opposite end of the dialogue. Przywara and Stein were thus brought together as intellectual compatriots due to the fact that they both shared an intense desire and need to creatively confront ancient and medieval

---

9. For the best account of Przywara's life in English see O'Meara, *Erich Przywara*. For a shorter piece on Przywara's life and work see my "Why We Need Erich Przywara," *Communio* 44, no. 1 (Spring 2017): 144–72.

10. For a short introduction to Stein's life and writings see Sarah Borden, *Edith Stein* (New York: Continuum, 2003). In Stein's own words see Edith Stein, *Life in a Jewish Family (1891–1916)*, ed. Dr. L. Gelber and Romaeus Leuven, OCD, trans. Josephine Koeppel, OCD (Washington, DC: ICS Publications, 1986); and Edith Stein, *Self-Portrait in Letters (1916–1942)*, ed. Dr. L. Gelber and Romaeus Leuven, OCD, trans. Josephine Koeppel, OCD (Washington, DC: ICS Publications, 1993).

thought with modern and contemporary thought. And because of this shared desire they, in many ways, partook in a common project.

To phrase it differently, both Przywara and Stein took a creative dialogical stance towards the *philosophia perennis*. This creative dialogical approach implied that when the great thinkers of the Christian tradition were confronted by or transposed upon modern and contemporary thinkers they were not left unaltered by this dialogue and, conversely, modern and contemporary thinkers were also altered. This is necessarily the case whenever two different thought-worlds come together in a transposed confrontation in an act of living creative mindfulness. In other words, when one looks at the thinking of Przywara and Stein one finds not a repristination of Aquinas or Augustine, or a mere modernization of these thinkers, where they are totally and completely read through modern lenses. What one rather finds, though Przywara achieves this to a higher degree, is a personalized love and feel for the great thinking of perennial philosophy that grasps its significant (and not to be ignored) contributions to the question of being, with a simultaneous love and feel for the contemporary spirit and breakthroughs of the present moment.

Moreover, one finds in both thinkers a strikingly difficult balance that does not fall prey to an iconoclastic disregard for the tradition (Heidegger's totalizing *Seinsvergessenheit*). Nor do they fall prey to a mere dead canonical repetition of the past as in many versions of neo-Thomism. Both thinkers were imbued with a love and regard for the tradition, but they realized that it is only truly love when it is appropriated personally in a living creative and active response that is continually open to new horizons. Yet, these new horizons do not just drop out of the sky but are, in turn, made possible by the horizon of the tradition.[11] In sum, one finds in Przywara and Stein a third way between integralism and modernism that is utterly essential after Catholic thought's first failed attempt to encoun-

---

11. This, to many, may sound very similar to Gadamer's "fusion of horizons" and in many ways it is, insofar as all seek a nonviolent and harmonious reading of the tradition that does not read the tradition from a hermeneutic of violent rupture. (I am thus in complete agreement with Milbank's reading of Gadamer's thought presenting "a version of supplementation" that is nonviolent. See Milbank, *Theology and Social Theory*, 312.) Nevertheless, it is also very different because both Przywara and Stein do not have an understanding of being as entirely historical (although Przywara is in many ways a deeply historical thinker and is much closer to Gadamer than is Stein in this matter) as does Gadamer who is, in many ways, following Heidegger in this view. In fact, Przywara in the 1960s reviewed Gadamer's *Wahrheit und Methode* in an approving manner. See O'Meara, *Erich Przywara*, 13.

ter philosophical modernity in the modernist crisis. Przywara and Stein were brought together by this shared spirit of dialogue and confrontation, of reverence and daring, combining the ancient in the new and the new in the ancient, in a continued asking into the depths and heights of the mysterious question of being.

In this common project, Przywara and Stein must be seen as pioneers and trailblazers, as they were some of the first Catholic intellectuals to take up such daring and creative projects. And in this they must be mentioned among the ranks of other notable Catholic thinkers who sought to throw off the deadening weight and shackles of neo-Thomism, such as Maurice Blondel and Pierre Rousselot in France, Joseph Maréchal and Emile Mersch in Belgium, and Max Scheler, Dietrich von Hildebrand, Karl Adam, and Romano Guardini in Germany. (One could also add, at an earlier date in England, John Henry Newman to this list.) And although all of these thinkers pursued very different paths and approaches, one does find a common bond of dissatisfaction with the answers being given from both sides of the modernist crisis. Moreover, all of the above thinkers were convinced that a mere defensive repetition of Aquinas, in line with the Baroque commentators, was a dead end. No, rather what was needed was a creative engagement and not a mere mummified reaction. What was needed was a "transposition" (Maréchal), a dialogue and confrontation of the venerable tradition with the discoveries of modern and contemporary thought. Each of these thinkers, in one way or another, carried out a kind of "transposition." And, in so doing they opened vistas as yet unseen and unknown for Catholic philosophy and theology, thus paving the way for a fruitful engagement of the Catholic tradition with modern and contemporary thought, beyond the very limited answers given by modernists and integralists. For Przywara and Stein, contra the narrow-minded approach of a canonically interpreted Aquinas, the *philosophia perennis* was viewed *not* as finished product but as a *living task* that needed to be responded to.[12]

---

12. Stein says, "We know today that Thomism did not spring from the mind of Saint Thomas as a ready-made system of philosophic concepts. We have learned to see it as a living intellectual structure which we can observe in the successive stages of its organic growth. It is a method of thought which must be personally appropriated in order to gain new life within us. We are also aware that the great thinkers of the Christian Middle Ages wrestled with the same problems which concern us today and that they have therefore much to tell us that may prove of great help in our present situation." Edith Stein, *Finite and Eternal Being: An Attempt at an Ascent to the Meaning of Being*, trans. Kurt F. Reinhardt (Washington, DC: ICS Publications, 2001), 6.

And such is the first requisite hermeneutic tactic needed for any tenable Catholic strategy towards philosophical modernity.

Seeds of Disagreement

Such was Przywara and Stein's overarching shared response and hermeneutic tactic vis-à-vis the powerful wake of the modernist crisis and their crossroad moment. However, their intellectual relation went much deeper, indeed, reaching into a mutual influence on each other's magna opera: *Analogia Entis* (1932) and *Finite and Eternal Being*. Moreover, since the following three chapters seek to flesh out the very different strategies towards philosophical modernity and the *analogia entis* in these two texts, something needs to be said concerning Stein's interpretation of the relation between these texts. It must be noted, in view of the following three chapters, that Stein's remarks in her preface to *Finite and Eternal Being* concerning Przywara are tremendously illuminating and important for my purposes here for two principal reasons. First, they open the fissure through which their differences grow ever wider. Second, they reveal aspects of Stein's own self-interpretation as a thinker through which she, in turn, views her relation to Przywara, which is partly the reason why Stein misreads Przywara on certain points. I begin with her general remarks concerning the texts and then turn to a synopsis of Stein's thoughts on her relation to Przywara which I view as problematic, thereby signaling at this point to their problematic nature, by way of setup, as I take up these problems in the remainder of Part 1.

In the preface of *Finite and Eternal Being*, Stein refers to her six years of acquaintance with Przywara as a "lively exchange of ideas" and as "powerful stimulus" to her thought.[13] Moreover, out of the other thinkers mentioned

---

13. Stein, *Finite and Eternal Being*, xxix. Przywara and Stein first met in 1925, due to Dietrich von Hildebrand mentioning Przywara to Stein. Przywara relates that he became acquainted with Stein while he was "preparing with Daniel Feuling and Dietrich von Hildebrand a complete edition of the works of Newman in German. Von Hildebrand said to me at once that he wanted Stein to work on the most important texts [Stein translated Newman's letters from the Anglican period]." Cited in O'Meara, *Erich Przywara*, 121. Over the next six years they would exchange letters and meet. Their time of mutual contact proved very significant, especially for Stein, as Przywara was, one could argue, the only person who really sought to promote Stein's name as a Catholic intellectual. Furthermore, Stein was encouraged by Przywara to write her autobiography, *Life in a Jewish Family*. Nor was it un-

in the preface who exerted an influence on the text, namely, Heidegger and Conrad-Martius, Przywara receives the most attention. Yet the intellectual exchange between Przywara and Stein was not a simple one-way street. Przywara also sought Stein's consultation on his early manuscript of *Analogia Entis*. Upon receiving the draft Stein remarked, "The second part should have been the first, and the first second."[14] Furthermore, in Stein's preface to *Finite and Eternal Being* she notes that Przywara remarks, in his own preface to *Analogia Entis*, that Stein's confrontation of Husserl and Aquinas has "proved significant for his own study." Stein thus thinks that through this intellectual exchange each "decisively influenced" the other's text.[15]

Turning to the content of Stein's remarks in the preface, she sees the "problem" of both works to be "the same." Yet Stein does not immediately identify what the "problem" is. Nevertheless, it can soon be gathered that Stein is speaking of the *analogia entis* as she remarks that in both works "analogy is shown to be the fundamental law that rules over all existents and that therefore also determines the method of investigation."[16] Broadly speaking, then, the matter of thought for both works is the mysterious question of the *relation* between created and uncreated being, finite and eternal being, immanent and transcendent being, the being of man and the being of God. In other words, how construe this relation?

If this is the ultimate problematic of both works, how then does Stein see her methodological point of departure differing from that of Przywara's? And how, finally, does she see the style of her thinking as different from his? Stein sees the primary difference to be each thinker's methodological approach to consciousness vis-à-vis being. That is, as will be seen, Przywara begins with a formal metaphysical investigation of the relation between consciousness and being showing it to be nonabsolute and, there-

---

common for Stein to go to Przywara for advice. One such piece of advice that Stein accepted from Przywara was a translation of Aquinas's *Quaestiones disputatae de Veritate*. This was a significant undertaking that occupied four years of her life (1925–1929). Moreover, it was during the time of this translation that Stein made her first real extensive contact with the thought of Aquinas. The time of this translation must thus be seen as subsequently crucial for Stein's intellectual development and thus for *Finite and Eternal Being*. Martin Grabmann wrote the Introduction for Stein's translation of *De Veritate* and was very praising of Stein's balance and mingling of the language of contemporary philosophy with that of the language or idiom of scholasticism. Stein also states concerning this translation that it "paved the way for her return to philosophy." Stein, *Finite and Eternal Being*, xxvii.

14. Cited in O'Meara, *Erich Przywara*, 122.
15. Stein, *Finite and Eternal Being*, xxix.
16. Stein, *Finite and Eternal Being*, xxix.

fore, co-dependent upon one another, i.e., a nonidentical yet mutual belonging-together of consciousness and being in a world. Przywara's methodological point of departure is, therefore, to show that at the heart of the relation of being and consciousness resides a formal *difference*, or rift, in all *absolute* approaches to the question of the relation between being and consciousness (be they idealistic/*a priori*, or realistic/*a posteriori*). Stein sees such an approach to be the "elaboration of a philosophical system," while she views her approach as exhibiting a "conscious self-restraint" that "aims at an ontology [a doctrine of being]."[17] That is, Stein discusses consciousness only "as a way and means to gain access to the world of existents as a particular genus of being. The investigation, however, is not based in its entirety on the mutual relationship existing between consciousness and the data of the objective world." In other words, the investigation is not based on securing the formal relation of *difference* existing *between* consciousness and being, as it is for Przywara.[18] In sum, Stein views her approach to be a phenomenological-ontology, which discusses being as always already given to consciousness and, therefore, as always experientially engaged by/with being (and, therefore, in Stein's view humbler).[19] Przywara's presents,

---

17. Stein, *Finite and Eternal Being*, xxix.

18. Stein, *Finite and Eternal Being*, xxix. Ian Leask interestingly and, in my view, erroneously reads this passage of Stein as a rejection of Husserl's "correlationism" and transcendental project. Indeed, Leask even sees this as Stein stating that her position is closer to Przywara's than to Husserl's. However, such a reading is both unwarranted and misleading, starting with the fact that Stein's discussion of Przywara is clearly marked and delineated. It begins on the top of page xxix and ends on page xxxi, stopping at the start of the first full paragraph. Leask's misreading that Stein is here speaking about her differences with Husserl, and not Przywara, can be put to rest by simply noting that the sentence preceding the above quote reads, "The investigation of this book does not encompass the entire breadth of the problem as it has been presented in the first volume of the *Analogia Entis* [that is, Przywara's *Analogia Entis*: Husserl is nowhere mentioned in this context]." The next sentence is then the one that I quoted, as well as Leask, which begins, "Consciousness is discussed as a way and means to gain access to the world of existents." Stein, *Finite and Eternal Being*, xxix. As such, it is clear from the preceding sentence that Stein is still speaking of Przywara here. Not to mention that the section on Przywara goes on for another page and a quarter and has a clearly demarcated ending. That being said, there may be something to Leask's misreading of Stein, which is symptomatic of Stein's own misreading of Przywara, a reading that gives Przywara too much of a Husserlian coloring. For this misreading see Ian Leask, *Being Reconfigured* (Newcastle, UK: Cambridge Scholars Publishing, 2011), 100–101. O'Meara also has the same reading as mine concerning this passage. See O'Meara, *Erich Przywara*, 123.

19. As O'Meara correctly states, "There is, however, a difference in emphasis, for her [that is, Stein's] thinking is more situated in the subject." O'Meara, *Erich Przywara*, 123.

on Stein's reading, more of a formal, disengaged, metaphysical presentation of being and consciousness that ends in a "system."

There are numerous problems with this reading, two of which I will signal to here. First, Stein does not seem to fully grasp that Przywara's method is rooted in, and an expression of, the object of his investigation, namely, the dynamic "suspended middle" or tension of creaturely being or becoming. This is why what Przywara nominates a "creaturely metaphysics" must be seen as a formal *description* of the very condition of our becoming and therefore not an armchair metaphysics that is disengaged from the living moving reality of the creature-in-becoming. To say it otherwise, the formal epistemological suspended relation described by Przywara between consciousness and being is a faithful mirroring of the suspended movement or tension present in creaturely becoming and thus not a nonfluid closed system. Which is to say that thought itself takes place within, and is an expressing of, the dynamic and nonidentical makeup of creaturely being or becoming. Second, it is true to say that Przywara has a very systematic element in his work, but it is more true to say that there is present what I will call a "systematics of impurity," which seeks to deconstruct all forms of absolute metaphysics in favor of a radically suspended creaturely metaphysics. Hence, Stein does not seem to fully grasp how robustly Przywara is elaborating a metaphysics of difference and relation that construes difference as harmonious (and therefore not violent) with unity, that is, being as a musical analogical unity-in-difference. To say it otherwise, Przywara's thought analogizes being, seeing it as a manifold relational play of likeness and unlikeness, sameness and otherness, identity and difference. Przywara's thought, then, breaks open and reveals as illusionary all metaphysics of self-presence or totality. His thought is, therefore, at the farthest remove from being another mere "philosophical system."

Stein goes on to mention three other agreements "in principle" between her and Przywara which are found in both works. First, she finds there to be agreement in how both construe the relationship between the creature and the Creator. (If she is thinking again explicitly of the *analogia entis*, it is not clear.) Second, regarding Plato/Aristotle and Augustine/Aquinas she thinks that both she and Przywara embrace a hermeneutic of a both/and rather than a hermeneutic of an either/or. Lastly, she believes there to be agreement concerning how both construe the relation between philosophy and theology. However, she thinks it necessary to make "some qualifying remarks" regarding the latter. I will take up these "qualifying remarks" in the following chapter, which deals with the relation between *philo*sophy and *theo*logy, as I find Stein's remarks to be extremely important in seeing some of the many great differences that exist between Przywara's and Stein's approaches.[20]

How does Stein view the differences in style between her and Przywara? And how, in turn, does Stein self-stylize herself as a thinker and how does she stylize Przywara as a thinker? Stein sees "the procedure" of *Finite and Eternal Being* as differing from *Analogia Entis* insofar as Przywara's "creaturely thinking" proceeds under the categories of "historical immanence" (*innergeschichtliche Denken*), while hers strives towards "suprahistorical truth."[21] Stein, interestingly, views these differing methodological approaches as an expression of different mentalities of varying kinds of thinkers.[22] Stein does not see the above different mentalities as contradictory but as complementing each other's weaknesses. That is, Stein sees both approaches as moving towards a "progressive approximation towards 'supra-historical truth.'"[23] Stein, in turn, concludes that some thinkers (e.g., Przywara) have to gain access to "objects" (*Sachen*) by means of concepts elaborated and thought by other thinkers. The "strength" of such a thinking lies in "understanding" (*Verstehen*) and in being able to obtain deep understanding of "historical constellations." Conversely, there are other kinds of thinkers (e.g., Stein) who only gain access to things by "a direct investigation of the actually given world of things." These types of thinkers only make contact with other minds by measuring them according to what they have

---

20. Stein, *Finite and Eternal Being*, xxx.
21. Stein, *Finite and Eternal Being*, xxx.
22. O'Meara notes concerning Przywara's and Stein's styles that "Stein's tone is unassuming but is perhaps also more independent and self-confident than Przywara's broad, demonstrative union of typologies and aphorisms." O'Meara, *Erich Przywara*, 123. Yet I am not sure what confidence has to do with their differing styles. Both, in my view, equally speak in their own voice. Just because Przywara is often speaking in a broad historical manner and in constant conversation with the great thinkers never makes one doubt that what one is reading is distinctively Przywara's own particular idiosyncratic metaphysical vision of the *analogia entis*. In other words, Przywara speaks in his own voice even if he does not do so always directly. No one says that Heidegger lacked confidence because he was always speaking in dialogue with the great thinkers. And no one ever doubts when Heidegger speaks on Kant that he is really speaking on his construal of how the ontological difference remained unthought in Kant. In other words, Heidegger makes Kant speak as if he were Heidegger. Przywara, in many ways, employs the same hermeneutic tactic at times. One could indeed argue that this way really shows more confidence. But, again, I am not really sure that confidence has anything to do with different styles, in the sense that O'Meara is using it.
23. Stein, *Finite and Eternal Being*, xxx.

thought by the "exertion of their own intellect." This last trait, according to Stein, is the "characteristic mark of all born phenomenologists."[24]

Significant conclusions can be drawn from Stein's above comments: conclusions that pertain to the scope and project of *Finite and Eternal Being*, as well as Stein's general approach to being itself in the text. Not to mention her reading of Przywara. It is clear that, despite Stein's later engagement with medieval metaphysics, she always remains, to her mind, a phenomenologist. As such, the project of *Finite and Eternal Being* remains a phenomenological-ontology. Thus, Stein never elaborates a metaphysics of being. And by this I mean Stein always thinks being in immediacy to the personal I. Such an approach is tied with Stein's phenomenological preoccupation with essence and, therefore, "supra-historical truth." Following from this (as with Husserl), being is not directly related to history and its dynamic happening. This is why she can so easily equate Przywara's thinking with merely elaborating further our "understanding" of "historical constellations" and not being itself. But, for Przywara, such "historical constellations" tell us something about being itself, because creaturely being is through and through dynamic and, therefore, must be thought within the living stream of the venerable tradition. In other words, for Przywara, there is no pure phenomenological gaze upon pristine eternal essences as there was for many of the early phenomenologists (e.g., Scheler). Our gaze is always creaturely and, therefore, suspended between being and becoming, essence and existence, truth and history, unity and difference. In other words, our gaze is never total, but analogically chiaroscuro. It can be seen, then, that Stein's starting point and self-stylization is a phenomenological one, which in turn manifests her penchant for thinking being in a more static, constant, essentialist, and eternal manner. Therefore, in the end—it will be argued—Stein's "conscious self-restraint" of elaborating an "ontology" or doctrine of being is far more ambitious than Przywara's alleged "philosophical system" because it always already presumes a secure foundation of immediate access of the I to being. In contrast, Przywara's "systematics of impurity" begins with a mediatory difference between being and consciousness, which undercuts the privileging of the I's secure immediate contact with being. In other words, Przywara's thought thinks being's difference and distance by seeing being as analogically different, while Stein's thinking moves in a more foundational, essentialist, and exemplarist direction.

---

24. Stein, *Finite and Eternal Being*, xxx.

The Modernist Crisis

* * *

To conclude: the neo-Scholastic revival and the modernist crisis in the Catholic Church were seminal events definitively influencing the intellectual landscape of early-twentieth-century Catholic thought. Indeed, the development of twentieth-century Catholic thought cannot be properly understood without an understanding of these events (*subplot*). And nor can Przywara and Stein's shared project be understood without understanding it as taking place in the wake of these seminal events. This shared project was specifically expressed in their common desire to creatively confront the tradition with modern and contemporary thought. In this, Przywara and Stein were pioneers in twentieth-century Catholic philosophy, as they broke free from the deadlock of the narrow alternatives presented by the opposing sides of the modernist crisis. Further, in this shared project, an initial and common response was taken towards philosophical modernity in an attempt to once again make Catholic philosophy a living option amidst the crossroad moment in which they stood within the intellectual life of the Catholic Church. Przywara and Stein were thus correct in seeing that if philosophical modernity was to be engaged, then the only way to do so was creatively. In other words, what all of the magisterial Catholic trailblazers taught Catholic thinking, in the wake of the modernist crisis, is that it is an obligation for Catholic thought to engage philosophical modernity if it is to continue to live. The first step in this crossroad moment needed to be a step of creative engagement or "transposition" beyond the dialectic of the modernist crisis. Yet because of the Goliath- and Medusa-like character of philosophical modernity, the question immediately becomes: How enact and perform this engagement? How ensure a full range of Christian metaphysical vision, given the challenges of philosophical modernity that I laid out in the Introduction? It is difficult enough to creatively engage philosophical modernity, but how do so successfully in light of the pleromatic range of Christian vision? Seeds of the directions of Przywara's and Stein's respective responses to philosophical modernity were thus hinted at in the conclusion of this chapter. The following three chapters reveal the very fundamental differences and trajectories between Przywara's and Stein's approaches to philosophical modernity. And it is in light of these strategic approaches to philosophical modernity that the current viability or nonviability of their thinking for funding a robust postmodern pleromatic analogical Christian vision must be understood and judged.

CHAPTER 2

*Philo*sophy and *Theo*logy: Modernity and Countermodernity

> Where is the Life we have lost in living?
> Where is the wisdom we have lost in knowledge?
> Where is the knowledge we have lost in information?
> The cycles of Heaven in twenty centuries
> Bring us farther from God and nearer to the Dust.
> T. S. Eliot, "Choruses from 'The Rock'"

The preceding chapter served the function of setting up the formal and critical dialogue between Przywara and Stein enacted in Part 1. It did so by capturing something of the Catholic intellectual crossroad moment in which the thinking of Przywara and Stein occurred vis-à-vis the question of philosophical modernity. Their shared project of a necessary Catholic creative confrontation with philosophical modernity was accented. Moreover, chapter 1 further signaled to the seeds of division in this shared project in terms of how this necessary confrontation was to be intellectually performed. This chapter directly concerns the different strategies taken towards philosophical modernity in Przywara and Stein in regard to the question of the relation between philosophy and theology.

    I will argue that Stein's conception of Christian philosophy is too rationalistic and guided by modern philosophy's foundationalist project of the "dream of reason," that is, establishing a secure foundation of philosophy as a "rigorous science." To say it otherwise, Stein creatively transposes or passes on the Husserlian task of philosophy's aim of "total knowledge" to her own idiosyncratic interpretation of Christian philosophy. In doing so, a conception of Christian philosophy tinged with the rationalism of philosophical modernity is presented. Stein's conception of Christian philosophy is thus forgetful of the reality that, first and foremost, philosophy is (and always remains) a participatory loving-towards Wisdom. On the other hand, I will argue that Przywara presents a nonfoundational countermodern style of philosophy that respects the reality of *philo*sophy as a loving participation in and towards Wisdom. Przywara's view thus refuses the promethean temptation of aiming at "total knowledge," thereby reactivating a sapiential Christian vision of *philo*sophy respectful of mystery. In so doing a *philo*sophy that positively participates in mystery is presented. In a word, the end of *philo*sophy is a speculatively dramatic and aesthetic *reductio in mysterium*.

In treating the subject of the relation between *philo*sophy and *theo*logy, it will become apparent that Przywara's and Stein's respective strategies to this question prove to be a significant point of difference between the two thinkers. This point of difference acts as a kind of hermeneutic key that throws light on the ultimate strategic differences towards philosophical modernity intellectually performed by Przywara and Stein. The differences elaborated in this chapter will find a refrain in the two remaining chapters of Part 1. This chapter is thus foundational to my formal and critical dialogue and, therefore, essential to seeing the Christian postmodern visionary potential of Przywara's thinking. In a word, if the apostate divide between being and grace in philosophical modernity is to be overcome, philosophy must be returned to the "suspended middle" (*schwebende Mitte*) site of participatory analogical ordering and thus to the site of *theo*logical supplementation.

A Substantive Formulation of the Question of Reason and Revelation

Prior to entering into the formal comparison between Przywara's and Stein's understanding of the relation between philosophy and theology I would like to offer a general and substantive formulation of this problem for a twofold reason: first, for the simple reason that this question touches to the core how one understands the Christian narrative as well as the very nature of philosophy as such; and second, following from the first, once something of the enormity of this question is understood, it will become clear why Przywara's and Stein's respective answers to this question are fundamental to the *range* of their respective Christian visions.

What then is at stake in this question, what is the beating heart of the matter, and why is it such a dividing, divisive, and acrimonious question?¹ My answer lies in the fact that the question is inherently relational, thereby raising the possibility of either a harmonious unity or extreme discord between philosophy and Christianity. And, as such, this question touches upon the identity and essence of both philosophy (What is philosophy?) and Christianity (What is Christianity?), simultaneously. Thus, when one attempts to answer this question, one implicitly, or explicitly, gives an answer to one's conception of the meaning, essence, and reality of Christianity (even in a rejection of Christianity) and philosophy, concomitantly.

Seen from a more post-Reformation and post-Kantian perspective, one can then see how the relational nature of the question logically implies a theory of what revelation is (an implicit or explicit fundamental theology for those who are asking this question within the tradition of Christianity), as well as a metaphysics of being and thus one's view of the relation between the two.² Is finite being open to the infinite? Is there an interplay between time and eternity, immanence and transcendence? Is our understanding of being restricted to space/time? Is the *being* of the self transcendentally or dialectically self-legislative or open to mystery, transcendence, surprise, and otherness? These are the kinds of questions that come into play when one is speaking about a possible relation between philosophy and *theo*logy. Thus depending on how one construes these things, the possibility of a harmonious interplay of *theo*logy and philosophy (nature/grace) is possible *or* a more violent dissonance and disruption between the two.³ Consequent upon this, one's understanding of both the meaning of revelation (is it entirely personal/subjective or does it have historical/metaphysical import?) and metaphysics, in turn, gives rise to a certain epistemology. Is reason transcendentally or dialectically structured or is it dialogically and analogically open to the surprise of otherness? What is the nature of reason and rationality? Does reason mean a universally free and autonomous rationality or is this a form of irrationality that refuses to

---

1. For a fine treatment of this difficult question see Maurice Nédoncelle, *Is There a Christian Philosophy?*, trans. Dom Illtyd Trethowan (London: Burns & Oates, 1960).

2. Even for those thinkers who flatly deny revelation, a theory of revelation must still be given, that is, one must say what revelation *is* not. A perfect example of this is Feuerbach's anthropological reduction or projection theory of revelation.

3. For even when one denies the possibility of God or revelation, one does so on some sort of preunderstanding of being: being *is* nothing; all there is *is* what we can see, touch, taste, and prove. Yet here is an implicit metaphysics that is immanentist: metaphysics of some sort cannot be avoided.

open and submit itself to what is other than, but not contrary to, reason?[4] What role do history and tradition play in the answer to this question? And can two traditions such as the Judeo-Christian tradition and the Greek heritage meet without both traditions being corrupted, thus losing their particular identity?

In a more contemporary way one can say that what one encounters in the question of the relation of Christianity and philosophy is competing narratives (and I, of course, include competing narratives within Christianity itself). Thus in this war of narratives different views on how one narrates the meaning and identity of Christianity *and* philosophy and their respective places and roles in Western history come into question. This does not mean that each narrative is equally a "language game." But rather that in each narrative is an implicit or explicit narration of the truth of the meaning of being, i.e., being is such and such. Narratives do not exclude metaphysics but are unavoidably tied to a vision of things and thus a certain metaphysics of being. (Recall my remarks in the Introduction.) In summary, at stake in this question is the entirety of both Christianity *and* philosophy, and how one answers this relational question inevitably determines how one defines each tradition and discourse, and thus, the breadth of commerce between the two.

This is why this question has always been, and will always be, so inflammatory. This is to say, this question touches upon the beating heart of *both Christianity and philosophy* and thus so much of our Western history and narrative. Moreover, with the advent of philosophical modernity and the cutting of the gifting tie between being and grace this question becomes all the more urgent. Hence when this question reemerges, on the far side of what some have claimed to be "the end of history," "the end of metaphysics," then it demands to be grappled with. This question thus comes to our evening age of nomadic postmodern loss of identity like a kind of stranger or sojourner from a far land to a nomadic tribe that has left its home and been wandering for years in search of forgetfulness and misremembering. And upon the arrival of this stranger the tribe is reminded of all that it desired to forget and, indeed, had forgotten: even misremembered. But now with the arrival of this stranger the wandering tribe is forced to confront the question of itself, of its home, of its origin,

---

4. Think of Rahner's post-Kantian task in *Spirit in the World*: "what is to be explained is the intrinsic possibility of intellectual knowledge as the place for a theological event." Karl Rahner, *Spirit in the World*, trans. William V. Dych (New York: Continuum, 1994), 23.

and identity, and beyond that the place of this origin within this nomadic, some might even say, apocalyptic hour. So too is the question of the relational interplay between Christianity/philosophy, reason/revelation, being/grace. In this question we are forced again to ask the guiding questions of the West that we have tried to forget: "What is Christianity?" "What is *Theo*logy?" "What is Philosophy?" "What is Revelation?" "What is Being or Metaphysics?" "What is Reason?" "What is History?" Do these questions relate to one another and how have they formed the very meaning and identity of the West in our autumnal and dramatic evening hour? To shirk these questions would be to abandon the possibility of a nonidentical retrieval of a pleromatic analogical metaphysics of glory. And to further shirk this question would be to enter into narcissistic self-referential state of refusal to question into the very questions that have formed us: whether one likes it or not.[5]

A Christian Philosophy Tinged with Rationalism

In the previous chapter Stein's comments on her relation to Przywara, in the preface to *Finite and Eternal Being*, were briefly dealt with. In one of these comments Stein referred to their "agreement in principle" in regard to the relation between philosophy and *theo*logy. However, Stein also stated that some "qualifying remarks" were required on this matter.[6] It is now time to look at these comments and Stein's conception of Christian philosophy as a whole in order to see, in detail, the reasons for the above-mentioned differences between Przywara and Stein.

---

5. These questions are not just raised by Christian thinkers, but they are questions that have to be raised by all serious thinkers. In this I am thinking about, in many ways, the admirable atheistic materialist thinkers, such as Žižek and Badiou who, in their intellectual honesty, realize that there has to be a serious engagement with Christianity, theology, or revelation if one is to confront the realities of "savage Capitalism" by developing a nonreductive materialism. On this matter see the fine essay of John Milbank, "Materialism and Transcendence," in *Theology and the Political: The New Debate*, ed. Creston Davis et al. (Durham, NC: Duke University Press, 2005), 393–426. Likewise the whole debate concerning the "secularization thesis" touches upon the importance of this question in thinkers like Löwith, Blumenberg, Illich, Taylor, and Milbank, to name but some.

6. Edith Stein, *Finite and Eternal Being: An Attempt at an Ascent to the Meaning of Being*, trans. Kurt F. Reinhardt (Washington, DC: ICS Publications, 2001), xxx–xxxi.

Modernity and Countermodernity

Stein's Definitions of Philosophy and Christian Philosophy

Turning to the text: the urgency of this question, for Stein, is immediately attested to by its placement in *Finite and Eternal Being*.[7] Her treatment of Christian philosophy is found straightaway in the Introduction of the text.[8] And, by far, the most extensively treated subject is Christian philosophy.[9] In my reading, this is due to the fact that the viability of Stein's project, as a whole, rests on an adequate treatment of this question. This is due to the fact that the task of the text is a comprehensive synthesis of the truths of philosophy with the truths of revelation, as will be seen. The subject of Christian philosophy is central to Stein's project and, therefore, tied closely to her project's viability.

In order to get to the heart of Stein's conception of Christian philosophy, it must be seen how she defines philosophy. This is because the formal definition one gives to philosophy will greatly affect the kind of relation philosophy has with Christian revelation. And, in the end, one's definition of philosophy will determine what kind of Christian philosophy is pos-

---

7. The question of Christian philosophy and the relation between theology and philosophy was to take on tremendous importance in the life and work of Stein. Why? First, Stein took significant time after her conversion to find her equilibrium in respect to how she was going to, or not going to, live out her former intellectual vocation in light of her newfound faith. As such, Stein's person was wholly invested in the question of Christian philosophy. This personal investment had to be all the more acute, because she must have felt a strong need to justify and defend her new position to her philosophical contemporaries, most notably, Husserl and Heidegger. Second, Stein's intellectual task became defined by her project of confronting the thought-world of the Middle Ages with that of the new philosophical movement, phenomenology. Third, Stein's personal interest in the question of Christian philosophy must have been all the more enhanced by the fascinating fact that Stein herself saw firsthand something of the "French debate" on Christian philosophy, as she attended the famous conference at Juvisy in 1933 concerning this topic (this is where Stein met Maritain). Thus Stein was privy to the tumultuous stir that this debate aroused in the Francophone world: a stir that must have only confirmed her personal need to wrestle with this question. These three factors make Stein an intriguing contributor to the debate on Christian philosophy and must be seen as contributing to Stein's idiosyncratic, fascinating but, ultimately, problematic vision of Christian philosophy.

8. For the Introduction see Stein, *Finite and Eternal Being*, 1–29. The Introduction is given over to addressing basic problems that Stein feels require clarification prior to launching into the text, such as the problem of being in history (section 2), and certain linguistic challenges (section 3) pertaining to confronting medieval and modern idioms.

9. For the section on Christian philosophy see Stein, *Finite and Eternal Being*, 12–29. The Introduction consists of twenty-nine pages, eighteen of which are given over to Christian philosophy.

sible. With all de-fining there is a limiting and con-fining of possibilities and, therefore, it must be asked what possibilities are foreclosed by Stein's definition of philosophy.

To advance a definition of Christian philosophy Stein draws heavily from Maritain's *An Essay on Christian Philosophy*.[10] This text was originally a paper given at the University of Louvain in December 1931. Thus it was a central text in the French debate on Christian philosophy. And, because of Maritain's status as an intellectual in France, it was seen by many to be *the* representative view of the Thomistic position concerning Christian philosophy. And, given

---

10. Jacques Maritain, *An Essay on Christian Philosophy*, trans. Edward H. Flannery (New York: Philosophical Library, 1955). According to Maritain, his answer to this problem was endorsed by Garrigou-Lagrange, Marcel, and Gilson. Gilson viewed Maritain's solution as completely compatible with his own, which sought in history the final justification for Christian philosophy. Gilson thus saw Maritain as aiding in filling out his own approach by presenting a more formal resolution to the question of Christian philosophy. However, for the finest treatment of this debate within the French context, which complicates the aforesaid, see the magisterial essay by Henri de Lubac, "On Christian Philosophy," *Communio* 19 (1992): 479–507. In this essay de Lubac treats Maritain, Gilson, Blondel, and Marcel and their respective interpretations of Christian philosophy. De Lubac rightly sees Maritain's view as being the weakest endorsement of Christian philosophy (for reasons not unlike my own to be given below). This is to say, Maritain is unable to open up an intrinsic relation between philosophy and grace because, as will be seen, he defines philosophy as inherently independent and rational: whereas in order to have a robust Christian philosophy it is necessary for Christian philosophy to submit itself and be open to heteronomy and service. Thus Maritain's view of Christian philosophy is, in the end, very weak and something through which he is merely subjectively "comforted" from the outside. De Lubac, "Christian Philosophy," 496. On the other hand, Gilson's view goes much deeper. That is, for Gilson, Revelation is seen as the "generator of reason." Such a view is deeply fulfilled and completed by Blondel's "philosophy of insufficiency," which opens up an intrinsic space in philosophy to the supernatural, thereby revealing philosophy's role as a servant. De Lubac concludes the essay with an extraordinary meditation on some of the last words written by the great Rousselot before he was killed at Éparges near Verdun in February 1915. These words concern the "renaissance of reason" brought about through faith in the Incarnation. De Lubac, "Christian Philosophy," 498. If then it was Rousselot that rediscovered this ancient Christian teaching before his untimely death, it was Gabriel Marcel who, according to de Lubac, really incarnates and puts into practice this forgotten teaching in his profoundly experiential philosophy. Marcel's philosophy thus contemplates and lives from out of the realities of Incarnation, Eucharistic presence, faith, hope, and love. Marcel thus opens up a deeply Christian philosophy that inhabits the intersection of being and grace (or the mystery of being). But, in so doing, Marcel is also able to speak to non-Christians from out of the depths of his singular reflections on experience and the person, which are true for everyone precisely because he is dealing with the irradiation of the supernatural, which has penetrated and transformed all of being since the time of the Incarnation.

Stein's heavy appropriation of this text, I think it is safe to assume that Stein is also of this opinion. The core of Maritain's solution lies in his distinction between the "nature" and "state" of philosophy.[11] And it is this primary distinction that is taken up in her discussion on Christian philosophy, not though without an alteration as will be seen. According to Maritain, and Stein, the nature of philosophy is entirely determined by its object, or objects. These objects are fully accessible by the natural faculty of the mind, meaning that philosophy is defined, in its nature, as inherently rational and natural (as opposed to supernatural) and thus independent and distinct from *theo*logy. Thus the answer to Christian philosophy, for Maritain and Stein, is *not* to be sought in the "nature," or on the formal level, but rather in the "state" or situation of philosophy, meaning that philosophy is formally defined by its autonomy vis-à-vis *theo*logy and pertains solely to its various rational and natural objects. The question must thus be asked: Does the exclusion of the possibility of a formal relationality or *possible* openness to revelation, on the part of philosophy, not result in an *a priori* foreclosing of the insertion of mystery and otherness into the very heart of the definition of philosophy?[12] Is philosophy ultimately about a fully comprehensive rational enquiry into things or is it about a loving participation in Wisdom and a *reductio in mysterium*? This question has to be kept in mind as it will be central to understanding Przywara and Stein's respective interpretations of philosophy.

Stein's appropriation of Maritain, however, is not pure, for in it her Husserlian lineage comes to light. For Stein, in the preceding account of philosophy, something essential is missing, namely, that philosophy is a science (*Wissenschaft*). Moreover, like Husserl, she views philosophy's task as clarifying the foundation of the sciences. Thus, Stein's account of the nature of philosophy is not complete until philosophy meets the demands of a "rigorous science" and teleologically aims at the ideal of the "dream of reason,"[13] that is, a science that is complete and has arrived at total evidence or "total knowledge."[14] Such a science would have explained the entire existing states-of-affairs, without flaw or wrinkle. However, such an ideal is historically and practically untenable. In the world of experience

---

11. Maritain, *Essay on Christian Philosophy*, see especially 11–33.

12. This is not to deny that the formal objects of philosophy and *theo*logy are different, as they surely are, but rather it is a question about the formal relationality between the two discourses.

13. See Edmund Husserl, "Philosophy as a Rigorous Science," in *Phenomenology and the Crisis of Philosophy*, trans. Quentin Lauer (New York: Harper & Row, 1965), 71–147.

14. Stein, *Finite and Eternal Being*, 25.

there will always be flaws, blemishes, errors. Science will, in practice, never obtain absolute clarity. Yet, despite this acknowledgment this ideal is still retained and remains the guiding aim and paradigm of science for Stein.

In Stein's account of the nature of philosophy Husserl's understanding of science predominates. Yet what is more puzzling is that she seems to uncritically conflate Maritain's distinction between "nature" and "state" with her Husserlian distinction between science as an Idea, i.e., nature, and science on the level of history, and experience, i.e., state.[15] Nowhere does Stein signal to any problem with such an uncritical conflation. This is problematic on many accounts. However, I can only mention one here. Maritain's distinction between "nature" and "state" is rooted in what the ancients call *abstractio formalis*, that is, an abstraction that draws out what is intelligible *in* reality. That is, it disregards the existential aspect of a thing to concentrate on the pure intelligible essence. However, such an abstraction is ruled by the Thomistic method of distinguishing in order to unite. Thus, in Maritain's way of thinking, he is mindful not to create an idol, or a real reality, out of the pure essence. In Maritain's view it was such a Cartesian monster that created the ideal reality of a pure nature of man separated from grace. Such a construction is going to enable a pure Cartesian philosophy separated from grace and *theo*logy.

Husserl, on the contrary, prizes such a separation because it furthers modern philosophy and science's project of autonomy. Furthermore, Husserl's understanding of the Idea of science is contrary to Maritain's understanding of nature. Husserl's ideal is independent of reality and science in its actual state and thus is truly able to act as a teleological goal of/for the theoretical project of reason, or in more phenomenological terms, for the progressive filling out of meaning. Husserl's idea is more Cartesian and modern and has a Hegelian tinge to it. Maritain's sense of nature then is rooted in the *actual* and reality, while Husserl's idea is teleological and is thus rooted in the *possible* and is, therefore, infinite, i.e., the Ideal guiding aim or teleological goal of science, an aim or goal that acts always as the lodestar or paradigm.[16]

How then is this conflation finally worked out? At first glance it would seem that, despite Stein's Husserlian reading of philosophy, she, in many

---

15. For an example of this conflation see Stein, *Finite and Eternal Being*, 15.

16. For a short but interesting discussion on Husserl's teleology and the possible see Richard Kearney, *The God Who May Be: A Hermeneutics of Religion* (Bloomington: Indiana University Press, 2001), 84–87.

ways, continues to follow Maritain in his presentation of Christian philosophy concerning how faith or revelation contributes to philosophy. Stein follows Maritain on two accounts. First, on the level of the intellect, grace purifies and strengthens, making the intellect less susceptible to error. Second, on the doctrinal level or, according to Stein, on the level of philosophy as a science, revelation enriches by a donation of content. Revelation throws an entirely new light on being and existents. This light has set "new tasks" for philosophy to solve, problems that philosophy would have never known without the content of revelation.[17] This is seen, for example, in how the Eucharist has compelled philosophy to distinguish between substance and accident. To this point a rather common version of Christian philosophy is presented by Stein in line with Maritain's.

Stein, however, pushes her unique presentation of Christian philosophy further by seeing it as a *perfectum opus rationis*. Stein borrows this phrase from Maritain, who thinks he is quoting Aquinas. However, as F. Gaboriau, X. Tilliette, and Chantal Beauvais following them have pointed out, Maritain misquotes Aquinas.[18] Aquinas never employs the word *perfectum* but rather *usus*. The misquotation on Maritain's part probably has to do with a lapse in memory. Why then is this significant for my reading? For one reason, the word *perfectum* facilitates Stein's more Husserlian reading of Maritain and, via Maritain, Aquinas. Second, the way Maritain reads *perfectum* (here I am in agreement with Beauvais) is in keeping with

17. Stein, *Finite and Eternal Being*, 21.
18. See Chantal Beauvais, "Edith Stein and Modern Philosophy," in *Husserl and Stein*, ed. Richard Feist and William Sweet (Washington, DC: Council for Research in Values and Philosophy, 2003). All page numbers are cited from the online version, found at http://www.crvp.org/book/Series01/I-31/chap-10.htm/. Beauvais's essay on Stein is excellent. In this essay Beauvais argues that Stein walks a fine balance between—borrowing from Ricoeur—a "strong modernity" (desire for absolute foundation) and "weak modernity" (a weakening of the epistemic priority of the subject). That is, Stein holds fast to a cogito-centered philosophy as a rigorous science, but decenters its autonomy by demanding a theological supplementation. Thus, due to this Stein belongs to a "weak modernity." But, in the end, Beauvais concludes that Stein and Husserl belong to the "same spiritual family": a conclusion to which I concur. Beauvais, "Edith Stein," 13. But rather than lauding the balance in Stein—as Beauvais seems to do—Beauvais's fine argument confirms me in my belief that one has to go much further than Stein does. That is, one must move beyond the categories of both a "weak" and "strong" modernity. We need to go beyond modernity as a whole to see which options are viable today: options that cannot rest on the foundational urge of modern philosophy. In other words, if one is to be truly postmodern, then one has to be sure not to be basing one's postmodernity on modern premises, thereby dialectically tying oneself to modernity. This approach to postmodernity will become more fully clear in Part 2.

Aquinas's usage of *usus*, that is, of the philosopher's using his reason rightly and thus not a teleologically perfected reason. It is even interesting to note that in the context in which Maritain mentions the phrase, he is qualifying it by saying that it should not be understood in a *rationalist sense* and that Aquinas had a much humbler understanding of reason than did Descartes or Spinoza.[19] In a word, Stein's context and use of *perfectum* is much more in line with a rationalistic interpretation of reason in the vein of Descartes and Spinoza than it is with Aquinas's humble understanding of *usus* (as well as Maritain's humbler intention of his misquoted *perfectum*). Thus it is an oddity of history that Maritain's misquotation of *perfectum* played into Stein's hands and aided her more modern and Husserlian interpretation of Christian philosophy.

What exactly does Stein mean by claiming that Christian philosophy is a *perfectum opus rationis*? What is meant is that Christian philosophy does not just designate the "mental attitude" of the philosopher, nor is it "merely the doctrinal system of Christian thinkers." Rather Christian philosophy is "*the idea* [italics mine] of a *perfectum opus rationis*."[20] This is to say that Stein (facilitated by Maritain's mistaken quotation) places *perfectum* under the banner of the Husserlian ideal of science's aim towards "total knowledge." This means that Christian philosophy must aspire to absolute knowledge and thus a complete synthesis of the truths of reason with the truths of revelation. Therefore, philosophy needs revelation if it is to accomplish its theoretical task. Here it can be seen how Stein creatively reinterprets Husserl's foundationalist task, that is, she undercuts it insofar as it is no longer the task of a pure autonomous philosophy. Nevertheless, the torch is now passed on to Christian philosophy to aim at the ideal of "total knowledge," which now uses *theo*logy as a kind of handmaiden in order to attempt a synthesizing of all truth. Christian philosophy is thus teleologically oriented towards this ideal or *perfectum*: but an ideal that comes about by Christian philosophy's appropriation of *theo*logical truth. "A Christian philosophy in this sense [that is, in the sense of an idea of a *perfectum opus rationis*] must aspire to a unity and synthesis of all the knowledge we have gained by the exercise of our natural reason and by revelation."[21] Stein seeks to retain the Husserlian task of reason's theoretical project, while decentering its autonomy in the name of Christian

19. Maritain, *Essay on Christian Philosophy*, 14.
20. Stein, *Finite and Eternal Being*, 25.
21. Stein, *Finite and Eternal Being*, 25.

philosophy now understood as the "idea of a *perfectum opus rationis*." Yet again Stein, as in the case of science, recognizes that due to our finitude, such a task is impossible while we are *in via*, but when we reach the fatherland, or beatific vision, we will see in one glance the task of reason's aims fulfilled.[22] This is the essence of Stein's conflation of Husserl and Maritain and, via Maritain, Aquinas: a conflation that is not without significant worries.

A Critical Assessment of Stein's Understanding of Christian Philosophy

I offer three objections regarding Stein's conception of Christian philosophy. First, regarding Stein's (and Maritain's) formal definition of philosophy understood as a fully rational enquiry that is determined by its objects which are natural and accessible to the intellect, one may easily ask: Is not this definition too rationalistic and logocentric?[23] Second, following from this, philosophy is defined as autonomous vis-à-vis *theo*logy, and thus the *possibility* of a dynamically formal relationality with *theo*logy is foreclosed to philosophy by definition.[24] Third, love, wonder, and participation are nowhere mentioned in Stein's and Maritain's definition of philosophy. In the end, philosophy is defined in a modern sense as a strict rational science, thus excluding all of the aforementioned possibilities.[25] Relationality, oth-

---

22. Stein, *Finite and Eternal Being*, 26.

23. Logically following from this definition of philosophy is a formal exclusion of the possibility that the primary concern of philosophy, being, is a mystery. Being, according to this definition, is fully accessible and knowable and, therefore, grasped/captured, in its essence, by a clear concept (there is an essentialization of being in this definition). Therefore, mystery, wonder, difference, and otherness are excluded *a priori* from our understanding of being and it is defined as inherently rational and graspable in a too narrow sense. In my view, the four thinkers, in the twentieth century, that best accentuated the mystery of being were: Przywara, Heidegger, Balthasar, and Marcel. In contemporary discourse today, Desmond likewise strongly emphasizes the overdetermination and wonder at the heart of the truth of the mystery of being.

24. One could say this of myth, art, and poetry as well, for if philosophy is fully autonomous, then it is monological and forgets its dialogical conversation with its others.

25. I think that, in the end, Maritain's reading of philosophy is more sapiential than Stein's, even if I am not ultimately satisfied with Maritain's presentation of Christian philosophy, as it too easily falls into a narrow Thomistic vision of philosophy in line with the Baroque Thomistic commentators.

erness, and a sapiential vision of philosophy are occluded in this narrowly rationalistic definition of philosophy.

These problems are only further exacerbated by Stein's idiosyncratic and ultimately Husserlian reading of Christian philosophy, now understood as the "idea of a *perfectum opus rationis*." Such an aim, and definition, of Christian philosophy prohibits philosophy from being a loving-towards and participation in Wisdom. Philosophy is understood, in its essence, as a science that aims at full clarity, disclosure, and "total knowledge," rid of all doubt and error. This view of philosophy is governed by the desire for absolute security and clarity, which is philosophy's teleological perfection. Such a view is paradigmatic of the governing impulse of the "dream of reason" inaugurated by Descartes and reaching its pinnacle in Hegel, where love is replaced by absolute knowledge. Such a paradigm is still fully at work in Husserl's understanding of philosophy as a "rigorous science."[26] The goal, in the end, remains the same, that is, a secure rational science freed of all doubt and whose teleological goal is absolute evidence.

Such a vision is alluring to Stein even if she realizes, like Husserl, that this goal will never be reached while we are *in via*. This vision prohibits, by definition, a vision of philosophy as a sapiential loving-participation in Wisdom because its desire is to overcome its present state of imperfection (loving and participation) and reach "total knowledge." And where there is "total knowledge"—as Hegel clearly saw—there is no longer love or participation because when philosophy becomes Absolute the Concept reigns supreme in its fully disclosed and translucent clarity: a clarity that, in its mirroring light, dispels religion, participation, and mystery. Am I then insinuating that Stein is a Hegelian and that this is ultimately her vision of philosophy? No, I am not. But what I am suggesting is that Stein's transposition or grafting of the modern and Husserlian conception of philosophy as a "rigorous science" onto her conception of Christian philosophy (even if the autonomy of modern philosophy is now somewhat decentered in a "weak modernity") runs the risk of being *haunted* by the specters of modern philosophy's rationalistic urge to foundationalism. Not to mention modern philosophy's unwarranted love affair with security, which manifests itself in a promethean urge for complete evidence (and thus a latent Hegelianism). Stein's conception of Christian philosophy runs the risk of a Christian form of rationalism where the singular place and truths of

---

26. Even if he denies the system-building mania of German Idealism and says that, in many ways, science has yet to begin.

*theo*logy are instrumentalized by using them to work towards the "idea" of Christian philosophy understood as a "*perfectum opus rationis*." In other words, in Stein's conception of Christian philosophy does not *theo*logy become the handmaiden of philosophy's synthesizing task, thereby reversing Peter Damien's famous expression? In the end, the question must be asked: What place is left for wonder, love, participation, mystery, and theological truth in a philosophy whose aim is total disclosure?

Stein's Misreading of Przywara

It is time to turn to Stein's "qualifying remarks" concerning Przywara's understanding of the relation between philosophy and *theo*logy in order to see how they are symptomatic of Stein's conception of Christian philosophy and her misreading of Przywara. Her remarks on Przywara's understanding of the relation between philosophy and *theo*logy confirm my suspicion (as signaled to in the previous chapter) that Stein's interpretation of Przywara does not do justice to, nor fully grasps, the radicality of Przywara's project of a "systematics of impurity" enacted in *Analogia Entis*. This project, I will show, is far from Stein's interpretation of Przywara elaborating another "philosophical system."

Stein's worry and "qualifying remarks" are concerned with the fact that Przywara speaks of a union between *theo*logy and philosophy within a single metaphysics, and that she was not able to understand fully what Przywara meant by this.[27] She agrees with Przywara that philosophy reaches its "perfection" through *theo*logy but not *as theo*logy, and that the formal primacy belongs to *theo*logy insofar as the Christian philosopher must ultimately submit to the authority of the *magisterium*. Here she is referring to an ecclesial theology and thus the binding nature of dogmatic statements, not the individual practice of theology by various theologians, who are themselves also bound to the *magisterium*. However, Przywara is talking about far more than just the dogmatic primacy of theology, as will be seen.[28]

What then is the heart of the problem? I believe it to be twofold. First, it is my suspicion that Stein believes that Przywara's union of philosophy and *theo*logy, in a single metaphysics (to be explained in the following), admits too much theological content into philosophy. This endangers the

27. Stein, *Finite and Eternal Being*, 25.
28. Stein, *Finite and Eternal Being*, 25.

autonomy of philosophy protected by her formal definition of philosophy and the project of Christian philosophy understood as the "idea of a *perfectum opus rationis*." Second, Stein misconceives the radicality of Przywara's understanding of metaphysics, thereby missing the profundity of his construal of the relation between philosophy and *theo*logy in a single metaphysics, though in fact these two points dovetail.

Beginning with the first claim, it must be noted that the very paragraph that mentioned Stein's inability to fully understand what Przywara means by the unity of *theo*logy and philosophy in a single metaphysics is the very same paragraph where she first gives her final formulation of Christian philosophy as the "idea of a *perfectum opus rationis*." In fact, the sentence admitting that the formal primacy belongs to *theo*logy, understood as the *magisterium*, is followed by this qualification, a qualification that directly pertains to Przywara's understanding of the formal primacy of *theo*logy or her worry therefrom:

> It is therefore our conviction that the term Christian philosophy designates not only the mental attitude of the Christian philosopher, nor merely the actual doctrinal system of Christian thinkers but above and beyond these the idea of a perfectum opus rationis. A Christian philosophy must aspire to a unity and synthesis of all knowledge which we have gained by the exercise of our natural reason and by revelation.[29]

The context and content of the above quote show clearly that Stein is worried that if one were to take Przywara's model, which formally sees the philosophical as fulfilled and perfected (but not destroyed, as will be seen) by the *theo*logical, then one would have to abandon the idea of philosophy as a strict and "rigorous science," now understood as a Christian philosophy that aims at a unity of all truth and total knowledge. In a word, Przywara's view would subvert modern philosophy's "dream of reason" newly appropriated by Stein's rationalistic conception of Christian philosophy: a conception that seeks to appropriate theological truth for a comprehensive synthesis that aims at "total knowledge," thereby making *theo*logy the handmaiden of Christian philosophy so conceived.

Such a suspicion is further confirmed by turning to the endnote at the conclusion of the sentence in which Stein voices her inability to fully understand Przywara's meaning of the unity of philosophy and *theo*logy

---

29. Stein, *Finite and Eternal Being*, 25.

in a single metaphysics, namely, endnote 42.[30] The endnote is concerned with Przywara's definition of metaphysics as a "going behind" into the "background" of "*physis*," meaning that metaphysics is not concerned with beings but with being qua being.[31] This is in accord with Aristotle's definition of metaphysics as first philosophy. Stein too thinks that metaphysics is concerned with the meaning of that which is or *ousia*, and thus is a searching for the ultimate causes of things according to the natural powers of the intellect. This is also how she seems to read the heart of Przywara's understanding of philosophical metaphysics. And thus, according to Stein's reading of Przywara, metaphysics becomes theological once it invokes *theo*logy and this is the distinction between the two. To further confirm the suspicion that Stein is worried about Przywara's blurring philosophy and *theo*logy, it is telling that she ends the endnote with a quote from Fr. Roland-Gosselin concerning the difficulty of demarcating the division between philosophy and *theo*logy. Yet, in this endnote, Stein does not mention that Przywara calls his metaphysics a "creaturely metaphysics." Nor does she mention how such a designation radically qualifies Aristotle's definition of philosophy. Moreover, Stein's failure of mentioning what Przywara means by a "creaturely metaphysics" is symptomatic of Stein's rather simplistic view of Przywara's distinction between philosophical metaphysics and theological metaphysics. In other words, because Stein seems to miss what Przywara means by metaphysics she simultaneously misses the possible relation between philosophy and *theo*logy opened by a radically "creaturely metaphysics" and thus the dynamically formal relationality lacking in her understanding of the relation between philosophy and *theo*logy.

What, then, does Przywara mean by a "creaturely metaphysics"? Here it is impossible not to anticipate some of what will be discussed in the following. Przywara's employment of the previously mentioned definition of metaphysics is used as a springboard in order to contaminate/deconstruct/subvert any attempt at an absolute metaphysics in favor of a radically "creaturely metaphysics." The starting point of his "creaturely metaphysics" is the formal "suspended tension" between being and consciousness. Such a "suspended tension" seeks an analogical space or middle that avoids, or disallows, absolutizations of self-identity, as in, for example, a meta-noetics that begins with consciousness and attends to

---

30. Stein, *Finite and Eternal Being*, 25; the corresponding endnote 42 occurs on 552.
31. Stein, *Finite and Eternal Being*, 552.

essences (Husserl), or a meta-ontics that begins with being-in-the-world as historically existing (Heidegger).

Przywara firmly holds to this method of tension because it is the very condition of our becoming. Thus his method is rooted in, and is a descriptive expression of, its object; namely, the real "suspended" space of our creaturely being. Therefore, at the heart of creaturely being lies a space of opening, a difference, a real distinction between essence and existence that thrusts beyond itself in an open transparency. And it is this real metaphysical difference between essence/existence that is epistemologically expressed in the formal problem of a "creaturely metaphysics," namely, the formal tension between being/consciousness. This formal problematic of a "creaturely metaphysics" radically alters the above-mentioned Aristotelian definition of metaphysics. Przywara's formula for his creaturely metaphysics reads essence in-and-beyond existence (*Sosein in-über Dasein*). With this formula creaturely being is seen as *ecstatic*, insofar as man is never in complete possession of his being: essence is always in-and-beyond and is thus eschatologically *deferred*. Man's dynamic makeup of essence and existence is open-ended. Therefore, creaturely being is held radically suspended beyond any possible identity. If Stein were to have interpreted being, in the manner of Przywara, making the formal object of a "creaturely metaphysics" the suspended tension between being and consciousness, then she would have opened the possibility for a dynamically formal relationality (rooted in our concrete state of becoming) that views philosophy in its formal essence as open to the possibility of revelation, mystery, and otherness. (This will be clarified shortly.) However, Stein's vision of Christian philosophy, and her interpretation of Przywara, shows both a hesitancy and misreading of Przywara that, again, misses the real daring of his antifoundationalist and countermodern project.

A Sapiential and Participatory Vision of Philosophy

In turning to Przywara's interpretation of the relation between philosophy and *theo*logy it is time to see how his view avoids my concerns about Stein's rationalistic conception of Christian philosophy. Yet, it is not enough to see that Przywara's reading of the relation between philosophy and *theo*logy avoids a rationalist conception. For it must also be shown that Przywara provides a brilliant model of the relational interplay between *philo*sophy and *theo*logy. Przywara's model strikes an analogical balance between the two discourses, which is not only rare, but also provides a remarkably viable option for one seeking an antifoundationalist postmodern understanding of Christian philosophy. The reason for Przywara's profoundly viable vision is threefold. First, Przywara begins by defining philosophy as a loving participation towards Wisdom, thereby reactivating a sapiential and participatory style of *philo*sophy, counter to foundational and absolute models of philosophy. Second, Przywara allows for a formal space of opening or relationality that makes possible a *possible* dynamic relationality between *philo*sophy and *theo*logy.[32] Third, relative to the first two, this allows philosophy to respect wonder, mystery, and otherness, thereby viewing them as not antithetical to philosophy (or states to be overcome), but as, indeed, the positive fulfillment of philosophy. Upon this model philosophy is seen as positively being fulfilled and perfected, but not destroyed, by divine revelatory mystery. In a word, the site of the "suspended middle" is opened and *philo*sophy is performed by enacting an aesthetic and speculatively dramatic *reductio in mysterium*.

Philosophy as Radically Participatory

Przywara's vision of philosophy is dynamically Platonic and Augustinian (perhaps even Pseudo-Dionysian). Which is to say it is a radically participatory style of visionary philosophy that obtains itself in an act of transcendence beyond itself. Philosophy—in both its beginning and end—is a creaturely venture that is *defined* in the tradition of Plato as a loving participation in/towards Wisdom.[33] Within this view there is a *difference* implied in the very definition of philosophy itself, understood as *philo*-(Sophia). This means that the human being or philosopher's greatness is expressed in a humble *loving-towards* or participation in Wisdom. (Think of Socratic learned ignorance: I know that I do not know.) Wisdom, therefore, belongs to the divine, and to paraphrase Aristotle, *is not a human possession* (*Met.* 1, 2, 928b).[34]

---

32. It should be noted that Przywara is not saying philosophy lays claim to Revelation, but that philosophy is receptively open to the possibility of revelation. This will become clear later on.

33. For Przywara's discussion of the Platonic definition of philosophy as a "loving towards" Wisdom, see Erich Przywara, *Analogia Entis: Metaphysics: Original Structure and Universal Rhythm*, trans. John R. Betz and David Bentley Hart (Grand Rapids: Eerdmans, 2014), 161.

34. Even Aristotle, for whom this distinction was no longer really operative, was unable

Philosophy, then, is a loving participatory activity that, as creaturely, humbly outstretches itself towards Wisdom: but an outstretching that wisely acknowledges its limit(s). However, this limit should not be viewed as merely negative, but rather as positive because creaturely transcending is itself *transcended* by what is truly other than/to philosophy, namely, Wisdom. Therefore, it is precisely Wisdom's transcendence and alterity that renders love and participation possible. (Think of Przywara's systematics of the in-and-beyond, which forecloses the possibility of identity.) This model thus guards against the titanic urge to storm Olympus, delusionally believing that Wisdom—which belongs only to the gods/God—can be captured and possessed by creaturely hands or concepts. Przywara enacts a de-absolutization of philosophy, which prohibits a usurpation of the divine by philosophies that aim at absolutization or identity with the divine. Philosophy, understood as *philo*-(Sophia), is already understood relationally. That is, insofar as philosophy is distinct from Wisdom, it is not identifiable with Wisdom or the divine. Philosophy thus *distinctly* participates, via love, in or towards the divine, in virtue of the divine's transcendence.

Hence philosophy, understood on a participatory and sapiential model, already implies by its very definition of philosophy as *philo*-(Sophia) that philosophy is inherently relational and therefore not fully autonomous. This is why it is possible for Plato, in the *Phaedo*, to liken philosophy to a mystery rite (*Mysterien-Akt*) and to funerary mysteries and the priesthood of Apollo's swans.[35] This is also what enables Aristotle to speak of philosophy's closeness to the mystical and the priestly act of leisurely contemplation.[36] In this sapiential vision of philosophy, philosophy is intimately related to myth, religion, and mystery, thereby rendering an admirable exchange between its others possible, in contradistinction to philosophy defined from a rationalistic and autonomous viewpoint.[37] By

---

to fully erase the profound commerce and unity between *mythos* and *logos* found in his teacher Plato. Traces of this are thus still found in Aristotle's work. For example see Aristotle, *Met*. I. 2, 928b, 18, where Aristotle says the lover of Wisdom is the lover of myth.

35. See Plato, *Phaedo* 69cd.

36. See Aristotle, *Met*. I, 2, 982b, 18, I, 981b, 24f.

37. One could easily say that Przywara was always concerned with countering the rabid trend of desacralization, the evacuation of the holy, the mysterious, and the religious from the world, so prevalent in modernity and his time. This is why Przywara's disciple, Balthasar, will say (referring to one of Przywara's later work's, *Mensch: Typologische Anthropologie*, that "Walter F. Otto, Martin Buber and Erich Przywara turned in indignation against the cynicism of the Jungian method of therapy, which evacuates and degrades to the level of mere psychic archetypes man's relation to authentic images of Being, indeed, images of God." Hans Urs

defining philosophy according to a participatory, sapiential, and creaturely model, a possible space for otherness and relativity to what is other than/to philosophy is already opened up within philosophy itself. Such a possibility was occluded from Stein's (and Maritain's) definition.

By advancing a sapiential model of philosophy, as paradigmatically expressed in the unity of *mythos* and *logos* in Plato and with traces still present in Aristotle, it is easy to see how this sapiential vision was seen by Christian thinkers as finding its ultimate expression in philosophy's participation in *theo*logical Wisdom or revelation. This is why Aquinas could refer to *theo*logy as the *maxime sapientia*.[38] That is to say, insofar as the very subject matter of *theo*logy is God's own self-utterance, Wisdom itself speaking, *theo*logy can be seen as the maximum participation (analogous to philosophy's sapiential participation) in Wisdom possible for man in this world. Seen in this light, *theo*logy can be said to be that which *philo*sophy was always moving towards and that through which *philo*sophy finds its consummation and fullest participation in Wisdom, because *theo*logy's subject matter is the divine solely for the divine's sake.[39] This merely touches the surface of the analogical ordering of *philo*sophy to *theo*logy. Nevertheless, it does, at the minimum, show the possibility of a transition and possible union-in-difference between the two discourses: a union that demands further justification.

A Promethean Usurpation of the Divine: Theopanism/Pantheism

Prior to entering into a fuller discussion of this unity-in-difference between *philo*sophy and *theo*logy it is necessary to look more deeply at what Przywara is countering, namely, absolutizations or totalizations in all of their insidious forms of manifestations, endemic in philosophical modernity. The absolutizations that Przywara is seeking to avoid by his analogical balance are degenerate or immanent forms of theology that work by way of negation by collapsing the *difference* between *theo*logy and *philo*sophy. These take two forms. First, there is theopanism (a term coined by Rudolf Otto), which proceeds by way of devolution from above to below. Theopanism commences

---

von Balthasar, *The Glory of the Lord*, vol. 1: *Seeing the Form*, trans. Erasmo Leiva-Merikakis et al. (San Francisco: Ignatius Press, 1982), 500.

38. See Aquinas, *Summa. Th.* I, q. 5, a. 6, corp.
39. See Aquinas, *In Boeth. De Trin.*, q. 5, a. 4, corp.

with theology and ends with a philosophy parasitic on theological content now emptied of itself, thereby collapsing *theo*logy into philosophy (e.g., Hegel's dialectical sublation of *theo*logy).[40] Historically, theopanism is tied to the theology of the Reformation, which sees God as working and doing all things. Here the reality and agency of the creature is forgotten, as in Luther's sole agency of God and Barth's Lutheran doctrine of *Alleinwirksamkeit*. (Contra to this compare Aquinas's venerable understanding of secondary causality.) In theopanism, God becomes the all and, in the end, *theo*logy is entrapped within philosophy rendering *theo*logy and God's transcendence, as well as the activity of the creature, null and void. God is understood as: "God as creature."[41] Second, there is pantheism, which proceeds by way of evolution from below to above; here the all becomes God. God is understood as: the "creature as God."[42] Philosophy (understood as absolute) becomes a theology immanently contained, ending in a theologically immanent *mythos* or mysticism. Historical examples that Przywara gives are the cosmic mysticism of Spinoza and Bruno, the Dionysian chthonic world of Nietzsche and Jewish messianism, reaching its apex in Talmudic mysticism where God becomes God in and through the working of man or the law.[43]

In truth, both theopanism and pantheism are expressive of the same reality given through different methods and accents, with the end result being the same. In theopanism/pantheism the analogical middle or distance between God and the world and *theo*logy and *philo*sophy is forgotten. Transcendence is collapsed into immanence. God is part of the world and *theo*logy is part of philosophy, thereby destroying the reality of both God and the creature and *theo*logy and *philo*sophy. Analogical difference is forgotten, and where analogical difference is forgotten the freedom of God and the freedom of the creature (and correlatively the freedom of *philo*sophy and *theo*logy) are lost. When this freedom *between* God and creature is lost then, logically, a savage metaphysical monism or identity ensues, thereby uniting with the Titanic/Luciferian refusal of the creature *to be* a creature. *God is the creature because the creature is God.* And in the same way *theo*logy is always contained immanently within philosophy, because

---

40. For Przywara's discussion of theopanism see Przywara, *Analogia Entis*, 165.
41. Przywara, *Analogia Entis*, 165.
42. Przywara, *Analogia Entis*, 165.
43. See Przywara, *Analogia Entis*, 166. One could, no doubt, today add to this list the late Heidegger's immanent theology based in a neo-pagan mythos parasitic upon Christian truth and Levinas's mysticism, where God can only be God in and through man, ethically understood.

philosophy is conceived of as absolute and *not* creaturely. Hence where analogical difference is lost, so too is freedom. And when freedom is lost, real relationality is foreclosed and thus a true union of harmonious unity-in-difference. Therefore, the formal models of theopanism/pantheism, and their various historical instantiations heightened within philosophical modernity, must be rejected and countered by an analogical relation between *theo*logy and *philo*sophy.

In the above understanding of theopanism and pantheism, there are many unacknowledged and secret alliances, affinities, dependencies at work (both within the formal investigation and historical topography) in regard to the *question of God in modern philosophy*. Moreover, upon deeper inspection, it becomes clear that the *conatus* of modern philosophy and its desire for absolutization is rooted in a dependence upon certain theologies that themselves have already lost the distinction between God and humankind. (Think of my description of philosophical modernity in the Introduction.) Such theologies give rise to, and find confirmation in, puristic forms of absolute metaphysics. For example, as was seen, there is an affinity between Reformation theology and pure forms of *a priori* metaphysics as expressed in German Idealism. Przywara goes so far as suggesting that theopanism is the formal ground of such a metaphysics. Further, taking another example, it is possible to argue that the formal ground of pure *a posteriori* metaphysics is found in various forms of Jewish messianism. If this is indeed the case, is it possible to say that Przywara's "creaturely metaphysics" finds a formal ground in a specific theology? The answer is undoubtedly yes. A "creaturely metaphysics" finds its formal ground in a Catholic *theo*logy, which alone is able to secure a God who is both in-and-beyond the creature and a *theo*logy that is both in-and-beyond philosophy. This claim, of course, requires further clarification and justification. However, upon having elaborated on the dreadful pair theopanism/pantheism, it is clear why such Promethean/Luciferian endeavors must be staunchly rejected, a rejection that simultaneously brings-into-relief the urgent necessity of Przywara's project, as well as the need to elucidate its intricate brilliance and proposed solution.

The Generic Difference between Philosophy and Theology

In the above it has become apparent that the problem with theopanism/pantheism is that the differences between God and the creature and *theo*logy and *philo*sophy are forgotten. This problem thus demands a reassertion of difference (on a descriptively formal level), which becomes concrete in the analogical workings of a "creaturely metaphysics" and Catholic *theo*logy. I begin by securing the generic differences (generic differences obliterated in theopanism/pantheism) between *theo*logy and *philo*sophy.⁴⁴ Consequent upon Przywara's sapiential definition of philosophy as *philo*-(Sophia) it follows that what remains decisive is precisely the *philo* of philosophy, which signifies the participant and *not* the participated. The creature and not God must be seen as the formal object of *philo*sophy. Here it is important to recall (as with Stein's reference to Przywara's definition of metaphysics in endnote 42) that Przywara begins with Aristotle's definition of metaphysics, which concerns itself with the ground, end, and definition of things. And, therefore, a going *behind* into the *background* of things in which the question of being qua being arises, emerges, or surfaces. But, as was seen, Przywara complicates this definition by recognizing the promiscuous impurity of the question. That is, upon immediately asking into the question of being qua being, the question of the questioner questioning being is simultaneously posed. The question of the act of consciousness of the one who is asking into the ground, end, and definition of being qua being is also raised. This brings one to the formal problematic of a "creaturely metaphysics" that treats the formal duality of being and consciousness.

In the history of metaphysics this problem has been given two basic solutions: either a privileging of being (a meta-ontics) or a privileging of consciousness (a meta-noetics). Przywara, however, does not wish to fall into either mode of absolutization. And therefore, being and consciousness remain in a rhythmic state of co-belonging, a between or a suspended tension/middle that keeps open this analogical space of difference and rhythmic tension of unity-in-movement. The formal object described by a "creaturely metaphysics" is rooted in, and is an expression of, the very condition of our (*be*)coming expressed in the mysteriously beautiful maxim of Pindar, namely, "become what you are."⁴⁵ Here it can be said that Przywara's formal description of being and consciousness is expressive of the real metaphysical distinction between essence and existence in man, which can be characterized as an Augustinian and dynamized understanding of the real distinction, uttered in the descriptively dynamic formula: *Sosein*

---

44. For Przywara's discrimination between philosophy and theology see Przywara, *Analogia Entis*, 162–64.

45. Przywara, *Analogia Entis*, 124.

in-über Dasein. Although this anticipates much of what will be discussed in the next chapter, this will prove essential for my discussion here in order to see how *theo*logy solves the inherent tensions present in *philo*sophy or metaphysics.

It can now be asked—in a Heideggerian manner—how does the question of God enter philosophy? The answer to this question becomes apparent in the fact that metaphysics asks into the ground, end, and definition of things and therefore is a reaching into the hinterland of the question of being qua being. Yet, if this definition was complicated by the formal problematic of a "creaturely metaphysics" expressed in the suspended tension between being/consciousness, then the question of God (as a question of the final ground, end, and definition of a "creaturely metaphysics") will be asked only "insofar as" God is related to the creature.[46] This means that natural theology is implicit in the definition of metaphysics as such and that God is sought as the ground, end, and definition of the creature. This implies that the divine is only treated, in metaphysics, in relation to the creature because the formal object of *philo*sophy is the creature and *not* God. *Theo*logy's formal object, on the other hand, is God and God's own self-expression or utterance. That is to say, as compared to the "philo" of *philo*sophy, what is distinctive about *theo*logy is the "theo."[47] Thus the creature, for *theo*logy, comes under investigation "insofar as" it is the *topos* or site of the divine's self-utterance.[48]

Does this mean that *theo*logy treats the creature only as a negative limit concept and that *philo*sophy likewise does the same with God? The answer to this question, for Przywara, is undoubtedly no. If this was the answer, then it would constitute the rupture between *philo*sophy and *theo*logy endemic in modernity. An example of this would be methodological atheism à la Heidegger's project of a closed finitude that collapses essence into *existence*, thereby absolutizing creaturely becoming, which, in turn, *a priori* closes the creature and philosophy off from the analogical suspended and open provisionality of philosophy and the creature in the name of a creature (*Dasein*), which is incurvated in upon itself by care in the world, thereby whispering to itself "I am that I am." Thus such a position of absolutization is plainly self-refuting. And on the side of theology, one would have a *theologia archetypa* that treats God merely as he is in

46. Przywara, *Analogia Entis*, 163.
47. Przywara, *Analogia Entis*, 162.
48. Przywara, *Analogia Entis*, 163.

himself and thus not also as he is in *relation* to us. Which, to say the least, would be an arid and deficient form of theology lacking dynamic breadth and pertinence.[49] Not to mention that "limit" itself is a concept that only has meaning for man and therefore loses all applicability when applied to God: the Unlimited or Absolute.

Rather what is opened up in the above discrimination is a commonality founded in generic or formal difference: namely, the "insofar as." In *theo*logy the creature is treated "insofar as" the creature is the *topos* of the divine's self-utterance. And God is treated, in *philo*sophy, "insofar as" the creature (and a "creaturely metaphysics") is seeking its ground, end, and definition. Thus, on the generic or formal level, one finds that in emphasizing the formal difference between *philo*sophy and *theo*logy a space of commonality has been opened "insofar as" both *theo*logy and *philo*sophy treat God and the creature according to their varying methods and discourses. However, this is commonality that escapes the danger of univocally collapsing *philo*sophy and *theo*logy into one because the unity is founded upon a formal *difference*.

Some conclusions may be drawn from the aforesaid that aid in transitioning over to offering a substantive solution to the problem of the relation of *philo*sophy and *theo*logy. First, the question of the relation between *philo*sophy and *theo*logy can only be treated if there is a clear discrimination between the two. However, this discrimination is not equivocal, i.e., no relation, nor is it dialectical, i.e., the *Aufhebung* of *theo*logy into philosophy, nor is it univocal, i.e., complete identity without difference. Rather the unity is founded within difference. There is a true commonality that does not collapse the difference and is thus analogical. There is a likeness grounded in unlikeness. This opens the way for *theo*logy to be authentically seen as both in-and-beyond *philo*sophy. Second, *philo*sophy itself must be conceived as creaturely and thus not *a priori* closed to *theo*logy, understood in a natural *and* supernatural sense. (Recall that this formal relationality to *theo*logy was foreclosed by Stein and Maritain's definition of philosophy.) This is the case, not for some hidden apologetic or *theo*logical reasoning, but because this is the only way that respects man's radical contingency and becoming. That is, Przywara keeps open man's unity-in-movement, suspended middle, between of essence/existence, consciousness/being, in a hovering provisionality, where man is opened ecstatically beyond himself. Man is eschatologically deferred (*Sosein in-über Dasein*). Third, follow-

---

49. See Aquinas, *In Boeth. De Trin.* q. 5, a. 4, ad 8.

ing from the previous two, this requires that I return to Przywara's claim that Catholic *theo*logy is the formal ground of a "creaturely metaphysics." (This is the formal primacy with which Stein was concerned.)[50]

The Troubling Question of Natural Theology

If the above questioning is going to be adequately answered, then a certain path has to be taken, namely, it is necessary to broach the troubling and difficult question of *theologia naturalis*.[51] Following from this it is also necessary to again accent the general movement of Przywara's "creaturely metaphysics" in order to fully understand how the question of natural theology is both raised and answered. This answer, in turn, reveals the need for *theo*logical supplementation to the inherent formal tension present in philosophy and metaphysics as such. Once this is done one will then be able to understand how Przywara conceives Catholic *theo*logy as the formal ground of a "creaturely metaphysics" that then opens up the profound analogical unity-in-difference between *philo*sophy and *theo*logy. It can then finally be seen how *philo*sophy was all along headed towards a *theo*logical *telos* and thus pointed the way to a *reductio in mysterium* that does not destroy *philo*sophy, but indeed fulfills and consummates its deepest longing, namely, to participate in the mystery of Wisdom.

It has just been seen that for a "creaturely metaphysics" the question of natural theology is implicit to the very nature of metaphysics. Przywara's definition of metaphysics was, at the commencement, in line with Aristotle. Metaphysics concerns itself with the ground, end, and definition of things, which thus requires a going behind into the background where the question of being qua being emerges. However, this definition was qualified and complicated by the formal tension and question of a "creaturely metaphysics" being the question of the formal duality between being and consciousness expressive (on a descriptively formal level) of the condition of man's complete contingency and becoming. This condition was revelatory of the real difference or distinction *between* essence and existence in man (*Sosein in-über Dasein*). In this movement Przywara's desire to avoid all forms of absolutization also became apparent. Further, this desire was merely seek-

---

50. Przywara, *Analogia Entis*, 166.

51. This is why Barth called the *analogia entis* the "invention of the Antichrist": because he saw it containing a natural theology and thus an idolatrous conception of God.

ing to be true to the concrete condition of becoming and contingency that is characteristic of man's moving state. This demanded that metaphysics remain true to and respectful of difference, namely, the differences between essence/existence and consciousness/being. When this remaining true is enacted, then man's between or suspended middle condition is respected and man is kept radically open, de-absolute, provisional, ecstatic, and eschatologically open-ended or deferred. Such a condition of man is the very condition of *philo*sophy understood as a "creaturely metaphysic." Thus in all of this, what is revealed is that the creature and philosophy are *not fixed states but between states of transition*. That is, they are suspended open and dynamic states. This, in turn, implies that the creature and *philo*sophy are relations that are transcending because they themselves are *transcended* (the constant movement to the above and beyond). Now if this is the transitional state of a "creaturely metaphysics" then the question of God, in a "creaturely metaphysics," must also reflect this dynamic state.

If it has been seen that the formal object of philosophy is the creature, but that metaphysics likewise deals with the ground, end, and definition of things, then this likewise implies that the question of God will be raised in a creaturely way (i.e., the question of God is raised in relation to the creature: the ground, end, and definition of the creature). The question of God is raised as the first truth and beginning (*prima veritas/principium*) of the creature as well as the defining end (*finis/telos*) of the creature's rhythmic moving or becoming. Thus metaphysics' question of ground, end, and definition, now de-absolutized by the formal problem of a "creaturely metaphysics," formally carries within it the very question of the creature's relation to God. In keeping with the formula of a "creaturely metaphysics" of essence in-and-beyond existence, the question of God emerges as the question of God beyond-and-in the creature. It can now be seen how the question of God arises from within the very formal configuration of the question of metaphysics as such, and from the inherent tensions kept open by a suspended and transitionally provisional "creaturely metaphysics." Moreover, a "creaturely metaphysics" then points the way to a God who is both beyond-and-in the creature and therefore contains a natural theology that gestures to a transcendent God (and thus also a *theo*logy that is both beyond and in *philo*sophy, as will be seen). What then of this God who is both beyond-and-in the creature? Or how secure his transcendence, if indeed this can be done?

Here, however, one is on shaky ground because, in truth, there is no ground whatsoever. Przywara has demolished all ground upon which philosophy and the creature could stand. Here there is no foundation or security, but rather radical contingency, betweenness, a hovering suspended middle (*schwebende Mitte*). In Augustinian terms, the creature is and is not, *est non est*. And *philo*sophy, as a creaturely endeavor, is just as inherently unstable as the creature. There is no firm foundation of a *Cogito* or speculative identity that grounds being and thought. Being and thought are analogically double, ungrounded, and rhythmically and relationally open-ended between poles of absolutization. Both the creature and *philo*sophy point the way to something *other than themselves*. Here though a danger and temptation resurface insofar as God can be glimpsed in the movement of creaturely becoming, and theology (understood as natural theology) can be discerned in the contours of philosophy. The creature and philosophy are always tempted to close the creaturely suspended middle and idolatrously attribute these traces of God and theology, in the creature and philosophy, to the creature and philosophy themselves. When this is done the devious usurpations of theopanism and pantheism reemerge, as expressed in totalizing philosophies that contain insidious immanent theologies whose formal grounds are rooted in degenerate forms of theology that are forgetful of the difference between God and man. This idolatrous road of mirroring and parodying the divine, however, was rejected for its Promethean/Luciferian equation of the creature with God. It remains to ensure that a "creaturely metaphysics" does not fall into a more covert and subtle mode of idolatry by too much stressing the "in" in the formula of God beyond-and-*in* the creature. In today's philosophical parlance it must be asked: Is this not just another ontotheological formula that chains and ties the divine to metaphysics and its idolatrous speculations and formulas that merely conjure the divine in a theurgic manner? Przywara too is deeply concerned with this "Heideggerian question" well prior to Heidegger posing the question in 1957. Przywara, though, gives a decidedly un-Heideggerian answer that is far more profound than Heidegger's critique of the entirety of the history of Western metaphysics and the relegation of the *theo*logical tradition.

If a God beyond-and-in the creature has arisen from the formal grounds of a "creaturely metaphysics" and the inherent thrusting and open tensions of creaturely becoming, how is it possible to ensure and stress the *beyond* rather than the *in*, and is this possible within the confines of a "creaturely metaphysics"? If one were to stop here, would not the beyond of God be tied to the "from" of the creature and, in so being, contradict the final formula of a "creaturely metaphysics" of a God *beyond*-and-in the creature? (Here it is important to recall that if the transcending movement of the creature and *philo*sophy is to truly be transcendent then this movement itself must be asymmetrically *transcended*.) The answer given to these questions must be, without a doubt, yes. For if the divine is to be truly divine then it must be free, free to choose how it appears and free *over* its own manner of appearing. The divine must be independent of any creaturely strictures, thereby avoiding the idolatrous fashioning of human hands and concepts.[52] In fact, does this not demand an asymmetrical reversal? And an asymmetrical reversal where the divine is not seen as coming from the creaturely but, indeed, where the creaturely is seen as coming from the divine? In other words, has not a "creaturely metaphysics" pointed the way the entire time in its groundless transitional state and increasing relativization to the need for a *theo*logical supplementation that would complete and fulfill its formal suspended tensions that point beyond, thus ensuring that this beyond is truly *beyond and transcendent of philosophy and the creature*?

Philosophy and the creature all along have gestured in their open *expec*tancy to a relation and participation in otherness that they themselves cannot command. And thus to a free and ungroundable God who reveals himself as he wills and creates *ex nihilo*. Does not, then, a "creaturely metaphysics" require its formal ground to be found in Catholic *theo*logy, which alone secures the transcendence of God and *theo*logy? The answer to this question may now be given as a resounding yes. This formal ground which is *theo*logical does not, however, destroy philosophy, but rather consummates, liberates, and fulfills it. And it does so by securing a participation in an asymmetrical transcendence that is truly free, namely, a participation in the self-revealing Creator *ex nihilo*. At this point it is important to underscore and stress what Przywara is *not* saying. Przywara is not giving a "proof" for revelation. Nor is he tying revelation to the need of the creature. (For if he did, a "creaturely metaphysics" would itself contain its own immanent theology.) Rather, he is showing that philosophy and the creature are in their provisional essence, at the minimum, open to the *possibility* of revelation, and that it would be contradictory to *a priori* close them off to this possibility, while, simultaneously, *theo*logy would perfect the deepest longing of philosophy's desire to participate in Wisdom. We have now arrived at the place where we may begin to understand how a *philo*sophical and *theo*logical metaphysics work together in a harmonious analogical unity-in-difference.

52. Przywara, *Analogia Entis*, 161.

Analogical Ordering/Theological Supplementation

The key to understanding what Przywara means by the union of philosophy and *theo*logy in a single metaphysics, which at first sight sounds opaque (as it was to Stein), can be made comprehensible in two ways. First, the movement of Przywara's thought must again be accentuated. Second, one must thoughtfully think into the formal *theo*logical/analogical axioms he uses to explain the relation between philosophy and *theo*logy. The two axioms are grounded in the work of Aquinas and are as follows. The first pertains to the noetic (consciousness) and reads, *fides non destruit, sed supponit et perficit rationem*; while the second pertains to the ontic (being) and reads, *gratia non destruit, sed supponit et perficit naturam*.[53] Thus to reenter and accentuate the movement of Przywara's thought, and to think deeply into analogical workings of a real union and relationality in difference between *philo*sophy and *theo*logy, as expressed in these two axioms, will serve as my map through this complex question as well as my mode of clarification.

In the metaphysical movement of Przywara's thought there has been the continual emphasis and accentuation of the in-over or in-and-beyond dynamic. And what has become manifest in this movement is a motion of rising and dynamic intensity through which this dynamic is ever further caught up or taken up more and more in and towards the beyond. Further, this beyond is continually distancing itself from the creature. It is becoming increasingly transcendent: an asymmetrical reversal is occurring. This is due to the fact that what is being thought is relation and relationality and thus a *relativization of the creature*. This relationality was first seen in the dynamic suspended relation between essence/existence, consciousness/being, which, far from being a self-enclosed relation (and therefore not a real relation) or oscillation within itself (à la Heidegger's *Dasein*), is a genuine analogical suspended between that points beyond itself. Here there is no stasis, no firm ground or position from which one can start, as in the *Cogito*, as the first principle of modern philosophy's foundationalism. Rather there is a movement open to and expectant of the possibility of otherness. Following this ever further intensification the need arose for an even fuller relativization where the question of natural theology was arrived at. This question pointed to the need for the beyond to arrive from

---

53. For Przywara's discussion of these axioms see Przywara, *Analogia Entis*, 169–70. For references in Aquinas, see Aquinas, *De Ver.* q. 14, a. 10, ad 9; Aquinas, *Summa Th.* I, q. 1, a. 8, ad 2; q. 2, a. 2, ad 1.

truly beyond. The creature's and philosophy's transcendent movement—pointing beyond—was thus open to being vertically transected or transcended by a God and *theo*logy that were both beyond-and-in philosophy, and thus truly free, thereby perfecting and fulfilling philosophy's inherent tensions without being tied to these tensions in an idolatrous manner. Catholic *theo*logy proved to be the formal ground (exhibiting a formal primacy) over a "creaturely metaphysics." For Przywara, the *en-telecheia* (as opposed to the teleology of Stein, which aimed at "total knowledge" via the appropriation of *theo*logical truth) of *philo*-(Sophia) is *theo*logy, understood as the site where philosophy finds its fulfillment, liberation, and perfection.

At this point certain objections can certainly be raised. Such as, has not Przywara usurped the place of philosophy, in the name of the primacy of *theo*logy? In what way can *theo*logy exhibit primacy over philosophy and be said to be its *entelecheia*?[54] Is this not just a pious wish of a priest who was really a theologian rather than a real philosopher? And are we not merely returning to the Middle Ages where philosophy was the handmaiden of *theo*logy? Further, are we not forgetting the great emancipation of philosophy becoming pure: commencing with Scotus and Suarez and brought to fruition in Descartes (where philosophy really begins), consummated in Hegel's speculative appropriation of *theo*logy, where all becomes Rational philosophy and mystery gives way to the aura of the Concept, right down to Heidegger's pure, true, and autonomous philosophy and methodic atheism? Such objections miss the nuance and movement of Przywara's thought and his "pleromatic analogical hermeneutic of a nonidentical repetition" of the past and thus his originality, which is original because it is rooted in a tradition that is newly rethought (and therefore living) and thus prudent enough not to dispense with the great glory and the Wisdom of the past (as T. S. Eliot saw so clearly, the way forward is the way back), without also succumbing to a canonical repetition. Przywara surely takes us forward. But the way forward may have to present itself as a deconstruction of the ruse of a purely autonomous philosophy unrelated to its others (be they myth, religion, poetry, and especially *theo*logy). And by way of this deconstruction, Przywara is able to take us to a more postmodern place where a true conversation with otherness and difference takes place. And, in the case of Przywara, this postmodern site consists in a reimagined "suspended middle" that subverts the apostate divide between

---

54. For Przywara's discussion of the theological *entelecheia* of philosophy see Przywara, *Analogia Entis*, 174.

being and grace in philosophical modernity by speculatively establishing the analogical ordering of *philo*sophy to the dynamic exchange of the gift of *theo*logical supplementation.

How, then, explain the analogical working relation between *philo*sophy and *theo*logy in a single metaphysics bound in a harmonious unity-in-difference? It is explained by the fact that the formal object of *philo*sophy is the creature. And that what is formally revealed in a "creaturely metaphysics" is an open analogical tension or movement to an over, above, and beyond. Therefore a formal opening and transparency to (at the minimum) the possibility of revelation shows itself. A "creaturely metaphysics" is formally provisional and not *a priori* closed to the possibility of the otherness of revelation. Such a metaphysics thus finds its end, fulfillment, completion, perfection, and concretization by turning to the one concrete, factual, and historically existing order of grace and redemption. With accepting the concrete and historical actuality of revelation and redemption, one is now able to treat the final end of the creature and philosophy formally described hitherto.

In other words, one is now able to treat the objects of a "creaturely metaphysics" in their finality, namely, consciousness and being *as redeemed*. This is how Przywara construes a final *theo*logical metaphysics, namely, as treating the finality of the creature as redeemed. The object of metaphysics remains the same, namely, *the creature*. However, metaphysics has now found its perfection and finality in and through *theo*logy, but not *as theo*logy. (Recall that Stein agreed with this, but could not understand how a provisional and final *theo*logical metaphysics work together in a single metaphysics.) Furthermore, recall that the formal object of *theo*logy is God treated solely for God's sake. Here however, in a final *theo*logical metaphysics, the formal object is still the creature, but now accenting the *end* of the creature as historically existing in the *one concrete order of grace and redemption*.[55] Przywara's strong emphasis on the concrete

---

55. For the supernatural end of the creature see Przywara, *Analogia Entis*, 170. Przywara's stress on the concrete order of sin and redemption is succinctly expressed in his 1941 essay, "Philosophy as a Problem," where he says, "A *properly Christian* perspective has the final word: for there is only one concretely existing world: the order between God and creature in this concretely existing world: the order between original sin in Adam and redemption in Christ, the crucified. The concretely existing face of philosophy (every philosophy, that is, found within the concretely existing world and its history) is not visible except from the perspective of this order (within which, as an objectively universal order, every concretely existing human being stands, whether he knows it or not). Consequently, the question of a 'Christian philosophy' is not the question of one particular philosophy among others within

order of grace and redemption is groundbreaking and prefigures other great attempts to break the neo-Scholastic hold on the understanding of an abstract pure nature separated from grace. In this, Przywara has made a tremendous contribution comparable to, and paving the way for, Balthasar and de Lubac. Indeed, it may even be argued that Przywara exhibited a more profound analogical balance between being and grace than did de Lubac and Balthasar.

However, the question must be asked: Is Przywara, then, merely playing a game of semantics where, in reality, he is now on the level of *theo*logy?

---

the ambit of philosophy as such—rather, the question of the relation between Christianity and philosophy is the question concerning the concretely existing shape of philosophy as such (within this single, concretely existing order that obtains between original sin in Adam and redemption in Christ)." Przywara, "Philosophy as a Problem," in *Analogia Entis*, 402–3; for the pages of this essay see 400–429. Here is Przywara's answer to Bonhoeffer's inability to understand the *analogia entis* and how, indeed, the *analogia entis* is rooted in the concrete order of grace and redemption while, nevertheless, still retaining an analogical ordering of nature (being) and grace (faith), which is always denied in the Reformed tradition. For Bonhoeffer's critique of Przywara see Dietrich Bonhoeffer, *Act and Being: Transcendental Philosophy and Ontology in Systematic Theology*, ed. Wayne Whitson Floyd Jr., trans. H. Martin Rumscheidt (Minneapolis: Fortress Press, 2009), 152–53. Here Bonhoeffer denies any type of creation (and thus being) that is outside of Christ. For Balthasar's stance on this matter, which is in the vein of Przywara, see Hans Urs von Balthasar, *Theo-Logic*, vol. 1: *Truth of the World*, trans. Adrian J. Walker (San Francisco: Ignatius Press, 2000), 12. Likewise, for Balthasar's admirable attempt to bring Przywara and de Lubac into conversation with Barth, see Balthasar, *Karl Barth*. In this work Balthasar, in order to defend Przywara against Barth's criticism (along with Bonhoeffer's criticism which follows Barth's) against the *analogia entis* as a kind of metaphysical construct that lays hold of God outside Revelation, rightly stresses the *analogia entis* as always already taking place and occurring in the one concrete order of grace and redemption. To do so, Balthasar draws from Przywara's later works in which he thinks this emphasis becomes more stressed and apparent. It may be well true that Przywara more clearly expresses this in his later works, such as is seen in the above 1941 essay, which is also cited by Balthasar in *The Theology of Karl Barth*. See Hans Urs von Balthasar, *The Theology of Karl Barth: Exposition and Interpretation*, trans. Edward T. Oakes, SJ (San Francisco: Ignatius Press, 1992), 257. However, this stress is already clearly present in the first edition of *Analogia Entis* as well, and is there for any keen reader to perceive without much effort. That said, it well may be the case that Przywara does not stress this enough in his writings in the 1920s. And as it is most probable that Barth himself did not read *Analogia Entis* when making his famous criticism and, indeed, that Barth's criticism is directed towards *Polarity: A German Catholic's Interpretation of Religion*, then Balthasar's claims are justified. Balthasar is also completely right that "we may say that nothing whatever can be found of that ogre that Barth has made of the analogy of being." Balthasar, *Karl Barth*, 257. For references to Przywara in *The Theology of Karl Barth*, see Balthasar, *Karl Barth*, xvii–xviii, 8, 35, 30, 39, 98, 190, 225–26, especially 255–57, 319, 328–29, 343, 360–61.

For did Przywara not also say that *the*ology too treats the creature insofar as it should not just be a mere *theologia archetypa*? This is a very valid question, but a question that would still nevertheless miss the fact that the entirety of this discussion is ruled by the formal *the*ological axioms: faith does not destroy, but presupposes and perfects reason (consciousness), *and* grace does not destroy, but presupposes and perfects nature (being). Here, I think, is where Stein must have missed the analogical dimensions (and therefore Przywara's double analogical logic) of these two axioms, which, as analogical, are double and thus speak of both the philosophical *and the*ological, thereby opening up a belonging-together in an analogical unity-in-difference: an analogy of discourses. For if Stein understood this, then she could have explained how a *philo*sophical and *the*ological metaphysics work together in the union of a single metaphysics. These two axioms are also sorely misunderstood by thinkers who immediately foreclose the possibility of a Catholic or Christian metaphysics as unphilosophical because it is based on faith. This is a misunderstanding precisely because the analogical working of these two axioms respects *both being and grace* and are, therefore, simultaneously human and divine. It is true that one may not accept these axioms because they speak of grace and faith and thus have to be taken on faith. But this is a faith that, in the Catholic view, does not destroy but perfects reason and being. And, therefore, even if one does not accept this faith, it can still be seen *how a contradiction does not ensue* and how the structure of a Christian or Catholic metaphysics can work and be taken as a hypothesis, even if one does not, ultimately, agree with this hypothesis or structure. This demands further justification.

Returning to a description of the movement of Przywara's thought: a single metaphysics commences with a provisional "creaturely metaphysics" that decenters all forms of absolutization and foundationalism in philosophy. This is done by showing that man and philosophy, in and of themselves, are inherently unstable (the Augustinian *est non est*). They possess no ground in and of themselves. This was expressed in the formal problem of a "creaturely metaphysics," namely, the suspended duality between being and consciousness, which was rooted in the real metaphysical difference in man between essence and existence: *Sosein in-über Dasein*. This in-over or in-beyond structure presented itself along the way in intensifying modes. This intensification reached a high point in the question of natural theology, where the divine came into the picture as the ground, end, and definition of man and thus a God beyond-and-in philosophy (as well as theology in-and-beyond philosophy). God can then be arrived at (in keeping with

Vatican I) as a kind of positive limit concept and can be affirmed by man's searching reason as the *principium* and *finis* of the creature.

Here, however, a certain danger ensued, for philosophy and the creature could themselves not secure the transcendence they were aiming for in the in-and-beyond structure, which revealed the creature and philosophy to be transitional. Philosophy was in danger of tying God too much to the "from" and "in" of the creature, thus running the risk of idolatry reminiscent of theopanism/pantheism. If this metaphysical movement of thought (which has hitherto confined itself solely to metaphysics without once invoking the aid of *theo*logy or revelation) towards the beyond is to be truly beyond, then it must pass into what is other to it, namely, Catholic *theo*logy, which alone carries with it the means of securing God and *theo*logy's transcendence. This is accomplished in light of a God who is beyond all grounding and idolatry because this God is free, self-revealing, and the Creator *ex nihilo*. Philosophy's relational and analogical in-and-beyond structure is fulfilled because it is itself surpassed and transcended by a beyond that is truly beyond because the creature is now seen for what it truly is, namely, a relation, or a free *gift* granted in an asymmetrical relation by the ever-greater God.

Enter now a speculative *theo*logical metaphysics that was opened up by the provisional autonomy of a philosophical metaphysics. (It is autonomous because no *theo*logical motifs were invoked, but it is also provisional because man's being and philosophy were shown to be nonabsolute and therefore relative *transitional states*.) This provisional *philo*sophy is thus opened up towards a final speculative *theo*logical metaphysics in which philosophy and the creature find their liberation, end, and perfection. *Theo*logy has thus revealed itself to be the inner telos of the philosophical (and therefore always in a certain sense, in philosophy, as the beyond of philosophy) as the aim or goal that *philo*sophy was reaching toward. Moreover, analogously to the way that man possesses a natural desire for God, so too does *philo*sophy possess, as Betz felicitously notes, a "natural desire" for *theo*logy. Nevertheless, it is a natural desire for an end and fulfillment that, paradoxically, remains out of philosophy's power to obtain. For it cannot lay claim to revelation (or it would be just another form of immanent theology), but it does point towards the holiness of the temple (*fanum*) in the manner of the *pro-fanum*.[56] The two belong together in an analogical

---

56. For Przywara's brilliant discussion of the profane and sacred see Przywara, *Analogia Entis*, 182.

ordering or unity-in-difference, which should not be torn asunder in the name of an enlightened state of secularization: for the pro-fane cannot be understood but as a pointing towards and relationally passing-over into the sacred.

The entirety of the philosophical and creaturely realm is thus shown to be presided over by the supernatural, divine, and *theo*logical, which indeed, super-form (*überformt*) this entire realm, exhibiting both a formal (idea) and actual (reality) primacy as the inner telos of the philosophical.[57] Moreover, from the vantage of the finality of a *theo*logical metaphysics, it can be seen that the *theo*logical is—in an Aristotelian sense—the *telos* because it is that which refers back to a "setting-into-action" (*energia*) by the *theo*logical, and thus, a giving of "power-as-possibility" (*dynamis*) to the philosophical and its desire for the divine, revealed in its potential for obedience to the *theo*logical (in old Scholastic terms the *potentia oboedientialis* of the creature's readiness to receive grace, or in this analogous instance, *philo*sophy's expectant openness to receive the grace of the *theo*logical).[58] *Philo*sophy thus receives its fullest and final actualization by a passing-over into what is other to it—but a passing-over that is *intrinsic* to *philo*sophy's very essence (as given as a "power-as-possibility"), which is itself a transitive ascending movement (participation) in the giving and active energy of the *theo*logical.

But perhaps this Aristotelian example gives the impression that the philosophical and *theo*logical (and thus the guiding *en-telecheia* of the *theo*logical) are too much tied on a quantitative univocal and horizontal plane of immanence. To avoid this worry, Przywara accentuates and inflects the ascending, vertical movement of rising intensification (an intensification itself given by the pull of the *theo*logical) through his superb example of Augustine's Christianized form of neo-Platonism. This example is given in Augustine's renowned formula: "as the body is to the soul, so is the soul to God."[59] This formula explodes any possible interpretation of belonging together on a univocal plane of immanence according to differing quantitative degrees (akin to Deleuze's interpretation of being and desire).[60]

---

57. Przywara, *Analogia Entis*, 174.
58. Przywara, *Analogia Entis*, 174.
59. Przywara, *Analogia Entis*, 175.
60. For a fine essay that argues against Deleuze's univocal interpretation of desire and being in favor of an analogical interpretation of being, which signals and points to the implication (an implication that still demands more elaboration at the conclusion of this text) of the *analogia entis* for political thought as a means of resistance against the devious

Rather one sees here the gesture towards a participatory analogy where the belonging-together of the terms is bound by a common element (the "as ... so") in a formally higher and qualitatively *different* primacy.[61] In other words, if the higher term of the soul over the body, or God over the soul, does not exhibit a formally higher primacy, then the relation is lost because it is through this higher primacy that the lower term (whether the body or the soul) first attains its actualization: an actualization that is not through itself (in itself) but in virtue of the beyond itself, that is, in what is *different* and *beyond* itself.

It is thus via an analogical participation of qualitative degrees of difference (exhibited in a unity-in-difference) through which the lower terms obtain their participatory and, therefore, relative-identity, in what is other to, and higher than them. (The soul is higher than the body and is that in which the body finds its actualization, and God is higher than the soul and is that in which the soul finds its actualization.)[62] This, in turn, can be analogously applied to *theo*logy's primacy over the philosophical through which philosophy passes over into the *theo*logical. There is, however, no rupturing violence. Nor is it as if philosophy simply fails and is insufficient to its task. Rather there is a harmonious flowing of philosophy into *theo*logy. There is no *tertium quid*. This is far from some frustrating acceptance or acquiescence on philosophy's part, but rather a positive fulfillment and perfection of philosophy's transitive essence. *Philo*sophy is a participatory passing-over into the otherness of *theo*logical Wisdom. Yet this does not destroy philosophy but fulfills, perfects, and consummates the ascending participatory *ex*pectant metaphysical desire of *philo*sophy, a desire that itself was given by the *theo*logical and all the while guided by *theo*logy's acting and guiding *telos* which only comes as an eventful revelatory surprise, or gift.

In sum: a single metaphysics begins with a relative-autonomous philosophical "creaturely metaphysics" that travels the whole breadth of the philosophical (because no theological motifs were invoked in the formal

---

hegemony of Capitalism's univocal power over the world, see Daniel M. Bell Jr., "Only Jesus Saves: Toward a Theopolitical Ontology of Judgment," in *Theology and the Political*, 200–230. Also, for an application of Desmond's metaxological metaphysics, read as being in alliance with an analogical understanding of being, and thus offering resistance to the Capitalist stress on identity, see Creston Davis and Patrick Aaron Riches, "The Theological Praxis of Revolution," in *Theology and the Political*, 22–51.

61. Przywara, *Analogia Entis*, 174–75.
62. Przywara, *Analogia Entis*, 174–75.

description of creaturely contingency) and arrives at a place of open eschatological expectancy: to a beyond towards which philosophy looks, but cannot obtain. And in this looking towards, philosophy is paradoxically desiring and open (obedient) to the possible surprise of otherness, or revelation. Such a philosophical metaphysics passes over into concrete fulfillment when it enters into alliance with Catholic *theo*logy, in the one concrete order of grace and redemption, a concrete order to which a philosophical metaphysics was always formally open and, further, an order through which *philo*sophy finds its perfection and finality in the actuality of revelation and the speaking God. Such a perfection and finality, though, carry with them the whole breadth of the philosophical, because the philosophical was the *pre*supposed. And, as the *pre*supposed, *philo*sophy was that upon which the *theo*logical builds, as grace builds on being or nature. Simultaneously, a philosophical metaphysics, as the pre*supposed*, was also that which was always already *supposed* by a final *theo*logical metaphysics. Hence, *theo*logy was that to which a philosophical metaphysics was *always already* heading towards. *Philo*sophy then was *always already* presided over, super-formed, and set-into-action by the guiding *theo*logical *telos*. Nevertheless, this is all one movement within a single harmonious metaphysics because grace, faith, and *theo*logy do not destroy but presuppose and perfect metaphysics.

*Philo*sophy, then, is finally liberated and freed into its participatory essence. *Philo*sophy, as a loving-towards and desiring of Sophia, now participates in the *maxime sapientia* of *theo*logical mystery because *philo*sophy participates in the grace of the free, groundless, and ungraspable God of grace and creation: He whose Wisdom is mystery (*Si comprehendis, non est Deus*). In a word, *philo*sophy as sapiential and participatory is a *reductio in mysterium*. *Philo*sophy gives itself up in order to find itself, because, as sapiential, *philo*sophy never was itself except by participating in what was not itself, that is, Wisdom or the divine. *Philo*sophy's wealth is its poverty and its poverty is its wealth through which its dignity is released, in and through service and love for the otherness of Wisdom. By losing itself, *philo*sophy finds itself as it always was and should be. *Philo*sophy finds itself as a humble and loving participant that is now united, in an analogical peaceful unity-in-difference, with the otherness of *theo*logical Wisdom (without confusion and without separation). This unity is expressed in the one movement of a provisional and final metaphysics working together and bound by an analogical unity-in-difference through which the human and creaturely participate in the divine. Thus, on both sides of this asymmetrical relation, there is a freeing and loving respect of difference that allows the co-belonging of the two discourses: an analogy of discourses. Such is Przywara's sapiential and participatory vision of *philo*sophy and *theo*logy belonging together in a single harmonious creaturely metaphysics super-formed and participating in the divine. This *vision* is very different from Stein's vision of philosophy aiming towards a rationalistic total disclosure of all truth. Stein's vision, and *telos*, of philosophy remains a modern one, even if it gestures to a weakened modernity. Przywara, on the other hand, leads us in a far more postmodern direction of the "suspended middle" by deconstructing modern philosophy's *conatus* for a secure foundation and total disclosure in favor of a sapiential and participatory vision of *philo*sophy. In Przywara's vision, *philo*sophy is inherently relational and granted, asymmetrically, by the ungroundable God of revelation and creation *ex nihilo*, and thus receptive of otherness and mystery: the mysterious gracing of otherness.

Concept and Mystery: A Reductio in Mysterium

Before this chapter concludes I would like to touch on Przywara's discussion of concept and mystery.[63] My reason for this is twofold. First, in Przywara's discussion of concept and mystery his profound contention and counter-Hegelian way of thinking comes strongly to the fore. Moreover, because Hegel's system must be seen as the apex of modern philosophy's *conatus* for foundationalism and self-presence where mystery is fully overcome in favor of the Concept, Przywara's brilliant counter- and anti-Hegelianism strikes at the core of modern philosophy's project of the "dream of reason." Second, in this discussion Przywara's dramatically speculative, aesthetic, and pleromatic Christian vision is especially on display via his leading of *philo*sophy and *theo*logy into a *reduction in mysterium.*

It has just been shown that Przywara's "creaturely metaphysics" achieves a radical decentering and relativization of philosophy and man, thus showing the utter uncertainty and unstableness of man and philosophy (the Augustinian *est non est*). This unstableness and uncertainty came to expression in the dynamic metaphysical formula: *Sosein in-über Dasein*. This formula was revelatory of man's concrete condition of becoming and

---

63. For Przywara's extraordinary treatment of concept/mystery and *reductio in mysterium*, see Przywara, *Analogia Entis*, 181–88.

the real metaphysical difference/distinction between essence and existence in man. This formula was then reflected in the formal epistemological problem of a "creaturely metaphysics," namely, the suspended tension or duality between consciousness and being. Thus epistemology is reflective and descriptive (that is, situated in the analogical between of man's existence) of the real metaphysical difference between essence/existence and is therefore just as insecure as man and philosophy's groundless condition.

In other words, if man's *being*-in-becoming is creaturely, then so too is truth, seen from a creaturely perspective. Truth, as a transcendental of *being*, is likewise analogous, between, or suspended and therefore non-absolute and relative. Truth is analogical: meaning it is *between* being/becoming, essence/existence, consciousness/being, time/eternity, history/truth, philosophy/*theo*logy, identity/difference, and likeness/dislikeness, and thus never pure or absolute. Here there is no pure phenomenological grasp of eternal essences, no *Cogito*, no transcendental apperception, and no speculative identity. Truth is a promiscuous mixing where there is a shading at play of light and shadow: a seeing in a glass or mirror darkly. For the analogical suspended between gaze, truth *is* chiaroscuro, or a speculatively dramatic and aesthetic belonging-together of concept and mystery. Thus, like creaturely being, epistemology and creaturely truth must exhibit the same inherent tension and dynamic, namely, the relational and transitive in-and-beyond structure. Moreover, like God and *theo*logy, mystery must be seen as both in-and-beyond the concept and thus the fulfillment and *telos* of the concept. Mystery thus plays *in* the concept stretching it *beyond* itself by taking it up *into* itself. *Philo*sophy and *theo*logy are, in the end, about a visionary *reductio in mysterium*.

In the foregoing, Przywara's sapiential and participatory vision of *philo*sophy was laid out, thereby showing the intrinsic co-belonging of the *pro-fanum* and *fanum*, of the *pro*fane and the sacred. How then does the profanity of the philosophical concept lead into and break off before the *mysterium* of the sacred, of the holy, of that which is set apart, occult, and closed? What is their relation (if any), and what is their dynamic? The realm of mystery was broached first in the philosophical when a formal concept of the divine or God was arrived upon as the *principium et finis* of the creature (i.e., the ground, end, and definition of the creature). Thus, in arriving at a metaphysical concept of God, as the *principium et finis* of the creature, one arrives at what the neo-Scholastics called the "*mysterium naturale*."[64] Here the

---

64. Przywara, *Analogia Entis*, 181.

metaphysical concept touches upon the divine and the *mysterium* implicit within metaphysics as a creaturely desirous searching into the ground, end, and definition of being qua being—that is to say, of the mystery of natural theology implicit within metaphysics as such. What, then, of the manner of this metaphysical and conceptual touching upon mystery? How understand this mystery, and what relation does the philosophical concept have vis-à-vis mystery?

Here, it must be remembered, that as with a God beyond-and-in the creature and a theology beyond-and-in philosophy, one is at the enigmatic, liminal, and analogically paradoxical site or *topos* where philosophy, as a provisional endeavor, ends. Here one is at a site that touches upon the *telos* of the divine and the *theo*logical which *philo*sophy cannot itself obtain, but is, nevertheless, implicit within *philo*sophy as a guiding beyond. This is the point of extreme suspendedness and intensification where one's relation to the beyond is at a point of a passing-over into the beyond, and thus expectantly open to a relation coming fully from an asymmetrical beyond which is divine. It is a space of open-endedness, an eschatological site of expectancy before the possibility of otherness. At this liminal space one is touching upon a mystery that is both beyond-and-in the metaphysical concept. It is a mystery precisely because here one is dealing with man's metaphysical desire, questing, and searching—arising out of the *cor inquietum*—for the divine. This is adequately expressed in the profound Augustinian maxim, "so that He who is to be found should be sought, He is hidden, *ut inveniendus quaeratur occultus est*."[65]

In other words, within Przywara's conception of natural theology there is already implicitly present the hiddenness of the mystery of the living God. Upon the conceptual arrival at God, as the ground, beginning, and end of man, there is present the pointing beyond and transcendence of God in the conceptual formula God *beyond*-and-in the creature. The beyond points towards, or better, is expressive of the hiddenness of God. *Philo*sophy and its concept(s) (provisionally understood) stand at the liminal space of intersection with the divine pointing towards a mysterious transcendence that cannot be fully grasped. Moreover, *philo*sophy and the metaphysical concept(s), like the *pro-fano*, break off before, and point towards, the inner and hidden sanctuary of the divine. And insofar as *philo*sophy and its metaphysical concept(s) of the divine, expressed in the dynamic conceptual formula God-beyond-and-in the creature, seek

---

65. Przywara, *Analogia Entis*, 181.

to respect and keep open the transcendence of the divine (as far as this is possible for philosophy to do), then *philo*sophy and its dynamic formal concept(s) must be seen as a "guarding of mystery (*occultus est*)": contra the various hydra heads of theopanism/pantheism and their immanent theologies seeking to undercut the mystery of divine transcendence.[66] The philosophical concept, far from encapsulating the divine, breaks off before the transcendent (like the path that breaks off before the temple precincts) hiddenness of the mystery of the divine. *Philo*sophy (and its metaphysical concept[s]) is a leading into mystery, that is, a *reductio in mysterium*. But is this utter mystification and irrationalism? Before I answer this, let me turn to the *theo*logical concept and its relation to mystery.

The function of the metaphysical concept(s) of the divine is twofold. First, the metaphysical concept functions as a "guarding" and breaking off before the closed doors of the mystery of the divine. Second, if the metaphysical concept(s) functions in a breaking off, then this likewise implies a leading *into* the mystery of the divine. It then follows that the concept will find its fulfillment and perfection when it itself is *initiated* into mystery. That is, when the concept is itself "overwhelmed *into* mystery" (*In das Geheimnis übermächtigt wird*).[67] This occurs when the concept is taken up into the "*mysterium supernaturale*" of *theo*logical Wisdom.[68] If then the philosophical concept breaks off before mystery, then in the *theo*logical concept "mystery is the fullness *of* the concept."[69] The concept finds its fulfillment and liberation (as did the creature and *philo*sophy) when it passes over into the grace of the *theo*logical and the mysterious Wisdom flowing from the infinity of the ungraspable God of revelation and creation. Here the creature and the concept are themselves grasped by mystery, where the very subject matter of the *theo*logical comes from the divine speaking the mystery of the Divine Self. Here the Augustinian maxim that was touched upon tangentially by the philosophical concept and the desirous search for God finds its completion, namely, "so that He who has been found might be sought, *He is unending* [italics mine] *ut inventus quaeratur, immensus est*."[70]

Further, the fullness of the concept thus sojourns within the positivity of the mystery of divine infinity. It is a visionary grasping of the ungrasp-

---

66. Przywara, *Analogia Entis*, 181.
67. Przywara, *Analogia Entis*, 181.
68. Przywara, *Analogia Entis*, 181.
69. Przywara, *Analogia Entis*, 183.
70. Przywara, *Analogia Entis*, 181. For the reference to Augustine, see Augustine, *In Jo. Tract*. LXIII, i.

able, the *Si comprehendis, non est Deus*, the *Deus tamquam ignotus*, a knowing in unknowing, the "super-luminous darkness" of Denys.[71] It is an analogical play (chiaroscuro) between the *theo*logical metaphysical concept(s) of a *theologia positiva* and the ever-receding mystery of a *theologia negativa*. For *theo*logy too, and its concept(s) of God, must ultimately be a *reductio in mysterium* in the tradition of Augustine, Denys, and Aquinas. The speculative *theo*logical metaphysical concept(s) of God inhabits, is taken up into, the realm of mystery. The concept can only be itself by surpassing itself into the dynamic positivity of the divine infinity of the unending mystery of the speaking God. The concept is not destroyed, but fulfilled by continually being taken beyond itself in the flowing dynamic positivity of God's life and mystery. And only thus can the concept be saved from falling into the erroneous irrationalism of a Rationalism that thinks it can encapsulate and grasp the flowing infinite divine life by dialectically sublating mystery and arriving at the fullness of the Concept, now understood as Absolute Knowledge. This is Przywara's definitive reversal of Hegel, in light of a critical retrieval of the Augustinian-Dionysian-Thomistic tradition, which sees the fullness of the concept as residing in, and being taken up, into the mystery of God's unending life of flowing dynamic positivity.

Thus, this is far from mystification and irrationalism; rather it is a speculatively dramatic and aesthetically beautiful analogical balance of a true positive knowing in unknowing. It is being grasped by a mystery that has been implicit within metaphysics and its concept(s), because metaphysics and its concept(s) have been relationally open, in their transparent and eschatological openness, to mystery and otherness. Mystery and otherness are not foreign to the transitive state of the creature, metaphysics, and the concept and thus, there is no risk of a *deus ex machina*. Moreover, in this understanding, God is not grasped in the manner of the irrational-Rationalism of Hegel, that is, in a concept of God, in the sense of "God's self-concept."[72] Nor is this some kind of state of religious fanaticism of a fideistic chaotic rapture of faith/reason that is unable to decide between the demonic and angelic. Here there is genuine metaphysical vision: a *knowing in unknowing*. These two aforesaid forms of irrationalism are surpassed because what occurs here is a respect for the abiding fullness of the positive

---

71. Przywara, *Analogia Entis*, 182. For the reference to Augustine, see Augustine, *Serm.* CVII, iii, 5; for the reference to Aquinas, see Aquinas, *In Boeth. de Trin.* q. 1, a. 2, cor et ad. 1; for the reference to the Areopagite, see Pseudo-Dionysius, *Myst. Th.* I, 1.

72. Przywara, *Analogia Entis*, 184.

and living infinity of God's plenitudinous life, devoid of all negativity and lack. If there is a concept of God, then it is one of the very *living* infinity of God, which is the only way to approach God's true self-concept, so to speak.

Further, at the very point where the philosophical creaturely concept(s) of God seems to fail and break off before the mystery of God, this can only be interpreted as a failure from the creaturely vantage. When seen from the side of God, what seems to be a "disintegration" is in fact a positive "likeness" to God. Which is to say that the "overflowing dynamic" of the creature, and its attempt to understand God in a multiplicity of concepts, is a revelatory likeness of God's own positive dynamic life of eternal overflowing.[73] This is rooted in the extraordinary insight of Aquinas that God mirrors his divine simplicity in the multitude and mutability of created things.[74] Through our seemingly insufficient and diverse conceptions of God, something of the positive simplicity of the living and infinite life of God is analogically grasped. God is thus grasped, as the act of all things, as within all things (*interior omni re*), as transcendent of all comprehension and beyond all things (*exterior omni re*).[75] God's immanence is grasped in virtue of his transcendence and mystery, positively and analogically mirrored in our diverse concepts of God: though a mirroring and analogical likeness of he who is, ultimately, *beyond all likeness*. God's immanence to the visible, creaturely, and mutable is possible because he himself is invisible and eternal act and thus a mystery that is positively beyond-and-in our metaphysical and diverse conceptions of God. To put it as simply as possible, it is because of God's transcendent never-to-be-closed distance from creation that God's act is supremely and intimately present within all created things and our creaturely conceptions of the divine. This, in turn, allows us to positively mirror and participate in the divine infinity with our diverse conceptions of the divine, while never closing the distance in an idolatrous mirroring. This is because our conceptions are always analogically mediated through the multiplicity of created things (and creation as a whole). And, thus, our creaturely concepts bespeak the never-to-be-encapsulated flowing and dynamic infinity of God.

Mystery thus holds sway and plays in the concept, in virtue of its transcendence beyond the concept (both in its philosophical and theological

---

73. Przywara, *Analogia Entis*, 184.

74. Przywara, *Analogia Entis*, 184. For the references to Aquinas, see Aquinas, *De Ver.* q. 1, a. 4, ad 3; *De Ver.* q. 27, a. 1, ad 7; and *Summa Th.* I, q. 13, a. corp.

75. Przywara, *Analogia Entis*, 185. For the references to Augustine, see Augustine, *De Gen. ad Litt.* VIII, 26.

sense). This guards against two forms of rationalism (and thus also irrationalism, because many forms of irrationalism are reactive to degenerate forms of monological reason closed off to mystery and otherness). First, there is the rationalism of the philosophical concept, which works from the below or immanence and seeks to encapsulate and comprehend by putting its conceptual finger on the pulsating life of the divine by dialectically arriving at the "self-concept" of a dialectically Trinitarian counterfeit God à la Hegel and his confrères.[76] Contra such a rationalism Przywara asserts that the end of even the most rigorous philosophy must be a *reductio in mysterium* where the philosophical concept(s) breaks off into the mystery of the divine that is beyond-and-in the concept, thus respecting and giving way to divine transcendence. Second, there is a theological rationalism that would seek to derive all truth from the above in light of the theological concept. This form of rationalism runs the risk that faith has no metaphysical ground on which to stand and is thus about obscure feelings of the divine, which frustrates reason and thus is a kind of "false mysticism."[77] Contra this, it was seen that the way into the mystery of the *theo*logical was truly a positive way and was a passing over from the philosophical concept(s) into the fulfillment of the concept in the *theo*logical. In theological mystery was found the fullness of the concept, thus freeing and releasing the concept into the mysterious vibrancy of the positive flowing life of divine eternity. Here was a true positive knowledge of the divine that was reflected in our creaturely and diverse conceptions of the divine. Our diverse conceptions thus showed forth the positivity of the simplicity of the God who is pure act (that is, he whose essence is his existence) and eternal overflowing, analogically mirrored and mediated in and through creaturely plurality.

Yet this positive way is opened up to the negative way, or better, was made possible by the transcendent mystery of God who is exterior to all things. God is thus able to manifest the intimacy of his presence, in immanence, without collapsing the living eternity of God into the immanent creaturely sphere or concept. For, in the end, this positive knowledge was always already bathed in the dazzling super-luminous darkness of divine glory. Here all true knowing is an unknowing of a God whose existence can be known *but never his essence* (the *Si comprehendis, non est Deus*, and *Deus tamquam ignotus*). For the *telos* of *theo*logy, like *philo*sophy, is the *reductio in mysterium* towards the ever-greater God. But this is not

76. Przywara, *Analogia Entis*, 184.
77. Przywara, *Analogia Entis*, 188.

the road of mystification and irrational mysticism. Rather it is the same road of the analogical binding of the harmonious unity-in-difference seen before. Here the concept(s) (both in its provisional metaphysical guise and its speculative *theo*logical metaphysical guise) is bound with mystery. The concept thus walks step by step with mystery, until the concept itself is truly fulfilled and taken up into the positivity of the flowing mystery of divine life. The concept is never destroyed and left behind, but finds itself in surpassing and surrendering itself to the mystery that was always present in and guiding it, as the positive beyond of the concept. In this view reason and the concept reach their highest exaltation. That is, in Przywara's view, reason and the concept are worthy and capable of participating in (truly knowing in an unknowing) the mystery of God's supernatural life. Yet here, as well, faith and mystery are themselves made truly knowable (but of course never fully knowable) and comprehensible in a nontotalizing way. The presupposed groundwork of the metaphysical, and its concept(s), render knowable theological truth. Yet this knowability of the metaphysical and its concept(s) passes over into a participation in the mystery of theological truth by aiding a speculative *theo*logical metaphysics. All of this is again accomplished through the unity and movement of a single philosophical-*theo*logical metaphysics. This single metaphysics, bound by an analogical unity-in-difference, serves the one, ungraspable, free, transcendent, and loving God of creation (being/metaphysics), grace (revelation/faith), and glory, thereby uniting concept and mystery in a speculatively dramatic and aesthetic musical play of analogical balance.

*   *   *

To conclude: We have discussed many essential points in this chapter, points that will find a continual refrain throughout the remainder of Part 1. This chapter began with bringing-into-view the substantive and relational significance of the question of reason and revelation within Christian discourse and the Occidental tradition, thereby showing the current urgency and need to deal with this encompassing and seminal question. Moreover, the enormity of this question was emphasized to further show how Przywara's and Stein's respective answers to this question are essential to the *range* of their Christian vision.

Stein's solution to the problematic of the relation between philosophy and *theo*logy was seen to be premised on modern principles tainted with foundationalism. This is immensely important as Stein's modern approach to Christian philosophy will be consistent with both her interpretation of being (chapter 3) and the *analogia entis* (chapter 4). Stein's modernity, even if weakened, marks the entirety of her discourse and renders it less viable to our postmodern condition. On the other hand, Przywara presents a participatory countermodern style of *philo*sophy that opens up to a robust and expansive dialogue with *theo*logy. This approach renders Przywara's voice viable and needful in any attempt to develop a specifically pleromatic Christian vision in light of our postmodern condition. His voice is viable because through it a "suspended middle" site of an analogical ordering of *philo*sophy to *theo*logical supplementation is reactivated beyond philosophical modernity. Likewise, as with Stein, Przywara's approach to the relation between *philo*sophy and *theo*logy remains consistent with his interpretation of being (chapter 3) and the *analogia entis* (chapter 4). Thus in the question of the relation between philosophy and *theo*logy, in Przywara and Stein, the trajectory of their respective strategies to philosophical modernity is set into motion. In short, these respective strategies serve as hermeneutic keys to their viability or nonviability of aiding a specifically pleromatic style of Christian postmodern discourse, sought for in Part 2.

CHAPTER 3

Visions of Being: Foundation and Nonfoundation

For as you begin, so will you remain.
                         Friedrich Hölderlin, "The Rhine"

A small mistake in the beginning is a big one in the end.
                         Thomas Aquinas, *On Being and Essence*

In the preceding chapter we arrived at certain strategic positions towards philosophical modernity that will aid in opening up an understanding of Przywara's and Stein's differing interpretations of being. These positions concerned the style or vision of philosophy being performed in regard to what kind of relation was elaborated between philosophy and *theo*logy. In Stein we saw a very modern approach to philosophy. This came to expression in Stein's weakened rationalistic and foundationalistic interpretation of Christian philosophy. This interpretation passed on the Husserlian vision of philosophy as a "rigorous science" to the task of Christian philosophy whose teleological aim is "total knowledge" or complete evidence. It is now time to see how Stein's foundationalistic tendencies surface and resurface in relation to her thinking on being, or to see that "Stein is a *modern* philosopher, because she does not altogether give up a cogito-centered philosophical project."[1] The question of this chapter (in the portion pertaining to Stein) will be: How does Stein's modernity, which came to expression in her view of Christian philosophy,

---

1. Chantal Beauvais, "Edith Stein and Modern Philosophy," in *Husserl and Stein*, ed. Richard Feist and William Sweet (Washington, DC: Council for Research in Values and Philosophy, 2003), http://www.crvp.org/book/Series01/I-31/chap-10.htm/.

manifest itself in her interpretive vision of being which searches for a solid foundation?

On the other hand Przywara's style of philosophizing pointed towards a dynamic thinking of analogical difference that was at the heart of his ancient and surprisingly new sapiential and participatory vision of *philo*sophy which revealed the teleological aim of his project to be *theo*logical Wisdom and supplementation (the "suspended middle"). This ultimately manifested itself in seeing *philo*sophy and *theo*logy as a *reductio in mysterium*. Przywara's countermodern and antifoundationalist project thus opened itself up towards postmodern vistas. Thus the question of this chapter (in the portion pertaining to Przywara) is: How is Przywara's countermodernity rooted in his dynamic metaphysical vision of being, understood as analogical difference? This was already partly explored in the previous chapter. However, in the preceding chapter, Przywara's metaphysics of analogical difference was only treated in view of its enabling an understanding of his conception of the relational interplay between *philo*sophy and *theo*logy, and not directly in view of his core vision of being. The latter is the aim of this chapter. I thus focus on those aspects of Przywara's thinking that get to the beating heart of his interpretation of being, while also filling out some important details that could not be attended to in the previous chapter.

Following from this, it is not necessary to go into the same depth for Przywara as it will be for Stein, because many pieces of his analogical metaphysics were already laid out in the previous chapter. Pieces were already laid, because in order to understand the relation between *philo*sophy and *theo*logy it was first necessary to understand something of his metaphysics of being, which is ineluctably tied (analogically ordered) to *theo*logy. This was not the case with Stein. One could understand Stein's treatment of Christian philosophy without an extensive engagement with her philosophy, which, in turn, demands a fuller treatment of her philosophy in the present chapter. Nevertheless, there will be moments of repetition in my presentation of Przywara, but they will be nonidentical forms of repetition. These nonidentical forms of repetition will make possible a presentation of the full dynamic breadth of Przywara's "systematics of impurity."

A Vision of Being-as-Foundation

We have seen in the foregoing investigation of Stein's notion of Christian philosophy that it exhibited something of modern philosophy's *conatus* for foundationalism and a teleological goal of "total knowledge." It is time to see how this *conatus* and goal resides at the very beginning of Stein's phenomenological-ontology, thus determining both its direction and end. In other words, we must explore how the paternity of Descartes and Husserl casts a shadow over Stein's project of a phenomenological-ontology. This is particularly evident in a Steinian rendition of the *Cogito* and its tendency towards immediate certainty, security, and evidence. In so doing Stein shows her inability to fully rid her thought of the egological foundationalist project endemic in modernity. In seeking to establish this, it is good to recall that Stein always saw herself as a phenomenologist and thus a follower of the egological approach of early phenomenology. This approach to being, then, always remains experientially and immanently based (given and reduced to the I). Which is to say that her "ontology" or "doctrine of being" is an immanent investigation of being that never oversteps itself to the beyond of transcendence, to the exteriority of metaphysical desire and the loving distance of speculation. Likewise, recall that Stein's intention in doing this was an attempt in "conscious self-restraint" as opposed to Przywara's elaboration of an alleged "philosophical system." When all is said and done it will become clear that Stein's anthropocentric phenomenological-ontology is far more ambitious than Przywara's metaphysical "systematics of impurity" because it fails to adequately think being's difference, distance, and mediation.

The Founding I

Stein's founding gesture and methodological "starting point" is the indubitable fact of the being of the I.[2] This founding gesture will determine, in one way or another, the entire project and direction of the remaining text. For is that not exactly the point of a foundational "starting point" from which one's method is grounded and launched, a launching that is itself

---

2. Edith Stein, *Finite and Eternal Being: An Attempt at an Ascent to the Meaning of Being*, trans. Kurt F. Reinhardt (Washington, DC: ICS Publications, 2001). "The Starting Point of the Inquiry: The Fact of Our Own Being" is the title of section 2 of chapter 2 of *Finite and Eternal Being*. Stein nominates chapters 2 and 3 Augustinian and chapter 4 Aristotelian.

paradoxically secured by the positing of the very method that is seeking a secure point of departure? In other words, in seeking a "starting point" of an inquiry, what comes first: the epistemological method or the inescapable ontological fact of our own being? (I will return to this question below.) Stein says,

> Whenever the human mind in its quest for truth has sought an indubitable certain point of departure, it always encountered the inescapable fact of its own being or existence. . . . When Descartes in his Meditationes de prima philosophia [*Meditations on the First Philosophy*, i.e., metaphysics] made the attempt to reconstruct philosophy as a trustworthy science on the foundation of indubitable certitude, he started out methodologically with his familiar effort of a universal doubt. He eliminated everything which—owing to possible deception or illusion—could be subject to doubt. What remained as an irreducible datum was the fact of doubt itself, generally speaking, the fact of thought itself and of the being implicit in the thinking: Cogito, sum.[3]

Stein goes on to speak of the kinship between Descartes and Husserl's method insofar as Husserl's project of laying the methodological foundations of phenomenology sought a "suspension of judgment" [*Urteilsenthaltung*] from the naïveté of the "natural attitude."[4] Husserl's phenomenological reduction demanded that one abstain from any judgment of the existence of the natural world. What remains after this abstention of judgment is the "area of *consciousness* understood as the *life of the ego* [*Ichleben*]." Once one methodologically arrives at this reduced site of consciousness, what can no longer be doubted, for Husserl and Stein, is the act of conscious perception. Stein finds in all of this the "I live" of Augustine, thus clearly interpreting Descartes's "I think" and Husserl's "being conscious" or "experiencing" as touching upon the same reality as Augustine.[5] Stein then sees the three aforementioned philosophers as touching upon the immediately implied ontological fact of the *am* (being) of the I that comes to expression in perception, thinking, and living. By seeing it this way Stein does not view the *Cogito, ergo sum* as a conclusion, but rather as immediate and "primordial knowledge" given through the absolute coinci-

---

3. Stein, *Finite and Eternal Being*, 35–36.
4. Stein, *Finite and Eternal Being*, 36.
5. Stein, *Finite and Eternal Being*, 36.

dence of being and consciousness.⁶ Consciousness is, at its deepest heart and ground, knowledge or consciousness of one's own being. This kind of knowledge is "primordial," "unreflected," and should not be understood as a "first principle" from which one can then, in turn, "measure" all other truths.⁷ Nevertheless, this reduced-conscious-knowledge of being, given in the I, is indubitable, certain, and a "primordial starting point" from which one grounds and founds philosophy and philosophical enquiry.⁸

Stein here is, in many ways, very close to some aspects of the early Balthasar and Rahner and quite far away from Przywara's analogical subversion of the *Cogito*. Balthasar says: "Insofar as consciousness understands itself as being, it has in principle understood being as such, in an intuition so original, with an evidence so unsurpassable, that nothing can be more certain than this understanding. Being and consciousness coincide so immediately that any distinction between them would be totally futile. In this insight, being is understood, not as a predicate of a subject that escapes further specification and transcends knowledge, but as the subject itself, indeed, as the subject of subject."⁹ Surprisingly, in this latent Idealism of the early Balthasar, which is manifested from time to time in his work, he stands very close to Rahner (his intellectual nemesis).¹⁰ This is easily

---

6. Ian Leask interestingly reads Stein's immediate starting point as being similar to the counter-intentional move of Michel Henry's "auto-affection" and the seeing of what cannot be seen by the eyes of flesh, namely, flesh itself. Although Leask's reading is instructive and interesting, it is far too forced. Stein here is not moving in a counter-intentional direction, as does post-Heideggerian French phenomenology. This is because Stein is here entirely faithful to the modern, and specifically Husserlian use of method. The reduction is used to arrive at the immediacy of the I as a secure starting point. Does Stein, however, arrive at a mere replication of the *Cogito*? No, she does not, as will soon be seen. But she does still arrive, through the reduction, to an I that is indubitable and a firm foundation from which philosophy builds, despite the fact that her rendition of the *Cogito* is more felt, personal, and ontological. However, despite the more ontological and personal character of the Steinian I, it is still an heir of the Cartesian and Husserlian method which seeks foundation and certainty. Therefore, one is still dealing with a reduced-conscious-knowledge, which has not yet abandoned reflexivity and ground in a counter-intentional move. See Ian Leask, *Being Reconfigured* (Newcastle, UK: Cambridge Scholars Publishing, 2011), 82–86.

7. Stein, *Finite and Eternal Being*, 36.

8. Stein, *Finite and Eternal Being*, 36.

9. Hans Urs von Balthasar, *Theo-Logic*, vol. 1: *Truth of the World*, trans. Adrian J. Walker (San Francisco: Ignatius Press, 2000), 166.

10. A few serious qualifications need to be made here concerning my critique of Balthasar. It must be noted that the early Balthasar was much more influenced by Przy-

seen when one turns to *Spirit in the World*: "Knowing is the being-present-to-self of being, and this being-present-to-self is the being of the existent," or "Knowing is the subjectivity of being itself. Being itself is the original, *unifying* unity of being and knowing in the unification of being known." In Balthasar's phenomenology of truth, Rahner's "metaphysics of knowledge" or transcendental Thomism, and Stein's phenomenological-ontology, one finds a deep and understandable reaction to the narrow-minded and rationalistic manual neo-Scholasticism/Thomism that emphasized a naïve and totally uncritical objectification of being. All three thinkers seek to elaborate an intimate, immediate, and deeply intuitive grasp or *Vorgriff* of being that shows being to be subjectivity and presence-to-self. In so doing, they all advance a needed ontological interpretation of the I, the *Cogito*, or subject, which loosens the epistemological hold of modern philosophy. This, in turn, allows for a personalization and spiritualization of truth and being over against formalism and positivism, which infected so much of neo-Scholasticism. Despite all of this, the question needs to be forcefully asked: Is this the only way to overcome the naïveté of narrow-minded Scholasticism, and has not too much been capitulated to the privileging and fetishizing of the subject characteristic of modern thought, which first came to full expression in Descartes's founding *Cogito*, reaching its apex in Hegel's spiritualization of being where the object becomes subject? Or

---

wara than the later Balthasar, who was more influenced by the Heideggerian Thomism of Gustav Siewerth and Ferdinand Ulrich. This can be seen in the text of *Truth of the World* (1947), where, for example, Balthasar follows Przywara in this understanding of analogical polarity expressed in the real distinction between essence and existence. Moreover, he also interprets essence in the same manner as Przywara, as being open-ended and eschatological, while also seeing the *analogia entis* to be the central means of guarding the God/world distinction. All of this equates to a very profound meditation on the positive truth of the mystery of being, which points to a more postmodern thinking of difference, mystery, and otherness. Thus, on many points, Balthasar remains very far away from both Rahner's and Stein's anthropological foundationalism and reduction of being to the subject. However, one of the weaknesses of Balthasar's work (despite its many inspiring strengths and brilliance) is his eclecticism, which, in this case, involves an appropriation of idealist themes that are incompatible with the Przywara-inspired portions of the text. Przywara, then, is by far the more consistent and rigorous metaphysical thinker of the two. That said, despite Balthasar's inconsistencies at times, Przywara and Balthasar remain, in my view, the two strongest opponents of the foundational and anthropological undertakings of much of twentieth-century Catholic thought. This undertaking has revealed itself as a failed Catholic *aggiornamento* that has become too complicit with the anthropocentric rationalism and secularity of modernity and thus has failed to move in the direction of the robust postmodern pleromatic Christian position for which I am advocating.

to phrase this otherwise, in Derridean terms, are we not running the risk here of a metaphysics of presence that lays its stress on being understood as identity intuitively and immediately grasped within the subject, thus reminiscent of Parmenidean being and its equation with thought or Hegelian dialectics, which ultimately stresses identity and self-presence, making mediation a mere moment towards speculative self-identity? Rather, what is needed, it is my contention, is an analogical countermovement and subversion of the *Cogito* that frees a space to once again think being's difference, otherness, exteriority, mediation, and mystery.

With that said: After Stein founds her philosophical project upon the immediate intuitive insight of the being of the I, she continues by drawing three conclusions: "If, in turning upon itself, the intellect contemplates the simple fact of its own being, it reads in this fact a threefold question: (1) What is that being of which I am conscious? (2) What is that self which is conscious of itself? (3) What is that intellectual movement in which I am and in which I am conscious of both myself and the movement?"[11] All three questions thus further reveal the immanent sphere of Stein's phenomenological-ontology, and its subjective mode of questioning, which has by no means fully abdicated the reflexive nature of modern philosophizing.[12]

Calling Foundation into Question

I concentrate my critique on three areas that have been broached above. First, Stein's privileging of the Cartesian (and Husserlian) method, which, in turn, reveals a desire for indubitability, immediacy, ground, clarity, certainty, and evidence. Second, Stein's modern reading of Augustine in which she mistakenly sees Descartes and Husserl as belonging to the same spiritual family. Third, how the preceding two critiques converge in Stein's project of a phenomenological-ontology grounded in the clarified certainty of the *Cogito*, thereby running the risk of being a philosophy tainted by self-presence.

First, in the above exposition of Stein's view of the *Cogito* it is clear that Stein shares something of modern philosophy's *conatus* to ground philosophy on a firm and solid foundation that is itself transparent and

---

11. Stein, *Finite and Eternal Being*, 37.
12. One can also note Stein's similarity with Transcendental Thomism and its emphasis and investigation of the dynamism of the intellectual act.

self-evident. This is a result of the mind's search for truth and an indubitable starting point. According to Stein, philosophers who have sought and desired this foundation have always arrived at the inescapable fact of the being of the I (e.g., Augustine, Descartes, and Husserl). However, here, an *aporia* was arrived at that brought me to the question of what comes first: the epistemological/methodological enquiry or the ontological fact of the I as a firm and indubitable foundation? Which founds which: the method or the I? It would seem that the method itself founds the I, which, in turn, retrospectively and belatedly founds and grounds the validity of the method. There is thus something at work here analogous to the mutually engendering "reciprocal causality" between faith and reason, as brilliantly discussed by Rousselot in *The Eyes of Faith*. Yet, here what is at work is far more pernicious insofar as it is the modern *faith and belief in method*, a faith that secures and grounds the ontologically evident fact of the being of the I. A question must be asked that cannot be fully developed here: Does not modern method seek to take the place of faith in Christian revelation in a parodic fashion?

Is not a kind of faith still at work in the founding gesture of modern philosophy? This time, however, the faith lies not in God but in the power of man to posit a subjective method that itself grounds all truth—a method that is, paradoxically and retrospectively, secured by the methodologically reduced *Cogito* understood as a firm ground.[13] Furthermore, it is only be-

13. This is one of the many strange characteristics of the *Cogito*, namely, that subjective method would become the founding generator of the myth of a universally valid reason. As Descartes says, "I have never contemplated anything higher than the reformation of my own opinions, and basing them on a foundation *wholly my own* [italics mine]." René Descartes, *A Discourse on Method*, trans. John Veitch (London: Everyman's Library, 1994), 12. Yet the entirety of Descartes's project is itself based in belief in certainty, for it is impossible for philosophy to escape some kind of belief. As de Lubac states, "The philosopher always starts from a theoretical given. Consciously or not, he always implements the contributions of two realms, scientific and religious. He always depends, not only on experience, but—in the largest sense of the word—*on belief*. 'The philosopher's reflection,' wrote Sylvain Lévi, 'Always raises itself with the aid of materials furnished by general beliefs, by the convention of the day, by the tradition, whether or not it invokes these things, whether or not it claims to liberate itself from them.'" Moreover, de Lubac will go on to say that this is why "Descartes's wet-nurse is more responsible than he himself believed for all that he drew from his *cogito*." Henri de Lubac, "On Christian Philosophy," *Communio* 19 (1992): 484–85. Thus there is simply nothing like the myth of an unaided reason that Descartes's subjective method founded. Rather it was first Descartes's *belief and faith* in certitude that was floating around in the air or *zeitgeist* of the epoch of the dawning of modernity—or apparently contained in the milk—which first compelled him to seek a sure method, which, in turn, discovered the

cause modern man demanded certainty, security, indubitability, and a firm foundation that the *Cogito* was ever posited or discovered. It was only the voluntaristic aloofness of the God of nominalism and late-Scholasticism and the vacancy and emptiness this left that enabled something like the *Cogito* to emerge.[14] Thus, the *Cogito* is thought within the infinite spaces (Pascal) where God himself is no longer more intimate to man than man is to his own self (as God is in analogical distance, which secures the space of distance needed for love and the intimacy of presence). Perhaps even God is a demonic deceiver and life itself a dream, a nightmare, an irreality.[15] Or, if God is not a demonic deceiver, then he becomes a mere idolatrous securer of the modern method and the *Cogito*. Metaphysics thus becomes predetermined and prefigured by the methodological quest for certainty, evidence, and ground. And all of this is arrived at through the universal method of doubt, which, in turn, arrives at the reduced certainty of the *Cogito* which retroactively grounds the method that has first enabled the discovery of the *Cogito*.

Subjective method predetermines metaphysics in modern philosophy. This is why Stein states that when Descartes attempted to "reconstruct philosophy as a trustworthy science on the foundation of indubitable certitude, he started out *methodologically* [italics mine] with his familiar effort of a universal doubt." This is also why Husserl starts out with the method of

---

Cogito. Likewise think of Luther's inability to live within a faith that was not totally certain of salvation. Was it then this inability or loss of trust in God and revelation that demanded man to turn to himself as the giver of certainty?

14. For a superb genealogy of the fateful turn in late-Scholasticism away from an analogical vision of being towards the neutrality of a univocal vision of being that lays the groundwork of modernity, see "The Parting of the Ways," in Hans Urs von Balthasar, *The Glory of the Lord: A Theological Aesthetics*, vol. 5: *The Realm of Metaphysics in the Modern Age*, trans. Erasmo Leiva-Merikakis (San Francisco: Ignatius Press, 1991), 9–47. Clearly here Radical Orthodoxy is very indebted to Balthasar's reading of the hermeneutic key of late-Scholasticism being its rejection of analogy in favor of the univocity of being which plays into the utter breakup of spirituality, metaphysics, and *theo*logy: a breakup that gave birth to the arid intellectual atmosphere of late-Scholasticism, and the privatized, anti-intellectual, and sentimental nature of the *Devotio Moderna* exemplified, for example, in the horrific work *The Imitation of Christ*.

15. As Pascal says, "When I see the blind and wretched state of man, when I survey the whole universe in its dumbness and man left to himself with no light, as though lost in this corner of the universe, without knowing who put him there, what he has come to do, what will become of him when he dies, incapable of knowing anything, I am moved to terror, like a man transported in his sleep to some terrifying desert island, who wakes up quite lost and with no means of escape." Blaise Pascal, *Pensées*, trans. A. J. Krailsheimer (London: Penguin, 1995), 59.

phenomenological reduction and the suspension of judgment concerning the natural world.[16] Stein remains a believer and heir of modern philosophy's desire to be a firm foundational science, which implies an embracing of modern philosophy's prioritizing of method as the starting point of philosophy, metaphysics, or ontology. Thus, as in her interpretation of Christian philosophy, she accepts the principles of modern philosophy, namely: method, foundation, immediacy, indubitability, certainty, clarity, distinctness, and evidence.

Second, it was seen that Stein equated Augustine, Descartes, and Husserl as philosophers of the same pedigree, the same bent of mind, the same spiritual family. These three thinkers represent the search for indubitability and firm foundation that resulted in the discovery of the I and the am implicit therein. However, as with Stein's conflation of Aquinas (via Maritain) with Husserl, there is here another conflation, this time, however, of a more worrisome nature. It consists in conflating the great pleromatic Christian visionary, Augustine, with the rationalistic modernity of Descartes and Husserl. I examine this conflation by briefly drawing from Gilson's superb essay, "The Future of Augustinian Metaphysics," in the fine collection of essays titled *Saint Augustine: His Age, Life, and Thought*.[17]

In this essay Gilson thoroughly dismantles any possible conflation of the Augustinian "method" with Cartesian method, or Augustine with Descartes. Gilson rightly notes that Augustine was a Christian philosopher and elaborated a "Christian philosophy," while Descartes was a Christian *and* a philosopher *but not a Christian philosopher*.[18] This difference cannot be underscored enough as it is the determining point of departure for Augustine who is diametrically opposed to Descartes. For Augustine's *methodos* (in the Greek sense of way or journey) is one of faith (*credere—intelligere—videre*) and thus a method that is lived and "concrete" and in-

---

16. Stein, *Finite and Eternal Being*, 36.

17. Przywara also contributed to this wonderful volume an essay titled "Saint Augustine and the Modern World."

18. Étienne Gilson, "The Future of Augustinian Metaphysics," in *Saint Augustine: His Age, Life, and Thought*, trans. Edward Bullough, 290. For another strong account of why Augustine cannot be understood as a Cartesian, see Michael Hanby, *Augustine and Modernity* (London: Routledge, 2003). For a view that spans the entire breadth of Augustine's corpus and that reads the earlier Augustine as having idealist leanings (due to his reaction to Manicheism), but later develops a strong mediatory philosophy rooted in the "*totus Christus*"; see Erich Przywara, "The Religious Gnoseology of Saint Augustine," in *Analogia Entis: Metaphysics: Original Structure and Universal Rhythm*, trans. John R. Betz and David Bentley Hart (Grand Rapids: Eerdmans, 2014), 505–19.

volves the entire man: body, soul, feelings, emotions, intellect, will, *and grace*.[19] If there is a method of doubt in Augustine it is one that arises out of the *cor inquietum* and the darkness of life cut off from the grace of the living God. While conversely, Descartes's "method of doubt" is ruled by the vacuity of a formalistic abstraction, namely, "Mathematical Method."[20]

In the end, "the radical preventative of doubt is much less the *cogito* than the act of faith. Whoever believes in God and His word holds a truth infinitely richer and more fruitful than the *cogito*: 'I believe, therefore I know' is better as a first principle than 'I think, therefore I am.'"[21] Descartes begins with a love and *faith* in mathematical method, which makes metaphysics subservient to method, thus enacting a reverse circumincession of faith and reason, as found in Christianity. By doing this, Descartes inaugurates a philosophy entirely cut off from faith and revelation (although already paved by late-Scholasticism). This, in turn, reduces being to the pure objectivity of clear and distinct ideas where God is proved via the *Cogito*. God is immanently tied to the *Cogito* by viewing God, in an instrumental manner, as the guarantor of the new religion of certainty and foundation.[22] Thus the founding of the order of autonomy or the *saeculum* takes place where philosophy is torn away from faith, *theo*logy, and revelation, while, conversely, Augustine begins with faith in God, thus exhibiting a profoundly beautiful circumincession of reason illuminated by faith (and thus not contrary). This, in turn, founds philosophy in trust and faith in the ungroundable God. Security and certainty lie in trust and faith and, therefore, there is no ground of the *Cogito* (secured first by method). Rather, there is the *cor inquietum* and its restless moving state ever-compelled forward by a desire for the living infinity of God (the *homo abyssus* and the *Deus abyssus*). Nor is there a rationalistic "proof" for God's existence that grants certitude because, "When we ask Augustine to prove to us the

---

19. Gilson, "Augustinian Metaphysics," 302. Augustine was the first to coin the term/notion of Christian philosophy.

20. Gilson, "Augustinian Metaphysics," 294. For two works that deal with the drastic and revolutionary effects of extension, spatialization, and the institution of writing over lived speech and the oral tradition, see Catherine Pickstock, *After Writing: On the Liturgical Consummation of Philosophy* (Oxford: Blackwell, 1998), 57–100; and Michel de Certeau, *The Mystic Fable: The Sixteenth and Seventeenth Centuries*, trans. Michael B. Smith (Chicago: University of Chicago Press, 1992).

21. Gilson, "Augustinian Metaphysics," 303.

22. As Pascal is claimed to have stated, "I cannot forgive Descartes: in his whole philosophy he would like to do without God; but he cannot help allowing him a flick of the fingers to set the world in motion; after which he had no more use for God." Pascal, *Pensées*, 330.

existence of God, he asks us in turn first to believe in it; can we make the same request to our contemporaries without losing our qualifications to be philosophers?"[23]

Never, then, shall the two meet or be synthesized. One is a/the father of modernity who ushered in modern ontologism (to come to full fruition in his disciple Malebranche), Idealism, and the *saeculum*. The other is the quintessential pleromatic Christian philosopher who acts as a living witness to the vibrant vitality and daring of the great pleromatic Christian tradition, thus inspiring those of us who seek a "pleromatic analogical hermeneutic of a nonidentical repetition" of the past, that is, of that which is ever ancient and ever new (as in the Beauty that Augustine ceaselessly sought). Stein's conflation shows a tremendous insensitivity to the unbridgeable difference between Descartes and Augustine (as did her conflation of Aquinas [via Maritain] with Husserl). Once again, Stein's Christian philosophy risks a modernization of Christian thought on principles that she does not seem to see are entirely antithetical to Christian thought, because they themselves arose out of a degeneration of Christian thought which then took the form of a willful and autonomous rejection of the place that grace and revelation play in the philosophical act. The vacuous monstrosity of the *Cogito* (it is monstrous because it is extra-linguistic, anti-incarnational, anti-hermeneutical, anti-historical, and anti-*theo*logical in its assertion of autonomy) could not be thought if Descartes did not desire to build all things anew by sweeping away the tradition, grace, and the Wisdom of the *theo*logical from the space of philosophy.[24] Stein is not sensitive enough to the post-Christian apocalyptic nature of philosophical modernity and does not see fully the dangers of founding a Christian philosophy on the spirit of Descartes (or Husserl). Stein's modernity is again evident and opposed to Przywara's profound, one could say, postmodern Augustinianism as revealed in the extraordinary vision of his countermodern sapiential and analogical elaboration of the relation between *philo*sophy and *theo*logy.

Third, how then do my above two critiques converge in Stein's project of a phenomenological-ontology centered in a version of the *Cogito*? First, let me clearly state that Stein's understanding of the I or the *ego* is not fully compatible with the *Cogito* of Descartes. Stein is pushing the *Cogito* in the direction of ontology and the am implicit in the I. Her I or *ego* is phe-

---

23. Gilson, "Augustinian Metaphysics," 290.
24. For a brilliant analysis of the formal vacuity of the *Cogito* see Pickstock, *After Writing*, 57–100.

nomenologically interpreted as a deeply felt and primordially experienced knowledge. This I touches on something of a pristine matinal immediate knowledge prior to "reflective" thinking.[25] Stein's I is not then as formalistic as the I of Descartes nor is it a complete reflexive positing of the I as in Idealism. But because of the phenomenological *method* it is still reflexive and remains a *conscious knowledge* despite the added and much-needed element of feeling. It is, then, a more ontological I that adds an experience (feeling) of consciousness to reflexivity, which thus pushes this I more in the direction of a personalization of being and truth.

Clearly it is a step forward from Descartes, Idealism, and Husserl insofar as it is rediscovering the ontological implications of the I and knowledge. What then are the limitations to Stein's approach? It is precisely that Stein has not gone far enough, as her thought is too deeply determined and constricted by the principles of modernity. To begin with, Stein's discovery of a more ontological and personal I is still rooted in the reduction and thus haunted by the predetermination of being by modern mathematical method, or the method of doubt that predestines being to be sought as foundation, ground, indubitability, security, clarity, and evidence—all of which is given in the immediacy of intuitive knowledge. Stein still follows the aforesaid method and principles of modernity, which desires philosophy to be a firm science of foundation, which ultimately ends in a pursuit and teleology of full and total disclosure based on an indubitable starting point, as was seen in her conception of Christian philosophy. Stein's thought may play between a weak and strong modernity, but ultimately her thought is too constricted by ground, foundation, certitude, and immediacy and thus she risks totality, even if this is not her intent.

Being's Redundancy

The culmination of Stein's vision of being comes to fulfillment in her understanding of "transcendental truth."[26] In this discussion it will be seen how Stein arrives at a thoroughly phenomenological definition of being as evidence, givenness, manifestation, and/or revelation. Which is to say, a tautologous definition of being's redundancy is arrived at: the meaning of being

---

25. Stein, *Finite and Eternal Being*, 36.
26. For Stein's discussion of transcendental truth see Stein, *Finite and Eternal Being*, 294–98.

understood as the being of meaning. By characterizing being as manifestation, Stein, in a manner not unlike Heidegger and Hegel, privileges man or "*Geist*" as the preeminent *locus* of being's manifestation of truth. This privileging of man as the preeminent site of being's showing (phenomenologically conceived) immanently ties being to "*Geist*," where being is essentialized (intellectually and conceptually captured) and its excessive exteriority is forgotten in favor of the *circulus* of immanent phenomenological seeing which spiritualizes the truth of being. Such an anthropocentric view of being can only be overcome by an analogical metaphysics of mediation and exteriority that relativizes man by seeing difference at the heart of being, as will be seen.

Stein advances beyond a mere formal or logical definition of truth by arriving at the ontological depths of truth's disclosure. In so doing, her approach begs comparison with Heidegger's famous essay "On the Essence of Truth" insofar as both are seeking the ontological ramifications of phenomenology and truth's disclosive element.[27] Stein is thus carrying further her project of a phenomenological-ontology. Following the logic of the phenomenological reduction that discovered the ontological disclosure of the am in the I, Stein now seeks to lay bare the logic of manifestation present in all beings or existents. This reveals a preestablished harmony between beings and spirit (note the Leibnizian and Idealist connotations). In other words, Stein is moving towards a synchrony between being and spirit that seeks to grasp the unitariness (*ens commune*) of being in a philosophy of the revelation of meaning. Which is another way of saying, a philosophy of meaning in its unitary totality.[28]

Stein never wavered in the fact that subjectivity is the privileged way to investigate being, nor did she ever abandon the methodological/epistemological anteriority of the subject, as Beauvais rightly sees.[29] Nor does it make a difference that Stein acknowledges the ontological anteriority of being, or that she is sometimes called a "realist phenomenologist" who was suspect of Husserl's idealist turn. Why? Stein never abdicates phenomenology's method, the formal nature of which consists in identity, as Przywara clearly saw so early on.[30] This is why the entire history of phe-

---

27. See Martin Heidegger, "On the Essence of Truth," in *Basic Writings: From Being and Time (1927) to The Task of Thinking (1964)*, ed. David Farrell Krell, trans. John Sallis (San Francisco: HarperCollins, 1977), 115–38.

28. This will become fully clear in the following chapter.

29. Beauvais, "Edith Stein," 3.

30. See Erich Przywara, "Edith Stein and Simone Weil: Two Fundamental Philosophical Themes," in *Analogia Entis*, 603.

nomenology is one fierce struggle to think alterity and difference. Whether it is in Stein's early phenomenology of empathy, Heidegger's historization of phenomenality and essence which privileges the adventing or futurity of being (absence/withdrawal), Levinas's counter-intentional rendering by the face, or the superlative giving of givenness in Marion, all of which is one tiresome and losing battle against phenomenology's formal principle of identity expressed in its method of a direct and *immediate* noetic encounter with essence. Nor can this battle be won unless one drops the epistemological/methodical prioritizing of the reduction-to-consciousness. Thus whether one privileges a noetic phenomenology (as in Hegel) or a noematic phenomenology (as in Husserl), the formal methodological principle remains the same, namely, identity.

This is important to note here because the inner logic and tension of phenomenology are being hit upon from its inception to the present day—that is, phenomenology's struggle with identity and its failed attempt to think alterity, which has resulted in a totalitarian proclamation of the death of philosophy and the end of metaphysics. Thus phenomenology's preoccupation with the capturing of being in essence and the belief that philosophy is, at its heart, phenomenology must be eschewed. This must be done, in favor of a reinvigoration of an analogical metaphysics of mediation and alterity that must be pursued if philosophy is going to be salvaged from totality. Heidegger tried to do this with his historical thinking of essence. In the note appended to "On the Essence of Truth," he states that "the question of the essence of truth finds its answer in the proposition *the essence of truth is the truth of essence*."[31] This statement finds fuller formulation in the first volume of *Nietzsche*, where he concisely but unsatisfactorily says:

> For, supposing that the essence of truth did change, that which changes could always still be "one" which holds the "many," the transformation not disturbing the relationship. But what is preserved in the metamorphosis is that which is unchangeable in the essence, which essentially unfolds in its very transformation. The essentiality of essence, its inexhaustibility, is thereby affirmed, and also its genuine selfhood and selfsameness.[32]

31. Heidegger, "Essence of Truth," 137.
32. Heidegger, *Nietzsche*, vol. 1: *The Will to Power as Art*, ed. and trans. David Farrell Krell (San Francisco: HarperSanFrancisco, 1984), 147–48.

Here is an immanentist attempt to think the logic of the *analogia entis* on a historical plane of immanence that thinks being as the history of being's phenomenality or essence unfolding as a play between the One and the many. Being is thus trying to be thought as a unity-in-difference, movement-in-silence/rest, unity-in-movement, where being's hidden essence withholds itself in an ever-deferred inexhaustible promise. Heidegger tells us that this promise is not negativity, but rather being's withheld and sacred promise to man, which in its deferred eschatological futurity parodies the ever-receding mystery of God's Infinite life (as expressed in negative *theo*logy) and the economic promise of God, in Christ, of the coming of the Kingdom (as expressed in Christian eschatology). Thus genuine difference is never reached because being's essence is its historical and temporalized withdrawal. Being is thus trapped in a unilateral line of the essence or essencing of being's different repetitions. This is done through the dialectic of being expressed in unconcealment/concealment, difference/self-sameness. In other words, being is univocal, not analogical, and thus Heidegger has not escaped an essentialization of being and identity characteristic of phenomenological identity, now exemplified on the historical plane of immanence. Being still stands in need of man in its (the *es gibt*) impersonal and playful game of univocal hiding.

Levinas takes a step beyond Heidegger (only in the end to take two steps back) when he realizes that metaphysics must precede ontology or, in other words, phenomenology.[33] But Levinas uncritically takes up Heidegger's metanarrative of the history of metaphysics, being one of phenomenological totality or egology where transcendence and exteriority are never reached. Levinas's thinking is thus the dialectical inversion of Heidegger, where he banishes being from his discourse (as Heidegger did in his last public lecture) because he views being, as Heidegger does, as the temporalization of essence. Thus Levinas never has recourse to the richer traditions of Western thought, because Levinas accepts Descartes's secularization of philosophy, as well as the notion that being is ruled by phenomenological identity. And when God does come to mind in Levinas's thought, it is only within and through man. So if in Heidegger's thought being stands in need of man, in Levinas's thought God stands in need of man. All analogical relation of distance is eschewed in favor of identity.

---

33. See Emmanuel Levinas, *Totality and Infinity: An Essay on Exteriority*, trans. Alphonso Lingis (Pittsburgh: Duquesne University Press, 1969), 42–48.

Foundation and Nonfoundation

As for Marion, he really does not advance any further than Heidegger or Levinas: for where Heidegger once said being, and Levinas says the Other, Marion now says givenness. Like Levinas, Marion takes up Heidegger's view of the history of being as one of egological and phenomenological totality, which has never thought the giving of givenness (although he qualifies this somewhat in his later work). Marion does this by seeing the metaphysical distinction between essence and existence expressing the quintessential metaphysical dichotomy that is overcome in Husserl's thought on givenness. But this is because Marion is drawing from Descartes's understanding of the distinction between essence and existence, which is ultimately rooted in Suarez's understanding or denial of the real distinction (his *distinctio sola rationis*), which is univocal.

Marion's understanding of the real distinction may be adequate to the denial of the real distinction in post-Scotistic thought, but it is surely not adequate to Przywara's and Balthasar's reinterpretation of the real distinction, which is, in my view, in keeping with the spirit of Aquinas. And Marion has no excuse for this shallow reading of essence/existence, as he is a reader of both Przywara and especially Balthasar. Nor does Marion overcome phenomenological identity by stating that the subject receives itself from the giving of givenness because there still has to be some sort of reduction performed by a subject, if the givenness is to be received with the right will, as Marion says it must. In other words, in all of Marion's attempts to construct a completely receptive subject, there is still *a prior subject*, which, in the performance of the reduction, must allow givenness to show and give itself. Marion's thought remains one of identity because he has not released himself fully from the phenomenological method. Givenness still stands in need of Marion's spectral, but ultimately Cartesian, subject.

Thus, as of yet, no *pure* phenomenologist has overcome the formal principle of the phenomenological method, namely, identity (as Przywara diagnosed so early on). For if they did they would no longer be phenomenologists, but metaphysicians of analogical exteriority and creation who take what is best from phenomenology, but ground it in the analogical and rhythmic distinction between essence/existence, thereby viewing thought and language themselves as analogical communicational spaces of transcendence.

With that said: My interest here is to lay bare the guiding logic of phenomenology present in Stein's discussion of transcendental truth, which despite its ontological implications remains a discourse on being's redundant sameness or identity. What exactly does Stein mean by transcendental truth? The answer given to this question is Stein's first formulation—in *Finite and Eternal Being*—of a preliminary definition of being's meaning in her attempt to ascend to being's meaning. Stein *dis*covers this definition through a phenomenological reinterpretation of the metaphysical understanding of transcendental truth, now understood on a disclosive model of truth. Upon this view, what is most proper and transcendental to all individual beings or existents is their "Being-ordained to the spirit" (*Zuordnung*), which belongs to all genera of existents and is thus the most overarching transcendental aspect of existents.[34] Yet in discovering the disclosive nature of existents, one is no longer merely speaking of beings but, indeed, of being itself; in a very special sense, however, this being-ordained pertains to being. "'*To be* manifest' (or revealed), '*To be* ordained'—these verbal forms imply being, and not a special mode of being, but being as such. In short, *being means* (though perhaps without thereby exhausting its full meaning) a *being manifest for or a being revealed to the spirit* [*Sein ist Offenbarsein für den Geist*]."[35] In this definition of being as "a being manifest for or a being revealed to the spirit" is implied a very special privileging of a certain genus of being, namely, *Geist*, as "spirit is a genus in a preeminent sense because it is of the nature of spirit to be open to all existents, to be filled with that which is, and to have its life (i.e., its actual being) in the most intimate contact with that which is."[36] This is Stein's syncretism of a preestablished harmony between being-as-meaning and spirit.

Being is defined as for man, and man is defined as for being. Each belongs together in a phenomenological correlation. But what does this mean for being's definition, and correlatively, what does this mean for man's definition? Being here is entirely equated with manifestation, revelation, meaning, evidence, and essence. Being at its core is essence and this is Stein's pure essentialism. If existents/beings in their factual existence (which for Stein are still in existence without thought) have a meaning, it is in and through their disclosive potential through which man, in turn, discovers being in its transcendental appearing. Being is the appearing of essence, which is for man. And man is open to being/essence in its disclosive breadth, offering a site for meaning's appearance. It is in the synchrony of being and *Geist* that being/meaning/essence appears, because being is tautologously defined as meaning, appearing, evidence, and essence. Being

34. Stein, *Finite and Eternal Being*, 297.
35. Stein, *Finite and Eternal Being*, 298.
36. Stein, *Finite and Eternal Being*, 298.

is phenomenologically defined. The meaning of being is the being of meaning. Being is identical with meaning and meaning is identical with being in the syncretistic and immediate intuitive encounter of the mind with the essence of being. Being is essence. Existence is thus left out of the equation, as if existence, in and of itself, is a brute factical thereness that cannot be taken into the realm of Cartesian *clarté*, intelligibility, and meaning. Being is thus defined and captured in essence, and the mysterious analogical/nonidentical play of essence and existence is forgotten, where difference and the nonconceptualizable lie at the heart of creaturely being's abiding *mysterium* in its ever-transcending play of a knowing in unknowing. Being and thought thus stand together in a kind of Parmenidean identity of the well-rounded sphere of meaning.

What then does this mean for a definition of man? Stein here is moving to a more ontological definition of man—as again does Heidegger—where man is seen as *Geist* and an open locus of the appearing of being-as-meaning. However, her discourse on man's openness to being is still founded upon the anteriority of phenomenological method, which, as was seen, predetermines being as foundation, security, and indubitable clarity. Method thus still founds man's openness to being, marking being at the outset as the light of the clarity of essence and intelligibility. Man's secure being, discovered by method and the foundationalism of the being of the I, remains the prerequisite whereby being's transcendental appearing must be thought. For the first and primary appearing of being takes place within the clarified subjective encounter of presence-to-self, which never escaped the reflexive nature of modern philosophizing in its privileging of method. Once again, Stein's attempt to get to the ontological, and a definition of man as openness to being, is truncated by her phenomenological method because her ontology is an immanent investigation of being, founded in the security of subjectivity-as-foundation. Hence, following the formal method of phenomenology, Stein's thinking (despite its profound effort) is still haunted by the specters of identity prevalent in the anthropocentric and epistemological direction of modern thought.

This again is most evident in Stein's search for an ontological I that seeks to be "an indubitable certain point of departure" that grounds philosophy on a firm foundation. This is accomplished through an equation of being with the I; an I given in intuitive immediacy reached via the method of phenomenological reduction. Stein, then, is too much a modern philosopher of immediacy, which logically demands an equation of being with the I or the being of the I. Upon this premise or principle of immediacy one is necessarily pushed in the direction of a univocalization of being where being is understood as the primordial givenness of the being of the I to the self. Being is thus thought by way of identification and identity (I = being, being = I). Being becomes subjectivity and is anthropologically reduced by the phenomenological method of immanent experiential and intuitive seeing. This is still the mark of the reflexive transparency of the self, characteristic of modernity and phenomenology's formal principle of identity expressed in its method of an *immediate* noetic encounter with essence. Once the logic of immediacy is taken up, this of necessity disallows a thinking of difference at the heart of being. When this is done, the first being that must always be thought is the *being of the I* given absolutely in the immediate coincidence of phenomenological seeing. And only from this point of departure can the manifest otherness of being be thought. But here being's otherness can only be being's redundancy: the meaning of being is the being of meaning because being is reduced to the I through its essentialization.

Thought remains trapped in the circularity of the seeing of givenness/essence, which can only be arrived at through a prior and firm given, namely, the I methodologically and phenomenologically reduced (the dubious circumincession of method and the *Cogito* as seen above). Upon this model the analogical doubling (nonredundancy), mediation, differencing, and mysterious play of the otherness of analogical being are forgotten in favor of a univocal philosophy of immediate self-presence and being's redundant disclosure (being/meaning, meaning/being, being = essence, essence = being). Self-presence thus becomes the ground and mode of departure for any thinking of being's disclosure. Stein is thus unable to shake the univocal and foundational philosophy of immediacy bequeathed to her by Descartes and phenomenologically reinterpreted by her master Husserl. (It was merely logical that Husserl would write *Cartesian Meditations* ending with a monadological Idealism.) It must be concluded with Beauvais that "Stein is a *modern* philosopher; because she does not altogether give up a cogito-centered project" and in refusing to give up on this project, "Stein and Husserl belong to the same 'spiritual family.'"[37] And it further must be concluded with Przywara that "Edith Stein remains—even as an interpreter of Saint Thomas—the most authentic disciple, indeed the 'daughter,' of Husserl's 'phenomenological method.' Accordingly, she transfers all real existents to the level of the 'essential.'"[38]

37. Beauvais, "Edith Stein," 13.
38. Przywara, *Analogia Entis*, 598.

Stein, then, is not pushing modernity to its breaking-point by a creative pleromatic refashioning of the tradition, as is Przywara's postmodern thinking of analogical difference. Rather, Stein is, like Rahner, reading and basing Christianity and Christian thought on the anthropological foundationalism of modern philosophy, thus manifesting the spirit of the thinkers of the Catholic *aggiornamento* who seek to bring Catholic thought up-to-date. But by so doing, these thinkers merely tied Catholic thought to a firm and unshifting anthropocentric foundation (which logically denies the movement of history and tradition and thus cannot be up-to-date). Rather, a thinking and undertaking of a pleromatic hermeneutic of retrieval and *ressourcement* is needed that would deeply question the principles of philosophical modernity and the *saeculum*, and thereby not become unwittingly complicit with the anthropocentric *apotheosis* of man in modern philosophy. Catholic thought must be challenged to think a postmodern Christian understanding of analogical difference.

An Abyssal Vision of Being

In turning to Przywara's core vision of being I proceed in three metaphysical steps. First, I revisit Przywara's starting point, in light of its contrast with Stein's foundational starting point. Second, I then treat the inner logic of analogical *being*, contra various logics of totality. Third, I conclude by showing how Przywara's abyssal thinking performs a definitive analogical deconstruction of the *Cogito*.

Epistemology Unmoored

Przywara grounds epistemology in the ungroundable suspended tension *between* essence and existence, thereby giving objective anteriority to creaturely being's being-in-becoming, while nevertheless giving methodological and epistemological primacy to a meta-noetic point of departure. This is necessarily so because the formal epistemological problematic of a "creaturely metaphysics" is the formal suspended tension *between* being and consciousness. That is, in every metaphysic is implied the question of the questioner who questions into being. Moreover, because being and consciousness *are* creaturely, they belong together. This co-belonging is expressed in a privileging of the act of consciousness which reaches out "towards being" in a mutual "to one another" (*Zueinander*),³⁹ that is to say, in the structure of "world."⁴⁰ Przywara thus deploys, on a metaphysically formal level, the characteristically phenomenological meta-noetic point of departure (note: this is done only on a metaphysically objective, exterior, and formal level and thus not in the subjective method of the reduction) of a mutual co-belonging of being/consciousness. However, it must be forcefully underscored, in this nod to phenomenological correlation (and Husserl in particular), that this epistemological method is itself a faithful mirroring—or *description*—of man's creaturely condition of becoming, that is, "the *in fieri*" of man.⁴¹ To state it more succinctly, the formal epistemological object of a "creaturely metaphysics," namely, the *Zueinander* or suspended tension (*Spannungs-Schwebe*) between being and consciousness is nothing more than an expression of the real metaphysical difference of essence in-and-beyond existence, now expressed on the level of method: "the object become method."⁴² Thought, from the outset, is *inserted* within the mysterious difference between essence and existence that constitutes man's dynamic analogical being-in-becoming. Przywara's thought thus deconstructs, from its inception, any firm ground on which epistemology and metaphysics can/could stand.

Przywara's engagement with phenomenology, and his taking up of the problematic of being/consciousness or correlation/world, is done for a twofold reason. First, to allow what is best in phenomenology to be seen, namely, the co-belonging of consciousness and being (which is simply a mark of created being). Second, at the same time, it is done to deconstruct and subvert phenomenology from within with metaphysical exteriority. This is to assert that neither Husserl (who absolutizes essence) nor Heidegger (who absolutizes existence by collapsing essence *into* existence) is truly faithful to the phenomenological problematic of correlation. This is so, because neither Husserl nor Heidegger, in the end, grounds phenomenology in the real (exterior) metaphysical difference between essence/existence. It can be said, then, that Przywara is more faithful to the phenomenological discovery of "world" than is Husserl, Heidegger, or Stein. This is accomplished by systemizing or exteriorizing "world" in a dynamic "systematics of impurity" that pulls phenomenology's penchant for identity from under

---

39. Przywara, *Analogia Entis*, 123.
40. Przywara, *Analogia Entis*, 123.
41. Przywara, *Analogia Entis*, 124.
42. Przywara, *Analogia Entis*, 124.

its feet. It is only in the mysterious interplay between essence and existence that holds the phenomenological "world" together by *holding them apart*, i.e., an epistemological method that is metaphysically determined or exteriorized by man's between, suspended, wayfaring, and sojourning condition. Man's being is a between being that is never absolutely *there* (Pindar's "Become what you are," or Saint John's "what we will be has yet to be revealed" [1 John 3:2]).[43] Man's *being* is, therefore, an abyssal and mysterious composite or analogical and dynamic rhythm bound by difference (unity-in-difference). Epistemology and "world" are exteriorized because they themselves are inserted within the between of man's being which, as between, is itself an exterior ecstatically deferred and abyssal *mysterium*.

Thus this formal epistemological and metaphysically objective approach is anything but a metaphysical objectification or representation. Rather it is a breaking open of creaturely being's abidingly dramatic and aesthetic *mysterium*. This is done by inserting thought into the very heart of creaturely being's dynamic *relation between* essence and existence (*Sosein in-über Dasein*). So what appears to be, at first sight, another metaphysical representation or speculation (the formal problematic of being/consciousness and the real distinction) is a systematic deconstruction ("systematics of impurity") of all systems of identity (including phenomenological identity). Identity, totality, and foundation are eschewed in favor of an Augustinian abyssal, exterior, and dynamic reinterpretation of the seminal Thomistic distinction between essence/existence. This is taken up and expressed, on an epistemological level, in the "new" phenomenological problematic of "world" now held apart metaphysically (exteriorized) by man's moving and between being. Thus, in one fell and brilliant swoop, Przywara de-absolutizes a pure meta-ontic starting point (an absolutization of being) and a pure meta-noetic starting point (an absolutization of thought), thus implicitly and explicitly addressing the formal starting points taken up in metaphysics as such: in premodern thought, modern thought, and contemporary phenomenology.

Przywara thus pulls away any and all firm foundation on which philosophy could hope to stand, in favor of a hovering, suspended, never-to-be-closed flowing vibrancy of analogical exteriority and mediation. This

---

43. Przywara quotes this phrase from Pindar in order to help make concrete his idiosyncratic formula *Sosein in-über Dasein*. Przywara, *Analogia Entis*, 124. Likewise, Betz aptly uses this biblical quote from John to make Przywara's nonfoundational view of man more concrete. Betz, Introduction, 64.

style of thought is "a radical humbling" of thought in favor of a radically "creaturely metaphysics" grounded in the nonground of being's analogically mysterious *relation*. This is why Balthasar will say that Przywara "like no other broke to pieces all the putative absolute formulas outside and in the Church as though they were nothing but toys, razed every 'high tower set against God,' literally decimated all concepts."[44] Przywara thus constructs a radically nonfoundational analogical philosophy of creaturely being's mysterious nonidentical rhythm that dissolves all systems of identity and self-presence, thus marking his metaphysics with a real postmodern flair as an authentic metaphysics of difference and relation, analogically understood.

The point has now been arrived at where my previous claim that Przywara's systematic thinking is, in fact, humbler than Stein's "conscious self-restraint" in elaborating an "ontology" instead of a "philosophic system" (her critique of Przywara) can be substantiated.[45] The question of the point of departure for thinking can be said to be, in many ways, the question of thought. This question determines, in one way or another, the entirety of the direction of one's philosophy. Think of Balthasar's profoundly pertinent words at the beginning of the first volume of *The Glory of the Lord* (words reminiscent, in a critical way, of the beginning of the *Science of Logic*). "Beginning is a problem not only for the thinking person, the philosopher, a problem that remains with him and determines all the subsequent steps; the beginning is also a primal decision which includes all the later ones for the person whose life is based on response and decision."[46] Stein begins her philosophy ("primal decision") with Descartes and Husserl's methodological doubt through which she arrives at a reduced space of consciousness. Here the *being* of the I first makes its disclosive appearance in the *I think* and *I perceive*, thereby marking being as immediate self-presence of the I methodologically and intuitively arrived at. The being implicit in the I then becomes the firm foundation from which thinking grounds and bases itself. In other words, thinking grounds itself in the firm foundation of the subjectivity of self-presence, which is methodologically and reflexively secure. This ground remains in Stein's move towards the

---

44. Betz, Introduction, 7.
45. Stein, *Finite and Eternal Being*, xxix.
46. Hans Urs von Balthasar, *The Glory of the Lord*, vol. 1: *Seeing the Form*, trans. Erasmo Leiva-Merikakis et al. (San Francisco: Ignatius Press, 1982), 17.

synchrony of being and spirit in the logic of phenomenological manifestation where being is defined as the being of meaning. Stein's phenomenological discourse is thus ruled by the spirit of modernity where the inner logic of her thought leans towards and is haunted by words such as *foundation, clarity, security, immediacy, intuition, essence, univocity, self-presence*, and *identity*. Stein never abdicates the formal methodological principle of phenomenology, which is identity. Thus Stein never escapes the danger of foundation and identity, which is the inner logic of her point of departure. Her "conscious self-restraint" is, in the end, self-refuting because its subjective and methodological starting point always risks being haunted by totality. Therefore, Stein's admirable and creative attempt to get beyond Husserl is waylaid from the outset in her faithfulness to Husserlian and modern method.

On the other hand, if, at first sight, Przywara's method seems far too formal/objective and metaphysical (in the derogative sense of the term) and thus another metaphysical exercise of system-building and metaphysical representation, then, in reality, this could not be further from the truth. For Przywara advances a "systematics of impurity" ("primal decision") which, from the very first movement, disallows and militates against every form of identity and metaphysics of self-presence. Moreover, the reason that Przywara takes up a formal/objective and epistemological problematic, in his "creaturely metaphysics," is to save the phenomenological discovery of "world" from identity by exteriorizing it in the abyssal metaphysical difference between essence/existence. And because epistemology is rooted in man's analogical being-in-becoming (and thus man's lack of foundation, self-possession, and self-presence) it is metaphysically exteriorized in the *mysterium* of nonidentical analogical relation and betweenness. Epistemology is thus rooted in the *nonrepresentable* relational play between essence and existence.

The *circulus* of phenomenological seeing is broken up by a play of chiaroscuro between concept and mystery, knowing *in* unknowing. The excessive nature of phenomenality and its event-character is saved because whatever is given of essence-in-existence is also always above and beyond existence and thought and thus never fully disclosed. There is an aesthetic and dramatic reserve in the otherness of being's phenomenality that never does away with its eventful mystery. An analogical play of concept and mystery is advanced, which nonobjectifiably thinks and allows for being's metaphysical transcendence, exteriority, and mystery. Przywara's alleged "system," by Stein, is thus the breaking open of all closed systems in a rigorous logic and epistemology rooted in being's abidingly dramatic and aesthetic *mysterium*. Przywara's logic *of* being is thus, contra Stein, ruled by such postmodern words as *nonfoundation, chiaroscuro, mystery, insecurity, event, mediation, suspendedness, tension/middle/between, nonrepresentation, essence in-and-beyond existence, nonidentity*, and *analogy*. Przywara's thought is, therefore, ultimately humbler than Stein's because it breaks down foundation at every step, while Stein advances a logic that leans towards identity and foundation, even if this was not her intention. Stein's phenomenological logic of being *sees too much*, while Przywara's analogical logic of being sees everything *within* the moving, flowing event of dynamic mediation. It is an aesthetics of being's dramatic mystery, which always sees "in a glass, darkly" (1 Cor. 13:12).

Logics of Being

The very starting point of Przywara's thought, as abyssal, advances against identity and foundation. This advancement is rigorously reconfirmed through looking at his treatment of what he insightfully sees to be the three major expressions of the *logos* of being: logic, dialectic, and analogy.[47] It should be evident, at this point, that in Przywara's discussion of various logics of being there are, ultimately, only two real possibilities. The first possibility is to advance a divine logic of being that collapses the moving tension of creaturely being into a form of identity, thereby denying the creaturely nature of being's logic in favor of a Godlike standpoint and usurpation. While the second possibility consists in deploying a creaturely logic of being's concrete open and suspended condition, thus humbly accepting one's concrete creaturely condition of being-in-the-midst and eventful mediation. In Przywara's discussion of logic he is not interested in formal syllogistic logic (or if he is, it is only insofar as this is expressive of a metaphysical logic). Rather, Przywara is interested solely in metaphysical logics that pertain to the real reality of creaturely being vis-à-vis the divine. Metaphysical logic, thus, either accepts or denies the objective order of creaturely being's suspended between and abyssal condition.[48] "*Pure logic*" pretends to have an unmediated and thus an immediate access to truth,

---

47. For this discussion see Przywara, *Analogia Entis*, 192–97.
48. In this, Desmond's fourfold sense of being shares remarkable similarities with Przywara, to be discussed in Part 2.

which is a miming of a Godlike standpoint.[49] Pure logic "constitutes a desire 'to be like God.'"[50] This immediate standpoint is revealed in the lack of a prefix in logic as an unmediated interpretation of *Logos* reflected in the "intrinsic linearity of 'logy,'" which denies an understanding of *Logos* as being comprised by an eventful and "manifold problematic."[51] When this "manifold problematic" of *Logos* is denied, one gets a pure form of knowledge "modelled upon the ideal of divine knowledge, which comprehends everything from the One (from, namely, itself), and thus comprehends the fullness of reality from its idea."[52] Pure logic in its linear unmediated starting point denies the manifold nature of created being and reality by seeking to take a path that is itself denied to the creature, which is to say, a bird's-eye view of the whole in a logic of identity (A = A). Such a path is clearly impossible for creaturely thought, which, in its suspended/hanging condition, is denied a clear linear unmediated path. Rather, thought must follow an eventful promiscuous crisscrossing path within the manifold problematic of *Logos* itself (and thus never abandoning the realm of the sensible). Pure logic is thus another expression of absolutization and foundation, which seeks an *absolutum* of the pure concept and thus a desire of "knowing ... like God" (Gen. 3:5).

Dialectic, however, with the insertion of the prefix *dia*—which grammatically means an "in between" in the dual meaning of "through" and "apart" (*durch, zer*)—offers a thinking that takes place in the space between "possibilities which are antithetical" and thus opposed to one another.[53] If, then, one takes *dia*lectic to mean a "taking apart," then one is very far from the immediate identity of the concept in pure logic. Rather, one finds a "confirmation of a perduring 'in between' as an 'in between'—and 'solution' here means only the recognition of this in between."[54] Here historically, then, one encounters the aporetic and antithetical thinking found in Platonic dialectics in "knowing that I do not know," finding its fulfillment in the Christian Platonism of Augustine with a renewed "resurrection" of Platonic aporia in modernity with Kierkegaard (one could also think of Johann Georg Hamann).[55]

49. Przywara, *Analogia Entis*, 194.
50. Przywara, *Analogia Entis*, 194.
51. Przywara, *Analogia Entis*, 194.
52. Przywara, *Analogia Entis*, 194.
53. Przywara, *Analogia Entis*, 194.
54. Przywara, *Analogia Entis*, 194.
55. Przywara, *Analogia Entis*, 195.

If, on the other hand, one takes *dia*lectic to mean "through," one then historically encounters Aristotelian syllogistic logic which views antitheses, not as an ultimate aporia, but as a means of solving or dissolving the antitheses into "clear knowledge" and logical "proofs."[56] Such a movement towards identity, found in Aristotelian logic, finds its historical confirmation in Hegel. (Is this not why Hegel, in his *Lectures on the History of Philosophy*, sees Aristotle as a kind of precursor of his thought?) Contradiction and antitheses thus reveal the ultimate "'identity' of the one *Logos*," thereby showing the tremendous gap between the above meaning of aporetic dialectic and Hegelian dialectic.[57] In Hegelian dialectic, "It is the distance of a tension, the two terms drawn apart only that they might spring back together all the more passionately."[58] Both senses of dialectic, in and of themselves, are not satisfactory insofar as they remain caught between equivocity and univocity, contradiction and identity, that is, in a "passion raging between contradiction and identity, between extremest night and extremest day."[59] "'Dialectic', in and for itself, is a 'creaturely realism,' but one caught in a delirium, reeling irredeemably between a defiant self-recusing (into its own night of antitheses) and a passionate desire for fusion (understood not as a desire for self-submission, but a desire for self-mastery)."[60] Taken in its full meaning, then, dialectic gets caught in antitheses of extremes, which is a between of "delirium" and thus not an authentic open between that points beyond itself.

What of this beyond that is beyond equivocity/univocity, contradiction/identity? The simple answer is that one needs an authentic "creaturely realism" that is not caught in an antithetic, nor a self-deluding flight to the divine, as was the case in pure logic. Rather one needs a creaturely ana-logic that takes up its thinking within creaturely tensions that are rhythmic, musical, and thus ultimately peaceful without thereby doing away with the genuine dynamic and event-character of creaturely reality (a movement-within-rest and a rest-within-movement). Ana-logic or analogical logic means that thought takes place within the two meanings of the prefix *ana*, which according to Przywara's fascinating etymological interpretation of *ana*, signifies both an "according to an orderly sequence" *and* an "upward movement," meaning that all thinking is a "distanced obe-

56. Przywara, *Analogia Entis*, 195.
57. Przywara, *Analogia Entis*, 195.
58. Przywara, *Analogia Entis*, 195.
59. Przywara, *Analogia Entis*, 196.
60. Przywara, *Analogia Entis*, 196.

dience to the Logos."⁶¹ Analogical logic thus takes place in accordance with a transcendent above which works in all things and which thought, in turn, follows. To make this more concrete, Przywara gives the analogy of a river that can only be followed upstream because the source is itself active in the flowing of the river, thereby allowing one to find the origin.⁶² To interpret: thinking (or ana-logical logic) takes place in the flowing stream of creaturely eventful becoming, which is marked by the suspended correlation between essence/existence, being/consciousness. This tension, however, is not one of a mysticism of the pure concept, advocated in pure logic. Nor is it a mad delirium between two antitheses: equivocal self-separation from the divine and mystical fusion with the divine, both of which advance through contradiction. Rather it is an order of thought that follows the *Logos*, which works all things as beyond all things. Creaturely tensions thus always point beyond themselves to the Originating *Logos* who is in-and-beyond thought and creation and thus that which orders creaturely being and *logos* to a following of "distanced obedience."

Within this above discussion and the difficult density of Przywara's thought and language, a profoundly simple truth (and as simple, easily ignored) is seeking to be expressed, namely, the meaning of what it means *to be* a creature. Przywara's intense creaturely logic and metaphysics is a description, not only of the movement of creaturely becoming, but also, importantly, of the creature's experience of the divine as understood in orthodox Catholic tradition and spirituality (and thus an *experience* of that which is beyond all experience).[63] Thus all of the aforementioned logics of identity and equivocal separation from the divine are ultimately expressive of heterodox experiences of the divine where God and the creature are collapsed. Or God's closeness through distance is denied. (This will become clearer in the next chapter.) Przywara sets forth a nonfoundational logic (ultimately rooted in the principle of noncontradiction, as will be seen) that fights against identity on every front. Or, as Przywara

---

61. Przywara, *Analogia Entis*, 196.

62. Przywara, *Analogia Entis*, 196.

63. For a more explicit application of how the *analogia entis* works in reference to religious experience and spirituality see Erich Przywara, "Metaphysics, Religion, Analogy," in *Analogia Entis*, 422–25. Here Przywara explains how any religious and mystical experience must be rooted in the ever-greater dissimilarity of the Fourth Lateran Council. (See Henry Denzinger, *The Sources of Catholic Dogma*, trans. Roy J. Deferrari [Fitzwilliam, NH: Loreto Publications, 1954], 432.) Przywara's rooting of analogy in the Fourth Lateran Council (1215) will be made clear in the following chapter.

beautifully says (speaking of the above-mentioned delirium of dialectics), "'*Analogy*' is the inner balancing of this confusion: defiant self-recusing yields to humble self-discrimination, and a passionate desire for fusion to loving-surrender."[64] Thus, as with *philo*sophy that only obtained itself in its participatory abandon and service to the Wisdom of the *theo*logical, the creature only ever truly obtains itself through a humble self-differentiation that passes over into a nonidentical participation enacted through "loving-surrender" to God, bound by the never-to-be-closed distance between the Lord and the servant. Analogical logic is thus ultimately a logic of spirituality, humility, service, and love that safeguards against all forms of confusion and fusion with the divine.[65]

Subverting the Cogito

The question of the starting point for Przywara is not a question of a pure indubitable ground on which to stand and from which one can, in turn, build a system as expressed in modern philosophy's foundationalism, system-building mania, and self-positing thought. Rather, the "primal decision" of the starting point was seen to be an abyssal one that revealed the heart of creaturely being's abiding difference and *mysterium*. Such a dramatic and aesthetic vision of creaturely being further came to utterance in a rigorous ana-logical logic. This logic was a creaturely logic rooted in man's creaturely and abyssal mystery, which humbly differentiated itself from the divine by obediently following the Originating *Logos* that works and orders all things. All of this is another way of saying that what Przywara is ultimately advancing is a thoroughgoing dynamic de-substantialization, de-essentialization, and de-categorization of being enacted via an *analogization of being*. Analogy is not merely an attribute of being: "analogy *is* being."[66]

If "analogy *is* being" then, following Przywara's method which roots epistemology in the exteriority of metaphysics, it must be concluded that "thought *is* (noetically) analogy."[67] Moreover, if analogy can be termed

---

64. Przywara, *Analogia Entis*, 196.
65. This connection between the logic of the *analogia entis* and spirituality will become important in the final chapter, where I seek to lay out an "analogical-apocalyptic metaphysics of the saints."
66. Przywara, *Analogia Entis*, 314.
67. Przywara, *Analogia Entis*, 314.

a "principle," then it is precisely in the analogical sense that both being and thought are analogical in their living structure and moving nature.[68] Principle is, therefore, analogized as are being and thought, all of which then becomes expressive of the relational and de-substantialized nature of Przywara's singular interpretation of analogy. This principle is expressed in the principle of noncontradiction (analogically conceived, as will be seen in the next chapter), not as a principle of self-positing thought, but precisely as an expression of the dynamic state of nonidentity characteristic of creaturely being's nonidentical makeup of essence and existence. Creaturely being, in virtue of being nonidentical, finds its formulation in the principle of noncontradiction as working between identity and contradiction (pure logic/dialectic). The principle of noncontradiction thus respects man's analogical and open between. Thus, this principle is not transcendentally posited by thought, nor is it immediately conceived as an original pure starting point. Rather it is a starting point in virtue of *being* a starting point. This implies that it is a creaturely principle that is open, fluid, and moving because it is expressive of the nonidentical, analogical co-belonging of essence and existence in man. And, thus, it is a principle genuinely of the moving suspended between that is neither identity nor contradiction (a coalescing of unity-in-movement). In a word, if being *is analogy* then Przywara's analogical principle of noncontradiction is a nonfoundational deconstructing principle that is the ensign under which Przywara's "systematics of impurity" and thought marches in its war against foundation and the promethean onslaught of modernity's infatuation with self-presence.[69]

---

68. Recall that Przywara, in the 1962 preface, recognized the infelicitous choice of the word *principle* and the consequent misunderstanding that ensued from its use in regard to what he actually meant by the *analogia entis*. Further, as was seen, this was indeed why Przywara decided to change "principle" in the 1962 edition to "Original Structure," which is a far more felicitous choice than the word *principle*. In the above discussion I seek to partly clarify how "principle" is not to be understood in a modern foundational sense. This requires clarification because the word still occurs at the conclusion of the 1962 edition.

69. It need not be said that this also has wide-ranging and significant ramifications for one's interpretation of language, which cannot be gone into here. Przywara will say, in response to a Benedictine reviewer of *Analogia Entis*, "If being in itself is analogical, in the sense of the Fourth Lateran Council . . . , this necessarily applies to thought and language as well. But this means that both thought and language are an 'ever-transcending' movement. There is no such thing as possessive saturation in a concept or formula. Rather, one can only make every thought and word transparent 'beyond itself,' which is to say that I think and speak in a 'transcendental dynamic' way: always beyond every concept and every word

However, what I am interested in here is what this says about the *Cogito* in light of the present discussion with Stein, insofar as she never fully abdicated a *Cogito*-based philosophy. Before I cite a passage that will make clear Przywara's subversion of the *Cogito* it must be recalled that Przywara acknowledged the methodological anteriority of a meta-noetic starting point in his formal discussion of being/consciousness, which was itself a method rooted in its object, namely, the suspended condition of being's concrete becoming. Here, I think, it becomes fully clear why Przywara took this route (as partly alluded to above). He took it in order to show that there is no Cartesian interiority and that the *Cogito* is a mask, a ruse, a myth, indeed, a fundamental impossibility. Przywara says, no doubt with a bit of irony, "It was in this sense, then, that we discovered *analogia* as a principle within the *cogito*. It came into view not as something formal from which objects could be derived, but as a formality of movement."[70] What does this mean? It means that the immediate eternality, garb, or mask of the *Cogito* is trans-pierced with the moving earthliness of creaturely thought from the outset. This is to say, insofar as creaturely thought is marked, at the outset, by the suspended correlation of being and consciousness in a "world," the "final consequence is that even the truth which flashes out within the *cogito* does so 'transparently': not as an eternal immutable truth 'in the *cogito*,' but in-and-beyond the becoming of the creaturely correlation of consciousness and being."[71] Furthermore, the fundamental intention or "principle' of thought is one of analogical tension and suspension rooted in the nonfundamental nature of creaturely being, which always points beyond itself in its exteriorized and ecstatically abyssal nonground.

Truth, as conceived by the creature, is not fundamental or eternal, but creaturely, relational, mediated. Truth is an eventful and dramatic chiaroscuro that takes place within the very mystery of difference which *is* created analogical being. There can never be an interior ground that is the *Cogito* in its pretended eternal immediacy to truth, which puts on a divine mask. The only "I think" is an I that thinks as a being-in-the-midst of difference, relation, exteriorization, and suspension. It is the "I think" that thinks as always already within the dramatic rhythm of the mysterious mu-

---

in ever renewed movement." Cited in Betz, Translator's Preface, xvi. David Bentley Hart, in the spirit of Przywara, profoundly thinks through the analogical meaning of language in *The Beauty of the Infinite*, as will be touched upon in Part 2.

70. Przywara, *Analogia Entis*, 312.

71. Przywara, *Analogia Entis*, 312.

sicality of created being, which ever points beyond itself. "As this primordial dynamic, analogy is a rhythm—just as, according to Pythagoras, the cosmos vibrates with a 'resonant rhythm,' and just as according to Plato, God is the 'measure of all things and all actions.' Only in the sense of such a rhythm and such a measure is analogy a 'principle.' Ontically as being and noetically as thought, it is 'principally' the mystery of the primordial music of this rhythm."[72] Foundation and the *Cogito* are thus subverted and give way to a dramatic aesthetics of creaturely being's musical rhythm and mystery. In the words of T. S. Eliot, a "music heard so deeply that it is not heard at all, but you are the music, while the music lasts."[73] That is, until we ourselves give way and are taken up into the Eternal music and silence of the ever-greater living God in an asymmetrical analogical relation of love (Lord and servant).

*   *   *

To conclude: the foundational logic discovered in Stein's approach to Christian philosophy was further brought to light in her core interpretation of being. It was seen that Stein's vision of being was marked by foundationalism and immediacy due to her faithfulness to Husserlian and modern method. Stein's admirable and creative engagement with philosophical modernity is continually restricted by her reliance on Husserlian and modern method. Her Christian vision continually shows its modern paternity, even if weakened. Conversely, Przywara's nonfoundational logic, expressed in his analogical and sapiential relation between *philo*sophia and *theo*logy, was likewise confirmed in his core interpretation of being as analogy. This was seen to be an interpretation of being that was de-substantial, abyssal, and relational, thus exhibiting strong postmodern characteristics. Moreover, Przywara's interpretation of being was reflected in his method of the exteriorized unmooring of epistemology from ground in a suspended never-to-be-closed relation between being/consciousness which points beyond itself. This unmooring of epistemology struck at the core of modern foundationalism in an analogical deconstruction and subversion of the *Cogito*: a *Cogito* from which Stein's project was unable to fully release itself.

---

72. Przywara, *Analogia Entis*, 314.
73. T. S. Eliot, "The Dry Salvages," in *The Complete Poems and Plays* (New York: Harcourt, Brace & World, 1958), 136.

It is becoming increasingly clear that Stein's and Przywara's strategic positions towards philosophical modernity are fundamentally different. Przywara and Stein are two very different thinkers. Stein advances a phenomenological-ontology that is anthropocentrically based in a "primal decision" that roots her project in the *being of the I* and thus subjectivity, while Przywara advances a project of an analogical metaphysics of relation and difference based in a "primal decision" that roots itself in its object, namely, the nonrepresentable space between essence and existence and thus creaturely being's abiding abyss and *mysterium*. Przywara's candidacy for postmodern Christian election is growing stronger, while Stein's is weakened by her "weakened modernity." Lastly, everything that has been seen in the last two chapters will determine the final outcome of each thinker's ultimate interpretation of the *analogia entis*. Stein's and Przywara's respective logics remain consistent throughout. The beginning is present in the end.

CHAPTER 4

Differing Reimaginings of the *Analogia Entis*: Anthropocentrism and Theocentrism

> Thou mastering me
> God! Giver of breath and bread;
> World's strand, sway of the sea;
>   Lord of living and dead;
>   Thou hast bound bones and veins in me, fastened
>   me flesh,
>   And after it almost unmade, what with dread,
>   Thy doing: and dost thou touch me afresh?
> Over again I feel thy finger and find thee.
>   From Gerard Manley Hopkins,
>   "The Wreck of the Deutschland"

O admirabile commercium! / Creator generis humani / animatum corpus sumens / de Virgine nasci dignatus est: / et procedens homo sine semine / largitus est nobis suam deitatem. [O admirable exchange! / Humankind's Creator / taking on body and soul / in his kindness, is born from the Virgin: / and, coming forth as man, yet not from man's seed / he has lavished upon us his divinity.]
                     From the Antiphon at Vespers, January 1,
                       Feast of the Holy Mother of God

In the previous two chapters of Part 1, emphasis has been placed on a formally critical dialogue between Stein's and Przywara's interpretations of philosophy and being in order to lay bare their respective styles of philosophizing. We have examined their differing strategic positions towards philosophical modernity consequent upon their shared project of a needed creative Catholic engagement with philosophical modernity in the wake of the modernist crisis. In this concluding chapter of Part 1 the culmination of each thinker's style of philosophy and vision of being will come fully to light when it is seen how the previous findings play out in analogical relation between the creature and God. We will see that the findings of the previous two chapters are fully confirmed in Przywara's and Stein's respective reimaginings of the *analogia entis*.

Stein's interpretation of analogy will be based on a common term of reference or relation of meaning, namely, the *ens commune* (reflexively interpreted) shared between God and man: difference-in-unity, while, conversely, Przywara's view of analogy will transect all likeness between God and man within the ever-greater dissimilarity of the Fourth Lateran Council marking analogy—not as an exercise of metaphysical bridge-building—but as a relation of asymmetrical alterity and love: unity-in-difference. Steinian discourse remains tied to the principles of philosophical modernity, while Przywarian vision overcomes modern principles in a countermodern and postmodern fashion. Once this conclusion is reached it will then be possible to see why a choice has to be made between Przywara and Stein. This choice is again made in light of the *telos* of this text, which seeks a constructive pleromatic reimagining and synthesis of analogical metaphysical vision in light of our postmodern Christian context.

The *Analogia Entis* Reimagined as the *Ens Commune*

We have arrived at a site where we are able to see the problematic nature of Stein viewing the *analogia entis* as the "fundamental law" of *Finite and Eternal Being*.[1] This is because the end result of Stein's "conscious self-restraint" of elaborating a phenomenological-ontology turned out to be a far more ambitious project that is haunted by identity, as opposed to Przywara's alleged "philosophical system." Przywara's "philosophical system" was in fact a "systematics of impurity" or a rigorous deconstruction of all systems in favor of a humble deployment of an open systematics that grounded itself in the nonground of creaturely being's abiding and

---

1. Edith Stein, *Finite and Eternal Being: An Attempt at an Ascent to the Meaning of Being*, trans. Kurt F. Reinhardt (Washington, DC: ICS Publications, 2001), xxix.

openly suspended *mysterium*.² Now I call into question the statement in the preface where Stein claims that she and Przywara are in agreement concerning the relation between the creature and Creator.³ That is to say, if analogy is ultimately about how one construes the *relation between* God and man, does Stein see this relation in the same way as Przywara? The answer is clearly no. But why and how do they differ concerning this relation of all relations?

Stein's interpretation of the commonality between *Finite and Eternal Being* and *Analogia Entis* consists in, as has been seen, viewing analogy as the "fundamental law" under which each text proceeds. And, indeed, Stein even quotes Przywara's central thesis that analogy is rooted in the text of the Fourth Lateran Council, concerning its statement that whatever likeness there is between the creature and Creator, there always remains an ever-greater dissimilarity between the two.⁴ If Stein explicitly acknowledges this and indeed seems to grasp the heart of analogy as accentuating, not likeness, but rather likeness-in-dissimilarity, thus following Przywara's interpretation of analogy, why does she end up accentuating commonality and mutuality in her actual thought? The thesis I will again put forward is that Stein has many aims and intentions (such as moving beyond Husserl) within *Finite and Eternal Being* that are destined to remain unfulfilled due to her modern principles and starting point, which always constrict the breadth of her Christian vision. The greatest unfulfilled intention of *Finite and Eternal Being* is its inability to *fully* protect the ever-greater dissimilarity between God and man. This failure is rooted in the very logic of Stein's narration on philosophy and being, which now prohibits her from adequately guarding the abiding difference between God and man by collapsing the two into a *tertium quid*, namely, the *ens commune*.

I proceed in four steps. First, I begin by basing my thesis in a key passage where Stein reads the Thomistic real distinction between essence/existence as opening up a univocal interpretation of being, whereby she shows her intention of grasping being in a common concept that bridges

---

2. Stein, *Finite and Eternal Being*, xxix.
3. Stein, *Finite and Eternal Being*, xxx.
4. See Stein, *Finite and Eternal Being*, 37–38, and for endnote 11, see 38 (endnote 554), where Stein references the Fourth Lateran Council. The text from the Fourth Lateran Council reads: "*inter creatorem et creaturam non potest tanta similitudo notari, quin inter eos non maior sit dissimilitudo notanda*" (Henry Denzinger, *The Sources of Catholic Dogma*, trans. Roy J. Deferrari [Fitzwilliam, NH: Loreto Publications, 1954], 432). I will discuss more fully the meaning of this text and its significance for Przywara later on in this chapter.

the gap between finite and infinite being. Second, I then proceed to investigate how Stein seeks to elaborate a phenomenological point of access to analogy via her investigation of temporality and the I. Third, I then show how Stein immanently arrives at the idea of eternal being where a danger of reading the eternal I on the basis of her rendition of the *Cogito* arises. I conclude with the highpoint of *Finite and Eternal Being* where her logic of univocal being and mutuality comes fully into view in light of the previous three sections.

Ontological Bridge-Building

Stein does not just tacitly acknowledge the *maior dissimilitudo* as constituting the *analogia entis* but, indeed, explicitly acknowledges (cites the Fourth Lateran Council) the ever-greater dissimilarity between God and man, in keeping with Przywara's interpretation. Why then, it must be asked, does Stein's logic militate against the *maior dissimilitudo* despite her avowal of it? The answer to this question must be sought in two facets of Stein's thought. First, Stein's guiding intention of the text is to elaborate a theory of being's meaning (a phenomenological-ontology) in both its finite and eternal aspects. This marks her project as geared toward, from the outset, being's *essential* unity, univocity, likeness, and mutuality. Further, this is in keeping with the ambitious task of her Christian philosophy's aim at "total knowledge" through a synthesis of all rational and supernatural truths as well as the fundamental starting point of the being of the *I*. Second, these fundamental intentions of Stein's guiding logic fully come to expression in her univocal interpretation of the Thomistic real distinction, which prohibits an adequate thinking of creaturely being's difference from God.

In the context of the passage I am about to quote, Stein is discussing Aristotle's "epochal contribution" of act/potency and his situating *the* question of philosophy in "What is that which is?" or "What is meant by *ousia*?"[5] Stein sees Aquinas, in his youthful opusculum *De ente et essentia*, as taking up these epochal rational discoveries of Aristotle now with the aid of revelation, and especially the doctrine of creation. It is in this context that Stein tips her univocal hand by presenting a more Scotistic (*distinctio formalis*) or Suarezian (*distinctio sola rationis*) interpretation of the Thomistic *distinctio realis*.

---

5. Stein, *Finite and Eternal Being*, 3.

Already in this early treatise [*De ente et essentia*], Thomas had taken his most decisive step beyond Aristotle: He had within the realm of that which is [*Seiende*] distinguished between being [*esse*] and essence [*essentia*]. The equation of ὄν and ousia, from which Aristotle had started out, remains valid only for the First Existent [*Seiende*]. With this distinction being as such—as distinct from that which is [*Seiende*]—was understood for the first time as comprising both finite and infinite being as simultaneously encompassing the abyss which separates the former from the latter. From this vantage point, a way to seize upon the entire manifoldness of all that which is [*Seiende*] could be envisaged.[6]

Stein here is, of course, speaking of the seminal significance of the Thomistic discovery of the real distinction (*distinctio realis*), which became a veritable battleground within Scholastic philosophy and specifically Scotus and Suarez, who along with many other Scholastics denied the metaphysical validity of this crucial Thomistic discovery. What is at stake, historically, in this discovery is nothing less than a debate of how one understands the relation between the Creator and creature, or infinite and finite being.[7] Which is to say, that the implication of the real distinction, in line with Przywara (and Balthasar) is, indeed, the *analogia entis*. In this discovery the difference between God and the creature is metaphysically secured. That is, the *actus purus* (He whose essence is His existence in the unutterable dynamic simplicity of the absolute life of infinite Being) is qualitatively different and can never be equated with the borrowed, participated being of the creature, created *ex nihilo*. Further, in this discovery a definitive metaphysical demarcation has *occurred*, for the first time, that fully expresses the *doctrine of creation ex nihilo* which, therefore, guards the never-to-be-closed distance between God and creaturely being-in-becoming. This distinction is marked by the nonidentity and difference of essence and existence in man's flickering being arising out of nothingness.

Such is the import of Przywara's interpretation of the *distinctio realis* (and following him Balthasar), namely, that it marks the analogical dis-

---

6. Stein, *Finite and Eternal Being*, 4.

7. There is also the implication of this distinction for Christology in the scholastic schools as to how one understands the human nature of Christ in relation to his divine Personhood, or in other words, the hypostatic union. For an excellent summary of these Christological debates among the scholastic schools (Thomist, Scotist, Molinist, and Suarezian), see Karl Adam, *The Christ of Faith: The Christology of the Church*, trans. Joyce Crick (London: Burns & Oates, 1957), 194–204.

tance between God and the creature as a relation of asymmetrical alterity. In this interpretation of the *distinctio realis*, Przywara and Balthasar are and remain the two most faithful and creative interpreters of the brilliance and spirit of Aquinas in the twentieth century.[8] Why? Simply put, this distinction (because really and truly metaphysical) works against all forms of philosophical/theological anthropocentrism and theopanism/pantheism, which seek to collapse this abyssal difference into metaphysics of identity. This difference enables all other differences (here I leave out the question of Trinitarian difference) by respecting both the otherness of God and the otherness of creation by seeing relation as constituted by the whyless and transcendent freedom of God (He Who *Is* Absolute Being). This, in turn, gives the true otherness of creation in an unmerited, unnecessary donation of created being that opens a participatory relation of alterity, love, and exchange between God and man in the space of love's free traversal.

Stein's reading of Aquinas's radical discovery of the *distinctio realis* is curious as to how she finally conceives the import of its meaning. It rightly acknowledges that in Aristotle there is not an adequate difference or gap between essence and being. She is further right to see that this lack of distinction is because "Aristotle knew nothing of a *creation*."[9] And Stein is perfectly correct that this distinction can only be thought in the light of revelation and the doctrine of creation *ex nihilo*. Without this doctrine there is no adequate way of truly respecting the abiding difference between the otherness of God and the otherness of creation. Aquinas thus, in the light of revelation, creatively transposes the equation of being and essence, found in Aristotle, onto God: now allowing it to be mysteriously applicable to God alone. At the outset it seems that Stein is acknowledging a real metaphysical distinction between essence and existence in the creature that would be in line with Przywara's analogical intention. Indeed, if Stein ended the passage with the fact that the "equation" of being and essence "remains valid only for the First Existent," then this passage would not be curious at all, as it would simply fall in line with the view that the real distinction marks the inexhaustible difference between God and creation.

---

8. For Balthasar on the real distinction, see Hans Urs von Balthasar, *Theo-Logic*, vol. 1: *Truth of the World*, trans. Adrian J. Walker (San Francisco: Ignatius Press, 2000), especially 102–7, and Hans Urs von Balthasar, *The Glory of the Lord: A Theological Aesthetics*, vol. 4: *The Realm of Metaphysics in Antiquity*, trans. Erasmo Leiva-Merikakis (San Francisco: Ignatius Press, 1989), 393–97.

9. Stein, *Finite and Eternal Being*, 3.

However, Stein entirely switches the register of the import of the *distinctio realis* with a view, not to creation's abiding difference from God, but rather as allowing one to read both finite and eternal being as being comprised by a concept of common being: "being as such ... was understood for the first time as comprising both finite and infinite being as *simultaneously encompassing the abyss which separates the former from the latter* [italics mine]. From this vantage point, a way *to seize* [italics mine] upon the entire *manifoldness of all that which is* [*Seiende*] could be envisaged." How else is one to read this curious shift in this passage but as expressive of the fact that, in Stein's interpretation, the "epochal contribution" of Aquinas's *distinctio realis* is not the abiding difference it posits between God and creation, but rather the ability to apply the one term, "being," to both finite and eternal being? This thus marks the real distinction as an act of ontological bridge-building that encompasses "the abyss" which separates God from creation or creation from God. This, in turn, allows one to "seize" upon the unity of being and the "manifoldness of all that which is." I am forced to conclude that, for Stein, somehow (though she never elaborates why she makes this jump or asserts this) the *distinctio realis* is a means of elaborating a common concept of being (*ens commune*) that allows us "to seize" upon the meaning of being by bridging the never-to-be-bridged gap between God and creation. Being here is a *tertium quid* and/or *tertium comparationis* that neutrally encompasses God and man. It must be concluded that the ultimate epochal import of the *distinctio realis*, for Stein, is *not* metaphysical but *epistemic*.

Is not Stein guilty of what Barth accused Przywara of doing with analogy, namely, an exercise in metaphysical or ontological bridge-building that endangers the transcendence of God and revelation by making God subservient to being, now understood as a *tertium quid*?[10] If so, does this not remain consistent with Stein's penchant for foundationalism and her reflexive identical starting point founded on the subject's presence-to-self? Is not the weight of Stein's logic too heavy, thus moving her to accentuate mutuality and sameness between God and man over difference? This will become more fully clear when I deal with Stein's ultimate interpretation of analogy as a "common constitutive element of

10. It is not possible here to go into the full depth of Barth's objection to Przywara's *analogia entis*; however, for a definitive rebuttal of Barth's position see Betz, Translator's Introduction, and John Betz, "After Barth: A New Introduction to Erich Przywara's *Analogia Entis*," in *The Analogy of Being: Invention of the Antichrist or the Wisdom of God?*, ed. Thomas Joseph White, OP (Grand Rapids: Eerdmans, 2011), 35–87.

meaning."[11] However, at this point, it thus must be concluded that Stein does not uphold a real metaphysical difference between essence/existence (analogical difference) but rather a more Scotistic and Suarezian interpretation that views it as an epistemically formal, rational, and conceptual distinction, and therefore, univocal. This opens a way to capture the relation between the creature and Creator via unity and commonality and *not difference*. For Przywara, the *distinctio realis* functions as the real metaphysical moving dynamic relation that constitutes the abiding difference between God and creation and, thus, concomitantly, the *analogia entis*,[12] while, for Stein, the epochal import of the *distinctio realis* rests in its epistemic import to bridge and "seize" the manifold of finite/infinite being in a common term of reference and thus, concomitantly, the univocality of the *ens commune*.

Phenomenological Access to the Analogia Entis

Stein seeks to give an experiential and phenomenological account of the *analogia entis*. This is in keeping with the immanent approach of her phenomenological-ontology. She achieves this phenomenological point of access to the *analogia entis* through giving a description of the temporality of the ego or I.[13] Hence, subsequent upon securing the foundation of the immediate coincidence of being with the I, in the lineage of Husserl and Descartes, Stein now attempts to switch the field of play by elaborating the finitude of the I, in a manner reminiscent of Heidegger's *Being and Time*, contra the disguised eternality of the transcendental I. Stein, then, is again seeking to switch the field of play against the paternal presence of the Husserlian method. Yet is this really the case? Or, is it more likely that Stein only seemingly checkmates Husserl and his transcendental and parsimonious patrimony, in light of the fact that her turn to temporality

---

11. Stein, *Finite and Eternal Being*, 335–36.
12. For a short passage that grasps the metaphysical significance of the real distinction for Przywara, see Josef Pieper, *Faith, Hope, Love*, trans. Richard and Clara Winston (San Francisco: Ignatius Press, 1986), 96–97. For a reading that partially grasps the real distinction, but ultimately misses the mark of the theological import of the real distinction and the metaphysical significance of creation in Przywara, see Dietrich Bonhoeffer, *Act and Being: Transcendental Philosophy and Ontology in Systematic Theology*, ed. Wayne Whitson Floyd Jr., trans. H. Martin Rumscheidt (Minneapolis: Fortress Press, 2009), 73–78.
13. See *Finite and Eternal Being*, 38–43.

and finitude still takes place on the board first laid down by Husserlian method? That is, is not Stein really checkmated by Husserl, as the field of her discourse is still determined by the board predetermined and haunted by modern method? In Stein's move towards temporality and finitude, the Cartesian/Husserlian ghost again rears its ugly head, showing her inability to fully move beyond the shadows of the methodical ancestry of Descartes and Husserl.

In keeping with the introspective and immanent approach of phenomenology when one turns inwards, reflecting on the I's being and the intellectual movement constituting this reflection, a dual aspect of the I's being makes an appearance. This "dual aspect" is of "being and ... non-being."[14] This, in turn, effectuates an inability to "endure this dual perspective," namely, that the very being which I am, as well as my intellectual movement which constitutes this I, is "subject to change."[15] This leads to the conclusion that the I, and conscious life, are "inseparable from temporality."[16] The I that I am now is always distended between the past and the future. The flux of finite being is always an admixture of being and non-being, and, therefore, cannot be said to be pure or eternal being. In fact, it is in this very temporal distention that the idea of eternal being immanently arises within the being of the I.

From here Stein moves, once again, to a *rational legitimation* of her philosophical discourse by remarking that the ideas of mutable and immutable being "are ideas which the intellect encounters within itself; they are not borrowed from anything outside itself. A legitimate point of departure for a philosophy based on natural reason and natural knowledge is again found."[17] Once again we see Stein's need to legitimate and secure her discourse as a fully rational discourse that plots its narrative within the immanence of conscious life self-enacted through the interiority of phenomenological method. Enter the phenomenological approach to the *analogia entis*, where Stein's problematic avowal of the *maior dissimilitudo* comes to utterance:

> What is meant by analogia entis (as indicative of the relationship existing between temporal and eternal being) also becomes faintly visible at

---

14. Stein, *Finite and Eternal Being*, 37.
15. Stein, *Finite and Eternal Being*, 37.
16. Stein, *Finite and Eternal Being*, 37.
17. Stein, *Finite and Eternal Being*, 37.

this point. Actual being at the moment at which it is reveals something of the nature of being as such, i.e., of the fullness of being which knows of no temporal change. But precisely because this actual being is only for the moment, it is not at this moment the fullness of being: The very reason for its caducity [*Hinfälligkeit*] lies in its being momentary, and it is thus only an analogon of eternal being which is immutable and therefore plenitude of being at every moment. Momentary or temporal being, on the one hand, is merely a remote image or likeness [*Abbild*] related to the primordial prototype of its similitude but yet infinitely far removed from it by its dissimilitude.[18]

There are many things going on in this passage. First, on the most charitable reading, one might say that Stein is offering a phenomenological point of access, via temporality, to the Thomistic real distinction, which proffers a more ecstatic view of the self. However, there are too many issues that militate against this reading or, at least, render it problematic. And if these issues do not fully abrogate this reading then they, at the minimum, show forth again the many tensions that keep arising in *Finite and Eternal Being* and conflict with Stein's intent to move beyond Husserl and her faithfulness to the key principle of phenomenological method. First, we have just seen that Stein views the real distinction between essence and existence as an epistemic means of bridging and seizing upon both finite and eternal being in a univocal and common concept of being (*ens commune*) that encompasses the "abyss" and thus the "dissimilitude" spoken about above. Second, Stein does not begin her discourse with the fractured and impoverished "caducity" of the finite self, but rather with the indubitable, foundational, immediate, and secure coincidence of the *being of the I*. Thus Stein's attempt to ecstatically decenter the self paradoxically comes only after the identity of self-presence is secured. Difference is posited only after the secure ground of identity has first been established. Third, in the following investigation of temporality, as will soon be seen, Stein invokes Husserl's pure ego (*Reine Ich*) as a formal and necessary constituent of identity underlying our streams of experience. All of the above complicates the possibly generous reading of Stein fully elaborating the ecstatic difference between essence and existence through the phenomenological experience of temporality. This also prompts one to ask: Why would Stein not begin her discourse with an elaboration of temporality, thus more fully

---

18. Stein, *Finite and Eternal Being*, 37–38.

attempting to inaugurate difference at the outset instead of the univocal identity of being with the I? The answer again given must be the haunting of Steinian discourse by Husserlian and Cartesian paternity.

Further, this passage confirms that Stein is deploying a phenomenological reimagining of the *analogia entis*. This understanding of the *analogia entis* is seen through the lens of the immanent seeing or interiority of a phenomenological-ontology. Straight out of the gate, Stein is pushing analogy into an egological perspective of an analogy between the finite I with the eternal I. That is, all thinking of God and his transcendence takes place through the reflective, interior, and experiential seeing of the finite temporal I. The finite I, in turn, through its distention between the past and future, is able to immanently *dis*cover the *idea* (and therefore essence) of eternal being as plenitude and life: the eternal I. I will have much more to say about this later. However, at this point, what again must be underscored is that prior to Stein's turning to the temporally distended I is the "I think" and "I perceive" of the self immediately coinciding with the being of itself.

With the aforesaid in mind it needs to be noted that Stein's turn to temporality is her most creative and concerted attack on the transcendental tradition, and Husserl, in particular. Here the promethean nature of the ego, understood as a transcendental necessary divinity that "*imparts to itself* or *posits its own being*," is rightfully diagnosed and confronted.[19] Contra such a heterodox approach Stein, under the influence of Conrad-Martius and Heidegger, seeks to elaborate a view of the ego that "stands in need of time," and, therefore, a view of the being of the I as inherently "*received*" in contradistinction to the illusionary autonomy of the transcendental ego.[20] Stein boldly and correctly diagnoses the dangers of this transcendental tradition and sees how it is not compatible with a Christian vision of being. However, she is unable to fully administer the analogical *pharmakon*. Again using the metaphor of the game of chess: all of her moves on the board are first laid out by Husserlian method and thus constricted and constrained. Stein, fully cognizant of the dangers of the pretended godlike nature and masquerade of the transcendental ego, is not fully able to outwit this modern subterfuge and masked monstrosity within the narrowed field of play that is hermeneutically open to her. Because of this, Stein is in danger of transposing the modern transcendental self-sufficient deity of the

19. Stein, *Finite and Eternal Being*, 54.
20. Stein, *Finite and Eternal Being*, 54.

ego unto God: thereby thinking God on the phenomenological transcendental paradigm of complete and utter self-presence and transcendental self-consciousness: God as the supreme Ego or *the* Phenomenologist par excellence. In order to see this, the constricted moves on Stein's Husserlian board must be rehearsed.

Stein seeks, paradoxically, to decenter the transcendental ego, via distention and the diachronic placement of the ego into the temporal flow of the stream of experience, only after first securing the fundamental identity of the ego in its synchronic and intuitive self-presence. Further, shortly after this diachronic intermezzo, synchronic self-presence reemerges in her recourse to Husserl's methodological and formal construction of the *pure ego* (*Reine Ich*), which she embraces but also seeks to weaken. "Husserl calls that self which is immediately given in conscious experience the pure ego."[21] "Husserl says of the pure ego that It has no content and cannot be described as it is in itself. 'It is pure ego, and that is all.' This means, then, that the pure ego is alive in every such statement as '*I* perceive,' '*I* think,' '*I* draw conclusions,' '*I* experience joy,' '*I* desire' etc."[22] Stein seeks to weaken this formal I (without thereby abandoning its synthetic work) via a phenomenological description of memory and recollection. It is impossible for a finite and temporal ego to have total recall, self-presence, or "self-possession."[23] This is due to the fact that our fundamental experience is constituted by temporality and a "powerlessness" to call into being and sustain past experiential contents (such as joy).[24] Such "lacunae," in the memory of the past, show that the ego is by no means eternal and omniscient.[25] From the ego's finite experience of time and its distention it can be concluded, with Heidegger, that the ego's being is "*thrown into existence* [*ins Dasein geworfen*]."[26] This being is opposed to an autonomous and intrinsically necessary "being *a se* (by itself)."[27]

---

21. Stein, *Finite and Eternal Being*, 48.
22. Stein, *Finite and Eternal Being*, 48. Stein, in this section, is drawing upon both *Ideas* and *The Phenomenology of Internal Time Consciousness*.
23. Stein, *Finite and Eternal Being*, 54.
24. Stein, *Finite and Eternal Being*, 54.
25. Stein, *Finite and Eternal Being*, 54.
26. Stein, *Finite and Eternal Being*, 54.
27. Stein, *Finite and Eternal Being*, 54. Stein is here at her best. Stein's phenomenological description of temporality that, unfortunately, could not be gone into in extreme detail here, is profoundly illuminating. And, once again, it needs to be said that Stein has certainly gone beyond Husserl and shown possible avenues of approach in opening up a kind of phenom-

Has Stein done enough to advance beyond Husserlian method, as opposed to other phenomenologists who have more fully questioned Husserl's transcendental starting point and the idea of phenomenology as a "rigorous science," such as Heidegger, Merleau-Ponty, and Marcel?[28] Stein continually shows herself to be a faithful follower of Husserlian method. This following seems to be rooted in her fear that, if philosophy were to give up this method, then it would cease to be a fully rational and scientific discourse (a foundational discourse that is called into question by the aforementioned phenomenologists). This fact was signaled to in the above quote, namely, "our ideas which the intellect encounters within itself; they are not borrowed from anything outside itself. This means that we have now found a legitimate point of departure for a philosophy based on natural reason and natural knowledge."[29] Following from this, Stein's avowal of the "pure ego" of Husserl ensures a formal principle of methodological certainty and identity that remains anterior to and, therefore, authorizes her discussion of temporality.

Such a principle is ruled by the methodological abstractness and formality of intuitive immediacy. This is why Stein says, following Husserl, that the pure ego, in its methodological immediacy, cannot even be described. It is thus this contentless I that remains the constituting element of all conscious streaming experience, and secures the identity of the I from flowing away into the *apeiron* of time and existence. "The ego is then, we conclude, always actual, always actually living present."[30] This, as opposed to the ruse of eternality of the transcendental ego, does not mean that this ego is eternal, but rather that the finite ego needs time for its contentlessness to be filled out with contents of experience. Nevertheless, behind this temporal flux of the ego, which is actualized through experience (content, distention), remains the pure ego (form-of-identity), which is founded on intuitive and conscious self-possession and presence. That is, the formal and methodological principle of identity that rules phenomenology re-

---

enological "proof," or better, "showing" of the "received," fragile, and contingent nature of creaturely being paramount for Christian philosophical discourse.

28. For a fine essay that gets to the differences between Marcel and Husserl concerning their respective and diverging approaches to phenomenology, see Paul Ricoeur, "Gabriel Marcel and Phenomenology," in *The Philosophy of Gabriel Marcel: The Library of Living Philosophers*, vol. 17, ed. Paul Arthur Schilpp and Lewis Edwin Hahn, trans. Susan Gruenheck (Chicago: Open Court, 1984), 471–94.

29. Stein, *Finite and Eternal Being*, 37.

30. Stein, *Finite and Eternal Being*, 52.

mains in this description of temporality. Yet, if the finite ego, for Stein, does not constitute full and total self-presence and self-possession, then it falls to the eternal I to fulfill this demand. Nevertheless, the finite ego is still thought and ruled by the paradigm of self-presence and self-possession. This demands the question: Is this because we are the *analogon* of eternal Self-Presence, or is Stein forced to think God as a kind of *analogon* of the methodically constructed I or pure ego because this is the only way left to weaken the transcendental ego on her predetermined board of play?

The Idea of Eternal Being/The Infinite Ego

Stein's moves are constricted by the Husserlian board of method, which she cannot fully escape. And because Stein strongly demurs at the idolatrous pretensions of the ego, of transcendental ilk, there is only one hermeneutic move that is left to her, in order to avoid the divinization of the finite I. That is, Stein must read the firm ground of the eternal-like immediacy of the finite I as itself a kind of image of the divine I. Yet here one is on very shaky ground. For, in this play of immediately reflexive mirroring of the being of the I to itself, how is one to adequately discriminate one's divine-like self-reflection from the reflection of the divine *in* the finite self? Moreover, due to the fact that the very nature of the transcendental I is precisely its masked eternality and intuitive immediate knowledge of itself, in the Cartesian and Husserlian lineage, then, this forces a question. What path of judgmental discrimination is open to Stein in order to ensure that she is not merely reading the masked eternality of the *Cogito*, which haunts her discourse, onto the *Deus semper maior*? Does Stein get caught in a mirror-play where the light of the internal self-reflection of the pretended eternality of the finite I refracts itself, thereby bending the image of the *Deus semper maior* in man into an image of the methodological finite I? And, further, does this result in reading the image of the finite I into/onto the image of God in itself? This question will come fully to light when I turn to the apex of Stein's discussion of the *analogia entis*; nevertheless, the answer can certainly be hinted at here.

In Stein's intensifying resistance to Husserl, seen in the finite ego's distention, it was concluded that this ego is not transcendentally self-sufficient, but a "received being." Yet, "Whence comes this received being?"[31]

31. Stein, *Finite and Eternal Being*, 55.

Anthropocentrism and Theocentrism

This question must be asked because of the Husserlian view that the ego constitutes its being from within "transcendental worlds" and is viewed as a necessary and autonomous being that denies every and all forms of heteronomy. But for Stein, as a Christian philosopher, it is only pure and eternal being that deserves such determinations, i.e., a being that is "by itself and in itself [*a se* and *per se*] eternally immutable, autonomous, and necessary."[32] It must, therefore, be asked "whether it is possible to make some valid predications concerning our relationship to pure being within the limitations of this finite realm of being."[33]

What mode do Stein's predications concerning the divine take? At this point it must be recalled that in order to legitimate her discourse as rational, it was stated that these ideas concerning the divine must arise solely from within the immanent sphere of the intellect or mind and are thus not to be "borrowed from anything outside itself."[34] Three points must be noted concerning this approach. First, all ideas are taken from within and arise from the interior self-reflection and experience of the being of the I on itself. Second, following from this, this once again shows that Stein is not attempting a metaphysical speculative reflection on the divine, but rather an immanent phenomenological-ontology that remains both reflexively and experientially based. Third, any predications that Stein arrives at will be, in keeping with phenomenology, ideas or essential predications that say nothing of the divine's existence, but only the divine's ideal status. Moreover, Stein thinks that the *idea* of pure being can be arrived at via an immanent reflection on the transitional state of the finite I. This investigation shows two things: first, that the finite ego is incapable of total recall of its experiential contents, and second, that it is through this experience of finitude that something enduringly present is also revealed, namely, the methodological construct of the pure ego. From this one can conclude that "the ego itself seems to be closer to pure being because it attains not only to the crest of being [like experiential contents such as joy, which need the ego to attain being] for one single moment, but is sustained in it at *every* moment."[35] From this affinity of the enduring, present nature of the finite ego with eternal being, one immanently arrives at the idea of eternal being:

---

32. Stein, *Finite and Eternal Being*, 55.
33. Stein, *Finite and Eternal Being*, 55.
34. Stein, *Finite and Eternal Being*, 37.
35. Stein, *Finite and Eternal Being*, 56.

The ego is capable of arriving at the idea of eternal being not only by way of envisaging the becoming and fading away of its experiences, but also on the basis of the experienced specific nature of its own being, which is confined to an existence from moment to moment. The ego shrinks back from nothingness and desires not only an endless continuation of its own being but full possession of being as such: It desires a being capable of embracing the totality of the ego's contents in one changeless present instead of its having to witness the continually repeated disappearance of all these contents almost at every moment they have ascended onto the stage of life. The ego thus arrives at the idea of plenitude [*Idee der Fülle*] by crossing out from its own being what it has come to know as privation.[36]

Here there is a turn away from the "caducity" of being, which was focusing on dissimilarity opened through the becoming and transient nature of finite being. This move away from the "caducity" of being is rooted in the fact that Stein inaugurates an attempt to secure difference, paradoxically, only after she has first secured her indubitable and immediate starting point of the coincidence of the being of the I. The underlying present I haunting Stein's discourse again manifests itself in her attempt to arrive at an idea of eternal being.

Stein has intimated that the idea of eternal being arises out of our transience and becoming in which experiential contents (her favorite example of joy) come to be and fade away, because the ego is itself unable to fully and completely hold on to these contents (a mark of our difference from the divine). Now, however, there is a turn towards the mutuality and affinity of the finite ego with eternal being. This is done by turning to "the basis of the experienced specific nature of its [the ego] own being." Yet what "nature" is being spoken of here? Is it not the nature of the Steinian version of *Cogito*, which she desired to be the firm foundation of her philosophical investigation? And is this not the ego that, at the outset, was possessed of foundation, identity, and immediate intuitive security? The answer must be yes, because Stein only sought to belatedly establish difference, via her discussion of temporality, rather than at the outset. This grounding identity must then, logically, make a reappearance. Such an ego desires a "full possession of being." But whence comes this desire, for has not Stein's ego precisely always been shadowed by the transcendental ideal of possession

---

36. Stein, *Finite and Eternal Being*, 56.

and self-presence?[37] Yet, if Stein recognizes that such a self-presence and divinization of the finite transcendental ego is heterodox and untenable, then she is left with no choice but to transpose this desire of self-presence, self-possession, and a full "possession of being" onto eternal being. This is necessarily the case if Stein is not prepared to abrogate the board of play of Husserlian method. "It [the finite ego] desires a being capable of embracing the totality of the ego's contents in one changeless present instead of its having to witness the continually repeated disappearance of all these contents almost at every moment they have ascended onto the stage of life." For is not such a being precisely the vision of transcendental consciousness that Stein forbids the finite ego and that she is worried about? Is Stein in danger here of transposing the dream of Idealism, namely, of the *intellektuelle Anschauung* onto God, thus thinking of God on a transcendental paradigm? In Stein's view it would seem that only God is capable of being the Transcendental Phenomenologist whose intellectual act and content is fully fulfilled in an everlasting eternal moment of intuition and self-presence. Thus what would be privation, for the finite ego, is only adequately fulfilled in the eternal moment of consciousness: of the infinite presence of the divine I to itself.[38] "The ego ... arrives at the idea of plenitude [*Idee der Fülle*]

---

37. Stein in elaborating and touching upon the "desire" of the intellect for the fullness of being is, again, not far away from Transcendental Thomism and its emphasis on the intellect's dynamic orientation towards absolute being à la Maréchal. However, Stein's thinking is not as hospitable as Rahner's thought to mystery, as seen, for example, in Rahner's thinking in the play back and forth between abstraction and conversion, which is the mark of "spirit in the world" opened onto the horizon of infinite and absolute being. This is because, for Rahner, this horizon remains unknown, and thus, in its unknownness is able to speak; see Karl Rahner, *Spirit in the World*, trans. William V. Dych (New York: Continuum, 1994), 406–8. Nor does Stein develop fully the affective and desiring nature of the intellect in the way that Rousselot—a precursor of Transcendental Thomism—does. For Rousselot, at least, harkens back to the Augustinian tradition, which sees love as propelling knowledge. As Rousselot says, "Reason itself is nothing other than a pure love of Being." Pierre Rousselot, SJ, *The Eyes of Faith: Answer to Two Attacks*, trans. Joseph Donceel, SJ (New York: Fordham University Press, 1990), 52. It would be interesting to more fully develop Stein's affinities and differences with Transcendental Thomism as I have here and there hinted at in this work. However, at this point it is sufficient to note that there are, indeed, similarities.

38. This presents a more-than-interesting and important theological question: What exactly does Stein think that the beatific vision is, or in what does it consist? Stein hints at an understanding of the beatific vision as fulfilling the teleological aim of human reason in its attempt to elaborate a full and total *Wissenschaft*. Thus when we are granted the light of glory it would, Stein thinks, allow "us to envision in one single glance what human reason has been trying to compile during millennia of its laborious efforts." Stein, *Finite and Eternal*

by crossing out from its own being what it has come to know as privation." But whence comes this privation and how arrive at the idea of plenitude?

The idea of plenitude is only reached, not through negation or privation, but from the model or ideal of the ego as fully self-possessive,

---

Being, 21. Stein states this in her discussion of Christian philosophy. Likewise, here Stein seems to imagine God as the supreme Phenomenologist whose I coincides with all of its contents in a completely fulfilled manner. This reading begs the question as to whether Stein does not envisage the beatific vision on a rationalistic model as the site of fulfillment for phenomenology's teleological goal of totality. Such a rationalistic vision of the beatific vision is fully countered in theologians such as Gregory of Nyssa, in his *The Life of Moses*, and taken up, in a contemporary manner, in Hart's *The Beauty of the Infinite*, where he combines Gregory of Nyssa's term *epektasis* with Przywara's *analogia entis* (as will be seen). Here Hart sees man as continually propelled outward towards the mysterious and never-ending divine infinity of God, which resides and continues on in eternity and the beatific vision. Likewise, Balthasar, in his understanding of divine becoming and futurity, sees the beatific vision as not expunging mystery—in a Hegelian manner—but rather as deepening mystery in a knowing that takes place within love. To prove this point Balthasar draws interestingly, not on Gregory of Nyssa here, but rather, as O'Regan states, Augustine's *Enarrationes in Psalmos*, 118, 26.6. See Cyril O'Regan, *The Anatomy of Misremembering: Von Balthasar's Response to Philosophical Modernity*, vol. 1: *Hegel* (New York: Crossroad, 2014), 141–44. Yet the most profound understanding of the beatific vision may not be given by a theologian but, indeed, by the greatest Catholic poet, namely, Dante. When Dante, in the *Paradiso*, comes to the *Empyrean* and sees the three circles of light, each of a different hue, he sees or discerns within these circles the human form of Christ. When Dante tries to contemplate the mystery of the Trinity and the hypostatic union therein he says, "that was not a flight for my wings." Dante Alighieri, *The Divine Comedy*, ed. David H. Higgins, trans. C. H. Sisson (Oxford: Oxford University Press, 2008), *Paradiso*, Canto XXXIII, line 139. The *Paradiso* ends in the words of union with the mystery of God's love, "But already my desire and my will were being turned like a wheel, all at one speed, by the Love which moves the sun and the other stars." Dante, *Paradiso*, Canto XXXIII, lines 142–45. Does not this vision of Dante give the exclamation point to the Balthasarian view that it is precisely the mystery of Christ that both saves and consummates negative theology? Will not this very mystery of the hypostatic union, now taken up into the eternally dynamic triune life of love, only be enhanced in our Eucharistic gazing upon the Body of Christ which, according to Dante, is the fleshed heart and center of the Love that is the Trinity itself? In this view, mystery can only be increased as the beatific vision is seen as a gaze of doxological reception into the very fleshed heart of God amid the mystery of the triune life. This theological detour is not insignificant, as it all-too-briefly shows how one's philosophical ideas become reflected in theological truths and mysteries. That is to say, where dynamic mystery resides at the heart of philosophical discourse (as it does for Przywara, Balthasar, and Hart, for example) then this affects one's theology, and, in this specific case, the beatific vision as open to mystery. On the other hand, if one's philosophical discourse is inhospitable to mystery, as is the tendency in Stein, then this likewise reflects itself in theological considerations, such as a more rationalistic interpretation of the beatific vision. This is why the *analogia entis* opens an analogy of discourses.

present, and enduring. ("The ego itself seems to be closer to pure being.") Thus, it is the affinity of the finite ego (in its sustained presence) to eternal being that underlies Stein's discourse through which the ego comes to an understanding of the idea of eternal presence. In crossing out temporal privations, the ego then once again encounters its secure ground from which it started and then projects the idea of eternal being from off of its self-present reflected ground onto God. Finitude is in danger of being a condition to be overcome in the ego's "desire" for the "full possession of being" that continually lurks in the ground and background of Stein's thought. Stein then, due to her Husserlian starting point and her version of the *Cogito*, is unable to fully elaborate the *positivity of finitude*, or in the words of Claudel, "the inexhaustible resources of our nothingness," which Chrétien so beautifully employs in his understanding of the positive "wound" of finitude.[39] By "crossing out" what Stein sees to be negative privations of our being, she is crossing out our unity with God *founded in and through our receptive difference from God*. Such a receptive difference is fully broken open by Przywara through his elaboration of our unity with God (essence and existence, which we share with God) as being the mark of our greatest difference from God, whose essence is his existence. The analogical dynamism of the nonidentity of essence and existence—to borrow from Chrétien—is our "wound," where we actively receive and serve in the midst of our positive *mysterium* and brokenness from out of our distance and difference from God. Przywara's logic, again, works by establishing unity through difference, distance, and asymmetry, while

---

39. See Jean-Louis Chrétien, *The Ark of Speech*, trans. Andrew Brown (London: Routledge, 2004), especially "Wounded Speech," 17–38. If there is one phenomenologist that comes close to fully calling into question Husserlian method, it is not Marion, but Chrétien. Chrétien's phenomenological voice is entirely unique and extraordinarily beautiful. Out of the "new" phenomenologists, Chrétien is by far, in my view, the most profound and enticing voice writing today. Claudel remains a key and enduring influence on Chrétien's thought in opening a poetics where "the eye listens" (a phrase he borrows from the title of Claudel's book on Flemish painting). For perhaps the greatest piece ever written on Claudel, see the haunting essay of Jean-Louis Chrétien, "Like a Liquid Bond," in *Hand to Hand: Listening to the Work of Art*, trans. Stephen E. Lewis (New York: Fordham University Press, 2003), 130–51. Yet one can pose a valid, but unfortunate question regarding Chrétien's work. That is, given the deeply idiosyncratic and theologically poetic voice of Chrétien, it can be asked: Will he ever be given the proper attention and acknowledgment he deserves in academia today? Is he thus fated to be forgotten, like the prophetic voice of the great Max Picard? (I am indebted to my dear friend Patrick Ryan Cooper for drawing this very apt analogy between Chrétien and Picard.) Chrétien, of course, knows Picard's work well.

Stein's logic works by establishing difference through unity, affinity, and mutuality.

This is why Stein must cross out our differences and temporal wounds in order to reach the idea of a fully transparent and self-possessed being, but a transparent being that is already inaugurated and founded in her discourse and version of the *Cogito*. In doing so, is Stein not merely seeing the transcendental shadows and images of the autonomous ego, which haunt her discourse, as an image of God in man, thereby imagining God on the model of the self-sufficient deity of the transcendental ego? My worries here are too great as to Stein's inability, due to her predetermined board of play, to fully expunge and exorcise these wraith-like shadows from her discourse, not to answer this question in the affirmative. This affirmative answer will become fully clear in the next section. Suffice it to say that there is enough here to not embrace the way in which Stein arrives—through her method of phenomenological immanence—at the idea of eternal being.

The Analogia Entis *Univocally Conceived*

Stein opens the discussion of her final formulation of the *analogia entis* by referring to the Thomistic view that, in the being of God, there are "no contraries of potency and act."[40] In God, all potency is fully fulfilled and actualized. In this reference to act/potency, in God, she is once again referring to the real distinction, which is null and void in God. His very essence is his existence, i.e., pure act. This signals to the "preeminence of the eternal and infinite, which is so difficult to grasp because, in the eternal and infinite, being can no longer be separated or distinguished from existence. On the other hand, in all finite things being and existence differ."[41] "Finally, the first being is called the *first existent* (*primum ens*). But *ens*—as in the case with all transcendental terms—is predicated only in an analogical sense, i.e., in the sense of that *analogia entis* which describes the peculiar relationship that exists between finite and eternal being and which permits us to apply the term "being" to both terms of the relationship on a *common constitutive element of meaning* [*gemeinsamer*

---

40. Stein, *Finite and Eternal Being*, 335. For the whole of this discussion see §4 of the fourth chapter, titled "The First Being and the *Analogia Entis*," 335–54.

41. Stein, *Finite and Eternal Being*, 335.

Sinnbestand] [italics mine]."[42] Here, once again, the enigmatic reading of the real distinction is encountered. Stein seems to allow for some sort of metaphysical distinction between finite and eternal being, but one that is mitigated, and perhaps even swallowed up, by an overarching epistemic interpretation that seeks to univocally apply the one term, "being," to both God and man.

Such an application, in turn, allows for both God and man to be set within an epistemic matrix of meaning. This allows Stein to bridge and encompass God and man in a phenomenological theory of meaning that seeks to elaborate the unitariness of being, understood univocally. Yet this passage differs from the passage pertaining to the real distinction insofar as Stein here explicitly states that the task and function of the *analogia entis* "permits us to apply the term being to both terms of the relationship on a common constitutive element of meaning." That is to say, the *analogia entis* is read in the same way as real distinction. The *analogia entis* provides the epistemic means of adjudicating the difficulty of the relation between God and man by plotting a relation of meaning between finite and eternal being. This is at risk of losing the abyssal difference and distance between God and man. Stein reads the *analogia entis* as providing the conceptual means of univocally uniting the being of God with the being of man. Thus in keeping with her logic of meaning the *analogia entis* is read, at the outset, on the basis of the *ens commune* and thus a *tertium quid*.

Przywara is perfectly correct to be worried about Stein's move here, which subsumes the *analogia entis* under the common banner of a *neutral idea* of being. This problem arises from the inadequacies of Stein's phenomenological point of departure, which views both finite and eternal being from within the phenomenological intuition of essence. Further, this method then views both finite and eternal being as different modes or degrees of being opened to the purview of essential seeing. Therefore, within this univocal point of reference, enacted through a phenomenological intuition of essence, the being of God is in danger of appearing merely as quantitatively different from finite being (as a kind of heightened mode or degree of being) as opposed to a robust qualitative difference and distance through which unity is founded and transected by an ever-greater dissimilarity.[43] Such a view endangers both the Fourth Lateran Council's

---

42. Stein, *Finite and Eternal Being*, 335–36.
43. For Przywara's critique of Stein see Erich Przywara, "Edith Stein and Simone Weil: Two Fundamental Philosophical Themes," in *Analogia Entis: Metaphysics: Original Structure*

accentuation on difference and dissimilarity of the *Deus semper maior*, and the *analogia proportionis* of Aquinas, which puts the exclamation mark on this Council. This is done by rigorously understanding analogy on the basis of two X's marked by a "double 'alterity' of one to another," thus ensuring that analogy is precisely only that, namely, an analogy that finally breaks off into an unknowing and mystery of otherness of the *Deus semper maior*.[44] I will have much more to say concerning Przywara's ultimate shape and construal of the *analogia entis*. However, Przywara's worry that Stein's vision of analogy endangers the difference stressed by the Fourth Lateran Council and the Thomistic *analogia proportionis* brings me back to the question of how Stein's explicit endorsement of the text of the Fourth Lateran Council and the *maior dissimilitudo* finally plays out.

That is, the question must be asked: Does Stein, under the strain and weight of her logic, show a real impatience towards the accenting of mystery and otherness stressed in the Fourth Lateran Council and the Thomistic *analogia proportionis*? And further, if the Fourth Lateran Council and Thomistic *analogia proportionis* were followed by Stein, would this not demand that Stein give up on her attempt to offer a unified phenomenological theory of being's meaning? And further, would not this following only allow a *kataphasis* to take place in the distance of *apophasis*, which is reflective of the analogical-binding of thought being taken up in the dy-

---

and Universal Rhythm, trans. John R. Betz and David Bentley Hart (Grand Rapids: Eerdmans, 2014), 602–3. My critique of Stein reaches many of the same conclusions as Przywara's, but does so by a different means. Namely, my avenue of critique began with the dangers of Stein's foundational view of Christian philosophy and then moved to her immediate starting point of the being of the I as a point of foundational immediacy from which all other intuitions of essences takes place. Przywara, on the other hand, bases his more fully in the formal principle of phenomenology, namely, identity, which is methodologically enacted in a direct noetic encounter with essence. And although I am in complete agreement with Przywara on this point and have referred to this principle throughout this work, my intent was to show more fully what is implicit in Przywara, namely, how this principle fully comes to light in Stein's version of the *Cogito* and is rooted therein. Thus, if I am in agreement with Przywara that Stein remains a faithful follower of Husserl, I have more fully tried to show these Husserlian hauntings in Stein's discourse (both in her interpretation of Christian philosophy and her version of the *Cogito*) than Przywara stresses in his short but insightful critique. Furthermore, if my critique of Stein differs from Przywara's it is in content and emphasis, but not in form. For in the latter I am in complete agreement with him as to the ultimate shape and limitations of Stein's discourse, and indeed, the limitations of phenomenological method in general, when left by itself without the aid of an analogically abyssal and exterior metaphysics.

44. Przywara, "Stein and Weil," 603.

namic movement of knowing in an unknowing, thereby marking thought itself as reflective of, and participating in, the *mysterium* of the positive and dynamic infinity of the God who is pure act, thus escaping all placement within univocal meaning?

Such hesitancy towards the mystery of the *analogia proportionis* comes to utterance in the following passage.[45] Stein's tactical move here seeks to show the need to fill out the metaphysics of Aquinas, and his understanding of *analogia proportionis*, with a phenomenological-ontology. In so doing she commences her move towards an ultimate phenomenological and personalistic reimagining of the *analogia entis*.

> Does this mean, however, that there is no distinction whatever between God's being (i.e., existence) and God's essence? Saint Thomas uses such phrases as "God is his goodness, his life," etc., or "God is his being." These predications endeavor to pronounce in the form of a judgement something which can actually no longer be pronounced in the form of a judgement. For every judgement requires an analytical articulation [*Zergliederung*], but that which is perfectly and absolutely simple does not permit of analytical articulation. At best we might perhaps legitimately say, "God is—God," and we might take such a statement as an admission of the impossibility of defining the divine essence by anything other than God himself. In other words, the name God denotes essence and being (i.e., existence) in undivided unity.[46]

45. Stein, *Finite and Eternal Being*, 337–42.

46. Stein, *Finite and Eternal Being*, 342. The context and placement of this passage is important. This passage follows Stein's brief discussion of analogy in Aristotle and Aquinas ("1. The Meaning of *Analogia Entis* in Aristotle and Saint Thomas Aquinas") where Stein quotes from Aquinas (*De Ver.* q. 2, a. 11, corp., art.), once again avowing the *maior dissimilitudo* protected by Aquinas's understanding of *analogia proportionis* where "The infinite distance between God and the creature is thereby not diminished." Stein, *Finite and Eternal Being*, 337. Yet this passage is directly preceded by the opening of §4 where, it was just seen, Stein sees the *analogia entis* as allowing one to "apply the term being to both terms of the relationship on a common constitutive element of meaning." Thus, Stein's admission of the *maior dissimilitudo* of analogy is first preceded and set into motion only after she has affirmed the functionality of analogy, as providing the grounds to establish a common point of reference and meaning (in the same way that Stein only seeks to decenter the self—via temporality—after the grounding of the self in intuitive self-presence). Further, with the ending of the discussion of God's simplicity (the coincidence of his being and essence), in part 2, Stein's continual impatience with pure metaphysical speculations in the manner of Aristotle and Aquinas comes to the fore. This was also seen in her attempt to enlist the *analogia entis* in a phenomenological direction.

Stein here is concerned with the radical state of unknowing and negative theology that the Thomistic notion of divine simplicity puts forward in its limiting of thought and a theory of meaning which she wishes to elaborate. Nor is it too much to hazard that Przywara's stress on the analogical mystery of knowing and participation *in mystery* is also implicated in this worry, given Stein's explicit but complicated endorsement of Przywara's touchstone of the Fourth Lateran Council. But, if this is not enough to confirm my suspicion of Stein's reservation concerning the implications the mystery of divine simplicity would have on a phenomenological philosophy or theory of being's common meaning, then it is enough simply to turn to the following sentence of this passage: "I shall now attempt to approach the ultimate ontological questions from an *entirely different point of view* [italics mine]."[47] Yet, what is this "point of view" that seeks an alternative to the difficulty of thinking the mystery of divine simplicity and the analogical-binding of *kataphasis* to *apophasis* through which reason is open to, and supplemented by, a participation in mystery (*reductio in mysterium*)? If Stein is to achieve a phenomenological theory of meaning where finite and eternal being come under the banner of a "common constitutive element of meaning" (i.e., the *analogia entis* as the *ens commune*) what hermeneutic road is open to her given the restricted board of play?

Stein is worried about the radical implication of divine simplicity, insofar as the divine simplicity surpasses "analytical judgments" that are unable to take hold of the mystery of divine being and its energy of simplicity, which marks ultimate predication of the divine as impossible. This is why scholars such as Beauvais and Secretan realize that Stein is not interested in the "classical expression of analogy that aims at creating a link between God and world by correlating essence and existence."[48] Rather, Stein is interested in an "analogy of the personal 'I.'"[49] Yet such a correlation of essence/existence works, in Przywara, by precisely enacting a unity with God by establishing difference and *mysterium* at the heart of creaturely being. This, in turn, provides a receptive site of openness to otherness that is rooted in man's obediential potency (this will be discussed shortly) towards the mystery of God's being *and* supernatural life. This interpretation sees man's fullness and completion as residing in *a participation in*

---

47. Stein, *Finite and Eternal Being*, 342.
48. Chantal Beauvais, "Edith Stein and Modern Philosophy," in *Husserl and Stein*, ed. Richard Feist and William Sweet (Washington, DC: Council for Research in Values and Philosophy, 2003), 7.
49. Beauvais, "Edith Stein," 7.

the positive mystery of God's dynamic flowing and replete infinity. Stein is uninterested in such a correlation between essence/existence, which in an adequately interpreted rendition of Aquinas stresses our unbridgeable difference from God.

Why this uninterest? The answer is to be found on two accounts that have been stressed throughout this formally critical dialogue. First, Stein advances an overly ambitious interpretation of Christian philosophy that aims to synthesize all of the truths of revelation with the truths of reason, therefore viewing philosophy as a foundational science that teleologically aims at or towards totality. Second, following from this, Stein's avowed task is to elaborate a theory of being's meaning plotted within a narrative grounded in the I's experiential and reflexive intuition of itself. Both of these points come to fruition here and assume a prominent place in Stein's ultimate performance of an egological analogy that seeks to lay out a "common constitutive element of meaning" between the being of God and the creature. Stein's narrative of being's meaning thus operates on a flattened and neutral board, namely, the univocality of the *ens commune*. To confirm this, one has to take Stein's theological "detour" (Beauvais),[50] where, for the first time in the text, she makes explicit use of revelation. But, as was seen, this theological "detour" is fraught with many dangers, not the least being an instrumentalization of theological truth, which is used to fulfill Christian philosophy's aim towards totality. How, then, is this instrumentalization and "detour" deployed in Stein's recourse to the naming of the divine by the Divine Self in Exodus 3:14?

Stein's demurral at the Thomistic metaphysical articulation of the simplicity of God's mystery is rooted in her desire to place our knowledge of God within a reflexive experiential base. Such a base, in turn, allows one to institute a common term of reference that allows for thinking our similarity with God. To do this, Stein must turn to the personal character of revelation, and the speaking God who declares his personal being as opposed to the unknowing of the *actus purus*. This is because Stein is worried that such mysterious simplicity crosses out all human conceptions, experiences, and predications, and, therefore, the possibility of being's unitary meaning, in both its finite and eternal guise. Revelation is needed in order to surpass the limits of a philosophical knowing that ends in the simplicity of unknowing. These fears are mitigated by turning to revelation and Exodus 3:14 where God does not declare himself as "'I

50. Beauvais, "Edith Stein," 6.

am being [*das Sein*]'" or "'I am he who exists' [*der Seiende*]," but "'I am who *I am.*'"[51] Stein here is entirely anticipating the great debate concerning the first Name of God, which was to explode on the scene anew in post-Heideggerian discourse.[52] In this post-Heideggerian debate all equations of God and being are thus viewed as expressive of antiquarian, substantialist, and onto-theological metaphysics, which have domesticated and "Hellenized" Christian discourse. This important debate can by no means be gone into here but it is, nevertheless, interesting to note that Stein shares certain sympathies and worries with Marion concerning the Thomistic naming of God (and thus, by implication, Gilson's thesis of the "metaphysics of exodus"), though Stein would by no means embrace Marion's stance of radical apophaticism.[53] Stein's answer is a personalist interpretation of the divine Name where God names himself as "I am" or, in other words, "*being in person.*"[54]

Revelation provides what reason cannot, namely, a radically personal understanding of a God who speaks in the first person singular. Stein, in her elaboration of analogy, seeks to supplement and correct the seemingly impersonal mystery of the *actus purus* of the Thomistic tradition. But in what manner does Stein do this? Is Stein demanding that revelation be interpreted exclusively on the basis of itself, thereby protecting it from unwarranted philosophical and conceptual intrusion, as enacted and inflected differently by theologians such as Barth and Balthasar? Or is Stein rather using theological truths and revelation to fulfill the task of Christian philosophy's aim towards totality and synthesis in order to elaborate a

---

51. Stein, *Finite and Eternal Being*, 342. It is by no means possible to raise, I dare say, the almost undecidable debate about the translation of this enigmatic Hebrew text that has provoked a whole plethora of translations in the twentieth century alone. Suffice it to say that Stein sees herself here as holding to the Augustinian interpretation and translation of this phrase. See Stein, *Finite and Eternal Being*, 595, endnote 22.

52. Though, of course, this debate has precedence in the great tradition as well, as it was Aquinas who first assigned the name of being to God as the primary instance of divine naming as opposed to Augustine, Pseudo-Dionysius, and Bonaventure.

53. For just some of the numerous literature on the debate of divine naming, see Paul Ricoeur, "From Interpretation to Translation," in *Thinking Biblically: Exegetical and Hermeneutical Studies*, trans. David Pellauer (Chicago: University of Chicago Press, 1998), 341–55; for a characteristically postmodern and post-Heideggerian reading see Richard Kearney, *The God Who May Be* (Bloomington: Indiana University Press, 2001), 20–38; and for the classic expression of this debate see Jean-Luc Marion, *God without Being: Hors-Texte*, trans. Thomas A. Carlson (Chicago: University of Chicago Press, 1991), 73–83, 102–7.

54. Stein, *Finite and Eternal Being*, 343.

unified theory of being's meaning? My answer, as already seen in the above, consists in the latter. Yet it remains to be seen how exactly Stein seeks to implement her theory of being's unified meaning via a personalist and egological reading of Exodus 3:14.

Stein thinks there is an impasse and limit to the Thomistic correlation between essence and existence of finite and eternal being, one that ends in a mystery of unnameability. Thus, in turning to revelation and the divine naming that occurs in Exodus 3:14, Stein believes that one encounters a counterbalance and possibility of both a renaming and an elaboration of a unified theory of being's meaning. How so? When one turns to Exodus 3:14 one encounters the reflexive experience of the divine I with itself coming to expression in language: the reflexive language of "I am."[55] "The name by which every person designates himself or herself qua person is the name 'I' [*Ich*]. Only an existent who in its being is conscious of its being and simultaneously conscious of its differentiation from every other existent can call itself an 'I.'"[56] Here one encounters an utterance that is expressive of absolute Personhood and Spirit (constituted by reflexive and/or conscious self-embrace) whose very egological life coincides with its being. Moreover, all of the contents of the divine Ego are fully actualized and present within a perfectly coinciding moment of self-presence: being *and* life. "In the case of that I whose very being is life we can at best understand that *I* and *life* (or *being*) are not two different things but inseparably one. They are the *personally formed plenitude of being.*"[57] God is absolute personal Spirit or *Geist*.

Here one does not encounter "lacunae" or nothingness within the ground of being which is personal Spirit, as was the case with the nothingness encountered within the being of the finite I beset by temporal distention. Further, as was seen with the discussion of transcendental truth, finite *Geist* was open to being's transcendental appearing (the synchrony of being and spirit), which thus marked and defined being as meaning (the meaning of being is the being of meaning). Here, then, in absolute, eternal, and personal *Geist*, which admits no separation of its being from its life, being is meaning and meaning is being: total synchronic disclosure, eternal self-presence. Such self-presence has only hitherto been intimated in the self-presence of the finite *Cogito*, which subtracts its temporal wounds and difference in order to analogically arrive at the *idea* of eternal being.

---

55. Stein, *Finite and Eternal Being*, 343.
56. Stein, *Finite and Eternal Being*, 343.
57. Stein, *Finite and Eternal Being*, 345.

Yet, as I argued, there is a problem: that is, the idea of plenitude was not really arrived at through subtraction, but rather by a return to the finite I's ground and starting point of secure immediate self-presence, which Stein only belatedly tried to decenter with her discussion of temporality.[58]

Stein's appeal to Exodus 3:14 is precisely a "detour" in order to re-inaugurate and institute her view of analogy as a "common constitutive element of meaning" or the *ens commune* and *not* a thinking fully of God on the basis of his own self-revelation or declaration. Her purpose is to elaborate a foundational view of Christian philosophy that aims towards a unified theory of being's meaning by synthesizing all of the truths of revelation with the truths of reason—thereby teleologically aiming towards full and total disclosure—now obtained in the infinite life of *Geist* revealed in her reading of Exodus 3:14. Such a move is made possible by viewing or seeing the common element of reflexive experience—the conscious self-embrace of the I—found in both the finite I *and* the infinite I, as precisely the *ens commune* or *tertium quid*. This is how Stein substantiates a unified theory of experiential and reflexive meaning, thereby bridging the gap between finite and eternal being.[59] The reflexive experience of the finite I becomes the Ariadne's thread Stein follows towards the divine I's reflexive experience given in the revelation of "*I* am": though, in this instance, the thread lacks its saving purpose. In Stein's appeal to Exodus 3:14 she thinks that she has found warrant for a common element of meaning sought for in her phenomenological reimagining of the *analogia entis*. That is, Stein has found the commonality between the finite and eternal I: the *ens commune* now situated in a reflexive and experientially based phenomenological-ontology and a view of Christian philosophy as "the idea of a *perfectum opus rationis*."

Here one is at the end because one has returned to the beginning of Steinian discourse and her narration on philosophy and being. In Stein's turn to revelation and Exodus 3:14, one finds the intentions of her Christian philosophy to synthesize theological truth and philosophical truth within the frame of a theory of being's unified meaning, elaborated through a phenomenological-ontology, fulfilled. Such a phenomenologi-

---

58. Stein again draws on this argument of subtraction in her section on Exodus; see Stein, *Finite and Eternal Being*, 344.

59. As usual Beauvais—following Secretan—is a more-than-able reader of Stein in hitting upon Stein's reinterpretation of the *ens commune* on the grounds of a reflexive and experiential sharing between the finite I and infinite I, though Beauvais does not seem to be at all worried about this move as am I. See Beauvais, "Edith Stein," 7.

cal-ontology grounded itself in the immediate, experiential, and reflexive version of the Steinian *Cogito*. From such a base Stein then proceeded to phenomenologically reinterpret the *analogia entis* and the *distinctio realis* in a univocal direction (*ens commune*) that sought a "common constitutive element of meaning." The univocal and epistemic direction and lens through which Stein read the *distinctio realis* and the *analogia entis* is now seen as accomplished by Stein's interpretation of the *ens commune* as the I's experiential and reflexive self-experience *comprising both finite and eternal being* (her unity and theory of being's overarching meaning),[60] all of which came fully to light in Stein's turn to Exodus 3:14 through which she sought to accomplish all of these aspirations by seeing, in this biblical text, *the same kind* of reflexive experience in the divine I that was found, at the outset, in her version of the *Cogito*: the starting point of her entire philosophical endeavor.

In doing so, Stein runs the risk of seeing God as the *analogon* of man rather than seeing man as a faint, flickering, and distant *analogon* of God. She thus runs the danger of compromising the *maior dissimilitudo* of the divine by transposing a version of the *Cogito*, and a vision of man as immediately and intuitively self-possessed and self-present, onto the infinite glory of God. Such a move makes the divine look too much like, and similar to, her egological vision of the self, which was haunted by the ghosts and traces of Husserl's transcendentalism. And thus the patrimony of the apocryphal story of *apotheosis* told in much of modern philosophy, which places an eternal and divine-like mask upon the finite I. By viewing the *analogia entis* on a univocal model or grid of the *ens commune* phenomenologically rendered and reduced by the methodologically secure base of the reflexive and experiential I, Stein ends up, however unwittingly so, tying God to the methodological I of modern philosophy. Stein was never fully able to abdicate the methodological and egological board of play set down by Husserl (and by implication the Cartesian and Transcendental tradition). And because of this Stein ends with an analogical vision of God too much in danger of viewing God from the ground of the anthropocentric view of modern philosophy's reflexively and experientially grounded site.

60. Stein explicitly says that this is what she is doing, when she states, "The relationship between the divine 'I am' and the multiplicity of finite existents is the primordial *analogia entis*. All finite being shares in *a common meaning* [italics mine] because it has its archetypal image [*Ur-bild*] in the divine 'I am.'" Stein, *Finite and Eternal Being*, 346–47. Thus once again showing that Stein's appeal to Revelation, in her view, enacts the link or commonality that enables a unified theory of being's meaning.

DIFFERING REIMAGININGS OF THE *ANALOGIA ENTIS*

The ghosts that haunt Steinian discourse thus, unbeknownst to her, carve out a space of secularity within her Christian philosophy that endangers the distance and glory of the *Deus semper maior*. This is done by, unknowingly, pulling God into an anthropocentric orbit or constellation that stresses unity, mutuality, commonality, identity, and sameness. The weight of Stein's narration on philosophy and being, which moved towards totality, foundation, and immediate self-presence, is too heavy. This is due to the fact that Stein's discourse is predestined by the prior and anterior field of play of modern method. Stein's analogical conception of God must, by necessity, be brought down by the gravitational pull of her reflexive and experientially based phenomenological-ontology. Throughout *Finite and Eternal Being*, Stein often signals to a proper diagnosis of the ills that trouble and beset modern philosophy. She is, nevertheless, unable to fully apply an adequate cure. Stein has already let the Trojan horse of Husserlian foundationalism and method into the walls of her discourse. And given these nocturnal specters that haunt Stein's discourse, her thought is overly laden by the anthropocentric and foundational principles of modernity. Another road must be taken, if one is to push forward and elaborate a pleromatic postmodern Christian vision. This road must radically question, encounter, and counter the secular post-Christian narrative pull of philosophical modernity. Przywara's analogical metaphysics of difference offers such a path of creative resistance.

One final possible objection must be briefly dealt with: Have I shortchanged Steinian discourse by not having dealt with her Trinitarian ontology, which seeks to move away from the egological underpinnings of her thought by enlisting *the* theologoumenon of the Christian tradition into her discourse? Are not my fears mitigated by the self-giving life of the three Divine Persons, which, in the second half of *Finite and Eternal Being*, are read as the paragon of all finite existents? Stein turns to the Trinity in order to more fully elaborate the meaning of being as consisting in a community of persons, as found in the intra-divine life. Stein sees herself following the Augustinian tradition by enlisting Augustine's psychological model of the Trinity and his theology of relations in Book 15 of *De Trinitate*, which "may well be called the fountainhead of all subsequent Trinitarian theology."[61] But, insofar as Stein models the divine self-knowledge on "immediacy," which is the "common element" between our "self-knowledge" and the divine knowledge (which was reached via

---

61. Stein, *Finite and Eternal Being*, 355.

methodological reduction), she runs the risk of being unable to see the very analogical mediation and/or relations within the Trinity itself. This mediation is enacted through the spiration and *condilectio* of the Holy Spirit as an authentic analogical mediation or between—between the Father and the Son. A thinker such as Milbank—drawing from Desmond—perfectly sees this enduring analogical between. Such a principle as a "third" or the Holy Spirit is thus the "principle of analogy," as Milbank profoundly states.[62]

This movement of analogy and mediation within the very intra-divine life prevents the gaze of the Father and the Son from being a pure self-reflective embrace, or a seeing of the same in the different (as in a mirror), and thus merely the embrace of the same difference. Rather, it is only when a third term, or better, Person, comes into play—the Holy Spirit—that the love between the Father and Son is precisely the spiration of the difference of an analogical between. This, in turn, shows the love between the Father and Son to be a love always already set within analogical difference and mediation and not just the self-reflected love of the Father and Son. Without this difference the between would be abolished in a moment of self-reflective seeing of sameness in difference, unity in equivocity, equivocity in unity, and thus neither real unity nor real difference (i.e., an analogical unity-in-difference, an enduring never-to-be-closed in-between). Such an analogical view of the Trinity, expressed in the mediating role of the Holy Spirit, allows for the real relationality or difference within the perichoretic dance of the Trinitarian life of Love. Here an analogical metaphysics reaches its apex because, if creaturely being was seen to be an analogy (made up of difference), it is because it is modeled upon the difference that the Trinity itself *Is*. Divine Being is thus co-primeval, co-extensive, and convertible with the difference of relation and analogical event, meaning that there is no divine unicity outside or behind the relations themselves: *God Is in Himself Relationship*. This is why Przywara ends the *Analogia Entis* with speaking of the relation in-between the creaturely and God as being defined by the sway of "the intra-divine itself, the hyper-transcendent expression of which is the theologoumenon of the intra-divine 'relations' (*relationes*), which *are* the Father, Son and Holy Spirit."[63] In the Trinity,

---

62. John Milbank, "The Double Glory or Paradox versus Dialectics: On Not Quite Agreeing with Slavoj Žižek," in *The Monstrosity of Christ: Paradox or Dialectic*, ed. Creston Davis (Cambridge, MA: MIT Press, 2009), 186–88.

63. Przywara, *Analogia Entis*, 314.

Being *Is* Event and Event *Is* Being. Here Being *Is* Relation and Relation *Is* Being. Here there is a Unity-in-Difference and a Difference-in-Unity. Yet none of this takes place or occurs before, behind, above, or underneath the *circumcessio* of the relations of Persons. The Trinity *Is* a performance of consubstantial and relational Love.

Such an analogical view of relation, in the Trinity, is protected in thinkers like Przywara, Balthasar, Desmond, Milbank, Hart, and O'Regan. On the other hand, Stein's logic of immediacy and the invocation of an "I, thou" model of the Trinity is in danger of missing the analogical mediation present—through the Holy Spirit—within the dynamism of the Trinity itself. Stein is thus in danger of seeing and emphasizing the I in the thou and the thou in the I, modeled upon the self-reflective gaze. Does this open Stein up to the charge of a weak and faint form of Sabellianism or modalism insofar as the dyadic gaze of the Father and Son has a tendency to return to the reflexive and immediate knowledge of the divine I or Father? Once again, my worries about the constraints of Stein's logic remain, even in her invocation of the Trinity.

The *Analogia Entis* as the *Commercium* of the *Analogia Caritatis*

In the following, as with the preceding discussion of Stein, Przywara's guiding logic and narration on philosophy and being will be followed to its consummation. This will be done by tracing the outcome of Przywarian optics as this comes to full light in his ultimate reimagining of the *analogia entis*. In seeking this continuity of vision and logic I will turn to the height and depth of his ultimate analogical vision.[64] In advancing my argument and preference for Przywara's construal of the *analogia entis* over Stein's, I proceed in four steps. First, I open with a brief excursus on the Fourth Lateran Council and Joachim of Fiore in order to show the paramount import of this council and the need for a contemporary analogical metaphysics in light of the recrudescence of Joachimism in modern discourse. Second, I then proceed to discuss Przywara's analogical interpretation of the principle of noncontradiction. Third, the preceding, in turn, sets up Przywara's vision of the *potentia oboedientialis* as constituting man's finite and creaturely being as being opened up towards, and by, the supernatural. Fourth, all three meet in Przywara's ultimate vision of the *analogia entis* as

---

64. See §6, Przywara, *Analogia Entis*, 198–237.

an asymmetrical and obedient relation of creaturely service to or towards the ever-greater Christian God of love.

An Excursus on the Fourth Lateran Council and Joachim of Fiore

There is no better place to begin an elucidation of Przywara's vision of the *analogia entis* than with the fountainhead and touchstone of Przywara's re-interpretation of *analogia entis*, namely, the Fourth Lateran Council (1215) and its resistance to Joachimite apocalyptic and pneumatic discourse, which seeks to undercut the *maior dissimilitudo* of the ever-greater God by enacting a confluence and identity between God and man. Through looking at this, one is then able to glimpse how the *analogia entis* can be deployed as a counter to the intensifying apocalyptic stage of philosophical modernity in light of my reading of philosophical modernity. (Recall my comments in the Introduction.) This confluence has had a large-scale recrudescence or reactivation within modern discourse, not the least being the titanic storming of Olympus by Hegelianism and its *apotheosis* of man, which evacuates and abolishes the divine distance and glory of God. God is thus viewed as becoming in and through the agon of history. And a history viewed as the very theogonic agon within God himself.[65] God's

---

65. This recrudescence of Joachimite discourse, especially in Hegelian discourse, has been noted by many thinkers in the twentieth century such as Przywara, Balthasar, de Lubac, Ratzinger, Löwith, Voegelin, and Jacob Taubes (the latter from a positive perspective). Yet the origin of this affinity between Hegel and Joachim originated in the nineteenth century with the Hegel critic and theologian Franz Anton Staudenmaier (1800–1856), the "fourth wheel" of the Tübingen School. (I am indebted to Cyril O'Regan for pointing out to me this nineteenth-century precedent of the Hegel/Joachim thesis in Staudenmaier.) For O'Regan's rehabilitation of Staudenmaier and his influence on Balthasar's resistance to Hegel's misremembering of the Christian tradition, see O'Regan, *Misremembering*, 1:276–90. Voegelin has done some very interesting work on Joachim's thought. Voegelin sees Joachim as "the Gnostic father of modernity" and very much the precursor of Hegel. For some illuminating and thought-provoking ideas on this matter, consult Eric Voegelin, *Science, Politics and Gnosticism: Two Essays* (Washington, DC: Regnery, 1968), 63–68; as well as Eric Voegelin, *History of Political Ideas*, vol. 2: *The Middle Ages to Aquinas* (Columbia: University of Missouri Press, 1997), 126–34. Voegelin himself was influenced by Przywara, de Lubac, and Balthasar as he attests to in one of his letters to Strauss. I will refrain here from mentioning O'Regan's important contribution and movement beyond Voegelin in regard to the Gnostic return thesis, as it will be spoken about in Part 2. For the groundbreaking text on Gnosticism in the twentieth century see Hans Jonas, *The Gnostic Religion: The Message of the Alien God and the Beginning of Christianity*, 3rd ed. (Boston: Beacon Press, 2001). This text was originally writ-

transcendent being, in Hegelianism, is thus sacrificed on the secularized altar of time, process, and progress and, in being, emptied of all genuine divinity. In returning to the Fourth Lateran Council and Przywara's analogical interpretation of this council, one is able to offer resistance to any and all forms of identity-metaphysics (whether premodern, modern, or covertly so in postmodern discourse) that would attempt to collapse the uncollapsible distance between the human and the divine. The meaning and import of the Fourth Lateran Council is just as relevant today, indeed more so, than it was in 1215. In light of this fact, this part must also be read as pertaining to the present moment and not just a mere historical medieval relic of a bygone past. For no one, more than Przywara, has accentuated the significance of this Council for present-day discourse and its current apocalyptic viability and applicability.

Przywara does not mention Joachim of Fiore (c. 1130/35–1202) in *Analogia Entis*. Nevertheless, insofar as the second chapter of the Fourth Lateran Council's dogmatic ruling on the *maior dissimilitudo* consists in a condemnation of Joachim's collective view of the Trinity, Joachim's presence is everywhere felt, insofar as the *maior dissimilitudo* is the linchpin of *Analogia Entis*.[66] Moreover, Joachim's presence is also felt by proxy via Przywara's great resistance towards Hegel's *Aufhebung* of mystery and *theo*logy through his critical retrieval of the Augustinian-Dionysian-Thomistic tradition and an elaboration of *philo*sophy and *theo*logy as a *reductio in mysterium*. This is to say, if Hegel can rightfully be seen as a Joachim *redivivus* then it follows: to resist Hegel is to resist Joachim and to resist Joachim is to resist Hegel, albeit in different but not altogether dissimilar ways. Thus, Przywara's brilliant contemporary analogical reading of the Fourth Lateran Council must be partly (or, perhaps, more than just partly) seen as a resistance to both the monistic collapsing of the analogical interval and the faulty appropriation of the Johannine tradition of love and spirit in German Idealism in general, and Hegel and his intellectual progenies in particular. German Idealism and Hegelianism are thus viewed by Przywara

---

ten prior to the great discovery of the Nag-Hammadi Gnostic library in Egypt (1945). Jonas later added two chapters to this work. Chapter 12, 290–319, deals with the Nag-Hammadi discoveries, while Chapter 13, 290–319, provisionally sets forth a Gnostic return thesis in Existentialism and Nihilism, and Heidegger in particular. I am indebted to Professor Peter Sampo—a student and disciple of Voegelin—and his superb lectures on Gnosticism in my undergrad years at Thomas More College of Liberal Arts for my entrance into, and still partial grasp of, Gnosticism.

66. Denziger, *The Sources of Catholic Dogma*, 431–32.

as a metamorphosing reactivation of Joachimism and its privileging of identity between God and man, as well as Joachimism's one-sided elevation of the fourth gospel, thereby undermining the synoptic gospels, Acts, and Paul's epistles in order to read history in a pneumatic direction of love's spiritual freedom.[67]

Przywara's burgeoning Christian apocalyptic resistance to counterfeit apocalyptic comes fully to light when one turns to his 1940 essay "The Scope of Analogy as a Fundamental Catholic Form," thus making explicit what was already implicit in *Analogia Entis*.[68] Here Przywara fully lays out the affinity between Joachimism and Idealism (as well as Western Theosophy à la Baader and Eastern Sophiology à la Berdyaev and Bulgakov) and, in particular, Schelling and Hegel, with regard to their radical identification of God and man.[69] With this return of Joachimism, in both its Eastern

---

67. The Johannine trope and distortion of the fourth gospel present in German Idealism, running through Fichte, Schelling, Hölderlin, and Hegel, is an important symptom through which the diagnosis of the return of Joachimism, in German Idealism, is partly reached for thinkers such as Przywara, Balthasar, and O'Regan: though all of these thinkers will have more positive readings of a genuine Johannine element—to a greater or lesser degree—in Hölderlin (an element totally denied by Heidegger in his ultra-philhellenic and post-Christian reading of Hölderlin; for this reading see Martin Heidegger, *Elucidations of Hölderlin's Poetry*, trans. Keith Hoeller [New York: Humanity Books, 2000]). For Balthasar's reading of Hölderlin see Hans Urs von Balthasar, *The Glory of the Lord: A Theological Aesthetics*, vol. 5: *The Realm of Metaphysics in the Modern Age*, trans. Erasmo Leiva-Merikakis (San Francisco: Ignatius Press, 1991), 298–338. However, for the most thoroughly Johannine (and anti-Heideggerian) reading of Hölderlin see Marion, *Idol and Distance: Five Studies*, trans. Thomas A. Carlson (New York: Fordham University Press, 2001), 81–138. In this book Marion, interestingly, compares the fate of Przywara to that of Hölderlin. Marion is indebted to Przywara's reading of Hölderlin; see Erich Przywara, *Hölderlin: Eine Studie* (Nuremberg: Glock und Lutz, 1949). In my opinion, Marion's chapter on Hölderlin, in this text, is one of the finest and most inspired pieces that he has written.

68. Erich Przywara, "The Scope of Analogy as a Fundamental Catholic Form," in *Analogia Entis*, 348–99.

69. Przywara, *Analogia Entis*, 360. For Przywara's treatment of Joachim and the Fourth Lateran Council in this essay, see especially 353–62. Bulgakov is an interesting case as to whether or not Przywara's inclusion of him in this list of thinkers of Joachimite descent is valid or not and, indeed, if Bulgakov is in danger of compromising the God/world distinction safeguarded by the *analogia entis*, as Przywara suggests. Betz and Hart show reservations with regard to Przywara's reading of Bulgakov when remarking in a translator's footnote, "Notwithstanding its merit, Przywara's reading of Russian Sophiology would seem to apply more to its (Joachimite)-Schellingian roots than its late flowering in Bulgakov." Przywara, "Scope of Analogy," 356–57. For another positive treatment of Bulgakov as an anti-Gnostic and anti-Hegelian thinker and his influence on Balthasar, see O'Regan, *Misremembering*,

and Western variants, Przywara sees Joachimism "in its final form: as the *unity of the Western and Eastern* in their absolute form: both a spiritualism of the Trinitarian person [West] and a pneumaticism of the Trinitarian cosmos [East] as the extreme consequence of the identification established by Abbot Joachim between divine and creaturely tritheism."[70] With the above said, it can be seen that the Fourth Lateran Council and its resistance to Joachimism is even more pertinent today than it was in 1215 insofar as what is being faced today is, precisely, the "extreme consequence" of Joachim's thought and its consummatory renaissance and resurgence in Idealism, and Hegelianism in particular. Moreover, given the fact that Hegel's influence on Christian discourse (both philosophical and theological) is monumental, it is easy to see why Przywara's analogical thought can act as a kind of Christian apocalyptic *pharmakon* and/or inoculation towards any philosophy/theology that shows symptoms of Hegelian and Joachimite descent.

In what then does the historical condemnation consist and what is its significance for Przywara? This council, in its second chapter, is responding to Joachim's accusation against Peter Lombard (the father of Scholasticism) and his emphasis on the Father, Son, and Holy Spirit's unity in their common essence. Joachim sees this emphasis on a common essence, in Lombard, not as a Trinity, but a "quaternity" in God. According to Joachim this, in turn, views the common essence shared between the Trinity as a kind of fourth term, thereby undermining the Trinity as such.[71] Joachim opposes Lombard's consubstantial view of the Trinity by presenting a view of the Trinity as "collective and similar" in the same way that "many men are called one people" or "many faithful one Church."[72] The unity of the

---

1:305–21. For further treatment of Bulgakov by O'Regan see Cyril O'Regan, *Theology and the Spaces of Apocalyptic* (Milwaukee: Marquette University Press, 2009), 50–60. For a reading that intimates, but does not develop, an affinity between Przywara and Bulgakov as re-enacting the theme of participation in theology post-1300s (along with other figures such as Balthasar, Rowan Williams, and Olivier Boulnois), see John Milbank, *Being Reconciled: Towards an Ontology of Pardon* (London: Routledge, 2003), 113. Milbank's thinking seems to be, in general, quite hospitable to Bulgakov's Sophiology insofar as it, in his view, by no means knows the binary Western opposition between nature/grace. See John Milbank, *The Suspended Middle: Henri de Lubac and the Debate Concerning the Supernatural* (Grand Rapids: Eerdmans, 2005), 77–78. As for my stance on Bulgakov, it must be said that I am still very much wrestling with this issue and thus undecided.

70. Przywara, "Scope of Analogy," 360.
71. Denzinger, *The Sources of Catholic Dogma*, 431.
72. Denzinger, *The Sources of Catholic Dogma*, 431.

Anthropocentrism and Theocentrism

Trinity is thus not consubstantial but "collective."[73] To elaborate this view Joachim draws from Acts 4:32, 1 Corinthians 6:17, 1 Corinthians 3:8, Romans 12:5, and Ruth 1:16. But the most important scriptural passage that Joachim refers to is John 17:22–23, "I will, Father, that they are one in us as we are one, so they may be perfected in unity."[74] Thus, as the Fourth Lateran Council suggests, Joachim's mode of argumentation moves from the collective unity of faith and love in the faithful, or Church, and then reads this kind of collective unity back into the Trinity itself.[75] Joachim presents a "tritheism" that denies the consubstantial sharing of the divine essence by the three divine Persons. Contra Joachim's view the council upholds Lombard's consubstantial view of the Trinity. And it is in this context that Przywara's beloved analogical formulation comes to expression, namely, *inter creatorem et creaturam non potest tanta similitudo notari, quin inter eos non maior sit dissimilitudo notanda.*[76]

This statement, for Przywara, dogmatically expresses the inner meaning and significance of a Catholic analogical metaphysics (grounded in creation *ex nihilo*). This understanding is to be found, implicitly or explicitly, in all mainline orthodox magisterial thinkers of the Christian tradition.[77] For Przywara, then, this statement and the analogical metaphysics that follows from it, is the *sine qua non* and fundamental principle that marks and makes possible orthodox Catholic thinking upon the relation between God and the creature. This analogically dogmatic expression thus protects against any and all forms of identity in their protean variations, starting with Joachim's pneumatic Trinitarianism of history, which thinks and advances a unity between man and God via the becoming of history's three stages—Father, Son, and Spirit—which then achieves a spiritual unity of man with Spirit in the third age (the spiritual monks of Joachim). Likewise, any identity of mystical fusion with God is refused that would see the highest stages of the mystical life (*unio caritatis* or union of grace) and divinization as consummating a union of confusion with the divine that would abolish creaturely difference. The same applies to modern forms of dialectical Trinitarianism of personal spirit and history that would arrive at a spiritual unity where man ultimately becomes God (Baader, Schelling, and Hegel).

---

73. Denzinger, *The Sources of Catholic Dogma*, 431.
74. Denzinger, *The Sources of Catholic Dogma*, 432.
75. Denzinger, *The Sources of Catholic Dogma*, 431.
76. Denzinger, *The Sources of Catholic Dogma*, 432.
77. Przywara thinks that this statement finds its fullest expression in the analogical thinking of Aquinas.

The list of protean forms of identity could go on, but the point is made that, for Przywara, the analogical import of the Fourth Lateran Council enacts a creaturely realism that places all forms of unity and similarity with God in the distance of dissimilarity, which transects all likeness within the realism of the event of distance which creation is. The creature/Creator relation of dissimilarity is thus the ineluctable and intractable condition of distance through which all talk of similarity, likeness, and union must submit. This realism of the creature/Creator analogical relation, as established by the Fourth Lateran Council, thus draws a line in the sand between authentic orthodox thinking and comportment towards God and inauthentic heterodox thinking and comportment towards God. A yes or no is demanded between accepting and embracing our condition of loving distance and radical obedience of creaturely service (*fiat*) towards the *Deus semper maior*, or a desire to be and know like God (*non serviam*), thereby seeking to abolish the glory and distance of the ineffable *Deus semper maior*.[78]

Plotted in this way the *analogia entis*, insofar as it implicates the entire rhetoric of Christian life, existence, and response (practice, forms of life, spirituality, and theory), sets history in an apocalyptic horizon of confrontation. Here history is viewed not as the primordial fall of being and its historical whyless game of hiding, sheltering, and withdrawing (Heidegger), nor as a history of Spirit's agonizing theogonic self-actualization on the progressive/necessary path towards Absolute Spirit (Hegel). Rather, history is man's apocalyptic and dramatic choice for or against God (think again of the apocalyptic laws from *Theo-Drama*, volumes 4 and 5).[79] Thus

---

78. Balthasar, following Przywara, but taking it in a more fully aesthetic direction (though the aesthetic dimensions are by no means lacking in Przywara), sees the abolition of distance as the destruction of God's glory, which, Balthasar laments, is largely lost in modern philosophical discourse. "Glory stands and falls with the unsurpassability of the *analogia entis*, the ever-greater dissimilarity of God no matter how great the similarity to him. In so far as German Idealism begins with the *identitas entis*, the way back to Christianity is blocked; it cannot produce an aesthetics of 'glory' but only of 'beauty': and the 'aesthetics as science,' which was rampant in the nineteenth century, is its fruit." Balthasar, *Metaphysics in the Modern Age*, 548–49.

79. See Heidegger's famous mythicizing of being in Martin Heidegger, *The Principle of Reason*, trans. Reginald Lilly (Bloomington: Indiana University Press, 1991), where he compares the play of being to the play of a "royal child" who plays because it plays, "without 'why,'" 113. Compare this with Balthasar's anti-Heideggerian and anti-Hegelian Christian apocalyptic view of history where he says, "It is the free thinking intellect that makes history and its deep decisions roll and echo down through the centuries. In this way history is the

Anthropocentrism and Theocentrism

Przywara's designation or ascription of Newman as a prophetic and apocalyptic thinker can just as easily be read as a description of Przywara's thought and the exigent apocalyptic import of the *analogia entis* for Christian history. The *analogia entis* is expressive of history read through the lens of a battle within the one concrete order of sin and redemption: a battle that consists in deciding *for or against* an integrated Catholic vision and response.[80] The passage from Przywara reads, "Newman saw man, the world, and history from the already almost prophetic perspective revealed to him by that final struggle between Christ and the Antichrist legible on the countenance of the modern world. He is thus the peculiar and unique *Augustinus redivivus* of modern times, and that because, amidst the torrent which bears all things to their doom, his gaze is calmly fixed upon the God of the end. *Deus Omnia in omnibus*."[81] For Przywara, the meaning, significance, and weight of the *analogia entis*, and by implication the Fourth Lateran Council, cannot be overemphasized or exaggerated. In the *analogia entis* all aspects of the Catholic faith (grounded in the fundamental creature/Creator relation of dissimilarity) are, in one way or another, touched upon. This, in turn, demands a decision, for or against, an integral and pleromatic vision of the Catholic faith: a decision that bears upon the entire rhetoric of Christian existence (theory, practice, spirituality, and forms of life). The *analogia entis* is an apocalyptic metaphysical/theological dividing line in the sands of time and history between a dramatic yes and a no to the Christian God of creation and redemption. The *analogia entis* is a specifically Catholic integrating pleromatic "fundamental form" of thought and life and, as with everything truly Christian, a sign of division and contradiction.

---

apocalypse (that is to say, the opening) of the decision of the intellect for or against God." Balthasar, *Metaphysics in Antiquity*, 39. Voegelin beautifully expresses something similar to Balthasar in his neo-Augustinian insight that history is a struggle "between *amor Dei* and *amor sui*, *l'âme ouverte* and *l'âme close*; between the virtues of openness towards the ground of being such as faith, hope and love and the vices enfolding closure such as hybris and revolt; between moods of joy and despair; and between alienation in the double meaning of alienation from the world and from God." Eric Voegelin, *From Enlightenment to Revolution* (Durham, NC: Duke University Press, 1975), viii.

80. Barth was thus right to see the question of the *analogia entis* as implicating the Antichrist, but was simply wrong about which side to fully stand on.

81. Erich Przywara, "St. Augustine and the Modern World," in *St. Augustine: His Age, Life and Thought*, ed. M. C. D'Arcy, trans. E. I. Wakin (New York: Meridian Books, 1957), 286.

DIFFERING REIMAGININGS OF THE *ANALOGIA ENTIS*

The Principle of Noncontradiction Analogically Conceived

As promised in the previous chapter, something must be said concerning Przywara's interpretation of the principle of noncontradiction as culminating his "systematics of impurity" by grounding the nonground of creaturely being and analogy in the principle of noncontradiction as the condition of all "activity of thought."[82] Przywara's interpretation of the principle of noncontradiction completes his formal topology of logics, as seen in the last chapter, by elaborating an open and suspended between/middle or mediating logic, contra all forms of logic that seek closure. Therefore, just as Stein's core logic and interpretation of being (foundational/immediate) funded her view of analogy, so too does Przywara's open logic of noncontradiction (nonfoundational/mediatory) fund his reenvisioning of analogy. Furthermore, in looking at this analogical interpretation of the principle of noncontradiction, I am able to—along with completing his discussion of logics—also open up Przywara's extraordinary reimagining of the Thomistic *potentia oboedientialis*, to be discussed in the following section.

In order to grasp the significance and stress that Przywara places on the principle of noncontradiction it is necessary to see how this principle militates against logics of closure and identity (pure logic/dialectic). It is precisely the principle of noncontradiction, understood as a creaturely and analogical principle, that enacts, or better, *is the very performance*, on a noetically formal level, of the open and suspended back-and-forth movement of creaturely being's abidingly relative and participatory condition. That is to say, because Przywara's epistemology is grounded in the nonground of creaturely suspension, becoming, and *mysterium*, which unmoors epistemology from foundation, it is the principle of noncontradiction that is fully deployed in this unmooring of epistemic foundationalism. This principle humbles thought by being a "negative reductive formality" that prohibits thought from stepping out of the bounds of our creaturely suspended condition of *in medias res*.[83] Thought can deny many things, but at the minimum, it reaches a place where "even if one denies everything one cannot deny 'this.'"[84] This "this" which one cannot deny is precisely the unavoidable creaturely and analogically suspended condition of creaturely being in which thought takes place and is expressed in/as the "negative

---

82. Przywara, *Analogia Entis*, 199.
83. Przywara, *Analogia Entis*, 199.
84. Przywara, *Analogia Entis*, 199.

reductive formality" of the creaturely and analogical principle of noncontradiction. The principle of noncontradiction is the indelible mark of the very analogical nature of thought's activity or movement. When one thus seeks to deny this position, one apostatizes from one's creaturely condition and dares to put on the mask of the divine and in so doing whispers to oneself the divine name "I am who I am."[85]

How then does the principle of noncontradiction fare when seen from the vantage of pure logic and dialectic? The principle of noncontradiction is set in contradistinction to the principle of identity expressed positively as "'what is (valid), is (valid).'"[86] This is opposed to the negativity, or minimum, of what cannot be denied of the principle of noncontradiction. Przywara judges logic(s), then, by whether or not they are ultimately ruled by the divine status of the principle of identity, which only pertains to the divine sphere, or, the creaturely status of the principle of noncontradiction, which holds sway and pertains exclusively to the creaturely sphere.[87] Such is the litmus test Przywara applies to pure logic and dialectic, a test that we already know was failed. Yet how specifically do pure logic and dialectic fail to uphold the principle of noncontradiction as the formal parameters of creaturely analogical thought in its activity and movement?

First, pure logic given its immediate and attempted divine-like starting point immediately subsumes the principle of noncontradiction under the banner and ruling hand of the principle of identity. It does so because it seeks, from the outset, an "initial foothold" and then, in turn, is in danger of treating this "foothold" as absolute.[88] This is so because pure logic is ruled by an *apriorism of being* (*Seins-Apriorismus*), which functions by, and through, a pretended intuitive immediacy to the realm of pure and eternal being. Such an approach colludes with the principle of identity by making the starting point of thought the pure realm of being and thus the divine "what is valid, is valid" of the principle of identity.[89] The creaturely principle of noncontradiction is thus waylaid from the outset in favor of a divine-like starting point that is impervious to the analogical nature of thought and thus the mediation of the senses. Such an apriorism of being is historically found in German rationalism, ontologism, and, very interestingly and correctly, for Przywara, in trends of neo-Scholastic thought

---

85. Przywara, *Analogia Entis*, 202.
86. Przywara, *Analogia Entis*, 199.
87. Przywara, *Analogia Entis*, 199.
88. Przywara, *Analogia Entis*, 199.
89. Przywara, *Analogia Entis*, 200.

whose "unconscious dependence upon German rationalism attempts to derive '*principles*' immediately from the principle of non-contradiction."[90] This neo-Scholastic attempt to derive principles from the principle of non-contradiction reifies and objectivizes the principle of noncontradiction, thus making it impossible to distinguish from the principle of identity. For Przywara the neo-Scholastics are guilty of making a last stand for the theory of "innate ideas," thus showing their infection with modern Rationalism.[91] Further, such an apriorism of being is fully in relief in the *Cogito* of Descartes and the mathematical method in its immediacy to eternal truth. The same goes for the absolute nature of Kant's categories; and, finally, also with Husserl's transcendental ego where God does not stand above consciousness, or the *Cogito*, but is rather the inner teleological goal of the *Cogito* itself.

The aforesaid approaches to logic thus deny the principle of non-contradiction. And they do so because they deny the minimum negative ground from whence thought sojourns or dwells, namely, the *in fieri* or wayfaring condition of the creature, meaning that thought is continually a "journey towards truth."[92] This apriorism of being, expressed in pure logic, divests and forbids the creature its "journey towards truth" by turning the principle of noncontradiction into a possessed objectified thing. Once this is done, the principle of noncontradiction is transmuted into the standing-still-point of the principle of identity where the thinker, through an immediate/intuitive grasp of the eternal realm of pure being and truth, coincides with this realm. Further, it should be noted that Przywara's stress on the "journey towards truth" does not lead to a relativism of truth, but to a relativization of the creature, which means that the creature always possesses truth according to its creaturely status, which is never divine. A creaturely realism is elaborated that realizes that thought takes place within the real metaphysical distinction between essence and existence and thus Przywara (and following him Balthasar) drew the logical epistemological conclusions of the creaturely condition of truth's analogical mediation. The neo-Scholastics, due to their infection by Rationalism, were afraid to draw these logical/epistemological conclusions.

Second, dialectic at the outset evinces a dislike towards the "shipwreck of the absoluteness of pure logic" and its pure intuitive/immediate ground-

---

90. Przywara, *Analogia Entis*, 200.
91. Przywara, *Analogia Entis*, 202.
92. Przywara, *Analogia Entis*, 201.

ing in the principle of identity. Such a dialectical view seeks to destabilize the "stability" of identity and seemingly, at the start, move more towards the instability and movement of the principle of noncontradiction.[93] However, insofar as this seeming instability and movement arises from "pure contradiction," the dialectical overcoming of pure logic and of the principle of identity appears in the final form as a dialectical ruse that swings back to the principle of identity initially inveighed against. Dialectic is a masked and invidious form of identity. The ultimate case in point of this is plainly Hegel. Contradiction is the "form in which self-identical 'ontic truth' or self-identical 'noetic being' is immanent to the mutable world from above, so much so that the world is the rhythm of dialectical unfolding."[94] The principle of identity reigns from the beginning, only to momentarily contradict itself in the absoluteness of contradiction by becoming itself in what was opposite to itself and thereby dialectically returning to self-identity. In such a Hegelian logic of "contradiction-identity" God is "usurped" in the most heinous way possible. This is to say, God is not usurped in the naïveté of pure logic which sees the divine as present within the creaturely in virtue of the creature's unwarranted and pretended grasp of the immediacy of eternal truth, nor does Hegelian dialectic usurp God by trying to grasp the very instance where the creature originates from God. Rather, Hegel presents the most fearful form of titanism because Hegel makes use of *the* theologoumenon and mystery of mysteries of the Christian tradition, namely, the Trinity. Hegel lays hold of, with counterfeiting hands and concepts, this Christian mystery by seeing "the origination of the creature" as "the (Trinitarian) 'origination of God' (the Son)."[95] Hegel, by inverting the Trinitarian Christian mystery, uses a Trinitarian schema to elaborate a developmental and dialectical view of God that empties itself in and through a dialectical identity with man. In Hegel, the principle of identity is not expunged, but dialectically exacerbated to the umpteenth degree.

Perhaps the aporetic dialectic, resuscitated in Kierkegaard's *Philosophical Fragments*, and then taken up in Heidegger's "existential phenomenology," fares better in expunging the principle of identity, insofar as here, being is replaced by becoming. Here, however, one encounters another ruse and clandestine form of identity hidden in Heideggerian thought. Why? Because if the pure logic of the principle of identity is really over-

---

93. Przywara, *Analogia Entis*, 202.
94. Przywara, *Analogia Entis*, 202.
95. Przywara, *Analogia Entis*, 202.

come in existential becoming, it is done with a "creature incurvated upon itself (as shaped by 'care' 'in the world')."[96] This means that only the "static" and "material" mode of the principle of identity is overcome. This is so because, on the "dynamic formal level," the principle of identity is in place.[97] For *Dasein*, in an infinite manner, is always on the way to its "own-most possibility." Thus *Dasein* plays an infinite circular dance with itself within a self-contained becoming of being "in the world."[98] *Dasein* always remains identical with itself in its "own-most possibility."

This means that "Hegelian contradiction is radicalized in the Heideggerian 'Nothing.'"[99] Heidegger's Nothing as Nothing proves "productive" or "producing" of "all things."[100] In so doing, *Dasein* secretly coincides and conspires with itself in a divine masquerade by uttering to itself "I am who I am."[101] Which is to say, Heidegger privileges possibility over actuality. And he does so in a way that cuts man off from any and all relation. *Dasein* is not an en-act-ment of, or by, an actuality outside and other to itself. Man's being, according to Heidegger, cannot be an analogical and participatory in-and-beyond that is relatively directed to what is beyond/other to man's being. By banishing actuality from his discourse Heidegger effectively cuts off the heteronomy of the divine. Man is infinite, in his possibility, because possibility is not enacted by anything but the surging sea of the infinite Nothing of possibility. In Heidegger, *Dasein*'s essence is his existence, and thus *Dasein* is an incurvated, autonomous, and tragically rebellious creature. Hegelian and Heideggerian dialectic remain two sides of the same coin. Hegel's dialectic is a theopanistic dialectic; while Heidegger's is a pantheistic dialectic. And both are ruled by the principle of identity. The principle of noncontradiction is ignored and thus man's analogical relativity to the divine.

The principle of noncontradiction has, up until now, been elaborated in opposition to the principle of identity, an identity that rules not a little of modern and contemporary philosophical discourse. Now it is time to see how the principle of noncontradiction is through and through analogical. First, the principle of noncontradiction is analogical insofar as, historically, it funds a discourse of the middle in Aristotle. It funds a middle between

---

96. Przywara, *Analogia Entis*, 202.
97. Przywara, *Analogia Entis*, 202.
98. Przywara, *Analogia Entis*, 202.
99. Przywara, *Analogia Entis*, 202.
100. Przywara, *Analogia Entis*, 202.
101. Przywara, *Analogia Entis*, 202.

Anthropocentrism and Theocentrism

the primordial opposition or battle for being waged by Heraclitus and Parmenides. For Heraclitus "all is movement."[102] This movement presides under the "symbol ... of eternally tangled tongues of flickering fire,"[103] while for Parmenides "all is rest," presiding under the "symbol ... of the sphere understood as the being of perfection in the stillness of consecration."[104] Both primordial thinkers deny and exclude the principle of noncontradiction because if all is stillness there is no creaturely change (Parmenides). And, conversely, if all is movement then there is no truth because the true can morph into the false and the false into the true. Yet both views are totally untenable because they bring about the "identity of opposites."[105] Heraclitus enacts an "explosive contradiction," while Parmenides enacts "the form of the motionless One."[106] Only then do analogy as a "middle" (*Nic. Eth.* V, 4, 1131b, 11) and the principle of noncontradiction offer an alternative of an authentic "equilibrium" for the basis of movement or "rest in motion."[107] Yet it must be noted that, in this interpretation of Aristotle, this "middle" or between is not a fixed reified thing, but acts as the "basis of movement," a "movement in rest," in which thought's activity takes place.[108]

Why? The answer is that the creature is an analogical dynamism of enacted possibility (possibility/actuality). The creature is not a pure contradiction à la Heraclitus and the chaotic shifting ground of prime matter and its unrealized infinite possibility. Nor is the creature a pure identity (Parmenides) where all possibility is enacted and realized, as in God. In the former and latter cases the principle of noncontradiction does not hold sway. Rather, as an enacted possibility, the creature is neither a chaotic possibility of contradiction, nor a pure actualized identity, but a movement in rest. The being of the creature presupposes an actuality that actualizes it and an *entelecheia* (the divine mover for Aristotle or the heavenly stars guiding the surging tumultuous sea) working within it, as above it. In understanding created being, as an analogical dynamism of possibility/actuality, one is back at the suspended character of creaturely being. Analogy, on the creaturely level, is an "*immanent dynamic middle directed to*

---

102. Przywara, *Analogia Entis*, 202.
103. Przywara, *Analogia Entis*, 205.
104. Przywara, *Analogia Entis*, 205–6.
105. Przywara, *Analogia Entis*, 206.
106. Przywara, *Analogia Entis*, 207.
107. Przywara, *Analogia Entis*, 206.
108. Przywara, *Analogia Entis*, 206. Przywara's interpretation of Aristotle is thus creative and has broken with the reified Aristotelianism of the neo-Scholastics.

an end."[109] And if man's being *is* precisely an "immanent dynamic middle directed to an end," then its analogical principle is that which is neither contradiction nor identity, but a hovering always open between, in which thought's activity indwells, namely, the principle of noncontradiction, analogically conceived. This enables one to say, at the minimum, that man's being *is not* God's being. Thought's site is thus the moving ground of thought's movement, namely, the open suspended *mysterium* of creaturely being. This site is dynamically open, because opened (enacted/directed), to what is beyond itself. Thought, and its nonfundamental fundamental principle, *is* analogical because creaturely being *is analogy/relation*, that is, neither pure contradiction, nor pure identity.

Such a view and use of Aristotelian metaphysics and the primacy of actuality over possibility, and thus the implication of the working of *entelecheia* in actuality, shows both a continuity and discontinuity between the pagan and the Catholic. Przywara interestingly notes (drawing from *Summa Th.* I, q. 13. a. 10, ad 5) that Aquinas declares that the pagan can and does arrive at a formal definition of God.[110] That is, a formal idea of God is discovered as enacting and causing all things, as above all things (the self-thinking circling thought of Aristotle). This view is not altogether different from the Catholic view of God's transcendence from the world (though Przywara is not implying that this is a fully transcendent God). But, materially speaking, such a God can be and, indeed is, an idol. This has its ground in Romans 1:21 where Paul distinguishes between knowledge (formal for Aquinas) and acknowledgment (material for Aquinas) of God. This ultimately means, from a Christian perspective, that "there is only the either-or between God and idol, and thus between *Catholic* and *pagan*."[111]

What Przywara is expressing above, with the use of Aristotelian metaphysics, is both continuous and discontinuous with Christian discourse. This is important to note here because, I would argue, Przywara's admiration for aspects of Aristotelian metaphysics is tenuous at best, and immensely critical at the worst. Przywara, then, must be seen as enacting a radically Christian reinterpretation of Aristotle. This is manifested in the fact that oftentimes, immediately following a discussion of Aristotle, Przywara invokes the Christianized neo-Platonism of Augustine (chapter 2). What then can be said concerning this continuity/discontinuity?

---

109. Przywara, *Analogia Entis*, 209.
110. For the footnote see Przywara, *Analogia Entis*, 212–13.
111. Przywara, *Analogia Entis*, 213.

Anthropocentrism and Theocentrism

The above view is continuous with Christian discourse insofar as there is a formal similarity between the pagan and Catholic conception of the divine. Nevertheless, it is also discontinuous and transcended by the transformation of metaphysics that takes place in Christian metaphysics insofar as only Christian thought acknowledges the tri-personal God, thus bringing together *knowledge and acknowledgment* of the divine, in a nonidolatrous manner. This means that the principle of noncontradiction finds its ultimate form in a Christian analogical metaphysics of creation. And this must be strongly stressed if one is to finally understand how he interprets this principle. What was glimpsed in Aristotle is completed in Augustine and Aquinas in a Christian metaphysical style. This is why the principle of noncontradiction, in Augustine (and Aquinas), is expressive of creation *ex nihilo* where the ground "'trembles above the nothing' and shows that those standing upon it are themselves 'nothing.'"[112] The principle of noncontradiction, viewed in a Christian manner, is the dynamically formal epistemic view of our nothingness from which we were/are called, and from which our created flickering being is continually held in being, by participation, from sinking back into the abyss of nothingness. Analogy is about, from the creaturely side, a being called from nothingness into a *"participatory being-related-above-and-beyond."*[113] To speak about this being called from nothingness into a participatory-relation is to speak of the creature's ability to receive and serve, from out of the resources of its poverty. In thus speaking about service, receiving, and participation, one is at the threshold of Przywara's beautiful discussion of the *potentia oboedientialis*, that is, of the creature ready to receive the unforeseen gift of supernatural grace.

Metaphysical Orientation to the Supernatural

In turning to Przywara's discussion of the *potentia oboedientialis*, one is at the heart of *the* question of Catholic philosophy and theology in the twentieth century, namely, the question of the relation between nature/grace. This question gets to the heart of meaning of man's openness and/

---

112. Przywara, *Analogia Entis*, 213.
113. Przywara, *Analogia Entis*, 213. I will speak, in the final section, about the objective priority of the above and beyond as the self-impartation of God to the creature as ruling this relation.

or orientation towards the supernatural (as alluded to in chapter 2). In regard to the present treatment, it must be said that Przywara's interpretation of the nature/grace question was groundbreaking in removing the encrustations of the neo-Scholastic view of a *natura pura* which was/is a rationalistic construct. Yet it must also be noted, so that this section can be read forward as well, that Przywara's conception of nature/grace was not merely groundbreaking, but was and remains more nuanced than many of the post-Conciliar treatments of nature/grace: treatments that either seek to secularize grace or abolish creatureliness by overemphasizing the supernatural. However, by far, the former has been the greatest danger or temptation in post-Conciliar thought. Przywara, as always, obtains a supreme analogical balance between the metaphysical and theological, which makes his thought timely and extremely relevant, to say the least.

In the background of Przywara's treatment of the *potentia oboedientialis* it is implicitly clear that he is refuting the rationalism of the two-tiered neo-Scholastic understanding of nature/grace and the doctrine of the *natura pura*. In the foreground, it is explicitly clear that what is being refuted is both a Protestant Lutheran/Barthian theopanistic understanding of grace and a Pelagian view of grace. The latter view, I will suggest, is resuscitated in Heidegger.[114] When dealing with these two critiques one is then able to see the analogical balance of Przywara's view of nature/grace as an analogically relational dynamism that respects both the active-potentiality and relative-independence of the creature, while, at the same time, recognizing the utter supremacy and *prius* of God and the unforeseen eventual surprise of grace, which can never be laid claim to by the creature.

This balance is rooted in the orthodox Catholic relational view of nature (metaphysics) and grace (*theo*logy) paradigmatically expressed, again, in the unsurpassable analogical maxims of Thomas Aquinas, *fides* (*gratia*) *non destruit, sed supponit et perficit rationem* (*naturam*) (chapter 2). This view eschews the Protestant narrative that sees sin as effectively abolishing the capacity of creation to be open to, and ready to receive, the supernatural. This Protestant narrative falls into a dualism (a kind of Marcionism) that fails to see creation as the first gift and proto-revelation of God which, in virtue of coming from God, is open to and going towards God, the God who is the *principium et finis* of the creature.[115] Such a denial of the glory

---

114. Przywara never explicitly makes this charge: he does though, in my view, strongly insinuate it.

115. Przywara, *Analogia Entis*, 228. See Aquinas, *De Ver.* q. 20, a. 4, corp.

of creation and the relative-independence of the creature, in the Protestant narrative, fails to acknowledge the important doctrine of Aquinas's *causae secundae*.[116] When one fails to respect the doctrine of *causae secundae*, one fails to see how the creature is "being prepared by God" (*De Ver.* q. 27, a. 2, corp.).[117] Indeed, the creature is given a participatory share in the positivity of infinite act and is able to "be the cause of goodness in others" (*De Ver.* q. 5, a. 5, corp.).[118] When this doctrine is denied, one becomes susceptible to the theopanistic bent of Protestant thought (à la Luther and Barth), which views God as working all things (*Alleinwirksamkeit*). The creature, in this view, becomes "the magic of impotence" and a mere chimera.[119] The creature is effaced before the all-working power of God, thus becoming indistinguishable from God himself and, as such, a function of God's own activity.[120] Once this is done the "relational edifice of the natural" is done away with and also the "positive potentiality" of the creature, which has been opened by God towards an "unlimited disposability."[121] And it is thus before God's "illimitable free decree" that the creature is sent out into/ unto a mission of free service for and towards its ever-greater God (note the Ignatian tonality).[122]

Protestantism is unable to see God being glorified in and through the relative-independence of the creature, which is genuinely freed into its relational otherness by the gift of creation, which, in turn, opens the possibility of elevation by supernatural life and thus free service. Protestant thought views this as a Catholic form of Pelagianism and, as such, an emancipation from God. But such a view would miss seeing the glorious and wonderful Catholic analogical paradox. That is, the more we are set free and independent (created different from God) the more we are close to God and dependent on him, as in the "Augustinian notion of being liberated by God (*gratia liberatrix*) for free service (*libera servitus*)."[123] It is only due to our created difference from God and releasement into freedom (which is a "free gift from above") that, in virtue of "the nothing of 'power-

---

116. This doctrine is utterly central to Przywara's analogical metaphysics of creation and the current discussion of the *potentia oboedientialis* of the creature.
117. Przywara, *Analogia Entis*, 227.
118. Przywara, *Analogia Entis*, 230.
119. Przywara, *Analogia Entis*, 223.
120. Przywara, *Analogia Entis*, 223.
121. Przywara, *Analogia Entis*, 227, 233.
122. Przywara, *Analogia Entis*, 225, 227.
123. Przywara, *Analogia Entis*, 229.

lessness,'" we are summoned to "service."[124] This shows that the greatest independence from God is precisely our greatest dependence upon God in "the distance of the servant from the Lord."[125] Creation and its effect of the *causae secundae* does not rid the creature of God, in a Pelagian fashion, but brings the creature closer to him, precisely in its relative-independence and distinctness from him: the closeness of the creature (servant) set free to freely serve God, who is Freedom itself (Lord and Master).

I have not fully answered the Protestant worry (and, indeed, also the neo-Scholastic worry of the integrity of philosophy and the *natura pura*) that an intrinsic orientation and receptive readiness of the creature to receive the supernatural presents, on the part of the creature, a titanic laying claim upon the unforeseen gift of grace. This worry sees grace being tied to the essence of the creature, out of necessity. Nevertheless, surely this answer can partly be glimpsed from the above. However, to fully answer this question, it is enough to turn to Przywara's answer to Pelagianism that refutes both Pelagianism and its modern variant in *Dasein*. This will, in turn, also refute the Protestant worry that the *potentia oboedientialis* is a kind of Catholic form of Pelagianism that lays claim to grace (as well as, by default, the *natura pura* tradition). Here I should briefly clarify: I am using the word *Pelagian* in its classic formulation, as an *emancipari a Deo* (which is what Augustine calls Pelagianism, *Opus Imperf. in Jul.*). Nevertheless, I am also answering the implicit Barthian concern that the Catholic *potentia oboedientialis* is a power intrinsic to man that captures grace and thus a form of Pelagianism. In sum, Przywara's refutation of Pelagianism (and its modern variant) is also a refutation of the Protestant charge that the Catholic understanding of grace is a form of Pelagianism.

If it has been seen that creation presents, or rather *is* a "relational edifice," it must be asked: How construe this relation or relationality? Throughout this work I have been stressing the intrinsic movement of Przywara's analogical metaphysics and its relational and participatory structure. This structure moves ever towards a beyond, but if this beyond is to be truly beyond, then the terms of the relation must be asymmetrically reversed and seen as coming from beyond, and thus, not from the creaturely side. Creaturely openness and movement is open because opened, and moving because moved (guided and directed). This was seen in the very analogical relation that obtained between *philo*sophy and *theo*logy

---

124. Przywara, *Analogia Entis*, 229.
125. Przywara, *Analogia Entis*, 229.

(chapter 2). The same template must be applied here, as one is ultimately speaking about the same thing, namely, the relation between nature/grace: analogical ordering/theological supplementation. Thus the creature has, in the transitivity of its eschatologically deferred essence ("what we will be has yet to be revealed," 1 John 3:2), an open-endedness and "provisionality" characteristic of its very nature.[126] This "provisionality" and open-endedness is given as a "free gift from above." This means that the limits of the creature are not "something irrevocably fixed in the essence of this potentiality, but rather a provisional halting point."[127] This "halting point" is given and ruled by the infinite freedom of God. God can do with his creature whatsoever he wills. ("The potential of obedience according to which the Creator can cause whatsoever he wishes to come about in the creature" [*De Ver.* q. 8, a. 12, ad 4].)[128]

This implies that God is able to breach these provisional and natural limits set within the relational structure of the creature. In doing so, two things happen and are simultaneously analogically safeguarded. First, the supernatural reality of the event of grace remains outside and beyond the creature's horizon and thus entirely unmerited, unforeseen, and unexpected, "for even a knowledge of the sphere of the supernatural is 'beyond nature.'"[129] The creature as a creature cannot and will never be able to foresee, demand, or lay claim to the mystery of the supernatural. Second, insofar as the creature is created relationally and the limits of its essence and potentiality are fluid, once the event of grace occurs—according to the free decree of the free self-revealing God of both creation (nature/reason/being) and redemption (grace/faith/revelation)—this grace does not violate or frustrate the creature. Nor does it do away with the reality of the creature's nature, which was itself made ready for, orientated towards, and open to, completion by the supernatural. The supernatural builds upon and "incorporates itself entirely into the relational structure

---

126. Przywara, *Analogia Entis*, 222.

127. Przywara, *Analogia Entis*, 223.

128. Przywara, *Analogia Entis*, 222–23, 229. It should be noted that this is, for Przywara, by no means a voluntarism of a God whose will is unfettered. For Przywara, in line with the Thomistic tradition, God is limited, not by anything outside himself, but by the very positivity of his own being and goodness. But since the term "limit" is something only applicable to the creature, this statement must be analogically qualified. Suffice it to say that the above statement does not point to the voluntaristic God of, say, Ockham or Descartes, but to a God that is both one with the positivity of his own being and goodness.

129. Przywara, *Analogia Entis*, 227.

of the natural."[130] The supernatural is the end of the creaturely, and the creaturely was always already "underway" towards the *entelecheia* of the supernatural.[131] Yet this end, on the part of the creature, could never be seen or laid claim to. It is and remains a free gift wholly beyond the creature's nature. But, paradoxically, insofar as the creature is created by God, gift is laid upon gift. (These gifts, though, are not the same; they are qualitatively different and bound together in an analogical harmony of unity-in-difference.) For it is only in the gift of grace and the supernatural that the gift of creation, the "*naturale desiderium*" and the restlessness of the "*cor inquietum*," finds rest in virtue of the "being opened" of the *potentia oboedientialis* through which the supernatural is incarnated.[132] In other words, what is expressed here is the reality that the intention of God, in creation, is to communicate his absolute love to, and for, the creature. This desire of God to communicate his love is thus inscribed into the very recesses of the creature's innermost being (first gift/first act of love). Thus to respond to this call, intrinsic to the creature's being, is to respond to the demand that God has placed upon the creature to love him, and this is why the creature is orientated towards the supernatural (the second gift/the completion of God's act of communicative love). God is the giver of both gifts, and thus the creature is placed under the demands of the *prius* of God's creative *and* redemptive love.

Here there is not a trace of Pelagianism. For the *prius* of gift always lies on the side of the one God, the giver of all gifts (to paraphrase James 1:17), Creator and Redeemer, *principium et finis* of the creature. The first gift is made ready and opened by the granting of other being relationally orientated through the *naturale desiderium*, *cor inquietum*, and the "active-potency" of the provisionally fluid essence of the creature. The *potentia oboedientialis* of the creature is, thus, ready to receive, not in a "magic of impotence," but in the openness of the "being opened" of "be it done unto me according to thy word" (Luke 1:38). Creation is analogically bound as an open site of relationality in, and towards, its completion through the unforeseen gift of the supernatural. Because the unsurpassable *prius* of the one ever-greater God of creation and redemption (and thus also and importantly history) is orchestrating the analogical dance of the *exitus et*

---

130. Przywara, *Analogia Entis*, 227.
131. Przywara, *Analogia Entis*, 227.
132. Przywara, *Analogia Entis*, 218, 227. For the *naturale desiderium* see Aquinas, *Summa c. Gent.*, III, 50.

reditus, creation and redemption, being and grace. Moreover, this all occurs within the one concrete stage of history, where the encounter between man and God eventfully occurs. This, in turn, means that this analogical-binding of the creature to grace exists only in the one concrete and historical reality of sin and redemption: a historical reality that plots history within a narrative between man's sin in Adam and redemption in Christ crucified: between the spirit of Christ and the spirit of the Antichrist.[133] For Przywara, as with Blondel, de Lubac, and Balthasar, man's condition is transnatural (i.e., no construct of *natura pura*) and thereby historical. Which means, from a Christian narratival standpoint, all philosophy is placed in the one concrete order and thus either redeemed or unredeemed. There is no possible neutrality here. Such is the Christian narrative grammar of the natural/supernatural. And such is a central aspect of Przywara's great challenge to contemporary thought and the post-Christian situation (as will soon be seen).

Concerning Heidegger, Przywara signals to the fact that Heideggerian *Dasein* is a form of modern Pelagianism. This is due to the fact that in the very paragraph in which Przywara particularly inveighs against a Pelagian reading of the "active potentiality" of the creature, he commences it with a critique of the Aristotelianism of Heidegger. This Aristotelianism of Heidegger seeks to establish potentiality as an origin unto itself.[134] In light of this, I would like to suggest that Przywara reads Heideggerian *Dasein* as a modern outbreak of Pelagianism. This is by no means a forced reading, as the whole of Przywara's brief critiques of Heidegger sprinkled throughout *Analogia Entis* views *Dasein* as a rebellious, closed, and autonomous creature. That being the case, Przywara's reading of Heidegger warrants a Pelagian indictment of Heidegger's thought. What then is Przywara's brief critique of Heidegger at the beginning of the paragraph that overthrows a misreading of the Catholic *potentia oboedientialis* as a form of

---

133. If the recurring use of the term "Antichrist" seems like Christian rhetorical flourish it should be noted that the magnificent Nietzsche likewise saw history as a battle between Christ and the Antichrist or Dionysius vs. the Crucified. Thus, the term "Antichrist" has found its way into the parlance of the increasing "apocalyptic tone" (Derrida) of Continental philosophy (I will say more about this "apocalyptic tone" in Part 2). See also Deleuze's use of the triptych priest (Kierkegaard), Antichrist (Nietzsche), and Catholic (Péguy). Gilles Deleuze, *Difference and Repetition*, trans. Paul Patton (London: Bloomsbury, 2014), 6. There are, of course, many other examples that could be cited like this in contemporary Continental philosophy.

134. Przywara, *Analogia Entis*, 228–29.

Pelagianism? And what, in the end, does this mean in the one concrete historical plane of grace and redemption?

In Przywara's understanding of the *potentia oboedientialis*, and his critique of Heidegger, one finds the starkest contrast and overthrow of Aristotelianism and the Pelagianism of Heidegger, which seeks to perform an *emancipari a Deo*. How so? Despite the privileging of act in Aristotle, *dynamis* still remains "an origin." (Agamben has a similar reading of Aristotle.)[135] And this, no doubt, is the ground and "prototype of Heidegger's 'productive Nothing.'"[136] This Nothing serves as the "primordial womb of the All" and thus a counter to the God that truly gives in the immensity of his freedom offering free gifts from above. Such a free gift from above opens a "fruitful possibility" from out of the "nothing of 'powerlessness'" that calls the creature out of nothing into its own relative and participatory being to the fruitfulness of service.[137] Nothing is thus productive of nothing outside the creative power of God, for only God creates *ex nihilo*. And, in this, God brings creation forth as what is truly other to him and thus the fruitful and active-potentiality of the creature ready to serve. Heidegger, in his "productive Nothing," seeks to cut possibility and potentiality away from the only true Origin: God himself. In so doing Heidegger enacts a Pelagian *emancipari a Deo* where the rebellious *Dasein* is alone with its own nothingness and thus a pretended origin unto itself, thus throwing off the Christian metaphysical inheritance which alone protects man from the apostasy of idolatry and the Pelagian self-assertion into which Heidegger woefully falls.

Created being is inherently relational and participatory. And it is this participatory relationality that bespeaks, through and through, the intrinsic orientation of man to supernatural fulfillment in the one concrete order of grace and redemption. This view overthrows illusionary autonomy in favor of the loving *fiat* of the creature, while, on the other hand, Heidegger's *Dasein*, and the privileging of possibility over actuality ruled by a methodological (a)theism, prohibits, *a priori*, the relative open-endedness of the creature. This results in an (auto)nomous creature that is willfully self-assertive and self-sufficient and, hence, in *Dasein*'s denial of all heteronomy, broadly speaking, Pelagian. Moreover, if one were forced to put each thinker's respective philosophy under an ensign (in light of the

---

135. Przywara, *Analogia Entis*, 229.
136. Przywara, *Analogia Entis*, 229.
137. Przywara, *Analogia Entis*, 229.

narrative of the one concrete order of grace and redemption, which will become paramount for Part 2) then the ensign, for Przywara, would be a metaphysics of the humble creaturely *fiat*: while, for Heidegger, it would be a philosophy of the revolting cry of *non serviam*.

To recapitulate: if one is to adequately think and do justice to the mystery of the relation between the natural and supernatural (being *and* grace), then one must strike a difficult analogical balance (a balance ultimately viewed from within the one concrete order of grace and redemption). Such a balance must respect the two sides of the relation. The first side realizes the relative independence of the creaturely sphere and its orientation towards, and openness to, the supernatural: thereby avoiding the theopanistic Protestant narrative. The second side realizes that the impetus, and governing motion, must be seen as coming from the other side of this relation, from the God who grants the "free gift from above," thereby overriding Pelagianism and the narrative of autonomy in modern and contemporary philosophy (my example of Heidegger). This rhythmic relationality is hard to obtain and retain. Moreover, it is open to critiques from both sides. From the Protestant side (and the neo-Scholastic *natura pura*) it risks a creaturely and metaphysical capture of grace. And for those who seek the autonomy of philosophy (again the neo-Scholastic *natura pura* or Heideggerian *Dasein*, etc.) it risks overriding or eliding the essence of the philosophical into the supernatural or theological. Yet, for Przywara, under the banner of the above Thomistic maxim of nature/grace, this is the only way to think the analogical relationality between God and man: thus saving the relative-independence of the creature by a robust metaphysics of creation, while concomitantly, placing this metaphysics of creation and its "relational edifice" under the *prius* of the supernatural. Przywara's thinking is thus a thinking and discourse of the event of relationality, the between, and the impossible/possible suspended middle (*schwebende Mitte*). Only in such a way can a discourse—as a discourse of discourses—of the analogical event of relationality between God and man be obtained and retained, set within the dramatic and apocalyptic stage of the history of sin and redemption.

The Commercium *of the* Analogia Caritatis

In turning to the consummation of Przywara's reimagining of the *analogia entis*, the movement of Przywara's thought must again be brought-into-view, underscored, and stressed. This is done in order to see how a definitive relativization of man occurs. It must be seen how the immanent analogy of man, as an "immanent dynamic middle directed to an end," or, man as analogy (*homo analogia*), is set at an infinite distance from the God of ever-dawning glory. Such a stance prohibits, in the most rigorous way possible, a view of analogy that captures God's dawning glory in a relation of mutual commonality expressed in the *ens commune* or a *tertium quid*. This sets Przywara's view of analogy at odds with Stein's view of analogy as a "common constitutive element of meaning" enacted through the *ens commune* of reflexive experience of the personal I. I argued that such a view risked an anthropocentric conception of God, which brought God dangerously close to the anthropocentric foundationalism and orbit of modern thought. There is no such danger present within Przywara's vision of analogy. Przywara is a pleromatic thinker of the ever-greater and infinitely dawning glory of the burning fire of God's love. Moreover, this glory is something positive because it is rooted in the unspeakable energy and positivity of God's living and flowing life of *Being*. It thereby results in a relation of love and service—ruled by God's infinite freedom—where the creature is sent forth on a mission of service where all is done for the glory of God (*ad maiorem Dei gloriam*). And because of this living in, and for, God's glory, the mystery of God is found in all things (in keeping with the Ignatian maxim). This is expressive of the analogical trace of the intimacy of God's ever-exceeding life of glory, aesthetically present within creation. Analogy, in the final instance, is a relation of love (*analogia caritatis*) where the creature dramatically pours its life out in service for its loving ever-greater Lord and Master. Here there is no glory of man apart from the glory of free service set free on a dramatic doxological mission of service that binds the creature—through distance and difference—to God's glory.

At crucial junctures in my argument for, and elucidation of, Przywara's analogical metaphysics, the asymmetrical reversal of the creaturely relation to the divine has always been enacted. This was done because it was/is necessary to see this relation of the beyond of the creature as coming from God, and *not* the *est non est* of the creature. This was the case with Przywara's understanding of natural theology (chapter 2) and was done in order to avoid the danger of an erotic titanism and idolatry. The risk of inclosing the above and beyond of the transcendence of the creature in upon itself was thus present. The creature was in danger of becoming the regulator of the God/creature relation. This danger bespoke the need for theological supplementation of the self-revealing God of revelation: a God free to reveal himself when and how he wills. Only in Catholic *theo*logy, being the formal ground of a creaturely metaphysics, was the above and beyond of the creaturely truly respected and kept open. *Philo*sophy became, or rather already was, a participation in theological Wisdom, thus viewing the terms of the relation as residing in the *prius* of God's freedom.

This paradigm was again invoked in the above with the discussion of the *potentia oboedientialis* of the creature. Here the creature's orientation towards, and natural desire for, the supernatural was placed under the *prius* of God's opening of the active-potentiality of the creature. The *prius* of God made ready the creature to receive the unforeseeable gift of grace as a "free gift from above," once again marking the above and beyond of the creature as coming from God: a being open because opened. This prohibited an erotic and Pelagian view of man's desire for the divine from overcoming the divine from the creaturely side. What is accented, without failing to acknowledge the erotic and transcending element of *naturale desiderium* and *cor inquietum*, is the active-potentiality of the *potentia oboedientialis*: a standing ready-to-receive, in anticipation of the unanticipatable. Emphasis was placed on the readiness-to-receive of the creature. This "being opened" is prepared by the free God as a "free gift from above" that sends the creature on a mission of service. There is an asymmetrical reversal of the terms of the relation between the creature and Creator, making sure that the *prius* falls on the side of God's glory. The creature is relativized and any unwarranted eroticism and/or willful Pelagian self-assertion, which seeks to control the relation between the Creator/creature from the creaturely side, is avoided. The same dynamic template, the same paradigm and the same relativization of the creaturely is at work in Przywara's ultimate construal of the *analogia entis*. For, if it were not, then the *analogia entis* would be an "*analogia **entis***" rather than a doubling or redoubling and thus an "***analogia** entis*."[138] What is decisive in the *analogia entis* is not being, but analogy, or being eventfully understood as analogy.

Yet what does this mean? For Przywara, there are two distinct yet mutually interrelated analogies. The first, as was shown in the discussion of the principle of noncontradiction, is an immanent analogy of the creature. This is expressed in the first part of the following formulation, namely, "*a dynamic back-and-forth between the above-and-beyond (of a transcending immanence) and the from-above-into (of an indwelling transcendence)*

---

138. Przywara, *Analogia Entis*, 236.

[*Zwischen Überhinaus* (*transzendierender Immanenz*) *und Von-Oben-hinein* (*immanierender Transzendenz*)]."¹³⁹ To understand the relation between these two analogies is to understand the "*concluding analogy*, which comprises the relation between the intra-creaturely analogy and the analogy between God and the creature."¹⁴⁰ The intra-creaturely analogy represents the *analogia attributionis* and—in Przywara's interpretation—emphasizes similarity. The latter represents the *analogia proportionis* and represents the ever-greater dissimilarity, dislikeness, and distance of the creature from God. The understanding of the interrelation of these two analogies (which will be seen importantly to comprise three movements of analogy in its final formulation) is crucial in seeing how analogy does not capture God in a univocal term or *tertium quid*. That is, insofar as the relation and likeness to God, in the *analogia attributionis*, is always placed within the ever-greater dislikeness and dissimilarity of the *analogia proportionis* and the Fourth Lateran Council.

The *analogia attributionis* represents the creaturely side of the relation insofar as the creature is similar to God, i.e., the creature itself is in relation to God in virtue of the fact that God is the *principium* and ground of the creature. The creature, as an effect or relation to God, points (in its analogical dynamism of the nonidentity of essence and existence and the suspended condition of thought's analogical condition suspended between being/consciousness) towards God.¹⁴¹ Yet, insofar as the creature's being is itself already a suspended middle and the *mysterium* of the *homo abyssus*, this relation breaks off into the mystery of God's otherness. This mystery is obtained and encountered in the *analogia proportionis* where the similarity of the creature is always already transected by the wholly otherness of God. The relation of the creature is "derived" and participatory from a God that is "from himself, in himself, and to himself."¹⁴² This analogy is one that must be seen as "strictly ... *a relation of mutual Alterity*."¹⁴³ Nevertheless, because Przywara's negative theology is not hyperousiological, it is rooted in the positivity of God's infinite and dynamic life and the energy of act (*actus purus*). This is why the *Being* of God can never be equated with the becoming (*est non est*) of the creature. This implies that the *negativum* is that which always allows for a *positivum*, that is, by qualifying the *positivum*

139. Przywara, *Analogia Entis*, 216.
140. Przywara, *Analogia Entis*, 231.
141. Przywara, *Analogia Entis*, 233. See Aquinas, *De Ver.* q. 23. a. 7, ad 9.
142. Przywara, *Analogia Entis*, 233.
143. Przywara, *Analogia Entis*, 231.

in the *negativum* of God's positive and replete life, which, for the creature, remains ungraspable and incomprehensible. "At its peak, the *positivum* of 'relation' reveals itself as the *negativum* of 'alterity'. As such the *negativum* of 'alterity' is the sign of fulfilment of the *positivum* of 'relation'. Incomprehensibility being the sign that it is God; comprehension, the sign that it is not God: *si . . . comprehendis non est Deus* [*In Ps.* LXXXV, 12]; *hoc ergo non est, si comprehendisti: si autem hoc est, non comprehendisti* [*Serm.* LII, vi, 16]."[144] There are positive statements about God but these positive statements always unsay themselves in negative statements: statements said within the expanse of infinite distance. This, in turn, makes sure that analogical statements are ruled by the *negativum* of incomprehensibility. But insofar as this *negativum* is rooted in the infinite positivity of God's dynamic life, it ensures that when one is speaking about God, it is always subservient and made possible by his incomprehensibility, and thus not an idol of human making and fashioning. God's incomprehensibility, rooted in the positivity of his infinite and dynamic life, is what secures the creature's true and positive relation to God.

Analogical discourse and creaturely relation flow from the primacy of Aquinas's *analogia proportionis* (in line with the Fourth Lateran Council) and thus respect and observe "the absolute dividing line of difference."[145] This marks analogical relation, thought, and language as between univocity and utter equivocity, both of which destroy authentic relation. Moreover, because this analogical relation observes "the ultimate dividing line of difference" the one term "being" is applied, not in the univocal manner of the *ens commune*, but in an analogical fashion. This means being refers to the "alterity (*diversas proportionis*)" of the one term "being," predicated of both God and creature.[146] This, however, needs to be more fully explained. If the one term "being," analogically set under alterity and difference, implies a similarity between God and the creature, then this similarity cannot be merely "balanced out" by the dissimilarity "in which this same *one* is in both God and creature (like and unlike, *simile 'et' dissimile*)." If this were the case a *tertium quid* would be enacted, which would make God subservient to the "suspended equilibrium" between likeness and unlikeness

---

144. Przywara, *Analogia Entis*, 232.

145. Przywara, *Analogia Entis*, 232. As Aquinas says, in keeping with the Fourth Lateran Council, "Although creatures bear within themselves a certain likeness to God, there is nevertheless present the greatest unlikeness." Aquinas, *De Ver.* q. 1, a. 10, ad 1 in contr. Cited in Przywara, *Analogia Entis*, 232.

146. Przywara, *Analogia Entis*, 232.

between God and the creature.[147] This view would make God subservient to a metaphysical construct, the *analogia **entis***.

This is simply not the case, and indeed cannot be the case for the thinker of God's dawning majesty. Rather, the *analogia entis* declares the unending transcendence of God and the mystery of his otherness. God is above and beyond every creaturely likeness or similitude, above the commonality of the *ens commune*, and above the quantitative univocal concept that follows from it. God is above and beyond genera, categories, and forms of predication. All analogical similarity is a gift of difference that is ruled by the absolute absolving *prius* of the God above the creature. All positive similarity, in being and knowing, is only given by and reduces everything "to the ultimate irreducible *prius* of God."[148] God is the wielder of the asymmetrical absolving relation of the ***analogia*** *entis*. Analogy is understood as a "relation of alterity" and is by no means captured as a term in a one-to-one relation, meaning that any analogy between God and the creature is precisely that: merely an analogy.[149] If creaturely being is itself an analogy, then this analogy is doubled over into an analogy of analogy in the concluding analogy of the relation between intra-creaturely analogy (*attributionis*) and the analogy between God and the creature (*proportionis*). The creaturely analogy is set at a distance (doubled over) by the second analogy of the infinite dividing line of difference.[150] Here any anthropocentric or metaphysical construct of a *tertium quid* or third univocal term (whether it is being, goodness, truth, beauty, etc.) is smashed to pieces by Przywara's Christian metaphysical hammer. All things are thus reduced to the irreducible *prius* of God: in the tradition of the Areopagite's "dazzling darkness," the "*Si comprehendis non est Deus*" of Augustine, and the "*Deus tamquam ignotus*" of Aquinas.[151]

    147. Przywara, *Analogia Entis*, 232.
    148. Przywara, *Analogia Entis*, 233.
    149. Przywara, *Analogia Entis*, 232.
    150. One may seriously ask here whether Marion's construal of the doubling of distance in *The Idol and Distance* is strongly influenced by Przywara's template of the *analogia entis*, given Przywara's presence in the text and Marion's knowledge of *Analogia Entis*. Does Marion try to salvage something of the *analogia entis* now understood in a post-Heideggerian direction in conversation with Przywara's student Balthasar? Of course, if in fact this is what Marion is doing, then it must be said that he clearly loses the brilliance and nuance of Przywara's argument in his overcapitulation to the Heideggerian narrative. Nevertheless, this would make an interesting study of some of the formal moves in Marion's elaboration of distance that seem to strongly overlap with Przywara's.
    151. Przywara, *Analogia Entis*, 232–33.

Anthropocentrism and Theocentrism

An important question must be posed, namely, is this being-taken-up into the mystery of silence and noncomprehension the last word? And, further, does such a "negative theology" provoke a silence of inactivity for Przywara? In other words, is Eberhard Jüngel right that the *analogia entis* so thoroughly safeguards God's transcendent otherness that it compromises his utter "nearness," as seen in the gospel narrative, thus succumbing to an overly negative, negative theology?[152] The simple answer is no. Because this analogical performance, for Przywara, finds its ultimate rhythm in three analogical scales of movement in which the Przywarian vision of the ***analogia entis*** comes to fulfillment. It commences with a "'positive relationship' of the 'similarity, however great' (*tanta similitudo*)" of the analogy of attribution.[153] The *analogia attributionis* thus showed itself as the positive of relation of the creature insofar as God, from the creaturely side, is shown to be the cause and ground of the creaturely. Yet, insofar as the creaturely revealed itself in the *mysterium* of the above and beyond, this creaturely relation was transected, overcome, and reversed by the "negative alterity" of the *maior dissimilitudo*. God is only the ground of the creaturely if he is above and beyond any common mutuality with the creature. This is the "suspended analogy" of the *analogia proportionis* under which the *analogia attributionis* is always subservient, i.e., to God the giver of all relation.

---

152. For Jüngel's thoughtful but ultimately insufficient critique of Przywara, see Eberhard Jüngel, *God as the Mystery of the World: On the Foundation of the Theology of the Crucified One in the Dispute between Theism and Atheism*, trans. Darrel L. Guder (Grand Rapids: Eerdmans, 1983), 282–85. Such an emphasis on Przywara's understanding of the descending *analogia attributionis*, as I am proposing here, is also—I would like to suggest—a response to Jüngel's thoughtful critique of Przywara. That is, Jüngel rightly sees that the Evangelical polemic against the *analogia entis* of Przywara was totally off the mark, largely because of Barth's inflammatory rhetoric. Jüngel realizes that the *analogia entis*—as conceived by Przywara—was never in danger of metaphysically collapsing the difference of God through a metaphysical construct. He thus sees that the *analogia entis* "protects the holy grail of mystery, and as such is really the opposite of what Protestant polemic has made it out to be." Jüngel, *God as the Mystery of the World*, 284. Rather, Jüngel is worried about the total opposite, namely, that if the *analogia entis* so thoroughly respects and protects God's mystery and unknowability, then it must be asked: What happens to God's "nearness" to man as expressed in the gospel understanding? Jüngel, *God as the Mystery of the World*, 282. This is what Jüngel believes to be the worry of the post-dialectical Barth (if there is such a Barth). In Jüngel's interpretation, Barth, in his turn to the *analogia fidei*, in the later volumes of the *Church Dogmatics*, still rejects the *analogia entis* of Przywara. But Jüngel thinks that in Barth's post-dialectical years, he does so for the opposite reason of God's nearness. And in this, Jüngel sees himself as following the later Barth on this matter.

153. Przywara, *Analogia Entis*, 234.

DIFFERING REIMAGININGS OF THE *ANALOGIA ENTIS*

Yet, and here is Przywara's particular brilliance, the *analogia attributionis* does not just simply disappear in the night of "dazzling darkness" of the *analogia proportionis*, but reappears in a third movement transfigured from above, that is, it is transfigured into the positivity of creaturely service and difference. This time, however, the *analogia attributionis* does not commence from below to above (i.e., the restlessness of the creature), as in the first instance, but in the asymmetrical reversal enacted through the "from above" of the *analogia proportionis* (i.e., through God's absolving alterity). The *analogia attributionis* now reappears fully as a from: from the "above to below" where the creature is "'sent forth' for the 'performing of service.'"[154] One could perhaps say it this way: whatever titanic, pagan, idolatrous, and unwarranted erotic residue or trace that was left in the ascending transcendence of the *analogia attributionis* has now been baptized and cleansed in the fire of God's ever-greater difference (as Creator and Redeemer). This, in turn, allows for the true positivity of creaturely difference to be seen and embraced as a gift of difference (analogical unity-in-difference). Thus it can be seen, once again, that Przywara accentuates the positive-potentiality and the *causae secundae* of the creature: because the creature can only be seen as that which is wholly sent forth from God into a graced mission of free service.[155] This is why, in Przywara's conception, the *analogia entis* is a specifically Christian or Catholic phenomenon where, in its three metaphysical movements, "Longing (in the ascending *analogia attributionis*) becomes a 'blinding rapture' (in the *analogia proportionis*), in order to become 'service' (in the descending *analogia attributionis*)."[156]

These three movements are analogically bound in the oneness and *prius* of the Christian God of creation *ex nihilo* and redemption. Only in this way is the unsurpassable glory of God in his otherness retained along with the *positivum* of creaturely difference and service. Here one enters the heart of the meaning of analogical unity-in-difference, which sets relation

---

154. Przywara, *Analogia Entis*, 235.

155. Betz is a masterful interpreter of Przywara, and I agree with nearly everything he writes concerning Przywara. However, in my view, if there is one underdeveloped aspect to his interpretation of Przywara it is that he underemphasizes the importance of descending *analogia attributionis* and the return of positivity after the baptism of ever-greater difference. Thus, I would put the question to Betz, in the spirit of camaraderie, does his emphasis on exonerating the *analogia entis* from a Barthian reading (which he does persuasively) perhaps prevent him from emphasizing more the positivity and return of the descending *analogia attributionis*?

156. Przywara, *Analogia Entis*, 235.

Anthropocentrism and Theocentrism

in the *negativum* of alterity of God's unsurpassable positivity of *Being*. This, in turn, sets free and enacts the *positivum* of the otherness of the creaturely into a "*communitas analogiae*," the "relation between God and creature . . . related as 'nothing' to the 'Creator out of nothing.'"[157] This relation of "nothing" is nothing more than the *admirabile commercium* of the *analogia caritatis* and thus an *event of loving freedom*: an event of love that takes place in the freedom of difference and love's free traversal. It is expressive of a creation freed into analogical difference by the glowing majesty of the God of freedom and love. Only in this analogical space of creation, granted freely by the ever-greater God, can the *commercium* of the wedding feast of the distance between the Lord and servant take place. The creature's life, lived within this *commercium* of analogical difference, is a life of dramatic performance and mission. Here every act, every thought, and every practice is united in the integral rhetoric of the Christian life of mission. Life, seen analogically, is a dramatic rhetoric of free doxological service. God is found in all things, in virtue of being above all things. God is found in a creation that has been granted in a whyless gift of love's difference. The last word, then, is not the metaphor or symbol of "night" of an overly negative, negative theology rooted in man's "unrest for God," as Jüngel thinks.[158]

Rather, it is a vision of the above three movements of analogy that ends in the descending *analogia attributionis*, where the entirety of the creature's life incarnates the nearness of God and his dramatic glory in performative service. But this is a God that is found in all things in virtue of his loving distance and freedom from all things. Przywara's last words are "service" and "love," not "night." The Christian vision and style of negative theology presented by Przywara is one of true knowing in unknowing, which participates in the ever-greater *mysterium* of God. This *mysterium* then spills over into an *enacting* of this *vision* of *mysterium* in the performance of a mission of free service. In other words, in this emphasis on mission and free service the tradition of the "*laus Dei*," in the Greek Church fathers, is being taken up, completed, and reimagined. Here Przywara invokes the Eastern themes of "to be light in light" and "*laus Dei*," obtained in the "blinding rapture" of the *analogia proportionis* of the ever-greater God, to whom all adoration is due.[159] Yet insofar as this vision of "blinding rapture" does not stop at a contemplative silence, but rather spills over into a life

---

157. Przywara, *Analogia Entis*, 237.
158. Jüngel, *God as the Mystery of the World*, 285.
159. Przywara, *Analogia Entis*, 235.

of *performing action and service*, the contemplative/doxological emphasis of the Eastern fathers is taken and transformed into a more Western and Ignatian direction.

The "*laus Dei*" becomes a Christian life of dramatic action, rhetorical performance, and service. Here there is more of an emphasis on finding God in all things in concrete and historical realities. The lived performativity of truth and praise, characteristic of a more Ignatian and Western approach, transforms the more eternal and doxological/contemplative orientation and approach of the East into a Christian performative metaphysics of doxological *praxis* and action. The nearness of God's loving distance is lived out in a spirituality of service and action, where God's loving mystery of distance is found and incarnated in all things (the concrete). This vision passes beyond the merely speculative or contemplative spirituality of an overly negative, negative theology into an integrating rhetoric of the whole of the creature's being. A creaturely metaphysics is a persuasive and performative metaphysics of dramatic action. The creature thus serves, adores, and glorifies the Lord in every facet of its incarnate and concrete life. This Christian pleromatic vision is thus a vision of integration that points the way towards a metaphysics of *praxis* grounded in a *vision* of the mystery/distance of God's creative and redeeming love. This, in turn, grants the nearness of God's presence in the incarnate concreteness of life and service. And here one chances upon the entry point into the undeveloped social and political implications of Przywara's thinking. That is, insofar as his analogical and creaturely metaphysics, based in a *vision* of God's loving distance and freedom, ends in a metaphysics and spirituality of dramatic service, then his thinking has the potential to unite Christian *vision and praxis* in an integral rhetoric of Christian social existence and apocalyptic challenging (to which we will return in the final chapter of Part 2).

The creature's task is to live and serve within this mystery of the *commercium* of God's presence in creation by seeing God in all things and, by so doing, capturing all things for the greater glory of the ever-greater God of glory beyond, and in, all things. This is Przywara's vision of the *analogia entis*, which breaks down all humanistic, personalistic, and anthropocentric conceptions of God. This is done in favor of a thinking that attempts to think, respect, and love the majesty of God's glory. This, in turn, implies a thinking of man not in the modern foundational sense of subjectivity, nor as the liberal subject endowed with "natural rights," nor the Capitalistic "last man" of "blinking" secular desires, nor autonomous *Dasein* or the schizophrenic fractured postmodern self—but, rather, a thinking of man as a free creature relationally constituted and sent forth on mission. The self is thereby an enacting and *performance of free doxological service*. This self is an "ecclesial" sojourner or "pilgrim" willing and ready to serve (to echo Catherine Pickstock echoing Jean-Yves Lacoste) where man's self is constituted *through mission and service*. Man's glory is God's glory because there is no glory outside of God's ever-dawning majesty, the *Deus semper maior*, whom man lovingly, obediently, and dramatically serves. In this radically relational/analogical vision of the creature, the creature performs a "metaphysics of action" and *praxis*.[160] Here, in a pleromatic fashion, vision itself is dramatically acted out in a self where vision becomes flesh.

* * *

In completion of the formal and critical dialogue, enacted in Part 1, and in view of pleromatic Christian postmodern potential, crucial contrasts between Stein's and Przywara's construals of the *analogia entis* must be made.

Stein's rationalistic interpretation of Christian philosophy and her immediate and foundational starting point were fully carried through in her final construal of the *analogia entis*. This was seen in the desire to use analogy as a means to bridge the infinite expanse between God and the creature. This was done in order to elaborate a common theory of being's meaning comprising both finite and eternal being. Moreover, this move was achieved by a return to the reflexive, personal, and immediate nature of her phenomenological starting point. From this point, Stein, by having recourse to revelation and Exodus 3:14, found the divine warrant for a common ground of meaning (*ens commune*) through an experientially personal and reflexive reading of the divine name "*I* am." Such a reading of the divine name risked bringing God into the foundational and anthropocentric orbit of modern philosophy's ground of self-presence. Stein, in her desire to elaborate a unified theory of being's meaning through the *ens commune*, experientially and reflexively conceived, risked reading God as a kind of graven image of modern subjectivity. This demanded a subtraction of temporality, difference, and human finitude from the finite I in order for this I to arrive at an *idea* of eternal being. The subtraction of finitude and temporal distention from the finite I merely returned the finite I to

---

160. Balthasar uses the phrase "metaphysics of action" for his discussion of the figure of Ignatius of Loyola. See Balthasar, *Metaphysics in the Modern Age*, 102–19.

its starting point of immediate self-presence. And here modern *apotheosis* and divine-like self-foundation haunted and lurked in her discourse. Stein's discourse begins with identity and immediacy and ends with a view of analogy that accentuates mutuality, commonality, and similarity in a unified theory of being's meaning rooted in reflexive subjectivity. God and and the creature are both comprised under the banner of the *ens commune*, experientially conceived. This view of analogy risks a modern anthropocentrism that does not fully safeguard the divine expanse of glory and difference of the ever-greater God. It risks a humanistic and personalistic elevation of man. Stein's logic and project remained consistent throughout. And despite her admirable and creative intentions, she is an heir of modernity's anthropocentric erring. A space of secularity was carved into her discourse that disallows her from fully funding a pleromatic Christian visionary counter to post-Christian philosophical modernity.

One the other hand, Przywara, from beginning to end, was and remained a supreme thinker of analogical difference, which undercut the foundationalism of modern thought with his "systematics of impurity." This resulted in a radically Christian view of difference and contingency, which revealed man to be a suspended *mysterium* and thus a relative participatory being (which was also his view of *philo*sophy as a creaturely metaphysics of participation). The general thrust of Przywara's thinking was a radical relativization and Christian decentering of the creature, a creature that is continually overtaken by the *prius* and majesty of God. The entire moving systematics of Przywara's thought found its consummation in a view of analogy as the **analogia entis**, which prohibited a view of analogy of the Steinian sort grounded in the *ens commune*. All analogy was placed under the radical alterity of God and the primacy of dissimilarity over similarity. This move, in the end, allowed Przywara to more fully respect the positivity of the creature insofar as this positivity was wholly funded by and through the ever-greater difference of God: a communion of unity-in-difference, as opposed to Stein's difference-in-unity and similarity. This style of thinking captures all things for God's glory in deep conversation with the great tradition through a pleromatic reimagining of this tradition in view of our dramatic hour of history. And because Przywara's knowledge of the living pleromatic Christian tradition is exemplary, he is able to fund a dialogue with modern and contemporary discourse without getting pulled into its post-Christian or anti-Christian orbit. Przywara's thinking holds the potential to fund a specifically Christian pleromatic vision as a radical counter to philosophical modernity and the nihilism of postmodernity.

PART 2

Constructive Reimagining

CHAPTER 5

Setting the Stage: Post-Conciliar Trajectories

Once, there was no "secular."
John Milbank, *Theology and Social Theory*

The function of this chapter is, as the title suggests, a setting of the stage of what is to follow in Part 2 as well as a transitional binding between Parts 1 and 2. In this stage setting I desire to accomplish two things. First, my reasons for preferring Przywara's vision over Stein's will again be presented here. This time, however, they will be presented in light of the circumstances of post-Conciliar Catholic thought, which I will codify under the banner of the *Communio/Concilium* divide, as it was from this perspective that the formal and critical dialogue was written. In other words, if it was seen that Przywara and Stein stood at a crossroad moment in Catholic thought in regard to their respective strategies towards philosophical modernity, then it will now be seen how each thinker's respective strategies towards philosophical modernity find affinities and refrains in the above two primary directions taken in post-Conciliar Catholic thought (*Concilium*/modern/anthropocentric, *Communio*/countermodern/theocentric). This is also done in light of the subplot of this work. Second, once the following connection is secured, then this allows me to—in light of the *telos* of this text—plot a line of lineage between Przywara's visionary trajectory, via his affinity with *Nouvelle Théologie/Ressourcement/Communio*, and non-identical forms of repetition of analogical vision in Desmond, Milbank, Hart, and O'Regan, that is, insofar as all these thinkers, in their countermodern strategy, exhibit a strong elective affinity with the retrieval of the polyphonic and pleromatic Christian tradition enacted in *Nouvelle Théologie/Ressourcement/Communio*. Further, the aforementioned thinkers are also extremely leery of the anthropocentric and transcendental approach of *Concilium*-minded thinkers in general. This is clearly seen in Milbank, Hart, and O'Regan (it is implicit in Desmond), all of whom are highly suspect of Rahner's transcendental turn. In thus refocusing the narrative, in light of these issues, it can then be seen why Stein's discourse is limited in its resistance towards philosophical modernity, while, on the other hand, Przywara's thought and vision is fully viable and is able to aid a robust and capacious Christian postmodern vision and grammar, thereby sharing an affinity with the above postmodern Christian thinkers. All of this sets the stage for my contemporary and constructive reimagining of the *analogia entis*, via a postmodern and post-Conciliar retrieval and expansion of Przywara's analogical vision, in light of the dramatic hour in which we now find ourselves.

The Trajectory of Twentieth-Century Catholic Thought

The first part of the twentieth century exhibited one of the greatest outbursts of creative Catholic thought in the history of Christianity. Further, this was a time of a genuine high culture in the history of the Catholic intellectual tradition. It was a kairotic time, a milestone and crossroad moment. It was the best of times and the worst of times. This time of creative energy presented a supreme challenge to Catholic self-understanding and identity as to how Catholic thought was to engage or not engage the historically unique and monumental event of philosophical modernity and the Enlightenment post-Christian counternarrative. All of this came to a head in the modernist crisis. Przywara's and Stein's thinking sought to meet this challenge head on. The meeting of this call is what brought them together and was the necessary first step if Catholic thought was to survive this Goliath-like encounter. However, their respective answers are also what set them apart. Indeed, it is not too much to say that their respective strategies and answers to the question of philosophical modernity, at this time of crossroads, are microcosms of the two primary strategies taken within twentieth-century Catholic thought, in the post-Conciliar period, towards philosophical modernity. This is to say, broadly speaking, an anthropocentric strategy/direction and a theocentric strategy/direction.

Within this crossroad moment, it must be once again accentuated that Przywara and Stein were of one mind that the narrow-minded parameters and defensive position of much of neo-Thomism needed to be overcome. A creative strategy of dynamic and creative encounter with philosophical modernity was needed if Catholic thought was not to moan its own dirge. In this, Przywara and Stein are aligned with the creative maneuver of "transposition" enacted by a host of Catholic thinkers pre–Vatican II in their attempt to overcome "Paleo-Thomism": from the early Scheler, Guardini, von Hildebrand, Adams, Rahner, and Balthasar for German speakers, to Blondel, Rousselot, Marcel, Gilson, de Lubac, and the *ressourcement* thinkers in France, to Belgian thinkers such as Maréchal, Schillebeeckx, and Emile Mersch. (This list of philosophers and theologians is of course by no means exhaustive.) All were of one mind that Catholic philosophy and theology must be rejuvenated and that the deadlock between modernism/integralism must be broken along with the tradition of Baroque Scholasticism in order for Catholic thought to both survive and thrive.

However, once narrow-minded sawdust Thomism was surmounted through a vindication of many of the thinkers suspected of modernism or neo-modernism by the *aggiornamento* of Vatican II and its opening to the modern world, new problems and questions immediately emerged.[1] It was soon seen that the devil was found in the details of how exactly Catholic philosophy and theology were to open themselves towards, and respond to, philosophical modernity (and modernity as such). Moreover, if two of the central questions of the modernist crisis can be said to be (1) How were the Church and its thought to engage philosophical modernity? and (2) How is one to understand the question of nature/grace?, then it must be said that both of these questions co-implicate each other and open up into the question of Catholic self-understanding and the style of engagement chosen. (This implies, of course, the very understanding of the Catholic Church itself.) As such, these questions did not die away as a historical anomaly of the modernist crisis, but wholly reemerged in the new setting of the post-Conciliar context and are still being asked today. In other words, the questions of Przywara and Stein's time are also the questions of our post-Conciliar context, albeit in a nonidentical setting. We are not fully beyond this deep-seated identity crisis of Catholic self-interpretation, vision, and style, which seems to be continually intensifying; nor are we fully beyond the question of the monumental post- or anti-Christian event of philosophical modernity (and modernity as such). In other words, *we are*

---

1. Though this form of Thomism has never been fully overcome and, indeed, one can say that, in certain circles, it is even experiencing a rebirth of sorts today.

not beyond the question of what style of Christian vision is needed today in this dramatic intensifying hour of Christian history.

For the sake of a need to gain an overview of post-Conciliar Catholic thought, the best way to formulate the differences that surfaced, post–Vatican II, is to look at the *Communio/Concilium* divide. This divide is investigated in order to gain a broad topography and general foothold in post–Vatican II Catholic discourse. The prime purpose of this is *not* to tell the full story of Catholic thought in the twentieth century, and specifically post-Conciliar Catholic thought, but rather to situate Stein and, especially Przywara, in regard to this story. If this is going to be done, then part of this story must be told, a story that if I were telling the whole story would have to be greatly complicated. Moreover, I am well aware that there are many objections to such a view of the *Communio/Concilium* divide, not the least being that this is a gross oversimplification of the issues haunting post-Conciliar discourse. Nor I am insensitive to this objection. Further, it is not my intention to deepen this divide on ideological motives. But the fact is that this divide is real and there are substantive differences between the two camps that cannot be avoided. In my view, then, the question of this "divide" is a question of the expanse of Christian thought and vision, and thus a question of a distinctively Christian pleromatic vision and style of thinking that would *seek to effectively go beyond both sides of this divide.* This is another way of saying that, in this divide, pleromatic enfleshed Christian vision has been fractured.

That said, in this going beyond there are, no doubt on my part, greater similarities with *Communio* thinkers, in general, insofar as their view of grace or the supernatural funds a robust Christian vision that more effectively counters the narrative pull of secularity (more will be said on this), though there are certainly profound and essential elements in *Concilium* thinkers that are lacking in *Communio* thinkers, most importantly, a sustained social critique and engagement with political theology, as will be seen. I will return to this divide again at the conclusion of this book by programmatically suggesting a way to move beyond it with the resources of Przywara's thinking through what I provisionally termed in the Introduction an "analogical-apocalyptic metaphysics." In the following I will hint at strengths and weaknesses to both approaches, tipping the scale, in the end, towards *Communio* thinkers. Nevertheless, *Communio*-minded thinkers require supplementation in order for a dramatic pleromatic enfleshed vision to be realized. Thus, as a whole, this divide must be gone beyond in order to regain an integral and whole vision of Catholic thought and life.

Post-Conciliar Trajectories

What then are the facets of this divide? *Concilium* was a theological journal founded in 1965 by Karl Rahner, Johannes Baptist Metz, Anton van den Boogaard, Paul Brand, Marie-Dominique Chenu, Edward Schillebeeckx, Yves Congar, and Hans Küng. This journal was/is intent on propagating the *aggiornamento* spirit of Vatican II. *Communio*, on the other hand, was founded in 1972 by Hans Urs von Balthasar, Henri de Lubac, Joseph Ratzinger, and Louis Bouyer (Marion and Claude Bruaire being founding members of the French branch with the aid of Balthasar). *Communio*, one might say, stresses more the continuity of Vatican II with the living glory of the pleromatic Christian tradition (in keeping with Ratzinger's both famed and infamous "hermeneutic of continuity"). As such, six demarcations of this "divide" can be discerned. However, it again needs to be noted that these distinctions are by no means hard-and-fast rules, as it is impossible to deal entirely with the intricacies of this debate here. They rather serve as general guidelines aiming to facilitate a broad topography and trajectory of post-Conciliar Catholic thinking in my partial and limited tale of post-Conciliar thought.

(1) In general, it can be said that *Concilium* thinkers advance a more naturalized, secular, and kenotic view of grace. This view sees grace as a kenotic dissemination into the world that ends in a depletion (or sometimes a total disappearance) of Christian vision, form, and content. This interpretation, in turn, gives far more autonomy to the secular order and post-Christian secular discourse, because grace has been, paradoxically, secularized and thus belongs to the autonomy of the post-Christian secular sphere already while, on the other hand, *Communio* thinkers emphasize more the transforming power of grace and the supernatural, marking being and the world with the imprint of grace, thus seeing the whole of reality as ordered to completion by and through grace. By so doing, they open up a fuller Christian vision filled with distinctive form and content. The world is inherently on its way to, and intrinsically orientated towards, the always already-transformative working power of divine grace. The supernatural is always already working on and forming the transnatural relative state of the natural order in light of the historical transformation wrought by the Incarnation.

Such a view is differently and controversially stated by Milbank in *Theology and Social Theory*, where he is discussing the two primary interpretations of nature/grace that seek to overcome the dualism of the two-tiered version of neo-Thomism. He calls it "a difference that can be crudely indicated and misleadingly summarized by saying that whereas the French version 'supernaturalizes the natural,' the German version 'naturalizes the supernatural.'"[2] Milbank's statement is slightly misleading, but the general thrust is perfectly correct. It is misleading because the German version he is speaking of is really Rahner (as he himself acknowledges). But to see Rahner as representative of the German position is misleading, because there are, of course, Przywara and the Swiss German speaker Balthasar, who are clearly at odds with Rahner's naturalizing of the supernatural. (Milbank would, of course, acknowledge this.) Thus to state it as a German/French "divide" is, indeed, misleading, as he himself attests. However, Milbank is perfectly correct to discern a general partition in the debate over nature/grace, especially as things began to work themselves out post–Vatican II. And he is also right in discerning that this divide consists in a secularization or "naturalization of the supernatural," on the one hand, and a supernaturalization of the natural, on the other. Thus it is not inappropriate to apply what Milbank says above to the *Communio/Concilium* divide, the former falling on the latter side, and the latter falling on the former side of Milbank's statement.

(2) Following from this, it is often said that *Communio* thinkers are revelationally based, while *Concilium* thinkers are correlationally based (a term that is most clearly and fully expounded in the work of Tillich). And here I am thinking, in particular, of David Tracy's comment in his introduction to *God without Being*, in which he makes this apt distinction.[3] Thus it can be said that *Concilium* thinkers are more fundamental and anthropocentrically based, while *Communio* thinkers place more emphasis on the event of revelation, and thus exhibit a more theocentric basis and direction.

(3) These previous two distinctions have a direct bearing on ecclesiology and the place and function of the Church in the modern world. For is the mission of the Church to entirely spill all of its form and content out into the world, thereby abdicating Christian grammar, vision, and form, as seemingly proposed by Schillebeeckx's "*extra mundum nulla salus*"?[4] Or, further, is the Church to empty itself, as in Bonhoeffer's protestant variant of Schillebeeckx's phrase, in a dialectic of secularization (a view that has

---

2. John Milbank, *Theology and Social Theory: Beyond Secular Reason*, 2nd ed. (Oxford: Blackwell, 2006), 207.

3. See David Tracy, foreword to Jean-Luc Marion, *God without Being: Hors-Texte*, trans. Thomas A. Carlson (Chicago: University of Chicago Press, 1991), x–xii.

4. These words of Schillebeeckx come from his final message at a theological symposium held in his honor at the University of Leuven in December of 2008.

had more than a little influence in Catholic thought)? Does the Church, and hence the Christian thinker, lose the power to speak from within the gift of Christ's distinctive Name, thus falling subject to anonymity? Does this not happen if the Church is fully equated with the world where "secularization" is viewed as the new "stage in the historical evolution of Christianity," as Schillebeeckx suggests?[5] And, here, does not all Christian form become totally mute and undiscernible? As O'Regan profoundly and provocatively poses the dilemma, in a very Balthasarian and Lubacian vein, "The battle is now more nearly *within* the church than *between* the church and the world, although the battle inside the church is the battle between the church viewed as church and the church viewed as world."[6] *Communio* thinkers, on the whole, favor the former, while *Concilium* thinkers, on the whole, propose the latter. Such questions of ecclesiology are central for Catholic thought, and, in the interest of this book, implicate the question of the nonecclesial or ecclesial nature of philosophy, and, by further implication, the question of the possibility of Christian philosophy bound to a certain historic tradition and community that lives in a creative fidelity and (re)membering of this living tradition in its nonidentical continuation. (Recall the ecclesial situatedness of analogical vision I laid out in the Introduction.)

(4) It can be said that *Communio* thinkers, as a whole, are more concerned with liturgy, while *Concilium* thinkers and liberation theology place a much-needed emphasis on the question of social justice and political theology. The latter is exemplified in a strong critique of bourgeois Catholicism and the complacency of Christians unwilling to challenge the *status quo* of the ideological framework of Capital's abstract empire and power. This is by no means to say that *Communio* thinkers are wrong to emphasize the supreme importance of liturgy, but it is to say that the element of social

---

5. Cited in Henri de Lubac, *A Brief Catechesis on Nature and Grace*, trans. Brother Richard Arnandez, FSC (San Francisco: Ignatius Press, 1984), 194–95.

6. Cyril O'Regan, *The Anatomy of Misremembering: Von Balthasar's Response to Philosophical Modernity*, vol. 1: *Hegel* (New York: Crossroad, 2014), 290. For a perfect example of these differing views on the Church, see de Lubac's superb critique of Schillebeeckx's interpretation of *Lumen Gentium* and the Church as "sacrament of the world" in de Lubac, *A Brief Catechesis*, 191–234. For an interpretation that reads the integral revolution of nature/grace, enacted by Blondel and de Lubac, as pointing the way towards Metz's view that the "Church is of the world: in a certain sense the Church is the world: the Church is not Non-World." See Gustavo Gutiérrez, *A Theology of Liberation: History, Politics and Salvation*, trans. Sister Caridad and John Eagleson (London: SCM Press, 1971), 97–100.

critique in *Communio* thinkers is extremely insufficient and underdeveloped. Milbank is spot on that "liberation theologians" are "right to point out that thinkers like de Lubac and Balthasar do not fully follow through the implications of their integralism, precisely to the degree that they fail to develop a social or a political theology."[7] Moreover, O'Regan expresses a similar view to Milbank when he acknowledges that Balthasar's treatment of social justice is very underdeveloped as compared to Metz. O'Regan thus fully recognizes the need for the aspect of social justice in Balthasar's apocalyptic *theo*logy to be more fully developed. (I will return to this key point in the final chapter.)[8]

Yet, for both O'Regan and Milbank, it is not a matter of abandoning the vision and breadth of de Lubac's and Balthasar's Christian vision, but rather of showing how this vision of grace more fully funds a political theology (Christian Socialism for Milbank) and a critique of secularity, than does the Rahnerian "naturalized" vision of grace endorsed by liberation theologians.[9] For O'Regan the above problem is a matter of showing that Balthasar's maximalist eidetic apocalyptic is more capable of funding a socio-political or theo-political critique than Metz's more minimalist eidetic apocalyptic discourse.[10] Moreover, it can be said that a serious confrontation with Marxism, Benjamin, Bloch, and the Frankfurt School is severely lacking in *Communio* thinkers, as opposed to the deep dialogue that Metz and liberation theologians have embarked on with these thinkers. Radical Orthodoxy thinkers and O'Regan have certainly moved in this direction,

---

7. Milbank, *Theology and Social Theory*, 209.

8. I will say more about these terms later, but suffice it to say that Balthasar makes use of the entire range of the Christian tradition and especially the Trinitarian backdrop of all of history, while Metz, due to his abiding by Kantian strictures, does not say much on the Trinity and focuses more on the death of Christ and the "dangerous memory" that follows from this death. His approach is thus minimalist in the range and reach of his apocalyptic discourse. However, it is still very clear that O'Regan has a profound appreciation for Metz's work. See O'Regan's wonderful and balanced treatment of Metz in O'Regan, *Misremembering*, 1:426–66.

9. For a fine critique of liberation theology's view of grace and the Church, which, at the same time, realizes the many positive aspects of liberation theology's critique of Capitalism, see Daniel M. Bell Jr., *Liberation Theology After the End of History: The Refusal to Cease Suffering* (London: Routledge, 2001), especially 56–62.

10. O'Regan, in acknowledging Balthasar's underdeveloped social critique, gives hints to how it could be developed but he has, as of yet, to turn fully to this direction in his work. Thus it can be said that the need to develop a maximalist Christian apocalyptic critique of Liberalism/Capitalism is an urgent one in light of Capital's seemingly unstoppable triumph. I will return to this urgent need in the last chapter.

but there is still much to be done in order to fund a critique of Liberalism/Capitalism and the "bio-political" order within a distinctively Christian grammar and vision. Lastly, the great debate between Carl Schmitt and Erik Peterson on the possibility of political theology needs to be attended to by *Communio*-minded thinkers if these issues are to be adequately dealt with. Indeed, I would suggest that Peterson's theo-political vision is the missing component in seeking to establish the apocalyptic and theo-political range of pleromatic enfleshed Christian vision and thus a radical Christian martyrological challenge to the apostate economized political order.[11]

(5) Further, it can be generally stated that *Concilium* thinkers have a much more positive view of modern philosophical discourse and the turn to the subject and, thus, the possibility of situating Catholic philosophy and theology within this framework, than do *Communio* thinkers. This is expressly seen in Transcendental Thomism and the post-Kantian seeking for an anthropological foundation of revelation (Rahner's "what is to be explained is the intrinsic possibility of intellectual knowledge as the place for a theological event") within the dynamism of human knowing cognizant of the limits of Kantian critique.[12] This is also seen in the reliance of Metz and liberation theology on Marxist thought, Bloch, Benjamin, and the Frankfurt School. Metz and liberation theologians thus use the aforesaid thinkers to *fully fund* their philosophical and theological vocabulary, while, conversely, *Communio* thinkers—though by no means avoiding a dialogue with modern and contemporary thought, especially Balthasar—tend to be rightly suspect of the anthropological base of Transcendental Thomism and the basing of theological discourse within the framework of the turn to the subject. Likewise, the dialogue with Marxist thought, Bloch, Benjamin, and the Frankfurt School enacted by *Concilium* thinkers and liberation theology is viewed suspiciously by *Communio* thinkers (and especially Ratzinger).[13] Thus on the whole it can be said that *Con-*

---

11. I intend to take up my Peterson thesis fully in the near future. However, I will briefly return to him in the last chapter of this work, signaling to his importance.

12. Karl Rahner, *Spirit in the World*, trans. William V. Dych (New York: Continuum, 1994), 23.

13. Ratzinger, as head of the Sacred Congregation for the Doctrine of the Faith, of course condemned many aspects of liberation theology in 1984. This condemnation is very complex and cannot, unfortunately, be gone into here. Interestingly, there are now recent signs that, under the Pontificate of Pope Francis, there is a rapprochement with aspects of liberation theology. This is seen in Pope Francis's correspondence with Leonardo Boff as well as his 2013 meeting with Gutiérrez. For some of Ratzinger's views on Marxism, liberation theology,

cilium thinkers exhibit a very positive view of philosophical modernity in its ability to fund Christian discourse, while *Communio* thinkers are more suspicious and tend to look to a resourcing and rereading of the Christian tradition, especially in the thought of patristics and the High Middle Ages.

(6) This brings me to my final point, namely, the stance towards the tradition. On the whole, *Communio* thinkers think that the way forward is the way back (to draw from Eliot). And that the breadth of the living tradition possesses the power and resources to move Catholic thought into the dramatic future. While, conversely, *Concilium* thinkers think that modernity offers the ability and opportunity to bring Catholic thought up-to-date by grounding Catholicism in the move towards the subject and the general secularization enacted through the Enlightenment, Marxism, and modern thought. Catholic thought should thus not be afraid to embrace many of these aspects of modernity in an attempt to reroot Catholic thought within the history of modernity, understood as a history of the event of secularization. However, if O'Regan is right, as I am convinced he is, that the tradition is "a dynamic field of memory, the Christian tradition—as with any tradition or discourse—is constantly threatened by forgetfulness. In a certain sense forgetfulness is coincident with the Christian tradition itself. There was never a time in which we do not find either a straightforward forgetting of the mystery of Christ, or memories which are themselves sophisticated modes of forgetting the essential."[14] The question thus becomes: Is the event of modernity complicit in this forgetting and misremembering of the Christian tradition? The answer given by Przywara, Balthasar, de Lubac, Milbank, Desmond, Hart, and O'Regan is yes—to a great degree—the major discourses that prevail in modernity are complicit in a wide-scale forgetting and misremembering of Christian thought and tradition. What is needed, for these thinkers, is a countermodern or postmodern Christian vision or grammar. This Christian vision resources the

---

Utopia, and chiliastic models of politics, see *Church, Ecumenism and Politics: New Essays in Ecclesiology*, trans. Robert Nowell (Slough, UK: Saint Paul Publications, 1988), especially Part III, "The Church and Politics," 143–255. Ratzinger, in many places in this text, rightly critiques an unwarranted eschatological consciousness and I am, more often than not, at one with these critiques. What I am troubled by is that he nowhere signals to what a robust Christian theo-political philosophy/theology should look like. And, due to this, he exemplifies the underdeveloped social critique lacking in *Communio*-minded thinkers, which I would like to overcome. I also find this fascinating, due to how much, in his theology, he was influenced by Erik Peterson.

14. O'Regan, *Misremembering*, 1:9–10.

tradition, not as a mausoleum, but as a site of remembrance that remembers differently, in order to think the ever-ancient and ever-new freshness of this living tradition in a pleromatic style, thus meeting head on our post-Christian condition.

In sum, this divide is important for gaining an initial foothold in post-Conciliar Catholic discourse. Yet this divide itself needs to be overcome in a full-blooded Christian vision that would be intimately united with Christian practices and forms of life incarnated in Christian social action and *praxis*, as will be discussed later. However, at this point this divide serves the purpose of suggesting and establishing lines of lineage and elective affinities, from a post–Vatican II standpoint, with Stein's and Przywara's differing trajectories at their time of a historic crossroad moment in Catholic thought.

Przywara's and Stein's Thinking Viewed from a Contemporary Vantage

After having offered this brief topography of post-Conciliar Catholic thought, I am now able to more adequately justify and answer how Part 1 opens into Part 2. In other words, I can justify how the groundwork (Part 1) serves and is read for the *telos* of the text (Part 2). Stein's and Przywara's projects both sought to offer an answer to the question of how Catholic thought was to engage philosophical modernity and contemporary philosophical discourse. For both were of the strong opinion that if a forceful and creative answer is not given, then Catholic thought will be dispensed with into the rubbish heap of history. Thus both thinkers exhibited profound daring and creative energy to meet this question in the wake of the modernist crisis at the crossroad moment for Catholic thought in which they stood. Likewise, both viewed this answer as consisting in a form of reimagining of the *analogia entis*. Yet the similarities stopped there. In fact, the actual application of this profound and necessary shared spirit and project could not have been more different, once one turned to the actual contours, logics, and respective narrations on philosophy and being. The question thus becomes, in light of the reemergence of the question of Catholic thinking's encounter with philosophical modernity in the new post-Conciliar context: Which thinker funds and facilitates a more positive and distinctive Christian style and pleromatic *vision* of reality? Which style is capable of adequately thinking difference and relation, as well as resisting the narrative secular pull of philosophical modernity which seeks to abolish the distinctive vision of Christian metaphysics in its close alliance with *theo*logy?

The answer is already self-evident, as confirmed throughout Part 1, that this thinker is, in my view, Przywara. This answer presupposes my stance towards philosophical modernity and my desired expanse of Christian vision as I set forth in the Introduction, which is to say that modernity in general is a discourse that needs to be overcome because of its wide-scale forgetting and distortion of the Christian tradition. Post-Christian secularity as a whole needs to be strenuously resisted. Further, a distinctive Christian pleromatic and dramatic vision is specifically needed in this Christian hour where "epic" and "lyric" styles of Christian discourse are no longer applicable. Both claims are more than controversial and contested. Yet one might add that the very contested nature of these claims is what partly gives them credence as distinctly Christian claims: claims of Christian difference. These claims—as a certain folly and *skandalon*—are dismissed as foolishness by the secular mind that inhabits the uninterested marketplace of ideas unaffiliated to any event or faithfulness to a living community and sacred tradition. But such unaffiliated and uninterested thinking is precisely what is countered by a Christian thinking bound to the foolishness of the *Mysterium Crucis*.

Thus, because of the above view that philosophical modernity represents a grand-scale event of the misremembering of Christianity, and correlatively, the Christian view of analogical being relationally bound to the supernatural, Stein's discourse must be viewed as insufficient to fully challenge this event. Insofar as her discourse is haunted by methodological modernity and the anthropocentric turn, a space of secularity was opened in Stein's Christian philosophy, a style of philosophy that has a foundational base and rationalistic tinge to it. Her discourse was thus in danger of instrumentalizing theological truth and pulling the ever-greater God into an anthropocentric orbit. Therefore, in light of the above topography of the *Communio/Concilium* divide, and specifically the above differences concerning grace, revelation, and the differing strategies towards modernity, it must be said that Stein's discourse shows more affinities with *Concilium*-minded thinkers. This is especially seen in Stein's positive assessment of the Cartesian and Husserlian method and the self-conscious grounding of her philosophy in reflexivity. Her approach shares remarkable similarities with Rahner's transcendentalist route, as has been signaled to along the way. Her philosophy, at the end of the day, must be characterized as a Catholic thinking that is foundational and anthropocentric rather than expressly theocentric.

What is important here is not the fine details of the similarity, but rather the general trajectory, spirit, vision, and strategy towards philosophical modernity that Stein shares with Rahner and *Concilium*-minded thinkers. This is to say, what I am calling into question is the general strategy in these thinkers towards philosophical modernity. Furthermore, let me be clear, I am not insinuating that if Stein had lived she would have fallen into this camp, nor that if she had it would have made a difference. My question again pertains to the expanse of Christian metaphysical vision, which is narrowed by the fundamental anthropocentric tendencies and secular thrust that Stein shares with *Concilium* thinkers in general. In light of Stein's strategy towards philosophical modernity, her thinking does not possess the requisite expansive power to move us in the direction of a robust postmodern Christian vision. Another road must be taken at the crossroad of Catholic thought in which Stein stood and in which we nonidentically stand today.

This road is the pleromatic visionary road of Przywara. Przywara, as a thinker of God's unsurpassable glory, shattered all such anthropocentric pretense in favor of a decentered Christian view of the self, understood as a creature sent on a dramatic performance of mission and service by the ever-greater God. Przywara's strong countermodernity, which emphasized the relative and participatory nature of *philo*sophy in service to the grandeur of God and revelation, offers a robust and specifically Christian vision of reality. This vision is, in turn, able to counter the narrative pull of philosophical modernity and post-Christian secularity. Further, Przywara's trajectory and countermodernity shows an elective affinity with *Nouvelle Théologie/Ressourcement/Communio*-minded thinkers in general, and Balthasar in particular. With that said, if one is seeking to trace and advocate a postmodern Christian vision, as I am seeking to do in Part 2, then Przywara's thinking proves overwhelmingly viable, living, and pertinent to such a task. Given Przywara's sharing a general trajectory with *Nouvelle Théologie/Ressourcement/Communio*-minded thinkers, a line of paternity can thus be traced and plotted with forms of nonidentical repetitions of Przywarian analogical metaphysics in Desmond, Milbank, Hart and, in an apocalyptic register, O'Regan. This is due to the fact that Desmond, Milbank, Hart, and O'Regan all deploy a countermodern strategy towards philosophical modernity that has a strong elective affinity with *Nouvelle Théologie/Ressourcement/Communio*-minded thinkers, in general. We have now arrived at a site where a shared Christian postmodern analogical vision can be traced, elaborated, and synthesized. In Part 2, a constructive reimagining, retrieval, and synthesis of the breadth of Christian analogical metaphysical vision is enacted, via a retrieved expansion of Przywara's vision, in light of our postmodern and post-Conciliar context, ending with a proposed reimagined analogical path forward for Christian thought today in our ever-intensifying dramatic hour of Christian history.

CHAPTER 6

The Postmodern Scene of Thought: Breaking Heidegger's Spell

> *Philosophy today is paralyzed by its relation to its own history.* This paralysis results from the fact that, philosophically examining the history of philosophy, our contemporaries almost all concur to declare that this history has entered the perhaps interminable epoch of its closure.
>
> Alain Badiou, *Manifesto for Philosophy*

In the preceding chapter, the trajectory of twentieth-century Catholic thought was laid out in order to see why Przywara's discourse is to be preferred over Stein's discourse. Lines of lineage and trajectories were thus laid in post-Conciliar Catholic thought. The line of trajectory preferred was one that exhibited a robust countermodernity, thus making way for a postmodern Christian vision and grammar. Thus, if one is seeking a postmodern Christian vision, then postmodernity itself has to be dealt with. That is what I propose to do here. And this means one thing, namely, breaking the spell of the most dominant voice of postmodernity: Heidegger. Only through breaking this spell can a space for a postmodern Christian vision be freed. In this chapter I propose to do this by looking at Heidegger's fabulation of being and his insidious influence on contemporary thought, especially of the religious and Catholic brand. Further, in order for this spell-breaking to be successful it is not enough to merely look at Heidegger's story. Rather, it is also necessary to look at theologically inclined modes of philosophy in contemporary Continental discourse that are under Heidegger's influence. Only in this way can it be seen how Heidegger's thinking truly limits, truncates, and prevents an authentic asking of the question of God, as seen in the generous tradition of Christian thought.

THE POSTMODERN SCENE OF THOUGHT

I end by looking at Desmond and Badiou, in their respective responses to Heidegger, reading them as two successful attempts to move beyond Heidegger in contemporary Continental discourse. This, in turn, sets up chapter 7 where I seek to establish a common postmodern analogical vision through examining nonidentical forms of Przywarian optics in Desmond, Milbank, and Hart. But in order to do this, Heidegger's spell must first be broken. Lastly, in reading this chapter all of my remarks concerning postmodernity in the Introduction need to be kept in mind.

Heidegger's Fabulation of Being

Being's History

"Our Epoch can be said to have been stamped and signed, in philosophy, by the return of the question of Being. This is why it is dominated by Heidegger. He drew up the diagnosis and explicitly took as his subject the realignment, after a century of Criticism and the phenomenological interlude, of thought with its primordial interrogation: what is to be understood by the being of beings?" says Badiou in *The Clamor of Being*.[1] Phenomenology was destined to become ontological and Heideggerian. Heideggerian discourse thus came to dominate Continental philosophy. Yet it is a strange paradox of history that the great thinker of the *Seinsvergessenheit* ends his discourse, in his last public lecture of 1962, "Time and Being," by seeking to eradicate the word *being* in favor of the *es gibt*.[2] The one who was to mourn the "forgetfulness of being" fell into a deeper mode of forgetting and misremembering, thus giving rise to the erasing and crossing-out of being in much of postmodern Continental discourse.

The century that began with the promise of a new beginning and the reemergence of the question of being ends with the proclamation of the "end of philosophy" and the "death of metaphysics." Thinking becomes necessitated by the need to take a "step back" out of philosophy *towards* a poetic thinking *back and into* the history of being, understood as a history of being's own withdrawal and forgetting.[3] Heidegger thus proposes a thinking of being's

---

1. Alain Badiou, *Deleuze: The Clamor of Being*, trans. Louise Burchill (Minneapolis: University of Minnesota Press, 2000), 17.
2. See Martin Heidegger, *On Time and Being*, trans. Joan Stambaugh (Chicago: University of Chicago Press, 2002).
3. For the famed "step back" see Martin Heidegger, "The End of Philosophy and the Task

withdrawal, which can only be thought within the poetic space of being's nonobjective giving, opened in the conversation between thinkers and poets. This dialogue, in turn, seeks to refound the site of the holy in the "fourfold" in the time of the eclipse of the sacred and the nihilistic "enframing" of technology (primarily Hölderlin who thinks the task of poetry and the poet, as well as Rilke and Trakl).[4] Heidegger tells the story—which is a mythicizing meta-history of being's forgottenness and thus a narrative of mourning—of *Aletheia*, which is at first sheltered in the poetic thinking of *physis* found in Heraclitus and Parmenides, which then begins to become occluded in Plato and Aristotle (more so in Plato than Aristotle for Heidegger). This story, then, becomes the long history of the forgetting of being's giving, in favor of the gift of presence in beings: giving gives way to the gift in its shimmering presence.[5] The fate of thinking and the West centers around this fateful turn towards presence and substance where being is thought as such. This is seen in being's various epochal and historical transmutations of the temporal essencing of essence: from the Platonic Idea, Aristotelian substance, the Christian idea of God and creation *ex nihilo*, the Cartesian *Cogito*, Hegel's Absolute Spirit, right up to Nietzsche's will-to-power and the transcendental thinking of Husserl.

History is one prolonged history of being's fated withdrawal from thought, and thought's task becomes the exclusion of the Christian interruption and aberration in order to return thought to the lightness of *Lichtung*, of the clearing in its Greek origins, seen as the free space of open-

---

of Thinking," in *On Time and Being*, 55–73. For more on the death of philosophy see Jacques Derrida, "Violence and Metaphysics," in *Writing and Difference*, trans. Alan Bass (Chicago: University of Chicago Press, 1978), 79.

4. For some of Heidegger's musings on poets and poetry, see Martin Heidegger, *Poetry, Language, Thought*, trans. Albert Hofstadter (New York: HarperCollins, 1971), especially "What Are Poets For?," 89–139; Heidegger, *Elucidations of Hölderlin's Poetry* (Amherst, NY: Prometheus Books, 2000); and Heidegger, *On the Way to Language* (New York: Harper & Row, 1971), especially his treatment of Trakl in "Language in the Poem," 159–200. For Heidegger's thinking on "enframing" see Martin Heidegger, "The Question Concerning Technology," in *Basic Writings* (New York: HarperCollins, 1993), 311–41.

5. For perhaps Heidegger's most important thinking on *Aletheia*, see Martin Heidegger, *Parmenides*, trans. André Schuwer and Richard Rojcewicz (Bloomington: Indiana University Press, 1992). Here the history of *Aletheia* or the history of being is said to be an "apostasy." Heidegger, *Parmenides*, 54. Further, in these lectures Heidegger's anti-Christian sentiments particularly come out insofar as the Christian God—the Creator and Redeemer—is described as one who "dominates" and "calculates" all beings as created, as opposed to the Greek gods who were ruled by the fate of being. Heidegger, *Parmenides*, 110–11. Heidegger's view of the Christian God is thus worlds apart from an analogical conception of the mystery of creation as a whyless loving and freeing *commercium* of being into its relational otherness.

ness. In this openness, being's history can be rethought without entrapping being in the history of its presence, which has consummated itself in nihilism and the closure of the sacred. Thinking becomes a poetic response which, in an Eckhartian form of *Gelassenheit* and Angelus Silesius's "Rose without why," lets beings be outside the nihilistic causal and objective thinking of Western philosophy and the representational subjectivism of modernity.[6] Metaphysics, totalized as the history of being's forgetting, is closed, and the epoch of the thinker in conversation with the poet is opened and announced by Heidegger.

This, however, does not simply mean that metaphysics can be dispensed with, as metaphysics is itself the trace of the withdrawal of being itself. Moreover, to dispense with this history would be to dispense with being itself as the history of Western thought. Thus it is not so much about going beyond this history (at least at first) as a going back into history to think the forgetting of forgetting otherwise than it has been thought before. The thinker stands in the gap of being's withdrawal to remember the giving that was forgotten in the gift. Only in such a way can one lie in wait and prepare for the futural turn of being into another possible transmutation. This is a futural transmutation that Heidegger's thought itself prefigures, but which he himself cannot command ("Only a god can save us"), cannot foretell, as he seeks to shelter and shepherd the whyless play of being that plays like a "royal child." Heidegger's thinking is *provisional* and prefigures a turn towards a new advent of being that would overcome nihilism. However, this advent is only partially aided by us, as we ourselves must wait for impersonal being to turn, to change, to transmute, and come otherwise so that being can come again beyond and otherwise to the history of nihilism, understood as the history of Western metaphysics. Such is what is heralded by the prophet of being and his late thinking marked by "pathmarks." These "pathmarks," though, are only provisional and announce the turnabout in the fate of being itself, which has only started to occur in the thoughtful experience of the event of Heidegger's thinking.[7]

    6. For Heidegger's treatment of the "rose without why," see Heidegger, *The Principle of Reason*, trans. Reginald Lilly (Bloomington: Indiana University Press, 1991), 32–40. For Heidegger's discussion of *Gelassenheit*, see Martin Heidegger, *Discourse on Thinking*, trans. John M. Anderson and E. Hans Freund (New York: Harper & Row, 1966). For one of Heidegger's most impressive texts, on the meaning of thinking, see Martin Heidegger, *What Is Called Thinking?*, trans. J. Glenn Gray (New York: Harper & Row, 1968).

    7. For Heidegger's meditation on the meaning of thinking as a "path," see Martin

It is only through an understanding of the above that the real significance of Heidegger's 1957 lecture "The Onto-theo-logical Constitution of Metaphysics" can be understood, that is, by situating it within Heidegger's metanarrative on being.[8] This is to say, if onto-theology is to be given any real meaning, then it must be done with the intent that Heidegger used it. Otherwise it is merely a generic label that can be, and indeed is, applied to everything. Moreover, reading onto-theology within the context of Heidegger's intended use, that is, as a constitutive feature of being's history of forgetting, allows for two things. First, it gives onto-theology a definitive meaning, which takes Heidegger's narrative of being more seriously than those who view it as a formal framework and criteria that can be applied in exonerating certain figures in the metaphysical tradition of the charge of onto-theology (this is often done by Thomists who read it as an abstract formal criterion that can then be checked off as *not* applying to Aquinas). Second, reading Heidegger's onto-theological critique within the seriousness of the Heideggerian framework of being's history allows one to precisely not take such a critique too seriously, insofar as this critique is situated within Heidegger's fabulous story of being and thus is exactly that, a mere story, albeit a story with extreme visionary power and persuasion. In the end, there are two stances towards Heideggerian thinking, namely, those who take the Heideggerian critique of onto-theology seriously and those who do not. Therefore, reading the onto-theological critique this way allows me to set up the respective responses of the three constellations of thinkers I treat below as a means of setting up the current scene of the turn to religion and how this scene is respectively colored as a response to Heidegger.

Onto-theo-logy

In what does Heidegger's onto-theo-logical critique of metaphysics consist? For Heidegger, onto-theology is anything but an abstract formal scheme or set of rules that test the conceptual adequacy of a thinker's thought of the divine. Heidegger is a historical thinker through and through. And

---

Heidegger, "Preface to the German Edition," in *Pathmarks*, ed. William McNeill (New York: Cambridge University Press, 2005), xiii.

8. See Martin Heidegger, "Onto-theo-logical Constitution of Metaphysics," in *Identity and Difference*, trans. Joan Stambaugh (New York: Harper & Row, 1969), 42–74.

this means that history must be interpreted *as being's own history*. This history, as was just seen, is the history of being's withdrawing absence, which gives way to the gift of beings in their unavoidable presence. For Heidegger, no thinking can escape this fate of being, which is also the fate of thinking the divine in an onto-theological manner. Not even Heidegger can fully escape such a thinking, insofar as he stands at the crossroads of a thinking that must, out of historic necessity, think the history of being as the history of forgetting. His thought only heralds the turnabout in being's historical destiny: a turnabout of being's historical and impersonal sending, which remains unthought because it is still coming and thus uncertain and eschatologically withheld. This implies that to ask if a thinker escapes onto-theology is a foolish question that misses the fateful sending of being as presence in Greek thought to which, as Westerners, we are all subject, whether we like it or not. This is why the context of "The Onto-theo-logical Constitution of Metaphysics" is central, as oftentimes it is ignored that the whole conversation takes place with Hegel *the* historical thinker who, for Heidegger, consummates the forgetting of being in Absolute Thought. Absolute thinking is thus the prime instance of a thinking of being as presence-to-thought. And such thinking is the epitome of onto-theo-logical thinking of the divine, understood as the Absolute of Thought.[9]

It is only in this historical context, in conversation with Hegel (understood as *the* historical thinker), that the question of how the deity and theology enter into philosophy is posed. Yet all of this has its ground and beginning in the fact *that being first gives itself as presence*. This presence launches the history of metaphysics as a thinking of the being of beings, and thus as ground. This, in turn, leaves being as unthought amidst and within the historical game of being's "royal" hiding. In other words, it is only in light of the historical dispensation of being as presence that the question of onto-theology makes sense. If being had not sent itself as presence to Greek thinking, then there would never have been something like onto-theo-logy. How and why being was sent in such a way one cannot *say*. For to seek an answer to this question would be to place being within the causal matrix of Western thought that Heidegger is trying to overcome. At most, what one can say is that being has *occurred*. And it is this occurrence, this *event*, which is the fate and task of Western history and thought. Being, therefore, occludes itself as origin, or hides itself at the origin of Western

---

9. For the discussion of Hegel see Heidegger, "Onto-theo-logical Constitution," especially 42–57.

thought and history. Thus is Heidegger's fiction, and only in this story of historical sending does something like onto-theo-logy occur. This means that onto-theo-logy is not a formal criterion that one either meets, or fails to meet, in thinking the divine in an idolatrous or nonidolatrous manner. It is only because being sends itself as presence that being is thought in terms of beings and thus tied to ground and grounding. Such a move of grounding being in beings requires a further grounding of the *being* of beings in another being. This is how, historically, the deity enters into philosophy—namely, as the ultimate ground of all grounding, the *causa sui*, which serves the highest function as the ground of being and beings because being has dispensed itself as presence in beings. This, in turn, requires one to give an account, i.e., metaphysics. God, due to the historical sending of being as the being of beings, i.e., presence, gets caught in a causal matrix of grounding and the logic of giving account. God, in the history of metaphysics, thus serves a logical and rationalistic function of representational thought. "Before the *causa sui*, man can neither fall to his knees in awe nor can he play music and dance before this god."[10]

Heidegger thus proposes that in light of the "step back" out of metaphysical thinking, which has begun to occur in his thinking, we abandon the idol of the God of the philosophers in favor of a god-less thinking. This thinking thinks in the hour of darkness and the exclusion of the holy as one lies in wait for the turnaround in the fate of being, a fate that remains uncertain in the face of the all-consuming representational thinking of technology. Indeed, such an a-theistic "god-less" approach may be closer to the divine God than the idolatrous causal God of grounding: the God of philosophers.[11] Yet the entire question of onto-theo-logy is bound to take place within the historical sending of being's dispensation of presence, through which the unthought history of being's difference from beings occurs. Being sent itself as presence and thus withdrew, in its very sending, thus giving rise to the errant path of Western metaphysics and its conceptual construct, the *causa sui*. This is Heidegger's historical fiction and the story he tells, a story that is *the story of being's very history*.

Heidegger's story is fabulous, visionary, and powerful. But it is precisely the fabulousness of the story that, in its tragic beauty and prophetic resonance, is, as a whole, riddled and transmuted with submerged Christian symbolism. This inverted and submerged Christian symbolism should,

---

10. Heidegger, "Onto-theo-logical Constitution," 72.
11. Heidegger, "Onto-theo-logical Constitution," 72.

to the discerning eye of the Christian thinker, render it highly suspect. Yet more than a few Christian thinkers have been enamored by Heidegger's visionary grand hermeneutic of the forgetfulness of being. And, in so being, they have set up Christian discourse within the Heideggerian framework. This is because Heidegger offers a historical narrative that gives a genuine aesthetic and dramatic (apocalyptic) *vision* and grammar through which things can be seen and interpreted in a time of the dissolving of the visionary power of the *mysterium* of the Christian story. Thus, not unlike Hegel, he offers a real vision filled with symbolism, borrowed from Christianity, now enlisted in the service of a secular eschatology and counternarrative. This is partly and importantly why Christian thought must return to its visionary power as opposed to "epic" and "lyric" styles of Christian discourse. In other words, the Christian thinker must have recourse to its dramatic *apokalypsis* if it is to counter these counterfeit forms of visionary *apokalypsis*.

Przywara is perfectly right: "That Heidegger is determined to take these features [unconcealment/concealment and being's arrival] as the features of *his* [italics mine] 'truth in the Logos in thought' is avenged from the very first, but especially in the final phase of his thought, in that it presents not a thinking dedicated to a 'philosophy of the Logos,' but an attempt at a 'new *mythos* and *mysterium*' into which he 'initiates' his disciples in the role of a real 'mystagogue.'"[12] Where Christian thinkers fail to think the visionary drama of the Christian story and "demythologize" its revelatory mystery, Heideggerian initiation is waiting in the vacuum of a rationalized and domesticated Christianity. Thus for a Christian thinker of visionary and pleromatic stamp, the mystagogical and initiatory nature of Heidegger's thinking, with its neo-pagan/post-Christian appropriation of Christian symbolism, is highly problematic. Further, if Badiou is right about the heavily committed and decisional nature of thought, and indeed that one *must choose* between Callicles and Socrates: How much more does this choice apply between Heidegger's new *mythos* and the Christian *mysterium* where, in the latter, truth is never one's own truth, but the Truth of the *Logos* that Christian thinking obediently and dramatically follows at a distance?[13] I would suggest that Heidegger's visionary narrative of being has

---

12. Erich Przywara, "Image, Likeness, Symbol, Mythos, Mysterium, Logos," in *Analogia Entis: Metaphysics: Original Structure and Universal Rhythm*, trans. John R. Betz and David Bentley Hart (Grand Rapids: Eerdmans, 2014), 455.

13. See Alain Badiou, "Thinking the Event," in *Philosophy in the Present: Alain Badiou*

reversed—in a submerged and subtle way—more powerfully than any other thinker (next to Hegel) the great Christian Alexandrian slogan of *spoliatio Aegyptiorum* into a *spoliatio Christianorum*. As such, when one takes up the Heideggerian narrative one takes up the implications, choices, intent, and visionary inverted Christian symbols of his thinking as well: that is unavoidable. A choice is demanded within thought for or against Heidegger's magical and mystagogical cult of being, which is complicit in a large-scale, yet submerged, "misremembering" of the Christian tradition of thought.

Postmodern Thought as a Reponse to Heidegger: Three Constellations

In seeking to lay out the trajectory of contemporary postmodern Continental thought, it is necessary to focus this question, for the purposes of this work, on the revival of religious discourse and/or the theological "turn" that has taken place in Continental thought. This "turn" has two features. First, the theological and creedal (and by creedal I mean, in this instance, specifically, Catholic) element in its French variant. This is expressed in what the late Janicaud has called the "theological turn" in French phenomenology as seen in thinkers like Marion, Chrétien, Lacoste (as well as the more heterodox thinking of the late Henry).[14] Second, this religious "turn" finds a heavy noncreedal element in its English-speaking variant, in thinkers like Caputo, Mark C. Taylor, and Kearney, all of whom, in one way or another, plead for a postmodern "religion without religion." (All of these thinkers are "Catholic," but all have distanced themselves from an explicit confessional or ecclesial context, and hence I am placing them in the noncreedal category.) Above and beyond these two constellations of thinkers lies a third group that must be added. This group is strongly conversant with, and implicated in, the religious "turn" in Continental thought. However, the latter group does not easily fit within the parameters of the above two groups. This constellation has two features. First, it consists in the postmodern Christian metaphysical thinking of Desmond (Catholic), Hart (Eastern Orthodox), and the Radical Orthodoxy thinkers (largely an

---

and Slavoj Žižek, ed. Peter Engelmann, trans. Peter Thomas and Alberto Toscano (Malden, MA: Polity Press, 2009), 15.

14. See, generally, Dominique Janicaud et al., *Phenomenology and the "Theological Turn": The French Debate* (New York: Fordham University Press, 2000), for the contours of this debate.

Anglo-Catholic phenomenon). The second aspect of this constellation is seen in atheistic thinkers like Žižek and Badiou (and Agamben in a slightly different register) and their fascinating nonreductive materialist dialogue with Christianity. That being said, I am proposing to examine all three constellations of thinkers in their respective responses to Heidegger, as their different responses to Heidegger will color and shape their religious and theological discourse through and through. This shows the strictures that the Heideggerian visionary narrative places on the possible range of Christian vision and discourse.

The Theological "Turn" in French Phenomenology

The ancestry of the theological "turn" in French phenomenology is rooted in the late Heidegger's thinking on givenness and withdrawal set within the frame of poetic nuance or saying. Moreover, this turn is also rooted in the thinking otherwise of Levinas and the counter-intentional rending of intentionality by the face of the other, beyond and other to, being. There is also the source of revelational-based *Nouvelle Théologie*, and especially the influence of de Lubac and Balthasar. However, my interest here is this group's response to Heidegger. It needs to be noted that Marion, Chrétien, and Lacoste all have varying responses to Heidegger and they thus do not present a single voice (Henry is different insofar as he is more *sui generis* and is not implicated here) in their respective responses. Nevertheless, there are certain structural similarities that can easily be discerned. That is, all of the aforementioned thinkers are in agreement that the Heideggerian critique of metaphysics has brought an end to metaphysics as such and that we are now living in a post-metaphysical epoch. This means that in the relation between Christian *theo*logy and philosophy, post-metaphysical phenomenology (conceived as post-Heideggerian and post-Levinasian) assumes pride of place over the long-held status of metaphysics as the primary propaedeutic to *theo*logy. In this they are heirs of Heidegger (even if Heidegger thinks that his thinking has moved beyond phenomenology to thought). This view is most strongly expressed by the most renowned of the group, Marion.[15] But it is clearly endorsed by Chrétien

---

15. For Marion's argument for phenomenology as first philosophy, see Jean-Luc Marion, *In Excess: Studies of the Saturated Phenomenon*, trans. Robyn Horner and Vincent Bernard (New York: Fordham University Press, 2002), 1–29.

and Lacoste as well. Moreover, all situate their respective discourses as a critical response to the ineluctable Heideggerian dilemma: Marion by seeking to think God as Agape outside of being's history (or later givenness and the gift outside being), Lacoste by trying to think a liturgical phenomenological subject outside of the secularized and paradoxically pagan conception of Heidegger's view of man, and Chrétien by rethinking the call and response as inherently religious, and language as a doxological act through which we humbly offer God back the gift of the world through our "wounded speech" as opposed to man's response to the call of impersonal being in Heidegger.[16]

No doubt all go beyond Heidegger in much-needed ways, the most important being the deep dialogue opened up by these thinkers in their "turn" towards the distinctive power of *theo*logy and Christian revelation to shed light on, and interpenetrate, phenomenological investigation. And the converse side of this is that phenomenology is not just confined to the limits of what appears, but is open to more exalted forms of phenomena that are in excess of the categories of thought, thus saturating thought above and beyond the concept, to speak the language of Marion.[17] Phenomenology is open, though by no means exclusively so, to the possibility of thinking themes of revelation beyond the apostate divide of philosophical modernity. This is a profound move beyond the early methical atheism of Heidegger as well as the mytho-poetics of being enacted in the late Heidegger. Yet despite all of this, the question must be forcefully asked: Has this group, in general, capitulated too much to the Heideggerian critique of metaphysics? And, in so doing have they accepted, as a *fait accompli*, that the great pleromatic metaphysical tradition of Christian thought was culpable and complicit in thinking God in terms of being in an idolatrous

---

16. For Lacoste's response to Heidegger see Jean-Yves Lacoste, *Experience and the Absolute: Disputed Questions on the Humanity of Man*, trans. Mark Raftery-Skehan (New York: Fordham University Press, 2004), especially, but by no means exclusively, 32–37. Lacoste's work is dedicated to the memory of de Lubac, thus manifesting the genealogical presence of *Nouvelle Théologie* in the theological "turn" in French phenomenology. For Chrétien's response to Heidegger see Jean-Louis Chrétien, *The Call and the Response*, trans. Anne A. Davenport (New York: Fordham University Press, 2004), especially, but not exclusively, "The Other Voice," 44–82; and Jean-Louis Chrétien, *The Ark of Speech*, trans. Andrew Brown (London: Routledge, 2004), especially "Offering of the World," 111–49.

17. For Marion's thought on saturation, see Jean-Luc Marion, *Being Given: Toward a Phenomenology of Givenness*, trans. Jeffrey L. Kosky (Stanford, CA: Stanford University Press, 2002), especially 199–220; and Marion, *In Excess*, especially his treatments of the event, 30–53, the idol, 54–81, the flesh, 82–103, and the icon, 104–27.

manner, and hence, that a Christian metaphysical thinking of God as *Being* is now forbidden us?

To answer this, I will take the most extreme example of the group, that is, the early Marion. I am well aware that just treating Marion does not do justice to some of the differences and divergences with the other two. But insofar as Marion is the most renowned and extreme of the group, I am forced, in light of space, to let his voice be representative. That being said, I am also working under the above-said assumption that the absence of any metaphysics in the work of Lacoste and Chrétien is due to a capitulation to the Heideggerian critique of metaphysics, which Marion takes to the extreme. Thus the work of Lacoste and Chrétien finds resonance and structural similarities with the extreme stance of Marion, albeit not to the same degree. In other words, the varying capitulation to the Heideggerian critique in these thinkers is a quantitative distinction and not qualitative. And they thus can be treated as a certain direction and constellation within the contemporary response to Heidegger.

No Christian or Catholic thinker has thought through more rigorously the consequences of the Heideggerian critique of onto-theology and what a post-metaphysical Christian theology would look like than Marion. Nor has any thinker taken more seriously the charge of idolatry within metaphysics and the Christian tradition than Marion. Yet despite the brilliance, rigor, and originality of Marion's thinking and critique, the question must be seriously and forcefully posed: Has not Marion fallen into another form of idolatry that demands God give up the very energy and unspeakable infinity of his *Being*, merely because a Heideggerian reading of being's history demands it? To hold such a view is simply another way of putting strictures and limitations on God. This time, not as an attempt to think God as being, but God as beyond being, now conceived within the very story of being fabricated by Heidegger. Such thinking precisely makes God subservient, not to an inadequate metaphysical construct (a worry this book strongly shares), but rather to a style of thinking that makes God subservient to one particular thinker's view of being. But, as Przywara rightly saw, this view of being was Heidegger's own personal truth. Thus to think God otherwise to Heidegger's critique, on the basis of Heidegger's critique, is to make God subservient to one thinker's interpretation of being and the fabulous story that comes with it. To do so is to capitulate that Christian thinking has no say on history. Indeed, that there is no such thing as a Christian interpretation of history (a Christian philosophy or *theo*logy of history). History, for Marion, in *The Idol and Distance* and *God* *without Being*, is taken to mean the history of metaphysical idolatry and the *Seinsvergessenheit*. Here Christian thinkers, and especially Aquinas, in *God without Being*, are fully accused of idolatry in light of the Heideggerian history.[18] It is true in *The Idol and Distance* that there is still a very faint trace of the *analogia entis*, insofar as Marion brings Heidegger's *Ereignis* into conversation with Balthasar's fourfold distinction of being. Here Marion reads the "it gives" in its whyless inane game of play as a faint, vague, and distant icon of Christian distance. That is, insofar as the Christian thinker must be within the indifference of being in order to forgive it its inanity, thus making it a faint icon of the Christian distance between the Father and Son.[19]

However, such an approach of reading being as an ever-so-faint icon of God is wholly abandoned in *God without Being*. This is due to being's extreme vanity (already prefigured in being's inanity in *The Idol and Distance*).[20] Furthermore, any talk of a faint relation of God to being is dropped in favor of an extreme negative theology or hyperousiology, where God is understood as Agape and thus wholly other to being. Being is, therefore, always and necessarily an idolatrous attribute, ascription, or description of God. Further, in this extreme hyperousiology the glory of creation is not given any weight insofar as the analogical relationality of the freeing of creation, into the gift of its difference, is not viewed as positive. And because being is not viewed as created, but rather as the inane history of being's idolatrous mirror of vanity, then God is set over the world in a distance, which is far too neutral, aloof, and perhaps even Jansenistic. As such, there is no possibility of an analogical unity-in-difference. And, correlatively, there is no possibility of a genuine *commercium* of love, set within the *prius* of God's alterity and ever-greater positivity of *Being*, which

---

18. For Marion's charge of idolatry against Aquinas see Jean-Luc Marion, *God without Being: Hors-Texte*, trans. Thomas A. Carlson (Chicago: University of Chicago Press, 1991), 77–83. For Marion's retraction of the charge of idolatry against Aquinas and his more nuanced, but still insufficient treatment of Aquinas, see Jean-Luc Marion, "Thomas Aquinas and Onto-theo-logy," in *Mystics: Presence and Aporia*, ed. Michael Kessler and Christian Sheppard (Chicago: University of Chicago Press, 2003), 38–74.

19. For Marion's treatment of Balthasar's "fourfold distinction" in conversation with Heidegger's *Ereignis*, which is arguably the most fascinating portion of the text, see Jean-Luc Marion, *The Idol and Distance: Five Studies*, trans. Thomas A. Carlson (New York: Fordham University Press, 2001), especially "Distance and Its Icon," 198–253. And for specific references to Balthasar, see 245–46, 249.

20. For Marion's treatment of the vanity of being, see Marion, *God without Being*, especially 119–25. For the "inanity" of being see, again, Marion, *Idol and Distance*, 198–253.

sets free the positivity of created being-in-becoming as a gift of difference. Following from this, the site of creation *is not* viewed as a free and genuine exchange between God and man. In Marion, all genuine analogical relationality, opened by Przywara and the great tradition, is made impossible, because being is *Ereignis* and thus God is not, and cannot be, *Being*.[21]

There are three main weaknesses in Marion's attempt to think God outside and beyond Heideggerian being. First, Marion seeks to base Christian philosophy and *theo*logy wholly within the Heideggerian framework and thus Heidegger's view of the history of being. Further, if being and history are read in a Heideggerian manner, then a Christian transformation of metaphysics is prohibited, *a priori*, from offering a counternarrative to Heidegger's visionary narrative. Second, following directly from the first, he flatly ignores the seminal Christian metaphysical doctrine of creation *ex nihilo*, which is metaphysically expressed in the *analogia entis*. Such an ignoring of creation and the *analogia entis* prevents him from also ascribing to the analogical axiom of Christian thought, namely, grace does not destroy, but presupposes and perfects nature (or being). Third, following from the previous two, he fails to grasp the implication of the return to the concrete historical interpretation of grace in the one concrete order of grace and redemption, as found in Przywara and his fellow *Communio* confrères, de Lubac and Balthasar. For if Marion acknowledged this, then he would have the basis for a Christian view of history that would see Heidegger's view of history as an anti-Christian competing visionary narrative that fails to see history as an apocalyptic opening for or against the Christian God.

Marion, then, is complicit in another form of idolatry, insofar as he demands God give up his ever-greater majesty of *Being* because one historical thinker proclaims it must be so. Such a view both constricts and restricts Christian philosophy and *theo*logy by tying them—and indeed demanding—that Christian philosophy and *theo*logy think within Heidegger's historical narrative, if idolatry is to be avoided. At the end of the day, one has to conclude with both Desmond and Balthasar concerning the limits of Marion's attempt to think a post-metaphysical theology. Desmond says, "I do not subscribe to the view that Heidegger has a corner on being, and that to think God we must do so without being

---

21. For a balanced critique of Marion's failure to think analogy, see David Bentley Hart, *The Beauty of the Infinite: The Aesthetics of Christian Truth* (Grand Rapids: Eerdmans, 2003), 237–41.

(Marion), as if Heidegger had a lock on being."[22] And further as Balthasar rightly states, "J. L. Marion seems in his two works *L'Idole et la distance*... and *Dieu sans l'être* to concede too much to the critique of Heidegger."[23] For to "concede" Heidegger too much is to concede being and history and thus foreclose the possibility of a distinctive Christian grammar of being and history, as found in the vision of an analogical metaphysics, and thus the possibility of a countergrammar and story to Heidegger's grand visionary tale.

Marion, as the extreme representative of the post-metaphysical phenomenological thinkers of the theological turn, cannot and does not represent an adequate response to Heidegger. Marion, along with Chrétien and Lacoste, capitulates too much to the critique of Heidegger. This is manifested insofar as the relation between philosophy and *theo*logy is accepted to be, as a fate of history, post-metaphysical and post-Heideggerian. They are thus unable to draw from the great reserves of pleromatic Christian Wisdom and its metaphysical tradition. Without these reserves, they are unable to offer a robust resistance to Heidegger's discourse, within a Christian metaphysical framework and history, due to their limited post-metaphysical grammar and phenomenological framework. Heidegger's visionary master narrative greatly limits the expanse of Christian vision in these profound but, ultimately, insufficient thinkers.

The Noncreedal Turn to Religion

In turning to the noncreedal turn to religion, in its English-speaking variant, one discovers the same surrender to the Heideggerian narrative of the end of metaphysics and onto-theology as found above. This is expressly seen in the work Caputo, Mark C. Taylor, and Kearney, all of whom exude a tremendous allergy to anything which, to their thinking, smacks of metaphysics and presence. All three are prime exemplars of postmodern thinkers seeking to rethink and restructure thinking on God, or better, the divine *after* the closure of metaphysics, inaugurated by Heidegger. As with the other thinkers of the theological turn, they likewise take a critical stance to Heidegger on many issues. However, in the essential, they

---

22. William Desmond, *God and the Between* (Oxford: Blackwell, 2008), 8.
23. Hans Urs von Balthasar, *Theo-Logic*, vol. 2: *Truth of God*, trans. Adrian J. Walker (San Francisco: Ignatius Press, 2004), 135.

remain heirs and sons of Heidegger. This is to say, the above thinkers fully and completely embrace and herald the "death of metaphysics," a death that is viewed in a positive light as a necessary historical and iconoclastic smashing of metaphysical idols. Hellenized Christian theology has been chained to metaphysics for too long, amidst and within the erring centuries of Western thought. The Western tradition of Christian thought must suffer a "twilight of the idols" so that the false God who *Is* can be replaced by the god who never comes and is, thus, always coming.

Taylor and Caputo seek to accomplish this with the aid of Derridean deconstruction, through which they seek to free the divine from the economy of presence in light of the undecidability of *différance*. Moreover, since both Taylor and Caputo seek to apply deconstruction to religion, theology, and God, they can both be said to share a common project. However, this project differs on one primary point. Taylor in *Erring: A Postmodern A/Theology* pushes deconstruction in favor of a death of God theology[24] and thus, in Caputo's view, turns "*différance* against God," thereby seeking a closure that deconstruction itself does not, and cannot, permit.[25] Caputo seeks to accentuate what is to his mind the affirmative side of deconstruction and its openness and passion for the impossible. Such openness is paradigmatically expressed in the Augustinian question, "What do I love when

---

24. See Mark C. Taylor, *Erring: A Postmodern A/theology* (Chicago: University of Chicago Press, 1984). This is a watermark text in postmodern theology or a/theology and can thus be seen as paving the way for Caputo's religious use of deconstruction. Taylor's text is a seminal text because it creatively seeks to combine deconstruction with Altizer's "death of God theology." The purpose of this, for Taylor, quoting Altizer, is to enact "'a true revolution'" against orthodox Christianity that is not "'simply an opening to the future but also a closure of the past. Yet the past which is negated by a revolutionary future cannot simply be negated or forgotten. It must be transcended by way of a reversal of the past, a reversal bringing a totally new light and meaning to everything which is manifested as the past, and therefore a reversal fully transforming the whole horizon of the present. Modern revolutionary assaults upon the whole movement of profane or secular history can now serve not only as models but also as sources for a revolutionary theological assault on the history of faith.'" Taylor, *Erring*, 9. Taylor seeks to enact this "reversal," called for by Altizer, by perversely rereading and deconstructing what are to Taylor's mind "the four notions essential to the Western theological network": God, the self, history, and the book. Taylor, *Erring*, 13. The end result is a totally heterodox Christology that, in a Blakean manner, seeks to marry heaven and hell, Christ and the Antichrist, in a postmodern carnivalesque and transgressive revel. It is unfortunate that there is not space enough to properly critique Taylor's parasitic and perverse logic and project here.

25. John D. Caputo, *The Prayers and Tears of Jacques Derrida* (Bloomington: Indiana University Press, 1997), 14.

I love my God?"[26] Now, however, this question is read through the lens of deconstruction as an expression of the love and desire for the impossible, of the *tout autre* that will never come. Kearney, on the other hand, takes a negative view of deconstruction and undecidability in favor of a more ethically minded thought. Kearney thinks it important to ask what the perpetually deferred openness of deconstruction's unnameability/undecidability is actually open to: a god or a monster? Kearney's thinking, then, is heavily influenced by Levinas and liberation theology. And in this influence is seen a deep concern for the poor, widows, strangers, and orphans.[27] However, despite these minor differences, all three are of one mind that we have definitively and irrevocably entered a post-metaphysical era, thereby explicitly accepting the Heideggerian critique. In so doing all three frame their respective discourses in this Heideggerian shadow.

In light of my interests here, I propose to look at Kearney's work for the following reasons. First, because Caputo will be treated in chapter 8, he will not be treated here. Further, seeing how there is a good amount of overlap between Caputo and Taylor in their deconstructive reading of religion, theology, and God, Taylor will not be treated, in order to avoid overlap. These are the negative and practical reasons for treating Kearney. Second, the positive reason for choosing Kearney is that he is by no means as extreme as Caputo and Taylor. He is also able to properly discern weaknesses in Caputo's and Marion's respective approaches. Following from this, Kearney seeks to offer a middle ground within contemporary Continental thought and the turn to religion by presenting what I will term a "weak metaxology."[28] Because of this, Kearney's work broaches a liminal

---

26. Caputo, *Prayers and Tears*, xxii. This question of Augustine, put to the use of deconstruction, is a continual refrain throughout most, if not all, of Caputo's work after his turn towards Derrida away from Heidegger, though, of course, this question of Augustine was first enlisted by Derrida in *Circumfession*, this time, however, putting the emphasis on my or *meum* and not God.

27. Kearney cites liberation theology as a source of his thinking. See Richard Kearney, "Maybe Not, Maybe: William Desmond on God," in *Between System and Poetics: William Desmond and Philosophy after Dialectic*, ed. A. F. Kelly (Burlington, VT: Ashgate, 2007), 197.

28. Concerning the relation between the two thinkers, Desmond says that "I have learned from his [Kearney's] stress on eschatological possibility." William Desmond, "Maybe, Maybe Not: Richard Kearney on God," in *After God: Richard Kearney and the Religious Turn in Continental Philosophy*, ed. John Panteleimon Manoussakis (New York: Fordham University Press, 2006), 56. It should be noted that Desmond's essay first appeared in *The Irish Theological Quarterly* in 2003, and was then later reprinted in *After God*. Likewise, Kearney in *The God Who May Be* borrows Desmond's neologism "metaxology." Kearney says "we share

space in the constellation of thinkers I have placed him in. He is able to point in another direction that he himself cannot take. However, this direction is taken by his fellow Irishman and fellow metaxological thinker, namely, Desmond, as will be seen. To state it simply: Kearney's thinking is more nuanced than Caputo's and Taylor's, but still overly laden with the commonplace narrative of onto-theology. He thus sets up the need for the move beyond Heidegger, enacted in the third constellation of thinkers, but a move that he himself never fully makes.

In what then does Kearney's more nuanced move consist? It consists of situating the question of God in the very heart of the extremes of postmodern discourse. He takes up a "middle way" between the "extremes of absolutism and relativism" present within post-Heideggerian thinking on the divine.[29] These extremes are exemplified in the unconstrained apophaticism of Marion and Levinas, both of whom hold to a God of radical transcendence. This God is so transcendent that absolutely nothing can be said concerning it. The other extreme is manifested in thinkers like Caputo, Žižek, Campbell, Lyotard, and Kristeva, all of whom force God into some sort of underground of abyssal unnameability.[30] Kearney seeks to maneuver a "middle way" between the hyper-transcendent deity of negative or apophatic theology and the chaotic and monstrous underground of the kataphatic postmodern theologians. In so doing he advances a hermeneutic philosophy that is thoughtful of the mediating place of metaphor (Ricoeur's influence). This is expressed in his philosophy of religion, which sees God neither in terms of nonbeing nor being, but instead as the possibility-to-be. Kearney nominates his approach "onto-eschatology" and "narrative eschatology."[31]

Kearney discerns the need for a balance between univocity and equivocity and between kataphatic and apophatic theology. This, for him, is what is missing in the extremes of post-Heideggerian thinking on the divine. Indeed, if one were just to read Kearney's critique, one might think he is pleading for some faint form of the *analogia entis* as a relational me-

---

[Kearney and Desmond] a common determination to choose a middle way (Greek, *metaxy*) between the extremes of absolutism and relativism." Richard Kearney, *The God Who May Be: A Hermeneutics of Religion* (Bloomington: Indiana University Press, 2001), 6. Moreover, for an interview by Kearney with Desmond, see *The Desmond Reader*, ed. Christopher Ben Simpson (Albany: State University of New York Press, 2012), 229–44.

29. Kearney, *God Who May Be*, 6.
30. Kearney, *God Who May Be*, 7.
31. Kearney, *God Who May Be*, 8.

diation between univocity/equivocity and the kataphatic/apophatic. However, this is clearly not so. And the reason for this is that the parameters within which Kearney seeks to address the question of God are already set. They are the parameters of Heidegger's critique of onto-theology. Kearney's allegiance to Heidegger is extremely evident in his facile dismissal of Augustine, Bonaventure, Aquinas, and Gilson as onto-theologians.[32] Thus the best that Kearney can do is set up his discourse on the divine as a mediation between the extremes of post-Heideggerian discourse on the divine and nothing more.

Further, because Kearney's discourse on the divine finds itself between the extremes of post-Heideggerian discourse, then the most he can offer is a "weak metaxology" and thus a view of God as the possibility-to-be: "God neither is nor is not but may." This is his answer to the extremes of post-Heideggerian kataphatic and apophatic discourse. Yet, such a god is an erotic god that needs and desires man if this god is to come or (be)come. As Kearney provocatively says in his essay "Enabling God,"

> I want to propose . . . a God who needs man and desires us, who dwells in the room next door, as Rilke daringly puts it "Du, Nachbar Gott," waiting for our signs, just as we wait in turn. Here is another kind of God—one who cannot come or come back, who cannot be conceived or become incarnate, until we open the door, until we give the cup of cold water, until we share the bread, until we cry "I am here? Where are you? Why don't you come?"[33]

Kearney's "onto-eschatology" seeks a god of mutuality, reciprocity, equality, and sameness with man. Such a god is finite, erotic, and historical. It is a vision of a becoming god that stands in need of man to come and (be)come.

This view is the polar opposite of the Christian God of creation and grace, who, in the mystery of his transcendence and freedom (the *prius* of God's analogical relationality), freely gives creation to be. Not because the Christian God needs man to be or (be)come, but simply because he desires creation to be, without any need and why. Here is a needless desire, and needless giving, manifested in God's gift to creation. It is this whyless free giving that analogical thought respects, as it thinks within the *commercium*

---

32. See Kearney, *God Who May Be*, 22–25.
33. Richard Kearney, "Enabling God," in *After God*, 65.

of creation-as-gift. God does not need to create, but in the mystery of his agapeic love he freely *desires* to. Here one returns to the sojourning site of analogical thought, namely, the *reductio in mysterium* of the ever-greater mystery of God's love. The love of this God is a mystery of non-necessitated freedom, an agapeic and desirous giving. Such a giving love is, and will always be, wholly incomprehensible and mysterious.

Kearney's view of God is opposed to such whyless giving. Nevertheless, he was able to diagnose certain weaknesses in post-Heideggerian discourse on the divine. But because his proposed solution assumed the very assumption of the extremes of the impasse that he was trying to overcome, namely onto-theology, his discourse was unable to succeed from the outset. The most Kearney was able to offer in his "weak metaxology" was a god that "neither is nor is not but may." Such a god is wholly erotic and needful and could not (be)come without us. Moreover, Kearney's view of the divine is a perfect example of the inherent limitations of thinking the divine in a post-Heideggerian fashion. From the Christian analogical viewpoint such an understanding of the divine is wholly deficient for the following reasons. First, as with Marion, it places Heideggerian strictures on how one can and cannot think God. Second, such strictures prohibit a nonidentical re-turn to the great pleromatic Christian metaphysical/theological tradition and its generous and spacious thinking on God. Third, Kearney's god as erotic, needful, and historically finite is indiscernible from the fabric of the human image and the human imagination. This god is, therefore, cut from the same cloth as man. God, for Kearney, is a neighbor of man, mutually one with man. This god waits for man to let him be god: the god of our making and of our eschatological imagination. But such a god is a god of human fabrication and, therefore, an idol.

To conclude: neither of the first two constellations of thinkers are able to overcome Heidegger due to the fact that, from the very outset, they capitulate and give too much credence to Heidegger's narrative of the end of metaphysics and onto-theology. By doing so, the parameters of thinking God are constricted and restricted within the Heideggerian framework: God *must not be thought as Being*. The Heideggerian framework and spell needs to be broken. One must move beyond those who contentedly attend metaphysic's wake, a wake at which all complacently conspire in the talk of the otherwise or beyond of being. Such is the task of the third constellation of thinkers.

Breaking Heidegger's Spell

Heidegger Called into Question

For the majority of Continental postmodern thinkers, to not take seriously Heidegger, and his critique of the death of metaphysics and onto-theology, is to not take seriously the historicity of thought and its unavoidability. To fail to think post-metaphysically is a failure to think within the exigency of the historic demands placed on thought within our apocalyptic time of "ends." Anything else would be nothing less than pure metaphysical nostalgia.[34] Yet, for a minority of Continental thinkers, to subscribe wholly to Heidegger's critique is to subscribe to a discourse that has become dominant and commonplace. This subscription is the very manifestation of the withering and dying of thought. In other words, in philosophy, once again a certain form of thought becomes the *lingua franca*. Thought itself becomes domesticated and limited to an *afterword*. And thus any thought or thinking can only be spoken after, and via, the repetition of the previous thinker who has set the boundaries and limits of thought. This happened, historically, with Aquinas and neo-Scholasticism and with Kant's critique and neo-Kantianism, to give a few examples. And it has happened again today, in an exceptionally powerful way, with the dominance of Heidegger's visionary thinking, as seen in the first two constellations of thinkers.

The third constellation of thinkers I propose to treat demand that thought *decisionally* challenge Heideggerian dominance in an attempt to bring philosophy back to the space of the *foreword* of thought, unbeholden to any school: as all "schools" are always and necessarily the dying of thought. Such a stance, in turn, reopens thought to the dynamic of tradition in an attempt to move beyond Heideggerian strictures. This move is enacted, in different ways, by Hart and Milbank in their demand that philosophy return to its theological and metaphysical roots, in an attempt to overcome and out-narrative the dominant post-metaphysical narrative of postmodernity.[35] A similar move is enacted in Desmond's "overcom-

---

34. For example, I am thinking of Kearney's critique of Desmond's thought exhibiting "nostalgia for metaphysical speculation," thus showing Kearney's strong post-metaphysical commitments. Kearney, "Maybe Not, Maybe," 194.

35. For Milbank's critique of Heidegger, see Milbank, *Theology and Social Theory* (Oxford: Blackwell, 2006), 298–304. For Hart's critique of Heidegger and some reservations concerning Milbank's critique of Heidegger in *Theology and Social Theory*, see Hart, *Beauty of the Infinite*, 40–43. Hart agrees, at the end of the day, with Milbank that Heidegger presents an ontology of violence. But he thinks that Milbank's conclusions are a bit hasty and that his argument is not the most persuasive. Moreover, it can be said that out of Przywara, Desmond, Milbank,

ing the overcoming of metaphysics," as seen in his Catholic metaxological metaphysics of creation.[36] Here Desmond seeks to rethink the question of being in dialogue with the vibrant dynamic of the tradition, outside of Heidegger's "lock" on being and the nihilism of postmodernity. Yet the overcoming of Heidegger is not limited to these Christian thinkers, but is also exhibited in the radical leftwing thinking of Badiou and, in a less powerful way, Žižek.

For my purposes here I propose to treat Desmond and Badiou. Despite the fact that they are extremely different thinkers, they exhibit profound overlap on certain positions. This overlap is perhaps most conspicuous in regard to their position towards Heidegger. My reason for choosing Desmond and Badiou is straightforward. They both offer a robust challenge to Heidegger, but do so from wholly different positions. Desmond's resistance is enacted from out of the tradition of the great Christian metaphysical thinking on God (especially Augustine), while Badiou's resistance is enacted from out of a radically unique atheistic and materialistic leftwing position. The latter position is unique because it proffers a Platonic materialism and a "Platonism of the multiple." Moreover, Badiou's philosophy has increasingly become conversant with the universalism of Christian discourse and the event of the Resurrection, paradigmatically expressed in the discourse of Saint Paul. Thus in taking these two thinkers as representative of Heideggerian resistance one is able to come at Heidegger from both sides, so to

---

and Hart, Hart is the most favorable to Heidegger and, indeed, that his work, like Balthasar's aesthetics, has a certain Heideggerian flavor to it. Like Balthasar—following Siewerth and Ulrich—Hart seems to be intrigued with the kenotic potential of Heideggerian being. Moreover, Hart himself, in his discussion of Milbank, takes up Balthasar's critique of Heidegger in *Metaphysics in the Modern Age* (see Hans Urs von Balthasar, *The Glory of the Lord: A Theological Aesthetics*, vol. 5: *The Realm of Metaphysics in the Modern Age*, trans. Erasmo Leiva-Merikakis [San Francisco: Ignatius Press, 1991], 429–50, and especially for Balthasar's critique that the whylessness of Heideggerian being ultimately results in a "mathematical necessity," 625)—without mentioning Balthasar—that, in the end, Heidegger's thought is unable to see being as a gratuitous and whyless giving, but rather as a fated necessity. Hart, *Beauty of the Infinite*, 43. Here, as in other places, Hart is very indebted to Balthasar. Further, if one looks at Przywara, Milbank, Desmond, Balthasar, and Hart as counter-Heideggerian thinkers, which they all certainly are, it should at least be noted that Przywara, Milbank, and Desmond offer greater suspicion towards the potential of Heidegger's thought, whereas Balthasar and Hart—without taking over Heideggerian premises—are much more intrigued with the aesthetic and kenotic potential of Heidegger's interpretation of being. My thinking tends more in the direction of the suspicion of Przywara, Milbank, and Desmond on this matter.

36. I will argue in the next chapter that Desmond's metaxology is a dynamic form of analogy remarkably similar to Przywara's.

speak, that is, from both a Christian and materialist/atheistic direction. This is done in order to return thought to its decisional foreword in the time of thought's uncritical acceptance of the status of an (after)word.

The shared critique of Heidegger, in Desmond and Badiou, stems from the fact that they are both profound thinkers of being. Indeed, it can be said that they have written the two most important contemporary works on being: *Being and the Event* (1988) and *Being and the Between* (1995). Moreover, both thinkers are attempting to think being in a situation that is analogous to Heidegger's, that is, in a time of the forgetting of being. This time, however, the forgetting is not due to neo-Kantianism and early phenomenology (Husserl). But, rather, it is due to the hegemony of Heidegger's own forgetting in his late poetic thinking, which begins to proclaim the turnabout in being away from metaphysics *into* the second coming of being. This, for Desmond and Badiou, has resulted in a *second* forgetting of being itself. Thus both Badiou and Desmond set up their discourse as a critical response to Heidegger. Furthermore, although these critical responses are chronologically after Heidegger, and are situated partially against Heidegger, Badiou's and Desmond's discourses can in no way be said to be "post-Heideggerian" (in the sense of the first two constellations of thinkers). Why? Simply put, both thinkers offer an alternative to Heidegger's "fourfold," alternatives that are by no means premised or built upon Heidegger (except perhaps slightly schematically). Badiou seeks to set up the compossibility of thought's four generic conditions (matheme, poem, inventive politics, and love) by de-suturing the suture of thought to the poem enacted by Heidegger.[37] This de-suturing of thought to the poem and a rejection of historicism is, for Badiou, one of the primary tasks of thought today that will free philosophy for its "(re)turn."[38]

Likewise, Desmond sets up a "fourfold" configuration of being (univocal, equivocal, dialectical, and metaxological) that seeks to offer an alternative to the Heideggerian configuration of being and a return to metaphysics that, like Badiou's, is not subjected to Heidegger.[39] Both, then,

---

37. For the suture of thought to one of its generic conditions, see Alain Badiou, *Manifesto for Philosophy*, ed. Norman Madarasz, trans. Norman Madarasz (Albany: State University of New York Press, 1999), especially 61–67.

38. For the (re)turn of philosophy see Badiou, *Manifesto for Philosophy*, 113–38.

39. Deleuze could also be said to be a thinker who does not fall into the Heideggerian snare. As Badiou says, "The conviction that 'together' [Badiou and Deleuze] we could at least highlight our total and positive serenity, our active indifference, concerning the omnipresent theme of the 'end of philosophy.'" Badiou, *Clamor of Being*, 4.

offer and present non-Heideggerian ways to think being beyond and free from Heideggerian premises and categories. This, however, does not mean that Heidegger should simply be bypassed or ignored. Badiou and Desmond fully recognize the brilliance, originality, and rank of Heidegger as a thinker of being. Nevertheless, this does not mean that one has to think being beholden to Heidegger. Hence neither Desmond nor Badiou seeks to overcome Heidegger within the parameters of Heideggerian thought, as was seen with Marion and Kearney. For if Badiou and Desmond did seek to take the hermeneutic stance of Marion and Kearney, namely, of overcoming Heidegger from the inside, they realize they would fail. Both rightfully recognize that Heidegger's visionary thinking is too powerful to be overcome from within. It cannot be hermeneutically outwitted (much like Hegel's system). And, therefore, they switch the terms of the debate outside of a Heideggerian framework. Badiou and Desmond hence bring to the fore a very important element of thinking, namely, its need to *decide* and thus its decisional character and right (for lack of a better term) to a foreword. And both have, indeed, chosen and made thoughtful decisions that if philosophy is to be possible today, then it must be so outside and otherwise than the parameters of thought set by Heidegger's grand and powerful hermeneutic. In this, Badiou and Desmond stand apart from the vast majority of their post-philosophical contemporaries and have broken the *status quo*. Both then are examples of necessary philosophic courage and decision in a supreme time of indecision where thought is itself "paralyzed by its relation to its own history."[40]

Within the thoughtful decisions of Badiou and Desmond, against Heideggerian dominance, certain remarkable features can be discerned in these two very different thinkers. In all of these features what is at work is the belief that philosophy, ontology, or metaphysics is still possible. These features represent overlapping ways in which Badiou and Desmond seek to overcome the Heideggerian belief that philosophy is over and done with. They are as follows:

(1) The question of being is still and will always remain *the* question of philosophy.
(2) Historicism needs to be broken with.
(3) The extreme bias and anti-Platonic stance, exhibited in the Nietzschean and Heideggerian tone of postmodernity, needs to be overcome.

---

40. Badiou, *Manifesto for Philosophy*, 113.

(4) The question of Truth has to be reraised.
(5) The question of eternity, long forgotten in philosophy, must also be reasked. (This, for Badiou, is a philosophical eternity while for Desmond it is both religious and philosophical.)
(6) Philosophy needs to reopen itself to a dialogue with Christianity (this is the case with the later Badiou).
(7) The linguistic turn in philosophy is not absolute.
(8) The great classical questions of philosophy and the tradition need to be revived.

Within every one of these overlaps the answers given by Badiou and Desmond, in most cases, could not be more different. However, I am not interested in these differences here, but in the overlap, and how this overlap works itself out in a resistance to Heidegger, other than a resistance based within Heidegger's own terms. These eight features stand, for Badiou and Desmond, as ways in which the terms of the debate against Heidegger can be decisionally switched, thus freeing philosophical discourse for the possibility of a space outside the Heideggerian narrative of the "end of philosophy." Badiou and Desmond thus remind their contemporaries of the painful fact that philosophy and metaphysics can be done and are, indeed, still being done.[41]

*   *   *

---

41. It need not be said that within the context of this text Desmond's Catholic metaphysics is to be preferred to Badiou's atheistic materialism. But it should be noted, in passing, that Badiou is, on my estimation, one of the greatest of the soixante-huitard thinkers. Moreover, he is the most favorable dialogue partner, in contemporary Continental discourse, with Christian thought, because of his profound attempt to elaborate a "materialism of grace." Žižek is not far off the mark in saying that Badiou can be read "as the last great author in the French tradition of Catholic dogmaticists from Pascal and Malebranche on." Slavoj Žižek, "Paul and the Truth Event," in *Paul's New Moment: Continental Philosophy and the Future of Theology* (Grand Rapids: Brazos, 2010), 88. Moreover, Milbank is likewise not far off the mark when he suggests that Badiou points towards a restoration of the "European tradition" of "universality in terms of the concealed underlying homology of socialism, materialism, Platonism, and Christianity." John Milbank, "The Return of Mediation," in *Paul's New Moment*, 238. Badiou is an affiliated thinker and thus a thinker who genuinely believes in something in the time of supreme indecision and unbelief. He thus stands contra the Liberal/Capitalist Empire of unbelief, nonfiliation, and sterile wasted desires. Badiou's unique materialism needs to be taken seriously by Christian thought in the latter's absolutely necessary battle against Capitalism's anti-Christian spirit.

In the foregoing, the contemporary stage of postmodern thought has been set. This was done with a view to the current religious and theological turn within Continental philosophy, situated as a response to Heidegger. In looking at this turn, three constellations of thinkers were presented and judged according to the adequacy of their respective responses to Heidegger. This was done because Heidegger's thought sets up, frames, and dominates the contours of the debate in the religious turn. This was seen, specifically, in regard to Heidegger's hermeneutic of being's forgetting, the end of philosophy and onto-theology. This meant that the question of God must, for many, now be raised in a decidedly nonmetaphysical fashion. This was the conviction of the first group of the so-called "theological turn" in French phenomenology, which, as a Catholic phenomenon, seeks to open a space of dialogue between phenomenology and theology by trying to think the Christian God post-metaphysically in light of the closure of metaphysics proclaimed by Heidegger. Marion was taken to be representative of this group and their shared desire to think God otherwise to Being. But for the reasons given above, Marion's view was seen to be inadequate insofar as it presents a naïve acquiescence to Heidegger's thought and thus a giving up on an analogical Christian metaphysical grammar and a Christian view of history.

The second, noncreedal constellation of thinkers of the religious turn were, likewise, convicted of the same naïve and uncritical acquiescence to Heidegger's grand hermeneutic. Among this group Kearney was chosen, as he alluded to certain weaknesses and extremes within post-Heideggerian thinking on God. Yet because Kearney's thinking frames his answer directly in the midst of post-Heideggerian discourse, he takes up the very premises that are the causes of the weaknesses he himself has discerned. His discourse is set up for failure at the outset. The most one can do in his "weak metaxology" is fabricate a god that neither is nor is not, but may be. The thinking of the second group remains wholly entrenched in the Heideggerian narrative, which tells one how one should think and not think the divine or God.

It was only when the third constellation of thinkers was arrived at that a space of freedom was secured outside the web of Heideggerian discourse. From this third constellation of thinkers Badiou and Desmond were chosen in order to enlist both a Catholic and a materialist in resistance to Heidegger. Badiou and Desmond forcefully brought thought back to its decisional character of the foreword, thereby freeing thought from Heideggerian strictures. For Badiou and Desmond being can be, and indeed needs to be, thought outside of Heidegger, if philosophy is to find a new beginning in this indecisional time of ends. Therefore, a stance needs to be taken to think either within or without the Heideggerian framework. Such a stance to think outside of Heidegger and the closure of metaphysics is taken and enacted by Desmond, Milbank, and Hart, all of whom return to styles of analogical metaphysics. Moreover, the return of analogical metaphysics results in, and is made possible by, a deep conversation with the theological and metaphysical tradition. This is done in order to once again think God, not as otherwise to being, but indeed as the mystery of *Being* itself. This space of reopening beyond Heidegger opens the possibility of a renewed and nonidentical dialogue with Przywara's *analogia entis*. In other words, once the spell of Heidegger is broken and a new path is made, then so too is opened the prospect of tracing a postmodern pleromatic Christian vision. This Christian grammar will now be traced in Desmond, Milbank, and Hart in conversation with Przywara. The result is an expansive and spacious way forward for Christian thinking, beyond the impasse of the rationalism of philosophical modernity and the largely nihilistic coloring and empty discourse of postmodernity.

CHAPTER 7

The Resurgence of Analogical Metaphysics: Desmond, Milbank, and Hart

> The realities which are the objects of our faith are not foreign to the sensible world. . . . Christ, who embraces all of them, fully belongs to both our world and the one above. He sanctifies all of our sensible world, to which he belongs, and which, created in him, the Word, was also renewed by him, the Emmanuel. It follows that our faith is not only the power of believing in certain truths of the supernatural order: it is also, *and at the same time*, a new power of interpreting the visible world and natural being; a renaissance of reason. It is a perfection of the mind, which takes faith up at its foundations, thus restoring, deepening, and enlarging it . . . the whole category of *ens*, objective form of the objects of spirit, is elevated and supernaturalized by it.
>
> Pierre Rousselot, quoted in Henri de Lubac, "On Christian Philosophy"

Chapter 5 saw the choice made for a countermodern trajectory within post-Conciliar Catholic discourse. In this preference for a countermodern discourse a line of paternity and descent was suggested, commencing with Przywara, through *Nouvelle Théologie*, ending with the countermodern and postmodern discourses of Desmond, Milbank, and Hart (as well as O'Regan as will be seen in the following chapter). This choice and preference for a countermodern trajectory took one to the question of postmodernity in chapter 6. This chapter was, in essence, a call to break Heidegger's spell. This spell-breaking was accomplished in two movements. First, a breaking of the fabulation of being enacted in Heidegger's story of the "end of metaphysics" and the historic necessity following from this, namely, "onto-theo-logy." Second, theologically inclined modes of philosophy were examined and judged in regard to their adequate or inadequate response to Heidegger. Three constellations and trajectories were laid out. The first two were seen to be wholly indebted to the Heideggerian narrative, thus resulting in an insufficient, cramped, and empty discourse on a "God" unable to be thought in terms of *Being*. The third constellation was shown to be adequate to breaking the Heideggerian spell by switching the terms of the debate outside of the reach of the Heideggerian web. A space was thus freed, in postmodernity, to think a capacious Christian metaphysical vision outside of Heideggerian strictures. Chapter 7 proposes to think this specifically postmodern Christian space, exemplified in the styles of analogical vision deployed by Desmond, Milbank, and Hart. By treating forms of postmodern analogical vision as nonidentical forms of repetition of Przywarian optics, the postmodern viability of Przywara's thought is shown and enhanced, while, at the same time, a general analogical vision and grammar is also secured and synthesized, thereby showing the path of a specifically Christian vision, grammar, and response to philosophical modernity and postmodernity. Moreover, chapter 7 must be seen as the fruit of chapters 5 and 6, insofar as it seeks to trace the contours of a postmodern analogical vision. Chapter 7 is also the centering or torso chapter of Part 2, insofar as it sets up the transition into the tracing of apocalyptic vision, which becomes crucial in the two remaining chapters.

Lastly, in treating Desmond, Milbank, and Hart one encounters variations of the kind of style of analogical metaphysics I am advocating for, as seen in my remarks on metaphysics in the Introduction, as well as my reading of Przywara set forth in Part 1. Here one encounters distinctive Christian visions of being taken up within a storied or narrative optics that acts and serves as a counternarrative, rhetoric, or grammar contra the narratives of modernity and postmodernity. Within these respective narratives a "pleromatic reimagining" of the Christian metaphysical tradition is under way. Yet in all three thinkers the resourcing of metaphysics is not a resourcing of metaphysics in general, but a resourcing of a certain *style* of metaphysics. And the metaphysical style thoughtfully chosen is, like Przywara (and Balthasar), an analogical metaphysics or the *analogia entis*. For all three thinkers, then, it is only an analogical metaphysics that has withstood the burning purgatorial fires of modern and postmodern suspicion. Moreover, only an analogical metaphysics is strong enough to withstand the seemingly all-embracing visionary dialectical totality of Hegel and the aesthetic visionary pull of Heidegger. On the far side of history, and the death of metaphysics, the *analogia entis* has risen triumphant out of the ashes and cinders of the fires of suspicion like the legendary phoenix. This is what brings these three thinkers so close to each other and also so close to Przywara—the first thinker, in the twentieth century, to powerfully voice the perennial potential and fundamental importance of the *analogia entis* and its radically pleromatic Christian vision.

Przywara and Desmond as Kindred Spirits

The most remarkable case of overlap in the similarity of styles in Desmond, Milbank, and Hart with Przywara's analogical vision is undoubtedly and unequivocally Desmond's. Why? Because Desmond is not a reader of Przywara, as are Milbank and Hart. And thus there is no direct genealogical connection between the two thinkers. Desmond's first encounter with Przywara's thought was the doctoral stage of this present work. Nor is it possible to make a connection of an indirect influence, via Balthasar, as Desmond has just begun to read Balthasar recently, well after the body of his work has been completed.[1] Hence why this great overlap that I will argue for? If there is no direct or indirect link linking Desmond to Przywara, then one must look back at Desmond's and Przywara's sources to make a connection between their remarkable similarity in vision and thought. One outstanding figure looms large as an ancestral and genealogical link between Przywara and Desmond, namely, the celebrated Augustine.[2] The great genealogical link between Przywara and Desmond must be said to be the imbibing of the glorious spirit of the bishop of Hippo. And thus the vision of man as an inherently becoming and restless between being, a *homo abyssus* related to the *Deus abyssus* and the vision of a God, that if comprehended, is not God. The Augustinian spirit, I contend, marks the shared vision that animates the work of both Przywara and Desmond.[3]

---

1. O'Regan also remarks on the similarities between Balthasar and Desmond concerning their critique of Hegel, yet recognizing that there is no direct influence of Balthasar on Desmond's thought. See Cyril O'Regan, *The Anatomy of Misremembering: Von Balthasar's Response to Philosophical Modernity*, vol. 1: *Hegel* (New York: Crossroad, 2014), 568, 575.

2. Aquinas must also be listed as an important connection, but he does not play as important a role in Desmond's thinking as he does in Przywara's. Nevertheless, the influence of Aquinas is certainly there in Desmond's thinking as well.

3. Desmond has been known to characterize his work as a postmodern form of Augustinianism.

Moreover, it can be said that since Przywara's *Analogia Entis*, the work of Desmond, in especially *Being and the Between* and *God and the Between*, is the most complete and open systematic vision of a Catholic metaphysics produced.[4] Yet in what does this agreement consist and what are the thematic overlaps between Desmond and Przywara? I proceed in three steps. First, I set forth the similarities in Przywara's and Desmond's conception of metaphysics. Second, I then move on to show how this conception of metaphysics works itself out in their respective topologies of being and open systematics. Third, from there I look at how the preceding two come to fruition in an analogical/metaxological conception of the God/creature relation.

Lastly, it needs to be said that there are, indeed, many differences between Desmond and Przywara, but none so deep that they would mitigate the common spirit and overlap in vision. Furthermore, if this were a fuller treatment of the two thinkers, then these differences would have to be dealt with. However, seeing how this is not my main interest here, these differences will not be thematically dealt with, though I will allude to an important one at the conclusion of this discussion. I briefly mention one significant difference on the formal level. The main formal difference between Desmond and Przywara is that Desmond's work is far more expansive and comprehensive in its scope, while Przywara's is far more schematic, condensed, topographical, and suggestive. This is seen in four important areas. First, in Desmond's treatment and dialogue with figures in the Western tradition, he takes great pains to argue for or against central figures in the history of philosophy, while Przywara's treatment of Western figures is suggestive and topographic. Second, this element is further seen in the extensive elaboration that Desmond gives of his fourfold sense of being in comparison to Przywara's treatment of various logics of being that span a couple of pages of *Analogia Entis*. Third, if it was seen that Przywara

---

4. Betz likewise acknowledges the similarities between Desmond and Przywara in a footnote in the Translator's Introduction to *Analogia Entis*. See Betz, introduction, in Erich Przywara, *Analogia Entis: Metaphysics: Original Structure and Universal Rhythm*, trans. John R. Betz and David Bentley Hart (Grand Rapids: Eerdmans, 2014), 33. This is also something that has been discussed between the two of us in private correspondence. In my interview with John Milbank I asked if he would agree with my assessment that out of the great Catholic thinkers in the twentieth century, Desmond's thinking resonates most with Przywara's. To this assessment he unequivocally replied: yes. For Milbank's full response see my interview, "Between Philosophy and *Theology*: The Theological Implications of William Desmond's Thought: An Interview with John Milbank," in *Radical Orthodoxy: Theology, Philosophy, Politics*, forthcoming.

sought to save what is best in phenomenology by rooting it in a metaphysics of analogical difference that kept open the suspended correlation between being/consciousness, then the same could be said of Desmond's work. However, if Przywara accomplished this on a formally descriptive and systematic level, Desmond also embarks on this, partly, through an implementation of phenomenological description. Nevertheless, this is a phenomenological description that is always metaphysically rooted in our being-between. Thus Desmond's stance towards phenomenology is similar to Przywara's insofar as it avoids phenomenological methodology and identity. But it is also different insofar as his approach embarks on intense phenomenological descriptions; phenomenological descriptions that do not take place in Przywara's schematic and dynamically formalistic style. Fourth, the more comprehensive approach of Desmond is also paradigmatically seen in his extensive treatment of creation *ex nihilo*. And although creation *ex nihilo* is the linchpin of Przywara's *analogia entis*, it is never treated extensively. In passing, these are a few formal differences between Przywara and Desmond, all of which show ways in which Desmond could be said to develop more fully certain aspects of Przywara's thought, thereby rendering it in a different key.

Metaphysics

It was just said that both Desmond and Przywara have imbibed the spirit of the great Augustine, but to inhale and drink from the Augustinian spirit is to also drink from the springs of Plato's thought. And nowhere is this indebtedness to Plato, in Przywara and Desmond, more evident than in their unceasing reminder that metaphysics will always be—due to its very essence—a loving participation in Wisdom. This loving participation continually bathes in the wonder that ever animates metaphysical mindfulness as a thinking *within* the very mystery of being itself. Moreover, both Przywara and Desmond think that metaphysics often goes whoring in an attempt to divest and deflower being of its mystery by capturing it in univocal concepts. For Przywara and Desmond, then, metaphysics must, like Hera at the spring of Nauplia, once again bathe within the original *thaumazein* of the Platonic pathos if metaphysics is to return to its primordial site, a site it should never have departed from.[5] Further, it was seen that,

---

5. For Desmond's discussion of Plato and wonder, see William Desmond, *Being and*

for Przywara, philosophy was and always remained a creaturely activity, a ceaseless loving-towards Wisdom, a continual journey towards truth that leads to a *reductio in mysterium*, understood as a metaphysical guarding of the mystery itself. The same must be said of Desmond. For Desmond too, like Przywara, metaphysics is a "*being beholden*" and a being true to being's excess and (over)determination. Such a "*being beholden*," like Przywara's reversal of Hegel's Concept, means a "*being taken hold of*" and "seizure" of the mind, of the concept, by being's overwhelming mystery.[6]

Thought, or metaphysical mindfulness, is a being-taken-up into and by the mystery of otherness, both in and beyond the mind's wayfaring, sojourning condition. Thinking, as a thinking within the metaxological between (like the analogical *schwebende Mitte*), is a communicational space of otherness and transcendence within man's ineluctable in-between condition which is open because opened. Both Przywara and Desmond think that thought's dwelling space is the very indwelling of a mystery that, in keeping with their Augustinian spirit, is both interior and exterior to thought's in-between moving condition. Metaphysics concerns a loving and participatory respect for being's abiding otherness and mystery, which is never reducible to the clarity of consciousness. In this, Desmond and Przywara stand at odds with the foundational *conatus* and turn to the subject in modern thought. And they both harken back towards the Platonic and Augustinian sapiential vision of metaphysics as a loving participation in Wisdom. This is opposed to a thinking that would seek to capture lady Wisdom, where she is forced to disrobe before the voyeuristic eye of instrumental and univocal thought. Being's mystery is guarded from beginning to end in Przywara's and Desmond's thinking, and it is not reducible to consciousness's self-identical clarity, or dialectical identity.

Does this mean that Desmond seeks to return to a totally uncritical and naïve realism that seeks to wholly set the objectivity of being over against thought? The answer is already implicated in the above, but needs to be further fleshed out. With Przywara, it was seen that he sought to unmoor epistemology from any and all foundation. Such a move placed all epistemology within the *prius* of metaphysics, conceived as taking place within the real creaturely and metaphysical difference between essence and existence. This move did not deny the correlation of being/conscious-

---

the Between (Albany: State University of New York Press, 1995), 8; for metaphysics' need to experience a "born-again" perplexity, see 33–38.

6. Desmond, *Being and the Between*, 10.

ness, but rather prevented the correlation from becoming absolute by reducing one to the other in the same. A similar move is at work in Desmond's understanding of metaphysical mindfulness. For Desmond—like Przywara—the question is not one of asking if there is a relation between being and thought, as Idealism and phenomenology hold, but rather: How construe this relation? "I agree that it is tautologously true that knowledge of being is not possible without knowing; hence obviously a certain mindfulness is a condition of the possibility of knowing being. How, in Heaven's name, could one know being outside of *knowing* being? Idealism saw this platitudinous truth as a great revolutionary breakthrough, but it tells us almost nothing."[7] For Desmond, it is obvious that there is a correlation between being and knowing or, in Przywara's language, of the meta-ontic and meta-noetic. This is not in question. But the question is precisely: What does this mean? Does it mean Descartes's *Cogito*, Kant's categories, or Hegel's substance become subject? The answer, as with Przywara, is a resounding no to such possibilities.

The answer given by Desmond is extraordinarily similar to that of Przywara's, in that it consists in a metaxological or analogical answer, in a new form of realism, namely, a creaturely realism. Our knowing is thus "made possible by the *being* we are."[8] And the kind of being we are is precisely, as with Przywara, an inherently contingent, moving, dynamic, and suspended-between being. And, correlatively, this implies that in the very *relation* between being and knowing, as nonidentically open, resides the relative site and/or space where otherness and heteronomy are inserted. "We are made possible as a coming to be, as a coming to be mindful, by an origin prior to the original self or transcendental ego."[9] Epistemology is unmoored from foundation by seeing the relation between being and knowing as residing within the very kind of energy of our given being, that is, dynamically middle beings that are nonidentical and nonoriginary. Thought, rooted in our being-between, is not a one-to-one correlation between being and consciousness, but an open site of self-transcendence where the heteronomy of being's otherness and mystery inserts itself within our enacted or "actualized" being.[10] Our being-between is a *given related being*. And thought's correlation to being, grounded in our dynamically given

---

7. Desmond, *Being and the Between*, 27.
8. Desmond, *Being and the Between*, 28.
9. Desmond, *Being and the Between*, 28.
10. Desmond, *Being and the Between*, 28.

being-between, is reflective of our being. Metaphysical mindfulness is a dynamic site of communicational transcendence open to what is other to itself: both interiorly and exteriorly. Thus, as with Przywara, man's being is inherently relational. And thought is thus metaxologically relational or communicative. That is, thought is an open site of transcendence that is open to being's mystery, because man's being is enacted and opened by an origin other to and prior to man. Both Przywara and Desmond, at the end of the day, present a realism of creaturely knowing, which is grounded in the very suspended and between condition of created abyssal being. In this condition, metaphysical mindfulness is open and respectful to being's ==ever-exceeding mystery== of otherness. This is because our being itself, as given to be, is inherently and peacefully split, opened, doubled (be-tween) by the otherness which has first given us to be prior to becoming.

Topologies of Being and Open Systematics

In Desmond's extreme respect, and love, for being's abiding mystery it is necessary to note that, as was the case with Przywara, this is by no means a capitulation to obscurantism or irrationalism. Like Przywara, Desmond is also a rigorous and systematic thinker. But everything turns on how one construes the word *systematic*, or even more worrisome, the word *system*. Here one encounters the second great overlap with Przywara, namely, that Desmond likewise presents something similar to what I have termed Przywara's "systematics of impurity." This is to say, a systematics of thought that seeks to de-absolutize and relativize thought in the face of metaphysical closure or totality. In so doing Desmond—as a metaxological thinker—like Przywara, walks an extremely fine line and balance between determinability and indeterminability, or better, (over)determinability: between intelligibility/knowing and unknowing, a *knowing in unknowing*. In a word, Desmond thinks *between* system and poetics and presents, like Przywara, an open system that *rigorously* thinks and guards being's dramatic and aesthetic mystery.[11] This open system serves two functions, one negative and the other positive. Yet both elements are inextricably intertwined. First, the purpose of an open systematics is to discern, in certain modes

---

11. See the fine collection of essays in *Between System and Poetics: William Desmond and Philosophy after Dialectic*, ed. A. F. Kelly (Burlington, VT: Ashgate, 2007). Pickstock, Milbank, and O'Regan all contributed essays to this work.

of thinking, the tendency towards closure and an inability to keep man's being-between open all the way through, while, at the same time, realizing that there are elements of truth in these modes of thinking (the first three senses of being, to be mentioned below). But, at the same time, it must be realized that these elements themselves cannot be absolutized. The second function is precisely thinking man's relational and between being, in a manner that is true to the openly in-between condition of man, which is to say, of thinking man as related to other being/beings and to the source and origin of all being, namely, God: the "Agapeic Origin."

In doing so, Desmond, like Przywara, resorts to a systematic topology of being. This is what is termed the four senses of being: the univocal, equivocal, dialectical, and metaxological. It is unfortunate that these senses cannot be gone into more deeply here as Desmond himself treats them in extreme detail and rigor (as noted above).

In the first sense of being, namely, the univocal sense of being, it must be said that "univocity stresses sameness," determinability, intelligibility, and unity: "*to be is to be intelligible.*"[12] Here there is a desire to make being and beings secure and reducible. Being, in its many senses, is reconstructed and set within the firm foundation of clarity and security. This clarity and security is manifested in the privileging of rational categories. Thought seeks to flee from the lived equivocities of life and enigma of being made up of seemingly irreconcilable differences outside the secure aura of intelligibility. However, intelligibility, unity, and determinability, expressed in univocity, are clearly necessary. Nevertheless, taken solely by itself, the univocal, brought to its logical conclusion in, for example, the *mathesis* of Descartes, presents an absolute hegemony of the univocal and functional reason. Univocal reason left solely to itself seeks to domesticate being's mystery in clear and distinct conceptual identity. And, thus, "the will to absolute univocity is self-subverting, and cannot evade its own opposite, equivocity."[13]

Univocity, absolutized, throws us back on the enigmatic question of the equivocal and, therefore, the differences from which the determination of the wholly univocal mind seeks to escape. The equivocal sense of being stresses being's enigmatic becoming, "sensuous appearing" and the show of being. The equivocal sense stresses being's aesthetic and poetic sense. "Equivocal becoming" shows forth a "*promiscuity*" and "confusion"

---

12. Desmond, *Being and the Between*, 16.
13. Desmond, *Being and the Between*, 82.

of being that escapes easy capture in the neat and tidy "schema" of rational categories.[14] Here being's singularities and differences are at play in a web or matrix of the mixing of opposites in nature's becoming, seen as a poetic and aesthetic showing. This aesthetic view of being/beings is opposed to the *mathesis* of strict univocal mindfulness. Furthermore, this equivocity, seen in nature's aesthetic show, is also and importantly seen in the equivocal being par excellence: man. For man's being is saturated with "doubleness," "ambiguity," "free imagination," and indeed "*self-deception*."[15] Equivocal man's desire loves the mingling of light and darkness in the chiaroscuro play of the dramatics of existence. Man, in loving, knows not what he loves, or necessarily even why he loves, but man loves and desires nonetheless. Thus the metaphysical perplexities that arise within the equivocal sense of being must be respected. Further, these equivocal perplexities are integral to man's concrete existential condition. But to end or stop with the equivocity of man, thereby absolutizing it, is to risk skepticism and nihilism—a skepticism and nihilism most extraordinarily voiced by Macbeth: "a tale told by an idiot, full of sound and fury, signifying nothing."[16]

In the first two senses of being, the univocal and equivocal, there is a stress, either on unity or difference, determination or indetermination. Neither was able to give an account of the other. Therefore, neither was able to think relation or mediation. Either there is identity or there is difference and never the twain shall meet. How then proceed forward? Clearly one cannot return to the self-identical *stasis* of the fixed univocal position. Nor is it possible to stay with the movement of the mixing confusion of the equivocal. But perhaps since the equivocal shows something of the mind's movement and restlessness within the enigmatic movement of becoming, it can, at the minimum, loosen thought up for something beyond the impasse of the univocal and equivocal. Such is the task of dialectic and its stress on mediation.

Desmond notes four important aspects of dialectic in relation to beings/being. First, dialectic *reinterprets* "unity" (the univocal) and doubleness (the equivocal). Second, in dialectic, there is the "notion of becoming as immanent transcendence." Third, there is an emphasis placed on an immanent "organic development," which is stressed over a mechanical view

---

14. Desmond, *Being and the Between*, 92.
15. Desmond, *Being and the Between*, 108–9.
16. William Shakespeare, *Macbeth*, Act 5, scene 5, 28.

of development. Fourth, there is an accentuation on "being as mediated," though with a privileging of the "self-mediation."[17] Nevertheless, the end of dialectical mediation still privileges closure and totality. At its best, dialectic recognizes the dynamic nature of thinking as a movement of mediation between determinacy and indeterminacy, which takes place in a world of change, becoming, and process. This mode of thought takes place in the milieu of coming to be and passing away. Dialectic, in seeking an attempt at dynamic mediation, is a fuller and deeper attempt to articulate the play back and forth between determinacy and indeterminacy in beings. This back-and-forth play is never achieved in the univocal and equivocal senses. Yet dialectic, once absolutized, loses the dynamic finesse of mediation and the play it was seeking to achieve. This is done through returning to a new form of univocity via the speculative movement of self-return in Hegel. Being's otherness, partially conceived in dialectic, is fully overcome and recuperated in a thinking of the whole expressed in thought's autonomous and wholly erotic self-determination. Dialectic, in the Hegelian sense, does not and cannot keep its promise.

Enter the metaxological, which seeks to be true to *real relationality* overcome in the absolutizations of unity (univocal), difference (equivocal), and self-mediation (dialectical). Thus, the first three senses of being ultimately lose the openness of the open and the in-between character of man within a community of beings marked by intermediation. Within this intermediation the mystery of being's otherness and relationality is preserved, because being's communication is not reducible to the return of self-mediation. The excess of being's communication to metaphysical mindfulness remains just that, an excess of transcendence. This excess is *in* thought as always *beyond* thought in the abiding difference of its otherness. Moreover, in a "*logos* of the *metaxu*" being comes together in a unity-in-difference, which, in the given milieu of being's happening, is the happening of a community of being-between.[18] Such a site of dynamic happening is a festivity that is expressive of being's agapeic sharing. Being is a feast of community-in-difference that is always in excess of itself. The very happening of the between itself is the free gift of the releasement of being-as-creation by an Agapeic Origin truly other to, and transcendent of, creation itself. Desmond's account of the between, as the given site of being's genuine otherness, difference, and relation, is an account of a

17. Desmond, *Being and the Between*, 142.
18. Desmond, *Being and the Between*, 178–79.

relational metaphysics of creation. His metaphysics is a performance of agapeic mindfulness. Agapeic mindfulness, in turn, rigorously and metaphysically thinks the metaxological intermediation of being and beings while, at the same time, poetically singing the other(s) of thought. Agapeic mindfulness is a doxological act of praise lauding the given goodness of the being-in-metaxological-relation: the relational gift of free creation. Desmond presents a relational metaphysics of creation in its beauty and poetry. Being *is* a kind of poetry. And Desmond's thinking metaxologically thinks and sings the glory of the God of creation. This God is intimately present within creation as lovingly and infinitely above creation.

At this point the tremendous overlap between Desmond and Przywara should be completely evident. Let me briefly summarize. Both thinkers present topologies of being within an open systematics respectful of being's abiding mystery. In doing so, both seek to de-absolutize and relativize created being and created thought within the in-between contingency of creation as relationally open. Przywara did this through his discussion of pure logic, dialectic, and analogy seeking to be true to unity, difference, and the dynamic nature of dialectical mediation. This was accomplished by keeping all three *relatively together* in a dynamically open analogical unity-in-difference. Desmond, likewise, accomplishes something remarkably similar in his fourfold sense of being. Here too the positive aspects of the first three senses of being were taken up in a relativized form in the metaxological relation of a community-within-difference. Both thinkers, as analogical/metaxological thinkers, seek to authentically think real relationality, thereby respecting the mystery of man's dynamically suspended and between condition. By keeping man's being authentically open, they also keep open the site for the insertion of being's otherness into man, and thus a communication and genuine knowing (unity) of being, but one that is never wholly reducible to thought or experience. Being, in being known, is only known as other to thought (being's difference founds the unity-of-knowing). Being remains in excess of knowing and experience and thus transcendent in the mystery of its otherness. Knowing, at its deepest, is a genuine knowing of mystery, or better, *a knowing within mystery*. For both thinkers, then, man's very being is analogical or metaxological through and through. And so too is metaphysical thinking a metaphysical thinking that takes place within the suspended between-being, which we mysteriously *are*. The mystery of the *homo abyssus* is dynamically related to the mystery of the *Deus abyssus* and, thus, their profound Augustinianism.

THE RESURGENCE OF ANALOGICAL METAPHYSICS

The Metaxological as a Dynamic Form of the Analogical

A similarity in vision and style has been argued for in respect to Przywara's and Desmond's work. This was seen in two aspects: first, in their conceptions of philosophy as a loving participation in Wisdom, which safeguards being's abiding mystery; second, in regard to their respective interpretations of man as a between, mediatory, and dynamically suspended being. Further, the implication of this was seen in terms of the effect this had on the relation between being and knowing, that is, in an epistemology of an abyssal and suspended creaturely realism. All of these aspects find their pinnacle in the God/creature relation. How, then, does Desmond view this relation of all relations?

For Desmond, due to the very nature of our being-between in a complex site of interrelations, and the showing of transcendence in immanence, it is impossible to have any straight "univocal speech of ultimate transcendence."[19] Rather all human thinking and language must arise out of the concrete milieu of created being and be a crisscrossing of relations. Any knowledge of God is a between knowledge. This between knowledge traces the signs of transcendence from within the immanence of the between itself. But insofar as the between itself is not a fixed site, but a moving open passage, this moving site points to the beyond of the between. The between is a site of relational passage and passing on and over into the relational source of the given being of the between. Yet how think the relation of immanence to transcendence? And, further, how think transcendence within the between without thereby reducing the transcendence of God to the between in a monistic way?

The answer to this question, for Desmond, is attempted in classical analogy and as such has "something in common with" what he calls "metaphysical metaphor." For Desmond metaphysical metaphor is precisely an attempt to think in the dual meaning of "*meta*" as "*beyond*" and in the "midst."[20] There is a similar in-and-beyond structure at work in metaphysical metaphor, as there was with Przywara's *in-über*. That is, if metaphysical metaphor seeks to read the communication of transcendence within immanence by offering an "ontological image" of transcendence, then it does so through a "metaphorical is" that is attentive to a metaphysical connection or relation between beings.[21] This relation is mindful of a community

---

19. Desmond, *Being and the Between*, 208–9.
20. Desmond, *Being and the Between*, 211.
21. Desmond, *Being and the Between*, 210.

of beings beyond radical univocity or complete equivocity (the example of "the king is a lion").²² Metaphysical metaphor is a way of thinking the play and relation between immanence and transcendence. This relational play carries and ferries across the between, understood as a dynamically open and moving middle, in a way that is not reducible to complete univocity, equivocity, or dialectical closure.

Analogy seeks the same middle road as a thinking in the middle, and in its classical variant analogy is particularly concerned with addressing "our efforts to speak of ultimate transcendence in such a fashion that no reduction of immanence follows."²³ It is important to note that Desmond, from the beginning, interprets "traditional" analogy in the most charitable light, which is to say that Desmond *does not* see analogy as a mere semantic or logical game, but, rather, as a *metaphysical* thinking that seeks to avoid reducing God to the creature in a one-to-one relation. The intention of analogy is always a metaphysical thinking that does not obviate or reduce the difference between God and man. This puts Desmond in line with Przywara over Stein and any attempt to interpret analogy on a univocal base of the *ens commune*, understood as an act of metaphysical bridge-building. "In analogical likeness, the co-implication of the two is a conjunction but never a reduction of difference."²⁴ For Desmond, in keeping with the Fourth Lateran Council and Przywara, "Every likeness is also an unlikeness."²⁵

However, if the best intention of analogy is to guard a relation of likeness in unlikeness, then Desmond is also rightly worried that certain forms of analogy reinsert a strong univocal element and a freezing of the terms of the relation in static mathematical poles. This is the case with Aristotle, who does not always avoid "a logicization of the analogy of being."²⁶ The primary concern of analogy needs to be a thinking of the relationality of relations. And this means that, as for Przywara, these relations themselves cannot be fixed poles, but dynamized real relations. Indeed, "The metaxological metaphor might be seen as a dynamized version of analogy."²⁷ For Desmond, a metaxological metaphysics is related closely to an analogical metaphysics, that is, if the latter is conceived dynamically as a thinking of the between and the open real relationality between God and man. Such

22. Desmond, *Being and the Between*, 209.
23. Desmond, *Being and the Between*, 211.
24. Desmond, *Being and the Between*, 211.
25. Desmond, *Being and the Between*, 212.
26. Desmond, *Being and the Between*, 214.
27. Desmond, *Being and the Between*, 212.

was brilliantly the case with Przywara. Once again, there is a profound overlap between Przywara and Desmond. Both offer dynamized versions of analogical or metaxological being by taking what is best in the dynamism of dialectic, though all the while keeping dialectic open in analogical/metaxological relationality. In so doing, both stress that the ultimate emphasis has to be placed on the dynamically different relation between God and man. How, then, does Desmond ultimately achieve this dynamically different relation between God and man?

Przywara and Desmond are deeply conversant with Plato and Aristotle in their thinking on analogy. It would be interesting to compare their respective overlaps and differences in interpretations of Plato and Aristotle. Unfortunately, this is impossible here. Yet what must be noted concerning Desmond's and Przywara's relation to Plato and Aristotle is that they both think they need to be completed by having recourse to a Christian metaphysics of creation. For only then can the dynamically different relational dynamism between God and man be adequately secured. For both thinkers, classical Greek thought does not possess the potential to think man as a dynamic image of God, because God is not fully dynamic *creativity*. God is not a free fashioner of what is truly other to him. Both thinkers then are, like Aquinas, thinkers of creation and thus creation's secondary causes. Desmond says, in keeping with Aquinas and Przywara, "creation is like the Creator to the extent that it becomes creative for its own right, for itself." Creation is not a mere chimera, a weightless appearance or "epiphenomenon," but a creativity that participates in the ability to give, to share, create, perform, and enact goodness.[28] But this ability to give and share in creativity, in dynamic imitation of God's creative *Being* and energy, is not a usurpation of God. Nor is it a controlling of the God/creature relation on the part of the creature. Rather creative imitation and participation are rooted in the asymmetricality of the God/creature relation, insofar as it is God, as freely absolute, that genuinely gives the creature this potential and energy of creative fidelity (to borrow from Marcel) and participation. "Agapeic creation is asymmetry per se, in that the relation is the other as other, and not for a return to self-relation. The transcendence of the origin is hence not incompatible with its solidarity with creation."[29]

Accordingly, God is only thought as related to creation when this relation is not viewed as necessary. "This hyper-transcendence suggests an

---

28. Desmond, *Being and the Between*, 213.
29. Desmond, *Being and the Between*, 215.

asymmetrical relation of God to world: world is God dependent; God is not world dependent."[30] But, paradoxically, it is this very difference and wielding of the relation between God and man, on God's part, that secures the genuine otherness of creation as created. God's relation to man is a free relation and only as such can man then be free for himself to share, participate, and serve through his own activity and relative-autonomy. This is the glorious paradox of a Catholic analogical metaphysics of creation and participation. It is only through the asymmetrical unlikeness and utter transcendence of God that creation is given its metaphysical weight and glory. And not only does this asymmetry of God to creation give creation its metaphysical weight; but it also gives the ability of God (because God freely wields this power) to be truly present and intimate to creation, as what is not creation. Creation is saturated, both with its own excess, and with the excess of what is transcendent of and other to it: God. God and creation are a genuine dynamic relation of communion-in-difference: an "agapeic feast." Creation is itself a veritable marriage feast or *commercium* of the love between the created and Uncreated. Creation is a song of the difference of love and love's free traversal.

Desmond and Przywara are remarkably similar thinkers. And they are thinkers that live within a spirit of creative fidelity to the pleromatic tradition of Christian thought. This is especially seen in the way they have enhanced the Catholic tradition's thought on God and creation by dynamically reimagining it within their respective relational metaphysics of creation: analogically and metaxologically conceived. We have discerned three major overlaps: first, their view of philosophy as a sapiential participation in mystery; second, their view of being as inherently dynamic, suspended, and between (this view, in turn, marked all metaphysical knowing as a knowing *within* the mystery of being); third, their radically asymmetrical view of the God/world relation presided over by an ever-greater dislikeness of God, which allows creation to be given as truly other to God. Thus such asymmetrical relationality does not denigrate creation, but is and becomes a thinking of the weight and glory of creation and a thinking of real communion and exchange between God and man.

My purpose here has been by no means to assert that Przywara and Desmond are identical or the same. But they do share a remarkable vision and similarity in style that is in agreement on the most essential issues. And as my focus here was to establish this unity in thought, I have not

---

30. William Desmond, *God and the Between* (Oxford: Blackwell, 2008), 253.

focused on their differences in approach. Nor have I focused on how they arrived at this similar vision of reality in different ways. However, I would like to conclude by making a passing remark on what I see to be an important distinction between Desmond and Przywara. This distinction does not put them at odds, but offers a different perspective on the same reality. The distinction concerns their respective *methodological* approaches to nature/grace.

Przywara is more explicitly a philosophical *and* theological thinker, insofar as he fully deals with the formal relationality between nature/grace and *philo*sophy/*theo*logy within a narrative of the one concrete order of grace and redemption. Within this narrative, Przywara argues for the need of metaphysics to be completed and supplemented by the *theo*logical and grace. Desmond is by no means insensitive to these issues, nor are they unimportant to him. But it is by no means his focus. Desmond does not seem to be interested in formally arguing for the relation between nature and grace. And, in this, Desmond belongs to a *methodology* of a more Augustinian bloodline, while Przywara's approach belongs to a *methodology* slightly more Thomistic, insofar as he directly takes up the nature/grace, philosophy/*theo*logy relations as a formal problem.

Desmond's methodology, as Augustinian, is performative of the union between nature/grace. This is enacted through a metaphysical mindfulness always already worked on by grace. In this sense, it is also more Marcelian insofar as it can be said to be a Christian philosophy of incarnation that works within the irradiation of the light of grace (though far more systematic than Marcel's thought). Desmond's thinking then, like Augustine's and Marcel's, is testimonial. His thinking does not argue for a Christian philosophy, nor does it formally think the relation between nature and grace. Rather, it shows this relation in action. And it is clear that, like Marcel, Desmond accepts and embraces the paradox of Christ. And because of this the same thing can be said of Desmond that de Lubac says concerning Marcel's thought: that in this embracing of Christ, "it is no less true that the results can present themselves as directly intelligible in such a way that even the unbeliever could adhere to them. If someone explains myself better to me than I have succeeded in doing myself, why should I spurn this explanation, whose value I directly perceive?"[31] Desmond's methodological approach to the one concrete order of nature and grace is thus performative and testimonial.

---

31. Henri de Lubac, "On Christian Philosophy," *Communio* 19 (1992): 502.

Przywara's methodology, on the other hand, thinks the one concrete order of nature and grace from the other side. That is, he seeks to formally perform, describe, and argue for this relation and the need for philosophy to be completed by grace and theology. It is true that one can also wholly accept everything Przywara says concerning the suspended contingency of creaturely being as intelligible. But things become more controversial when he argues for a theological supplementation and completion of philosophy by the theological, even though this does not destroy the essence of the philosophical, but alone preserves it. If Desmond's strength in approaching the nature/grace issue is the lived performative testimonial side, then Przywara's strength is his formally dynamic and performatively descriptive approach to nature/grace. What do I mean? I mean insofar as all of Przywara's thought takes place within the one concrete order of grace and redemption he still sees the value of making a formally dynamic distinction between the two. This, though, is by no means a neo-Scholastic abstraction of a *natura pura*, because Przywara's analogical distinction between the two orders aids one in better seeing the relational dynamism between the two. Further, making a formally dynamic distinction in thought enables one to stress and see more the intrinsic orientation and openness of the creature to the supernatural, and correlatively, *philo*sophy's inherent need for theological completion. Yet both approaches precisely stress the one concrete and dramatic unity of nature/grace, though they do so from different methodological angles. And as no thinker can do everything, both approaches are needed in creating a polyphonic counternarrative to post-Christian secularity. One methodology is slightly more Augustinian, testimonial, and performative, thereby showing this dynamic as lived. And the other methodology is formally performative, speculative, and *descriptive* and, thus, slightly more Thomistic. This latter view helps one see the relational dynamic within thought as a faithful description from life and the one dramatic concrete order. Yet insofar as both methodologies are, at the end of the day, descriptive and expressive of, in different ways, the one concrete and dramatic historical order of grace and redemption, they ultimately represent a much-needed return to the *Augustinian integrative, sapiential, and dramatic style of Christian pleromatic vision*. Both Przywara and Desmond manifest the truth of the words with which de Lubac concludes his extraordinary essay "On Christian Philosophy":

> Try as man may to reject Christ, he always ends up confronting himself—his intelligence as well as his heart—such as he has been trans-

formed in his very nature by Christ. And to philosophize one cannot begin from anything else, one cannot employ anything else along the way. If the spirit is not closed into itself... it cannot escape itself either. Time is irreversible. Every philosopher of today, provided he be perspicacious enough to pass beyond positivism and enter truly into philosophy, is, whether he wishes it or not, and perhaps in just proportion to his perspicacity, a Christian philosopher.[32]

Milbank's Discourse of the Suspended Middle (*schwebende Mitte*)

It is by no means controversial to claim that John Milbank is one of the most polarizing and controversial theological voices writing today. Yet from whence comes this controversy? The controversy springs from, at least, three aspects of his work. These three aspects are essential to his theological project and are what give it its weight and fecundity. The controversial points are as follows. First, Milbank offers a robust Christian counternarrative to the genesis of modernity. Second, his integral interpretation of nature/grace gives supremacy to the supernatural order. Third, he returns to an analogical and participatory metaphysics of creation.

A Genealogical Narrative

In Milbank's theological project he unabashedly and unapologetically thinks that theological discourse holds a needful and necessary say in philosophy, art, politics, social theory, and, indeed, all public discourses. In this claim he tirelessly affirms a distinctively Christian discourse and narrative that challenges the meaning of modernity and the advent of secularity: the both famous and infamous "Once, there was no 'secular.'"[33] Milbank, in seeing modernity as a contingent historical event, seeks to challenge this narrative and imagine it otherwise. This is done by employing a diverse number of voices: Paul, Augustine, Gregory of Nyssa, Proclus, Maximus the Confessor, Aquinas, Eckhart, Cusanus, Vico, Jacobi, Hamann, Bulgakov, Blondel, de Lubac, Przywara, and Desmond, to name but some. In so doing Milbank seeks to set forth an imaginative Christian coun-

---

32. De Lubac, "Christian Philosophy," 505.

33. John Milbank, *Theology and Social Theory: Beyond Secular Reason* (Oxford: Blackwell, 2006), 9.

ternarrative ("counterhistory," "counterethics," and "counterontology").[34] This counternarrative seeks to explain, in a comprehensive genealogical manner, the genesis of modernity as arising out of the degeneration and deterioration of theological themes, thus showing that modernity is reliant upon these degenerative theological forms, indeed, that modernity itself parodies, deforms, and inverts many essential Christian truths.

Milbank's task is to set up a theological vision otherwise than the narrative of modernity and postmodernity. This task is enacted through a recapturing of the integral vision of nature/grace and a deployment of the polyphonic nature of the Christian tradition and countermodern moderns (Jacobi, Hamann, and Blondel, for example).[35] In this, Milbank's project must be said to be similar to, and influenced by, the genealogical task of Balthasar expressed in *Herrlichkeit*.[36] Both Milbank and Balthasar seek to genealogically counter the overthrow of Christian vision in modernity by nonidentically (re)membering an integral Christian vision rooted in an ecclesial community, practices, and forms of life. Such an attempt seeks to once more offer the full breadth of the Christian vision or mythos as an alternative to the violence of the ancient, modern, and postmodern worlds. But insofar as this vision, and reason, is rooted in an ecclesial community, practices, and forms of life, reason—Christian reason—is situated within narrativity and not an "abstracted universal reason."[37] And this is one of the main reasons why Milbank's *theo*logy is properly labeled postmodern. Milbank enacts a postmodern form of Augustinianism (as he himself

---

34. Milbank, *Theology and Social Theory*, 383.

35. For Milbank's treatment of Jacobi and Hamann see John Milbank, "The Theological Critique of Philosophy: In Hamann and Jacobi," in *Radical Orthodoxy: A New Theology*, ed. John Milbank et al. (London: Routledge, 1999), 21–37.

36. Milbank though is oftentimes very critical of Balthasar. And there are crucial differences in genealogical readings, for example, with regard to Cusanus, Eckhart, and the great Oratorian Bérulle (the spiritual director of Descartes). Milbank views these three thinkers in a more positive light (especially Eckhart) and is largely following de Lubac's reading of them. On the other hand, Balthasar is critical on certain points regarding these thinkers, especially with regard to Eckhart endangering the *analogia entis*: a reading with which I concur. But perhaps Milbank's most serious charge against Balthasar is that he suggests, in the transition from Balthasar's aesthetics to dramatics, that there is a turn away from a more metaphysical register to a mythic one. O'Regan would not see this turn as a move towards the mythic, but rather, to the apocalyptic register, as he lays out in *Misremembering*. And I concur with O'Regan's reading here. For Milbank's critique of Balthasar, see John Milbank, *The Suspended Middle: Henri de Lubac and the Debate Concerning the Supernatural* (Grand Rapids: Eerdmans, 2005), 66–78.

37. Milbank, *Theology and Social Theory*, 392.

confesses and admits), in that he once again seeks to put forward the Augustinian view of two cities. This is done through a Christian narrative, rhetoric, grammar, and ontology that show the "ontological priority of peace over violence." This, for Milbank, is the guiding vision and intuition of Augustine. And it is only Christianity that can give this peace through and within the ecclesia of the *Civitas Dei* over against, and counter to, the *civitas terrena* and the violence of its *libido dominandi*.[38]

Nature/Grace

The second controversial point of contention in Milbank's discourse is his interpretation of nature/grace. In order to set up the above counternarrative, vision, and genealogy against the secularity of modernity, Milbank draws heavily from the integral revolution of nature/grace enacted by Blondel and de Lubac (and Przywara as will be seen).[39] In so doing he seeks to elaborate a "suspended" (hence his drawing from, and admiration for, Przywara and Desmond) discourse of relational participation of the natural in the supernatural. So, as was seen with Przywara, Milbank opens himself to attacks from both sides. For some, this thinking wholly usurps philosophy and the secular sphere, allowing them no independence and autonomy from God and the supernatural order, while, for others, this discourse is far more philosophical, cultural, and political than theological.

However, Milbank would not have it any other way, as this is precisely what he is seeking to do, namely, to propose "a new sort of ontology—indeed, in a sense a 'non-ontology'—articulated *between* the discourses of philosophy and theology, fracturing their respective autonomies, by tying them loosely and yet firmly together."[40] In this, Milbank's task is very similar to Przywara's analogical relationality between *philo*sophy and *theo*logy. His view of a "non-ontology" arises from an attempt to articulate a Christian metaphysical grammar that sees grace as inherently incarnational and thus needing, so to speak, history, culture, politics, and philosophy. This is because without culture, history, politics, and philosophy, grace

---

38. Milbank, *Theology and Social Theory*, 392.

39. For Milbank's most sustained treatment of de Lubac see Milbank, *Suspended Middle*. And for his treatment of Blondel see Milbank, *Theology and Social Theory*, 210–20. Blondel is arguably the central figure of *Theology and Social Theory*.

40. Milbank, *Suspended Middle*, 5.

merely remains "nominal" and not "mediated."⁴¹ And, as such, grace is and remains incomprehensible and without any "real effect."⁴² Like Przywara, de Lubac, and Balthasar, Milbank is a theologian of culture and thus one who thinks *the mediation of grace*. This marks his discourse as a between, suspended, and hovering discourse that plays back and forth between the relational and participatory site of mediated analogical exchange between philosophical and theological discourses. This site is a "non-ontological" space between that thus seeks to think the *event of grace* as a paradoxical mediatory interruption.

The interruption of the Word, in history, forever transmutes and transfigures our relation to all cultural discourses, but in such a way that the Word truly and authentically mediates himself within these discourses, thereby fulfilling and completing them. This, in turn, creates a genuine Christian culture, whereby Christian experience, thought, and practice are made incarnate (mediated); as grace does not destroy, but presupposes and perfects nature and, in this case analogously, culture. This mediated interplay *between* nature and grace prompts Milbank to speak from both sides of the philosophical and theological. This speaking is never precisely a pure philosophical or a pure theological speaking. It is a speaking within the always already transnatural and analogically relational exchange between the two discourses. Milbank's discourse is a radically "suspended middle" discourse, a discourse of a thinking of the event of the between. And, in this, he is of the same ilk as Przywara (and in a slightly different way Desmond).

An Analogical and Participatory Metaphysics

The third point of contention in Milbank's discourse is that, in order to fund both his narrative countergenealogy and his suspended discourse of nature/grace, he has recourse to a participatory analogical metaphysics. In so doing Milbank, like Przywara, strongly believes that *theo*logy must be metaphysical. And, like Desmond, Milbank simply demurs at the proclamation of the death of metaphysics. To be more precise he thinks, like Przywara, that metaphysics must analogically participate in the theological and become a theological metaphysics. This means two things in respect to both Milbank's narratival countergenealogy and his suspended discourse

---

41. Milbank, *Suspended Middle*, 5.
42. Milbank, *Suspended Middle*, 13.

on nature/grace. First, to hold a narrative-style *theo*logy does not mean that the metaphysical is excluded. Second, rather, metaphysics is wholly necessary to narrative in order to explicate "the beliefs in this narrative."[43] Here Milbank, due to his postmodern situation, more fully thinks the relation between narrative and metaphysics than does Przywara. Milbank can be said to develop more fully the narrative impulse in Przywara's work expressed in the latter's accenting of the one concrete history of grace and redemption. In other words, Christianity is a particular story and narrative derived from certain cultural practices and settings. From this cultural setting arises a complexity that requires an interpretation of these cultural practices and forms of life. This interpretation then must open up into the doctrinal, propositional, and theoretically speculative level. This, in turn, becomes a necessary part of the Christian story and one that cannot be easily set aside without endangering the integrity and uniqueness of the Christian vision and story. This approach walks a fine line between a purely propositional and dogmatic understanding of the Christian religion and a totally experiential interpretation of the Christian religion. Narrativity is a complex reality and includes a deeply theoretical and speculative aspect, which implies that "if history is to return, so also is ontology, which has been shamefully neglected by theology."[44] Milbank, then, does not desire to set up a sharp distinction between narrative and metaphysics because all stories are stories of being.

Why then does an analogical metaphysics fit with Milbank's narrative *theo*logy? The answer is that only an analogical metaphysics respects the harmony and mediation of unity within difference. This analogical harmonious difference is ultimately rooted in the Trinitarian God, a God who is a dynamic mediation and between. The Trinity is analogical insofar as the unity between the Father and the Son is given in and through the gift of difference which *Is* the Holy Spirit. The Holy Spirit opens a between that is a dynamic mediation of unity and difference. This mediation of the Spirit passes beyond both unity and difference, insofar as it is an aesthetic harmony of unity-in-difference. This unity-in-difference must then be seen as a harmonious musical mediation. Moreover, this harmonious musical mediation, in turn, marks Trinitarian analogical mediation or the "between" in the Trinity as "absolute."[45] Yet, "The harmony of the Trinity is therefore

43. Milbank, *Theology and Social Theory*, 392.
44. Milbank, *Theology and Social Theory*, 390.
45. Milbank is indebted to Desmond's metaphysics of the between in the way in which

not a harmony of a finished totality but a 'musical' harmony of infinity."⁴⁶ The harmony of Trinitarian mediation is passed on freely to creation and is completed in the Incarnation where God, through Christ, freely speaks to us. As creatures created by the Trinitarian God of dynamic mediation we have been authentically and creatively set free by God and addressed by this same God in the mystery of the Incarnation. This creative differentiation, grounded in the Trinitarian God, and deepened in and completed by the historical interruption of the Word, is passed on to the community of the church through the gift of the Holy Spirit.⁴⁷ To fashion a tradition, narrative, practice(s), forms of life, and theoretical speculation is to partake, and participate in, the very dynamic fashioning of the aesthetics of God's peaceful and harmonious life of infinite creative music. The truth of Christianity, in the open totality of its narrative, is not an abstract "correspondence" to truth but a truth that is a performative "*participation* of the beautiful in the beauty of God."⁴⁸

The Christian tradition, narrative, and its theoretical or speculative thinking become an aesthetic practice. Here truth, in the Christian tradition, means to creatively and nonidentically repeat the giving of the gift of harmonious difference passed on by the analogical music of the Trinitarian

---

he seeks to apply a thinking of the between to the Holy Spirit in order to develop an image of the Trinity as analogically dynamic. See footnote 120 in Milbank, *Theology and Social Theory*, 431. But for where this influence becomes even more explicit, see Milbank, *The Monstrosity of Christ: Paradox or Dialectic*, ed. Creston Davis (Cambridge, MA: MIT Press, 2009), especially "The Double Glory or Paradox versus Dialectic," 111–233; and for specific references to Desmond, see 112, 131, 135–36, 139, 146, 150, 153, 159, 163, 166–67, 171, 198, 203.

46. Milbank, *Theology and Social Theory*, 431.

47. One is able to see a similarity between Balthasar and Milbank here as both desire to ultimately root tradition in the dynamic life of the Trinity. This is not surprising, as both thinkers are what O'Regan would term "pleromatic" apocalyptic theologians, insofar as they draw upon the entire range of Christian vision and especially the Trinity: Balthasar says, "The motif of *traditio* 'handing on,' beginning in God and extending to the creation through him who is 'the beginning of God's creation' (3:14), will prove to be a fundamental theme of the theo-drama, constant through all acts. *Traditio* begins within God (as the doctrine of the Trinity formulates it), and this prevents God's self-giving to the world to be interpreted mythologically: God is not swallowed up by the world. It is not through the self-giving to the world that God becomes a lover. And this same *traditio*, this same self-giving within the Godhead, also means that God does not merely hover above the world as the *hen* of philosophy, as the *noesis noeseos*: rather, the divine self-giving becomes the prototype and archetype of his self-giving to the world and all the *traditio* follows from it." Cited in O'Regan, *Misremembering*, 1:256.

48. Milbank, *Theology and Social Theory*, 434.

life. This life is given again in and through the goodness and beauty of creation, only to reappear, in an unimaginable way, with the Word's interruption of history. The Truth of the Word is then passed on within and through the performance of an ecclesial community: an ecclesial community that is a continuation of the Incarnation, now baptized by the Spirit's life-giving mediation and Pentecostal fire. Human fashioning and creativity are a participation in the very aesthetic mediation of God's Trinitarian life as this life freely spills itself out into creation, the Incarnation, and the church. For the Christian, to creatively fashion and reimagine this tradition and narrative in an affiliated faithfulness to the ongoing event of this continuing tradition, is to embrace an analogical metaphysic of participation. This means that the created participation of the creature shares in the very life of the Trinity as passed on through the Incarnation and the church. Such a metaphysics is narratival and creative and an aesthetic and performative theological metaphysics, which nonidentically repeats and hands on the tradition in creative conformity to the pleromatic tradition. *Theo*logy, and a theological metaphysics, becomes an aesthetically ecclesial performance, whereby the gift of harmonious and creative differentiation is handed on, handed over (*traditio*), continually within the Christian tradition and community, as this community is itself rooted, ultimately, in the creative mediation and creative differentiation of Trinitarian analogical *Being*.

Accordingly, if an analogical metaphysics of participation achieves such a status in Christian narrative then it can neither be excluded from how one conceives the one concrete story of grace and redemption or nature/grace, insofar as it is within this one story that grace's mediation and the Christian narrative unfold. This is what propels Milbank's strong critique of a neutral, nonparticipatory metaphysics or a univocal epistemic metaphysics of the *ens commune*, which unhooks created being from a participatory share in God. Such a dualistic view, which gives unwarranted autonomy to the creature, is perfectly expressed in Scotus's univocal metaphysics. This metaphysics asserts that finite beings univocally are, in the same way that God is.[49] Such a view, by denying the utter giftedness and

---

49. Milbank's critique of Scotus is one of the most controversial, if not the most controversial, aspects of Milbank's narrative genealogy. And in his indictment of Scotus, as a univocal thinker, he is no doubt partially indebted to Balthasar's treatment of Scotus as a thinker forgetful of the *analogia entis*. See Hans Urs von Balthasar, *The Glory of the Lord: A Theological Aesthetics*, vol. 5: *The Realm of Metaphysics in the Modern Age*, trans. Erasmo Leiva-Merikakis (San Francisco: Ignatius Press, 1991), 16–21. For a critical but balanced treatment of Milbank's view on Scotus, see James K. A. Smith, *Introducing Radical Orthodoxy:*

nonsubsistence of creation, opens a site for the institution of secularity, which denies the participatory analogical metaphysics of Aquinas and the great tradition. And, correlatively, what is also denied in this view is the deep interpenetration of nature and grace held by the tradition. For Milbank, like Przywara, "Christian thought which flowed from Gregory of Nyssa and Augustine was able fully to concede the utter unknowability of creatures which continually alter and have no ground in themselves."[50] Here "finite being is not on its own account subsistently anything, but is only granted to be in various ways."[51] For Milbank, as in the Augustinianism of Przywara and Desmond, man is a mystery or a *homo abyssus*. And further, like Przywara and Desmond, this inherent mystery of man is rooted in an analogical metaphysics of creation *ex nihilo*. And, in line with this tradition, Milbank also grasps the very weight this gives to creation, in keeping with Aquinas's secondary causes.

The utter giftedness of creation does not make creation a mere chimera, but as with Przywara and Desmond, the analogical paradox is invoked, whereby man's relative and participatory autonomy is what allows man to share in creation and make the human world. "A creature *is* a creature by mediating the power to create even if it does not hold this power absolutely to itself, any more than it holds being of itself."[52] One is back to the glorious Catholic analogical paradox that was found in Przywara and Desmond, in keeping with the great tradition, namely, that only in creation's utter dependence on the free God does creation genuinely receive itself as a free gift as other to God. This, in turn, allows creation—as creation—to share and participate in God's dynamic creativity. Creatures as creatures fabricate culture, history, and politics and produce truth. Creatures can, and indeed do, mediate, share, and pass on the good. This is what the *analogia entis* respects and attempts to think, namely, the utter contingency and giftedness of creation and the unsurpassable glory of God, as this God gives creation its own glory as a genuine sharing in God's glory, as what is freely other to God in its free and gifted participation in God.

Mapping a Post-Secular Theology (Grand Rapids: Baker Academic, 2004), 96–100. Of course Gilson and Gustav Siewerth also have their own fierce critiques of Scotus.

50. John Milbank, *The Word Made Strange: Theology, Language, Culture* (Oxford: Blackwell, 1997), 44.

51. John Milbank and Catherine Pickstock, *Truth in Aquinas* (London: Routledge, 1999), 34.

52. Milbank, *Theology and Social Theory*, 432.

THE RESURGENCE OF ANALOGICAL METAPHYSICS

The preceding finds its apex and pinnacle in Milbank's interpretation of Przywara's *analogia entis* as bespeaking the same truth, and same reality, as de Lubac's *Surnaturel*.[53]

In his book on Barth, von Balthasar brought together de Lubac's account of the supernatural with Erich Przywara's restoration of the analogia entis to refute both a liberal theology starting from a human foundation below, and a Barthian commencement with a revelation over against a nature at once utterly depraved and merely passively open to the divine (in the sense of passivity "opposed" to human activity, not a radical passivity with respect to God in the heart of the active self). These two refutations imply a "suspended middle" and a non-ontology, since Przywara's analogy and de Lubac's supernatural belong neither to natural theology nor to doctrine, while at the same time they belong to both and encompass both. Natural analogies for God remotely anticipate even the divine essence, while the discourse of grace must perforce still deploy names that initially refer to the created order.[54]

Here one sees the importance of Przywara and the *analogia entis* for Milbank's thinking—indeed, so much so that he uses Przywara's phrase the "suspended middle" (*schwebende Mitte*) for the title of one of his most seminal works. This is to say, an analogical discourse of the "suspended middle," as bespeaking the truth of the one concrete order of sin/grace and redemption, seeks to think the paradox of grace in its mediatory and relational interaction with being. This is the heart of Milbank's narrative *theo*logy, namely, to overcome any and all dualistic understanding of nature/grace that results in secularity and an abandoning of the full extent of Christian vision. And, as for Przywara, this means taking up a participatory analogical metaphysics rooted within the one concrete order of sin and redemption, where philosophy is shown to be insufficient unto itself. Nor

---

53. In this, Milbank is following Balthasar's bringing together of Przywara and de Lubac in *The Theology of Karl Barth*.

54. Milbank, *Suspended Middle*, 31–32. Milbank's assessment in the above is clearly right on and, indeed, the theme of being and grace, centered in the *analogia entis*, can be said to be the leitmotif of *The Theology of Karl Barth*. And indeed it can be said to be Balthasar's most sustained treatment of this troubling question of twentieth-century Catholic thought. See Hans Urs von Balthasar, *The Theology of Karl Barth: Exposition and Interpretation*, trans. Edward T. Oakes, SJ (San Francisco: Ignatius Press, 1992), especially "The Concept of Nature in Catholic Theology," 251–325, and "Christocentrism," 327–64.

can *theo*logy deny or exclude metaphysics, as both metaphysics and *theo*logy—analogically conceived—precisely become a thinking of the *event of relation* between the two discourses. This thinking of the event of relation between the two discourses is neither a purely philosophical thinking nor a purely theological thinking. It is a middle discourse, a *between* discourse of analogical paradox and, as such, it is true to both discourses in their inherent and historic relationality. Milbank's story is a Christian story and thus an analogical story of paradox, a story of *the mediation of being through grace and grace through being*. This event of mediation between the two discourses is performed within a participatory and performative narrative *theo*logy situated within the one concrete order of sin/grace and redemption. By elaborating such a view, Milbank has gone a long way in reasserting a distinctively Christian vision and he must be invoked as another powerful voice along with Przywara and Desmond through which the lineaments of a distinctively Christian analogical and pleromatic metaphysical vision can be discerned.

Hart's Analogical Beauty of the Infinite

Beside Desmond and Milbank, Hart is the thinker most directly indebted to Przywara, as he is the co-translator of *Analogia Entis* (John Betz being the other). And Hart directly cites Przywara's conception of the *analogia entis* as being his as well. "I should note, in choosing the term *analogia entis*, I am using it in the very particular sense it was given in the last century by the remarkable Erich Przywara."[55] However, like Milbank, Hart also seeks to elaborate a postmodern Christian *theo*logy given his and Milbank's differing historical circumstances from Przywara's. In doing so, Hart, following Milbank, seeks to set up a narrative *theo*logy that seeks to out-narrate all other narratives within the framework of a Christian "ontology of peace" understood as the true story of being.[56] Moreover, also like Milbank, he does not seek to elaborate a narrative theology—like the "Yale school" of narrative theology, which seeks to banish the metaphysical from narrative discourse—as he distrusts "too absolute a distinction between narrative

---

55. David Bentley Hart, *The Beauty of the Infinite: The Aesthetics of Christian Truth* (Grand Rapids: Eerdmans, 2003), 241.

56. Hart says, "John Milbank provides the question from which part I of this essay sets out, and his particular approach to a Christian 'ontology of peace.'" Hart, *Beauty of the Infinite*, 29.

and metaphysics in theology . . . narratives are narratives of being."⁵⁷ And the competing war of narratives, rhetorics, and grammars, in postmodernity, is precisely the time for Christianity to reassert itself in a nontriumphalist and peacefully persuasive way, as the true grammar and vision of being and reality. Christian thinkers should not be afraid of postmodernity, but rather see it as an opportunity to return "theology to its original condition," namely, to "that of a story, thoroughly dependent upon a sequence of historical events to which the only access is the report and practice of believers, a story whose truthfulness may be urged—even enacted—but never proved simply by the process of scrupulous dialectic."⁵⁸ In keeping with Milbank, this means a tale of two cities, two narratives: one heralding metaphysical peace and the other heralding metaphysical violence.

The Uniqueness of Hart's Project

Hart, as an Eastern Orthodox theologian and metaphysician, does not attack secularity and modernity in the exactly same way as Milbank. Nor does he deploy the *analogia entis* to the exact same purposes as Przywara, insofar as Hart, like Balthasar, deploys the *analogia entis* to its full aesthetic potential. Further, though there are significant overlaps with Balthasar's theological aesthetics and *The Beauty of the Infinite*, there are also many differences and these differences come about due to ecclesial commitments. Hart is an Eastern Orthodox theologian, and thus his interests are not shared fully with more Western-minded thinkers such as Przywara, Balthasar, and Milbank.⁵⁹ Nevertheless, these differences do not prohibit a large amount of overlap, which, at the end of the day, enables a similar vision and complementary approach. However, these differences are by no means inconsequential. And if they were to be ignored, then such a stance would damper the plurivocity of the Christian tradition. How then characterize Hart's endeavor in *The Beauty of the Infinite* relative to his

---

57. Hart, *Beauty of the Infinite*, 31.
58. Hart, *Beauty of the Infinite*, 4.
59. It must also be taken into consideration that Hart is a convert to Orthodoxy, and this is certainly one of the main reasons why he knows Western sources so well and is able to bring the two traditions into such a fruitful dialogue. Yet Hart still does a fabulous job of muting, in his post-conversion theology, themes and questions that simply do not arise in the Orthodox tradition (such as nature/grace)—themes and questions that he is clearly very familiar with.

Eastern Orthodox commitments? For my purposes here, two important features can be discerned.

The first important point is that, for Hart, there is by no means the same urgency to take up the greatest twentieth-century debate in Catholic theology/philosophy, namely, the ever-recurring question of nature/grace. For Hart, coming out of the intellectual heritage of the Greek Orthodox tradition, and his heavy reliance on patristics, this question simply never arose—and, from the Eastern Orthodox perspective, simply never should have arisen. Hence Hart's complete silence on this issue in *The Beauty of the Infinite* and the total absence of figures such as Blondel and de Lubac. In light of this, Hart simply seeks to perform what is to his mind the non-divide between nature and grace, as expressed in the patristic tradition and Eastern Orthodox thinkers in general. Hart's stance, for different motives and reasons, is analogous to what was seen in Desmond insofar as the formal import of this question does not arise as it does in Przywara and Milbank. Nor does Hart explicitly deploy the *analogia entis* as a means of healing the nature/grace divide as do Przywara, Balthasar, and Milbank.

The second point is in regard to sources and how these sources come to construct the originality of the text, *The Beauty of the Infinite*. How is one to ultimately construe the vision of the text given Hart's drawing from diverse sources, both Western and Eastern? Such significant drawing from Western philosophy, and Hart's intense engagement with contemporary Continental philosophy, makes his text a rarity in the Eastern tradition. And this rarity is partly what marks it with both its ecumenical and postmodern flair.[60] In order to answer the above question, the most central sources of the text need to be identified to see how Hart's unique postmodern and Eastern Orthodox approach to *theo*logy is achieved in energetic conversation with Continental thought and Western sources.

I begin with the Western sources. First, as seen above, Hart's endeavor is indebted to the uniquely postmodern metaphysical form of narratival *theo*logy elaborated by Milbank. Hart's project must be partly seen as a continuation of Milbank's creative vision and endeavor to out-narrate all other narratives in a postmodern Christian persuasive rhetoric of an "ontology of peace."[61] Underlying Milbank's work is a deeply aesthetic and

---

60. Hart's approach to *theo*logy is not without precedent though. Hart can be said to be doing, for Eastern theology, what Balthasar did for Western theology in his deep engagement with Russian thought, specifically seen in his valorization of Vladimir Solovyov and Sergei Bulgakov.

61. Hart, *Beauty of the Infinite*, 29.

imaginative vision of *theo*logy, but this aspect is not always fully explicit in his oeuvre.[62] Hart can be said to be more fully fleshing out this element in Milbank's thought. In broaching the question of the aesthetic, one arrives at another great influence on Hart's thought, that is, the new aesthetic *style* of *theo*logy so profoundly exhibited in Balthasar's expansive mosaic of thought. Hart's thinking, then, is a thinking in continuation of the needed aesthetic paradigm shift enacted in *theo*logy by Balthasar. And no less important than the influences of Milbank and Balthasar is Hart's critical engagement with the central figures of contemporary Continental thought. This engagement ranges from Hart's intensely and glowingly critical admiration for Nietzsche, to his more reserved admiration for the kenotic potential of Heideggerian being, to his less reserved criticism of French postmodern thinkers of the sublime: Lyotard, Derrida, Deleuze, Nancy, and Levinas.[63]

Hart critically converses with these postmodern thinkers because he rightly sees that Continental thought grows out of a deep-seated reaction to expressly Christian forms of thought and hence the Christian tradition.[64] "Modern Continental philosophy is very much the misbegotten child of

---

62. I hold that the aesthetic element is essential to grasp Milbank's guiding vision, but it cannot be said to be the leitmotif as it is in Hart. Nevertheless, Hart is still indebted to Milbank, as well as Pickstock's liturgical aesthetics in his "aesthetic turn."

63. Hart says, and I think rightly so, of Nietzsche, "For Christianity, however, which has heard all of Dionysus's claims before, Nietzsche may well represent an even more momentous turning in the thought of the West, to wit: the appearance at long last of a philosophical adversary whose critique of Christianity appears to be as radical as the *kerygma* it denounces. Nietzsche grasped, even more completely than Celsus (the only other significant pagan critic of the faith), how audacious, impertinent, and absolute was Christianity's subversion of the values of antiquity: thus allowing theology to glimpse something of its own depth in the mirror of his contempt. In short, with Nietzsche the voice of unbelief at last swells to the register of the voice of faith and so, curiously, does faith honor." Hart, *Beauty of the Infinite*, 94. For Hart's treatment of postmodern thinkers in *The Beauty of the Infinite* see the following: Heidegger, 213–33, Lyotard, 47–49, Derrida, 53–57, Deleuze, 56–72, Nancy, 73–75, Levinas, 75–92. The fact that the most pages are spent on Deleuze and Levinas is by no means accidental. Deleuze is the postmodern thinker who fares best in Hart's critique, while Levinas is particularly singled out as a kind of gnostic thinker, who encapsulates what is worst in French postmodernism insofar as he lacks the affirmative spirit that is found in Deleuze and Nietzsche. The latter two, in their own ways, say yes to being. For Hart, rightly so, Levinas is a thinker of denial and evil. This is because Levinas has no conception of the good and is, therefore, of no real use to Christian thought or theology, in general.

64. In this he is similar to: Przywara, Balthasar, de Lubac, Desmond, Milbank, and O'Regan.

theology, indeed a kind of secularized theology; even at present its governing themes everywhere declare its filiation."[65] If Christian thought is to be true to itself, it must be true to its own history, even and perhaps most especially when this history has become one of revolt, failure, and deformation. Hart sees deeply that Christian thinking is wholly implicated in the tradition of Continental thought and its erring and winding path away from its Christian heritage. To embark on this critical conversation is to take up the battle for the Christian spirit and its history exemplified in two narratives, two grammars of being: "Dionysus against the Crucified."

Lastly, Przywara must be mentioned as the great remaining Western influence on the vision enacted within *The Beauty of the Infinite*. And, indeed, it is somewhat surprising that given the great presence of Przywara in the text, and the fact that Hart himself admits holding to Przywara's idiosyncratic vision of analogy, that Przywara is not specifically acknowledged in Hart's recognition of his influences, as are Milbank and Balthasar.[66] Yet, Hart's omission by no means lessens the presence of Przywara in the text. Nor does it mitigate the fact that Przywara's analogical metaphysics gives the template for his thinking upon the beauty of the infinite. In sum, Western sources play a more than significant role in Hart's metaphysical and theological thinking. Hart's narrative is complex and nuanced and cannot simply be classified as a classic text within the Eastern Orthodox tradition. Hart's thinking oversteps confessional boundaries and is applicable for more Western-minded Christian philosophical/theological thinkers because of its deep dialogue with the Western tradition.

Concerning the Eastern sources: Hart specifically mentions the importance of the giants of modern Eastern Orthodox thought: Vladimir Solovyov, Sergei Bulgakov, Pavel Florensky, Vladimir Lossky, Dumitru Staniloae, Pavel Evdokimov, and Alexander Schmemann. These thinkers influence the "style of thought" of *The Beauty of the Infinite* in a way that is "too deep properly to measure."[67] Along with modern Eastern Orthodox sources, there is also the overwhelming influence of the patristic tradition in both its Eastern and Western variants. But among the patristic thinkers there is one figure that wholly takes pride of place as *the* influence on Hart's thought, the great Cappadocian father: Gregory of Nyssa. It is in Nyssa's account of desire—understood in Gregory's term *epektasis*—

---

65. Hart, *Beauty of the Infinite*, 30.
66. See Hart, *Beauty of the Infinite*, 29.
67. Hart, *Beauty of the Infinite*, 20.

that Hart brings his specifically Eastern contribution to the Western (and specifically Przywarian) vision of the *analogia entis*, and thus the nuance through which one understands and *sees* the beauty of divine infinity. Despite Hart's diverse sources, he remains within the confessional commitments of the Orthodox tradition and thus his metaphysical participatory *theo*logy centers around beauty, or "*philokalia*," conceived heavily under the influence of Nyssa.[68]

The sources of Hart's text partly allow for the unique vision presented in *The Beauty of the Infinite* to be seen, which is to say that Hart's text must be seen as an exercise in postmodern transgression. This time, however, transgression is qualified by Christian vision and thus, transgression is viewed as ultimately peaceful and iconic. What do I mean? I mean that in Hart's drawing upon diverse sources of Eastern and Western thought, as well as the great atheistic thinkers of postmodernity, he is clearly trying to call into question certain boundaries within Christian theological and philosophical discourse: boundaries within Christian discourse, which is afraid of a real dialogue between East and West (from either side), and also certain retrograde theological stances that are afraid of dialogue with the nihilism of postmodernity and its many positive aspects. This is, partly, why Hart is a postmodern theologian. But Hart is not a postmodern theologian who falls prey to dissonance or relegates Christian thought to the postscript of undecidability. Rather what Hart invokes and deploys throughout his diverse and varying sources is a harmonious and polyphonic vision, which is extremely difficult to obtain. (In this, Hart begs comparison with Balthasar and Chrétien.) Hart challenges boundaries, but he does so in such a way that is not destructive, but productive, because in this postmodern challenging of boundaries he always keeps the essential vision, which remains indebted to the Eastern tradition. In so doing Hart proffers a Christian vision of created being as bathed in a shimmering iconicity reflective of the beauty and energy of divine infinity. In this vision, Hart is one with the spirit of the Cappadocian fathers, and especially Gregory of Nyssa, though he accomplishes all this with a postmodern panache, which properly challenges too narrow a vision of Christian discourse and Christian dialogue. *The Beauty of the Infinite* must be viewed as one of the most important and significant works in contemporary theology, across confessional divides.

---

68. Hart, *Beauty of the Infinite*, 30.

The Przywarian Template

For Hart, as with Przywara, Desmond, and Milbank, the "only real difference" is "the analogical" and analogical difference is the only possibility of liberation from the violence of metaphysical "totality."[69] In seeking to uphold analogical difference amidst the wars of identity and metaphysical totality—univocity/Apollo and equivocity/Dionysus—both of which close the beauty of being's transcendence, Hart deploys Przywara's brilliant reinterpretation of the *analogia entis*. For Hart, as with Przywara, the *analogia entis* is the solution to the age-old war between "an Ephesian and Eleatic topology of being,"[70] neither of which can explain the enigma of the relation between being and becoming: identitarian *stasis* or aleatory chaos. The *analogia entis* is the Christian answer to this enigmatic war of paganism. This Christian analogical answer is the unifying of a metaphysics of participation with the "biblical doctrine of creation" ultimately rooted within the Trinity.[71]

This epochal unification "made it possible for the first time in Western thought to contemplate both the utter difference of being from beings and the nature of true transcendence."[72] As with Przywara, Desmond, and Milbank, the doctrine of creation *ex nihilo* is the indispensable touchstone around which Christian metaphysical thinking turns. And only if metaphysics draws from biblical revelation can metaphysics be free of the violence of metaphysical totality. The *analogia entis* is expressive of the utter and free gratuity of creation as created within the expanse of loving distance given by the God who is and remains ever greater. Creation is a non-necessary event that reveals creation as the utter giftedness given by the God who *Is Love*. The term "analogy of being" is "shorthand for the tradition of Christian metaphysics, developing from the time of the New Testament through the patristic and medieval periods."[73] As with Przywara, the *analogia entis* is rightly seen as the great metaphysical treasure and the height and the depth of the Christian tradition's thinking on being and God. The *analogia entis* is the great metaphysical Christian thought that gives Christian thinking its pulsating vibrancy, its ever-new rhetoric of peaceful metaphysical challenging. Without this, Christian thought is seduced into foreign thoughts

---

69. Hart, *Beauty of the Infinite*, 8.
70. Hart, *Beauty of the Infinite*, 39.
71. Hart, *Beauty of the Infinite*, 241.
72. Hart, *Beauty of the Infinite*, 241.
73. Hart, *Beauty of the Infinite*, 241.

or forms of being: Gnosticism, Latin Averroism, Nominalism, Cartesianism, Kantianism, Idealism, Heideggerianism, as these forms of thinking are not easily compatible with the message of Christianity and its unique story of redemption. And as with Przywara and Milbank (Desmond implicitly), analogy is expressive of a specifically Christian grammar of creation and revelation that is able to discern "counterfeit doubles" of Christian thought. Hart, like Przywara, rightly extols the *analogia entis* as the Christian gift to metaphysics, a gift that can free it from the idolatry of totality, for those who choose to listen and think the beautiful truth it expresses. And, as for Milbank, the *analogia entis* is the metaphysical linchpin around which a persuasive rhetoric of an "ontology of peace" holds together.

Hart's central optic in *The Beauty of the Infinite* is grafted off the Przywarian optic. The latter is the template of Hart's aesthetics, an aesthetics that is not possible without analogical being's transcendence. I offer three features of Hart's explicit use of this Przywarian template.

First, Hart fully accepts Przywara's argument that the *analogia entis* does not establish an analogy between the creature and God within a univocal or generic category of being, which would capture God within the sameness of being's univocality. Rather, Hart sees clearly that what Przywara is enacting is an "analogization of being" in its difference from God.[74] Analogy is a total subversion of any form of essentialism (the danger with Stein) that would seek to close the analogical difference between God and creatures in the idolatry of the *ens commune*. As such, this analogization of being militates against the absolutisms of equivocity, univocity, and dialectical closure. Perfectly in line with Przywara, "the analogy of being is an emancipation from the tragedy of identity, which is the inmost truth of every metaphysics or theology (whether dialectical and dualist or idealist and monist) that fails to think being analogically."[75]

Second, Hart fully takes up Przywara's view of man as a nonidentical composite of essence in-and-beyond existence (though ultimately Hart puts a different stress on this, as will be seen). Our being has no ground in itself and is an event of gratuity and participation, which analogically mirrors God's one perfect and simple act of self-giving and embracing love. In the creature, essence/existence "is a dynamic synthesis of the incommensurable 'what' and 'that' of our being."[76] The same emphasis is placed

---

74. Hart, *Beauty of the Infinite*, 242.
75. Hart, *Beauty of the Infinite*, 245.
76. Hart, *Beauty of the Infinite*, 245.

on the dynamic *in fieri* of the becoming of the creature as always beyond itself, moving towards its eschatologically deferred essence in-and-beyond existence. Like Przywara and Desmond, Hart moves to a more ecstatic interpretation of the self, an ecstatic interpretation that can be read and developed from the work of both Augustine and Gregory of Nyssa.

Third, as with Przywara, the *dissimilitudo* takes priority over the *similitudo* in the creature's relation to God.[77] That is, God freely and asymmetrically wields the relation in the freedom of creation *ex nihilo*. The more the creature becomes as creature, in its difference from God, the more it grows in a unity-in-difference with God, as what is truly other to God. God's infinite difference from creation is again, paradoxically, what allows for his very intimacy and proximity to creation: as the act of all beings, which is most interior to them, as exterior to them. Divine transcendence gives the glorious intimacy of presence and is thus the farthest apart from the identity of dialectical alienation. The distance of God is the very sign of his love and the event of love's free traversal. In these three essential aspects, Hart is a faithful interpreter of Przywara. And it is with this faithful interpretation that Hart lays the groundwork of *The Beauty of the Infinite*.

Analogy's Aesthetic Range

Like Balthasar, Hart is immensely indebted to Przywara for his understanding of analogy. And further, like Balthasar, Hart seeks to deploy the *analogia entis* to its full aesthetic potential.[78] Przywara's conception of analogy is the fertile ground for the fully aesthetic interpretation of the *analogia entis* given by Balthasar and Hart. The *analogia entis* is inherently aesthetic because it precisely consists in the truth that God is wholly free. And creation is a gracious gift given by a God who is himself a Trinity: a triune life of manifestation. God's own immanent life is a life of analogical expression. Here being is always already differing in the shining forth of the Son, in the seeing of the Father, within the fullness and alighting of the Holy Spirit. Here, in this divine analogical rhetoric, and perichoretic dance of Trinitarian being, being is "to be manifest; to know and love, to be known and loved—all in one act, where there is no 'essence' unex-

---

77. Hart, *Beauty of the Infinite*, 246.
78. Again the aesthetic direction of Milbank's and Pickstock's work must be mentioned as an influence on Hart's aesthetic turn.

pressed, no contradiction awaiting resolution."[79] Creation *freely* spills out of this uncreated manifestation of light and love, as the freeing light of love. Creation is a free continuation and expression of this lightness of being, which is by no means "unbearable"—to think otherwise the extraordinary title of Milan Kundera's wonderful novel—when seen and embraced in its gracious gratuity.[80] Creation is "an 'aesthetic' expression of Trinitarian love" that replaces "*eidos* by the *eikon*."[81] Creation is God's poem, his poetic utterance and rhetoric, an aesthetic display of what is not God. Creation is an expression of God's beauty, glory, and goodness. God's affirmation of the goodness of creation, in Genesis, must not be viewed as a moral affirmation, but rather as a fully "aesthetic evaluation."[82]

Creation is a shimmering iconic event that reflects, in a creaturely manner, the beauty of God's free love. "Creation is only a splendour that hangs upon that life of love and knowledge, and only by grace; it is first and foremost a surface, a shining fabric of glory, whose innermost truth is its aesthetic correspondence to the beauty of divine love, as it is eternally expressed by the Trinity: a sacramental order of light."[83] This implies a move to an analogy of expression, seen in an *analogia delectationis* and an *analogia verbi*.[84] This turn towards these two aesthetic forms of analogy aids Hart in elaborating a metaphysically robust linguistic *theo*logy that is conversant with post-structuralism. However, Hart's view overcomes a nihilistic view of supplementarity, absence, and endless deferral. And in so doing language is taken back, or rather up, into the analogical transcendence of language by enacting a theological style of language that doxologically imitates, nonidentically repeats, and responds endlessly to the Trinitarian rhetoric of creation. Analogical discourse does not arise out of lack or absence of the other who will never come. But rather, in view of God's excessive transcendence, language happens in the ever-new occurring event of creation. Analogical language is an expression of creation, understood as an adventing gift that bespeaks God's transcendent love. Language must vary and continuously supplement itself in a praising

---

79. Hart, *Beauty of the Infinite*, 243.

80. See Milan Kundera, *The Unbearable Lightness of Being*, trans. Michael Henry Heim (London: Faber & Faber, 1984).

81. Hart, *Beauty of the Infinite*, 253, 251.

82. Hart, *Beauty of the Infinite*, 253.

83. Hart, *Beauty of the Infinite*, 252.

84. For Hart's discussion of *analogia delectationis*, see Hart, *Beauty of the Infinite*, 250–60; and for his discussion of *analogia verbi*, see 300–318.

response to the gift of divine transcendence in creation. Language is propelled on and forward into the infinity of God as unknown. This unknownness of God, in turn, calls forth the language of poetic and doxological supplementary praise and response.

Hart's project of *The Beauty of the Infinite* seeks to lay out a theological analogical/participatory metaphysics that is, from beginning to end, aesthetic. In doing so, Hart seeks to offer a Christian aesthetic education that presents a vision of being and creation as a gift of divine Trinitarian rhetoric over and beyond the violence of metaphysics. Such a view is harmonious and peaceable through and through. Presented here is a Christian apologetics that relies not on dialectical reasoning or triumphalism, but rather on a Christian reasoning of aesthetic performance and story. Such a vision is seen through the eyes of faith and love and is thus a unique vision, which requires a certain openness and education to see. This vision, although drawing from diverse sources, ultimately has an Eastern and iconic golden color to it. It is a peaceful Christian vision of the shimmering iconicity of creation and thus a powerful and distinctive Christian vision of being that runs counter to modernity and the nihilism of postmodernity.

Some Differences and Questions

In Hart's Eastern vision of being, Gregory of Nyssa is the hero of Hart's narrative. For Hart, Nyssa is the first and still the greatest systematic thinker of the infinity of the divine. Hart thus strongly demurs at the interpretation of Nyssa as a mere Christian neo-Platonist, an interpretation, Hart thinks, that truly fails to see the radical caesura and daring Christian revolution that Gregory enacted towards neo-Platonism. Hart finds this Christian revolution to consist in two interrelated aspects. These two aspects are Nyssa's thinking on divine infinity and man's desire for this divine infinity: *epektasis*. It is in the latter account of desire that Hart seeks to set up a counter-Christian narrative to Nietzsche's will-to-power: *epektasis* versus will-to-power.[85]

Further, it is in view of Nyssa's ecstatic, yearning, and erotic view of desire, ever stretched forth and drawn on into the infinity of difference which God Is, that Hart finally reads the essence in-and-beyond existence of Przywara. Desire's flight, or intensive striving towards God's infinity,

---

85. Hart, *Beauty of the Infinite*, 29.

is an infinite traversal of man towards God. Here God's distance is never overcome, but is always placed at an ever-new distance of God's thundering and living infinity. Desire is a continual journey of passage, as a passing on and over into divine infinity. And it is through desire's flight into infinity that we see God, in a light darkly. Here desire finds no rest or final "satiety" but ever pushes forward in a continual possession as dispossession: an "endless pilgrimage toward God" where man ever stretches out in a flight of desire towards the distance of the infinity of divine music.[86] Here the creature is continually, and ever, created anew.

Hart thus views the becoming of the creature and the oscillation between essence and existence, in Przywara, through the lens of Nyssa's *epektasis*. This means that the perpetual becoming of the creature is an "ecstasy," an "eros for God's infinity" that is "our feeding on being."[87] This is different from Przywara's descending *analogia attributionis*, where erotic desire is purged and transmuted in the active-potentiality of the creature in its radical openness and readiness to receive the gift of grace, that is, the gift of the creature's absolute readiness to serve and be sent on a dramatic mission of doxological service. Here one sees the difference between a more Catholic Western vision of man's relation to God and a more Eastern conception of man's relation to God. One emphasizes more the erotic element (Hart), and the other emphasizes more the receptive and active readiness to receive of the Scholastic *potentia oboedientialis* (Przywara). Przywara's vision arises out of a more Scholastic and Ignatian vision of service and the *fiat* (the let it be done unto me), whereas Hart's is more, dare I say, Platonic, Cappadocian. For Hart the *laus Dei* consists more in yearning, while for Przywara the *laus Dei* finds its culmination in the readiness to receive and active-service. Thus one is able to see how Hart puts an Eastern Orthodox inflection and twist on the Western/Ignatian/Przywarian vision of the *analogia entis*.

In the spirit of ecumenical dialogue and profound respect for Hart's Eastern vision, I end with some open questions concerning Hart's theological-metaphysical aesthetics. In Hart's noninterest in the question of nature/grace and his continual referral to creation as a "grace," is there still not a need for a more robust distinction between the free aesthetic graciousness of creation and God's supernatural life given through the grace of redemption? I am not saying Hart necessarily denies this, but his lan-

---

86. Hart, *Beauty of the Infinite*, 206.
87. Hart, *Beauty of the Infinite*, 244.

guage can, at times, lend itself to a view that there is simply no qualitative difference between participation in God's being and participation in God's supernatural life. This can lend itself to an overly spiritualistic and mystical vision of man characteristic of certain Eastern interpretations that forget the weightiness of concrete humanity. In this, the question must be asked: Could Hart's thinking benefit from a deeper discussion of the weightiness of Aquinas's secondary causes and the Scholastic *potentia oboedientialis*? Further, in Hart's profound emphasis on the aesthetic and the beautiful, has he forgotten something of the deep *circumcessio* of the transcendentals (truth, goodness, and beauty), which, in this *circumcessio*, cannot prioritize one over the other in the same way that one of the three divine Persons cannot be prioritized? And finally in Hart's erotic vision of man, is there still not a slight residue of Platonism/neo-Platonism, which is perhaps in need of more agapeic regulation? It is clear that Przywara, Desmond, and Hart all push towards an ecstatic view of the self (Hart under the influence of Nyssa and Przywara and Desmond under the influence of Augustine). But the question must be asked: How is this ecstatic view of the self inflected? What ecstatic vision of man is ultimately privileged: yearning or service? In Przywara and Desmond it is agapeic service, while Hart seems to tilt more in the direction of yearning and desire. Could Hart's discourse benefit from accenting more service and obediential openness, as is the case with Przywara and Desmond (though neither Przywara nor Desmond neglects desire, yearning, and restlessness, but the former is always clearly subservient to the agapeic)? This is to say, could Hart's discourse not benefit by placing more of an emphasis on the ecstatic nature of the self, interpreted as a being of active readiness, obedience, and service: a being of the dramatics of the *fiat* where yearning ultimately gives way to the openness of being-a-servant?

*   *   *

In this chapter a common vision, path, and narrative has been shown to exist between Przywara, Desmond, Milbank, and Hart. The common path presented is one of a distinctive countermodern, postmodern, and Christian analogical vision and style. This vision and style is highly expansive and spacious in the scope of its vision. Such a vision rejects both the foundationalism of philosophical modernity and the cramped and truncated discourse of post-Heideggerian postmodernism. This rejection of philosophical modernity and the nihilistic bent of postmodernity rests in the committed belief that there is something distinctively powerful and persuasive about a Christian thinking of being, understood as a creative dialogue and (re)membering of the pleromatic tradition. In other words, there is a distinctive Christian narrative of being, and Przywara, Desmond, Milbank, and Hart all tell it in their singular voices centered in an analogical style/vision, differently inflected.

For Desmond, Milbank, and Hart, like Przywara, metaphysics is analogical, and only in being analogical can it express and truly think real relationality, mediation, and the peaceful harmony between unity and difference, as a mediated unity-in-difference. Moreover, all three thinkers developed a performative metaphysics that was participatory, relational, and grounded in the Christian doctrine of creation *ex nihilo*. And it was only when metaphysics drew and drank from this revelational source of creation that metaphysics was set free from any and all metaphysical necessity and the tragic idolatry of totality. Thus for all three thinkers the relation between God and man is a free asymmetrical relation that is lovingly and freely wielded by the God of love. God, in his infinite glory, was set at an infinite distance from the world, from creation. However, this distance was by no means the aloofness of the god of voluntarism, nor of the god of dialectical self-alienation. Rather it was the site of the freedom of creation, as what is other to God. This site of distance is thus the site of freedom and the site of love's free exchange and traversal.

In light of God's free transcendence, God is more intimate and proximate to creation than creation is to itself. Creation is the space of God's free glory, his poem and his rhetoric. Here creation truly participates in God's glory, God's creativity, God's poetry, as what is truly and freely other to God. The relation between Creation and God is a feast of a communion-in-difference: a *commercium*. In this analogical vision of being and the guarding of the God/world relation, all three thinkers exhibited a profound overlap with the vision of Przywara. Milbank and Hart were directly influenced by Przywara, whereas Desmond independently drank from some of the same sources as Przywara, especially Augustine. Moreover, ways to enhance Przywara's narrative were also signaled to along the way. This was seen in Desmond's more expansive approach, which is able to fill out in more detail many of the schematic overlaps between Przywara and Desmond, while Milbank and Hart, thanks to their postmodern situation, more explicitly thought the relation between narrative and metaphysics. We have also seen that Hart, like Balthasar, develops more fully the aesthetic potential of the *analogia entis*. Further, all three thinkers continue to profoundly think and expand the performative nature of metaphysics that Przywara's style of thinking dramatically advanced.

In sum, these three thinkers, each in his unique way, show how Przywara can be reimagined in a postmodern key. That said, it is now clear why Desmond, Milbank, and Hart have been chosen as nonidentical repetitions of Przywara. They all show forth ways to elaborate a Christian analogical grammar and vision, contra the secularity of modernity and the nihilism of postmodernity. The tracing and synthesizing of a certain Christian vision and style is underway. In turning to O'Regan's profound thinking on the meaning of apocalyptic, this tracing of Christian vision is intensified. And we will see how the spacious Christian visions of Przywara, Desmond, Milbank, and Hart all exhibit a strong elective affinity with O'Regan's interpretation of pleromatic apocalyptic *theo*logy in its visionary deployment against philosophical modernity and the nihilism of postmodernity.

CHAPTER 8

Enlisting Apocalyptic *Theology*: Cyril O'Regan's Pleromatic Vision

> In him was life, and the life was the light of men. And the light shines in the darkness; and the darkness grasped it not.
>
> John 1:4–5

I have sought to proffer a certain style of philosophy, and philosophizing, through tracing, establishing, and synthesizing a certain vision, metaphysical rhetoric, and grammar, a way of viewing the whole of reality from within a specifically Christian analogical perspective. This chapter intensifies the search for Christian vision as a counter to the titanic nature of philosophical modernity and the nihilism of postmodernity. And it does so by entering into conversation with O'Regan's extraordinary vision of apocalyptic *theo*logy in its pleromatic instantiation. In doing so, this chapter lays the groundwork for my final move of showing the relational elective affinity between analogical vision and apocalyptic vision in my proposed "analogical-apocalyptic metaphysics." A few introductory and clarifying remarks are in order as to why I enlist O'Regan's postmodern Balthasar-inspired performance of apocalyptic *theo*logy.

First, in my view, O'Regan presents the most enticing and viable option and/or path forward today for a postmodern Catholic *theo*logy. And he does this by emphasizing the pivotal importance of *Christian vision* in its aesthetic, dramatic, and expansive nature (though intimately tied to practices and forms of Christian life, as will crucially be seen). Second, this path is closely aligned with the countermodern trajectory of Przywara, Desmond, Milbank, and Hart, all of whom, in different ways, propose a rhetorical style of Christian discourse. It is thus not happenstance that O'Regan is a keen reader of Desmond and Przywara and that he nominates the approach of Milbank and Hart's apocalyptic. Third, O'Regan, like no other Catholic thinker writing today, brings to the fore and diagnoses the massive inversion and perversion of Christian symbolism in philosophical modernity, thereby performing a much-needed exorcism of devious genealogical hauntings in Catholic and/or Christian discourse.[1] Without this exorcism a postmodern Christian space of vision cannot be secured. Fourth, O'Regan signals to the weaknesses prevalent in post-Conciliar Catholic thought, as alluded to in chapter 5. That is, he signals to the lack of distinctive Christian form and vision in more *Concilium*-minded thinkers and, therefore, their preference to not deploy the full ambit of the visionary Christian *mysterium*. However, on the other hand, with regard to *Communio*-minded thinkers (Balthasar in particular), he recognizes that their socio-political theology and *praxis*-based elements are sorely underdeveloped and lacking. This latter reason will prove essential for my programmatic elaboration of an "analogical-apocalyptic metaphysics" in the concluding chapter, as it is my contention that the only way forward for a postmodern Christian thought is to fully reunite vision and *praxis*: a union largely sundered in post-Conciliar Catholic discourse. Fifth, all of these aspects make O'Regan the perfect conversation partner in my attempt to reimagine Przywara's analogical vision in a postmodern mode, as there are both a confluence and an expansion of Przywarian optics in O'Regan's Balthasar-inspired rendition of pleromatic apocalyptic *theo*logy.

Lastly, since a post-Conciliar countermodern trajectory has been secured (chapter 5), as well as a postmodern Christian space of discourse (chapters 6 and 7), Christian thinking is now able to fully enter the postmodern fray. However, Christian thinking must do so by continually looking back at history and its own tradition (as a way forward) in order to regain its own vision, as this vision has itself been fractured into countless shards by philosophical modernity and its amnesia of Christianity, an amnesia and forgetfulness that the Christian tradition is also wholly implicated in and, in many ways, gave birth to. O'Regan is profoundly correct that all traditions—and in this case the Christian tradition—are subject to forgetfulness, or worse yet, to systematic distortion and misremembering. Hence one of the most crucial tasks of Christian thought today is to critically diagnose Christian forms of forgetfulness and misremembering

---

1. For more on this exorcism see the essays in my edited volume on O'Regan's work, *Exorcising Philosophical Modernity: Cyril O'Regan and Christian Discourse after Modernity* (Portland, OR: Cascade Books/Wipf & Stock), forthcoming.

in order for Christian vision to once again be whole. This is accomplished by embracing those truths that are non-negotiable in the Christian story and vision in the face of devious simulacra.

I proceed in four steps: First, I open with an elaboration of O'Regan's diagnosis of Gnostic return and how this transitions into his apocalyptic project. Second, I then contrast this project with Caputo's reading of Derrida's apocalypse *sans* apocalypse in his *Prayers and Tears of Jacques Derrida*. Third, I then proceed to set forth O'Regan's criteria for a pleromatic form or style of apocalyptic discourse. Fourth, I end with the guiding postmodern pleromatic apocalyptic vision of O'Regan, as presented and performed in *Misremembering*.

Gnostic Return and the Apocalyptic Turn

O'Regan's oeuvre is expansive. As a systematic and genealogical theologian heavily conversant with Continental philosophy and postmodern thought, O'Regan, like Milbank and Hart, is hard to compartmentalize into an easy category. Like Milbank and Hart, O'Regan is as much of a philosopher as theologian, or better, like any good theologian, he is just as competent and fluent in philosophical discourse as he is in theological discourse. That is to say, as a keen reader of both Przywara and Balthasar, O'Regan astutely realizes that one of the many marvels of the *analogia entis* is that it opens a site for an analogy of discourses and thus a middle spacing of relationality and dialogue between philosophical and theological discourses.[2] Moreover, O'Regan rightly understands that if theology is to have any traction, then it must be in dialogue with philosophy. For this dialogue with philosophical modernity and postmodernity, O'Regan, similar to Milbank, is by no means parsimonious in his enlisting of interlocutors who are able to set forth an expansive countervision to that of philosophical modernity and postmodernity. A partial list of figures enlisted in O'Regan's polyphonic advance against modernity and postmodernity includes: John, Irenaeus, Augustine, Maximus the Confessor, Bonaventure, Aquinas, Hamann, elements of nineteenth-century Tübingen theologians, Newman, Bulgakov,

---

2. O'Regan states, "One consequence of the analogy of being properly understood is the analogy of discourses in which philosophy continues to have an important role." Cyril O'Regan, *The Anatomy of Misremembering: Von Balthasar's Response to Philosophical Modernity*, vol. 1: *Hegel* (New York: Crossroad, 2014), 65.

Przywara, de Lubac and *ressourcement* theology, Balthasar, and for similar-minded thinkers today, Milbank, Hart, and Desmond.

O'Regan is best known for his work on Hegel (*The Heterodox Hegel*, 1994) and for his work on Gnostic return in modernity (*Gnostic Return in Modernity*, 2001; *Gnostic Apocalypse: Jacob Boehme's Haunted Narrative*, 2002; two of the seven projected volumes of the Gnostic return series have appeared). In *Gnostic Return in Modernity*, O'Regan seeks to rehabilitate and redo the approach of Ferdinand Christian Baur (1792–1860), one of the leaders of the Tübingen School of theology.³ In this redoing O'Regan complements, enhances, and moves beyond Voegelin's thought on Gnostic return by moving away from tracing this return to the pathological hubristic state of the Gnostic thinker, as Voegelin sought to do, to framing it within the question of a Gnostic narrative grammar, largely Valentinian gnosis and grammar. This Valentinian grammar is shown to take up and mime Christian symbolism and grammar and, in so doing, it turns Christianity insidiously on its head. In this unmasking of Gnostic grammar O'Regan employs the important term "*metalepsis*," defined as a transgressive disfiguration-refiguration of biblical narrative.⁴ In tracing this disfiguring Valentinian narrative grammar it is definitively shown that there is no such thing as a fundamental break between historical epochs (such as the modern and premodern). But, indeed, there is a genealogical continuity in the form of genealogical hauntings of discourses: and, in this specific case, the haunting by Valentinian gnosis in modernity (and Hegel in particular). Moreover, such a narrative grammar allows for the development and transformation of gnosis in modernity, with the Hegelian and modern emphasis on development and agon, as opposed to the more static models of premodern Valentinianism (even if development may be latently present in premodern gnosis, as O'Regan persuasively argues). What thus remains essential between premodern/modern gnosis is precisely *the narrative grammar* that systematically deforms and inverts Christian symbols and the biblical narrative.⁵

---

   3. For O'Regan's reasons for privileging the genealogical model of Baur's Gnostic return thesis over the experiential model of Gnostic return as seen in Johann Adam Möhler and Voegelin, see Cyril O'Regan, *Gnostic Return in Modernity* (Albany: State University of New York Press, 2001), 23–49. Though it is important to note that in O'Regan's redoing of Baur, Irenaeus remains, in my view, the guiding figure and impetus of O'Regan's narrative. For O'Regan's treatment of Irenaeus, see O'Regan, *Gnostic Return*, 143–67.
   4. See O'Regan, *Gnostic Return*, 92–93, 149.
   5. See O'Regan, *Misremembering*, 1:53–110.

ENLISTING APOCALYPTIC *THEOLOGY*

On a superficial reading, O'Regan's project may look like a simple historical or genealogical oddity with its interest in Gnosticism. But such a reading could not be further from the truth. Rather, I would contend that O'Regan's work is the most significant work being done today by any English-speaking Catholic theologian and, indeed, that his work is essential to the future of Catholic thought and necessary for any theologian or philosopher that desires the fullness of Catholic vision undistorted by devious simulacra and "counterfeit doubles." The seminal importance of this project is that it provides a diagnostic grammar through which Catholic thinkers can discern if a certain Christian discourse has been infiltrated by Gnostic themes and transmutations of Christian symbolism, intentionally or unintentionally. This task becomes all the more necessary because the greatest recrudescence of Gnosticism has occurred within German Idealism, and especially Hegel (as was partly touched upon earlier from a Joachimite perspective). And seeing how almost the whole of Catholic theology, in the twentieth century, is, in one way or another, in dialogue with Hegel, such diagnostic tools become vital in order to see if a certain discourse overcomes Hegel's Gnosticism, or succumbs to Hegel's brilliant visionary and panoptic cunning.

Such an endeavor is fully possessed and fed by the spirit of Irenaeus of Lyon, as manifested in *Against Heresies*, where Irenaeus thoroughly refutes the spirit of Gnosticism.[6] This Irenaean spirit is an absolutely essential ingredient, whether explicitly or implicitly, to any fruitful endeavor in Christian thought today.[7] This task and spirit is especially needful today, when everywhere the Christian thinker looks he sees the distorted, twisted, and secularized form of Christian themes that riddle contemporary Continental thought, whether it is in a phenomenological philosophy of truth as manifestation (revelation), hermeneutics as the privileged mode of interpretation (hermeneutics' biblical roots), or the secularized eschatology of Heidegger (the Christian *parousia*), or the use of negative and mystical theology (Heidegger, Levinas, Derrida, Caputo), to name but a few instances. O'Regan proffers a grammar that is able to discern a true likeness from a

---

6. Irenaeus's lineage and its apocalyptic potential are symbolic and real, as he is the disciple of Polycarp, the disciple of *the theologian* and apocalyptic visionary: the soaring eagle, John.

7. Przywara, de Lubac, Balthasar, Milbank, Hart, and Desmond can all be said to be Irenaean, insofar as they, to varying degrees, see the unmasking of "counterfeit doubles" as an essential element of their Christian thinking. Whether they draw directly from Irenaeus makes no difference. All that matters is that they are unmasking simulacra and thus partaking in Irenaeus's spirit.

systematic distortion. Once Christian thinking loses its Irenaean "discernment of spirits"—to make an apt Ignatian analogy—Christian thinking gives up the possibility of a recuperation of its truth and vision. This truth and vision have been fractured by a post-Christian secularity wholly dependent on the breakup of Christian vision from around the time of the thirteenth century onwards. The steps are short and slippery from Scotism, Nominalism, and the *Devotio Moderna* to Luther, Böhme, and Hegel's grandiose and systematic distortion of Christian mystery to Heidegger's submerged parody of Christian truth.

O'Regan thus rightly sees that Christianity is embroiled in the most massive form of misremembering Christianity has ever faced and, further, that modern thought has enacted a powerful reversal of the *spoliatio Aegyptiorum* into a *spoliatio Christianorum* in our post-Christian era. The coffers of the Christian tradition have been thoroughly plundered. And the very life and possibility of Christian vision are dependent on the diagnosis and countering of this reversal and plundering. To some this may seem an overstatement and exaggeration, indeed, a slightly "apocalyptic" overstatement. But, to others, such a serious seeing of what is at stake is precisely what sets genuine Christian thinking apart from simulacra and the forgetfulness of the Eternal *Logos* made flesh. O'Regan thus holds to the apocalyptic laws of "polarization" and "intensification" as laid out in volumes 4 and 5 of *Theo-Drama* (recall my remarks in the Introduction), and he further sees, like Milbank, that "reality is still saturated by evil invented in the angelic and human event of the fall. . . . As times advances, *this corruption worsens* [italics mine]—nor does the descent of the Son and the Spirit halt this worsening."[8] Part of the "worsening" of which Milbank is profoundly and prophetically speaking is extremely apparent in the wounding of Christian vision (always rooted in practices, worship, and forms of life) in modernity: a vision that is faring no better with the advent of postmodernity and its often (a)theistic religiousness. Is there a remedy? Is there a way forward through which one can regain Christian vision?

I would suggest that this remedy is discovered in the connection between O'Regan's earlier work, which focused on diagnosing a modern Gnostic grammar, and his later turn towards an apocalyptic register of

---

8. John Milbank, *Being Reconciled: Towards an Ontology of Pardon* (London: Routledge, 2003), 105. René Girard, in a less *theo*logical key, always holds to an apocalyptic intensifying and escalating view of history and violence as seen in his discussion of Clausewitz in *Battling to the End*.

Christian discourse. That is, O'Regan clearly understands that diagnosing Christian simulacra is merely part of the task of Christian thought in these times of post-Christian "worsening" and "intensification." Further, it is realized that the modern forms of Christian inversion in, for example, Hegel and Heidegger, offer a full visionary aesthetic and dramatic counter to Christianity that is compelling, luring, and seductive.[9] Thus if the task of the Christian is to strongly proclaim and speak forth the truth, then one must do so in a way that is itself compelling. And the only way to be compelling is to once again offer a vision that has the expansiveness of the aesthetic and dramatic dimensions of the *mysterium* of Christian *apokalypsis*, as counter to modern modes of inversion and misremembering.[10] Such an approach is by no means reactive, but proactive. If Christianity cannot match vision for vision, then it has failed to address the challenge of our dramatic and historic hour. This, I would suggest, is why O'Regan is now seeking a way to elaborate an apocalyptic grammar and vision that are able to counter narratives of visionary misremembering such as are exhibited in Hegel and Heidegger. Yet what is meant by the enigmatic and so often misunderstood and abused term "apocalyptic"?

O'Regan's first real tracing of apocalyptic discourse commenced in *Theology and the Spaces of Apocalyptic* and has now come to a full flowering in, as of yet, his magnum opus, *Misremembering*.[11] O'Regan is well aware of the difficulties and prejudices that beset any speaking of "apocalyptic." For perhaps no word is bound with such heavy imaginative baggage as the word *apocalyptic*. In the common imagination it evokes and conjures images of death, destruction, fire and brimstone, of crazed "prophets" naming the time and hour of Christ's second coming and people heading to the woods to wait for rapture.[12] Nor is this imaginative picture mitigated

---

9. O'Regan rightly says concerning Hegel, "Hegel's texts have a visionary—even mystical—quality lacking in most forms of modern Protestant and Catholic thought with their different propensities toward fideism and rationalism. And this vision is truly comprehensive in scope, having in view the entire dynamic enactment of the divine with the cosmos and humanity." O'Regan, *Misremembering*, 1:119.

10. Cyril O'Regan, *Theology and the Spaces of Apocalyptic* (Milwaukee: Marquette University Press, 2009), 127.

11. *Theology and the Spaces of the Apocalyptic* was initially "The Père Marquette Lecture in Theology," given at Marquette University in 2009. This work, given that it was first a lecture, provides an excellent introduction to *Misremembering*. The second volume of *Misremembering* is on Balthasar's response to Heidegger, and it is slated to appear shortly in two volumes.

12. The highly suspect heritage of Nelson Darby's dispensationalism and its tremendous influence on Evangelical Americans.

by the plethora of apocalyptic and post-apocalyptic films and literature that saturate pop culture today.[13] Moreover, O'Regan also realizes that "apocalyptic" likewise faces the critical suspicion of the enlightened mind and pristine rational credentials of modern academia. It would seem that "apocalyptic," then, must be mitigated to the frenzy of popular culture, as such a phenomenon, as a vital driving force, belongs irrevocably to the pre-demythologized unenlightened world. Further, O'Regan's claim that there is something like a present-day resurgence of apocalyptic discourse does not seem to fare well, insofar as certainly, on the whole, institutional Christianity has often taken a very critical stance towards apocalyptic and has frequently suppressed its oftentimes heterodox and chiliastic tendencies.[14] But the fact of the matter is that "apocalyptic" discourse will not go away and, indeed, keeps popping up, resurfacing like a protean reality, and is thus a force to be reckoned with and understood. Indeed, its form of discourse is paramount to understanding much of twentieth-century thought as well as contemporary Continental discourse and its "newly arisen apocalyptic tone"[15]—so much so that apocalyptic "in twentieth century and contemporary theology is nowhere and everywhere."[16] Yet how understand this discourse in its many nebulous facets, and does it have a certain currency in orthodox Christian thought today, or indeed, ever? And, further, if indeed apocalyptic discourse inhabits a certain space and currency within orthodox Christian thinking and tradition, then the question must be asked: Is this space the most fruitful way forward for Christian thought today?

All of this talk concerning "apocalyptic" simply begs for clear and distinct definition. Yet that is precisely what O'Regan does not give us.

---

13. For a partial list of Catholic and Protestant apocalyptic novels, some having more substance than others, think of: Robert Hugh Benson's *Lord of the World*, Walter M. Miller's *A Canticle for Leibowitz*, Michael O'Brian's *Father Elijah: An Apocalypse*, and the hugely popular Left Behind series by Tim La Haye and Jerry B. Jenkins. A list of apocalyptic and post-apocalyptic films would be too massive to give. Suffice it to say that, since the turn of the millennium, there has been an utter explosion of such films produced in Hollywood.

14. For an extraordinary scholarly achievement on some of these tendencies, consult Norman Cohn, *The Pursuit of the Millennium: Revolutionary Millenarians and Mystical Anarchists of the Middle Ages* (Oxford: Oxford University Press, 1970).

15. See the very important essay of Jacques Derrida, "On the Newly Arisen Apocalyptic Tone in Philosophy," in *Raising the Tone of Philosophy: Late Essays by Emmanuel Kant, Transformative Critique by Jacques Derrida*, ed. Peter Fenves, trans. John Leavey (Baltimore: Johns Hopkins University Press, 1993), 117–71. I will touch on this essay in the following.

16. O'Regan, *Spaces of the Apocalyptic*, 24.

Rather, O'Regan rightly realizes that when one is speaking of "apocalyptic," one is speaking of a vast and complex reality and discourse, which is not easily framed in an exact definition: for to define is always to delimit, to narrow and confine. There certainly are specific qualities to "apocalyptic" discourse and they can be discerned; however, they elude and avoid easy definitional capture. For if "apocalyptic" discourse is as much about a certain spirit (Derrida would say "tone")—or, better, vision—a critique and challenging of the *status quo*, then a narrow definitional framework would seem contrary to the nature of "apocalyptic" itself. This does not mean that O'Regan leaves one in the dark about the meaning of "apocalyptic." But it does mean that his method is one of a descriptive topology of various "apocalyptic" discourses, and not mere definitional placement. O'Regan's method is thus broad enough to include a wide array of thinkers and styles of thinking under the banner "apocalyptic."

This presents me with a methodological and practical dilemma here. That is, as I am confined by the particular interest of this work, I am not able to fully treat O'Regan's respective descriptions and treatments of certain apocalyptic thinkers, which fill out in the flesh his topography of forms of apocalyptic. For it is in these descriptions that one can better see what it is exactly that O'Regan means by apocalyptic and apocalyptic thinkers, by seeing the range of content or vision enacted by various thinkers. That said, my proposed hermeneutic answer to this dilemma is the following. In concentrating on *Theology and the Spaces of the Apocalyptic* I will have to confine myself to describing the topographical approach of O'Regan, which gives the skeleton but not the flesh of apocalyptic discourse. The fleshing out and capturing of the vision of apocalyptic will have to take place in an attempt to capture the overarching vision of *Misremembering*, in which a certain form of apocalyptic thought ("pleromatic") is being performed and retrieved. This means the "pleromatic" form of apocalyptic will be highlighted more than the "kenomatic" and "metaxic" forms (these terms will be explained). However, I will provide an excursus on the "kenomatic" form of Caputo's apocalypse *sans* apocalypse, in order to draw the stark contrast between a full ("pleromatic") and empty form ("kenomatic") of apocalyptic discourse. This unfortunately means that no examples of "metaxic" apocalyptic will be given here. This move is necessary, as it is the "pleromatic" form of apocalyptic discourse that lies in closest proximity to analogical vision, as well as the fact that Przywara, Balthasar, Hart, and Milbank can all be said to be "pleromatic" apocalyptic thinkers.

That said, for O'Regan, apocalyptic tendencies can be found in many of the major Christian thinkers in the twentieth century and contemporary Continental thought. Catholic apocalyptic thinkers include: Balthasar, Metz, Vattimo, and Caputo (although there are clear caveats in nominating Caputo and Vattimo as "Catholic" thinkers) as well as certain brands of liberation theology. Protestant representatives include Moltmann, Altizer, and Keller and, among Anglicans, Milbank. Nor does apocalyptic fail to find representatives in the Eastern Orthodox tradition in Bulgakov and Hart.[17] The question must be asked: What unites these various and diverse thinkers? The answer is that all of these thinkers exhibit a form of thinking that functions critically in regard to the prevailing *status quo* and prevailing forms of discourse. "As quintessentially critical forms of discourse ... modern and contemporary apocalyptic theology in all its variety, are united by their dissatisfaction with the regimes of discourse, practices, and forms of life of modern or contemporary Christianity as they flounder either by endless concession to secular culture or by getting caught in a reaction formation."[18] This is to say that, in one way or another, all forms of modern and contemporary forms of Christian apocalyptic discourse recognize that a radical change needs to occur, and that there is a deep cultural and spiritual crisis that is affecting Christian life, practice, and thought. However, it is more than clear that the answers given by the above thinkers are drastically diverse and often diametrically opposed. Nonetheless, they are all united by a sense of deep "dissatisfaction with present-day Christianity," however differently this form of "dissatisfaction" manifests itself.

Further, within the above group of diverse apocalyptic thinkers O'Regan rightly discerns two basic concerns through which one can divide these thinkers into two groups. The first group is primarily concerned with Christian *identity* in light of the drastic and deadly effect the Enlightenment project has had upon Christianity and its life, practice, and thought (e.g., Balthasar, Bulgakov, Milbank, and Hart), while the second group places more of an emphasis on *social justice* (e.g., Moltmann, Metz, liberation theology, Keller, and Caputo). This does not mean, however, that many of these thinkers do not attempt to bring these aspects together or that, indeed, such a synthesis of Christian identity and social justice is not crucial to a full Christian vision. (Recall my remarks on the *Communio/Concilium* divide, to which we will return in the following chapter.) But it

---

17. O'Regan, *Spaces of the Apocalyptic*, 24.
18. O'Regan, *Spaces of the Apocalyptic*, 26.

is to say that in making this distinction, O'Regan hits upon two fundamental points of emphasis within current apocalyptic discourse. By making this distinction between the two groups, one is then able to see how this distinction unfolds itself further on the epistemic front. In other words, O'Regan is able to pose the question of which viewpoint offers the greatest expanse of Christian vision, and is thus able to more fully synthesize the two concerns of Christian identity and social justice.[19]

To do this the idea of a "metaphorics of space" is set forth, understood on a mechanical rather than geometrical model.[20] That is, O'Regan seeks to see why it is that forms of apocalyptic theology are drawn to, or repelled by, certain discourses (or sources/texts, and importantly, but by no means exclusively, biblical texts). This is done in order to see which forms of discourses are able to offer a fuller and more expansive vision of Christian reality and thus better emphasize Christian identity, form, and content. Here O'Regan clearly tips his hand that he is in favor of the kind of theological apocalyptic that is maximally eidetic, and thus a form of Christian vision that is able to say the most about Christian life, practice, thought, and history. O'Regan thus hermeneutically judges other forms of apocalyptic from the space of the "pleromatic." The "pleromatic" space (derived from the Greek *pleroma* meaning fullness) consists in a high level of eidetic vision or disclosure, which offers a great deal of depth and meaning about God and his "intention" to, and for, the world.[21] Pleromatic forms of apocalyptic theology are heavily based in revelation, the Trinity, and the mystery of the cross and redemption, while also partaking in an extensive conversation with the great tradition in all of its aspects (practices, forms of life, as well as a deep engagement with metaphysical and speculative truth). In sum, pleromatic forms of apocalyptic theology draw from the entire spectrum of Christian tradition and view the whole of history from the background of divine disclosure and, in particular, the Trinity. Pleromatic apocalyptic offers a high level of visionary form and content. Representatives of this group again include: Balthasar, Bulgakov, Moltmann, Milbank, and Hart.

The kenomatic space of apocalyptic (derived from the Greek word *kenoma* meaning empty) is characterized by an utter lack of vision and content and is thus minimally eidetic. Such a form displays an extreme

---

19. O'Regan poses this question, but a full development of this needed union has yet to occur in his work, as already stated.
20. O'Regan, *Spaces of the Apocalyptic*, 26.
21. O'Regan, *Spaces of the Apocalyptic*, 27.

allergy to, in general, any confessional religion, dogmas, and institutions. Further, this form emphasizes complete and total interruption of all common forms of knowing, institutions, practices, and forms of life. Moreover, this often takes the form of an actual assault on confessional Christian apocalyptic, as is seen in Derrida's and Caputo's assault on the book of Revelation in particular. Proponents of this view are: Benjamin, Bloch, Derrida, and Caputo.[22]

The metaxic space of apocalyptic (derived from the Greek *metaxu* meaning "between") clearly works between maximally and minimally eidetic forms of apocalyptic discourse, insofar as it holds to some form of divine revelation, but is very careful not to offer too much description of this reality. Metaxic apocalyptic shies away from an understanding of God outside history and any thinking on the Trinity that would be, to the metaxic view, too speculative or metaphysical. Likewise, in keeping with the kenomatic form, it emphasizes interruption and newness. Metaxic apocalyptic is also oftentimes very critical towards institutional Christianity, practices, and dogma. Representatives of this form of apocalyptic include Metz, Keller, and Altizer (I would add Ivan Illich and René Girard to this list as well).

In sum, O'Regan utilizes these three spaces to judge the compatibility or incompatibility of these spaces with the fullness of Christian vision and reality. This is done in order to regain Christian identity and vision by proffering a diagnostic scheme that is able to gauge the adequacy or non-adequacy of the range of Christian vision. Further, this is accomplished by refiguring Christian discourse in an apocalyptic register: a register that is able to counter Christian simulacra with authentic and full Christian vision. However, this attempt remains a topological sketching and tracing in *Theology and the Spaces of Apocalyptic*. It is thus a programmatic approach that comes to completion in *Misremembering*.

A Destinerrant Trek through the Desert: Caputo's Apocalypse *sans* Apocalypse

Pleromatic apocalyptic discourse offers the fullness of Christian vision by drawing from the entire range of Christian truth, as it is disclosed to us by the freely speaking triune God of revelation and creation. From this disclosure, the pleromatic apocalyptic thinker seeks to interpret the en-

22. One could easily add Blanchot to this list.

tire drama of human existence and history from within, and through, the backdrop of this disclosure. Such a view offers a wide-ranging and full level of eidetic content. This discourse is clearly marked and identified as confessionally Christian, due to its acceptance of the entire ambit of Christian truth. Thus, one way to start understanding the reality of maximally eidetic pleromatic apocalyptic discourse is to start from its opposite, that is, from the nonvisionary (kenomatic) apocalyptic instantiated in Caputo: a vision that is *sans vision* and *sans vérité*. That is, I am proposing a messianic trek through the nomadism of postmodern thought, in order to better see the fullness of vision offered by pleromatic apocalyptic, in opposition to the empty nonvision of Caputo. Further, it is necessary here to recall that Caputo was placed in the second constellation of post-Heideggerian thinkers (as seen in chapter 6) insofar as he is representative of a thinking of the divine that is post-onto-theo-logical. Such thinking is in stark contrast to the spacious and generous thinking of Przywara, Desmond, Milbank, and Hart, as well as the equally spacious approach of O'Regan. Hence, through investigating Caputo's inconsistent apocalypticism my resistance to the cramped and limited nature of post-Heideggerian postmodernism, seen here in a deconstructive instantiation, is intensified in favor of the fullness of Christian vision offered in Przywara, Desmond, Milbank, Hart, and O'Regan.

Such a nonvision is eloquently set forth in the late anti-Heideggerian Caputo of *The Prayers and Tears of Jacques Derrida* (1997). This book is a landmark text in the terrain of the newly arisen religious turn in contemporary Continental thought. As such, it is a paradigmatic expression of the noncreedal "religion without religion" popular amongst postmodern thinkers and theologians like Caputo, Vattimo, and Kearney.[23] Caputo

23. For the early Heideggerian work of Caputo, see John D. Caputo, *The Mystical Element in Heidegger's Thought* (New York: Fordham University Press, 1986); and John D. Caputo, *Heidegger and Aquinas: An Essay on Overcoming Metaphysics* (New York: Fordham University Press, 1982). For Caputo's critique of Heidegger and his turn towards Derrida and Levinas, see John D. Caputo, *Demythologizing Heidegger* (Bloomington: Indiana University Press, 1993). For his thought on "religion without religion," see John D. Caputo, *On Religion* (London and New York: Routledge, 2001). And for Caputo's "dissatisfaction" with current Catholicism and confessional theology and his dialogue with another kenomatic apocalyptic thinker, Gianni Vattimo, see John D. Caputo, *After the Death of God* (New York: Columbia University Press, 2007), especially 70–74. In these pages Caputo clearly shows that, despite his nondogmatic and anti-confessional approach of a postmodern theologian, he still has ideas on what he thinks the "Church" should be, and, further, that John Paul II betrayed Vatican II by squashing its notion of "the people of God." It is clear that Caputo seeks a kenotic view of the Church

must be commended for seeking to raise again the question of religion in contemporary Continental thought. In so doing Caputo shows that to merely equate deconstruction with a naïve atheism and secularity is just as dogmatic as, to his way of thinking, confessional theology. Caputo offers a religious and messianic interpretation of Derrida that, despite its controversial nature, cannot be ignored. The arguments presented in *The Prayers and Tears of Jacques Derrida* present a viable portrait of Derrida as a thinker fueled by religious passion for the impossible, so much so that it is not too much to say that Caputo heralds Derrida as a kind of postmodern prophet *sans* prophecy. Further, Caputo rightly shows that many aspects of postmodern thought are, broadly speaking, religious, and in this instance, he rigorously and compellingly shows the affinity that deconstruction has with a kind of blind non-ocular and fideistic faith.

Yet despite this much-needed emphasis and intriguing inflection Caputo places on the religious quality of Derrida and deconstruction, the question must be asked: What sort of vision of religion is Caputo presenting? And does not this vision of nonvision act as a transcendental regulator of the three great monotheistic religions, and in the interest of this work, Christianity in particular? To phrase it otherwise, can one still be religious, in the traditional sense of religion and religious, if one accepts Caputo's religious deconstruction of religion? Or do we all have to become postmodernly religious, in the way Caputo conceives it? There is no better way to answer such questions than to look at Caputo's meaning of apocalypse *sans* apocalypse to see how *différance* allows only for a completely contentless religion, that is, a religion *without* any form, content, or vision and, therefore, a view of religion and Christian revelation that is an explicit critique of pleromatic Christian apocalyptic, confessional theology, and Christian philosophy in general. From the view of an apocalyptic thought, thought within the regulating parameters of *différance*, pleromatic apocalyptic (or an analogical metaphysics) must, of necessity, be a totalitarianism of the *ancien régime* that has failed to take seriously the guillotine-esque quality

---

which empties itself fully into the world, in a way that is not entirely unreminiscent of Schillebeeckx, as was seen in chapter 5. Here again this shows that the question of ecclesiology is inescapable. And that it is no accident that "Catholic" thinkers like Caputo and Kearney are often drawn to Catholic theologians who offer a fully kenotic view of grace and the Church. For Kearney's view of "religion after religion," see Richard Kearney, *Anatheism: Returning to God after God* (New York: Columbia University Press, 2010). See also my critical review of *Anatheism* in *Yearbook of the Irish Philosophical Society*, 2013, 161–67.

of *différance*, which has cut away any and all metaphysical or theological transcendence.

Yet how does Caputo seek to interpret the religious nature of Derrida's thought and, more broadly speaking, one of the most influential trends in contemporary Continental thought: deconstruction? Caputo's task is an impossible one, and thus in keeping with deconstruction. His task is a saying of the unsayable, within the horizon of presence and the infinite play of signifiers, in their continual deferment, postponement, translatability, and substitutability. For how else is the *tout autre* to be named, how else is it to come into the horizon of presence and writing without a certain violence? Things become even more complex since the *tout autre* being written about, in this text, is the founder of deconstruction himself: Derrida. The simple answer to the above questions is that Caputo wholly accepts and embraces this perpetual aporia of thought as thinking and writing's permanent condition. For to write is itself always a violence, a transgression, an impossibility, and Caputo would not have it any other way. Caputo's text on the religion of Derrida is precisely a text that embraces and loves the impossible—as impossible—and a faith in the coming of the *tout autre* that will never come.

Derrida appears in the text, but never purely, never fully and simply as himself, never as a *tout autre* that has laid bare his secret and, in this instance, his secret religion. Rather, Derrida always appears in the game of Caputo's translation of Derrida—a religious Derrida, who, like Augustine, is filled with prayers and tears. Caputo has "blurred" the lines between Derrida the man and deconstruction by focusing heavily on the late autobiographical works of Derrida.[24] Moreover, this text is muddled, befuddled, and ultimately unable to decide if Caputo is speaking of Derrida's religion or his own. Too many voices are at work for one to decide who is finally speaking. There is the voice of Derrida in Caputo and the voice of Caputo in Derrida, and the voice of Derrida "speaking of himself without speaking of himself" and Caputo's interpretation of this nonspeaking speaking Derrida.[25] When speaking about the religion of Derrida there is no fixed beginning, or end, but the ceaseless play of the voicing of voices (Caputo and Derrida) in their love for, and faith in, the impossible, as always already intertwined in textuality. "As to the 'Conclusion,' which I must not forget,

---

24. John D. Caputo, *The Prayers and Tears of Jacques Derrida* (Bloomington: Indiana University Press, 1997), xxv.

25. Caputo, *Prayers and Tears*, xxv.

I cannot say whether it is an edifying discourse or not, a gloss on Jacques or not, whether it has to do with his religion or mine. I do not know where to draw the line in this game of Jacks."[26]

In this "game of Jacks" Caputo seeks to show that Derrida is a thinker deeply misunderstood. And the central crux of this misunderstanding is precisely the inability to grasp the religious nature of Derrida's thought. By focusing on the religious aspect of Derrida's thought, Caputo seeks to show that deconstruction is a kind of faith, indeed, a postmodern religion *sans religion*. Deconstruction "is a passion and a prayer for the impossible, a defense of the impossible against its critics, a plea for/to the experience of the impossible, which is the only real experience, stirring with religious passion. By religion I mean a pact with the impossible, a covenant with the unrepresentable, a promise made by the *tout autre* with its people, when we are the people of the *tout autre*, the people of the promise, promised over to the promise."[27] Such a faith is "*sans savoir, sans avoir, sans voir*," thus seeking to trouble and fill with doubt all "positive religious faith" and their confessional beliefs in dogmas, institutions, and metaphysical and theological phantoms and idols.[28]

In seeking to tell the story of Derrida's turn or return to religion, the critical hermeneutic linchpin—where Caputo challenges most of the scholarly interpretations of Derrida's engagement with religion—is that he seeks to shift the focus from Derrida's famous engagement with negative theology (though he clearly acknowledges the importance of this dialogue) to the messianic and prophetic Jewishness of Derrida's thought.[29] Derrida's religion—if there is one—is a "messianic-apocalyptic" religion that calls for justice and a democracy yet to come, that will never come.[30] The religion of deconstruction thus seeks to trouble and bedevil any and all positive religions and their "concrete messianisms," which hold to a belief in the truth that their messiah has come.[31] This way of thinking seeks to protect one from the totality of "Truth" and the savage and dogmatic wars of religion where people are deluded that they possess *the* "Truth" and *the* Secret.

26. Caputo, *Prayers and Tears*, xxix.
27. Caputo, *Prayers and Tears*, xx.
28. Caputo, *Prayers and Tears*, xxi.
29. For Caputo's treatment of Derrida and negative theology, see Caputo, *Prayers and Tears*, 27–41.
30. Caputo, *Prayers and Tears*, xxvii.
31. Caputo, *Prayers and Tears*, xxviii.

However, Caputo's insistence that deconstruction is something "affirmative" and an "armed neutrality," and his belief that deconstruction, and its *différance*, is not a transcendental sufficient and enabling condition, which firmly puts things in place, is not altogether honest.[32] This is due to the fact that Caputo sees *différance* as a "quasi-transcendental condition," which, as a nonground, unmoors and destabilizes everything and can, therefore, never settle the question of God. "The effect of allowing *différance* its two cents is disturbing and subversive, for monotheists, atheists, and pantheists, for believers as well as unbelievers, for scientists as well as philologists, for *Seinsdenkers* as well as psychoanalysts."[33] But if deconstruction's task is precisely to leave things up in the air, questionable, open-ended, and translatable, why then does Caputo insist that the only thing (or one of the only things) not up for question is dogmatic faith and the great metaphysical tradition of Christianity? Why, if deconstruction cannot decide, does it decide on the great metaphysical speculations of Christianity? And how, in this instance, does *différance* not act as a kind of transcendental regulator of how one can, and cannot, think God? "But let there be no mistake: 'early on' deconstruction *does* delimit the *metaphysical side of theo*logy. Still, is that not an honorable and hoary religious project? Does it not have an honorable name, the name of 'dehellenizing Christianity,' more generally 'dehellenizing biblical faith'? Is it not an idea as old as Luther, and older still, tracing its origins back to the first chapter of First Corinthians, and older still than that, given that the prophets never heard of the science that investigates *to on he on*?"[34]

Caputo's argument does not hold water and is fallacious: either deconstruction does or does not delimit, or, if it does both, then it must be explained how it does so. Yet such an explanation is lacking in Caputo. And further, if it does delimit, then to excuse this delimitation as "honorable" still does not tell us why, and on what grounds, the "affirmative" and open-ended "quasi-transcendental" *différance* has the ability to judge amidst its self-proclaimed undecidability. Why in certain instances does *différance* have the ability to judge, decide, and conclude where, in other instances, it says things are up for question? What criteria does Caputo use to justify this move? He does not tell us, but merely says that it belongs to a certain project and "honorable" tradition, notably, Luther and

---

32. Caputo, *Prayers and Tears*, 12.
33. Caputo, *Prayers and Tears*, 13.
34. Caputo, *Prayers and Tears*, 5.

dehellenization. Yet from whence do dehellenization and Luther get their privilege over say a deep unity between Greek and Christian thought in Aquinas, for example? If one cannot decide, and deconstruction is meant to unsettle everything, why is not the tradition of dehellenization being unsettled as well, and why is it merely accepted as "honorable" and preferred to other traditions? Caputo's stance simply does not hold. Caputo has made a choice for the validity of dehellenization. And the tradition of dehellenization is held as more *true* to the essence of Christianity than a "Hellenized" version, whatever that may mean. Thus, in the end, Caputo (and Derrida) deploy *différance* as a kind of transcendental regulator and tell one what one can and cannot hold concerning faith, God, and Christianity. Here there is simply a naïve and uncritical acceptance of the Hellenization thesis of Christianity and the narrative of the onto-theological constitution of metaphysics that is at one with a Lutheran Protestant metanarrative. This choice and judgment, on Caputo's part, are particularly manifest in his treatment of the apocalypse and the empty non-vision of apocalypse without apocalypse. But, at this point, it is clear that *différance* does delimit, judge, as well as seek to prevent certain modes of thought and belief. With *différance* everything is not permitted; certain things are, indeed, set in their place.

Derrida's most famous treatment of apocalyptic is his 1980 essay "On a Newly Arisen Apocalyptic Tone in Philosophy," which was originally a talk given at Cerisy, at a gathering in honor of Derrida, where Caputo tells us, "Derrida addressed the eschatologists who had come together . . . to hear the apocalyptic call of/for 'the ends of man.'"[35] Indeed, it was not until 1980, as Caputo shows, that Derrida became aware that his continual deconstructive talk of *venir* and *à venir* sounded like and, indeed, expressed a certain apocalyptic tone. Moreover, interestingly, Derrida struck up this apocalyptic tone, not from a reading of the Bible, but from his reading of Blanchot.[36] And it was not until later that Derrida became aware of the citational reference of "Come" from the book of Revelation ("Come, Lord Jesus," Rev. 22:20). Thus in "On a Newly Arisen Apocalyptic Tone in Philosophy," Derrida seeks to address the apocalyptic tonality of his thinking and the newfound apocalyptic register in contemporary thought.[37]

35. Caputo, *Prayers and Tears*, 71.
36. For Caputo's treatment of the relation between Derrida and Blanchot on this matter, see Caputo, *Prayers and Tears*, 77–87.
37. See Immanuel Kant, "On the Newly Arisen Superior Tone in Philosophy," in *Raising the Tone*, 51–100. Kant's principal opponent, in this essay, was Johann Schlosser (1739–1798).

ENLISTING APOCALYPTIC *THEOLOGY*

Derrida does this in conversation with Kant's late essay "On the Newly Arisen Superior Tone in Philosophy." In this essay Kant, in an extremely polemical way, addresses certain Christian Platonists who, in a mystagogical fashion, think that they possess direct and immediate access to supersensible reality, and thus are privy to a certain secret that others are unable to access. This, to Kant's way of thinking, mystifies the enlightened nature of philosophy and its critique, thereby seeking to supplant it with a pseudo-philosophy and poetics. It is in this context that Derrida seeks to address the question of apocalyptic, and Derrida does so by addressing his relation to modernity and the Enlightenment, in what Caputo says is Derrida's "provocative delimitation of his relationship to the Enlightenment, an unsettling settling of account with modernity, as a kind of Derridean counterpart to the Foucauldian tract on Kant's 'What is Enlightenment?'"[38] One could say that it is Derrida's attempt to keep the element of Enlightenment critique, by also showing that there can be a postmodern apocalyptic tone of thought that does not have to pretend to possess secret knowledge, like the neo-Platonic Christian mystagogues of Kant's time. In other words, what if apocalyptic thought (conceived in a post*modern* deconstructive way) precisely shows us that there is no secret, no revelation, no ultimate truth? What if the revelation of revelations is that we are all adrift, wandering in the desert of *écriture*?

For Caputo, then, Derrida's apocalyptic turn is essential to understanding Derrida's religion, which is a "messianic-apocalyptic" religion. Such a religion is iconoclastic, demystifying, demythologizing, and part and parcel with a dehellenization of Christian discourse. And there is no better text to demythologize than *the* book of Christian vision, namely, the book of Revelation, as this book presents the full visionary potential of Christian discourse in light of the revelation of the Lamb slain from the foundation of the world (Rev. 13:8). Caputo, following Derrida, seeks to show that there cannot be, never was, or never will be such a thing as revelation. If there is going to be faith, then faith itself cannot be revelatory, metaphysical, institutional, or dogmatic. Faith must reside under the erasure of Blanchot's *sans*: faith *sans* faith, religion *sans* religion, messianism *sans* messianism, God s*ans* God, and apocalypse *sans* apocalypse. Faith and religion cannot and will never be allowed to be thought as connected with revelation, vision, knowledge, creeds, or metaphysical truth. Here no form, content, or knowledge can be ascribed to faith. Faith is wholly fide-

---

38. Caputo, *Prayers and Tears*, 88–89.

istic, a nonvision: "blindness, not vision—is all you have to go on."[39] Here there absolutely cannot be any sort of faith in the monotheistic sense, for no messiah will ever come to save man. For if a messiah did come, then he would no longer be a messiah but an idol entering into the economy of presence and thus ceasing to be he who is coming, which is the only trait of the messiah that Caputo will allow. There cannot ever be a last or final word, for if there was, then it would cut off the futural and, therefore, betray the impossible. The Christian apocalyptic vision of Christ as the messiah that has come, and is coming again, can never be allowed by the nihilistic apocalyptic of Caputo's religious deconstruction.

> This apocalypse without any vision, verity or un-veiling, this apocalypse sans apocalypse, is not John's, which calls determinately and identifiably for Adon Yeshoua.... It is nothing eschatological, theological, metaphysico-teleological, and if it is messianic, as it is, it is messianic without messianism... no Word of God whispering the words of revelation in Hebrew in the prophet's ear (too bad for the Egyptians and the goyim) or in Greek in the Evangelist's ear (too bad for the Jews). This is an apocalyptic without, the secret that there is no secret, a scrambled message, many of them, calling for something to come. This apocalypse without apocalypse belongs to and opens up a messianic time without any messianisms, without Yeshoua or any other identifiable Messiah, Jewish, Christian, Islamic.... So if John sings and dreams, prays and weeps, at the end of the Apocalypse, "Amen. Come, Adon Yeshoua," Derrida can only—but this is already quite a lot—sing, pray, and weep, at the end of "Pas," "Viens, oui, oui."[40]

Caputo lauds Derrida as a nonreligious religious prophet, a nonvisionary visionary, who sets forth an apocalyptic message without a message. This message tells the three great monotheistic religions, and Christianity in particular, with the emphasis placed on *apocalypsis*, that such forms of belief are no longer tenable. Christian and monotheistic beliefs are put under the transcendental regulation of *différance*. Believers are told how not to believe. Thus Caputo presents his nonvision of apocalypse as competing with Christian forms of apocalyptic, and, indeed, it is easy to see that Caputo thinks his version of apocalypse should be preferred to others.

39. Caputo, *Prayers and Tears*, 93.
40. Caputo, *Prayers and Tears*, 99–100.

Différance, in its thinking of difference, only allows for the univocality of the same, of the *sans*, that erases the difference of differing religions and their great traditions. And, in the case of Christianity, this means one's belief in the Person of Christ and thus one's ability to identify oneself as Christian within the gift of Christ's saving Name. Caputo seeks to dehellenize Christianity by rejoicing at the death of the God of "onto-theo-logic."[41] But he does more: he also seeks to de-Christianize Christianity by returning to a prophetic and pre/post-Christian time. Does he then try to turn Christianity more to its Jewish roots? I think he thinks so. But if so, then this is a postmodern Derridean Judaism *sans* Judaism, which is certainly not very Jewish. There is no more radical nonvisionary presentation of religion and Christianity, in contemporary thought, than the one set forth by Caputo's religious reading of Derrida. Caputo's uneven apocalypticism is an extreme example of kenomatic apocalyptic discourse.

This is why O'Regan rightfully says that, in the end, "the kenomatic space is a *pseudo-space* or at best a *virtual space*. The space of discourses about nothing has some 'nothing' features."[42] Moreover, O'Regan is also right to see that Caputo is at odds with himself, insofar as Caputo presents his version of apocalypse without apocalypse as "a defeater of the apocalyptic tradition that centers around the book of Revelation."[43] Indeed, Caputo is wrong to see his version of apocalyptic as a competitor to a pleromatic apocalyptic (a *theo*logical space). Because Caputo's apocalyptic discourse is not a space (it is a/theological), not a "position," but a set of deconstructive tactics aimed at disturbing discourses, including apocalyptic discourse.[44] But this is precisely where Caputo gets into trouble, for in the a/topological and a/positional space of deconstruction Caputo continually takes positions. He did so with the dehellenization project and the Lutheran tradition, and he does so by insinuating that an apocalypse without apocalypse is more adequate than traditional apocalyptic. Caputo thus tells us, in a rather dogmatic fashion, that the messiah cannot and will never come. Caputo, in the a/positional stance of deconstruction, risks betraying the "armed neutrality" of *différance* by taking too many positions. These a/positional positions thus end up making truth-claims on more or less adequate versions of Christianity and apocalyptic.

---

41. Caputo, *Prayers and Tears*, 113.
42. O'Regan, *Spaces of Apocalyptic*, 115.
43. O'Regan, *Spaces of Apocalyptic*, 114.
44. O'Regan, *Spaces of Apocalyptic*, 114.

"The incoming of deconstruction upon religion and theology, the advent of deconstruction in theology, turns theology around to the future, to what is coming, which returns theology to what was meant to be all along, *quid quod erat esse*, before the wilderness camp of the prophets was overrun by Eleatic ontotheologicians, before their prophetic, desert voices were drowned out by an excessively Hellenistic logos."[45] Caputo thus makes the a/positional tactics of deconstruction a position. This position, in turn, delimits an anti-revelational and anti-metaphysical nonspace or antispace for theology (or a/theology) in an attempt to return it "to what it was meant to be all along." Yet this is a decision on the *truth* of theology and the *truth* of its being ("to what it was meant to be all along"). Caputo thus attempts to show the inadequacy of confessional theology, thereby setting it at odds with the undecidability of deconstruction. In sum, Caputo makes far many more judgments on the essence of Christianity, faith, and apocalyptic than the proclaimed undecidability of deconstruction will allow. This shows forth the hidden nihilistic dogmatism of deconstruction itself. Deconstruction tells Christian thought it must give up its revelational and metaphysical base, and thus its Christian *identity*, and replace it with the a/positional position of a theology *sans theo*logy.

Pleromatic Apocalyptic Criteria

Caputo's extreme version of a kenomatic apocalyptic discourse is an a/topical site that not only seeks to unsettle Christian discourse but also makes claims on more adequate versions of Christianity and theology. Caputo's claims are wholly at odds with pleromatic Christian apocalyptic. For, if taken seriously, a kenomatic apocalyptic would fully make impossible Christian apocalyptic of the pleromatic kind, as the latter discourse is strongly based in revelation deployed as an interpretive vision through which the Christian thinker reads and sees the drama of human existence in and through the backdrop of triune revelation. Further, if accepted, a kenomatic discourse would prohibit the strong stress on Christian identity exhibited in pleromatic discourse, because pleromatic apocalyptic wholly draws from the perennial glory of Christian truth, tradition, practices, forms of life, and the metaphysical/speculative vision of the Christian story.

45. Caputo, *Prayers and Tears*, 115.

ENLISTING APOCALYPTIC *THEOLOGY*

Postmodern theology, of Caputo's brand, when seen from the point of view of pleromatic apocalyptic discourse (or a Christian analogical metaphysics), is expressive of another mode of misremembering in contemporary Continental discourse. This misremembering draws from many aspects of the Christian story and its symbols, but it does so for its own nihilistic purposes. These purposes then seek to create a new postmodern "religion without religion" that has little in common with the three great monotheistic religions, and Christianity in particular. Caputo's postmodern pseudo-apocalyptic discourse is another narrative amidst the numerous postmodern narratives. And this discourse, due to its extreme nature and its drawing from Christian symbolism, is able to aid one in refocusing on the need to refigure and creatively retrieve a distinctly Christian vision and identity of the pleromatic kind in its ultimate affinity with analogical vision. O'Regan goes a long way in beginning to retrieve Christian identity and vision by setting forth a programmatic task for Christian thinking amidst our "postmodern condition" at the conclusion of *Theology and the Spaces of Apocalyptic*. This vision is wholly at odds with Caputo's nonvisionary religion, as were the spacious approaches of Desmond, Milbank, and Hart in opposition to the first two constellations of postmodern thinkers spoken about in chapter 6.

In O'Regan's programmatic sketching, at the conclusion of *Theology and Spaces of Apocalyptic*, vision is presented as wholly essential to Christian discourse as a means for the Christian to reassert identity in the heart of our postmodern and post-Christian twenty-first century. Indeed, such a vision and stress on identity is a "necessity" in a time when all forms of identities are under attack as "particularistic."[46] In our post-Enlightenment world where the prevailing Enlightenment discourse, and its master narrative, has come under rightful critique and suspicion, O'Regan, like Milbank and Hart, promotes the task of Christian discourse to be one of nontriumphalist out-narration that reveals peace to be a key transcendental of the Christian interpretation of being. In the need to reexpress Christian identity and vision, in a bid to out-narrate other narratives, O'Regan sets forth pleromatic apocalyptic discourse as the privileged Christian mode of postmodern thinking. Pleromatic apocalyptic is fully adequate to the aforesaid task, which is "imperative" for Christian thought today.[47] This proposing of pleromatic apocalyptic as the way forward "by no means

---

46. O'Regan, *Spaces of Apocalyptic*, 127.
47. O'Regan, *Spaces of Apocalyptic*, 127.

implies the dispensability of retrievalist or argumentative modes of theology, but it does suggest that the visionary has become indispensable. For better or worse, Christians figure a way in which we make our way through the no-man's land in which everything is permitted except conviction."[48]

Pleromatic apocalyptic *theo*logy, however, is not another form of nostalgia, even as it looks to the past for guidance. It is a *rhetorical form and style* of *theo*logy in a number of different respects.[49] Further, as a rhetorical and proclamatory form of *theo*logy it is not altogether dissimilar to the extraordinary affiliated and believing materialism of Badiou. O'Regan keenly sees that, in the words of Badiou, "It is of the essence of faith to publicly declare itself."[50] Conviction thus voices itself from within an affiliated commitment, thereby proclaiming its faith in the brilliance of its life and vision. This is worlds apart from a private, subjective, and nonvisionary faith in the impossible that will never come, never eventuate itself in the economy of presence. Here, again in the words of Badiou, "Truth is either militant or it is not," with the caveat that this militancy rides under the banner of the transcendental peace in its nonviolent war against violence.[51] Pleromatic apocalyptic is the discourse that best enables the Christian, in a peaceful militancy, to radically speak forth the truth of Christian existence amidst the exigencies of the convictionless liberal moment in history in which we now stand.

Seven vital aspects of pleromatic apocalyptic are laid out. First, pleromatic apocalyptic discourse is a form of *theo*logy that seeks to persuade, not through argumentation, but through the power of its visionary beauty, and in this sense it shares an elective affinity with aesthetic modes of *theo*logy. Second, pleromatic apocalyptic discourse does not "exclude edification" or spirituality from its mode of expression. Third, an "adequate" pleromatic apocalyptic discourse has a "polemical and argumentative" side that is not fearful of saying no to secular culture which says no to Christianity. Fourth, pleromatic apocalyptic discourses must diagnose "simulacra" and "insufficient forms of Christianity." Fifth, to be "adequate" pleromatic apocalyptic discourse must pay attention to forms of life and practices where vision is "made flesh" in "exemplary" forms of life, witness, and service. Sixth, "genuine" apocalyptic discourse "moves towards a con-

48. O'Regan, *Spaces of Apocalyptic*, 127–28.
49. O'Regan, *Spaces of Apocalyptic*, 128.
50. Alain Badiou, *Saint Paul: The Foundations of Universalism*, trans. Ray Brassier (Stanford, CA: Stanford University Press, 2003), 88.
51. Badiou, *Saint Paul*, 88.

dition of ecstasy and anagogy" because its mode of discourse is "redolent" of the "future" of the triune God who utters himself as mystery.[52] Due to this, the Trinitarian God is worshiped and praised and Christians thus become the "doxological subjects" that they were intended to be all along.[53] Christians do not seek to discover God "by meticulously inspecting God's design, or plumbing history for its distinctions of how and when, but in practices and forms of life that have Christ as their measure and the Spirit as their power."[54] Seventh, pleromatic apocalyptic *theo*logy is a form of "pedagogy" in which Christians do not just see what is wrong with the world, but also see and acknowledge "oppression and persecution." "It is a vision of God that suggests that there is much more to do than enough, that witness even to the point of martyrdom is called for; and it is a vision in which it becomes obvious that God is the living imperative of praise that we cannot hold back, and that God is the victor over death as well as sin."[55]

Pleromatic apocalyptic *theo*logy, then, is not merely a theologically abstract exercise, but one that calls forth the need to make vision and word flesh. This is done in an attempt to regain and reassert Christian identity as a form of apocalyptic challenging, in the name of Christ, alighting and catching fire in the hearts and minds of Christians. Through this alighting, enabled through the power of the Spirit, *theo*logy seeks to reclaim Christian truth through the proclamation of the beauty of its dramatic witness, expressed in lived doxological forms of practice and life, melded with the glory of the speculative daring of the Christian tradition. In these various aspects the Christian sets forth the beauty of Christian form, along with a rigorous challenging and diagnosis of "insufficient forms of Christianity" and Christian "simulacra." All of this is done amidst the spirit of dissimulation and the lies that would make one forget or misremember Christ. This spirit, in the Christian view, is always a manifestation of the spirit of the antichristic lie that is ever present, and indeed intensifying, in the Christian struggle within history, understood as the one theo-dramatic concrete order of grace and redemption. Pleromatic apocalyptic boldly and unabashedly calls for the need to reassert the voice of Christian identity and vision. To see this programmatic sketch unfold I turn to *Misremembering*.

---

52. O'Regan, *Spaces of Apocalyptic*, 128.
53. O'Regan, *Spaces of Apocalyptic*, 128.
54. O'Regan, *Spaces of Apocalyptic*, 128–29.
55. O'Regan, *Spaces of Apocalyptic*, 129.

Cyril O'Regan's Pleromatic Vision

The Apocalyptic Vision of *Misremembering*

At first glance, and on a superficial reading, *Misremembering* might appear to be an exquisite scholarly contribution to the plethora of scholarly works on Balthasar that have appeared over the last fifteen years or so. Upon such a reading, the massive tome of *Misremembering* (528 pages, 649 including endnotes) would be seen as the first systematic and genealogical treatment of Balthasar's resistance to Hegel. It is clearly that on the surface, but the profundity and importance of the text consist in its depth of other merits.[56]

These other merits are that this text provides a veritable roadmap of how one is to *do* genuine postmodern Catholic *theo*logy. And it thus fully seeks to bring to light and vivify the programmatic statements at the conclusion of *Theology and the Spaces of Apocalyptic*. That is, it seeks to match orthodox Christian apocalyptic vision as a counter to the most egregious form of misremembering that Christianity has yet to encounter: Hegel's speculative visionary distortion of Christian symbolism. To accomplish this task, O'Regan enlists Balthasar, a theologian after his own heart. Yet the reading given of Balthasar is that of a visionary apocalyptic theologian. This reading focuses heavily on *Theo-Drama* 4 and 5 to bring the apocalyptic nature of Balthasar's thought into relief. For O'Regan, Balthasar, like no other, has matched Hegel point for visionary point.[57] To think in the wake of the Enlightenment, and Hegel's visionary response to the Enlightenment, is to think counter to Hegel. Indeed, it is the systematic and genealogical haunting of Hegel, in Christian theological discourse, that first must be exorcised if *theo*logy is to go forward. This text then, in the spirit of Irenaeus and his "son" Balthasar, must be partly and importantly seen as a systematic, genealogical, and visionary exorcism of Hegelian *Geist*.[58]

> It [Hegel's discourse] is haunted because in its post-Enlightenment discursive mansion it houses the ghosts of Christianity's premodern others,

---

56. This statement is by no means meant to denigrate the supreme scholarly contribution that O'Regan has made to Balthasar studies, but rather to assert that the text is about so much more.

57. O'Regan says, "Balthasar can be regarded as the most expressly anti-Hegelian of all contemporary theologians." O'Regan, *Misremembering*, 1:115.

58. For the treatment of Balthasarian fathers where O'Regan identifies four main influences on Balthasar's resistance to Hegel, see O'Regan, *Misremembering*, 1:275–330. The Balthasarian fathers whom O'Regan identifies are Staudenmaier, Irenaeus, Bulgakov, and Hamann.

among whom one finds apocalyptic, Neoplatonism, and Gnosticism. Hegelian discourse is a specter, because its discourse is already spectral. And when it becomes an issue as to how hostile the ghosts are to Christianity, attention falls on Gnosticism as the Ghost that is truly a Doppelgänger, and equally on the responsibility of the theologian to detect and refute it. Only such a refutation will make theology possible again, make it possible after modernity, make it legitimately postmodern, and for the same reason make it legitimately Christian.[59]

One of the central tasks of a postmodern orthodox Christian apocalyptic is a thoroughgoing detection of Hegelian ghosts and their Gnostic apparitions. If one is to begin to elaborate a postmodern orthodox Christian apocalyptic discourse, then the first step is an anti-Hegelian one. O'Regan's rigorous anti-Hegelian stance, which he takes up with Balthasar, joins him to a venerable tradition of anti-Hegelian thinkers such as Przywara, Voegelin, Milbank, Hart, and Desmond, all of whom have brilliantly discerned the extreme dangers of Hegelian thought.

Yet the problem remains: How resist Hegel? The simple answer, which is by no means easy to accomplish, is to offer a countervision that is just as expansive and comprehensive as Hegel's. Yet, there is an essential caveat, namely, this expansive and comprehensive vision must never deplete Christian mystery by allowing it to succumb to the Hegelian panoptic gaze. The story of the whole truth of Christian mystery must be retold, a retelling that is now inextricably intertwined with the amnesia of the Enlightenment, and the intentional misremembering of the Christian story and its distortion by post-Enlightenment thinkers like Hegel and his followers (as well as Heidegger, as O'Regan's volume 2 will treat). The Christian task is to break the spell of all master narratives that prohibit the Christian self from being a doxological self ecstatically open to the mystery of being and redemption. In order for this spell to be broken, the drama of the Christian story must return and the Christian self must again doxologically turn towards the breadth and expanse of Christian mystery. O'Regan tells an apocalyptic story of the possibility of a postmodern Christian thought that must be "an act of recollection of the memories of the Christian tradition

---

59. O'Regan, *Misremembering*, 1:47. In the reference to haunting, O'Regan is borrowing from the French Structuralist/Marxist thinker Louis Althusser's *The Specter of Hegel*, through which *hauntologie* enters postmodern discourse and is famously taken up in Derrida's *Specters of Marx*.

in which the phenomenon of God's self-gift to humanity is what makes possible Christian speech, action and forms of life."[60] Here is an explicit embracing of the aesthetic paradigm shift in theology that was enacted by Balthasar, continued on by Hart, and prefigured by Przywara and Milbank. Theology must pursue a path of creative and persuasive action that rests in a decision and "conviction that Christianity can make its case by rendering an account of itself in forms of speech, practice, and life that are intrinsically persuasive, because intrinsically beautiful, and would attend to the ultimate ground of its persuasiveness which is the glory of Christ rendered on the cross."[61]

Such a story, and its challenging of master discourses hostile to Christianity, must, of necessity, view history and the explication of its meaning within the one concrete story of grace and redemption, and thus a story told within the theo-dramatic utterance of revelation. History is not mere "forgetting" (Heidegger), nor pure "recollection" (Hegel), but "a history of memory against the general backdrop of forgetfulness and sharing space with forms of thought that miss the essential and thus can themselves be characterized as a species of misremembering."[62] History must be understood on the register of man's apocalyptic opening for or against the reality of the triune Christian God. History is "a record of desire, of response to the mystery of reality that is forever challenging, forever encouraging of question, forever discouraging of stock answers and amnesia."[63] At least this is how it should be, but clearly certain discourses have been more responsive to mystery than others, while others have failed miserably, not excluding many Christian discourses in their lack of response to mystery and thus its depletion.

In the retelling of the Christian story, the figure of the saint is wholly essential. This is because pleromatic apocalyptic discourse is also essentially about advocating witness, service, and making vision flesh (or vision arising from flesh and practice). And, in order to do this, the forgotten and misrepresented figure of the saint, in modernity, must also be remembered in this retelling of the story of Christianity. For O'Regan sees—like Bloy, Georges Bernanos, and Charles Péguy, and Balthasar following them—that the "representability of the saint is the crux of modernity."[64] This inability

60. O'Regan, *Misremembering*, 1:23.
61. O'Regan, *Misremembering*, 1:13.
62. O'Regan, *Misremembering*, 1:19.
63. O'Regan, *Misremembering*, 1:19.
64. O'Regan, *Misremembering*, 1:11. The figure of the saint figures in much of Bernanos's

of modernity to represent and accept the saint is also marked—as again seen by Bernanos, Péguy, and also Claudel—by an utter "prayerlessness" that is unable to accept the wounding of speech (Chrétien). All of this is again a manifestation of the difficulty that Christianity has living among the norms and prejudices of modernity.[65] Moreover, the saint, in her or his very essence, is a challenge to modernity because "the saint is an ecclesial person" who is wholly at odds with the rampant subjectivist individualism of modernity and the forgetting of community.[66] The saint is the one who accepts her or his singular and "unrepeatable" call to mission, service, and witnessing, in conformity to Christ, within his living Mystical Body.[67] For an apocalyptic orthodox Christian *theo*logy, which is concerned with witness, pedagogy, and anagogy, the Christian remembering of the iconic form of the saint is wholly essential to regaining Christian identity and vision: a vision arising from flesh and a fleshing out of vision. Here "be-

---

work. But perhaps must especially in *Under Satan's Sun* with the character of Father Donissan and *The Diary of a Country Priest* with the character M. Le Curé. See also Bernanos's extraordinary story "Joan, Heretic and Saint," in *The Heroic Face of Innocence*: *Three Stories by Georges Bernanos*, trans. R. Batchelor (Grand Rapids: Eerdmans, 1999), 1–22. Bernanos says, "For sanctity is an adventure; it is indeed the only adventure. Those who have once realized this have found their way into the very heart of the Catholic faith; they have felt in their mortal flesh the shuddering of another terror than the terror of death: the shudder of supernatural hope. *Our Church is the Church of the Saints*. But who worries about the saints? We want them to be old, full of experience and worldly Wisdom; and most of them are children. And childhood is alone against everyone." Bernanos, "Joan," 19. Bernanos's words here are, indeed, very similar to the famed ending of Léon Bloy's masterpiece *The Woman Who Was Poor*, where Bloy declares that there is only one unhappiness in life, namely, the unhappiness of not being a saint. The forgotten figure of the saint was a guiding thread in the work of all the great luminaries of the twentieth-century French Catholic literary revival, including Huysmans, Bloy, Claudel, Péguy, and Bernanos. And it is a bit of an understatement to say that Balthasar was deeply influenced, in his theology, by this recalling of the figure of the saint in the French Catholic literary renaissance. O'Regan powerfully picks up the thread of the theme of the saint in his apocalyptic *theo*logy. Balthasar also wrote a superb study on Bernanos titled *Bernanos: An Ecclesial Existence*, trans. Erasmo Leiva-Merikakis (San Francisco: Ignatius Press, 1996). For Balthasar's treatment of "The Metaphysics of the Saints," see Hans Urs von Balthasar, *The Glory of the Lord: A Theological Aesthetics*, vol. 5: *The Realm of Metaphysics in the Modern Age*, trans. Erasmo Leiva-Merikakis (San Francisco: Ignatius Press, 1991), 48–149. And for a particularly fascinating treatment, in "The Metaphysics of the Saints," see Balthasar's treatment of, perhaps, the most extraordinary Christian painter in the twentieth century, Georges Rouault, titled "Christ in the Clown," 201–4.

65. O'Regan, *Misremembering*, 1:131.
66. O'Regan, *Misremembering*, 1:79.
67. O'Regan, *Misremembering*, 1:79.

lieving and knowing is tied to praxis, and it is because this is so that the saint can be regarded as the exemplary instantiation of the specifically Christian form of knowing that is always illustrated in action, in Christian practices and forms of life."[68] The figure of the saint is essential to an apocalyptic *theology*, because it is through this exemplary form that the persuasiveness of Christian form is best rendered. The saint manifests Christian vision-in-action. The saint makes vision flesh in an iconic conformity to Christ: the Word made flesh. The saint is revelatory of Christian beauty and a memory that repeats forward the tradition and the Church. The saint shows forth a living enfleshed and acting humanity that is doxologically open before the expanse of being and Christian mystery.[69] The figure of the saint is a persuasive countering form to the utter depletion of Christian mystery in modernity, and the evacuation of Christian mystery in Hegelian misremembering.

Along with the diagnosing of Christian simulacra and the emphasis on the iconic figure of the saint, the vocation of the theologian is "remembering the living voices of the tradition as they witness to the mystery of the triune God revealed in Christ, as they attest to a logic of love. Balthasar understands this memory of memory and of the primary phenomenon to be creative, to involve a going on that is part of the traditioning process itself. Memory is as such a spiritual practice in Pierre Hadot's sense."[70] Such a practice or exercise of memory and the retelling of the Christian story is spiritual because here one is speaking of a "memory that is ecclesial."[71]

---

68. O'Regan, *Misremembering*, 1:78.

69. In the *disputatio* on the humanity of man, enacted in Lacoste's *Experience and the Absolute*, Lacoste presents the figure of the saint, the child, the fool (*du fol*), the "minimal man" as the key figure(s) for understanding our humanity. Here Lacoste phenomenologically shows that dispossession and poverty, rather than possession and appropriation (and here he phenomenologically points to an overthrowing of the illusions of natural property rights insofar as poverty is our native ontological condition prior to any right of property or appropriation), is what is most native and fundamental to our humanity. The figures of the saint, of the child, of the fool, of the "minimal man," through a voluntary choice of poverty—paradigmatically instantiated in liturgy and prayer—stand ontologically bare before the Absolute in a kenotic state of being-in-vocation. In other words, it is in this relation with the Absolute, instantiated in the displaced liturgical logic of the saint's humanity being laid bare before God, that we discover the true essence of the humanity of man, over and above the logic of the world, the logic of the Hegelian sage and the norms of modernity, which privilege rationality and the logic of appropriation. See Lacoste, *Experience and the Absolute* (New York: Fordham University Press, 2004), especially the whole of the last chapter, "Towards a Kenotic Treatment of the Question of Man," 168–94.

70. O'Regan, *Misremembering*, 1:111.

71. O'Regan, *Misremembering*, 1:13.

Such a memory is the "enacting" and performing of Christian vision that is not a nostalgic reminiscence but an active and creative dynamic, an "*ars memoria*," and thus part of the "traditioning process" itself.[72] The spirituality of Christian memory is apocalyptic because it takes place within the theo-dramatics of Christian revelation and history understood as a battleground of remembering Christ amidst the forces of misremembering.

The battle for Christian tradition then must be understood as *being true* to this tradition, because the ultimate horizon and meaning of tradition is Trinitarian. Tradition "is nothing less than the gift of the triune God, who grants the milieu and forms the medium in which response to the divine is shaped and articulated."[73] To interpret the tradition is to give and offer a response to the mystery of the transcendent triune life revealing itself on the apocalyptic stage of human history, where finite and divine freedom interact and mingle. This response cannot be a mere repetition, a mere "pass on" (*traditio*) but a "give back" (*redditio*), which is a creative receiving that gives back to the tradition in ever new ways.[74] Yet this process is one that must be rooted in the Church, understood as "Christ's self-gift."[75] The Church is always guided by the Spirit of Truth, which is the spirit of Christ, and thus enables new facets of Christ's mystery to be seen, interpreted, articulated, and responded to. Yet the whole of this process is not without danger, insofar as the entirety of Christian memory and the handing on and giving back of the tradition are not immune to forgetting and misremembering. Therefore, Christian memory is embroiled within the agon between the truth and the lie, the spirit of Christ and the spirit of the Antichrist. Christian memory is a spiritual practice and a "discernment of spirits," which, as part of the ecclesial "traditioning process," is always already immersed in a creative struggle for a faithful retelling of Christian vision and the Christian story. This retelling is one that is constantly endangered by the possibility (and actuality) of a distortion of Christ and the disfigurement of Christian symbolism. The spirituality of Christian memory, enacted within the tradition centered in the revelation of triune mystery and the self-gift of Christ to the Church, is the alighting and catching fire of apocalyptic vision.

To recapitulate: O'Regan seeks to elaborate a post-Enlightenment, post-Hegelian, and therefore, postmodern way of doing *theo*logy, which is

---

72. O'Regan, *Misremembering*, 1:14.
73. O'Regan, *Misremembering*, 1:31.
74. O'Regan, *Misremembering*, 1:135.
75. O'Regan, *Misremembering*, 1:248.

centered in vision and memory given through, and within, the gift of revelation. In doing so, *theo*logy seeks to address the evacuation of mystery accomplished by modernity and the master narrative of the Enlightenment. However, to respond fully to the Enlightenment, it is above all necessary to respond to the greatest visionary response given to the Enlightenment project, namely, Hegel's grandiose speculative response. In this response Hegel resurrects and recollects pre-Enlightenment discourses, and especially the discourse of Gnosticism. The first step towards the elaboration of a postmodern theological discourse is the countering-detecting and exorcism of Hegelian *Geist* from theological discourse and its systematic disfiguration and misremembering of Christianity.

The response to Hegel must then be a visionary one in which the full breadth of revelation, and the vision imparted through revelation, is deployed in a countering move. This countermovement embarks on a refiguration of the Christian story that seeks to break the spell of the displacement and overcoming of Christian mystery by both Enlightenment and Hegelian master narratives. This spell-breaking takes place within the conviction and belief that Christianity is still able to render itself persuasively through the intrinsic beauty of its dramatic form, practices, and ways of life. This persuasiveness is ultimately rooted in the Trinitarian horizon of history expressed in the Person of Christ, and the glory of the cross, passed on and repeated forward in the conforming iconic figure of the saint. Such a response calls forth a view of the Christian as a doxological self that openly and humbly receives the mystery of being and redemption: the redemption of being. O'Regan's response to philosophical modernity is thus genealogical, visionary, and rhetorical (dramatic and aesthetic), all the while attending to the importance of practices and forms of Christian life.

Crucial to this response to Christian mystery is the role that Christian memory plays in the retelling of the Christian story. Here Christian memory is understood as an ecclesial and spiritual practice. Memory itself is rooted in tradition, a tradition that is ultimately interpreted within a Trinitarian theo-dramatic horizon given in the self-gift of Christ to the Church. The theologian's response to tradition is a creative and dynamic response to triune and Christological mystery, ecclesially instantiated. Because of this, memory and vision take on apocalyptic dimensions. This is so because such a response is faced with closure, forgetting, and misremembering. In this closure, forgetting, and misremembering the Person of Christ and the dynamics of the living tradition can be, and are, disfigured and distorted by the dissemination of the lie, the spirit of the Antichrist, as this spirit is ever present along with the Bride in her journey towards the Lamb. Memory must become a spiritual apocalyptic practice that is able—in the act of creative remembering and giving back—to detect and discern true likeness from simulacra. Christian memory and the memory of the pleromatic orthodox theologian is thus performative, rhetorical, visionary, and a dramatic enactment or reenactment on the theo-dramatic apocalyptic stage of history, where the agon between the truth and the lie, Christ and the Antichrist, takes place. Such, in a nutshell, is the theological vision presented in *Misremembering*.

* * *

To conclude: my reasons for enlisting O'Regan's pleromatic apocalyptic *theo*logy are now explicitly evident. First, in relation to Part 2, O'Regan's discourse manifests the same countermodern trajectory as the discourses of Przywara, *Nouvelle Théologie*, Desmond, Milbank, and Hart (chapters 5 and 7). This is expressly seen because his apocalyptic *theo*logy is situated as a counter-response to both the Enlightenment project and Hegel's visionary response to the Enlightenment. Moreover, O'Regan's discourse also offers a spacious and expansive Christian response to the cramped nihilism and truncated thinking on the divine characteristic of postmodernity (chapter 6) that is remarkably similar to Desmond's, Milbank's, and Hart's responses towards postmodernity (chapter 7). This was specifically seen in the stark contrast between Caputo's kenomatic pseudo-space of apocalyptic and the full breadth of the *theo*logical space of pleromatic apocalyptic. Second, in regard to my postmodern and post-Conciliar reimagining of the *analogia entis* (chapter 9), O'Regan's apocalyptic and Balthasarian-inspired style of *theo*logy, for all of the reasons given and hinted at in this chapter, is the perfect conversation partner in my turn towards an "analogical-apocalyptic metaphysics." It is now time to bring my search for pleromatic Christian vision together in my programmatic proposal of an "analogical-apocalyptic metaphysics," understood as the most adequate and needed style of Christian discourse today.

CHAPTER 9

The *Analogia Entis* Reimagined:
A Christian Analogical-Apocalyptic Metaphysics

> For ultimately the priority of the mystery of Christ over the mystery of the Antichrist is the real inner meaning of all things.
> Przywara, *Deus semper major* III, quoted in
> Hans Urs von Balthasar, *The Theology of Karl Barth*

The crescendo and the climax of the story I have been seeking to tell has now arrived and so its end. Yet, an end is never merely an end, but always the commencement of a new beginning. The beginning of the end of the story, which will soon be told, is one that concerns the present and future. That is to say, it concerns the present and future direction of Christian thinking as we enter every day, more and more, into the unknown and ever-intensifying hour of our postmodern and post-Christian twenty-first century. What I would like to offer in this chapter is a vision and style of Christian metaphysics that I see to be crucial for the future of Christian thought, conviction, identity, practice, and vision amidst the multifaceted challenges facing Christian thought and belief today. Further, these unprecedented challenges are read within the apocalyptic laws of "polarization" and "intensification" of *Theo-Drama*, volumes 4 and 5, in keeping with my reading of philosophical modernity and postmodernity set forth in the Introduction. The first part of this chapter seeks to synthesize and bring together my search for Christian pleromatic vision by analogically binding the Christian creaturely participatory vision of the *analogia entis* with the Trinitarian theo-dramatic visionary backdrop of apocalyptic *theo*logy. The *analogia entis* is reimagined, apocalyptically, as a postmodern and post-Conciliar discourse of discourses in an "analogical-apocalyptic metaphysics." The second part of the chapter seeks to programmatically offer and set forth an essential aspect of the dramatic task of an analogical-apocalyptic discourse of discourses and hence an avenue for development for future thought enacted through an enfleshment of Christian analogical/pleromatic vision in a dramatics of Christian *praxis*, understood as a response to the post-Christian socio-political arena. In other words, a partial aspect of the theo-political potential of the *analogia entis* is opened.

Synthesizing Analogical and Apocalyptic Vision

It is not an infelicitous coincidence that the majority of the theologians that O'Regan nominates pleromatic apocalyptic thinkers (Balthasar, Milbank, and Hart, though this does exclude Moltmann) are also, and at the same time, analogical thinkers. Nor is it happenstance that all of the aforesaid thinkers have taken an aesthetic and rhetorical turn in *theo*logy in which the *analogia entis* plays an essential role. And further, nor is it unimportant that O'Regan holds that there is an elective affinity between aesthetic forms of *theo*logy and pleromatic apocalyptic discourse. Moreover, there is also a clear genealogical connection here as Balthasar, Milbank, and Hart are all, to varying degrees, indebted to, and in conversation with, Przywara's analogical metaphysics. Furthermore, there are reasons that Milbank, Hart, and O'Regan are all fond readers of Desmond's metaxological metaphysics. Likewise, it is not inconsequential that O'Regan is also himself an analogical thinker who draws from Przywara and Balthasar and the *maior dissimilitudo* of the *analogia entis*. In other words, a unity or similarity in vision is clearly presenting itself here, yet one that must be thought through and elucidated. What exactly are the connections here? And what role does the *analogia entis* play in this polyphonic unity of vision? This is to say, it must be seen why it is that there is an elective affinity between analogical metaphysics and pleromatic apocalyptic *theo*logy. This affinity leads towards my reimaging of the *analogia entis* and thus an "analogical-apocalyptic metaphysics" suspended within the eventful analogical site of *commercium* between *philo*sophy and *theo*logy in the one concrete stream of the history of sin and redemption.

In order to see these connections and the unity of vision being presented, I proceed in four steps: First, I begin by showing how the *analogia entis* reopens the expanse of Christian mystery—called for by pleromatic apocalyptic discourse—thereby showing an elective affinity between an analogical metaphysics and performative styles of theological aesthetics.

A Christian Analogical-Apocalyptic Metaphysics

Second, from this backdrop of Christian mystery, called for by an apocalyptic *theo*logy, I show how an analogical metaphysics is a rigorous way of detecting forms of discourse that offer themselves as inversions and refigurations of Christian discourse. Third, I then proceed to elaborate how an analogical metaphysics stages itself on the apocalyptic theo-dramatic stage of history. Fourth, from there I move on to show how an analogical metaphysics deeply entails an interpretation of the self as doxological and is, thus, especially concerned with dramatic practices and forms of Christian life, witness, and service, thereby offering a "metaphysics of the saints." I conclude by showing the rules of operation under which an "analogical-apocalyptic metaphysics" functions.

The Analogia Entis *and the Reenchanting of Christian Mystery*

Apocalyptic pleromatic discourse realizes that one of the drastic effects of philosophical modernity, and the Enlightenment project, is the domestication and evisceration of mystery and the inhospitable world that this has created for Christianity to live within, making extremely difficult Christian thought, practice, and forms of life. Moreover, if history itself can be seen as a "record of desire" that gauges one's response to the mystery of creation and reality, then it must be said that this response to the mystery of reality, advocated by an apocalyptic *theo*logy, is only fully present when this response is analogical. Why? The simple answer is that the vision presented in an analogical metaphysics is the only one that fully guards the transcendent mystery of a God who is freely and lovingly independent of the world. Such a discourse proffers a logic of God's glory. This is best expressed by Balthasar when he says, "Glory stands and falls with the unsurpassability of the *analogia entis*, the ever-greater dissimilarity of God no matter how great the similarity to him. In so far as German Idealism begins with the *identitas entis*, the way back to Christianity is blocked; it cannot produce an aesthetics of 'glory' but only of 'beauty': and the 'aesthetics as science,' which was rampant in the nineteenth century, is its fruit."[1] Philosophical modernity, as seen in the Introduction, is thus the denial of the Christian *analogia entis*.

---

1. Hans Urs von Balthasar, *The Glory of the Lord: A Theological Aesthetics*, vol. 5: *The Realm of Metaphysics in the Modern Age*, trans. Erasmo Leiva-Merikakis (San Francisco: Ignatius Press, 1991), 548–49.

The transcendent glory of God is what allows for the freeing of creation into its relational otherness, which, in its participatory being, shares and testifies to the freedom of God's whyless love, goodness, truth, and glory. Seen within this light, creation is always thought within the mystery of God's love; creation is thus: a mysterious "music" (Przywara), a "poem" (Desmond), a participation in creative beauty (Milbank), and God's aesthetic rhetoric (Hart). The *analogia entis* is a metaphysical discourse that always leads to a *reductio in mysterium* and thus takes place within the heart of the mystery of God's free and creative love. O'Regan is fully correct to see that any discourse that has as its "ambition to penetrate reality thoroughly compromises the *analogia entis* and collapses the creator-created distinction."[2]

The *analogia entis* thus safeguards and opens the expanse of Christian mystery by elaborating a metaphysics of creation that is rooted in the biblical narrative, and the creative transformation of a metaphysics of participation, which, for the first time in human history, allows one to think the ever-greater glorious transcendence of God: the difference between the *Being* of God and the borrowed received *being* of creation. But this transcendence of God is anything but a neutral aloofness of a self-thinking-thought or the anonymity of the One. This very transcendence of God is the space of infinite loving distance through which the glory of God is transmitted to creation. Only God's distance allows for the proximity of his shimmering presence. Only God's creative distance and difference allows for God to truly be in what is other to him, without confusing the two in an idolatrous and tragic identity. This indwelling of God's presence, in the immanence of creation, exhibits strongly aesthetic dimensions; because here creation is seen as a manifestation of God's twofold glory. First, God's glory is manifested in the creation of what is truly other to God, as a freeing and releasing of the gift of analogical difference: the gift of the otherness of creation. Second, creation, in virtue of its difference from God, is a true manifestation of God's abiding presence *within* his creation. But this presence is never reducible to creation itself. God is *in*, but also always and ever *beyond* creation, drawing creation on into the infinite expanse of God's transcendent glory in an endless traversal of the distance of love. Such a vision of the Creator/creature relation, held in an analogical metaphysics, is expressive of the dynamic beauty of God's love. Creation is

---

2. Cyril O'Regan, *The Anatomy of Misremembering: Von Balthasar's Response to Philosophical Modernity*, vol. 1: *Hegel* (New York: Crossroad, 2014), 77.

never over and done with. It is a dynamic and eventful site of the mystery of relation. Creation is a continuous act of analogical relation, exchange, and *commercium* where God brings himself into relation to man, in the immanence of his glory. But this is a glory that always exceeds the realm of its manifestation, thereby receding back into the realm of the burning mystery of God's dynamic positivity of *Being* and *Life*. Analogical thinking follows this dynamic by thinking and living within the mystery of God's presence, in immanence. This presencing of God's immanence initiates thought *into* analogical transcendence and the expanse of mystery: *into* a true knowing in unknowing through which thought participates and responds to the dynamic gift of the beauty of God's free and creative love.

An essential aspect of this movement is an aesthetic and performative appreciation of the mystery of the dynamics of creation, which itself thinks, participates, and shares in the mystery of *commercium* between God and man. This is why there is an essential affinity between theological aesthetics and an analogical metaphysics. Both are performative and respectful of God's mystery, set within a logic of being grounded in the nonground of created being's abiding *mysterium*, the corollary of which is a logic of God's free glory. Creation and creaturely being are given as a gift of difference from the ever-greater glory of God's free transcendence. Such a stance and affinity between theological aesthetics and analogical metaphysics thus proffers a performative vision where thinking takes place within the aesthetic site of the *commercium* of the *analogia entis*. Here thought is an enacting and performing of vision that is taken up within the beauty and glory of God's love. Furthermore, this is why an analogical metaphysics and theological aesthetics share an elective affinity with pleromatic apocalyptic discourse. This is so, because all three discourses proffer a *rhetorical performativity of vision* that is firmly set within the uniqueness of Christian story, vision, and conviction. This conviction, shared by all three discourses, in turn, offers the beauty of its peaceful truth as a means of countering other modes of vision and, in so doing, seeks to persuade by the intrinsic beauty of the Christian visionary story of analogical being. Analogical metaphysics, like forms of theological aesthetics and pleromatic apocalyptic discourse, seeks to reenchant Christian vision by offering a performative rhetorical thought that is fully responsive to the glory of Christian mystery and the expanse of its truth. This is done in opposition to any forms of metaphysical totality and Christian simulacra that would refuse a creative participation in the exchange with the beauty of God's freeing love. Such a refusal and rejection, from the analogically Christian perspective, always collapses the glorious beauty of the infinite distance between God and creation: a distance through which the dramatic and aesthetic exchange between God and creatures is acted out.

Thus it can be seen that, for an analogical metaphysics of creation, theological aesthetics, and pleromatic apocalyptic discourses, a re-enchanting of Christian mystery and vision is wholly essential for Christian thought. Rhetorical and performative Christian vision is paramount for all three modes of discourse as they all three seek to offer to the world the persuasiveness and beauty of Christian truth. And, as the *analogia entis* itself allows for an "analogy of discourses," it is by no means surprising that in Przywara, Balthasar, Milbank, Hart, and O'Regan, these three modes of discourse blend into one overarching vision by reinforcing each other in the uniqueness of Christian vision, while Desmond's Christian metaxological metaphysics can be seen as a powerful propaedeutic to both a theological aesthetics and pleromatic apocalyptic. These three forms of discourse are thus tied, and all three modes of discourse show elective affinities towards one another: affinities that are opened by an analogical unity-in-difference and the analogy of discourses that flows from this. The *analogia entis* gives the metaphysical ground, as nonground, from which the vision of glory and Christian mystery is reflected within styles of theological aesthetics and styles of pleromatic apocalyptic discourses. For, without an analogical metaphysics, styles of theological aesthetics and pleromatic apocalyptic discourses would be unable to offer a full vision of Christian glory that respects the difference of differences, namely, the God/world distinction (Moltmann's dialectical pleromatic apocalyptic is the exception here). It can be concluded that only forms of theological aesthetics and forms of pleromatic apocalyptic discourses that have the *analogia entis* as their metaphysical touchstone are fully adequate to the breadth of Christian vision needed for a full response to the depths of Christian mystery and the gifted reality of creation. Without the *analogia entis*, the Christian view of God is impossible and thus also Christian identity and vision.

The Analogia Entis *as a Rigorous Means of Detecting Christian Simulacra*

For pleromatic apocalyptic *theo*logy, one of its essential tasks is a diagnosing of forms of discourse that seek to reconfigure Christian truth in a transgressive manner, thereby producing "counterfeit doubles" and simulacra of Christianity. Certainly one way of detecting and countering Christian simulacra is genealogical, where one searches out a narrative grammar that is able to discern the hauntings of certain discourses by counterfeit doubles of Christianity (such as the reemergence of Gnosticism in modernity). O'Regan is masterful at such a necessary endeavor. The other way to search out counterfeit doubles is a metaphysical unmasking of idolatrous and anti-Christian discourses. Furthermore, underlying O'Regan's genealogical endeavor is an analogical metaphysics, as he invokes it at critical moments, thereby showing his indebtedness to Przywara and Balthasar. Moreover, there are genealogical strands in Przywara's work as well, insofar as he signals to certain premodern discourses haunting modern discourses, as was seen in his detecting of Joachimism in German Idealism. This marrying of genealogical detection with an analogical detecting of Christian simulacra is further seen in the works of Balthasar (especially in *Herrlichkeit*), Milbank, and Hart. In a word, these two ways of searching out Christian simulacra must reinforce each other in service to plenary Christian vision.

How then is the *analogia entis*, specifically, a rigorous metaphysical mode of countering and detecting forms of transgressive refigurations of the Christian story? Answer: the *analogia entis* opens up the expanse of Christian mystery by elaborating a specifically Christian metaphysical grammar and vision (the marrying of biblical creation with a transformed metaphysics of participation), which safeguards the free transcendence of God. It is thus able to detect and counter forms of metaphysics that compromise the God/world distinction in tragic and anti-Christian totality. The *analogia entis* detects and counters modes of metaphysics that are insufficient, foreign, and transgressive of the Christian story of being. Forms of discourse that are either transgressive, foreign, or insufficient to the Christian story of being include (without being exhaustive) Gnostic narratives, Joachimism, Nominalism/Voluntarism, Protestant Theopanism, and dialectical views of an agonic or theogonic god of development and process in German Idealism and Heidegger's historical mythicizing of being, to name some. In one way or another all of these discourses compromise the God/world distinction and are unable to keep the analogical balance of the freely given reality of creation in its peaceful goodness in relation to the asymmetrical God of transcendent love. Once again it is not surprising to see that analogical thinkers like Przywara, Balthasar, Desmond, Milbank, and Hart deploy an analogical metaphysics of creation against forms of metaphysical identity they view to be detrimental to a Christian view of God. Nor is it an accident that all of the aforesaid analogical thinkers specifically offer resistance to, and single out as particularly dangerous, the agonic or theogonic and developmental view of God presented in Hegel.

Again, an analogical metaphysics manifests an elective affinity with pleromatic apocalyptic discourse, insofar as both not only offer visionary responses to Christian mystery but also set forth, as one of their primary aims, a rigorous detection and countering of Christian simulacra. An analogical metaphysics shows itself again to be the most apt style of metaphysics to aid pleromatic apocalyptic *theo*logy in the battlefield of forgetting and misremembering of the truth of the Christian story of being. This is so because an analogical metaphysics is expressive of the full acceptance of the gift of creaturely existence, and its *fiat*, over against narratives of idolatrous totality and *non serviam*, as these latter discourses destroy the relation between the God of free glory and the creature that serves this glory with the entirety of its analogical and doxological being. A Christian analogical metaphysics is an essential part of the remembrance of the gift of the tradition amidst misremembering. An analogical metaphysics aids in telling the story of God's self-gift to humanity in creation and redemption, and the free and creative response to God's self-gift by the creature in its humble and joyful acceptance of the gift of creatureliness. The humble creatureliness of the *analogia entis*—as a creaturely logic and thus a logic respectful of God's surpassing glory—deploys itself as the most rigorous metaphysical mode of detecting anti-Christian metaphysical simulacra, which would dare to set man up in the place of God. In so doing, styles of analogical metaphysics join and aid pleromatic apocalyptic in its task of battling misremembering by proffering a creaturely metaphysics, rooted within the humble identity of a Christian grammar and vision of being, which is always at the service of the Divine Majesty.

The One Historical Concrete Order of Grace and Redemption: The Apocalyptic Stage

Pleromatic apocalyptic *theo*logy presents a view of history as taking place in the one concrete order of grace and redemption. This stage is interpreted as the dramatic interaction of finite and eternal freedom, as this stage is enacted within the "dynamic field of memory" that takes place among forgetting, misremembering, and intentional distortion of the Christian story and vision. The theologian's task in developing a genuine postmodern apocalyptic *theo*logy is, through a spiritual act of memory,

A Christian Analogical-Apocalyptic Metaphysics

to creatively remember and repeat forward the gift of the tradition in response to the mystery of divine revelation. But this is done in a tradition always already embroiled in the agon between the truth and the lie. Analogical metaphysics is likewise expressive of the one concrete order of grace and redemption, which sees the history of metaphysics as a battleground and a "record of desire" that tells the story of humble response and frightful revolt. This battleground ultimately consists in the agon between the truth of the creaturely *fiat* and lie of *non serviam*, through which the creature is seduced into thinking that it can usurp the place of God in a titanism of the spirit (monistic or identity-metaphysics as well as Heideggerian *Dasein*, for example). Thus an analogical metaphysics, set within the one concrete order of grace and redemption, already views history from an apocalyptic Christian standpoint, insofar as the history of metaphysics is viewed, ultimately, as an apocalyptic opening of the creature *for or against God* set within the theologoumena of sin and redemption. (Recall my signaling to the apocalyptic dimension of the *analogia entis* in the section on Joachim and the Fourth Lateran Council and my remarks in the Introduction.) An analogical metaphysics tells a Christian story that advocates a humble logic of creaturely love and service (recall Przywara's treatment of logics: pure logic, dialectic, and analogical logic) where the creature freely responds to the glory of infinite freedom through a doxological act of service and submission.

It is thus here, on the apocalyptic stage of history understood as the dramatic unfolding of human openness or closure to God that the *analogia entis*—as the "fundamental Catholic form"—truly shows its apocalyptic dimensions. Metaphysics, understood from the standpoint of the *analogia entis*, is not an abstract game or intellectual rumination, but an apocalyptic Christian story that gauges the level of response to the truth of the mystery of Christian analogical being. Analogical being is thus understood as the relational dynamic between the God of creation and grace and the creature created *ex nihilo* always already set within the one concrete story of grace and redemption. This story is a story of the choice between two abysses, two cities: a story of a faithful yes or a resounding no.

The first possibility is the acceptance of the wounded nothingness of our creaturely being, a being that is wholly an unmerited gift. To accept this being is to accept it from within the mystery of free abyssal love, a love that can never be fully understood because such a love is not causal: it is free and whyless. There can then be only one true response to this whyless love, namely, a losing of one's life in order to save and find it. This losing of one's life means the deepest acceptance and yes to: *being-a-creature*, and thus *being-a-servant, being-a-handmaiden*. Being-a-servant always entails the drama of a *being-sent*. For a creature is precisely the one who was, and will always be, sent forth from out of nothingness, emerging from the abyss of the fire of God's love in order to perform its mission of free and dramatic service. Yet this choice is never merely a subjective, interior, or pietistic choice, but an ecclesial, social, and affiliated choice, and thus made within the dynamic matrix of a community and tradition. This choice and acceptance of creatureliness is always a faithfully lived response to the full dynamics and living memory of Christian mystery, as this memory is creatively passed on ecclesially. It demands an ecclesial response, which creatively answers back, by and through a giving forward. This response is, therefore, a response to the entire spectrum of the Christian story in its shimmering and dappled mosaic (metaphysical/speculative/theological, spirituality/mysticism, liturgy, practices and forms of life, etc.). Being-a-creature is always already an explicit response to the entirety of the mystery of the Christian story, which takes place within the event of the mystery of being and grace acted out on the dramatic stage of history. This analogical story, and view of being, is one that tells the story of *commercium* and anti-*commercium*. This is why, at its deepest core, the analogical story of being is the story of the *analogia caritatis*: a love story of communion, a story of freedom and thus also a story of the betrayal and rejection of the freedom of love.

To reject *being-a-creature* is to reject the story of *commercium* that the *analogia entis* tells, on a metaphysical plane, concerning the drama of divine and human freedom. The rejection of the story of *commercium* is a story of an anti-*commercium* that parodies and inverts the Christian story of being. In the story of the anti-*commercium* the analogical movement of the creature, and the creature's nothingness arising out of the fire of God's abyssal love, is inverted in a countermovement of masking that seeks the self-apotheosis of the creature's relative nothingness. The gift of being, freely given by God, is appropriated as a "right" where one seeks to save one's life instead of losing it. Here the creature seeks only to serve himself. Such self-service is a nihilistic gesture that masks the abyss and gift of creaturely being with divine-like self-permanence and presence. This closed countermovement refuses the missionary and relational nature of created being. Man dares to be God, in a countermovement of anti-*commercium*, which betrays God's act of gratuitous love: thereby seeking to deify the nothingness and abyss of created analogical being in an act of self-exaltation that proclaims, "I am who I am."

A Christian Analogical-Apocalyptic Metaphysics

Here creaturely being is rejected and man is seen to be an autonomous foundation-unto-himself. This, in turn, creates the masquerade of the *civitas terrena*, which sets itself up as an opposed parody to the peaceful *Civitas Dei*. Being-as-gift is rejected and thus the relational dynamics of *commercium*/exchange of analogical logic. The Christian logic of analogical being, which is a creaturely logic of service that views man as the one sent forth to serve creation and God for God's greater glory, is replaced by self-service and self-worship. Service is rejected in favor of the *bellum omnium contra omnes*, where each seeks his own masquerading self-worship. The *analogia entis* tells an apocalyptic tale of the creaturely *fiat* and the *non serviam* of the creature: a tale of the agon between truth and the lie, *commercium* and anti-*commercium*, Christ and the Antichrist. An analogical metaphysics again shows its profound elective affinity with pleromatic apocalyptic *theo*logy in the boldness with which it speaks the truth of the Christian apocalyptic story, as it seeks to be true to its own tradition and identity amidst the forces of misremembering.

The Analogia Entis *as a "Metaphysics of the Saints"*

Pleromatic apocalyptic discourse could not be fully and essentially understood unless it was seen how it paid special attention to practices and forms of Christian life. These forms and practices are ultimately expressive of an ecstatic and anagogic uplifting vision of the Christian doxological self: a self in which vision was brought-into-flesh in a fleshing and acting out of Christian vision in witness and service. This was manifested most clearly in the figure of the saint, as this figure best rendered the beauty of Christian form and the persuasiveness of its story in the splendor of its truth. This is also precisely what the *analogia entis* does through its seeking to be true to the truth of the creaturely *fiat*. Here, then, it must be recalled that the *analogia entis* is especially concerned with the spirituality of the creature and what it means to be a creature. We have seen that the *analogia entis* was expressive of orthodox Christian spirituality, which was rooted in an experience of God, a God who was truly in experience, but also always ever beyond experience and human encapsulation.[3] The

---

3. O'Regan, like Przywara and Balthasar, also recognizes the *analogia entis* as constitutive of Catholic orthodox spirituality and mysticism. He says, "Nor finally, despite a high sense of human participation in the divine life, especially the divine life of the Trinity, does

analogia entis is a creaturely metaphysical logic that formally describes the religious orthodox experience of the Christian self in a logic of love. This is an experience attested and witnessed to, most fully, in the lives of the saints and their ecclesial missions within the "agapeic community" of the Church.

The *analogia entis* thus tells the story of a reverential obedience of the creature to the ever-greater God, a story that manifests itself in "humble self-discrimination" and "loving-surrender."[4] The "loving-surrender" of the humble *fiat* of the creature is the groundless-ground of orthodox Christian spirituality through which the creature receives the woundedness of its created and received being as a gift from the abyss of whyless love. The creature, in turn, responds with a "loving surrender," thereby offering back its borrowed, participatory, and analogical being as a doxological offering and oblation to the *Deus semper maior*. Yet, once again, this act of doxological offering, exemplified in the spirituality of the saint—and metaphysically protected by the *analogia entis*—is not a merely private and personal affair, but an ecclesial act that is performed in forms of speech (prayer/liturgy), practices, forms of life, active-service, and witness within the moving dynamics of a dramatic community and tradition. Spirituality, exemplified in the lives of the saints, is a communal and ecclesial performance. Analogical metaphysics—especially as it is presented in Przywara and Balthasar—is representative of orthodox spirituality and can thus be nominated "a metaphysics of the saints," grounded in a creaturely logic of the analogical offering of the *fiat*.

Catholicism support, either in the case of humanity in general, those with special charisms or those who engage in the mystical life, a view that would lessen the incommensurable distance between the divine and the human, the creator and the created. For instance, with the possible exception of Meister Eckhart, who focuses on the uncreated ground of the human soul and the indistinction between human beings as sons and the divine Logos, one would be hard pressed to name a single mystical theologian in the Catholic tradition who fails to assert that grace is a condition of human being's participation in the life of the Trinity. The ontological gap between uncreated and created remains intact, as does the ontological gap between creator and creation. The Victorines (twelfth century), William Saint Thierry (twelfth century), Bonaventure (thirteenth century), and Ruysbroeck (fourteenth century) all provide examples. But even in the Dionysian tradition in general, not excepting Scotus Eriugena, who was an influence on Eckhart, participation in the divine life supposes that participating human being is created." Cyril O'Regan, *Gnostic Return in Modernity* (Albany: State University of New York Press, 2001), 193–94.

4. Erich Przywara, *Analogia Entis: Metaphysics: Original Structure and Universal Rhythm*, trans. John R. Betz and David Bentley Hart (Grand Rapids: Eerdmans, 2014), 196.

A Christian Analogical-Apocalyptic Metaphysics

The analogical view of the self—as seen especially in Przywara's descending *analogia attributionis*—is a dramatic vision of the Christian doxological self, freed forth on a mission of the performance of service for the ever-greater God of glory. Here the Christian analogical logic of the doxological self gives its answer to the modern interiority of the foundational subject, as well as the postmodern spectral and decentered self. The Christian analogical-doxological self (paradigmatically expressed in the figure of the saint) is certainly nonfoundational and decentered, but this decentering is not spectral or schizophrenic. Rather, it is the analogical decentered self of participated creaturely being freely offering back the entirety of itself to God by accepting the mission of creaturely obediential service. The self receives itself in giving itself away, by embracing the pilgrimage and mission of ecclesial service. The Christian analogical-doxological self is understood on the basis of the dramatic performativity of *mission*, set within the dynamics of community and tradition.

Here, as with a pleromatic apocalyptic discourse, the figure of the saint and the Christian doxological self is held up as a sign of contradiction that, through the lived and testimonial truth of analogical-doxological being, is set forth in its beauty to manifest the truth of the Christian narrative. Thus again an analogical metaphysics is shown to be the most apt partner of a postmodern pleromatic apocalyptic *theo*logy, due to the supreme importance and attention it pays to spirituality, practices, and forms of life exemplarily expressed in the Christian figure of the saint. This is because the saint is the one who most fully and obediently offers herself or himself up in a community, through a creaturely doxological *fiat*, for the greater glory of God, thereby revealing the full meaning of what it means *to be a creature*. The figure of the saint thus always moves in the very heart of the apocalyptic struggle of human history, as a living iconic sign, that Christian memory is not dead. The saint is a living and repeating forward of the tradition, as the Bride painfully and slowly makes her way through history towards the Lamb, slain from the foundation of the world, under the ensign of the *Mysterium Crucis*. The saints, in losing themselves, find themselves by passing on and over into the glory of the scandal of *being* "crucified with Christ" (Gal. 2:19). Such is the figure of saint, as told by an analogical metaphysics, which shows its great elective affinity with pleromatic postmodern apocalyptic *theo*logy. Both discourses thus realize that this is a story that must be told, retold, and lived, if full Christian vision is to be regained in these times of "worsening" and "intensification."

THE *ANALOGIA ENTIS* REIMAGINED

Rules of Operation of an "Analogical-Apocalyptic Metaphysics"

In light of the elective affinity shown above, what kind of unity is there between analogical metaphysics and pleromatic apocalyptic *theo*logy? Under what rules would such a postmodern discourse of discourses function and operate?

An analogical-apocalyptic discourse is a postmodern discourse of discourses. That is to say, it is a relationally dynamic discourse that thinks within the site of the movement of relation, the relation *between philo*sophy and *theo*logy. It is a wholly nonfoundational, non-self-legitimizing postmodern discourse that sees and views the relation between philosophy and *theo*logy to be one of a suspended analogy of discourses. The analogical relation of discourses that takes place between philosophy and *theo*logy, in an analogical-apocalyptic discourse, is a discourse that is always already representative of one *trans*natural concrete historical order of grace and redemption, yet a *trans*natural historical order that is apocalyptic, through and through, insofar as history is viewed as an apocalyptic opening of the creature for or against God. An "analogical-apocalyptic metaphysics" judges history, and specifically the history of metaphysics, from the one final end of the creature, which is supernatural. History and metaphysics are read and judged from the standpoint of the creature's response or nonresponse to Christian revelation, which completes and perfects the mystery of created being. But, following Przywara's template (as seen in chapter 2), the primary concern (formal object) of an analogical-apocalyptic metaphysics is precisely *the mystery of created being's freedom and response* to God. An analogical-apocalyptic metaphysics is a Christian metaphysics that has as its formal object the mystery of the creature's apocalyptic response to the God of Christian revelation. But insofar as grace and *theo*logy never destroy the relative and transitional nature of *philo*sophy and creaturely being, but rather complete them, likewise an "analogical-apocalyptic metaphysics" is able to draw from and reinforce the full breadth of the theo-dramatic vision called for in a pleromatic apocalyptic *theo*logy, without thereby losing its creaturely metaphysical status.

Indeed, both discourses bespeak the entirely same truth and the entirely same message and vision, but they do so from different sides of the dynamic moving relational site of *philo*sophy and *theo*logy, relationally and analogically conceived. Pleromatic apocalyptic theology, as a mode of *theo*logy, is directly concerned with God's theo-dramatic revelatory "intention" towards the world and thus explicitly the Trinitarian backdrop

A Christian Analogical-Apocalyptic Metaphysics

of history (pleromatic apocalyptic *theo*logy's formal object). Further, an "analogical-apocalyptic metaphysics" is going to read the history of metaphysics in light of the *creature's* response or nonresponse to the Trinitarian apocalyptic backdrop of history. However, the full means of judging creaturely response to God cannot just come from an analogical metaphysics—for this discourse is not autonomous, but a discourse of discourses—but must be supplemented by the full revelatory vision offered by pleromatic apocalyptic *theo*logy. Thus a postmodern "analogical-apocalyptic metaphysics" would find its elective completion in pleromatic apocalyptic *theo*logy. However, a pleromatic apocalyptic *theo*logy would itself be aided by an analogical metaphysics, because it would gain a metaphysical means to describe the expanse of Christian mystery as well as a metaphysical means of detecting simulacra.

To state it simply, an "analogical-apocalyptic metaphysics" reads the apocalyptic drama of history from the side of *the mystery of created being's freedom* and thus, response or nonresponse to the mystery of revelation, as this revelation unfolds in the apocalyptic drama of history, while a pleromatic apocalyptic *theo*logy reads the same history from the *theo-dramatic* side of God's revelational intention towards the world. Yet the two sides can never be separated, as one focuses on created freedom, and the other on divine freedom. Only as such can the one Christian apocalyptic story be told, as this story is always already comprised by the interaction between finite/created and infinite/Uncreated freedom. An "analogical-apocalyptic metaphysics" is a discourse that is always already mediated and graced and thus one that is analogically related to pleromatic apocalyptic *theo*logy in an elective analogical unity-in-difference. "Analogical-apocalyptic metaphysics" and pleromatic apocalyptic *theo*logy thus hold the same apocalyptic vision, but narrate the one vision and story from different *narratival perspectives*: the former from the perspective of the dramatic act of the creature, the latter from the dramatic act of God. In this way, each aids and reinforces the other as they seek to participate and move within the full expanse of Christian mystery and vision. Such is the functioning mode of deployment of an "analogical-apocalyptic metaphysics." Further, such a discourse is a postmodern discourse of discourses, which functions in the moving site of relational analogical-difference in response to the theo-dramatic call of pleromatic apocalyptic *theo*logy. "Analogical-apocalyptic metaphysics" is thus always already functioning in response to the *other* of *theo*logical pleromatic apocalyptic. And the simple reason for this is that the call of the theo-dramatic Trinitarian act is always already anterior to the dramatic yes or no of the creature. An "analogical-apocalyptic metaphysics" is expressive of a "metaphysics of the saints," which is responsive to the anterior call of the theo-dramatic act of the triune God. An "analogical-apocalyptic metaphysics" is a graced and suspended tale, which tells the story of the *apocalyptic meaning of the fiat* counter to the *apocalyptic non serviam* of the creature, gauged through the resources of revelation, expressed in the theo-dramatic visionary story of a pleromatic apocalyptic *theo*logy.

Thinking the Task of an "Analogical-Apocalyptic Metaphysics": A Program

A Singular Inflection and the Task at Hand

After having seen the elective affinity between analogical metaphysics and pleromatic apocalyptic *theo*logy and the mode of operation under which an "analogical-apocalyptic metaphysics" is deployed, it is now time to see something of its task and singular contribution to contemporary Christian metaphysical discourse of a postmodern and post-Conciliar ilk. In other words, what is the singular vision, inflection, style, and task of "analogical-apocalyptic metaphysics"?

The singularity of an analogical-apocalyptic metaphysical discourse, as a constructive reimagining and expansion of Przywara's analogical vision, is its inflection on the apocalyptic meaning of the *fiat*. This is to say that from the viewpoint of an "analogical-apocalyptic metaphysics," the mystery of created being is read from the ultimate finality of the creature as graced and redeemed. This ultimate finality of the creature is expressive of the *trans*natural suspended condition of created being, as this condition unfolds on the apocalyptic dramatic stage of human history. History is the apocalyptic opening of the creature for or against the triune God of Christian revelation, the Lamb slain from the foundation of the world. An "analogical-apocalyptic metaphysics" finds its completion in and through a pleromatic apocalyptic *theo*logy, which provides the theo-dramatic content and revelatory apocalyptic "intention" of the triune God to the world. It is through this revelatory "intention" that an "analogical-apocalyptic metaphysics" gauges the inadequacy or adequacy of the creaturely metaphysical response to the Trinitarian, dramatic, and apocalyptic backdrop of history.

A Christian Analogical-Apocalyptic Metaphysics

The inflection, singular vision, and style of an "analogical-apocalyptic metaphysics" consist in a regaining of Christian vision by a particular meditation on the meaning of the openness or closure of the creaturely *fiat*. This means that the particular stance advocated by an "analogical-apocalyptic metaphysics" is a creaturely logic of dramatic doxological response and service, where the creature is seen and interpreted as the one sent on a performative mission of service for the greater glory of God. A creaturely logic of doxological service is, correlatively, a logic of God's ever-dawning glory, as the creature is precisely understood as an active and living response to God's glory. History is the apocalyptic story of this response ("My soul doth magnify the Lord," Luke 1:46) or nonresponse (*non serviam*) to the acceptance of creaturely service. The story of an "analogical-apocalyptic metaphysics" is the story of *commercium* or anti-*commercium*, the story of the acceptance or rejection of the love of the triune God of revelation and creation, as this love unfolds on the dramatic apocalyptic stage of history, where the agon between the truth and the lie takes place. An "analogical-apocalyptic metaphysics" is expressive of a dramatic "metaphysics of the saints" that inflects the singular aspect of the *fiat*, that is, of creaturely doxological service.

The task of an "analogical-apocalyptic metaphysics" is to regain the breadth of an integrated Christian vision, identity, and conviction by ceaselessly meditating on, and performing, the act of the creaturely *fiat*. This meditative performing is done amidst the battlefield of misremembering and forgetting of the truth of the *fiat* in the continuing story and history of the Christian triune God's loving *commercium* with creation. Special attention is paid to an integrated vision of Christian metaphysics that is continually fed from the entire range of the Christian story, which includes spirituality, the remembrance of the lives of the saints as iconic examples of the *fiat*, practices, and forms of life, as well as the great theological, speculative, and metaphysical aspects of the Christian tradition. An "analogical-apocalyptic metaphysics" takes place as a creative response to the entire range of the "traditioning process" of the Christian story within an ecclesial community. This metaphysics is not a mere armchair metaphysics, but is a response to the entire array of the "traditioning process" and hence special attention must be given over to promoting action and *praxis* (as was seen in the descending *analogia attributionis* and its inflection on dramatic Christian service, action, and *praxis*). Only in this way can the full truth of the creaturely *fiat* be expressive of the entirety of the Christian doxological self. In other words, an "analogical-apocalyptic metaphysics" calls for witness and active-service, through which the metaphysical apocalyptic vision of the *fiat* is made flesh and performed in a "metaphysics of the saints."

Concretely, this means that not only are metaphysical and speculative forms of simulacra called into question and detected by an "analogical-apocalyptic metaphysics," but also, and importantly, political and economic dimensions of simulacra that seek *to pervert and reconfigure Christian practice and forms of life*. This is to assert that an "analogical-apocalyptic metaphysics" would directly have to confront the question of political theology through a metaphysically inflected rendition of a theo-politics. It is by no means possible to adequately treat this here, as the remaining part of this chapter is programmatic. Nevertheless, I will briefly mention Erik Peterson, as the needed apocalyptic theo-political link connecting my Przywara-inspired "analogical-apocalyptic metaphysics" with O'Regan's Balthasar-inspired pleromatic apocalyptic *theo*logy. I will then conclude with programmatically showing the capability of the *analogia entis* to critique the anti-Christian system of Capitalism, as this critique would be part and parcel of a wider theo-political critique that is one of the central tasks of an "analogical-apocalyptic metaphysics."

Peterson is the thinker that has most deeply thought through the apocalyptic dimensions of a theo-politics and, indeed, how orthodox Christian apocalyptic cannot be fully understood without seeing the essentially political nature of the antichristic spirit of the lie. This is especially seen in his prophetic essay "Witness to the Truth," where, in embryonic form, is presented an entire theology of history written through a visionary optics rooted in the public and political nature of the book of Revelation. Further, in a similar vein to Balthasar's theo-dramatic apocalyptic reading of history, in volumes 4 and 5 of *Theo-Drama*, Peterson likewise sees history to be an ever-growing intensification between the forces of Christ and the forces of Antichrist. For Peterson, like Balthasar, Christian revelation is a "battlefield." Yet, unlike Balthasar, Peterson explicitly inflects his apocalyptic *theo*logy of history in a publicly and politically charged direction, ending in a theo-politics of the martyr, which seems to—controversially and brilliantly—deny legitimacy to any political order that does not recognize the eschatological sovereignty of the royal priesthood of the slain Lamb. And here Peterson supplements the element of the political lacking in *Communio*-minded thinkers, and he does so in a robustly revelational and Christian manner. Peterson further aids in supplementing what O'Regan rightly sees to be a weakness in Balthasar's apocalyptic *theo*logy, namely its underdeveloped political element. Peterson does this by accenting the public nature of Christian revelation as seen in the public and cosmic martyrological witness of the martyrs of the book of Revelation, in an attempt to show the illegitimate nature of the post-Christian political order.

This apocalyptic delegitimization of political power occurs *theo*logically. That is, it occurs in light of the event of Christ's revelation. With the appearance of Christ "the final, critical time has broken in."[5] In this eschatological "Endtime" a decision is required: an either/or for or against Christ. Christ's coming, then, establishes theologically, metaphysically, and historically the one concrete historical order of grace and redemption through which the "battlefield" of history is apocalyptically scripted and codified. Christ is the agonistic center of history, and it is his revelation, and the faithful witnessing of his followers, that prompts the satanic assault on Christ and his body. In a word, only after the appearance of Christ are the Antichrist and the satanic counterstrategy revealed.

Seen from this Christological and apocalyptic perspective any order of neutrality or anonymity expressed in a secular, "abstract," "timeless," pure mode of knowing is made impossible.[6] Christ's revelation epistemologically abolishes anonymity and neutrality in all forms of knowing. Knowledge, following Paul, is either searching the "deep things of God," in the Spirit, *or* the "deep things of Satan" (1 Cor. 2:10). In a word, through the concrete revelation of Christ knowledge becomes "*public*." All knowing, then, is situated and concrete and thus is unable to be "independent of the *hic et nunc* of the political order," and as such "it inevitably stands under the power of the Antichrist or the power of Christ."[7] This is so because on Peterson's interpretation of the satanic triumvirate of the book of Revelation, Satan symbolizes the metaphysical order, while the Antichrist symbolizes the political order and the false prophet the intellectual order. The Antichrist makes war on the Lamb, and his martyrs, specifically on the plane of a perverted political order, upon which the intellectual order of the false prophet is based. The political order of the Antichrist always seeks to make the "political symbol a cultic object." However, "In view of the revealing of Jesus Christ, the sphere of the political must also be revealed."[8] Either one professes worship and glory to the priestly eschatological kingdom of the

---

5. Erik Peterson, "Witness to the Truth," in *Theological Tractates*, trans. and ed. Michael J. Hollerich (Stanford, CA: Stanford University Press, 2011), 153.

6. Peterson, "Witness to Truth," 165–66.

7. Peterson, "Witness to Truth," 166.

8. Peterson, "Witness to Truth," 167.

slain Lamb, as seen in the sealed publicity of the martyrs of the book of Revelation, or one worships the demonic profanity of the post-Christian political order, where glory and worship are given to the counterfeit "cultic object" of political power.

In sum (and all too briefly), Peterson proffers an apocalyptic politically charged *theo*logy of history that seeks to delegitimize the post-Christian modern political order by reading history in light of Christ's revelation. This revelation renders political neutrality impossible, and thus any political order that does not recognize the eschatological sovereignty of the priestly kingdom of the slain Lamb is set under the banner of the cultic political order of the Antichrist. All veils are rent, and neutrality is shattered. The Antichrist makes political war on the saints, all of whom are sealed and washed publicly by the blood of the eschatological Lamb. Peterson's apocalyptic *theo*logy of history is a theo-politics of the martyr that publicly witnesses to the eschatological kingdom in the face of the demonic idolatry of the illegitimate existing political orders. And if an "analogical-apocalyptic metaphysics" is a "metaphysics of the saints," then in its theo-political dimensions this Christian metaphysics is expressly martyrological and thereby thinks the link between the metaphysical, political, and theological, which is inverted and perverted in the antichristic political order, as Peterson prophetically saw.

An "analogical-apocalyptic metaphysics" must then enter the theo-political arena. It thus calls for a fully integrated course of action that would unite intellectual critique with *praxis*-based ideology-critique. This metaphysics of the *fiat* extols a metaphysics of action, insofar as it seeks to integrate Christian spirituality, metaphysical/*theo*logical speculation, and *praxis*-based intervention. If these dimensions are ignored, then the Christian doxological self becomes a mere spectral, pietistic, and dualistic subject, unable to fully enter the battleground against social, political, and economic forms of misremembering of the truth of the Christian story. If the aforesaid dimensions are not dealt with, then an "analogical-apocalyptic metaphysics" would cease being a "metaphysics of the saints" and lose its formal object of the creaturely *fiat*, by giving up on the political, social, and economic nature of the *fiat* where the concrete yes to the triune God always takes place. This is to assert that the yes of the creature, understood from a Christian standpoint, always takes place in an ecclesial community and, of its very essence, has radical political and social implications that are inherently subversive of the *status quo* of the *civitas terrena* and its inborn desire for power and violence. An "analogical-apocalyptic

A Christian Analogical-Apocalyptic Metaphysics

metaphysics" takes place in, and pays special attention to, the political and social implications of the apocalyptic meaning of the *fiat*. This must necessarily be so, because the analogical-apocalyptic story of the *fiat* by no means resides wholly on an intellectual front but also, and importantly, on cultural, socio-political, and economic fronts that usurp and reconfigure Christian culture, practice, and forms of life, thereby making very difficult Christian practice and resistance.

Przywara's thinking on the *analogia entis* possesses the requisite resources to fund the above approach. Granted, these resources are latent and underdeveloped and thus must be expanded, reimagined, and rendered in a new key. Elements of Przywara's thought that must be developed to meet the above demands are as follows: First, Przywara wholly recognizes the ecclesial and communal nature of Christian philosophy, which is bound to the Augustinian *totus Christus*, yet he has never fully turned his attention to elaborating a form of Christian countering to socio-political and economic forms that are inherently anti-Christian.[9] In other words, the social implications of the *totus Christus* must be more fully followed through. Second, Przywara's understanding of the one concrete order of nature and grace prohibits any pure or modern form of autonomy. As Przywara sees, there is "no purely natural religion, no purely natural morality, no purely natural politics."[10] This is to say, there is no secular sphere that is separable from the yes or no to the one concrete order of grace and redemption, funded by an analogical participatory mode of metaphysics. Such a robust view of Christian grace, and the supernatural, gives the full resources for the development of a specifically Christian theo-political social critique. Third, because the *analogia entis* is metaphysically descriptive of orthodox Catholic spirituality—a logic of love—Przywara's thinking gives the resources to develop more fully the social nature of Christian spirituality, which is able to offer resistance to socio-political and economic forms of oppression. Fourth, Przywara's understanding of the *analogia attributionis* shows how a *vision* of God's surpassing mystery and glory spills over, not into inactivity, but into the mystery of the concrete and the historical expressed in a spirituality of Ignatian service, which seeks to find

---

9. The closest he has come to this is in his small but profound work *Idee Europa*, a work that has proved important to Pope Francis's understanding of Europe and the need for Europe to serve in a Christian manner. The Ignatian tone of service here is by no means coincidental.

10. Cited in Hans Urs von Balthasar, *The Theology of Karl Barth: Exposition and Interpretation*, trans. Edward T. Oakes, SJ (San Francisco: Ignatius Press, 1992), 257.

the mystery of God's transcendent love in concrete historical reality. This is especially exemplified in a metaphysics of dramatic service, action, and *praxis* towards which Przywara's third movement of the descending *analogia attributionis* pointed, as was shown in chapter 4. This latter point is pregnant with immense social and political implications that possess the potential to unite a robust Christian *vision* with concrete Christian *praxis*. These aspects of Przywara's work would need to be enhanced and developed in union with pleromatic apocalyptic, which recognizes the need to unite *vision and praxis*, sundered in post-Conciliar discourse.

*The Capitalistic Anti-*Commercium

In light of the above, it must be said that for an "analogical-apocalyptic metaphysics" it is absolutely essential to read the "signs of the times" as to which figurations of the dissemination of the lie, of the spirit of the Antichrist, present the greatest temptation, threat, and misremembering to the fullness of the Christian story and the integral *fiat* of the doxological Christian self. And here, no doubt, pride of place must be given to the prevailing anti-*commercium* of the world-spirit of Capitalism's economy of domination. This prevailing world-spirit then must be seen as one of the greatest current threats, within the "bio-political" world order, to the fullness of the Christian vision of a triune God, the self, desire, community, and this community's practices and forms of life. Through an all-too-brief critique of Capitalism I hope to signal to how Przywara's analogical vision can be placed in a new socio-economic and political key, with the aid of O'Regan's pleromatic apocalyptic *theo*logy, thereby rendering his vision viable in a contemporary light as a means of resistance to Capitalism's overwhelming hegemony, thus showing an aspect of its theo-political ability.

First, if it has been seen that an "analogical-apocalyptic metaphysics" narrates the Christian apocalyptic visionary story from the side of the dramatic action of the creaturely *fiat*, then it is also from this narratival perspective that its critique of Capitalism resides. This is to say, here—programmatically—the burden of an "analogical-apocalyptic metaphysics" lies in showing how Capitalism presents a dramatic no (anti-*commercium*) to the dramatic exchange of love enacted between finite and eternal freedom as acted out on the apocalyptic stage of history. Yet, in order to do this, the full visionary optics of the Christian story must be deployed against the Capitalistic capture of being. In other words, the entire matrix and glory of the living tradition must be invoked (spirituality, practices, and forms of Christian life, along with the sapiential, theoretical, and/or speculative dimensions of the Christian narrative) in a critique of Capitalism's global monopoly. The anti-Christian roots of Capitalism must thus be laid bare in order to show how, in its very essence, Capitalism is antithetical to the Christian story of being and the entire breadth and matrix of the "traditioning process." By laying bare such roots, one is able to better see how the openness of the Christian *fiat*, set within an ecclesial community, is obstructed on every point by the logic of domination of Capitalism's secular parody of the Christian story. (To give just one example, think of the commonly used and fitting perverse expression, *fiat* money, which exhibits a quasi-religious mystical reality, created *ex nihilo*.) An important aspect of this laying bare is tracing the complex genealogical emergence of Capitalism, from degenerative forms of Christianity, and the breakup of philosophy, theology, and spirituality from around the 1300s onwards. Milbank has made great genealogical strides in depicting the story of secularization and Capitalism as being wholly parasitic and subversive of Christian truth. Milbank would thus have to be invoked, as a genealogical aid, for an "analogical-apocalyptic metaphysics" of the *fiat*.

Second, following from the first point, this means that central to an "analogical-apocalyptic metaphysics" critique of Capitalism is a rejection of all extrinsic understandings of the nature/grace relation.[11] That is, the

11. Milbank is spot on in seeing that liberal rights theory presupposes the abstract construct of a pure nature unrelated to grace. Thus when Christian thinkers take up natural rights theory, which is so closely aligned to Capitalism's absolute "right" to private property, they give up their ability to offer a true Christian alternative to the secularism of liberalism/neo-liberalism and/or Capitalism. Such a view of absolute property rights has never been held in the entirety of the Christian tradition. As Pope Francis has recently remarked using two extraordinary quotes from Saint Ambrose and Saint John Chrysostom to combat the erroneous view of absolute property rights that runs counter to the entire Social Teachings of the Catholic Church, "A month before he opened the Second Vatican Council, Pope John XXIII said 'The Church shows itself as it wishes to be, everyone's Church, and particularly the Church of the poor.' In the following years, this preferential treatment of the poor entered the official teachings. Some may think it a novelty, whilst instead it is a concern that stems from the Gospel and is documented even from the first centuries of Christianity. If I repeated some passages from the homilies of the Church Fathers, in the second or third century, about how we must treat the poor, some would accuse me of giving a Marxist homily. 'You are not making a gift of what is yours to the poor man, but you are giving him back what is his. You have been appropriating things that are meant to be for the common use of everyone. The earth belongs to everyone, not to the rich.' These were Saint Ambrose's words, which Pope Paul VI used to state, in *Populorum Progressio*, that private property does not constitute an

very inability (and capitulation) by Christian thinkers to adequately critique the Capitalist empire, liberalism, and/or neo-liberalism, is rooted in a ceding of the one historical, analogical, and participatory interpenetration of nature/grace that is integral to the Christian story. In thus doing, Christians and Christian thinkers wholly embrace the separation of nature/grace enacted in modernity and liberalism. (Think of the example of the large-scale embracing of natural rights theory by Christian philosophers and theologians.)[12] In doing so, Christian thinkers succumb to a wholly

---

absolute and unconditional right for anyone, and that no one is allowed to keep for their exclusive use things superfluous to their needs, when others lack basic necessities. Saint John Chrysostom stated that 'not sharing your goods with the poor means robbing them and taking away their life. The goods we own are not ours but theirs.' . . . As we can see, this concern for the poor is in the Gospel, it is within the tradition of the Church, it is not an invention of communism and it must not be turned into an ideology, as has sometimes happened before in the course of history. The Church, when it invites us to overcome what I have called 'the globalization of indifference' is free from any political interest and any ideology. It is moved only by Jesus' words, and wants to offer its contribution to build a world where we look after one another and care for each other." Cited in Andrea Tornielli and Giacomo Galeazzi, "Francis: To Care for the Poor Is Not Communism, It Is the Gospel," *Vatican Insider*, January 11, 2015, http://vaticaninsider.lastampa.it/en/the-vatican/detail/articolo/38493/.

12. This is sadly seen in the attempt by many Catholic intellectuals, in the United States, to marry the project of liberal democracy and Capitalism with the Catholic faith. Indeed, it can be said that for many American Catholics to be a good Catholic is to be a good Capitalist, to be a good citizen of the *civitas terrena*. A prominent exponent of such a view is Michael Novak, among numerous others. Yet what must precisely be overcome is the belief that citizenship (as a project of modernity) trumps Christian identity. Stanley Hauerwas has penned a fascinating and provocative article on "The End of American Protestantism," which could perhaps just as easily read "The End of American Catholicism." This is to say, there is a very similar attempt by both American Catholics and Protestants to meld the secular modernity of Capitalism and liberal democracy with the Christian faith, the effect of which is to immediately wither the Christian faith, and its identity in Christ, into the narrow conformity of the *status quo*. Hauerwas says, "America is the exemplification of what I call the project of modernity. That project is the attempt to produce a people who believe that they should have no story except the story that they choose when they had no story. That is what Americans mean by 'freedom.' The institutions that constitute the disciplinary forms of that project are liberal democracy and capitalism. Thus the presumption that if you get to choose between a Sony or Panasonic television, you have had a 'free choice.' The same presumption works for choosing a President. Once you have made your choice you have to learn to live with it. So there is a kind of resignation that freedom requires." Stanley Hauerwas, "The End of American Protestantism," ABC Religion and Ethics, July 2, 2013, http://www.abc.net.au/religion/articles/2013/07/02/3794561.htm/. And it is precisely this ruse of freedom, which Capitalism and liberal democracy present, that makes it so easy to conform to these conformist projects of modernity. There is simply no real choice, because choice and freedom are viewed

A Christian Analogical-Apocalyptic Metaphysics

secular and modern view of the social, economic, and political spheres, which prohibits Christianity a public, prophetic, and apocalyptic voice. The radically social and public dimensions of the Christian message are thus ignored and forgotten. An "analogical-apocalyptic metaphysics" must counter this move by reasserting Christian identity, as expressed in the one concrete story of grace and redemption. Przywara, due to his analogical and participatory understanding of nature/grace, saw clearly, as noted above, that there is "no purely natural religion, no purely natural morality, no purely natural politics." All things refer back to Christ, where things are viewed from the perspective of redeemed/unredeemed, a yes/no to God's *commercium* and exchange in the economy of salvation. Przywara's vision of being and grace, in the one concrete historical order of nature and grace, has everything needed to fund (as does de Lubac and Balthasar's view of nature/grace) a specifically Christian metaphysical and theological challenge to Capitalism's perverse and apostate secular divorce of nature/grace.

The implications of the one concrete historical order of grace and redemption is that Christianity is inherently social, public, and political, and therefore cannot, and will not, abandon what it has to offer to socio-economic, cultural, and political realities. These realities must be viewed from the *one final supernatural end of man*: an end that is necessarily intertwined with, and presides over, man's social, political, and economic conditions. An "analogical-apocalyptic metaphysics" is a mode of discourse

---

negatively as the ability to simply choose (freedom of choice), and not the positive freedom of the obligation and ability to choose the good, the good of the community and the good of God. All choices, in Capitalism, are thus readymade choices or foreordained choices set up by the systems of Capitalism and liberal democracy, to which one must conform. And it is this ruse and the appearance of the minimum of choice/freedom (understood negatively as the freedom to choose) that satisfies the phantom belief in freedom. The masses have thus been given the bread and circuses of "free choice," which, in turn, makes one content and thus unwilling to challenge the *status quo* from the perspective of Christ and the prophetic voice of the Christian *ecclesia*. Jorge Bergoglio (now Pope Francis) is thus right to state that "the capitalist system also has its own spiritual perversion: to tame religion. It tames religion so that it does not bother Capitalism too much; it brings it down to worldly terms." Jorge Bergoglio, *On Heaven and Earth*, trans. Alejandro Bermudez and Howard Goodman (New York: Image, 2013), 151. The illusion of freedom and the taming of Christianity, by Capitalism and liberal democracy, have thus made it nearly impossible for present-day Christians to enact the social message of the Church, without which the Christian faith loses all life and vitality. The Christian faith is thus regulated to the private sphere, in an anti-social mode of forgetting and misremembering of the Christian story, which is wholly unprecedented in the history of Christianity.

that calls for the prophetic voice of the social dimensions of Christianity to be heard once again, bulwarked by the analogical understanding of nature/grace, which has been argued for throughout this work. Such an understanding thus sets the narrative within an apocalyptic standpoint of the communal, social, and public nature of the *fiat*. This is to say, the *fiat* of the creature is never purely an isolated individual act, but ever takes place within the matrix of social relations and political conditions. An "analogical-apocalyptic metaphysics" seeks to nonidentically repeat Przywara's vision by developing the social, economic, and political dimensions of Przywara's thought (and appeal would also have to be made to the resources of de Lubac and Balthasar and, as seen above, especially to Peterson; moreover, an uneasy alliance could also be found in Agamben's understanding of the "state of exception" and the "bio-political order," thus affirming the validity of his radical critique while shunning his profane messianic solution).

The *third* aspect of an analogical-apocalyptic metaphysics advance against Capitalism is, namely, a social and active spirituality. It has been signaled to that the *analogia entis*, as conceived by Przywara, is rooted in an orthodox spirituality of an experience of God's unsurpassable glory: an experience of God that is ever in and beyond man's experience, in keeping with analogical paradox. Likewise, it has been stated that Przywara renders the *laus Dei* in a more active, historical, and Ignatian key, which places the emphasis on rendering glory to God through active-service. Przywara's metaphysics is not an abstract or armchair metaphysics, but one that points towards a dramatic metaphysics of action/*praxis* or a "metaphysics of the saints," grounded in spirituality. Metaphysics, for Przywara, is partly descriptive of spirituality. Przywara's analogical metaphysics possesses the means to develop a more concrete, social, and active spirituality, where God's glory would be sought in advocating ways to fight for the marginalized, ignored, and forgotten victims of Capitalistic exclusion. No theological movement has emphasized more the need for spirituality to advance against Capitalism than liberation theology.[13] Przywara's thinking is by no means inhospitable to such concerns, but these aspects need to be developed. His analogical vision holds the resources to robustly unite orthodoxy with orthopraxis within an analogical balance of vision and *praxis* that recognizes the need to incarnate vision in action and spiritu-

---

13. See Gustavo Gutiérrez, *A Theology of Liberation: History, Politics and Salvation*, trans. Sister Caridad and John Eagleson (London: SCM Press, 1971), especially "A Spirituality of Liberation," 192–97, and "Poverty: Spiritual Childhood," 262–68.

A Christian Analogical-Apocalyptic Metaphysics

ality. In so doing, a Przywarian model could render a way forward towards a unity between the two, which would not supplant Christian vision solely with Christian activism, as is the tendency of certain modes of liberation theology. At the same time, Przywara's lack of development of such issues would have to be strengthened by an engagement with philosophies and theologies of *praxis*. Such a dialogue could both enhance Przywara's thought and, at the same time, correct one-sided tendencies of solely *praxis*-based philosophies and theologies. A nonidentical Przywarian model of an "analogical-apocalyptic metaphysics" would be fed by the analogical unity-in-difference of vision and *praxis*.[14] In sum, metaphysical and theological vision are necessary for spirituality, while at the same time, if metaphysical and theological reflection are not expressed and fed from action and spirituality, then they are sterile. Each must point towards and reinforce the other in an analogical movement of incarnation.

Fourth, following from the development of an active spirituality of service, which would seek to put forward strategies that promote God's glory by actively and practically fighting for the forgotten victims of Capitalistic dispossession: an "analogical-apocalyptic metaphysics" would likewise express this reality on a metaphysical front by exposing the roots of Capitalism's understanding of the being of the self. An "analogical-apocalyptic metaphysics" would have to show and uncover the metaphysical presuppositions of the Capitalistic subject (*homo economicus*) as exhibited in the violent and individualistic metaphysical battlefield of the *bellum omnium contra omnes*. It is here, on this battleground, that the Capitalistic subject is constructed as a subject formed and subjected to the logic of consumption. In this logic of consumption, under the Capitalistic axiom of maximal gain and profit, the self is mediated to itself through the fetishizing of the commodity as presented in the images of advertisement and media. The self is seen and interpreted as an aggregate of endless and wasted desires that need to unceasingly consume. It is through this logic of endless consumption that the self is constructed by the abstract logic of the system of Capitalism. This system manipulates the self by telling the self both what and how to desire, under the illusion of free choice. This, in turn, sets off a chain and proliferation of endless desire and consumption for finite

---

14. Here a dialogue with the Frankfurt School would clearly have to be opened, with their emphasis on the need to rethink theory based on the failure of revolutionary *praxis*. In other words, when *praxis* fails, then the theory that underlined this failure must be rethought.

fetishized commodities, which exercises a this-worldly religious and spiritual effect, which supplants the supernatural end of man and the universal destination of all goods (*Gaudium et spes*).[15]

Contra the constructed and monopolized self of Capitalism, and the wholesale capturing of being and desire by the system of Capitalism, is set forth the Christian view of the *homo abyssus*, that is, a self that is analogical/doxological and thus a self sent forth on a performance of an ecclesial mission of free service. Here the Christian self views the battlefield for the self and being, not as the *bellum omnium contra omnes*, but rather as the battleground for or against the misremembering of Christ: a Christ through whom the analogical Christian self receives its mission of ecclesial service. Przywara's decentered and Christian vision of the self could be rendered as a viable critique of the violent individualism of the constructed Capitalistic subject. Such a Christian view of the self is communal and ecclesial, a vision of the self that obtains its relative-identity through service to God and others. This is wholly opposed to the individualistic consumer logic of self-service, which denies any genuine self-giving and service requisite for any true community. On the Christian analogical/doxological model, freedom and desire are understood positively as a communal gift. Freedom is freedom to choose the good, the good of God, the good of the community, the good of being, and the good of creation ("freedom for"). All of this forms what Desmond beautifully calls an "agapeic community." Here freedom is only obtained through service and responsibility and is hence understood communally and relationally, while on the other hand, the Capitalistic model of freedom (rooted ultimately in a voluntaristic model of freedom) is understood negatively as the freedom to choose and a "freedom from." Desire and the self, on an analogical and doxological model, are always understood relationally and communally. Freedom and desire are an unmerited and shared gift, given by the ever-greater God, who frees creation into its relational otherness. Such a gift of the freeing of freedom ceases to be a gift when it is seen as an individualistic self-appropriated "right," rather than a communal and participatory sharing *in* freedom. The gifts of desire and freedom, analogically conceived, are only themselves

---

15. The great imaginative Marxist Walter Benjamin is thus perfectly correct to see Capitalism as an extreme religious cult, insofar as it seeks to satisfy all the needs that traditional religions tried to meet, though without any real dogma or theology, except in an inverted form. See Walter Benjamin, "Capitalism as Religion," in *Selected Writings*, vol. 1: *1913–1926*, trans. Rodney Livingstone (Cambridge, MA: Belknap Press of Harvard University, 2000), 288–91.

if they continually give themselves away, thereby avoiding all monopolization of freedom and desire which covetously hoards in self-pursuit, as in the Capitalistic logic of the maximization of profit. Here, no doubt, a meditation on the meaning of the Eucharist and the communal life of the Trinity, as excessive sharing, would have to be invoked in order to render a robust Christian social critique of Capitalism's anti-Christian premises. The analogical and doxological vision of the self, as an ecclesial self of the performance of dramatic mission, presented by Przywara, has radically social and political implications.

These implications would be developed in an "analogical-apocalyptic metaphysics," as a way of exposing the lie, which is the construction of the Capitalistic subject by the abstract logic of the Capitalist system. For underneath the two interpretations of reality are wholly antithetical visions of being. One is God-centered, peaceful, and communal; the other is man-centered in a violent, anti-communal, and anti-human way. In the latter view, man is blinded into rendering service and worship to the abstract power of Capital, by selfishly pursuing his phantom desires and phantom freedoms mediated to the constructed self through advertisement and media in an inglorious consumerist "society of the spectacle."[16]

Fifth, all of the aforesaid finds its consummation in the fact that an analogical-apocalyptic metaphysics is finally, and ultimately, a "metaphysics of the saints." It is a metaphysics of the *fiat*, in its ecclesial and communal nature, which attends to concrete practices, witnessing, and active-service. Such a witnessing was, in both an analogical metaphysics and a pleromatic apocalyptic *theo*logy, rendered most persuasive in the iconic figure of the saint: understood as a living manifestation of the truth of Christian vision and practice. The saint is the one who lives out most fully and iconically the *commercium* of God's love, which resides at the heart of the *analogia entis*, understood as an *analogia caritatis*. Thus if the heart of the vision of analogy is a metaphysical and theological description of the exchange between the love of the creature and the love of the Christian triune God, then it is the saint that is the living witness to the reality and vitality of such a vision. The saint takes center stage in the one concrete historical and apocalyptic story of grace and redemption. The saint, as an acting

---

16. Here I am, of course, borrowing from the famous title of the prophetic work *The Society of the Spectacle* by the French Marxist and critical theorist Guy Debord. See Guy Debord, *The Society of the Spectacle*, trans. Donald Nicholson-Smith (New York: Zone Books, 1994).

ecclesial person, is the embodiment of the *economy* of salvation and thus a different, alternative, and countereconomy of resistance and subversion to the Capitalistic economy: a "chaste anarchy," to use Caitlin Smith-Gilson's beautifully apt and powerful expression. Therefore, the special aspect and specific mode of an ideology-critique of Capitalism, instantiated by an "analogical-apocalyptic metaphysics," would be a meditation on the meaning of sanctity as an ecclesial, social, and political form of Christian resistance towards Capitalism.

Positively this means that any resistance towards Capitalism must reside in a reenacting and reimagining of Christian sanctity. Negatively, on the side of critique, Capitalism must be critiqued by an "analogical-apocalyptic metaphysics" by exposing the very structure and conditions of Capitalism's rending of the "representability of the saint" highly suspect. Yet this prohibiting of the "representability of the saint" is not a mere matter of the presentation of sanctity, but also and centrally, the very cultural, political, and material conditions of Capitalism that make it nearly impossible to lead a holy and Christian life in a consumeristic world. This is the case because, in a Capitalistic and consumeristic logic, grace is obstructed from being mediated through Capitalism's anti-Christian culture and dominating conditions seen in its economizing of the political, which inverts Christian community. This is manifested in today's postmodern world, as seen above, in a culture where the self is wholly mediated and constructed, not through grace, mission, community, and service, but through the images of media and advertisement in a "society of the spectacle." The social, economic, political, and material conditions that misremember and prevent Christian forms of practice and life must thus be wholly laid bare and countered by an analogical-apocalyptic "metaphysics of the saints."

Hence, in an "analogical-apocalyptic metaphysics," the analogical vision of the "metaphysics of the saints" (as suggested in Przywara's work and more fully expounded in Balthasar) incarnates the logic of analogical *commercium*. This incarnational logic is, in turn, deployed in its full breadth to counter Capitalism by creatively retrieving sanctity in its uniting of Christian identity in the practicing and living out of Christian vision. Moreover, in order for this deployment to be made concrete, lives of figures who could aid in better showing forth the strategy of an "analogical-apocalyptic metaphysics" would have to be invoked. Here I am thinking of, for example, Charles Péguy, Madeleine Delbrêl, Dorothy Day, Peter Maurin (and, in a different register, Simone Weil), all of whom point

A Christian Analogical-Apocalyptic Metaphysics

the way to a more prophetic, social, and apocalyptic mode of Christianity.[17] Such figures would have to be invoked in order to supplement an analogical "metaphysics of the saints" as a nonidentical repetition of Przywara, thereby rendering it in a more concrete social and political key, as a means of resistance to Capitalism. The above figures point the way to a *materializing* of Christian vision that shows forth the possibility of an authentic Christian materialism.[18]

Lastly, it needs to be stated how an "analogical-apocalyptic metaphysics" is not simply a reimagined enhancement of Przywara's analogical vision, but also a development of O'Regan's pleromatic apocalyptic interpretation of a postmodern Catholic *theo*logy. An "analogical-apocalyptic metaphysics" is an enhancement and development of O'Regan's pleromatic apocalyptic *theo*logy because it seeks to address the lack of an integral Catholic vision and response, characteristic of post-Conciliar Catholic discourse, as this absence was seen in the sundering of Catholic vision and Catholic *praxis*, alluded to in chapter 5. This lack of full integration was clearly diagnosed by O'Regan and Milbank, as they rightly acknowledged that in the work of thinkers like de Lubac and Balthasar (and I have added Przywara to this list), the socio-political side of their theology/philosophy was/is very underdeveloped, whereas thinkers like Metz and liberation theologians lacked the ability to adequately critique modernity and secularity with a robust understanding of grace and a Christian metaphysical/theological vision, while nevertheless developing much-needed political theologies in resistance to Capitalistic domination, therefore calling attention to the prophetic, apocalyptic, and social dimensions of Christianity. O'Regan acknowledges the need to address this divide but, in his development of pleromatic apocalyptic *theo*logy, he has yet to fully turn his attention to the healing of the rift between vision and *praxis*. An "analogical-apocalyptic metaphysics" seeks to address and overcome these inadequacies on both sides of this divide. It is my suggestion, and contention,

---

17. For an excellent account of the life and project of Day (and to a lesser extent Maurin), see Mark and Louise Zwick's introduction to *On Pilgrimage*, by Dorothy Day (Grand Rapids: Eerdmans, 1999), 1–64. And for a wonderful introduction to the life, person, and thought of Weil, see Gustave Thibon's introduction to *Gravity and Grace*, by Simone Weil (London: Routledge, 2002), vii–xxxvii.

18. Przywara, in his superb 1956 essay on Stein and Weil, says of Weil that she presents a "Christian materialism" that is a "genuine ... alternative to the contemporary rise of atheistic, dialectical materialism." Erich Przywara, "Edith Stein and Simone Weil: Two Fundamental Philosophical Themes," in *Analogia Entis*, 601.

that it is only through addressing these inadequacies and deficiencies, on both sides of the divide, that the fullness of Catholic vision can be *seen* and *enacted* in a fully Christian and integral postmodern and post-Conciliar response to our current dramatic place in history.

Further, the enhancement of O'Regan's pleromatic apocalyptic *theo*logy, enacted by an "analogical-apocalyptic metaphysics," would have to seek to bring into conversation the prophetic socio-political critic of capitalism, characteristic of minimalist eidetic forms of apocalyptic and their emphasis on issues of justice (such as Metz and liberation theology), with maximalist pleromatic forms of apocalyptic *theo*logy, such as is exhibited in Przywara and Balthasar, with their emphasis on Christian identity, the great Christian metaphysics/theological tradition, grace, and vision (here Peterson would again be wholly essential). The mode of conversation would thus be one in which the expansive range of pleromatic apocalyptic *theo*logy, expressed in a high level of Christian eidetic content and vision, would be shown as more adequate in developing a Christian socio-economic and theo-political critique. However, this critique has been woefully ignored by Catholic theologians of the pleromatic stamp. Inspiration, and a certain guidance, would have to be taken from minimalist apocalyptic attempts at political theology, their prophetic call for justice, as well as their strong challenge and critique of the *status quo*, Capitalism, and bourgeois Christianity. An "analogical-apocalyptic metaphysics"—as a nonidentical reimagining of Przywara's *analogia entis*—analogically related and ordered to pleromatic apocalyptic *theo*logy would turn special attention to this needful task in an attempt to offer a full vision of Catholic integration.[19] In this way both Przywara's analogical vision and O'Regan's pleromatic apocalyptic *theo*logy would be enhanced by bringing out more fully the possibility of an ideology-critique of Capitalism and the theo-political range, present within both discourses, in a call to incarnate vision *into praxis*. For, I would contend, without an integration of Christian vision and Christian *praxis*, one cannot fully nominate a discourse apocalyptic, in the sense of a critical discourse that seeks to reignite full Christian vision and memory in a battle against misremembering in all of its guises, in a postmodern, post-Conciliar Cath-

---

19. On the practical side, and in order for the above critique of Capitalism—from a pleromatic and an analogical-apocalyptic perspective—to gain traction, a deep dialogue would have to take place with the Marxist tradition and the Frankfurt School. This is a dangerous dialogue, but a needful one, as it has not been taken seriously by thinkers who possess a robust understanding of grace and Christian vision (though Milbank has, by far, gone the furthest in this direction, nor must Emmanuel Mounier be forgotten here).

A Christian Analogical-Apocalyptic Metaphysics

olic modality. This is so because the guises of misremembering span intensely high levels of theoretical/metaphysical/theological discourse, to narrative structures and genealogical hauntings, right down to the very flesh of practices, forms of life, cultural and socio-economic and political conditions. An "analogical-apocalyptic metaphysics" seeks to address this lack of full integration and the advance of the misremembering against the Christian story on all fronts.

* * *

The analogical narrative presented here has focused itself on the question of the abiding potential of a Christian analogical vision of being, concentrated in the enduring resources of Przywara's *analogia entis* constructively reimagined and conceived. This vision presented a way to face and counter the question of philosophical modernity, especially in regard to how philosophical modernity has been encountered and countered from within Catholic thought (the subplot of this analogical narrative). This analogical narrative is thus a kind of microcosm of the story of the struggles of Catholic thought with the Goliath of philosophical modernity, in an attempt to move beyond modernity, in a Christian way, by unlocking the postmodern pleromatic Christian truth of the *analogia entis*. Moreover, it was seen that both Rahner and Balthasar prophetically saw that Przywara's thinking has something to say and offer to the future of Catholic thought in its post–Vatican II situation. This book has been a ceaseless meditation on this *future*, on the enduring potential of Przywara's vision, and on the power of his thought and its gift to Christian thought. Yet this potential means nothing, if it is not rethought in light of challenges and circumstances that Przywara simply could not see and address. This book has sought to address and think these situations. And that is why nonidentical forms of Przywarian repetition were invoked, and why I further sought to enhance Przywara's vision and style in conversation with a visionary apocalyptic style of Catholic *theo*logy, in a reimagined synthesis of postmodern and post-Conciliar Catholic vision.

This led me to put forward what I have termed an "analogical-apocalyptic metaphysics" understood as a constructive and imaginative apocalyptic retelling of Przywara's *analogia entis*. Such a Christian metaphysics, I have suggested, is inextricably postmodern in its non-self-legitimizing nature, due to its analogical relation to revelation and pleromatic apocalyptic *theo*logy. Moreover, as postmodernly Catholic, an "analogical-apocalyptic metaphysics" is also an attempt to think *after* the post–Vatican II divide and the sundering of Catholic vision and Catholic *praxis* that took place in this divide. The guiding vision of this narrative is one of a Christian analogical style of metaphysics that is pleromatic and dramatically performative: an integration of *vision* and *praxis*. And it is my suggestion that, given the intellectual and political conditions of today's world—conditions that cannot be ignored by Catholic or Christian thinking—this is the most fruitful and authentic way to reactivate the Christian pleromatic tradition of metaphysical glory. Christian metaphysical glory, today, must be reimagined as a "metaphysics of the saints," which is to also imply that this glory is becoming increasingly dramatic, apocalyptic, and martyrological.

Christian metaphysical vision must look to this martyrological witnessing—must become this witnessing—if glory is to return on this vesperal side of history. Here Christian metaphysical vision is an enfleshing and performance of Christian vision. It is a vision and a rhetoric that calls for a doxological Christian self of performance and service, a self that loses its life in order to save it, set within the social matrix of an ecclesial community. It is a vision that is always incarnated in a materializing of vision, in practices, forms of life, witness, and doxological service. Only in this sense, when word and vision are made flesh, does the creaturely *fiat* take on apocalyptic dimensions. And only, in this sense, is an "analogical-apocalyptic metaphysics" truly, and fully, a glorious "metaphysics of the saints." For it is only when word and vision are made flesh, in the *fiat* of the creature, that the creature *becomes* the bearer of God's glory, as it is only through this *bearing* and *witnessing* that time begins to become full. The creature, as a bearer and witness of God's glory, thus labors in ecclesial service, amidst the apocalyptic struggle against the spirit of the lie and the spirit of the Antichrist, for the dramatic truth of the "fullness of time" (Eph. 1:9–10): when and where Christ "fills all in all" (Eph. 1:22–23).

Bibliography

Works by Erich Przywara

Works in English

Analogia Entis: Metaphysics: Original Structure and Universal Rhythm. Translated by John R. Betz and David Bentley Hart. Grand Rapids: Eerdmans, 2014.
"Christian Root-Terms: Kerygma, Mysterium, Kairos, Oikonomia." In *Religion and Culture: Essays in Honor of Paul Tillich*, edited by Walter Leibrecht, translated by Calvin Schrag, 113–19. New York: Harper & Bros., 1959.
The Divine Majesty. Translated by Thomas Corbishley, SJ. Cork, Ireland: Mercier Press, 1951.
Polarity: A German Catholic's Interpretation of Religion. Translated by A. C. Bouquet, DD. London: Oxford University Press, 1935.
"St. Augustine and the Modern World." In *St. Augustine: His Age, Life and Thought*, edited by M. C. D'Arcy, SJ, translated by E. I. Wakin, 251–86. New York: Meridian Books, 1957.

German Works

Analogia Entis I. Metaphysik. Ur-Struktur und All-Rhythmus. Einsiedeln: Johannes Verlag, 1962.
Crucis Mysterium: Das Christliche Heute. Paderborn: F. Schöningh, 1939.

Hölderlin: Eine Studie. Nuremberg: Glock und Lutz, 1949.
Mensch: Typologische Anthropologie. Nuremberg: Glock und Lutz, 1959.

Edited Works

An Augustine Synthesis. Arranged by Erich Przywara, SJ. New York: Sheed & Ward, 1936.
A Newman Synthesis. Arranged by Erich Przywara, SJ. New York: Longmans, Green, 1931.

Other Works

Adam, Karl. *The Christ of Faith: The Christology of the Church.* Translated by Joyce Crick. London: Burns & Oates, 1957.
Agamben, Giorgio. *Homo Sacer: Sovereign Power and Bare Life.* Translated by Daniel Heller-Roazen. Stanford, CA: Stanford University Press, 1998.
———. *The Kingdom and the Glory: For a Theological Genealogy of the Economy and Government.* Translated by Lorenzo Chiesa. Stanford, CA: Stanford University Press, 2011.
———. *State of Exception.* Translated by Kevin Attell. Chicago: University of Chicago Press, 2005.
Alighieri, Dante. *The Divine Comedy.* Edited by David H. Higgins. Translated by C. H. Sisson. Oxford: Oxford University Press, 2008.
Anselm. *St. Anselm: Basic Writings.* Translated by S. N. Deane. La Salle, IL: Open Court, 2005.
Aquinas, Thomas, and Joseph Bobik. *Aquinas on Being and Essence: A Translation and Interpretation.* Translated by Joseph Bobik. Notre Dame: University of Notre Dame Press, 1965.
———. *Summa Theologica.* Translated by Fathers of the English Dominican Province. Westminster, MD: Christian Classics, 1981.
Aristotle. *The Basic Works of Aristotle.* Edited by Richard McKeon. New York: Random House, 2001.
Augustine. *The City of God.* Translated by Marcus Dodds, DD. New York: Random House, 2000.
———. *The Confessions.* Edited by Philip Burton. Translated by Philip Burton. New York: Everyman's Library, 2001.

Bibliography

Badiou, Alain. *Deleuze: The Clamor of Being*. Translated by Louise Burchell. Minneapolis: University of Minnesota Press, 2000.

———. *Manifesto for Philosophy*. Edited by Norman Madarasz. Translated by Norman Madarasz. Albany: State University of New York Press, 1999.

———. *Saint Paul: The Foundations of Universalism*. Translated by Ray Brassier. Stanford, CA: Stanford University Press, 2003.

———, and Slavoj Žižek. *Philosophy in the Present: Alain Badiou and Slavoj Žižek*. Edited by Peter Engelmann. Translated by Peter Thomas and Alberto Toscano. Malden, MA: Polity Press, 2009.

Balthasar, Hans Urs von. *Bernanos: An Ecclesial Existence*. Translated by Erasmo Leiva-Merikakis. San Francisco: Ignatius Press, 1996.

———. *The Glory of the Lord: A Theological Aesthetics*. Volume 1: *Seeing the Form*. Translated by Erasmo Leiva-Merikakis. San Francisco: Ignatius Press, 1982.

———. *The Glory of the Lord: A Theological Aesthetics*. Volume 4: *The Realm of Metaphysics in Antiquity*. Translated by Erasmo Leiva-Merikakis. San Francisco: Ignatius Press, 1989.

———. *The Glory of the Lord: A Theological Aesthetics*. Volume 5: *The Realm of Metaphysics in the Modern Age*. Translated by Erasmo Leiva-Merikakis. San Francisco: Ignatius Press, 1991.

———. *Love Alone*. Translated by Alexander Dru. New York: Herder & Herder, 1969.

———. *Man in History: A Theological Study*. London: Sheed & Ward, 1982.

———. "On the Tasks of Catholic Philosophy in Our Time." *Communio* 20 (1993): 147–87.

———. *Theo-Drama: Theological Dramatic Theory*. Volume 1: *Prolegomena*. Translated by Graham Harrison. San Francisco: Ignatius Press, 1988.

———. *Theo-Drama: Theological Dramatic Theory*. Volume 4: *The Action*. Translated by Graham Harrison. San Francisco: Ignatius Press, 1994.

———. *Theo-Drama: Theological Dramatic Theory*. Volume 5: *The Last Act*. Translated by Graham Harrison. San Francisco: Ignatius Press, 1998.

———. *Theo-Logic*. Volume 1: *Truth of the World*. Translated by Adrian J. Walker. San Francisco: Ignatius Press, 2000.

———. *Theo-Logic*. Volume 2: *Truth of God*. Translated by Adrian J. Walker. San Francisco: Ignatius Press, 2004.

———. *The Theology of Karl Barth: Exposition and Interpretation*. Translated by Edward T. Oakes, SJ. San Francisco: Ignatius Press, 1992.

———. *Truth Is Symphonic: Aspects of Christian Pluralism*. Translated by Graham Harrison. San Francisco: Ignatius Press, 1987.

Barth, Karl. *Church Dogmatics I/1: The Doctrine of the Word of God.* Translated by G. W. Bromiley. London: T&T Clark, 2010.

———. *Church Dogmatics I/2: The Doctrine of the Word of God.* Translated by G. W. Bromiley. London: T&T Clark, 2010.

Basehart, Mary Catharine. *Person in the World: Introduction to the Philosophy of Edith Stein.* Boston: Kluwer, 1997.

Beauvais, Chantal. "Edith Stein and Modern Philosophy." In *Husserl and Stein*, edited by Richard Feist and William Sweet, 1–13. Washington, DC: Council for Research in Values and Philosophy, 2003. http://www.crvp.org/book/Series01/I-31/chap-10.htm/.

Bell, Daniel M., Jr. *The Economy of Desire: Christianity and Capitalism in a Postmodern World.* Grand Rapids: Baker Academic, 2012.

———. *Liberation Theology after the End of History: The Refusal to Cease Suffering.* London: Routledge, 2001.

Benjamin, Walter. "Capitalism as Religion." In *Selected Writings.* Volume 1: *1913–1926*, translated by Rodney Livingstone, 288–91. Cambridge, MA: Belknap Press of Harvard University, 2000.

Bergoglio, Jorge Mario, and Abraham Skorka. *On Heaven and Earth.* Translated by Alejandro Bermudez and Howard Goodman. New York: Image, 2013.

Bernanos, Georges. *The Diary of a Country Priest.* Translated by Pamela Morris. Glasgow: William Collins, 1981.

———. *The Heroic Face of Innocence: Three Stories by Georges Bernanos.* Edited by David L. Schindler. Translated by R. Batchelor, Pamela Morris, and David L. Schindler Jr. Grand Rapids: Eerdmans, 1999.

———. *Under Satan's Sun.* Translated by J. C. Whitehouse. Lincoln: University of Nebraska Press, 1994.

Betz, John R., "Beyond the Sublime: The Aesthetics of the Analogy of Being (Part One)." *Modern Theology* 21, no. 3 (2005): 367–411.

———. "Beyond the Sublime: The Aesthetics of the Analogy of Being (Part Two)." *Modern Theology* 22, no. 1 (2006): 1–50.

Blondel, Maurice. *Action (1893): Essay on a Critique of Life and a Science of Practice.* Translated by Olivia Blanchette. Notre Dame: University of Notre Dame Press, 2007.

Bloy, Léon. *The Woman Who Was Poor.* Translated by I. J. Collins. London: Purnell and Sons, Ltd., 1939.

Boersma, Hans. *Nouvelle Théologie and Sacramental Ontology: A Return to Mystery.* Oxford: Oxford University Press, 2009.

Bibliography

Boff, Leonardo, and Clodovis Boff. *Introducing Liberation Theology.* Translated by Paul Burns. Maryknoll, NY: Orbis Books, 1987.

Bonaventure. *The Mind's Road to God.* Translated by George Boas. Englewood Cliffs, NJ: Prentice Hall, 1953.

Bonhoeffer, Dietrich. *Act and Being: Transcendental Philosophy and Ontology in Systematic Theology.* Edited by Wayne Whitson Floyd Jr. Translated by H. Martin Rumscheidt. Minneapolis: Fortress Press, 2009.

———. *No Rusty Swords: Letters, Lectures and Notes (1928–1936).* Edited by Edwin H. Robertson. Translated by Edwin H. Robertson and John Bowden. St. James Place, London: William Collins, 1965.

Calcagno, Antonio. *The Philosophy of Edith Stein.* Pittsburgh: Duquesne University Press, 2007.

Caputo, John D. *Demythologizing Heidegger.* Bloomington: Indiana University Press, 1993.

———. *Heidegger and Aquinas: An Essay on Overcoming Metaphysics.* New York: Fordham University Press, 1982.

———. *The Mystical Element in Heidegger's Thought.* New York: Fordham University Press, 1986.

———. *On Religion.* London: Routledge, 2001.

———. *The Prayers and Tears of Jacques Derrida: Religion without Religion.* Bloomington: Indiana University Press, 1997.

Caputo, John D., and Gianni Vattimo. *After the Death of God.* Edited by Jeffrey W. Robbins. New York: Columbia University Press, 2007.

Cavanaugh, William T. *Being Consumed: Economics and Christian Desire.* Grand Rapids: Eerdmans, 2008.

Certeau, Michel de. *The Mystic Fable: The Sixteenth and Seventeenth Centuries.* Translated by Michael B. Smith. Chicago: University of Chicago Press, 1992.

Chrétien, Jean-Louis. *The Ark of Speech.* Translated by Andrew Brown. New York: Routledge, 2004.

———. *The Call and the Response.* Translated by Anne A. Davenport. New York: Fordham University Press, 2004.

———. *Hand to Hand: Listening to the Work of Art.* Translated by Stephen E. Lewis. New York: Fordham University Press, 2003.

Cohn, Norman. *The Pursuit of the Millennium: Revolutionary Millenarians and Mystical Anarchists of the Middle Ages.* Oxford: Oxford University Press, 1970.

Collins, James. "Edith Stein and the Advance of Phenomenology." *Thought* 17 (1942): 685–708.

———. "Przywara's *Analogia Entis*." *Thought* 17 (1942): 119–35.
Daigler, Matthew A. "Heidegger and von Balthasar: A Lovers' Quarrel over Beauty and Divinity." *American Catholic Philosophical Quarterly* 69, no. 2 (1995): 375–94.
Davis, Creston, John Milbank, and Slavoj Žižek, eds. *Theology and the Political: The New Debate*. Durham, NC: Duke University Press, 2005.
Day, Dorothy. *On Pilgrimage*. Grand Rapids: Eerdmans, 1999.
Debord, Guy. *The Society of the Spectacle*. Translated by Donald Nicholson-Smith. New York: Zone Books, 1994.
Deleuze, Gilles. *Difference and Repetition*. Translated by Paul Patton. London: Bloomsbury, 1994.
Denzinger, Henry. *The Sources of Catholic Dogma*. Translated by Roy J. Deferrari. Fitzwilliam, NH: Loreto Publications, 1954.
Derrida, Jacques. *Writing and Difference*. Translated by Alan Bass. Chicago: University of Chicago Press, 1978.
Descartes, René. *A Discourse on Method, Meditations and Principles*. Translated by John Veitch. London: Everyman's Library, 1994.
Desmond, William. *Being and the Between*. Albany: State University of New York Press, 1995.
———. *Ethics and the Between*. Albany: State University of New York Press, 2001.
———. *God and the Between*. Oxford: Blackwell, 2008.
Eliot, T. S. *The Complete Poems and Plays*. New York: Harcourt, Brace & World, Inc., 1958.
Fenves, Peter, ed. *Raising the Tone of Philosophy: Late Essays by Immanuel Kant, Transformative Critique by Jacques Derrida*. Translated by Peter Fenves and John Leavey Jr. Baltimore: Johns Hopkins University Press, 1999.
Gaboriau, Florent. *The Conversion of Edith Stein*. Translated by Ralph McInerny. South Bend, IN: St. Augustine's Press, 2002.
Gadamer, Hans-Georg. *Philosophical Hermeneutics*. Translated by David E. Linge. Berkeley: University of California Press, 1976.
———. *Truth and Method*. Translated by Donald G. Marshall and Joel Weinsheimer. New York: Continuum, 1975.
Garrigou-Lagrange, Réginald, OP. "Where Is the New Theology Leading Us?" *Angelicum* 23 (1946): 126–45.
Gilson, Étienne. *God and Philosophy*. New Haven: Yale University Press, 1941.

———. *Reason and Revelation in the Middle Ages.* New York: Charles Scribner's Sons, 1966.

Guardini, Romano. *The End of the Modern World.* Translated by Elinor C. Briefs. Wilmington, DE: ISI Books, 1998.

———. *The Faith and Modern Man.* Translated by Charlotte E. Forsyth. London: Burns, Oates & Washbourne, 1952.

Gutiérrez, Gustavo. *A Theology of Liberation: History, Politics and Salvation.* London: SCM Press, 2001.

Hanby, Michael. *Augustine and Modernity.* London: Routledge, 2003.

Hart, David Bentley. *The Beauty of the Infinite: The Aesthetics of Christian Truth.* Grand Rapids: Eerdmans, 2003.

Hauerwas, Stanley. *ABC Religion and Ethics.* July 2, 2013. http://www.abc.net.au/religion/articles/2013/07/02/3794561.htm/.

Hegel, G. W. F. *Phenomenology of Spirit.* Translated by A. V. Miller. Oxford: Clarendon Press, 1977.

———. *Philosophy of History.* Translated by M. A. J. Sibree. New York: Barnes & Noble, 2004.

Heidegger, Martin. *The Basic Problems of Phenomenology.* Translated by Albert Hofstadter. Bloomington: Indiana University Press, 1982.

———. *Basic Writings: From Being and Time (1927) to The Task of Thinking (1964).* Edited by David Farrell Krell. New York: HarperCollins, 1993.

———. *Being and Time.* Translated by John Macquarrie and Edward Robinson. Malden, MA: Blackwell, 2011.

———. *Discourse on Thinking.* Translated by John M. Anderson and E. Hans Freund. New York: Harper & Row, 1966.

———. *Early Greek Thinking.* Translated by David Farrell Krell and Frank A. Capuzzi. New York: Harper & Row, 1975.

———. *Elucidations of Hölderlin's Poetry.* Translated by Keith Hoeller. Amherst, NY: Prometheus Books, 2000.

———. *Identity and Difference.* Translated by Joan Stambaugh. New York: Harper & Row, 1969.

———. *Introduction to Metaphysics.* Translated by Gregory Fried and Richard Polt. New Haven: Yale University Press, 2000.

———. *Nietzsche.* Volume 1: *The Will to Power as Art*, and volume 2: *The Eternal Recurrence of the Same.* Translated by David Farrell Krell. San Francisco: HarperSanFrancisco, 1991.

———. *Nietzsche.* Volume 3: *The Will to Power as Knowledge and as Metaphysics*, and volume 4: *Nihilism.* Translated by David Farrell Krell. San Francisco: HarperSanFrancisco, 1991.

———. *On the Way to Language.* Translated by Peter D. Hertz. New York: Harper & Row, 1971.

———. *On Time and Being.* Translated by Joan Stambaugh. Chicago: University of Chicago Press, 1972.

———. *Parmenides.* Translated by André Schuwer and Richard Rojcewicz. Bloomington: Indiana University Press, 1998.

———. *Pathmarks.* Edited by William McNeill. New York: Cambridge University Press, 2005.

———. *The Phenomenology of Religious Life.* Translated by Matthias Fritsch and Jennifer Anna Gosetti-Ferencei. Bloomington: Indiana University Press, 2004.

———. *Poetry, Language, Thought.* Translated by Albert Hofstadter. New York: HarperCollins, 2001.

———. *The Principle of Reason.* Translated by Reginald Lilly. Bloomington: Indiana University Press, 1991.

———. *What Is Called Thinking?* Translated by Fred D. Wieck and J. Glenn Gray. New York: Harper & Row, 1968.

Hemming, Laurence Paul. *Postmodernity's Transcending: Devaluing God.* London: SCM Press, 2005.

Hopkins, Gerard Manley. *Hopkins: Poems and Prose.* New York: Everyman's Library, 1995.

Husserl, Edmund. *Cartesian Meditations: An Introduction to Phenomenology.* Translated by Dorian Cairns. Boston: Kluwer Academic, 1999.

———. *The Crisis of European Sciences and Transcendental Phenomenology: An Introduction to Phenomenological Philosophy.* Translated by David Carr. Evanston, IL: Northwestern University Press, 1970.

———. *Logical Investigations.* Volume 1. Translated by J. N. Findlay. Amherst, NY: Humanity Books, 2000.

———. *Logical Investigations.* Volume 2. Translated by J. N. Findlay. Amherst, NY: Humanity Books, 2000.

———. "Philosophy as a Rigorous Science." In *Phenomenology and the Crisis of Philosophy*, translated by Quentin Lauer, 71–147. New York: Harper & Row, 1965.

Ingarden, Roman. *On the Motives Which Led Husserl to Transcendental Idealism.* Translated by Arnór Hannibalsson. The Hague: Martinus Nijhoff, 1975.

Janicaud, Dominique, ed. *Phenomenology and the "Theological Turn": The French Debate.* New York: Fordham University Press, 2000.

Bibliography

John Paul II. *Fides et Ratio: On the Relationship between Faith and Reason.* Vatican translation. Boston: Pauline Books & Media, 1998.

Jonas, Hans. *The Gnostic Religion: The Message of the Alien God and the Beginnings of Christianity.* Boston: Beacon Press, 2001.

Jüngel, Eberhard. *God as the Mystery of the World: On the Foundation of the Theology of the Crucified One in the Dispute between Theism and Atheism.* Translated by Darrell L. Guder. Grand Rapids: Eerdmans, 1983.

———. *Theological Essays.* Volume 1. Edited by J. B. Webster. Translated by J. B. Webster. Edinburgh: T&T Clark, 1989.

Kearney, Richard. *Anatheism: Returning to God after God.* New York/Chichester, UK: Columbia University Press, 2010.

———. *The God Who May Be: A Hermeneutics of Religion.* Bloomington: Indiana University Press, 2001.

Kelly, Thomas A. F., ed. *Between System and Poetics: William Desmond and Philosophy after Dialectic.* Aldershot, UK: Ashgate, 2007.

Kessler, Michael, and Christian Sheppard, eds. *Mystics: Presence and Aporia.* Chicago: University of Chicago Press, 2003.

Kevern, John R. "A Future for Anglican Catholic Theology." *Anglican Theological Review* 76 (1994): 246–61.

Kisiel, Theodore. *The Genesis of Heidegger's Being and Time.* Berkeley: University of California Press, 1993.

Kundera, Milan. *The Unbearable Lightness of Being.* Translated by Michael Henry Heim. New York: Faber & Faber, 1984.

LaCocque, André, and Paul Ricoeur. *Thinking Biblically: Exegetical and Hermeneutical Studies.* Translated by David Pellauer. Chicago: University of Chicago Press, 1998.

Lacoste, Jean-Yves. *Experience and the Absolute: Disputed Questions on the Humanity of Man.* Translated by Mark Raftery-Skehan. New York: Fordham University Press, 2004.

Laqueur, Walter. *Young Germany: A History of the German Youth Movement.* New Brunswick, NJ: Transaction Publishers, 1984.

Leask, Ian. *Being Reconfigured.* Newcastle, UK: Cambridge Scholars Publishing, 2011.

Levinas, Emmanuel. *Otherwise Than Being: Or Beyond Essence.* Translated by Alphonso Lingis. Pittsburgh: Duquesne University Press, 1998.

———. *Totality and Infinity: An Essay on Exteriority.* Translated by Alphonso Lingis. Pittsburgh: Duquesne University Press, 2008.

Loyola, Ignatius. *Ignatius of Loyola: Spiritual Exercises and Selected Works.* Edited by George E. Ganass, SJ. New York: Paulist Press, 1991.

Lubac, Henri de. *Augustinianism and Modern Theology.* Translated by Lancelot Sheppard. New York: Crossroad, 2000.

———. *A Brief Catechesis on Nature and Grace.* Translated by Richard Arnandez. San Francisco: Ignatius Press, 1984.

———. *The Drama of Atheist Humanism.* Translated by Edith M. Riley. New York: Sheed & Ward, 1950.

———. "On Christian Philosophy." *Communio* 19 (1992): 478–507.

Lyotard, Jean-François. *The Postmodern Condition: A Report on Knowledge.* Translated by Geoff Bennington and Brian Massumi. Manchester, UK: Manchester University Press, 1984.

MacIntyre, Alasdair. *Edith Stein: A Philosophical Prologue.* New York: Continuum, 2006.

Macquarrie, John. *Heidegger and Christianity.* New York: Continuum, 1994.

Manoussakis, John Panteleimon, ed. *After God: Richard Kearney and the Religious Turn in Continental Philosophy.* New York: Fordham University Press, 2006.

Marcel, Gabriel. *The Mystery of Being.* Volume 1: *Reflection and Mystery.* Translated by G. S. Fraser. South Bend, IN: St. Augustine's Press, 2001.

———. *The Mystery of Being.* Volume 2: *Faith and Reality.* Translated by G. S. Fraser. South Bend, IN: St. Augustine's Press, 2001.

Maréchal, Joseph. *A Maréchal Reader.* Edited by Joseph Donceel. Translated by Joseph Donceel. New York: Herder & Herder, 1970.

Marion, Jean-Luc. *Being Given: Toward a Phenomenology of Givenness.* Translated by Jeffrey L. Kosky. Stanford, CA: Stanford University Press, 2002.

———. *God without Being: Hors-Texte.* Translated by Thomas A. Carlson. Chicago: University of Chicago Press, 1991.

———. *The Idol and Distance: Five Studies.* Translated by Thomas A. Carlson. New York: Fordham University Press, 2001.

———. *In Excess: Studies of Saturated Phenomena.* Translated by Robyn Horner and Vincent Berraud. New York: Fordham University Press, 2002.

———. *Reduction and Givenness: Investigations of Husserl, Heidegger, and Phenomenology.* Translated by Thomas A. Carlson. Evanston, IL: Northwestern University Press, 1998.

———. *The Visible and the Revealed.* Translated by Christina M. Gschwandtner. New York: Fordham University Press, 2008.

Maritain, Jacques. *An Essay on Christian Philosophy.* Translated by Edward H. Flannery. New York: Philosophical Library, 1955.

Maurin, Peter. *Easy Essays*. Eugene, OR: Wipf & Stock, 2003.
McDermott, John M. "Dialectical Analogy: The Oscillating Center of Rahner's Thought." *Gregorianum* 75 (1994): 675–703.
Metz, Johannes Baptist. *Poverty of Spirit*. Translated by John Drury. New York: Paulist Press, 1998.
Milbank, John. *Being Reconciled: Ontology and Pardon*. London: Routledge, 2003.
———. *The Suspended Middle: Henri de Lubac and the Debate concerning the Supernatural*. Grand Rapids: Eerdmans, 2005.
———. *Theology and Social Theory: Beyond Secular Reason*. Oxford: Blackwell, 2006.
———. *The Word Made Strange: Theology, Language, Culture*. Oxford: Blackwell, 1997.
Milbank, John, and Catherine Pickstock. *Truth in Aquinas*. London: Routledge, 2001.
Milbank, John, Catherine Pickstock, and Graham Ward, eds. *Radical Orthodoxy: A New Theology*. London: Routledge, 1999.
Milbank, John, and Slavoj Žižek. *The Monstrosity of Christ*. Edited by Creston Davis. Cambridge, MA: MIT Press, 2009.
Milbank, John, Slavoj Žižek, and Creston Davis. *Paul's New Moment: Continental Philosophy and the Future of Christian Theology*. Grand Rapids: Brazos Press, 2010.
Nédoncelle, Maurice. *Is There a Christian Philosophy?* Translated by Dom Illtyd Trethowan. London: Burn & Oates, 1960.
Newman, John Henry Cardinal. *An Essay in Aid of a Grammar of Assent*. London: Longmans, Green, 1909.
Nielsen, Niels C. "'*Analogia Entis*' as the Basis of Buddhist-Christian Dialogue." *Modern Theology* 3 (1987): 345–57.
———. "Analogy and Knowledge of God: An Ecumenical Appraisal (Roman Catholic and Protestant Interpretations in Relation to the Debate about the Analogy of Being between Erich Przywara, S.J., and K. Barth)." *Rice University Studies* 60 (1987): 21–102.
———. "Przywara's Philosophy of the '*Analogia Entis*.'" *Review of Metaphysics* 5 (1952): 599–620.
Nietzsche, Friedrich. *Beyond Good and Evil*. Translated by Marion Faber. Oxford: Oxford University Press, 1998.
———. *On the Genealogy of Morals and Ecce Homo*. Edited by Walter Kaufmann. Translated by Walter Kaufmann. New York: Random House, 1989.

———. *Thus Spoke Zarathustra: A Book for All and None.* Translated by Walter Kaufmann. New York: Modern Library, 1995.

———. *Twilight of the Idols and The Anti-Christ.* Translated by R. J. Hollingdale. London: Penguin Books, 2003.

Ockham, William. *Philosophical Writings: A Selection.* Edited by Philotheus Boehner, OFM. Translated by Philotheus Boehner, OFM. Indianapolis: Hackett, 1990.

O'Meara, Thomas F., OP. *Erich Przywara, S.J.: His Theology and His World.* Notre Dame: University of Notre Dame Press, 2002.

O'Regan, Cyril. *The Anatomy of Misremembering: Von Balthasar's Response to Philosophical Modernity.* Volume 1: *Hegel.* New York: Crossroad, 2014.

———. *Gnostic Return in Modernity.* Albany: State University of New York Press, 2001.

———. *Theology and the Spaces of Apocalyptic.* Milwaukee: Marquette University Press, 2009.

———. "Von Balthasar's Valorization and Critique of Heidegger's Genealogy of Modernity." In *Christian Spirituality and the Culture of Modernity*, 123–58. Grand Rapids: Eerdmans, 1998.

Otto, Rudolf. *The Idea of the Holy: An Inquiry into the Non-rational Factor in the Idea of the Divine and Its Relation to the Rational.* Translated by John W. Harvey. Oxford: Oxford University Press, 1950.

Palakeel, Joseph. *The Use of Analogy in Theological Discourse: An Investigation in Ecumenical Perspective.* Rome: Pontificia Università Gregoriana, 1995.

Pascal, Blaise. *Pensées.* Translated by A. J. Krailsheimer. New York: Penguin Books, 1995.

Peterson, Erik. *Theological Tractates.* Translated and edited by Michael J. Hollerich. Stanford, CA: Stanford University Press, 2011.

Picard, Max. *The World of Silence.* Translated by Stanley Godman. Chicago: Henry Regnery Company, 1952.

Pickstock, Catherine. *After Writing: On the Liturgical Consummation of Philosophy.* Oxford: Blackwell, 1998.

Pieper, Josef. *Faith, Hope, Love.* Translated by Clara Winston, Richard Winston, and Sister Mary Frances McCarthy, SND. San Francisco: Ignatius Press, 1997.

Plato. *Plato: The Complete Works.* Edited by John M. Cooper. Indianapolis: Hackett, 1997.

Pseudo-Dionysius. *Pseudo-Dionysius: The Complete Works.* Translated by Colm Luibheid. New York: Paulist Press, 1987.

Rahner, Karl. *Hearers of the Word*. Translated by Michael Richards. New York: Herder & Herder, 1969.

———. *Spirit in the World*. Translated by William Dych, SJ. New York: Continuum, 1994.

Ratzinger, Joseph Cardinal. *Church, Ecumenism and Politics: New Essays in Ecclesiology*. Translated by Robert Norwell. Slough, UK: St. Paul Publications, 1988.

———. *Daughter Zion: Meditations on the Church's Marian Belief*. Translated by John M. McDermott. San Francisco: Ignatius Press, 1983.

———. *Salt of the Earth: The Church at the End of the Millennium*. Translated by Adrian Walker. San Francisco: Ignatius Press, 1997.

Reinach, Adolf. "What Is Phenomenology?" *The Personalist* 50, no. 2 (1960): 194–221.

Rousselot, Pierre, SJ. *The Eyes of Faith: Answer to Two Attacks*. Translated by Joseph Donceel, SJ. New York: Fordham University Press, 1990.

Safranski, Rüdiger. *Martin Heidegger: Between Good and Evil*. Translated by Ewald Osers. Cambridge, MA: Harvard University Press, 1998.

Scheler, Max. 1973. *Formalism in Ethics and Non-formal Ethics of Values: A New Attempt toward the Foundation of an Ethical Personalism*. Translated by Roger L. Funk and Manfred S. Frings. Evanston, IL: Northwestern University Press, 1973.

———. *On the Eternal in Man*. Translated by Bernard Noble. London: Transaction Publishers, 2010.

———. *Ressentiment*. Translated by William W. Holdheim and Lewis B. Coser. Milwaukee: Marquette University Press, 1994.

Schilpp, Paul Arthur, and Lewis Edwin Hahn, eds. *The Philosophy of Gabriel Marcel*. The Library of Living Philosophers 17. La Salle, IL: Open Court, 1984.

Schindler, D. C. *Hans Urs von Balthasar and the Dramatic Structure of Truth: A Philosophical Investigation*. New York: Fordham University Press, 2004.

Scotus, John Duns. *Philosophical Writings*. Translated by Allan Wolter, OFM. Indianapolis: Hackett, 1987.

Sharkey, Sarah Borden. *Edith Stein*. New York: Continuum, 2003.

———. *Thine Own Self: Individuality in Edith Stein's Later Writings*. Washington, DC: Catholic University of America Press, 2010.

Siewerth, Gustav, and Andrzej Wierciński. *Philosophizing with Gustav Siewerth*. A new German edition with facing translation of "Das Sein als Gleichnis Gottes" (Being as likeness of God); and a study "'From Metaphor and Indication to Icon': The Centrality of the Notion of Verbum in Hans-Georg Gadamer." Translated by Andrzej Wierciński. Konstanz: Verlag Gustav Siewerth Gesellschaft, 2005.

Simpson, Christopher Ben. *Deleuze and Theology.* London: Bloomsbury T&T Clark, 2012.

——. *Religion, Metaphysics, and the Postmodern: William Desmond and John D. Caputo.* Bloomington: Indiana University Press, 2009.

Smith, James K. A. *Introducing Radical Orthodoxy: Mapping a Post-Secular Theology.* Grand Rapids: Baker Academic, 2004.

Snyder, Louis L., ed. *Documents of German History.* Translated by Louis L. Snyder. New Brunswick, NJ: Rutgers University Press, 1958.

Solovyov, Vladimir. *A Solovyov Anthology.* Edited by S. L. Frank. London: Saint Austin Press, 2001.

Spiegel, Herbert. *The Phenomenological Movement.* Volume 1: *A Historical Introduction.* The Hague: Martinus Nijhoff, 1971.

Stein, Edith. *Endliches und ewiges Sein: Versuch eines Aufstiegs zum Sinn des Seins.* Edith Stein Gesamtausgabe 11/12. Freiburg: Herder, 2006.

——. *Finite and Eternal Being: An Attempt at an Ascent to the Meaning of Being.* Translated by Kurt F. Reinhardt. Washington, DC: ICS Publications, 2001.

——. *Knowledge and Faith.* Translated by Walter Redmond. Washington, DC: ICS Publications, 2000.

——. *Life in a Jewish Family (1891–1916).* Edited by Dr. L. Gelber and Romaeus Leuven, OCD. Translated by Joesphine Koeppel, OCD. Washington, DC: ICS Publications, 1986.

——. *On the Problem of Empathy.* Translated by Waltraut Stein. Washington, DC: ICS Publications, 1989.

——. *The Science of the Cross.* Translated by Josephine Koeppel, OCD. Washington, DC: ICS Publications, 2002.

——. *Self-Portrait in Letters (1916–1942).* Edited by Dr. L. Gelber and Romaeus Leuven, OCD. Translated by Josephine Koeppel, OCD. Washington, DC: ICS Publications, 1993.

Taylor, Mark C. *Erring: A Postmodern A/theology.* Chicago: University of Chicago Press, 1984.

Teresia de Spiritu Sancto, ODC. *Edith Stein.* Translated by Donald Nicholl and Cecily Hastings. London: Sheed & Ward, 1952.

Tillich, Paul. *Systematic Theology.* Volume 1. Digswell Place, UK: James Nisbet & Co., 1964.

Tolkien, J. R. R. *The Monsters and the Critics: And Other Essays*. Edited by Christopher Tolkien. London: HarperCollins, 2006.
Tornielli, Andrea, and Giacomo Galeazzi. "Francis: To Care for the Poor Is Not Communism, It Is the Gospel." *Vatican Insider.* January 11, 2015. http://vaticaninsider.lastampa.it/en/the-vatican/detail/articolo/38493/.
Ulrich, Ferdinand. "A Dangerous Reflection on the Fundamental Act of the Creature." *Communio* 23, no. 1 (1996): 36–46.
Voegelin, Eric. *From Enlightenment to Revolution*. Edited by John H. Hallowell. Durham, NC: Duke University Press, 1975.
———. *History of Political Ideas*. Volume 2: *The Middle Ages to Aquinas*. Edited by Peter von Sivers. Columbia: University of Missouri Press, 1997.
———. *Science, Politics and Gnosticism: Two Essays*. Washington, DC: Regnery, 1997.
Weil, Simone. *Gravity and Grace*. Translated by Emma Crawford and Mario von der Ruhr. London: Routledge, 2002.
White, Thomas Joseph, OP, ed. *The Analogy of Being: Invention of the Antichrist or the Wisdom of God?* Grand Rapids: Eerdmans, 2011.
Zeitz, James V. "Erich Przywara on Ultimate Reality and Meaning: 'Deus Semper Major,' 'God Ever Greater.'" *Ultimate Reality and Meaning* 12 (1989): 192–201.
———. "Erich Przywara: Visionary Theologian." *Thought* 58 (1983): 145–57.
———. "God's Mystery in Christ: Reflections on Erich Przywara and Eberhard Jüngel [The Analogy of Being]." *Communio* 12 (1985): 158–72.
———. "Przywara and von Balthasar on Analogy." *Thomist* 52 (1988): 473–98.
———. *Spirituality and the Analogia Entis According to Erich Przywara, S.J.: Metaphysics and Religious Experience, the Ignatian Exercises, the Balance in Rhythm in "Similarity" and "Greater Dissimilarity" according to Lateran IV*. Washington, DC: University Press of America, 1982.
Zimny, Leo. *Erich Przywara: Sein Schrifttum (1912–1962)*. Einsiedeln: Johannes Verlag, 1963.
Žižek, Slavoj. *Living in the End Times*. London: Verso, 2011.

Index

absolutizations, 71, 74–79, 81, 83, 89, 125, 129, 256
Adam, Karl, 48
aesthetic, 14, 16–17, 28, 57, 73, 95, 98, 101, 125, 127–28, 132, 135, 174n78, 226, 240n35, 247, 253, 254–55, 265n36, 268–70, 274, 275–76, 280–86, 294, 311, 315, 322–26, 353
Agamben, Giorgio, 18, 190, 228, 346
agape, agapic, 17, 229, 231, 238, 254, 256–57, 260–61, 285, 332, 348
Altizer, Thomas, 234n24, 297, 299
Ambrose, Saint, 343n11
analogia attributionis, 194, 197–98, 199, 284, 333, 337, 341–42
analogia caritatis, 30, 191–201, 330, 349
analogia entis, 1–2, 16–17, 28–30, 33, 34–35, 50, 53n22, 88n55, 108n10, 118, 133n68, 174–75, 231, 236–37, 247–48, 271–74, 279–82, 290, 321–28, 331–33, 346–47
analogia proportionis, 158–59, 194–95, 198, 199–200
analogical-apocalyptic metaphysics, 8, 34–35, 288, 289, 321–23, 326, 334–36, 340–47, 349–54
analogical logic, 130–32
analogical metaphysics, 168–69, 173–74, 182–83, 186–87, 192, 245, 247–48, 250–53, 261, 267–73, 277, 286–87, 324–35, 340–41

analogical ordering, 85–94
analogy, 138–40, 158–59, 161, 176–77, 180–83, 257, 259–61, 280, 282
Anselm, Saint, 5, 15
anthropocentric foundationalism, 10, 121–22, 213, 216–17
anthropocentrism, 142, 206, 210; view of God, 165–66, 192, 196, 201–2
Antichrist, 189, 312, 318, 319–20, 338–40
apocalyptic, 22, 169–70, 171, 174–75, 226, 239, 293–97, 305–9, 311–12, 329, 336–40, 342–43
apocalyptic theology, 8–9, 20–21, 33–35, 212–13, 288–89, 297–99, 314, 316–17, 323, 333, 335–36, 340
apophatic theology, apophaticism, 162, 236–37
Aquinas. *See* Thomas Aquinas, Saint
Areopagite, 98n71, 196
Aristotle, Aristotelianism, 40–42, 45, 52, 71–75, 78, 81, 91, 130, 140–42, 159n46, 180–83, 189, 190, 221, 259–60
atheism, atheistic materialism, 32, 79, 45, 60n5, 79, 86, 225, 228, 229, 240–41, 243n41, 278, 301, 304, 351n18
Augustine, Saint, Augustinianism, 5, 6n9, 15, 25, 28, 40–42, 46–47, 52, 73, 78, 83, 89, 91, 94, 96–98, 99n75, 105n2, 106, 109–10, 112–14, 125, 129, 153n37, 154n38, 162nn51–52, 166, 170, 175, 182–83, 185–86, 196, 234–35, 237,

INDEX

240, 248, 250–51, 257, 262–67, 271, 281, 285–86, 290, 302, 341

Badiou, Alain, 21, 32, 60n5, 219, 220, 226, 228, 240–44, 311
Bakhtin, Mikhail, 22
Balthasar, Hans Urs von, 4n4, 6–8, 10, 13n12, 14, 19, 21, 31, 35, 39, 67n23, 74n37, 88, 107–8, 111n14, 119, 126, 141–42, 154n38, 162, 168, 169n65, 171n67, 172n69, 174–75n79, 178, 189, 196n150, 201n160, 207, 209, 210, 211–14, 217, 228, 231–33, 240n35, 247, 248, 265, 267, 269n47, 270n49, 272, 274, 275, 276, 277, 278, 281, 286, 288, 289, 290, 291, 292n7, 294n11, 296, 297, 298, 313–14, 315, 316n64, 317, 320, 321, 322, 323, 326, 327, 331n3, 332, 338, 345–46, 350–53
Baroque Scholasticism, 2, 40, 42n3, 48, 67n25, 207
Barth, Karl, 3, 3n2, 4n3, 6n9, 76, 81n51, 88n55, 143, 162, 175n80, 184–86, 197n152, 198n155, 272
Baur, Ferdinand Christian, 291
beatific vision, 153–54n38, 311
beauty, 16, 114, 174n78, 257, 269–70, 273–79, 282, 312, 317, 319, 323–26, 331, 333
Beauvais, Chantal, 65, 116, 122, 160–61, 164n59
being, 1, 19, 27–29, 42, 54, 116, 207, 242; analogical, 132–33, 135, 329; between-in-becoming, 28, 54, 95, 125, 248, 250, 252–54, 256–59, 279; consciousness and, 50–52, 72, 78–79, 82, 85, 87, 95, 106–7, 109, 115, 123–24, 126, 134, 135, 153, 194, 250, 251–53; eternal and finite, 29, 50, 140, 143, 145–47, 150–57, 163–65, 201–2; fabulation, 220–27, 246–47; forgetting of, 221–23, 224, 226, 241, 244; fourfold sense of, 128n48, 249, 254–57; of God, 14–15, 156–58, 159, 161–64, 165–68, 194–97, 198–99, 230–32, 238, 244–45, 247, 270, 324–35; grace and, 89–90, 273, 345; history, 220–25, 231, 232–33; of the I, 12, 27, 29, 105–9, 110, 112, 114–15, 121–22, 126–27, 140, 144–45, 146–51, 152; logos of, 128–32; of meaning, 120–21, 127, 140, 162–63, 223; mystery of, 250–53; presence of, 224–25, 233–34, 311, 324–35; thought, knowing and, 83, 132–33, 134–35, 252
Belgium, 48, 207
Benedict XVI, 6n9, 169n65, 209, 213
Benjamin, Walter, 18, 212–13, 299, 348n15
Bergoglio, Jorge. *See* Francis
Bergson, Henri, 41, 44
Bernanos, Georges, 315–16
Betz, John, 3n2, 7n10, 13n12, 90, 125n43, 171n69, 198n155, 249n4, 273
Blanchot, Maurice, 299n22, 305–6
Bloch, Ernst, 212, 213, 299
Blondel, Maurice, 42, 43n3, 44, 48, 62n10, 189, 207, 211n6, 264–66, 275
Bloy, Léon, 315, 316n64
Bonaventure, Saint, 5, 6n9, 15, 162n52, 237, 290, 332n3
Bonhoeffer, Dietrich, 88n55, 210–12
Borella, Jean, 19
Boulnois, Oliver, 172n69
Brémond, Henri, 43
Bulgakov, Sergei, 171, 264, 275n60, 277, 290, 296–98, 313n58
Buonaiuti, Ernesto, 43

Cajetan, 40
Callicles, 226
capitalism, 9, 18, 35, 60n5, 91–92n62, 200–201, 211–13, 243n41, 338, 342–52
Caputo, John D., 32, 34, 227, 233–36, 290, 292, 296–97, 299–310, 320
Cartesian philosophy, 11, 12, 42, 44, 64, 107n6, 109, 112, 119, 121, 134, 145, 147, 150, 165, 216, 221, 280
Catholic theology, 2–3, 33–34, 77–78, 81, 84, 86, 90, 93, 193, 275, 288, 292, 313, 351, 353
Chrétien, Jean-Louis, 32, 155, 227–30, 233, 278, 316
Christ. *See* Jesus Christ
Christian, Christianity, 18–19, 268–71;

Index

counterfeit doubles, 20, 33–34, 280, 292, 326–37; dehellenization of, 304–6, 308; identity, 297–98, 309–12, 316–17, 345, 350, 352; misremembering, forgetting, 22, 59, 169n65, 214, 216, 220, 227, 289–90, 293–94, 310, 313–20, 328, 331, 337, 340, 342, 345n12, 348, 352–53; mystery, 314–15, 317–20, 323–28, 330, 335; postmodern, 2, 22, 32–33, 166, 206, 217–20, 227–28, 236, 247, 275–77, 289–90, 314–15, 334–36, 353–54; simulacra, 292–94, 299, 311, 312, 317, 320, 325–28, 335, 338; symbolism, 225–27, 289–92, 310, 313–14, 318, 339; tradition, 23–25, 47–48, 214–16, 238, 243, 261, 265, 268–71, 276–77, 289–90, 293, 304, 314–15, 317–20, 328, 329, 333, 337–38; truth, 24–25, 76n43, 265, 292–94, 299–300

Christology, 6n9, 141n7

Claudel, Paul, 155, 316

Clement of Alexandria, 5

cogito, 19, 27, 65n18, 83, 85, 95, 103, 105–11, 113–14, 122, 132–35, 150, 155–56, 163–65, 178, 221, 252

commercium, 1, 16, 19, 30, 35, 137, 199, 200, 221n5, 231–32, 237–38, 261, 286, 322, 325, 330–31, 337, 345, 349, 350; anti-, 35, 330–31, 337, 342–53

communio, 31, 205–6, 208–14, 289, 338

Comte, Auguste, 18

concilium, 31, 205–6, 208–14, 216–17, 289

Conrad-Martius, Hedwig, 50, 147

counterfeit doubles, 20, 33–34, 280, 292, 326–37

countermodern, 8, 9–10, 26–27, 30–31, 33, 57, 102, 104, 114, 138, 205, 214, 217, 219, 246, 265, 285, 288–89, 320

counternarratives, 206, 226, 232–33, 247, 263, 283–84, 294

creation, 1, 19–20, 88n55, 99, 142–44, 174, 184–86, 187–89, 190, 192, 200, 231–32, 237–38, 240, 260–61, 269–70, 284, 286, 323–26, 327–28, 332n3, 337, 348; doctrine of, 140–41, 279–80; *ex nihilo*, 3–4, 17, 30, 94, 141, 173, 183, 190, 198–99, 221, 232, 250, 271, 279, 281, 286; gift of, 185, 188, 229, 237–38, 257, 271, 281–83, 326; metaphysics of, 14, 16, 183, 191, 239–40, 256–57, 260–61, 264, 324

creaturely: metaphysics, 52–53, 71–72, 77–79, 81–84, 86–90, 94–97, 123–32, 155–56, 176–77, 200–201; participation, 25, 75, 141–42, 183, 185, 190, 321; realism, 130, 174, 178, 252–53, 258

creatures, humans, relationship with God, 16–17, 29–30, 76–77, 79–80, 82–84, 96–97, 139–44, 155–57, 165–66, 173–74, 182, 185–87, 192–96, 258–61, 281, 286, 324–26, 329–30

Damien, Peter, 69

Dante, Alighieri, 154n38

Dasein, 180, 186, 189–91, 200, 329

Day, Dorothy, 350, 351n17

deconstruction, 234–35, 300–305, 307–9

Delbrêl, Madeleine, 350

Deleuze, Gilles, 21, 91, 189n133, 241n39, 276

Denys (Pseudo-Dionysius), 5, 98

Derrida, Jacques, 19, 21–22, 189n133, 234, 235n26, 276, 290, 292, 296, 299, 300n23, 301–3, 305–8, 314n59; deconstruction, 234–35

Descartes, René, 66, 68, 86, 105–15, 118–19, 122, 126, 144–45, 178, 187n128, 216, 221, 252, 254, 265n36

desire, 153–55, 200, 235, 237–38, 243n41, 255, 277–78, 347–49; for divine, 84, 90–92, 96, 105, 113, 129–30, 132, 155, 174, 188, 193, 201, 237, 244, 283–85, 315, 323, 329

Desmond, William, 8–10, 14, 20, 32–35, 67n23, 92n60, 128n48, 167–68, 205–6, 214, 217, 220, 227, 232, 235n28, 236, 239–64, 266–67, 268n45, 271, 273, 275–76, 279–81, 285–88, 291, 292n7, 300, 310, 314, 320, 322, 324, 326–27, 348

dialectic, 129–30, 178–80, 257

dialectical mediation, 254–56

difference, 28, 51–52, 73, 76–78, 80,

373

INDEX

92, 104, 122, 152, 195–96, 232, 280; *différance*, 21, 234, 301–2, 304–5, 307–8
Dionysian thought, 189n133, 276n63, 277, 279, 332n3
distinctio realis, 141–42, 144

Eastern church, Orthodox theology, 8, 171–72, 199–200, 227, 274–78, 283–85, 297
ecclesial, 25, 69, 201, 211, 227, 316, 318–19, 330, 333, 348–50; community, 16, 265, 270, 274, 332, 337, 340–41, 343, 354; memory, 23–24, 317–20, 330
ecclesiology, 211, 301n23
Eckhart. *See* Meister Eckhart
ecstatic view of self, 72, 80, 146, 281, 285, 314, 331
ego, 106, 114–15, 144, 147, 150–56; pure (*Reine Ich*), 146, 148, 149, 151; transcendental, 147–50, 153, 156, 178, 252
Eliot, T. S., 56, 86, 135, 214
Engert, Thaddäus, 43
England, 48
Enlightenment, the, 18, 21, 44, 206, 214, 297, 306, 310, 313–14, 318–20, 323
ens commune, 29, 116, 138–41, 143, 146, 157, 161, 164–65, 192, 201–2, 259, 270, 280
epistemology, 28, 123–28, 251–52
equivocal, 254–56, 279
eroticism, erotic, 17, 192, 193, 198, 237–38, 256, 283–85
eschatology, eschatological, 339–40; deferred, 28, 72, 80, 82, 118, 187, 281; expectancy, 23, 93, 96, 98, 108n10, 224, 226, 235–36, 238, 292, 338–40; onto-, 236–37
essence, 28, 64, 72, 117–19, 122, 221; existence and, 79, 81–82, 85, 95, 119, 121, 123–25, 139–40, 142–44, 155, 160–61, 163, 194, 251–52, 280–81, 285–86; nonidentity of, 28, 127, 133, 141, 155, 194; *Sosein in-über Dasein*, 28, 72, 78–81, 89, 94–95, 125
essentialism, 120–21, 280

eternal, 243; being, 29, 50, 140, 143, 145–47, 150–57, 163–65, 201–2
Eucharist, eucharistic, 23, 24, 62n10, 65, 154n38, 349
existence, 79, 81–82, 85, 95, 119, 121, 123–25, 139–40, 142–44, 155, 160–61, 163, 194, 251–52, 255; essence and, 79, 81–82, 85, 95, 119, 121, 123–25, 139–40, 142–44, 155, 160–61, 163, 194, 251–52, 280–81, 285–86
existentialism, 170n65, 179–80
ex nihilo, creation, 3–4, 17, 30, 94, 141, 173, 183, 190, 198–99, 221, 232, 250, 271, 279, 281, 286
experience, 29, 106, 131, 148–49, 151–52, 257, 331–32, 346; reflexive, 161, 163–65

Fabro, Cornelio, 41
faith, 89, 98, 101, 110–11, 113–14, 301, 303–7, 311
Feuerbach, Ludwig, 58n2
fiat, 35, 174, 190–91, 284, 285, 328, 329, 331–33, 336–38, 340–43, 346, 349, 354
Fogazzaro, Antonio, 43
forgetting, misremembering, 22, 59, 169n65, 214, 216, 220, 227, 289–90, 293–94, 310, 313–20, 328, 331, 337, 340, 342, 345n12, 348, 352–53
Foucault, Michel, 18, 306
foundationalism, 10, 19, 26–27, 33, 68, 85, 89, 94, 101–4, 109–15, 121, 127, 132, 135, 143, 166, 176, 201–2, 216–17, 251, 285–86, 333–34; anthropocentric, 10, 122–23, 192; egological, 27, 105; reflexive, 10, 11
Fourth Lateran Council, 29, 131n63, 133n69, 139, 140, 157–58, 160, 168–75, 194, 195, 259, 329
France, French, 43, 48, 62–63, 207, 209–10, 276; phenomenology, 32, 107n6, 227–33, 244
Francis, 213n13, 341n9, 343n11, 345n12
Frankfurt School, 212, 213, 347n14, 352n19
freedom, 76–77, 84, 93–94, 142, 185–86, 190, 192–93, 199–200, 237–38,

Index

260–61, 286, 323–25, 328–30, 334–35, 344–45n12, 347–49

Gaboriau, Florent, 65
Gadamer, Hans-Georg, 19, 47n11
Garrigou-Lagrange, Réginald Marie, 41, 43n4, 62n10
Geist, 116, 120–21, 163–64, 313, 319
German Idealism, 19–20, 46, 68n26, 77, 170–71, 174n78, 292, 323, 327
Germany, German, 43–44, 48, 207, 210; rationalism, 177–78
Gilson, Étienne, 62n10, 112–14, 162, 207, 237, 271n49, 350
Girard, René, 293n8, 299
givenness, 119, 122, 228–29
glory of God, 19, 29, 174, 192–93, 198–201, 202, 217, 257, 261, 271, 282, 286, 323–26, 328–29, 331, 333, 337, 340–43, 346, 347, 354; of Christ, 315, 319
Gnosticism, 20, 169–70n65, 276n63, 280, 290–94, 314, 319, 327
God, 96–98; anthropocentric view of, 165–66, 192, 196, 201–2; Being, 14–15, 156–59, 161–68, 194–99, 230–32, 238, 244–45, 247, 270, 324–35; desire for divine, 84, 90–92, 96, 105, 113, 129–30, 132, 155, 174, 188, 193, 201, 237, 244, 283–85, 315, 323, 329; divine naming, 160–65, 201; immanence, 75–76, 99–100, 118, 145, 151, 192, 258–59, 324–35; love of, 16–17, 29–30, 188, 192, 238, 279, 281–83, 286, 324–25, 327, 329–30; mutability, 98–99; Phenomenologist, 153–55; *prius*, 16, 30, 184, 188, 191, 193, 196, 198, 202, 231–32, 237; relation with humans, 16–17, 29–30, 76–77, 79–80, 82–84, 96–97, 139–44, 155–57, 165–66, 173–74, 182, 185–87, 192–96, 258–61, 281, 286, 324–26, 329–30; simplicity, 99, 159–62; transcendence, 28, 74–76, 82–84, 90, 96–97, 99–100, 142, 143, 147–48, 169–70, 182, 193–94, 196–97, 236–38, 251, 253, 258–61, 281–83, 324, 327
Gonzales, Philip John Paul, 4n3, 249n4

grace, 1, 19, 24–25, 31, 42, 42–43n3, 64, 87–89, 91, 93, 113, 184–89, 190–91, 207–10, 212, 232, 243n41, 272, 282, 315, 328–31, 334, 339, 345, 349–50, 351; nature and, 183–85, 187, 207, 209–10, 232, 262–63, 265, 266–68, 270–73, 275, 284–85, 341, 343–46
Greek Orthodox, 119, 275
Greek thinking, 59, 112, 221–22, 224, 260, 298–99, 305
Gregory of Nyssa, Saint, 5, 15, 154n38, 264, 271, 277–78, 281, 283–85
Guardini, Romano, 7n11, 48, 207

Hamann, Johann Georg, 129
Harnack, Adolf von, 15
Hart, David Bentley, 8, 10, 13n12, 15n14, 16, 31–35, 134n69, 154n38, 168, 171n69, 205–6, 214, 217, 220, 227, 239, 240n35, 245–48, 273–91, 292n7, 296–98, 300, 310, 314–15, 320, 322, 324, 326–27
Hauerwas, Stanley, 344n12
Hegel, G. W. F., 18, 20, 46, 64, 68, 76, 86, 94, 98, 100, 108, 116–17, 130, 169–74, 179–80, 221, 224, 226–27, 242, 247, 248n1, 251–52, 256, 291–94, 313–15, 319–20, 328
Heidegger, Martin, 7, 13n12, 15, 19–21, 31–33, 46–47, 50, 53n22, 61n7, 67n23, 72, 76n43, 79, 83, 85–86, 116–19, 121, 124, 144, 147–49, 170n65, 171n67, 174, 179–80, 184, 189–91, 219–47, 276, 292–94, 300n23, 314–15, 327, 329; fabulation of being, 220–27, 246–47; post-Heideggerian discourse, 15, 33, 107n6, 162, 196n150, 228, 233, 236–38, 241, 244, 285, 300
Henry, Michel, 32, 107n6, 227–28
Heraclitus, 181, 221
Hildebrand, Dietrich von, 48, 49n13, 207
history, 40, 54, 59–60, 169–71, 173–75, 189, 221–22, 230–31, 291–92, 298, 315, 328–29, 334–40; of being, 220–25, 231–33
Hölderlin, Friedrich, 7, 103, 171n67, 221
Hopkins, Gerard Manley, 137

INDEX

Husserl, Edmund, 12, 26–27, 41, 46, 50, 51n18, 54, 56, 61n7, 63–68, 72, 103, 105–6, 109–12, 114–17, 119, 122, 124, 126–27, 135, 139, 144–51, 148n43, 165, 178, 221, 241

I, being of the, 105–9, 110, 112, 114–15, 121–22, 126–27, 140, 144–52
Idealism, 107–8, 114–16, 122, 153, 252, 280; German, 19–20, 46, 68n26, 77, 170–71, 174n78, 292, 323, 327
identity, 117–19, 121–22, 125, 127–28, 146–47, 152–53, 173–74, 181–82, 251, 254, 327–28; Christian, 297–98, 309–12, 316–17, 345, 350, 352; God and man, 169–72; principle of, 176–80
idolatry, idolatrous, 81n51, 83–84, 86, 90, 99, 111, 150, 182–83, 190, 192, 195, 198, 225, 229–34, 238, 280, 286, 303, 307, 324, 327, 328, 340
Ignatian thought, 185, 192, 200, 201n160, 284, 293, 341–42, 346
immanence, 75–76, 99–100, 118, 145, 151, 192, 258–59, 324–35
Incarnation, 62n10, 209, 262, 266, 269–70, 347
integralism, 42, 42–43n3, 45, 47–48, 207, 212
Ireland, 43, 236
Irenaeus of Lyon, 290, 291n3, 292–93, 313n58
irrationalism, 98–99, 253
Italy, 43–44

Jesus Christ, 118, 211, 262, 263–64, 269, 307, 312, 318, 319–20, 333, 336, 345, 348, 354; glory of, 315, 319; Incarnation, 62n10, 209, 262, 266, 269–70, 347; *Logos*, 4, 23–24, 129–31, 132, 226, 293, 332n3; mind of, 23–24; revelation, 338–40; second coming, 294–95, 307; Word, 246, 267, 269, 270, 307, 317
Jewish, Judaism, 76, 77, 303
Joachim of Fiore, 18, 168–75, 327, 329
Johannine tradition, 170–71
John XXIII, 343n11

John Chrysostom, 343–44n11
John of Saint Thomas, 40
John Paul II, 44n5, 300n23
Jonas, Hans, 169–70n65
Jung, Karl, 74n37
Jüngel, Eberhard, 197, 199

Kant, Immanuel, 40, 44, 53n22, 178, 212n8, 213, 239, 252, 305n37, 306
kataphatic theology, 236–37
Kearney, Richard, 32–33, 227, 233, 235–38, 239n34, 242, 244, 300, 301n23
kenomatic apocalyptic theology, 33, 34, 296, 298–99, 300, 308, 309, 320
Kierkegaard, Søren, 18, 129, 179, 189n133
knowing, knowledge, 20, 98, 106–8, 115, 161–62, 257, 258, 339; being and, 83, 132–35, 252; total, 56–57, 63, 66, 68, 70, 86, 103, 105, 140, 161

Laberthonnière, Lucien, 43
Lacoste, Jean-Yves, 32, 201, 227–30, 233, 317n69
laus Dei, 199–200, 284, 346
Leask, Ian, 51n18, 107n6
Leo XIII, 40, 43
Le Roy, Édouard, 43
Lessing, Gotthold Ephraim, 18
Levinas, Emmanuel, 21, 76n43, 117–19, 228, 235–36, 276, 292, 300n23
liberal democracy, 344–45n12
liberalism, 18, 212–13, 243n41, 272, 311, 343n11, 344
liberation theology, 211–13, 235, 297, 346–47, 351–52
liturgy, 211–12
Logos, 4, 23–24, 129–32, 226, 293, 332n3
Loisy, Alfred, 43
love, 67–69, 192, 261, 331–32, 349; of God, 16–17, 29–30, 188, 192, 238, 279, 281, 282–83, 286, 324–25, 327, 329–30; participation in, 73–74, 194
Lubac, Henri de, 31, 43n3, 62n10, 88, 110n13, 169n65, 189, 207, 209, 212, 214, 228–29, 232, 262–64, 266–67, 276, 291, 292n7, 232, 262–64, 265n36, 266–67,

376

Index

272, 275, 276n64, 291, 292n7, 345–46, 351
Luciferianism, 76, 77, 83
Luther, Martin, 76, 111n13, 184–85, 293, 304–5
Lyotard, François, 21, 236, 276

magisterium, 69, 70–71
maior dissimilitudo, 29, 140, 145–46, 158, 159n46, 165, 169–70
man, definition of, 121, 180, 257, 271
Marcel, Gabriel, 62n10, 67n23, 149, 207, 260, 262
Maréchal, Joseph, 9, 48, 153n37, 207
Mariology, 3–4
Marion, Jean-Luc, 32–33, 43n4, 117, 119, 155n39, 162, 171n67, 196n150, 209, 227–33, 235–36, 238, 242, 244
Maritain, Jacques, 46, 61n7, 62–67, 75, 80, 112, 114
Marxism, 212, 213, 214, 341n59, 343n11, 348n15, 349n16, 352n19
Maurin, Peter, 350, 351n17
Maurras, Charles, 42n3
Maximus the Confessor, 5, 264, 290
medieval thought, 12, 14, 40–41, 43, 46, 61nn7–8, 86, 170, 279
Meister Eckhart, 222, 264, 265n36, 332n3
Mersch, Emile, 48, 207
messiah, messianism, 76, 77, 301, 302, 306–8, 346
metalepsis, metaleptic, 20, 291
metanarratives, master, 20, 21–22, 31–32, 118, 223, 226–28, 286, 310, 314, 319
metaphysics, 1–2, 5, 8, 14–17, 33, 45, 54, 70–71, 77, 93, 111–12, 222–23, 249, 346–47; analogical, 168–69, 173–74, 182–83, 186–87, 192, 245, 247–48, 250–53, 261, 267–73, 277, 286–87, 324–38, 340–41; analogical-apocalyptic, 8, 34–35, 288, 289, 321–23, 326, 334–36, 340–47, 349–54; of being, 58–60, 118–19; creation, 14, 16, 183, 191, 239–40, 256–57, 260–61, 264, 324; creaturely, 52–53, 71–72, 77–79, 81–84, 86–90, 94–97,

123–32, 155–56, 176–77, 200–201; metaphor, 258–59; onto-theology, 223–27; participation, 264, 267–73, 278, 279, 283, 286, 327; post-, end of, 228–30, 232–35, 238–40, 244–47; theological, 90–94; totality, 279–80
metaxology, metaxological, 92n60, 214, 235–40, 244, 249, 251–54, 256–64, 322, 326
Metz, Johannes Baptist, 209, 211n6, 212–13, 297, 299, 351–52
Milbank, John, 8–11, 19, 24n24, 31–35, 43n3, 47n11, 60n5, 167–68, 172n69, 205–6, 209–10, 212, 214, 217, 220, 239, 243n41, 245, 246–48, 249n4, 264–77, 279–80, 281n78, 285–91, 292n7, 293, 296–98, 300, 310, 314–15, 320, 322, 324, 326–27, 343, 351, 352n19
mindfulness, 15–17, 23–25, 250–53, 255–57, 262
misremembering, forgetting, 22, 59, 169n65, 214, 216, 220, 227, 289–90, 293–94, 310, 313–20, 328, 331, 337, 340, 342, 345n12, 348, 352–53
modernist crisis, 9–11, 25–26, 30–31, 39–49, 55, 206, 207, 215–16
modernity, modernism, 8, 17–21, 43–44, 49n13, 65n18, 94, 102, 114, 136, 166, 264–66, 315–16, 344n12
Moltmann, Jürgen, 297–98, 322, 326
mysterium, 1, 24–25, 26, 28, 125, 127–28, 155, 159, 176, 199, 202, 216, 226, 325; *reductio in*, 27, 57, 63, 73, 81, 93–101, 160, 170, 238, 251, 324
mystery, 94–101, 154n38, 158–61, 250–51, 314; Christian, 314–15, 317–20, 323–28, 330, 335

narratives, 40, 59–60, 161, 166, 236, 310; analogical, 353–54; biblical, 291, 324; Catholic Christian, 22–23, 25, 39, 57, 189–91, 197, 264–66, 270, 272–73, 286, 305, 333, 343; counternarratives, 206, 226, 232–33, 247, 263, 283–84, 294; genealogical, 264–66, 267–68, 291–92; Gnostic, 291, 327; metanarratives,

master, 20–22, 31–32, 118, 223, 226–28, 286, 310, 314, 319; metaphysics and, 1, 15n14, 19–20, 239, 262, 267–68; Protestant, 184–85, 191, 305; secular, philosophical modernity, 208, 215–17, 247; theology, 268, 272–74
natural theology, 81–84, 89–90, 96, 192
nature, 63–64; grace and, 183–85, 187, 207, 209–10, 232, 262–63, 265–68, 270–73, 275, 284–85, 341, 343–46; pure, 42–43n3, 184
negative theology, 118, 154n38, 160, 194–95, 197, 199–200, 231, 303
neo-Platonism, 91, 182, 214, 283, 285, 306, 314
Neo-Scholasticism, 9–11, 25, 30, 39–45, 55, 88, 95, 108, 177–78, 181n108, 184, 186, 191, 239, 263
Neo-Thomistic revival, 28, 40–43, 47–48, 62–64, 67n25, 98, 125, 139–41, 146, 156, 158, 160–63, 170, 176, 187n128, 191, 206–7, 209, 262, 263
Newman, John Henry Cardinal, 44, 46, 48, 49n13, 175, 290
Nietzsche, Friedrich, 18, 20, 22, 76, 189n133, 221, 276, 283
nihilism, nihilistic, 2, 18, 22, 170n65, 202, 221, 222, 240, 245, 255, 278, 282, 283, 285–88, 307, 309–10, 320, 330
nominalism, 111, 266–67, 280, 293, 327
noncontradiction, 133, 168, 176–83, 193–94
nothing, 180, 190
Nouvelle Théologie, 30–31, 44n4, 205–6, 217–18, 228, 229n16, 246, 320
Novak, Michael, 344n12

Oaks, Kenneth, 6n9
O'Meara, Thomas F., OP, 51nn18–19, 53n22
ontology of peace, 273, 275, 280
onto-theology, 223–27, 230, 237, 238, 244, 300, 305, 308
O'Regan, Cyril, 8–10, 17n16, 18, 20, 31, 33–35, 154n38, 168, 169n65, 171n67, 205–6, 211–12, 214, 217, 246, 248n1,

265n36, 269n47, 276n64, 287–300, 308, 310–20, 322, 324, 326–27, 331n3, 338, 342, 351–52
ousia, 71, 140–41

pantheism, pantheistic, 45, 75–78, 83, 90, 97, 142, 180, 304
papal policy, 41–44
Parmenides, 181, 221
participation, participatory, 16–17, 26–27, 78, 172n69, 194, 217, 335, 344, 348; analogical, 91–92, 180, 186, 341, 345; creaturely, 25, 75, 141–42, 183, 185, 190, 321; in love, 73–74, 194; metaphysics, 264, 267–73, 278, 279, 283, 286, 327; radical, 73–75, 202; toward/ in Wisdom, divine, 23, 57, 63, 67–69, 73–74, 81, 84, 93–95, 99, 101–2, 104, 132, 159–60, 193, 199, 250–51, 258, 260–61, 266, 280, 285, 324–25, 331n3, 332–33
Pascal, Blaise, 111, 113n22, 243n41
patristics, church fathers, 199, 214, 275, 277–79, 343n13
Paul, Saint, 25, 171, 182, 240, 264, 339
Paul VI, 343–44n13
Péguy, Charles, 189n33, 315–16, 350
Pelagian, Pelagianism, 184–86, 188–91, 193
perfectum opus rationis, 65–66, 68–69
Peter Lombard, 172–73
Peterson, Erik, 20n19, 35, 213, 214n13, 338–40, 346, 352
phenomenology, 12, 27, 46, 54, 61n7, 64, 249–50, 292; *analogia entis*, 144–50; French, 32, 107n6, 227–33, 244; ontology, 105–10, 112, 114–23, 126–28, 144–52, 157–59, 164–66
Philo-(Sophia), 73–74, 78, 86
philosophia perennis, 39, 46–48
philosophical modernity, 10–11, 12, 19–21, 25–26, 29–31, 39–40, 55–57, 77, 102, 114, 136, 169, 202, 205–8, 215–18, 247, 285–86, 290, 319, 353
philosophy, 42, 48; definitions, 26–27, 61–67, 73–75; sapiential model, 74–75; theology and, 56–69, 72–81, 85–94,

378

Index

96–102, 104, 135–36, 228, 232–33, 266–67, 290, 334
Pickstock, Catherine, 201, 276n62, 281n78
Pindar, 78, 125
Pius X, 41, 43, 44
Pius XI, 41
Pius XII, 41
Plato, 52, 73–75, 135, 221, 250, 260
Platonism, 242, 243n41, 285, 306
pleromatic apocalyptic theology, 296, 298–302, 308–12, 315, 320, 322, 323, 325–26, 328, 331, 333–36, 338, 342, 349, 351–54
political theology, 31, 35, 208, 211–13, 289, 338, 352
post-Christian, 19, 22, 33, 114, 166, 189, 202, 206, 209, 215–17, 226, 263, 293, 294, 308, 310, 321–22, 339–40
post-Conciliar, 6–11, 30–31, 35, 184, 205–9, 215, 219, 289, 320, 321, 336, 342, 351–53
post-Heideggerian discourse, 15, 33, 107n6, 162, 196n150, 228, 233, 236–38, 241, 244, 285, 300
post-Kantian, 58, 59n4, 213
postmodern Christianity, 2, 22, 32–33, 166, 206, 217–20, 227–28, 236, 247, 275–77, 289–90, 314–15, 334–36, 353–54
postmodernism, 16, 21–22, 65n18, 86–87, 94, 102, 123, 128, 136, 200–201, 220–21, 227, 239–47, 265–66, 275–76, 310
post–Vatican II Catholic discourse, post-Conciliar, 6–11, 30–31, 35, 184, 205–9, 215, 219, 289, 320, 321, 336, 342, 351–53
potentia oboedientialis, 91, 168, 176, 183–84, 193, 284–85
Promethean/Luciferian, 75–77, 83
Protestant theology, Protestants, 184–86, 191, 197n152, 210–11, 294n9, 295n13, 297, 305, 327, 344n12
Przywara, Erich, 5–6, 25–30, 32–33, 41, 45, 47, 51–52, 219, 247, 248, 292n7, 314, 315, 322, 324, 329, 332, 345–49, 351–54;

analogia entis, 6n9, 7n10, 12–13, 49–50, 69, 88n55, 133n69, 168–69, 186–87, 191–94, 202, 272–74, 279–82, 285–87, 321, 326, 331n3, 333, 336, 341–42, 353; apocalyptic theology, 288–89, 296, 300, 334, 338, 342; Catholic theology, 2–3, 33–34, 77–78, 81, 84, 86, 90, 93, 193, 267, 275, 288, 292, 313, 351, 353; Desmond and, 248–64, 266, 271, 273; *distinctio realis*, 141–42, 144; Hart and, 273–77, 279–81, 283–84; Heidegger and, 226, 230, 232, 239–40n35, 245; *maior dissimilitudo*, 170; Milbank and, 267–68, 271–72, 275; mystery, 160–61; nature/grace, 262–63; noncontradiction, 133, 168, 176–83, 193–94; *Nouvelle Théologie*, 30–31, 44n4, 205–6, 217–18, 246, 320; O'Regan and, 290–91, 327, 331n3; phenomenology, 124–26; philosophy and theology, relationship, 72–81, 85–94, 96–101, 104, 135–36, 262–63, 266–67; *potentia oboedientialis*, 91, 168, 176, 183–84, 193, 284–85; *Sosein in-über Dasein*, 28, 72, 78–79, 80–81, 89, 94–95, 125; Stein and, 45–51, 69–72, 138–39, 157–58, 205–8, 215–18; Trinity, 167–68, 179
Pseudo-Dionysius, 41, 73, 76, 98, 162n52, 170, 196
pure logic, 128–31, 177–80, 257
pure nature, 42–43n3
Pythagoras, 135

Radical Orthodoxy, 111n14, 212–13, 227–28
Rahner, Karl, 2, 6–7, 10, 30–31, 59n4, 107–8, 123, 153n37, 206–7, 209–10, 212–13, 216–17, 353
rationalism, 60–67, 98, 100, 178, 184; German, 177–78
Ratzinger, Joseph. *See* Benedict XVI
realism, 251; creaturely, 130, 174, 178, 252–53, 258
reason, 19, 21, 44, 57–59, 62n10, 63–66, 70, 89, 110–11, 153n37, 254; dream of, 56, 63, 68, 70, 94

INDEX

redemption, 87–88, 93, 187–89, 198, 200, 232, 262, 263, 268, 270, 272–73, 280, 284, 298, 312, 314–15, 319, 322, 328–31, 334, 336, 339, 341, 345, 349
reductio in mysterium, 27, 57, 63, 73, 81, 93–101, 160, 170, 238, 251, 324
reflexive foundationalism, 10, 11
Reformation, the, 76, 77
Reinach, Adolf, 46
religion, noncreedal turn to, 233–38, 300–309, 310
revelation, 57–59, 63, 65, 66, 84, 87, 90, 113, 142, 143, 161–64, 192–93, 201, 210, 213, 216, 217, 228–29, 272, 279–80, 286, 292, 298–301, 306–7, 309, 315, 318–19, 329, 334–37, 338–40, 353
Revelation, book of, 299, 305, 307, 308, 338–40
Ricoeur, Paul, 65n18, 236
Roland-Gosselin, Fr., 71
Rousselot, Pierre, 48, 62n10, 110, 153n37, 207, 246

saints, 315–17, 319, 331–33, 336–38, 340, 346, 349–51, 354
Scheler, Max, 41, 46, 48, 54, 207
Schelling, Friedrich, 20, 171, 173
Schillebeeckx, Edward, 207, 209–11, 301n23
Schleiermacher, Friedrich, 44
Schmitt, Carl, 18, 213
Schnitzer, Joseph, 43
Scholasticism, 2, 41, 91, 141, 172, 207, 284–85; Baroque, 2, 40, 42n3, 48, 67n25, 207; late, 111, 113; neo-Scholasticism, 9–11, 25, 30, 39–45, 55, 88, 95, 108, 177–78, 181n108, 184, 186, 191, 239, 263
science, 63–68, 70, 106, 112, 149, 161
Scotus, John Duns, 86, 119, 141, 270, 332n3
Secretan, Philibert, 160, 164n59
secular, secularization, 10, 22, 29, 31, 60n5, 91, 108n10, 118, 166, 170, 184, 200, 202, 205, 208–12, 214–17, 226, 229, 263, 264, 266, 271–72, 274, 276–77, 287, 292–93, 297, 301, 311, 339, 341, 343–45, 351
self, ecstatic view, 72, 80, 146, 281, 285, 314, 331
self-presence, 1, 12, 19, 52, 94, 109, 122, 126–27, 133, 146, 148, 150, 152–53, 163–64, 166, 201–2
service, 4, 24, 30, 62n10, 93, 132, 168–69, 174, 183, 185–86, 190, 192–93, 198–201, 217, 284–85, 315–16, 323, 327–33, 337–38, 341–42, 346–50, 354
Siewerth, Gustav, 108n10, 240n35, 271n49
Silesius, Angelus, 222
simplicity of God, 99, 159–62
simulacra, 292–94, 299, 311, 312, 317, 320, 325–28, 335, 338
Smith-Gilson, Caitlin, 350
social justice, 211–12, 235, 297–98, 317n69, 340–42, 346–47, 352
Socrates, 73, 226
Söhngen, Gottlieb, 6n9
Sosein in-über Dasein, 28, 72, 78–81, 89, 94–95, 125
Spinoza, Baruch, 66, 76
Spirit, 24, 163, 167–68, 174, 268–69, 318
spirituality, 4, 131–32, 200, 311, 318, 331–33, 337, 340–41, 343, 346–47
Staudenmaier, Franz Anton, 169n65
Stein, Edith, 9–13, 25–31, 39–40, 45–57, 60–72, 75, 78, 80–81, 85–87, 89, 94, 101–12, 114–17, 119–24, 126–28, 134–68, 176, 192, 201–2, 205–8, 210, 215–17, 219, 259, 280, 351n18
Suarez, Luis, 86, 119, 140–41, 144
supernatural, 19, 42, 62n10, 80, 87n55, 91, 101, 140, 160–61, 168, 183–91, 193, 208–10, 216, 246, 263, 264, 266, 272, 284–85, 316n64, 334, 341, 345, 348
suspended middle, 1, 52, 57, 73, 80, 82, 83, 86–87, 94, 102, 104, 191, 194, 264, 266–67, 272
symbolism, Christian, 225–27, 289–92, 310, 313–14, 318, 339
systematics, open, 253–57

Index

Taylor, Charles, 18
Taylor, Mark C., 32, 60n5, 227, 233–36
tertium quid, 29, 92, 139, 143, 157, 164, 192, 194–96
theocentric, 10, 30
theological metaphysics, 90–94
theology, 42, 69, 88–90; philosophy and, 56–69, 72–81, 85–94, 96–102, 104, 135–36, 228, 232–33, 266–67, 290, 334
theopanism, theopanistic, 75–78, 83, 90, 97, 142, 180, 184–85, 191, 327
theo-politics, 338–42, 352
Thomas Aquinas, Saint, 5, 15, 28, 40–42, 45–48, 50, 52, 65–67, 75–76, 85, 98–99, 112, 114, 119, 125, 139–43, 158–59, 161–63, 173n77, 182–85, 188, 195–96, 223, 231, 237, 239, 248n2, 260, 264, 271, 285, 290, 305
Tillich, Paul, 210
Tilliette, X., 65
titanism, titanic, 19–20, 74, 76, 169, 179, 186, 192, 198, 288, 329
Tracy, David, 210
tradition, 23–25, 47–48, 214–16, 238, 243, 261, 265, 268–71, 276–77, 289–90, 293, 304, 314–15, 317–20, 328, 329, 333, 337–38
transcendence, 28, 74–76, 82–84, 90, 96–97, 99–100, 142, 143, 147–48, 169–70, 182, 193–94, 196–97, 236–38, 251, 253, 258–61, 281–83, 324, 327
transcendentalism, transcendental tradition, 10, 30–31, 147–48, 150, 152–53, 165, 206, 213, 301–2

Trinity, Trinitarian, 4, 154n38, 166–68, 170, 172–73, 179, 183, 212n8, 268–70, 279, 281–83, 298–99, 312, 318, 319, 321, 331–32n3, 334–36, 349
truth, 21, 95, 117–18, 134–35, 178–79, 243, 251, 269, 303, 309, 311; Christian, 24–25, 76n43, 265, 292–94, 299–300; transcendental, 115–16, 119–20, 163
Tübingen School, 290–91
Tyrrell, George, 43

Ulrich, Ferdinand, 108n10, 240n35
univocity, 254–56, 279

Valentinian, 20, 291
Vatican I, 89–90
Vatican II, 40, 41, 207–9, 300n23, 343n11, 353
Voegelin, Eric, 169n65, 170n65, 175n79, 291, 314

Williams, Rowan, 172n69
wisdom, 5, 26–27, 56–57, 68, 73–75, 81, 86, 92, 93, 97, 114, 132, 193, 233, 250–51, 258, 316n64; toward/in, 23, 57, 63, 67–69, 73–74, 81, 84, 93–95, 99, 101–2, 104, 132, 159–60, 193, 199, 250–51, 258, 260–61, 266, 280, 285, 324–25, 331n3, 332–33
Word, 246, 267, 269, 270, 307, 317

Žižek, Slavoj, 32, 60n5, 228, 236, 240, 243n41

COMPLETE LIST OF SERIES TITLES

Conor Cunningham, *Darwin's Pious Idea:*
Why the Ultra-Darwinists and Creationists Both Get It Wrong (2010)

Stewart Goetz and Charles Taliaferro, *Naturalism* (2008)

Philip John Paul Gonzales, *Reimagining the* Analogia Entis:
The Future of Erich Przywara's Christian Vision (2019)

Nicholas M. Healy, *Hauerwas: A (Very) Critical Introduction* (2014)

Michel Henry, *Words of Christ* (2012)

Johannes Hoff, *The Analogical Turn:*
Rethinking Modernity with Nicholas of Cusa (2013)

Karen Kilby, *Balthasar: A (Very) Critical Introduction* (2012)

S. J. McGrath, *Heidegger: A (Very) Critical Introduction* (2010)

Edward T. Oakes, SJ, *A Theology of Grace in Six Controversies* (2016)

Adrian Pabst, *Metaphysics: The Creation of Hierarchy* (2012)

Marcus Pound, *Žižek: A (Very) Critical Introduction* (2008)

Aaron Riches, *Ecce Homo: On the Divinity of Christ* (2016)

Philipp W. Rosemann, *Charred Root of Meaning:*
Continuity, Transgression, and the Other in Christian Tradition (2018)

CENTRE OF THEOLOGY AND PHILOSOPHY

(www.theologyphilosophycentre.co.uk)

Every doctrine which does not reach the one thing necessary, every separated philosophy, will remain deceived by false appearances. It will be a doctrine, it will not be Philosophy.

Maurice Blondel, 1861–1949

This book series is the product of the work carried out at the Centre of Theology and Philosophy (COTP), at the University of Nottingham.

The COTP is a research-led institution organized at the interstices of theology and philosophy. It is founded on the conviction that these two disciplines cannot be adequately understood or further developed, save with reference to each other. This is true in historical terms, since we cannot comprehend our Western cultural legacy unless we acknowledge the interaction of the Hebraic and Hellenic traditions. It is also true conceptually, since reasoning is not fully separable from faith and hope, or conceptual reflection from revelatory disclosure. The reverse also holds, in either case.

The Centre is concerned with:

- the historical interaction between theology and philosophy.
- the current relation between the two disciplines.
- attempts to overcome the analytic/continental divide in philosophy.
- the question of the status of "metaphysics": Is the term used equivocally? Is it now at an end? Or have twentieth-century attempts to have a postmetaphysical philosophy themselves come to an end?
- the construction of a rich Catholic humanism.

I am very glad to be associated with the endeavours of this extremely important Centre that helps to further work of enormous importance. Among its concerns is the question whether modernity is more an interim than a completion—an interim between a pre-

modernity in which the porosity between theology and philosophy was granted, perhaps taken for granted, and a postmodernity where their porosity must be unclogged and enacted anew. Through the work of leading theologians of international stature and philosophers whose writings bear on this porosity, the Centre offers an exciting forum to advance in diverse ways this challenging and entirely needful, and cutting-edge work.

Professor William Desmond, Leuven